MONOLINGUAL

# OXFORD PICTURE DICTIONARY

## SECOND CANADIAN EDITION



Jayme Adelson-Goldstein

Norma Shapiro

8 Sampson Mews, Suite 204, Don Mills, Ontario M3C 0H5
www.oupcanada.com

Oxford University Press is a department of the University of Oxford.

It furthers the University's objective of excellence in research, scholarship, and education by publishing worldwide in

Oxford New York
Auckland Cape Town Dar es Salaam Hong Kong Karachi
Kuala Lumpur Madrid Melbourne Mexico City Nairobi
New Delhi Shanghai Taipei Toronto

With offices in
Argentina Austria Brazil Chile Czech Republic France Greece
Guatemala Hungary Italy Japan Poland Portugal Singapore
South Korea Switzerland Thailand Turkey Ukraine Vietnam

Oxford is a trade mark of Oxford University Press in the UK and in certain other countries

Published in Canada
by Oxford University Press



Oxford Picture Dictionary Monolingual Edition was originally published in 2008. This edition is published by arrangement with Oxford University Press.

**Library and Archives Canada Cataloguing in Publication**

Adelson-Goldstein, Jayme
Oxford picture dictionary / Jayme Adelson-Goldstein, Norma Shapiro. — 2nd Canadian ed.

Includes index.
Previous ed. written by Norma Shapiro and Jayme Adelson-Goldstein.
ISBN 978-0-19-543116-2

1. Picture dictionaries, English. 2. English language—Textbooks for second language learners. I. Shapiro, Norma II. Title.

PE1629.S49 2009 423'.17 C2008-907241-3

Oxford University Press is committed to our environment. This book is printed on paper which contains a minimum of 10% post-consumer waste.

5 6 7 - 13 12 11

Printed and bound in United States of America.

This second edition of
the Oxford Picture Dictionary
is lovingly dedicated to
the memory of Norma Shapiro.

Her ideas, her pictures, and
her stories continue to teach,
inspire, and delight.

The OPD team thanks the following artists for their storyboarding and sketches: Cecilia Aranovich, Chris Brandt, Giacomo Ghiazza, Gary Goldstein, Gordan Kljucec, Vincent Lucido, and Glenn Urieta

Illustrations by: Lori Anzalone: 13, 70-71, 76-77; Joe "Fearless" Arenella/Will Sumpter: 178; Argosy Publishing: 66-67 (call-outs), 98-99, 108-109, 112-113 (call-outs), 152, 178, 193, 194-195, 196, 197, 205; Barbara Bastian: 4, 15, 17, 20-21, 162 (map), 216-217 (map); Philip Batini/AA Reps: 50; Thomas Bayley/Sparks Literary Agency: 158-159; Sally Bensusen: 211, 214; Annie Bissett: 112; Peter Bollinger/Shannon Associates: 14-15; Higgens Bond/Anita Grien: 226; Molly Borman-Pullman: 116, 117; Jim Fanning/Ravenhill Represents: 80-81; Mike Gardner: 10, 12, 17, 22, 132, 114-115, 142-143, 174, 219, 228-229; Garth Glazier/AA Reps: 106, 118-119; Dennis Godfrey/Mike Wepplo: 204; Steve Graham: 124-125, 224; Graphic Map & Chart Co.: 200-201, 202-203; Julia Green/Mendola Art: 225; Glenn Gustafson: 9, 27, 48, 76, 100, 101, 117, 132, 133, 136, 155, 161, 179, 196; Barbara Harmon: 212-213, 215; Ben Hasler/NB Illustration: 94-95, 101, 148-149, 172, 182, 186-187; Betsy Hayes: 134, 139; Matthew Holmes: 75; Stewart Holmes/Illustration Ltd.: 192; Janos Jantner/Beehive Illustration: 5, 13, 82-83, 122-123, 130-131, 146-147, 164-165, 184, 185; Ken Joudrey/Munro Campagna: 52, 68-69, 177, 208-209; Bob Kaganich/Deborah Wolfe: 10, 40-41, 121; Steve Karp: 230, 231; Mike Kasun/Munro Campagna: 218; Graham Kennedy: 27; Marcel Laverdet/AA Reps: 23; Jeffrey Lindberg: 33, 42-43, 92-93, 133, 160-161, 170-171, 176; Dennis Lyall/Artworks: 198; Chris Lyons:/Lindgren & Smith: 173, 191; Alan Male/Artworks: 210, 211; Jeff Mangiat/Mendola Art: 53, 54, 55, 56, 57, 58, 59, 66-67; Adrian Mateescu/The Studio: 188-189, 232-233; Karen Minot: 28-29; Paul Mirocha/The Wiley Group: 194, 216-217; Peter Miserendino/P.T. Pie Illustrations: 198; Lee Montgomery/Illustration Ltd.: 4; Roger Motzkus: 229; Laurie O'Keefe: 111, 216-217; Daniel O'Leary/Illustration Ltd.: 8-9, 26, 34-35, 78, 135, 136-137, 238; Vilma Ortiz-Dillon: 16, 20-21, 60, 98-99, 100, 211; Terry Pazcko: 46-47, 144-145, 152, 180, 227; David Preiss/Munro Campagna: 5; Pronk & Associates: 192-193; Tony Randazzo/AA Reps: 156, 234-235; Mike Renwick/Creative Eye: 126-127; Mark Riedy/Scott Hull Associates: 48-49, 79, 140, 153; Jon Rogers/AA Reps: 112; Jeff Sanson/Schumann & Co.: 84-85, 240-241; David Schweitzer/Munro Campagna: 162-163; Ben Shannon/Magnet Reps: 11, 64-65, 90, 91, 96, 97, 166-167, 168-169, 179, 239; Reed Sprunger/Jae Wagoner Artists Rep.: 18-19, 232-233; Studio Liddell/AA Reps: 27; Angelo Tillary: 108-109; Ralph Voltz/Deborah Wolfe: 50-51, 128-129, 141, 154, 175, 236-237; Jeff Wack/Mendola Art: 24, 25, 86-87, 102-103, 134-135, 231; Brad Walker: 104-105, 150-151, 157, 206-207; Wendy Wassink: 110-111; John White/The Neis Group: 199; Eric Wilkerson: 32, 138; Simon Williams/Illustration Ltd.: 2-3, 6-7, 30-31, 36, 38-39, 44-45, 72-73; Lee Woodgate/Eye Candy Illustration: 222-223; Andy Zito: 62-23; Craig Zuckerman: 14, 88-89, 112-113, 120-121, 194-195.

Chapter icons designed by Von Glitschka/Scott Hull Associates

Cover Art by CUBE/Illustration Ltd (hummingbird, branch); Paul Mirocha/The Wiley Group (cherry); 9 Surf Studios (lettering).

Studio photography for Oxford University Press done by Dennis Kitchen Studio: 37, 61, 72, 73, 74, 75, 95, 96, 100, 180, 181, 183, 226.

Stock Photography: Age FotoStock: 238 (flute; clarinet; bassoon; saxophone; violin; cello; bass; guitar; trombone; trumpet; xylophone; harmonica); Comstock, 61 (window); Morales, 221 (bat); Franco Pizzochero, 98 (cashmere); Thinkstock, 61 (sink); Alamy: Corbis, 61 (table); Amana Images, 61 (soapy plates); Inmagine: 238 (oboe; tuba; French horn; piano; drums; tambourine; accordion); istockphoto: 61 (oven), 98 (silk), 99 (suede; lace; velvet); Jupiter Images: 61 (tiles); 98 (wool); 99 (corduroy); Foodpix, 98 (linen); Rob Melnychuk/Brand X Pictures, 61 (glass shower door); 238 (electric keyboard); Comstock, 99 (denim); Punchstock: 98 (t-shirt), Robert Glusic, 31 (Monument Valley); Roland Corporation: 238 (organ); SuperStock: 99 (leather); Shutterstock: Marek Szumlas, 94 (watch); United States Mint: 126; City of Edmonton Archives EA-10-2070: 198 (women win the right to vote); Tim Dixon: 198 (train) Locomotive 1392 is owned and operated by the Alberta Railway Museum in Edmonton, Alberta; Government of Nova Scotia: 198 (Halifax Explosion); Library and Archives Canada: 198 (Great Depression; WWII; Constitution Act); 198: The Associated Press (WWI); iStockphoto: 220 (goat); Parks Canada: 220–221 (all other parks photos) Parks Canada/W. Lynch/13.02.10.01(46), Parks Canada/W. Lynch/01.11.08.09(28), Parks Canada/K. Redmond/01.11.07.12(30), Parks Canada/J. Butterill/11.110.10.01(47), Parks Canada/N. Rosing/07.71.03.12(56), Parks Canada/W. Lynch/13.01.08.05(04), Parks Canada/K. Redmond/01.10.09.11(08), Parks Canada/ W. Lynch/07.71.03.17(02), Parks Canada/J. Woods/Cascade Creek Bridge, Parks Canada/H. Wittenborn/Long-liner Boat, Parks Canada/M. Morris/The Nabimu Caves.

# Acknowledgements

The publisher and authors would like to acknowledge the following individuals for their invaluable feedback during the development of this program:

**Dr. Macarena Aguilar,** Cy-Fair College, Houston, TX

**Joseph F. Anselme,** Atlantic Technical Center, Coconut Creek, FL

**Stacy Antonopoulos,** Monterey Trail High School, Elk Grove, CA

**Carol Antunano,** The English Center, Miami, FL

**Irma Arencibia,** Thomas A. Edison School, Union City, NJ

**Suzi Austin,** Alexandria City Public School Adult Program, Alexandria, FL

**Patricia S. Bell,** Lake Technical Center, Eustis, FL

**Jim Brice,** San Diego Community College District, San Diego, CA

**Phil Cackley,** Arlington Education and Employment Program (REEP), Arlington, VA

**Frieda Caldwell,** Metropolitan Adult Education Program, San Jose, CA

**Sandra Cancel,** Robert Waters School, Union City, NJ

**Anne Marie Caney,** Chula Vista Adult School, Chula Vista, CA

**Patricia Castro,** Harvest English Institute, Newark, NJ

**Paohui Lola Chen,** Milpitas Adult School, Milpitas, CA

**Lori Cisneros,** Atlantic Vo-Tech, Ft. Lauderdale, FL

**Joyce Clapp,** Hayward Adult School, Hayward, CA

**Stacy Clark,** Arlington Education and Employment Program (REEP), Arlington, VA

**Nancy B. Crowell,** Southside Programs for Adults in Continuing Education, Prince George, VA

**Doroti da Cunha,** Hialeah-Miami Lakes Adult Education Center, Miami, FL

**Paula Da Silva-Michelin,** La Guardia Community College, Long Island City, NY

**Cynthia L. Davies,** Humble I.S.D., Humble, TX

**Christopher Davis,** Overfelt Adult Center, San Jose, CA

**Beverly De Nicola,** Capistrano Unified School District, San Juan Capistrano, CA

**Beatriz Diaz,** Miami-Dade County Public Schools, Miami, FL

**Druci J. Diaz,** Hillsborough County Public Schools, Tampa, FL

**Marion Donahue,** San Dieguito Adult School, Encinitas, CA

**Nick Doorn,** International Education Services, South Lyon, MI

**Mercedes Douglass,** Seminole Community College, Sanford, FL

**Jenny Elliott,** Montgomery College, Rockville, MD

**Paige Endo,** Mt. Diablo Adult Education, Concord, CA

**Megan Ernst,** Glendale Community College, Glendale, CA

**Elizabeth Escobar,** Robert Waters School, Union City, NJ

**Joanne Everett,** Dave Thomas Education Center, Pompano Beach, FL

**Jennifer Fadden,** Arlington Education and Employment Program (REEP), Arlington, VA

**Judy Farron,** Fort Myers Language Center, Fort Myers, FL

**Sharyl Ferguson,** Montwood High School, El Paso, TX

**Dr. Monica Fishkin,** University of Central Florida, Orlando, FL

**Nancy Frampton,** Reedley College, Reedley, CA

**Lynn A. Freeland,** San Dieguito Union High School District, Encinitas, CA

**Cathy Gample,** San Leandro Adult School, San Leandro, CA

**Hillary Gardner,** Center for Immigrant Education and Training, Long Island City, NY

**Martha C. Giffen,** Alhambra Unified School District, Alhambra, CA

**Jill Gluck,** Hollywood Community Adult School, Los Angeles, CA

**Carolyn Grimaldi,** LaGuardia Community College, Long Island City, NY

**William Gruenholz,** USD Adult School, Concord, CA

**Sandra G. Gutierrez,** Hialeah-Miami Lakes Adult Education Center, Miami, FL

**Conte Gúzman-Hoffman,** Triton College, River Grove, IL

**Amanda Harllee,** Palmetto High School, Palmetto, FL

**Mercedes Hearn,** Tampa Bay Technical Center, Tampa, FL

**Robert Hearst,** Truman College, Chicago, IL

**Patty Heiser,** University of Washington, Seattle, WA

**Joyce Hettiger,** Metropolitan Education District, San Jose, CA

**Karen Hirsimaki,** Napa Valley Adult School, Napa, CA

**Marvina Hooper,** Lake Technical Center, Eustis, FL

**Katie Hurter,** North Harris College, Houston, TX

**Nuchamon James,** Miami Dade College, Miami, FL

**Linda Jennings,** Montgomery College, Rockville, MD

**Bonnie Boyd Johnson,** Chapman Education Center, Garden Grove, CA

**Fayne B. Johnson,** Broward County Public Schools, Fort Lauderdale, FL

**Stavroula Katseyeanis,** Robert Waters School, Union City, NJ

**Dale Keith,** Broadbase Consulting, Inc. at Kidworks USA, Miami, FL

**Blanche Kellawon,** Bronx Community College, Bronx, NY

**Mary Kernel,** Migrant Education Regional Office, Northwest Educational Service District, Anacortes, WA

**Karen Kipke,** Antioch High School Freshman Academy, Antioch, TN

**Jody Kirkwood,** ABC Adult School, Cerritos, CA

**Matthew Kogan,** Evans Community Adult School, Los Angeles, CA

**Ineza Kuceba,** Renton Technical College, Renton, WA

**John Kuntz,** California State University, San Bernadino, San Bernadino, CA

**Claudia Kupiec,** DePaul University, Chicago, IL

**E.C. Land,** Southside Programs for Adult Continuing Education, Prince George, VA

**Betty Lau,** Franklin High School, Seattle, WA

**Patt Lemonie,** Thomas A. Edison School, Union City, NJ

**Lia Lerner,** Burbank Adult School, Burbank, CA

**Krystyna Lett,** Metropolitan Education District, San Jose, CA

**Renata Lima,** TALK International School of Languages, Fort Lauderdale, FL

**Luz M. Lopez,** Sweetwater Union High School District, Chula Vista, CA

**Osmara Lopez,** Bronx Community College, Bronx, NY

**Heather Lozano,** North Lake College, Irving, TX

**Betty Lynch,** Arlington Education and Employment Program (REEP), Arlington, VA

**Meera Madan,** REID Park Elementary School, Charlotte, NC

**Ivanna Mann Thrower,** Charlotte Mecklenburg Schools, Charlotte, NC

**Michael R. Mason,** Loma Vista Adult Center, Concord, CA

**Holley Mayville,** Charlotte Mecklenburg Schools, Charlotte, NC

**Margaret McCabe,** United Methodist Cooperative Ministries, Clearwater, FL

**Todd McDonald,** Hillsborough Adult Education, Tampa, FL

**Nancy A. McKeand,** ESL Consultant, St. Benedict, LA

**Rebecca L. McLain,** Gaston College, Dallas, NC

**John M. Mendoza,** Redlands Adult School, Redlands, CA

**Bet Messmer,** Santa Clara Adult Education Center, Santa Clara, CA

**Christina Morales,** BEGIN Managed Programs, New York, NY

**Lisa Munoz,** Metropolitan Education District, San Jose, CA

**Mary Murphy-Clagett,** Sweetwater Union High School District, Chula Vista, CA

**Jonetta Myles,** Rockdale County High School, Conyers, GA

**Marwan Nabi,** Troy High School, Fullerton, CA

**Dr. Christine L. Nelsen,** Salvation Army Community Center, Tampa, FL

**Michael W. Newman,** Arlington Education and Employment Program (REEP), Arlington, VA

**Rehana Nusrat,** Huntington Beach Adult School, Huntington Beach, CA

**Cindy Oakley-Paulik,** Embry-Riddle Aeronautical University, Daytona Beach, FL

# Acknowledgements


**Janet Ochi-Fontanott,** Sweetwater Union High School District, Chula Vista, CA

**Lorraine Pedretti,** Metropolitan Education District, San Jose, CA

**Isabel Pena,** BE/ESL Programs, Garland, TX

**Margaret Perry,** Everett Public Schools, Everett, WA

**Dale Pesmen, PhD,** Chicago, IL

**Cathleen Petersen,** Chapman Education Center, Garden Grove, CA

**Allison Pickering,** Escondido Adult School, Escondido, CA

**Ellen Quish,** LaGuardia Community College, Long Island City, NY

**Teresa Reen,** Independence Adult Center, San Jose, CA

**Kathleen Reynolds,** Albany Park Community Center, Chicago, IL

**Melba I. Rillen,** Palmetto High School, Palmetto, FL

**Lorraine Romero,** Houston Community College, Houston, TX

**Eric Rosenbaum,** BEGIN Managed Programs, New York, NY

**Blair Roy,** Chapman Education Center, Garden Grove, CA

**Arlene R. Schwartz,** Broward Community Schools, Fort Lauderdale, FL

**Geraldyne Blake Scott,** Truman College, Chicago, IL

**Sharada Sekar,** Antioch High School Freshman Academy, Antioch, TN

**Dr. Cheryl J. Serrano,** Lynn University, Boca Raton, FL

**Janet Setzekorn,** United Methodist Cooperative Ministries, Clearwater, FL

**Terry Shearer,** EDUCALL Learning Services, Houston, TX

**Elisabeth Sklar,** Township High School District 113, Highland Park, IL

**Robert Stein,** BEGIN Managed Programs, New York, NY

**Ruth Sutton,** Township High School District 113, Highland Park, IL

**Alisa Takeuchi,** Chapman Education Center, Garden Grove, CA

**Grace Tanaka,** Santa Ana College School of Continuing Education, Santa Ana, CA

**Annalisa Te,** Overfelt Adult Center, San Jose, CA

**Don Torluemke,** South Bay Adult School, Redondo Beach, CA

**Maliheh Vafai,** Overfelt Adult Center, San Jose, CA

**Tara Vasquez,** Robert Waters School, Union City, NJ

**Nina Velasco,** Naples Language Center, Naples, FL

**Theresa Warren,** East Side Adult Center, San Jose, CA

**Lucie Gates Watel,** Truman College, Chicago, IL

**Wendy Weil,** Arnold Middle School, Cypress, TX

**Patricia Weist,** TALK International School of Languages, Fort Lauderdale, FL

**Dr. Carole Lynn Weisz,** Lehman College, Bronx, NY

**Desiree Wesner,** Robert Waters School, Union City, NJ

**David Wexler,** Napa Valley Adult School, Napa, CA

**Cynthia Wiseman,** Borough of Manhattan Community College, New York, NY

**Debbie Cullinane Wood,** Lincoln Education Center, Garden Grove, CA

**Banu Yaylali,** Miami Dade College, Miami, FL

**Hongyan Zheng,** Milpitas Adult Education, Milpitas, CA

**Arlene Zivitz,** ESOL Teacher, Jupiter, FL

The publisher, authors, and editors would like to thank the following people for their expertise in reviewing specific content areas:

**Ross Feldberg,** Tufts University, Medford, MA

**William J. Hall, M.D. FACP/FRSM (UK),** Cumberland Foreside, ME

**Jill A. Horohoe,** Arizona State University, Tempe, AZ

**Phoebe B. Rouse,** Louisiana State University, Baton Rouge, LA

**Dr. Susan Rouse,** Southern Wesleyan University, Central, SC

**Dr. Ira M. Sheskin,** University of Miami, Coral Gables, FL

**Maiko Tomizawa,** D.D.S., New York, NY

The publisher would like to thank the following people for their feedback during the development of the Canadian edition:

**Hosnie Abu-Abed,** The Palestine House, Mississauga, ON

**Darlene Barrowman,** Fulford Academy, Brockville, ON

**Mariette Baynton,** EF Vancouver, Vancouver, BC

**Hala Beidas,** The Palestine House, Mississauga, ON

**Joan Berndt,** Gladwin Language Centre, Abbotsford, BC

**Cecile Buhl,** Bow Valley College, Calgary, AB

**Eva Chaves,** Bishop Marrocco, Toronto, ON

**Janet Chriest,** Bow Valley College, Calgary, AB

**Luisa Cisterna,** Bow Valley College and Mount Royal College, Calgary, AB

**Paula Clark,** Study Abroad Canada, Charlottetown, PE

**Kathleen Denkewalter,** Burnaby English Language Centre, Burnaby, BC

**Janice Dumba,** Regina Open Door Society, Regina, SK

**Cheryl Fisher,** Newfoundland International Student Education Program, St. John's, NL

**Kelly Jordin Moffatt,** Halifax Immigrant Learning Centre, Halifax, NS

**Roshan Karanjia,** Delta Family Resource Centre, Toronto, ON

**Mary Klassen,** Bachelor of Arts in TESOL, Minnedosa, MB

**Nancy Lagacé,** L'Université du 3ème âge (Senior University) à L'Université Laval, Quebec City, QC

**Alejandra Lopez,** ESL SHOP, Toronto, ON

**Coralee Mathews,** Avon Maitland District School Board, Stratford, ON

**Denise McCorkell,** Canadian Forces Language School, Borden, ON

**Martha Miller,** EF Vancouver, Vancouver, BC

**Jo Raponi-Monk,** Sunnyside Adult Learning Centre, Toronto, ON

**Betty Rink,** Westman Immigration Services, Brandon, MB

**Stuart Schwartz,** Heartland International English School, Winnipeg, MB

**Heather Therrien,** Westman Immigrant Services, Brandon, MB

**John Vaccarella,** High School of Montreal, Montreal, QC

**Carole Whiston,** Columbia Square Adult Learning Centre, New Westminster, BC

**Eleanor Wiebe,** South Eastman English & Literacy Services, Steinbach, MB

**Agnieszka Witkowska,** Westman Immigrant Services, Brandon, MB


The publisher would like to thank the following for their permission to reproduce copyrighted material:

# Table of Contents

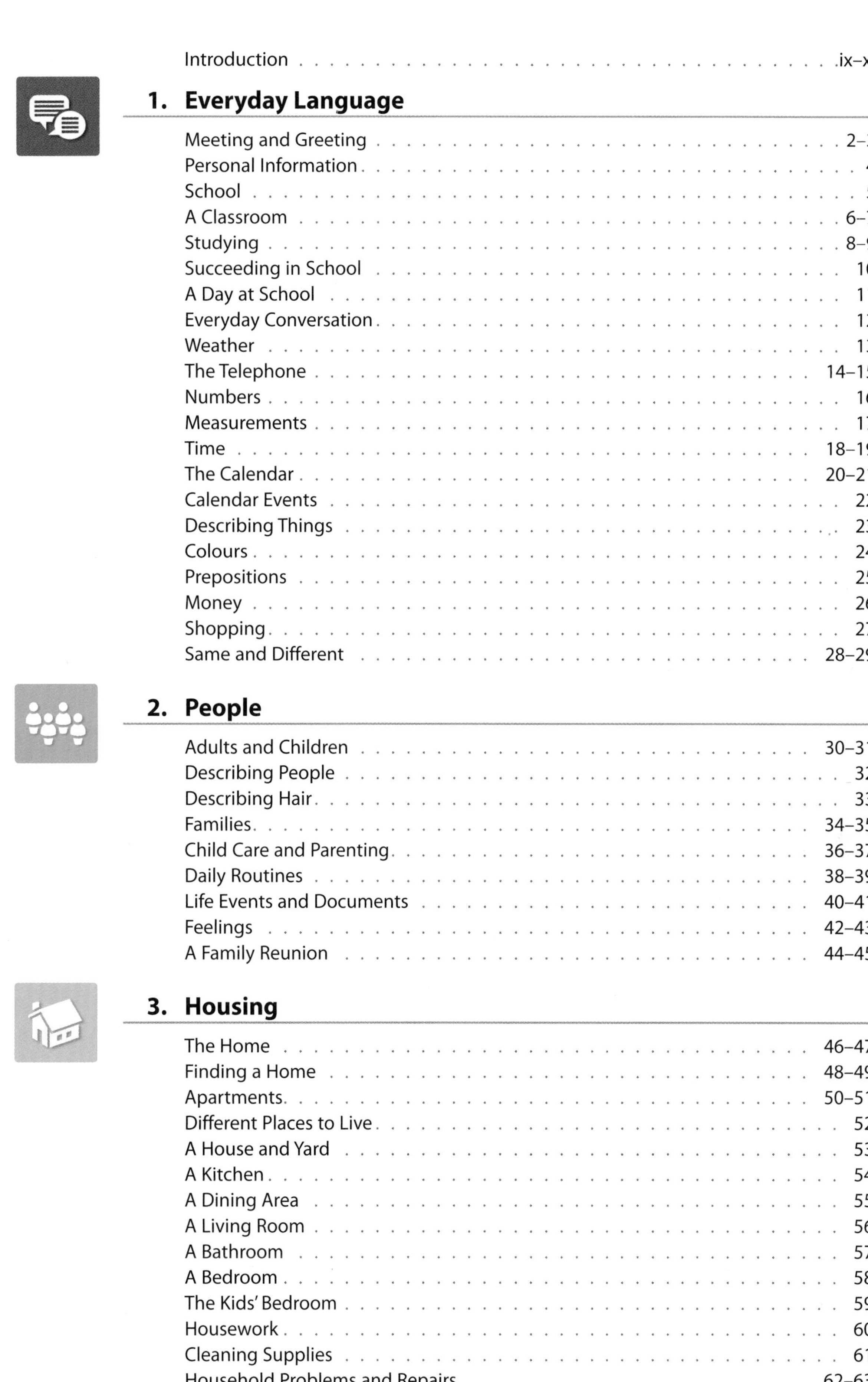

Introduction . . . . . ix–xi

## 1. Everyday Language

Meeting and Greeting . . . . . 2–3
Personal Information . . . . . 4
School . . . . . 5
A Classroom . . . . . 6–7
Studying . . . . . 8–9
Succeeding in School . . . . . 10
A Day at School . . . . . 11
Everyday Conversation . . . . . 12
Weather . . . . . 13
The Telephone . . . . . 14–15
Numbers . . . . . 16
Measurements . . . . . 17
Time . . . . . 18–19
The Calendar . . . . . 20–21
Calendar Events . . . . . 22
Describing Things . . . . . 23
Colours . . . . . 24
Prepositions . . . . . 25
Money . . . . . 26
Shopping . . . . . 27
Same and Different . . . . . 28–29

## 2. People

Adults and Children . . . . . 30–31
Describing People . . . . . 32
Describing Hair . . . . . 33
Families . . . . . 34–35
Child Care and Parenting . . . . . 36–37
Daily Routines . . . . . 38–39
Life Events and Documents . . . . . 40–41
Feelings . . . . . 42–43
A Family Reunion . . . . . 44–45

## 3. Housing

The Home . . . . . 46–47
Finding a Home . . . . . 48–49
Apartments . . . . . 50–51
Different Places to Live . . . . . 52
A House and Yard . . . . . 53
A Kitchen . . . . . 54
A Dining Area . . . . . 55
A Living Room . . . . . 56
A Bathroom . . . . . 57
A Bedroom . . . . . 58
The Kids' Bedroom . . . . . 59
Housework . . . . . 60
Cleaning Supplies . . . . . 61
Household Problems and Repairs . . . . . 62–63
The Tenant Meeting . . . . . 64–65

## 4. Food

Back from the Market . . . 66–67
Fruit . . . 68
Vegetables . . . 69
Meat and Poultry . . . 70
Seafood and Deli . . . 71
A Grocery Store . . . 72–73
Containers and Packaging . . . 74
Weights and Measurements . . . 75
Food Preparation and Safety . . . 76–77
Kitchen Utensils . . . 78
Fast-food Restaurant . . . 79
A Coffee Shop Menu . . . 80–81
A Restaurant . . . 82–83
The Farmers' Market . . . 84–85

## 5. Clothing

Everyday Clothes . . . 86–87
Casual, Work, and Formal Clothes . . . 88–89
Seasonal Clothing . . . 90
Underwear and Sleepwear . . . 91
Workplace Clothing . . . 92–93
Shoes and Accessories . . . 94–95
Describing Clothes . . . 96–97
Making Clothes . . . 98–99
Making Alterations . . . 100
Doing the Laundry . . . 101
A Garage Sale . . . 102–103

## 6. Health

The Body . . . 104–105
Inside and Outside the Body . . . 106–107
Personal Hygiene . . . 108–109
Symptoms and Injuries . . . 110
Illnesses and Medical Conditions . . . 111
A Pharmacy . . . 112–113
Taking Care of Your Health . . . 114–115
Medical Emergencies . . . 116
First Aid . . . 117
Medical Care . . . 118
Dental Care . . . 119
Hospital . . . 120–121
A Health Fair . . . 122–123

## 7. Community

Downtown . . . 124–125
City Streets . . . 126–127
An Intersection . . . 128–129
A Mall . . . 130–131
The Bank . . . 132
The Library . . . 133
The Post Office . . . 134–135
Driver Licensing Office . . . 136–137
Government and Military Service . . . 138–139
Civic Rights and Responsibilities . . . 140
The Legal System . . . 141
Crime . . . 142
Public Safety . . . 143
Emergencies and Natural Disasters . . . 144–145
Emergency Procedures . . . 146–147
Community Cleanup . . . 148–149

## 8. Transportation

Basic Transportation . . . 150–151
Public Transportation . . . 152
Prepositions of Motion . . . 153
Traffic Signs . . . 154
Directions and Maps . . . 155
Cars and Trucks . . . 156
Buying and Maintaining a Car . . . 157
Parts of a Car . . . 158–159
An Airport . . . 160–161
Taking a Trip . . . 162–163

## 9. Work

The Workplace . . . 164–165
Jobs and Occupations A-C . . . 166
Jobs and Occupations C-H . . . 167
Jobs and Occupations H-P . . . 168
Jobs and Occupations P-W . . . 169
Job Skills . . . 170
Office Skills . . . 171
Career Planning . . . 172
Job Search . . . 173
Interview Skills . . . 174
A Factory . . . 175
Landscaping and Gardening . . . 176
Farming and Ranching . . . 177
Construction . . . 178
Job Safety . . . 179
Tools and Building Supplies . . . 180–181
An Office . . . 182–183
A Hotel . . . 184
Food Service . . . 185
A Bad Day at Work . . . 186–187

# Contents

## 10. Areas of Study

Schools and Subjects . . . . . 188–189
English Composition . . . . . 190–191
Mathematics . . . . . 192–193
Science . . . . . 194–195
Computers . . . . . 196
The Internet . . . . . 197
Canadian History . . . . . 198
World History . . . . . 199
North America and Central America . . . . . 200–201
World Map . . . . . 202–203
Geography and Habitats . . . . . 204
The Universe . . . . . 205
A Graduation . . . . . 206–207

## 11. Plants and Animals

Nature Centre . . . . . 208–209
Trees and Plants . . . . . 210
Flowers . . . . . 211
Marine Life, Amphibians, and Reptiles . . . . . 212–213
Birds, Insects, and Arachnids . . . . . 214
Domestic Animals and Rodents . . . . . 215
Mammals . . . . . 216–217
Energy and Conservation . . . . . 218–219
Canadian National Parks . . . . . 220–221

## 12. Recreation

Places to Go . . . . . 222–223
The Park and Playground . . . . . 224
The Beach . . . . . 225
Outdoor Recreation . . . . . 226
Winter and Water Sports . . . . . 227
Individual Sports . . . . . 228
Team Sports . . . . . 229
Sports Verbs . . . . . 230
Sports Equipment . . . . . 231
Hobbies and Games . . . . . 232–233
Electronics and Photography . . . . . 234–235
Entertainment . . . . . 236–237
Music . . . . . 238
Holidays . . . . . 239
A Birthday Party . . . . . 240–241

Verb Guide . . . . . 242–244
How to Use the Index . . . . . 245
Index . . . . . 246–281
Geographical Index . . . . . 282–284
Research Bibliography . . . . . 285

## Teaching with the *Oxford Picture Dictionary* Program

The following general guidelines will help you prepare single and multi-level lessons using the OPD program. For step-by-step, topic-specific lesson plans, see *OPD Lesson Plans*.

### 1. Use Students' Needs to Identify Lesson Objectives

- Create communicative objectives based on your learners' needs assessments. (see *OPD 2e Assessment Program*).
- Make sure objectives state what students will be able to do at the end of the lesson. For example: *Students will be able to respond to basic classroom commands and requests for classroom objects* (pp. 6–7, A Classroom).
- For multi-level classes, identify a low-beginning, high-beginning, and low-intermediate objective for each topic.

### 2. Preview the Topic

Identify what your students already know about the topic.

- Ask general questions related to the topic.
- Have students list words they know from the topic.
- Ask questions about the picture(s) on the page.

### 3. Present the New Vocabulary

Research shows that it is best to present no more than 5–7 new words at a time. Here are a few presentation techniques:

- Say each new word and describe it within the context of the picture. Have volunteers act out verbs and verb sequences.
- Use Total Physical Response commands to build vocabulary comprehension.
- For long or unfamiliar word lists, introduce words by categories or select the words your students need most.
- Ask a series of questions to build comprehension and give students an opportunity to say the new words. Begin with *yes/no* questions: *Is #16 chalk?* Progress to *or* questions: *Is #16 chalk or a marker?* Finally, ask *Wh-* questions: *What can I use to write on this paper?*
- Focus on the words that students want to learn. Have them write 3–5 new words from each topic, along with meaning clues such as a drawing, translation, or sentence.

**More vocabulary** and **Grammar Point** sections provide additional presentation opportunities (see p. 5, School). For multi-level presentation ideas, see *OPD Lesson Plans*.

### 4. Check Comprehension

Make sure that students understand the target vocabulary. Here are two activities you can try:

- Say vocabulary words, and have students point to the correct items in their books. Walk around the room, checking if students are pointing to the correct pictures.
- Make true/false statements about the target vocabulary. Have students hold up two fingers for true, three for false.

### 5. Provide Guided and Communicative Practice

The exercise bands at the bottom of the topic pages provide a variety of guided and communicative practice opportunities and engage students' higher-level thinking.

### 6. Provide More Practice

*OPD* Second Canadian Edition offers a variety of components to facilitate vocabulary acquisition. Each of the print and electronic materials listed below offers suggestions and support for single and multi-level instruction.

***OPD Lesson Plans*** Step-by-step multi-level lesson plans feature 3 CDs with multi-level listening, context-based pronunciation practice, and levelled reading practice. Includes multi-level teaching notes for The OPD Reading Library.

***OPD Audio CDs or Audio Cassettes*** Each word in *OPD's* word list is recorded by topic.

***Low-Beginning, High-Beginning, and Low-Intermediate Canadian Workbooks*** Guided practice for each page in *OPD* features linked visual contexts, realia, and listening practice.

***Classic Classroom Activities*** A photocopiable resource of interactive multi-level activities, grammar practice, and communicative tasks.

***The OPD Reading Library*** Readers include civics, academic content, and workplace themes.

***Overhead Transparencies*** Vibrant transparenices help to focus students on the lesson.

***OPD Presentation Software*** A multi-level interactive teaching tool using interactive whiteboard and LCD technology. Audio, animation, and video instructional support bring each dictionary topic to life

***The OPD CD-ROM*** An interactive learning tool featuring four-skill practice based on *OPD* topics.

***Bilingual Editions*** *OPD* is available in numerous bilingual editions including Spanish, Chinese, Farsi, Urdu, Korean, and many more.

My hope is that OPD makes it easier for you to take your learners from comprehension to communication. Please share your thoughts with us as you make the book your own.

Jayme Adelson-Goldstein

eslinfo.ca@oup.com

**The second Canadian edition of the *Oxford Picture Dictionary* expands on the best aspects of the 1999 edition with:**

- New artwork presenting words within meaningful, real-life contexts
- An updated word list to meet the needs of today's English language learners
- 4,000 English words and phrases, including 285 verbs
- 40 new topics with 12 intro pages and 12 story pages
- Unparalleled support for vocabulary teaching

Subtopics present the words in easy-to-learn "chunks."

Colour coding and icons make it easy to navigate through *OPD*.

New art and rich contexts improve vocabulary acquisition.

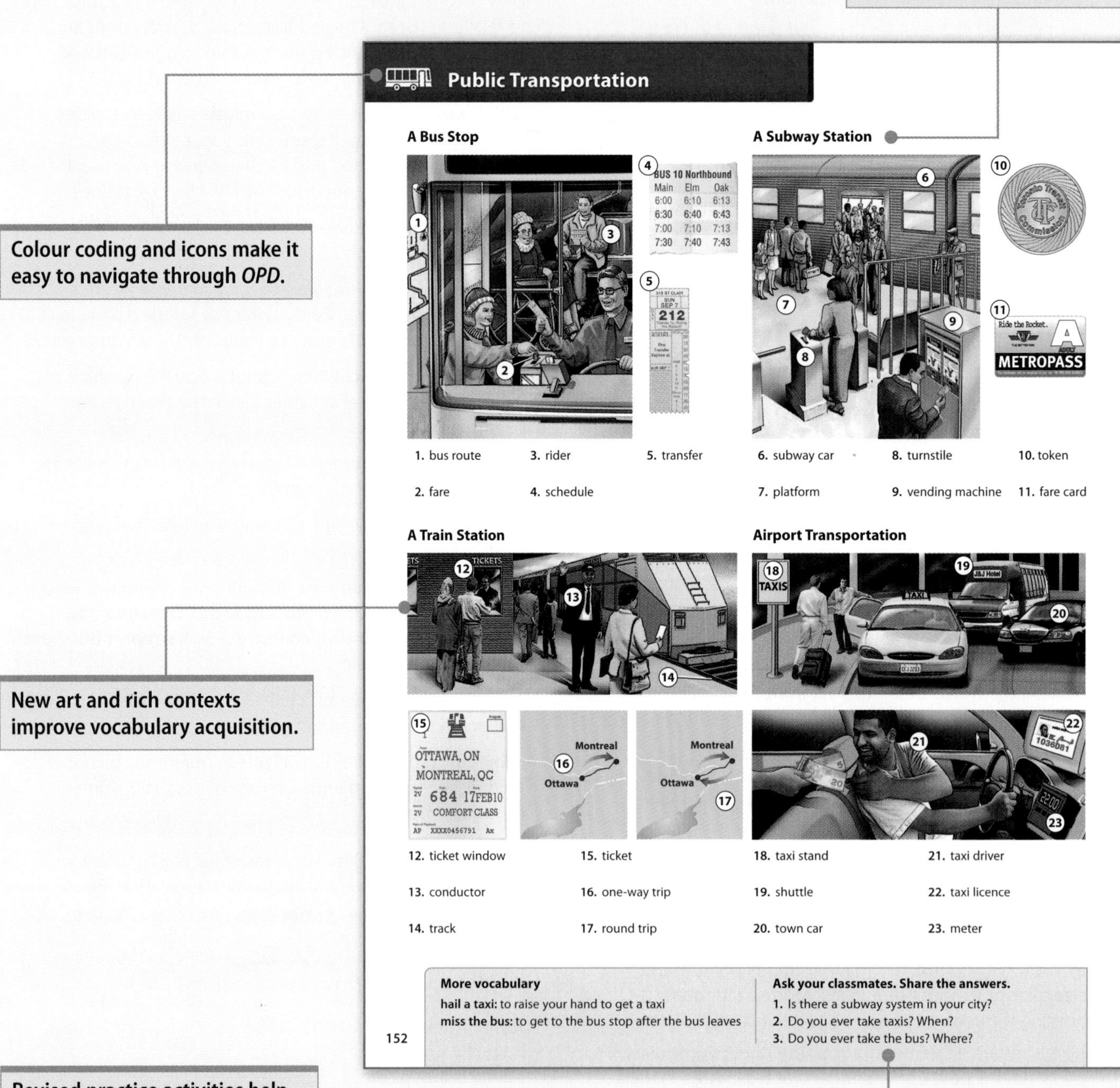


Revised practice activities help students from low-beginning through low-intermediate levels.

**NEW!** Intro pages open each unit with key vocabulary related to the unit theme. Clear, engaging artwork promotes questions, conversations, and writing practice for all levels.

Each intro page teaches key vocabulary items within the unit theme.

Practice activities make it easy to manage multi-level classrooms.

Back from the Market

1. fish
2. meat
3. chicken
4. cheese
5. milk
6. butter
7. eggs
8. vegetables
9. fruit
10. rice
11. bread
12. pasta
13. grocery bag
14. shopping list
15. coupons



**Listen and point. Take turns.**
A: *Point to the vegetables.*
B: *Point to the bread.*
A: *Point to the fruit.*

**Pair Dictation**
A: *Write vegetables.*
B: *Please spell vegetables for me.*
A: *V-e-g-e-t-a-b-l-e-s.*

**Ways to talk about food.**
*Do we need eggs?*
*Do we have any pasta?*
*We have some vegetables, but we need fruit.*

**Role play. Talk about your shopping list.**
A: *Do we need eggs?*
B: *No, we have some.*
A: *Do we have any...*

66 67

**NEW!** Story pages close each unit with a lively scene for reviewing vocabulary and teaching additional language. Meanwhile, rich visual contexts recycle words from the unit.

Pre-reading questions build students' previewing and predicting skills.

High-interest readings promote literacy skills.

Post-reading questions and role-play activities support critical thinking and encourage students to use the language they have learned.

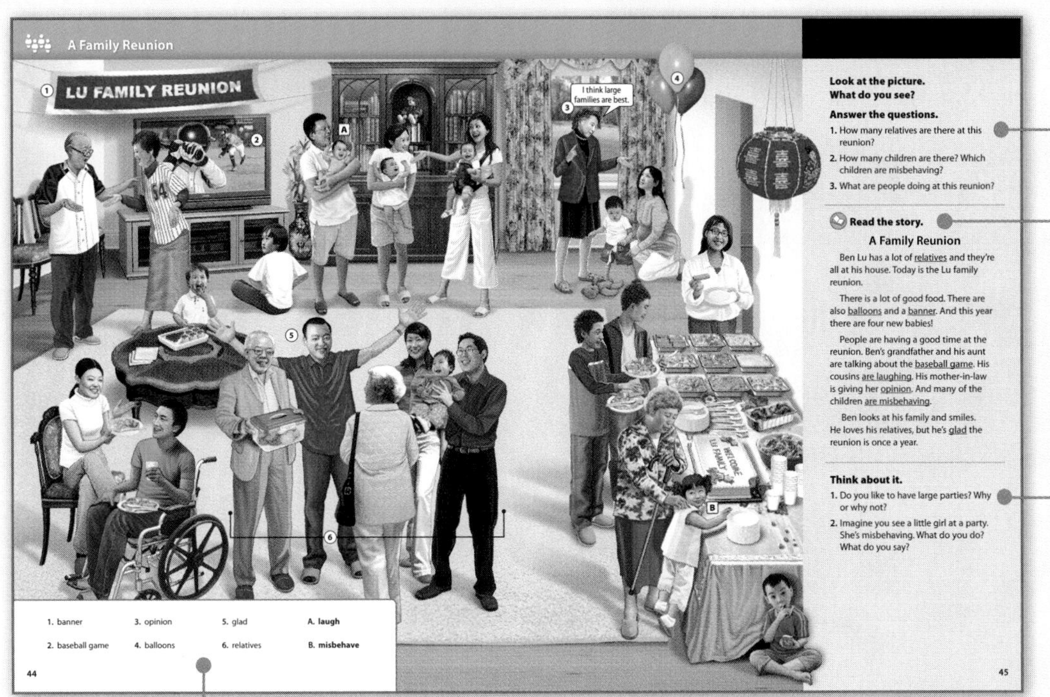

A Family Reunion



1. banner
2. baseball game
3. opinion
4. balloons
5. glad
6. relatives
A. **laugh**
B. **misbehave**

**Look at the picture. What do you see?**

**Answer the questions.**
1. How many relatives are there at this reunion?
2. How many children are there? Which children are misbehaving?
3. What are people doing at this reunion?

**Read the story.**

A Family Reunion

Ben Lu has a lot of relatives and they're all at his house. Today is the Lu family reunion.

There is a lot of good food. There are also balloons and a banner. And this year there are four new babies!

People are having a good time at the reunion. Ben's grandfather and his aunt are talking about the baseball game. His cousins are laughing. His mother-in-law is giving her opinion. And many of the children are misbehaving.

Ben looks at his family and smiles. He loves his relatives, but he's glad the reunion is once a year.

**Think about it.**
1. Do you like to have large parties? Why or why not?
2. Imagine you see a little girl at a party. She's misbehaving. What do you do? What do you say?

44 45

The thematic word list previews words that students will encounter in the story.

# Meeting and Greeting

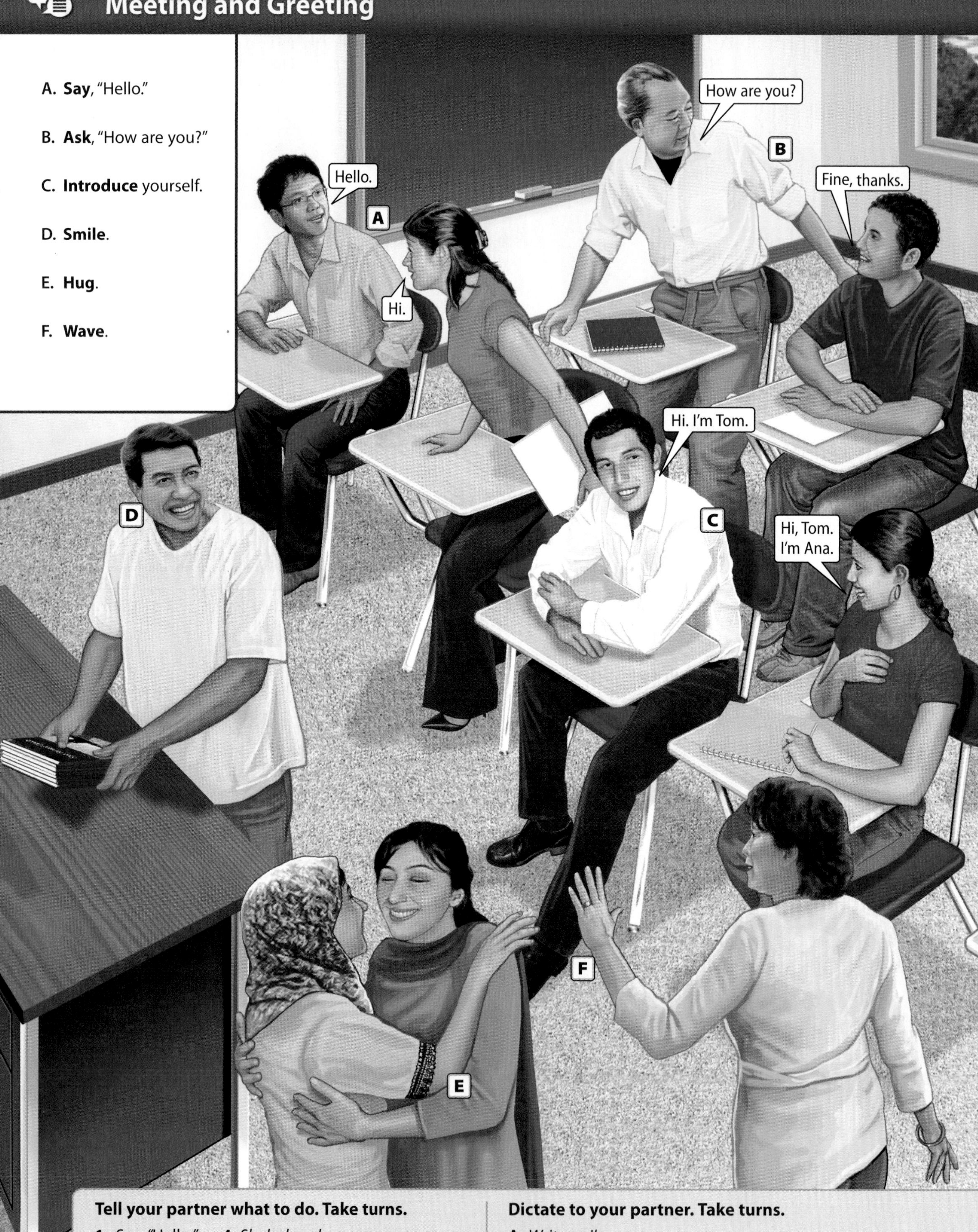
A. **Say**, "Hello."
B. **Ask**, "How are you?"
C. **Introduce** yourself.
D. **Smile**.
E. **Hug**.
F. **Wave**.
How are you?
Hello.
Hi.
Fine, thanks.
Hi. I'm Tom.
Hi, Tom. I'm Ana.
A
B
C
D
E
F

**Tell your partner what to do. Take turns.**

1. *Say, "Hello."*
2. *Bow.*
3. *Smile.*
4. *Shake hands.*
5. *Wave.*
6. *Say, "Goodbye."*

**Dictate to your partner. Take turns.**

**A:** *Write smile.*
**B:** *Is it spelled s-m-i-l-e?*
**A:** *Yes, that's right.*

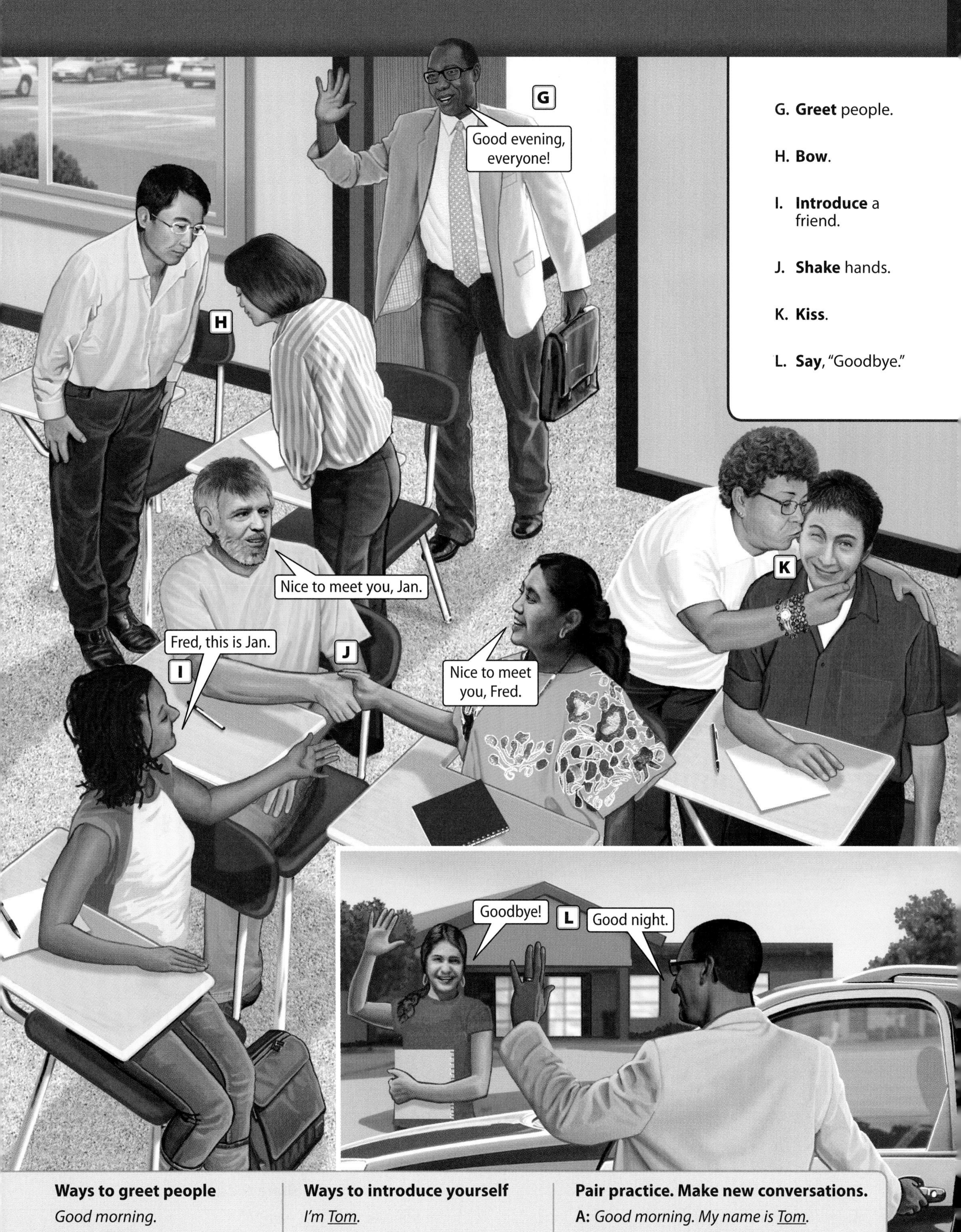


G. **Greet** people.

H. **Bow**.

I. **Introduce** a friend.

J. **Shake** hands.

K. **Kiss**.

L. **Say**, "Goodbye."

**Ways to greet people**

*Good morning.*
*Good afternoon.*
*Good evening.*

**Ways to introduce yourself**

*I'm Tom.*
*My name is Tom.*

**Pair practice. Make new conversations.**

**A:** *Good morning. My name is Tom.*
**B:** *Nice to meet you, Tom. I'm Sara.*
**A:** *Nice to meet you, Sara.*

# Personal Information

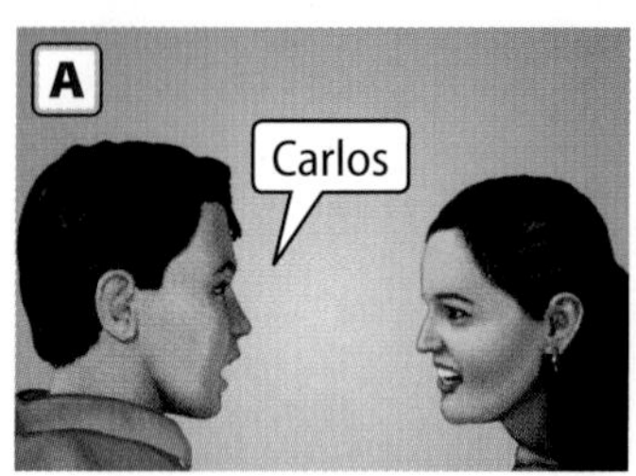


A. **Say** your name.

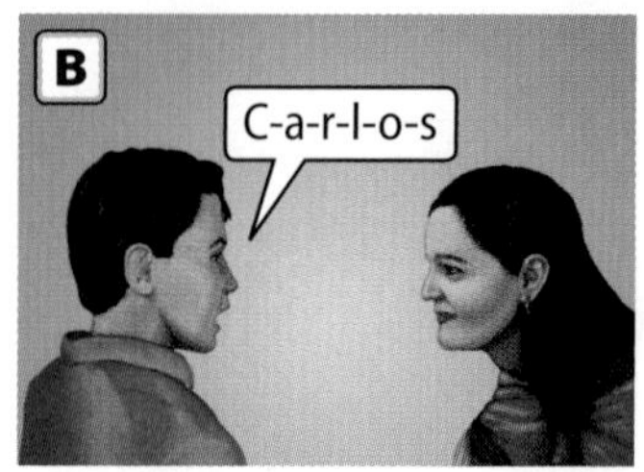


B. **Spell** your name.

C. **Print** your name.

D. **Sign** your name.

## Filling Out a Form

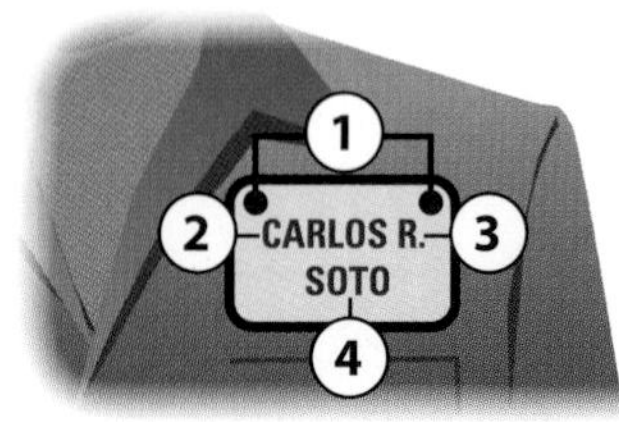

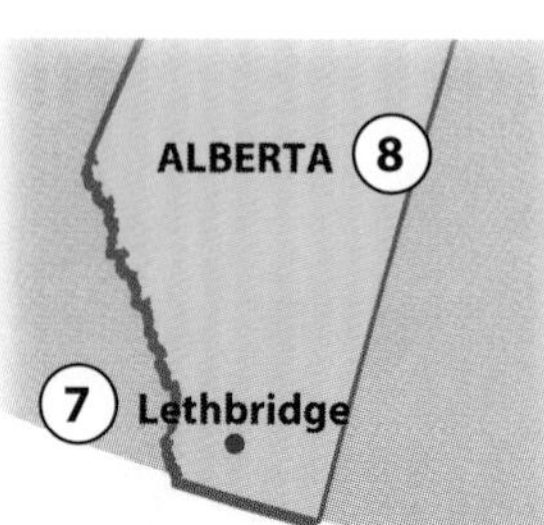

MR. CARLOS R. SOTO
446 PINE STREET #10
LETHBRIDGE, AB T1J 0N0
9


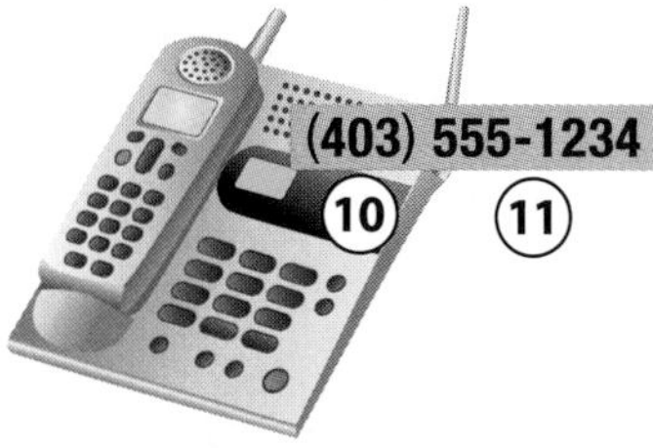


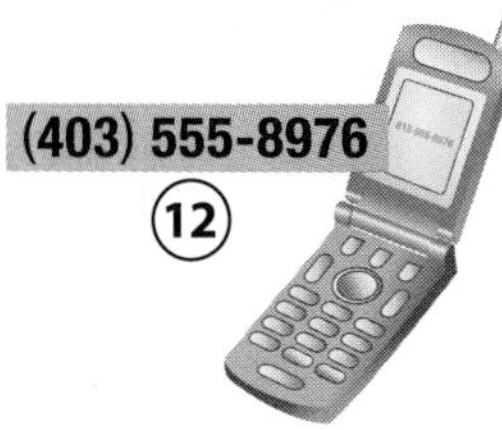

Employment and Immigration Canada
Emploi et Immigration Canada
SOCIAL INSURANCE NUMBER
NUMÉRO D'ASSURANCE SOCIALE
15
423 025 000
CARLOS R. SOTO
SIGNATURE Carlos R. Soto

19
Carlos R. Soto

### School Registration Form

1. name:

| ____ | ____ | ____ | ____ | ____ |
|---|---|---|---|---|
| **2.** first name | **3.** middle initial | **4.** last name | **5.** address | **6.** apartment number |

| ____ | ____ | ____ | ( ) | ____ |
|---|---|---|---|---|
| **7.** city | **8.** province | **9.** postal code | **10.** area code | **11.** phone number |

| ( ) ____ | ____ | ____ |
|---|---|---|
| **12.** cellphone number | **13.** date of birth (DOB) | **14.** place of birth |

___ - ___ - ___
**15.** social insurance number

**16.** sex: **17.** male ☐ **18.** female ☐

____________
**19.** signature

**Pair practice. Make new conversations.**

A: *My first name is* <u>*Carlos*</u>*.*
B: *Please spell* <u>*Carlos*</u> *for me.*
A: <u>*C-a-r-l-o-s*</u>

**Ask your classmates. Share the answers.**

1. Do you like your first name?
2. Is your last name from your mother? father? husband?
3. What is your middle name?

## Campus

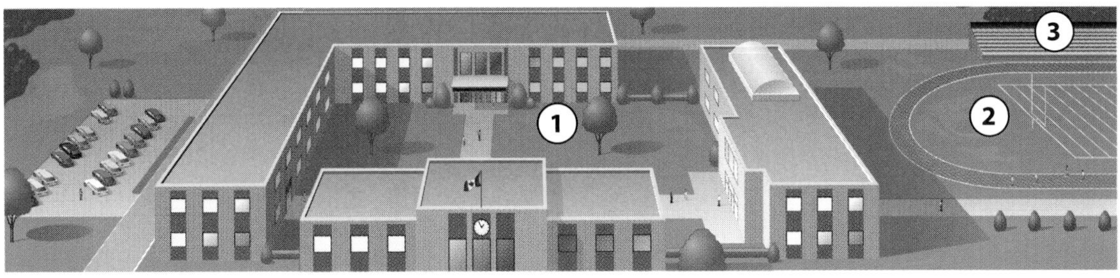

## Administrators

## Around Campus

1. courtyard
2. field
3. bleachers
4. principal
5. vice principal
6. counsellor
7. classroom
8. teacher
9. washrooms / restrooms
10. hallway
11. locker
12. main office
13. clerk
14. cafeteria
15. computer lab
16. teacher's aide
17. library
18. auditorium
19. gym
20. coach
21. track

**More vocabulary**

Students do not pay to go to a **public school**.
Students pay to go to a **private school**.
A church, mosque, or temple school is a **parochial school**.

**Grammar Point: contractions of the verb *be***

| | |
|---|---|
| He + is = He's | *He's a teacher.* |
| She + is = She's | *She's a counsellor.* |
| They + are = They're | *They're students.* |

# A Classroom

1. chalkboard
2. screen
3. whiteboard
4. teacher / instructor
5. student
6. LCD projector
7. desk
8. headphones

A. **Raise** your hand.

B. **Talk** to the teacher.

C. **Listen** to a CD.

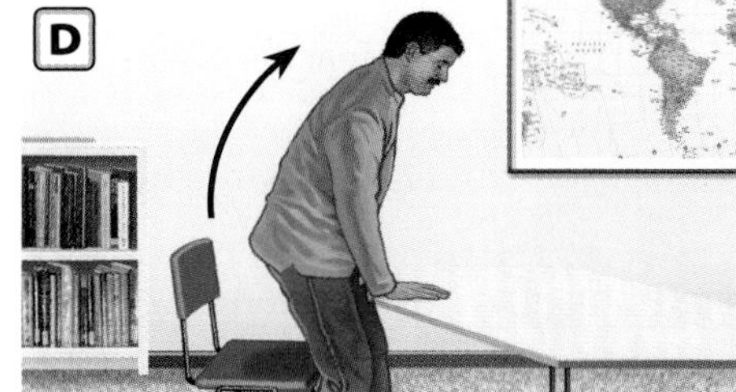

D. **Stand up**.

E. **Write** on the board.

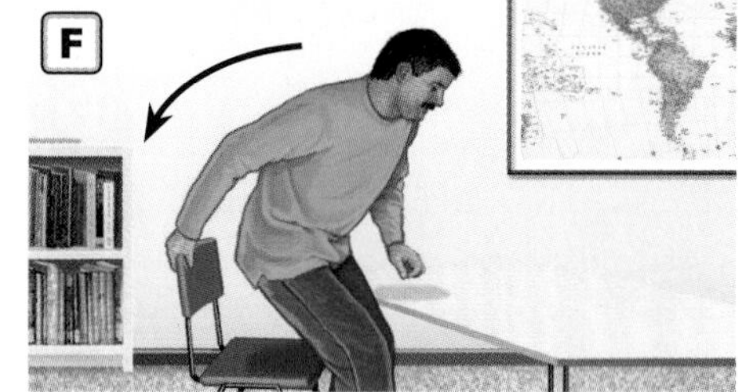

F. **Sit down**. / **Take** a seat.

G. **Open** your book.

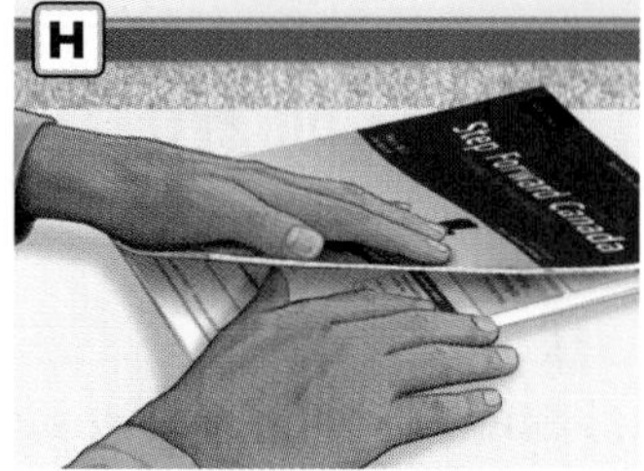


H. **Close** your book.

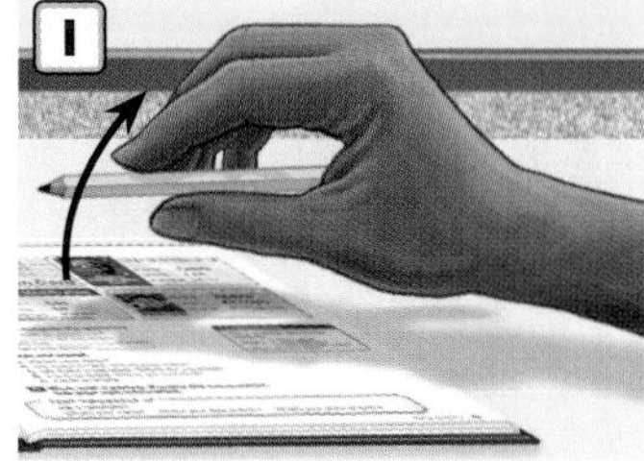

I. **Pick up** the pencil.

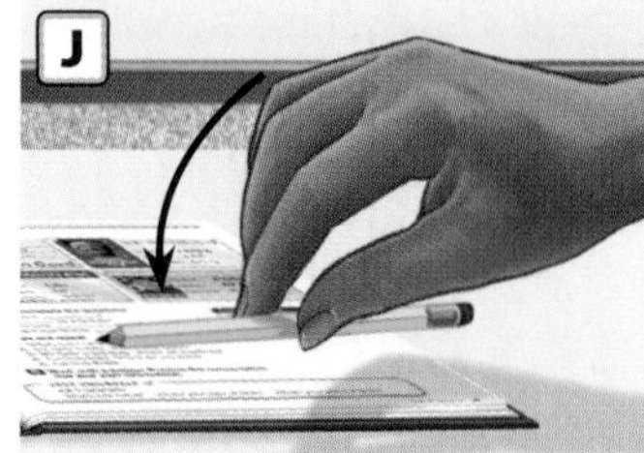

J. **Put down** the pencil.

9. clock
10. bookcase
11. chair
12. map
13. alphabet
14. bulletin board
15. computer
16. overhead projector

17. dry-erase marker
18. chalk
19. eraser
20. pencil
21. (pencil) eraser
22. pen
23. pencil sharpener
24. marker
25. textbook
26. workbook
27. 3-ring binder / notebook
28. notebook paper
29. spiral notebook
30. dictionary
31. picture dictionary

**Look at the picture.**
Describe the classroom.

**A:** There's a chalkboard.
**B:** There are fifteen students.

**Ask your classmates. Share the answers.**

1. Do you like to raise your hand in class?
2. Do you like to listen to CDs in class?
3. Do you ever talk to the teacher?

## Learning New Words

A. **Look up** the word.

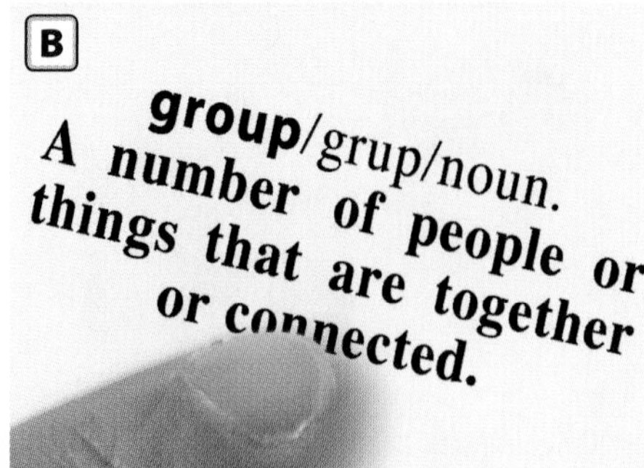


B. **Read** the definition.

C. **Translate** the word.

D. **Check** the pronunciation.

E. **Copy** the word.

F. **Draw** a picture.

## Working with Your Classmates

G. **Discuss** a problem.

H. **Brainstorm** solutions / answers.

I. **Work** in a group.

J. **Help** a classmate.

## Working with a Partner

K. **Ask** a question.

L. **Answer** a question.

M. **Share** a book.

N. **Dictate** a sentence.

## Following Directions

O. **Fill in** the blank.

P. **Choose** the correct answer.

Q. **Circle** the answer.

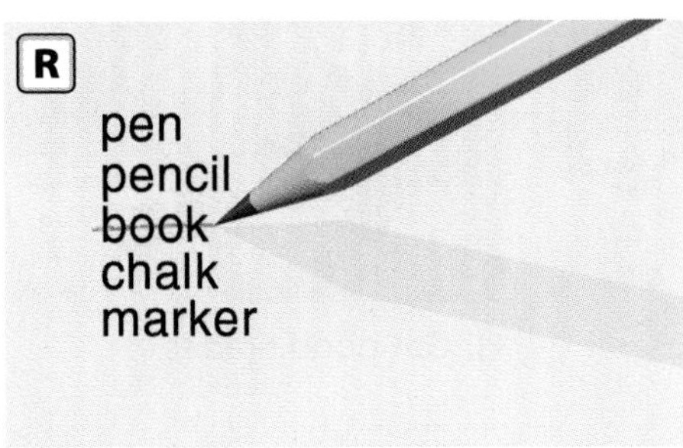


R. **Cross out** the word.

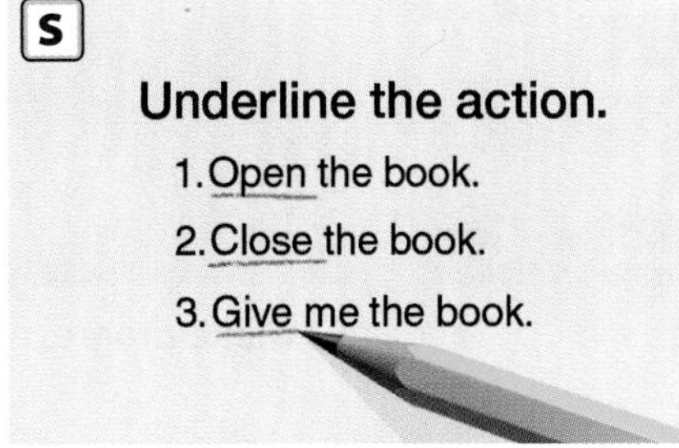


S. **Underline** the word.

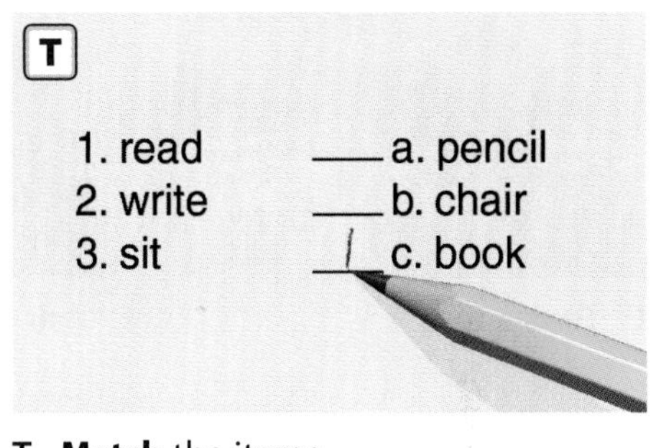


T. **Match** the items.

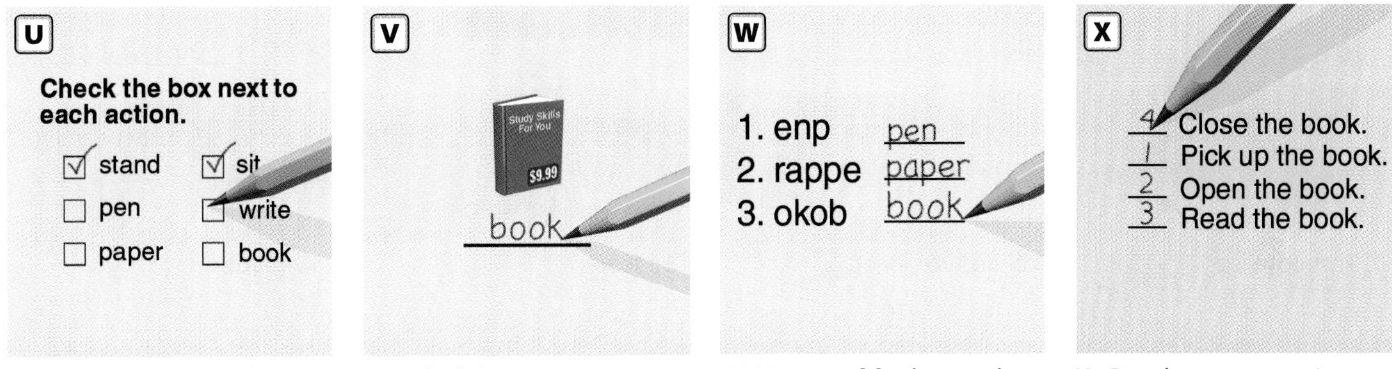


U. **Check** the correct boxes.

V. **Label** the picture.

W. **Unscramble** the words.

X. **Put** the sentences in order.

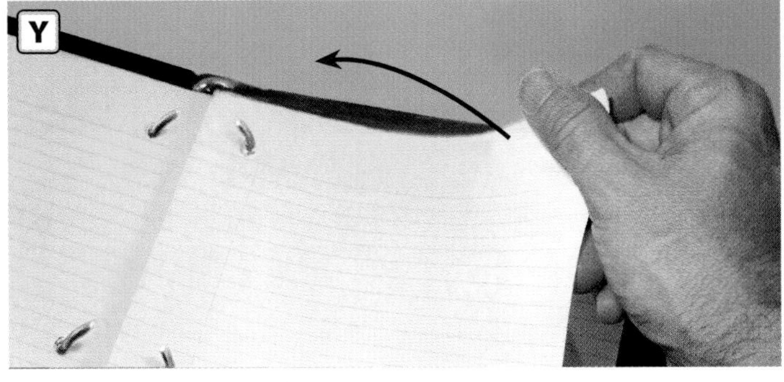


Y. **Take out** a piece of paper.

Z. **Put away** your books.

**Ask your classmates. Share the answers.**

1. Do you like to work in a group?
2. Do you ever share a book?
3. Do you like to answer questions?

**Think about it. Discuss.**

1. How can classmates help each other?
2. Why is it important to ask questions in class?
3. How can students check their pronunciation? Explain.

# Succeeding in School

## Ways to Succeed

A. **Set** goals.

B. **Participate** in class.

C. **Take** notes.

D. **Study** at home.

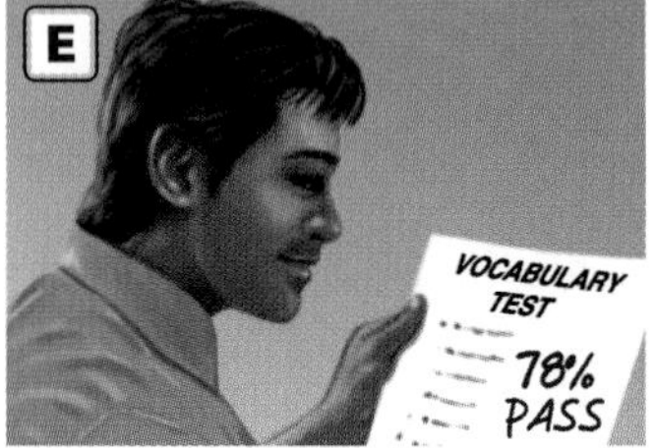


E. **Pass** a test.

F. **Ask** for help.

G. **Make** progress.

H. **Get** good grades.

## Taking a Test

1. test booklet

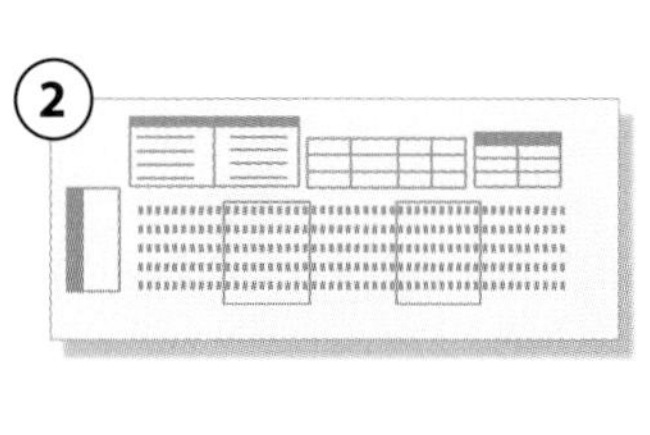


2. answer sheet

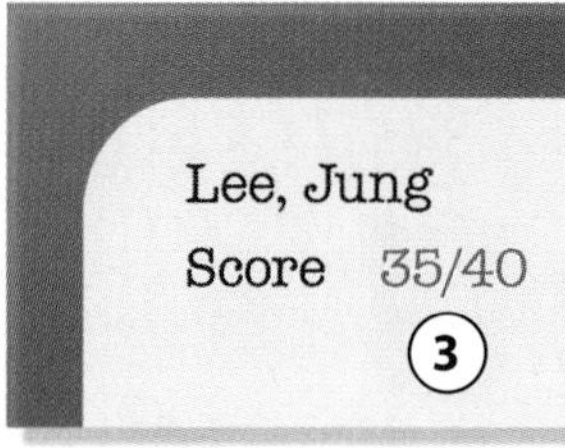


3. score

(4)

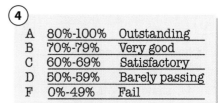

| | | |
|---|---|---|
| A | 80%-100% | Outstanding |
| B | 70%-79% | Very good |
| C | 60%-69% | Satisfactory |
| D | 50%-59% | Barely passing |
| F | 0%-49% | Fail |

4. grades

I. **Clear off** your desk.

J. **Work** on your own.

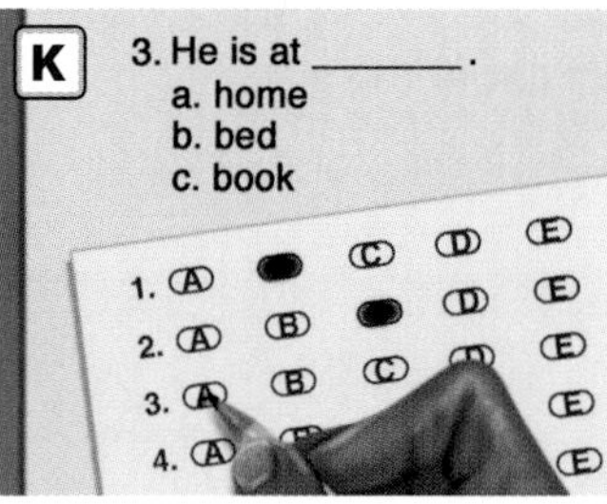


K. **Fill in** the answer.

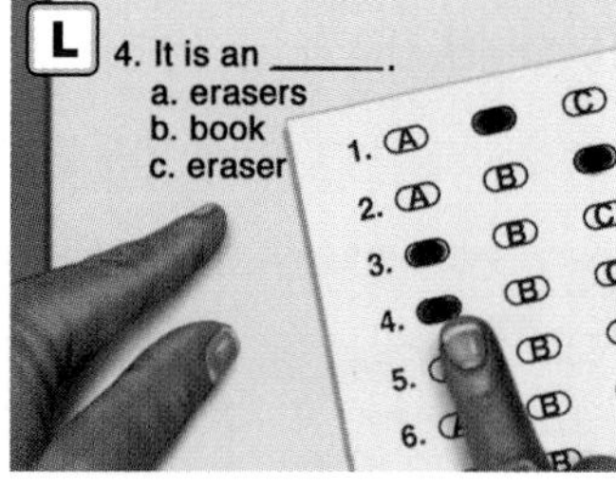


L. **Check** your work.

M. **Erase** the mistake.

N. **Correct** the mistake.

O. **Hand in** your test.

A. **Enter** the room.

B. **Turn on** the lights.

C. **Walk** to class.

D. **Run** to class.

E. **Lift / Pick up** the books.

F. **Carry** the books.

G. **Deliver** the books.

H. **Take** a break.

I. **Eat**.

J. **Drink**.

K. **Buy** a snack.

L. **Have** a conversation.

M. **Go back** to class.

N. **Throw away** trash.

O. **Leave** the room.

P. **Turn off** the lights.

**Grammar Point: present continuous**

Use **be** + verb + *ing*

*He **is** walk**ing**. They **are** enter**ing**.*

*Note: He is runn**ing**. They are leav**ing**.*

**Look at the pictures.**

Describe what is happening.

**A:** *They are entering the room.*

**B:** *He is walking.*

# Everyday Conversation

A. **start** a conversation

B. **make** small talk

C. **compliment** someone

D. **offer** something

E. **thank** someone

F. **apologize**

G. **accept** an apology

H. **invite** someone

I. **accept** an invitation

J. **decline** an invitation

K. **agree**

L. **disagree**

M. **explain** something

N. **check** your understanding

**More vocabulary**

**request:** to ask for something

**accept a compliment:** to thank someone for a compliment

**Pair practice. Follow the directions.**

1. Start a conversation with your partner.
2. Make small talk with your partner.
3. Compliment each other.

## Temperature

1. Fahrenheit
2. Celsius
3. hot
4. warm
5. cool
6. cold
7. freezing
8. degrees

## A Weather Map

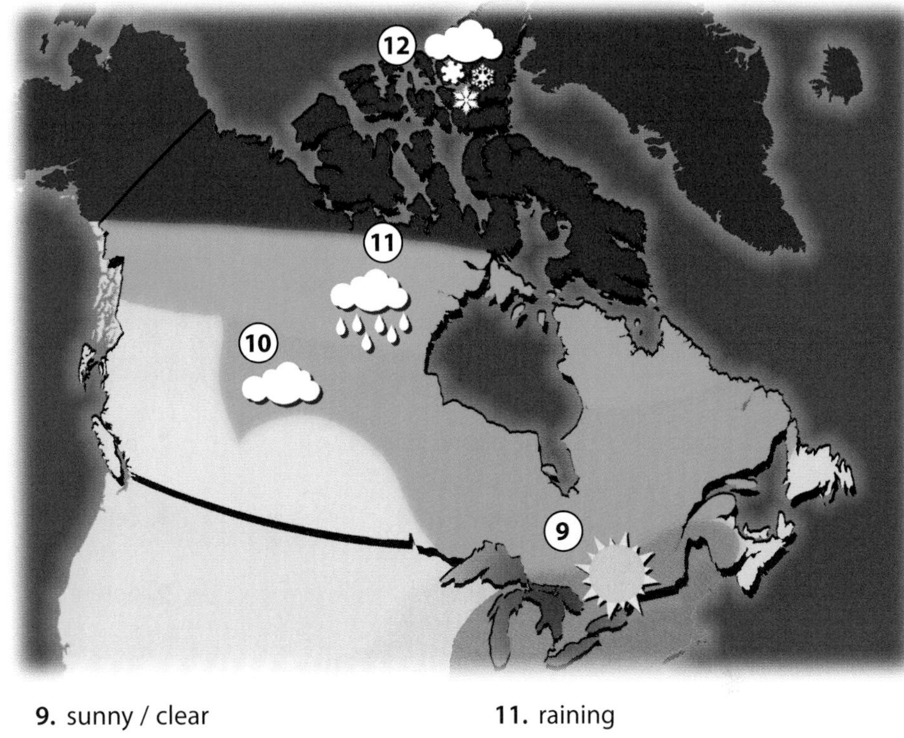

9. sunny / clear
10. cloudy
11. raining
12. snowing

## Weather Conditions

13. heat wave
14. smoggy
15. humid
16. thunderstorm
17. lightning
18. windy
19. dust storm
20. foggy
21. hailstorm
22. icy
23. snowstorm / blizzard

**Ways to talk about the weather**

*It's sunny in Toronto.*
*What's the temperature?*
*It's 30. They're having a heat wave.*

**Pair practice. Make new conversations.**

**A:** *What's the weather like in Yellowknife?*
**B:** *It's raining and it's cold. It's 2 degrees.*

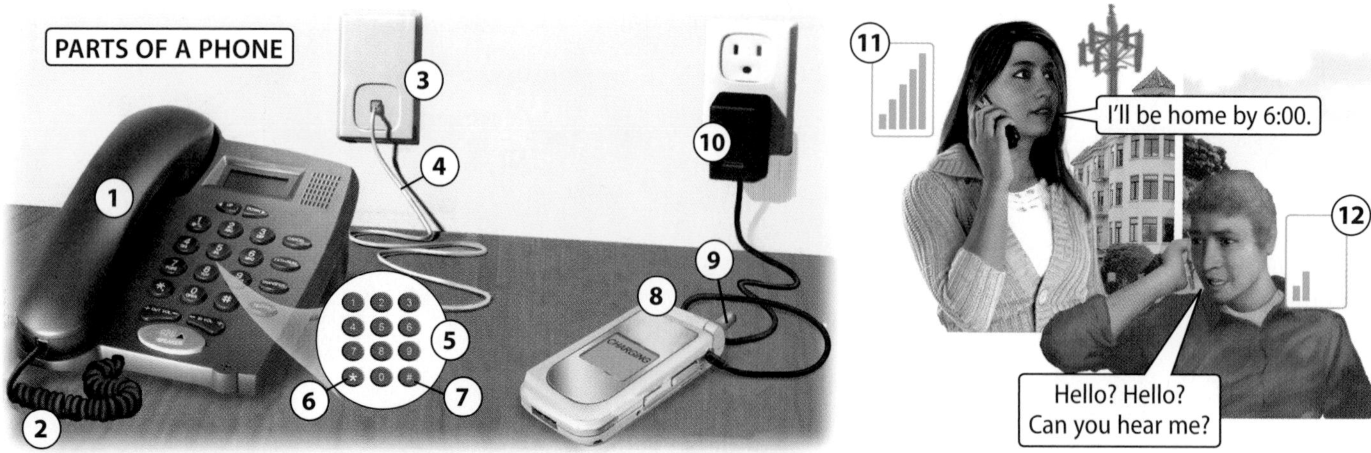


1. receiver / handset
2. cord
3. phone jack
4. phone line
5. key pad
6. star key
7. pound key
8. cellular phone
9. antenna
10. charger
11. strong signal
12. weak signal

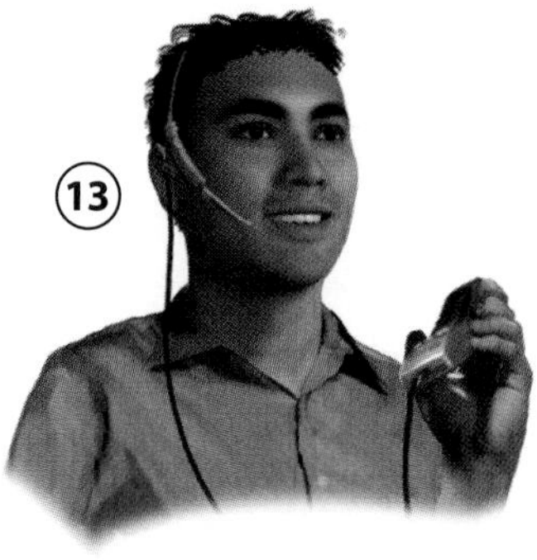


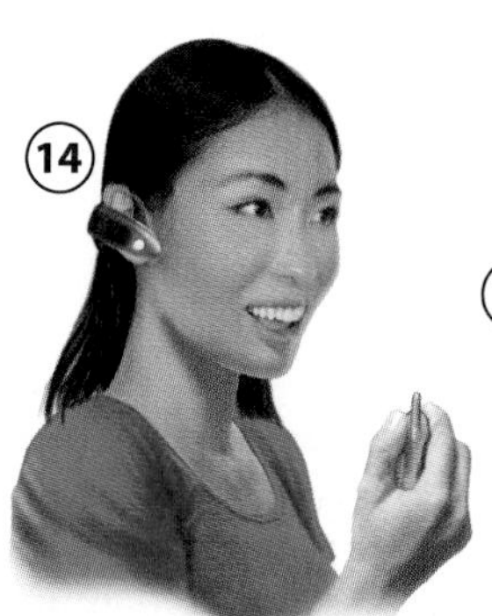


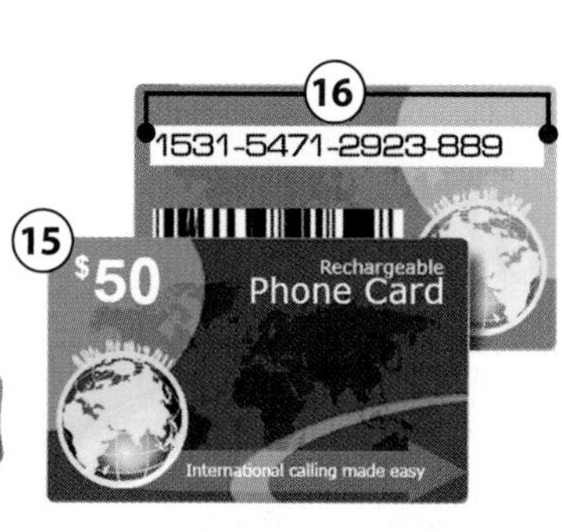


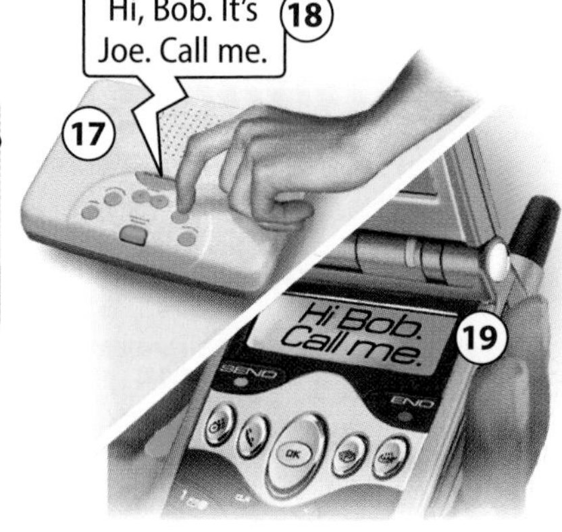


13. headset
14. wireless headset
15. calling card
16. access number
17. answering machine
18. voice message
19. text message

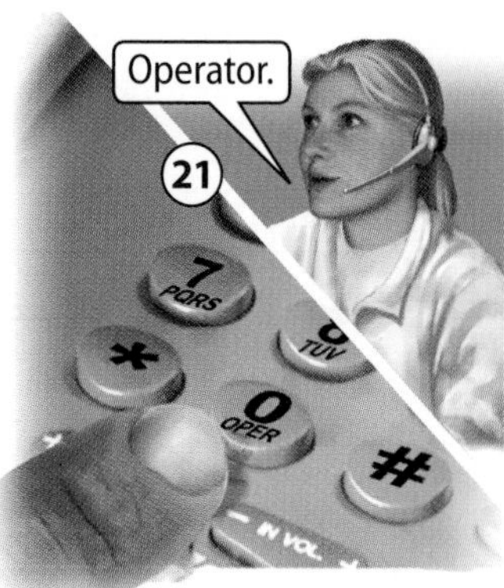

20. Internet phone call
21. operator
22. directory assistance
23. automated phone system

24. cordless phone

25. pay phone

26. TDD*

27. smart phone

## Reading a Phone Bill

28. phone bill
29. area code
30. phone number
31. local call
32. long distance call
33. country code
34. city code
35. international call

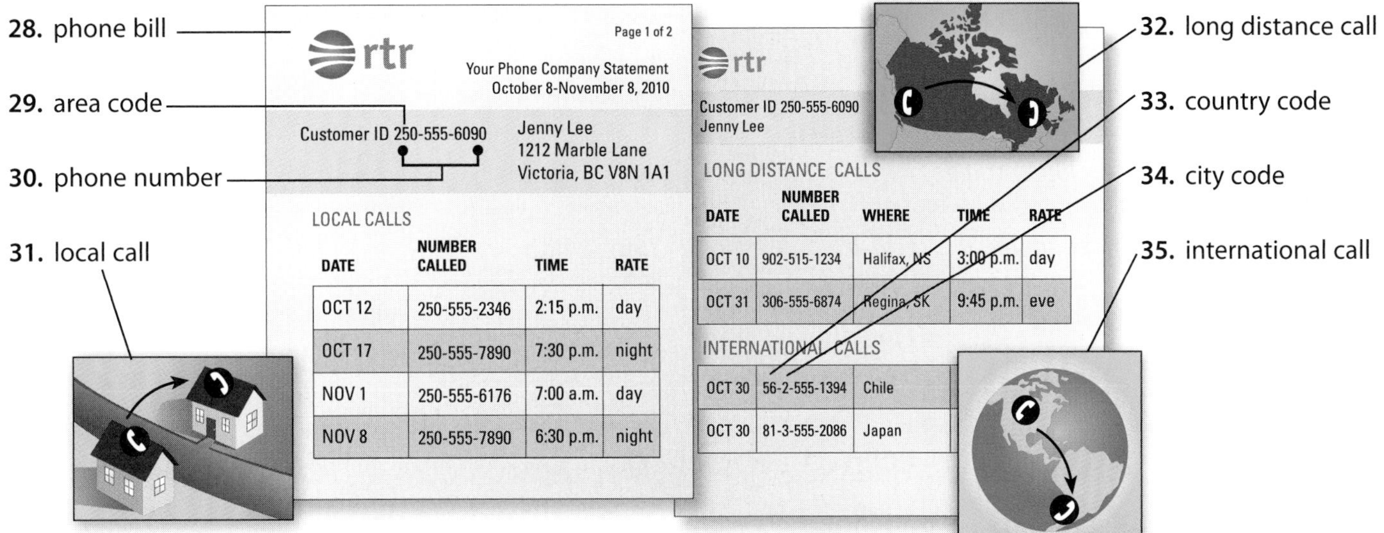

rtr

Page 1 of 2

Your Phone Company Statement
October 8-November 8, 2010

Customer ID 250-555-6090

Jenny Lee
1212 Marble Lane
Victoria, BC V8N 1A1

LOCAL CALLS

| DATE | NUMBER CALLED | TIME | RATE |
|---|---|---|---|
| OCT 12 | 250-555-2346 | 2:15 p.m. | day |
| OCT 17 | 250-555-7890 | 7:30 p.m. | night |
| NOV 1 | 250-555-6176 | 7:00 a.m. | day |
| NOV 8 | 250-555-7890 | 6:30 p.m. | night |

rtr

Customer ID 250-555-6090
Jenny Lee

LONG DISTANCE CALLS

| DATE | NUMBER CALLED | WHERE | TIME | RATE |
|---|---|---|---|---|
| OCT 10 | 902-515-1234 | Halifax, NS | 3:00 p.m. | day |
| OCT 31 | 306-555-6874 | Regina, SK | 9:45 p.m. | eve |

INTERNATIONAL CALLS

| DATE | NUMBER CALLED | WHERE |
|---|---|---|
| OCT 30 | 56-2-555-1394 | Chile |
| OCT 30 | 81-3-555-2086 | Japan |

## Making a Phone Call

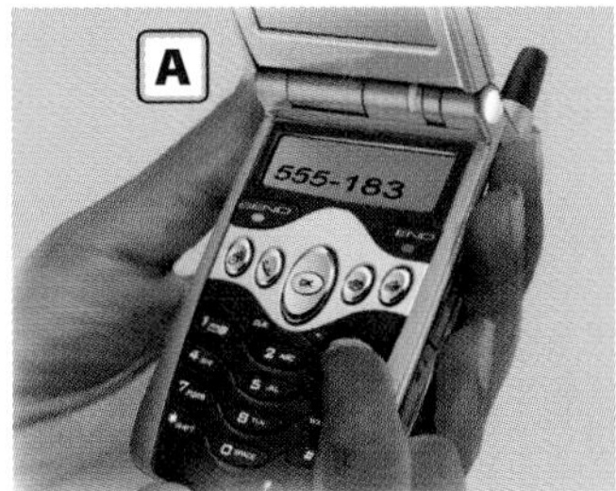

A. **Dial** the phone number.

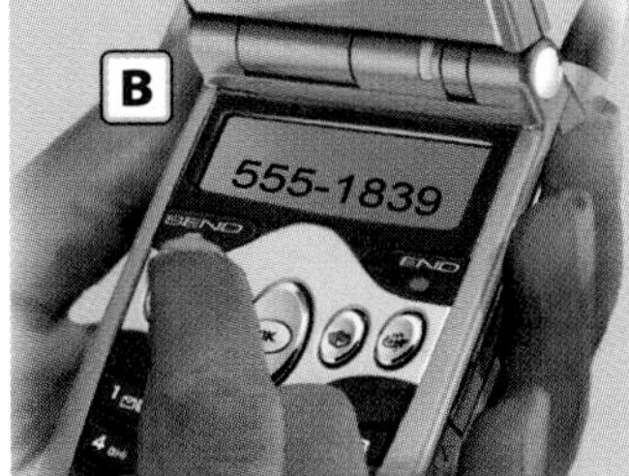

B. **Press** "send".

C. **Talk** on the phone.

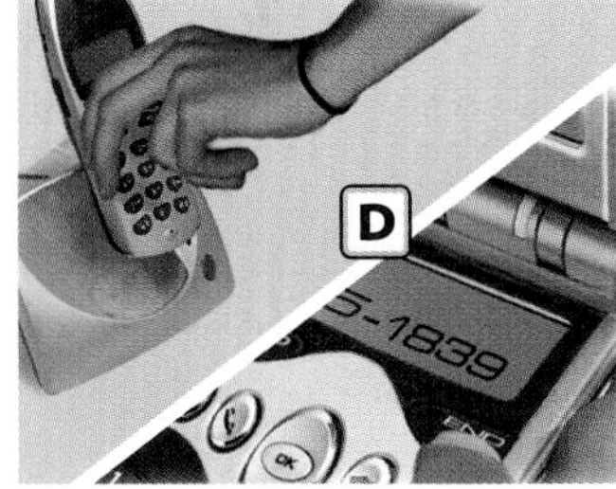
D. **Hang up.** / **Press** "end".

## Making an Emergency Call

E. **Dial** 911.

F. **Give** your name.

G. **State** the emergency.

H. **Stay** on the line.

*telecommunication device for the deaf

# Numbers

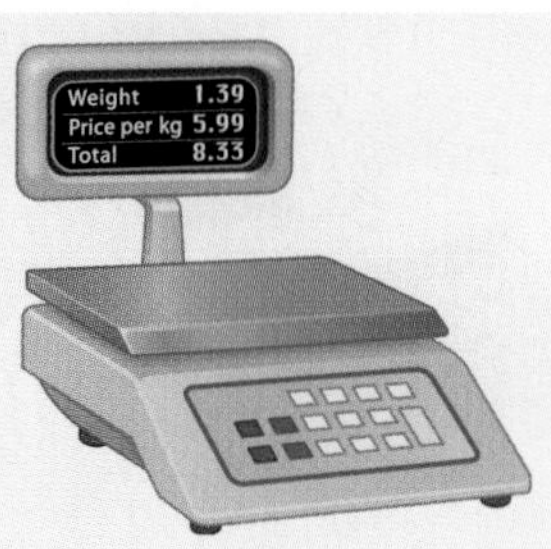

## Cardinal Numbers

| | | | |
|---|---|---|---|
| 0 | zero | 20 | twenty |
| 1 | one | 21 | twenty-one |
| 2 | two | 22 | twenty-two |
| 3 | three | 23 | twenty-three |
| 4 | four | 24 | twenty-four |
| 5 | five | 25 | twenty-five |
| 6 | six | 30 | thirty |
| 7 | seven | 40 | forty |
| 8 | eight | 50 | fifty |
| 9 | nine | 60 | sixty |
| 10 | ten | 70 | seventy |
| 11 | eleven | 80 | eighty |
| 12 | twelve | 90 | ninety |
| 13 | thirteen | 100 | one hundred |
| 14 | fourteen | 101 | one hundred one |
| 15 | fifteen | 1,000 | one thousand |
| 16 | sixteen | 10,000 | ten thousand |
| 17 | seventeen | 100,000 | one hundred thousand |
| 18 | eighteen | 1,000,000 | one million |
| 19 | nineteen | 1,000,000,000 | one billion |

## Ordinal Numbers

| | | | |
|---|---|---|---|
| 1st | first | 16th | sixteenth |
| 2nd | second | 17th | seventeenth |
| 3rd | third | 18th | eighteenth |
| 4th | fourth | 19th | nineteenth |
| 5th | fifth | 20th | twentieth |
| 6th | sixth | 21st | twenty-first |
| 7th | seventh | 30th | thirtieth |
| 8th | eighth | 40th | fortieth |
| 9th | ninth | 50th | fiftieth |
| 10th | tenth | 60th | sixtieth |
| 11th | eleventh | 70th | seventieth |
| 12th | twelfth | 80th | eightieth |
| 13th | thirteenth | 90th | ninetieth |
| 14th | fourteenth | 100th | one hundredth |
| 15th | fifteenth | 1,000th | one thousandth |

## Roman Numerals

| | | |
|---|---|---|
| I = 1 | VII = 7 | XXX = 30 |
| II = 2 | VIII = 8 | XL = 40 |
| III = 3 | IX = 9 | L = 50 |
| IV = 4 | X = 10 | C = 100 |
| V = 5 | XV = 15 | D = 500 |
| VI = 6 | XX = 20 | M = 1,000 |

A. **divide**

B. **calculate**

C. **measure**

D. **convert**

## Fractions and Decimals

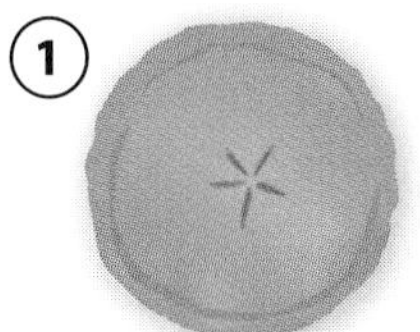

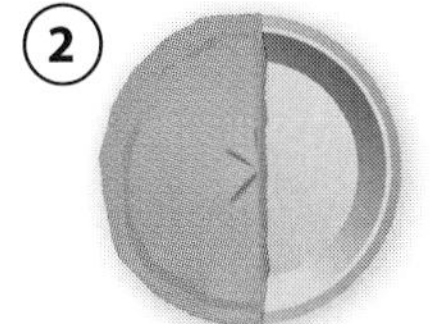

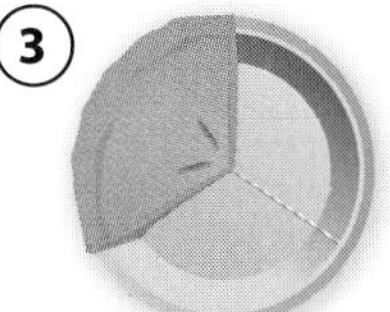

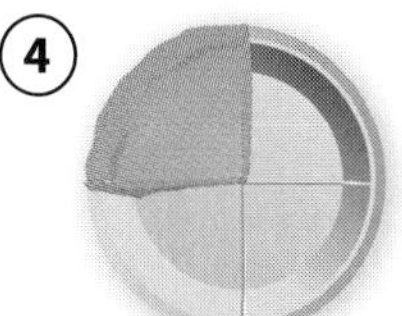

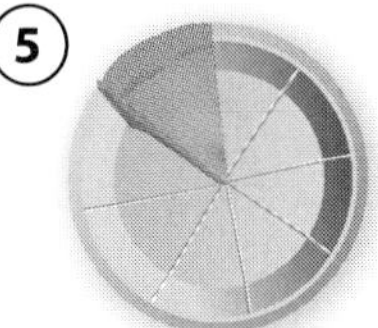

1. one whole
   1 = 1.00
2. one half
   1/2 = .5
3. one third
   1/3 = .333
4. one fourth
   1/4 = .25
5. one eighth
   1/8 = .125

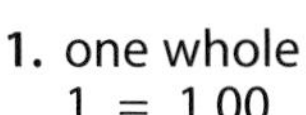

## Percentages

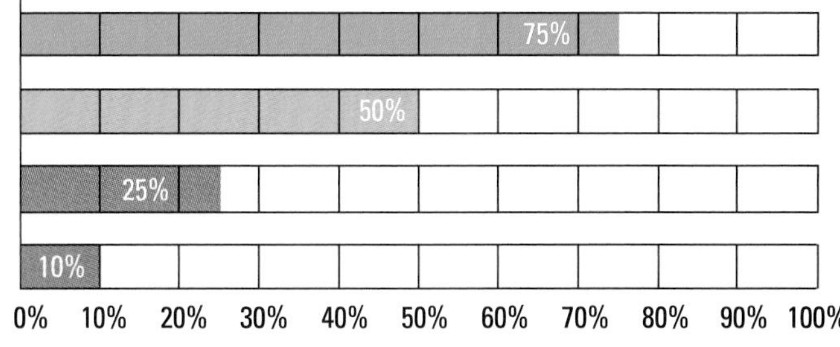


6. calculator
7. decimal point

## Measurement

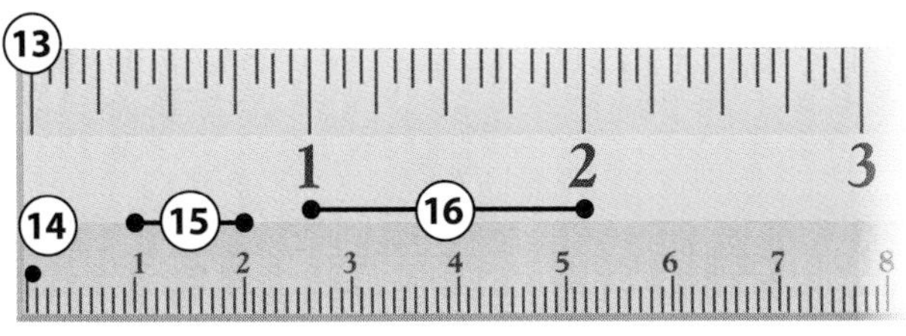


13. ruler
14. millimetre [mm]
15. centimetre [cm]
16. inch [in.]

## Dimensions

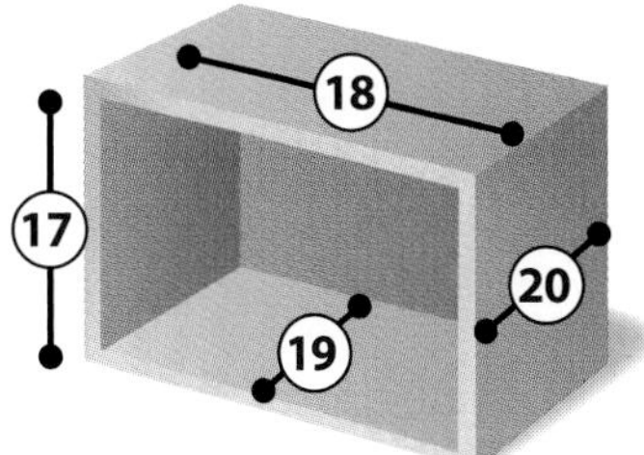

17. height
18. length
19. depth
20. width

### Equivalencies

10 millimetres = 1 centimetre
100 centimetres = 1 metre
1000 metres = 1 kilometre
2.54 centimetres = 1 inch
.91 metres = 1 yard
1.6 kilometres = 1 mile

# Time

## Telling Time

1. hour

2. minutes

3. seconds

4. a.m.

5. p.m.

6. 1:00
one o'clock

7. 1:05
one-oh-five
five after one

8. 1:10
one-ten
ten after one

9. 1:15
one-fifteen
a quarter after one

10. 1:20
one-twenty
twenty after one

11. 1:30
one-thirty
half past one

12. 1:40
one-forty
twenty to two

13. 1:45
one-forty-five
a quarter to two

## Times of Day

14. sunrise

15. morning

16. noon

17. afternoon

18. sunset

19. evening

20. night

21. midnight

**Ways to talk about time**

*I wake up at 6:30 a.m.*
*I wake up at 6:30 in the morning.*
*I wake up at 6:30.*

**Pair practice. Make new conversations.**

**A:** *What time do you wake up on weekdays?*
**B:** *At 6:30 a.m. How about you?*
**A:** *I wake up at 7:00.*

22. early

23. on time

24. late

25. daylight saving time

26. standard time

## Time Zones

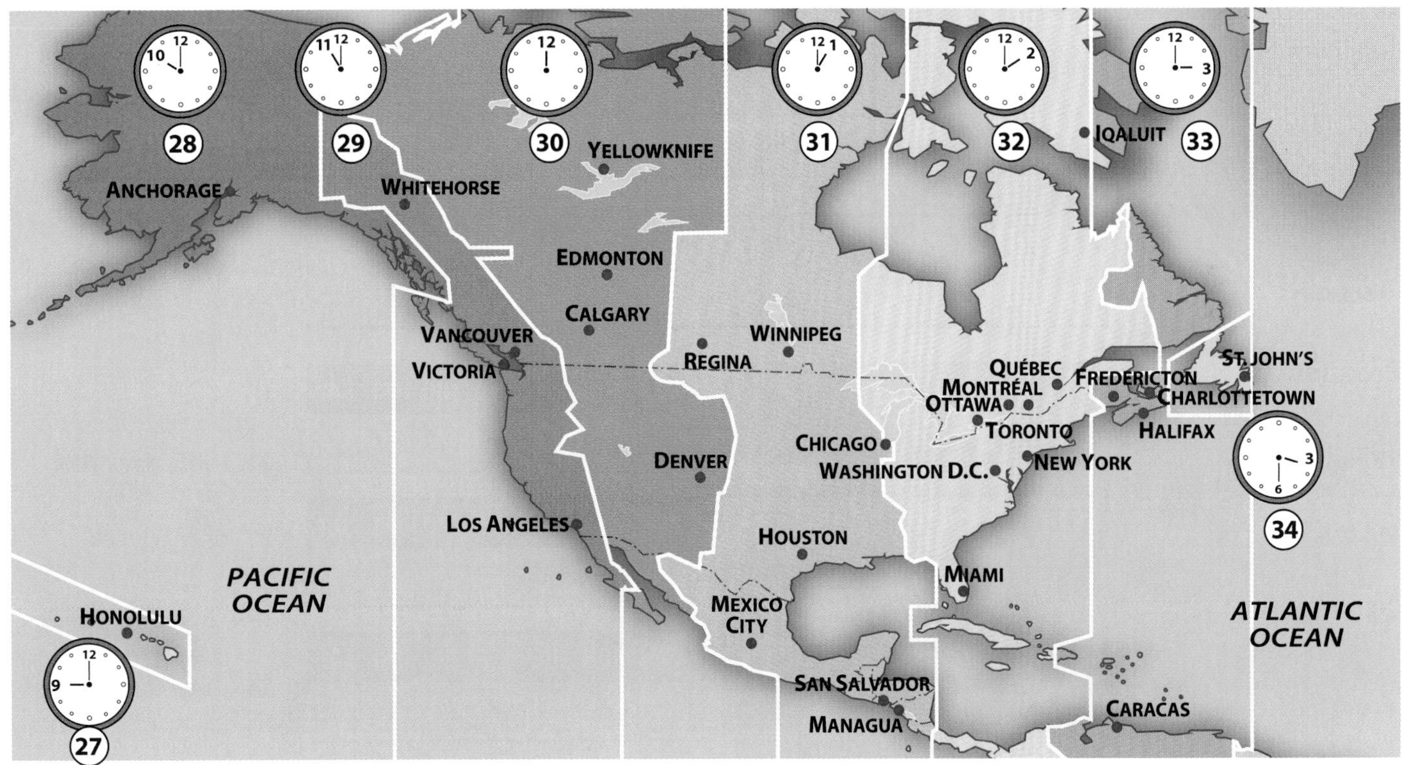


27. Hawaii-Aleutian time
28. Alaska time
29. Pacific time
30. Mountain time
31. Central time
32. Eastern time
33. Atlantic time
34. Newfoundland time

**Ask your classmates. Share the answers.**

1. When do you watch television? study? relax?
2. Do you like to stay up after midnight?
3. Do you like to wake up late on weekends?

**Think about it. Discuss.**

1. What is your favourite time of day? Why?
2. Do you think daylight saving time is a good idea? Why or why not?

# The Calendar

1. date
2. day
3. month
4. year

5. today
6. tomorrow
7. yesterday

## Days of the Week

8. Sunday
9. Monday
10. Tuesday
11. Wednesday
12. Thursday
13. Friday
14. Saturday

**MAY**

| SUN (8) | MON (9) | TUE (10) | WED (11) | THU (12) | FRI (13) | SAT (14) |
|---|---|---|---|---|---|---|
| 1 | 2 | 3 | 4 | 5 | 6 | 7 |
| 8 | 9 | 10 | 11 | 12 | 13 | 14 |
| 15 | 16 | 17 | 18 | 19 | 20 | 21 |
| 22 | 23 | 24 | 25 | 26 | 27 | 28 |
| 29 | 30 | 31 | | | | |

15. week
16. weekdays
17. weekend

## Frequency

18. last week
19. this week
20. next week

| | SUN | MON | TUE | WED | THU | FRI | SAT |
|---|---|---|---|---|---|---|---|
| 21 | ✓ | ✓ | ✓ | ✓ | ✓ | ✓ | ✓ |
| 22 | | ✓ | | | | | |
| 23 | | ✓ | | ✓ | | | |
| 24 | | ✓ | ✓ | | ✓ | | |

21. every day / daily
22. once a week
23. twice a week
24. three times a week

**Ways to say the date**

*Today is* *__May 10th__*. *It's the* *__tenth__*.
*Yesterday was* *__May 9th__*.
*The party is on* *__May 21st__*.

**Pair practice. Make new conversations.**

**A:** *The* *__test__* *is on* *__Friday__*, *__June 14th__*.
**B:** *Did you say* *__Friday__*, *the* *__fourteenth__*?
**A:** *Yes, the* *__fourteenth__*.

**25 JAN**

| SUN | MON | TUE | WED | THU | FRI | SAT |
|---|---|---|---|---|---|---|
| | | | | | 1 | 2 |
| 3 | 4 | 5 | 6 | 7 | 8 | 9 |
| 10 | 11 | 12 | 13 | 14 | 15 | 16 |
| 17 | 18 | 19 | 20 | 21 | 22 | 23 |
| 24/31 | 25 | 26 | 27 | 28 | 29 | 30 |

**26 FEB**

| SUN | MON | TUE | WED | THU | FRI | SAT |
|---|---|---|---|---|---|---|
| | 1 | 2 | 3 | 4 | 5 | 6 |
| 7 | 8 | 9 | 10 | 11 | 12 | 13 |
| 14 | 15 | 16 | 17 | 18 | 19 | 20 |
| 21 | 22 | 23 | 24 | 25 | 26 | 27 |
| 28 | | | | | | |

**27 MAR**

| SUN | MON | TUE | WED | THU | FRI | SAT |
|---|---|---|---|---|---|---|
| | 1 | 2 | 3 | 4 | 5 | 6 |
| 7 | 8 | 9 | 10 | 11 | 12 | 13 |
| 14 | 15 | 16 | 17 | 18 | 19 | 20 |
| 21 | 22 | 23 | 24 | 25 | 26 | 27 |
| 28 | 29 | 30 | 31 | | | |

**28 APR**

| SUN | MON | TUE | WED | THU | FRI | SAT |
|---|---|---|---|---|---|---|
| | | | | 1 | 2 | 3 |
| 4 | 5 | 6 | 7 | 8 | 9 | 10 |
| 11 | 12 | 13 | 14 | 15 | 16 | 17 |
| 18 | 19 | 20 | 21 | 22 | 23 | 24 |
| 25 | 26 | 27 | 28 | 29 | 30 | |

**29 MAY**

| SUN | MON | TUE | WED | THU | FRI | SAT |
|---|---|---|---|---|---|---|
| | | | | | | 1 |
| 2 | 3 | 4 | 5 | 6 | 7 | 8 |
| 9 | 10 | 11 | 12 | 13 | 14 | 15 |
| 16 | 17 | 18 | 19 | 20 | 21 | 22 |
| 23/30 | 24/31 | 25 | 26 | 27 | 28 | 29 |

**30 JUN**

| SUN | MON | TUE | WED | THU | FRI | SAT |
|---|---|---|---|---|---|---|
| | | 1 | 2 | 3 | 4 | 5 |
| 6 | 7 | 8 | 9 | 10 | 11 | 12 |
| 13 | 14 | 15 | 16 | 17 | 18 | 19 |
| 20 | 21 | 22 | 23 | 24 | 25 | 26 |
| 27 | 28 | 29 | 30 | | | |

**31 JUL**

| SUN | MON | TUE | WED | THU | FRI | SAT |
|---|---|---|---|---|---|---|
| | | | | 1 | 2 | 3 |
| 4 | 5 | 6 | 7 | 8 | 9 | 10 |
| 11 | 12 | 13 | 14 | 15 | 16 | 17 |
| 18 | 19 | 20 | 21 | 22 | 23 | 24 |
| 25 | 26 | 27 | 28 | 29 | 30 | 31 |

**32 AUG**

| SUN | MON | TUE | WED | THU | FRI | SAT |
|---|---|---|---|---|---|---|
| 1 | 2 | 3 | 4 | 5 | 6 | 7 |
| 8 | 9 | 10 | 11 | 12 | 13 | 14 |
| 15 | 16 | 17 | 18 | 19 | 20 | 21 |
| 22 | 23 | 24 | 25 | 26 | 27 | 28 |
| 29 | 30 | 31 | | | | |

**33 SEP**

| SUN | MON | TUE | WED | THU | FRI | SAT |
|---|---|---|---|---|---|---|
| | | | 1 | 2 | 3 | 4 |
| 5 | 6 | 7 | 8 | 9 | 10 | 11 |
| 12 | 13 | 14 | 15 | 16 | 17 | 18 |
| 19 | 20 | 21 | 22 | 23 | 24 | 25 |
| 26 | 27 | 28 | 29 | 30 | | |

**34 OCT**

| SUN | MON | TUE | WED | THU | FRI | SAT |
|---|---|---|---|---|---|---|
| | | | | | 1 | 2 |
| 3 | 4 | 5 | 6 | 7 | 8 | 9 |
| 10 | 11 | 12 | 13 | 14 | 15 | 16 |
| 17 | 18 | 19 | 20 | 21 | 22 | 23 |
| 24/31 | 25 | 26 | 27 | 28 | 29 | 30 |

**35 NOV**

| SUN | MON | TUE | WED | THU | FRI | SAT |
|---|---|---|---|---|---|---|
| | 1 | 2 | 3 | 4 | 5 | 6 |
| 7 | 8 | 9 | 10 | 11 | 12 | 13 |
| 14 | 15 | 16 | 17 | 18 | 19 | 20 |
| 21 | 22 | 23 | 24 | 25 | 26 | 27 |
| 28 | 29 | 30 | | | | |

**36 DEC**

| SUN | MON | TUE | WED | THU | FRI | SAT |
|---|---|---|---|---|---|---|
| | | | 1 | 2 | 3 | 4 |
| 5 | 6 | 7 | 8 | 9 | 10 | 11 |
| 12 | 13 | 14 | 15 | 16 | 17 | 18 |
| 19 | 20 | 21 | 22 | 23 | 24 | 25 |
| 26 | 27 | 28 | 29 | 30 | 31 | |

## Months of the Year

25. January
26. February
27. March
28. April
29. May
30. June
31. July
32. August
33. September
34. October
35. November
36. December

37

38

39

40

## Seasons

37. spring
38. summer
39. fall / autumn
40. winter

**Dictate to your partner. Take turns.**

**A:** *Write Monday.*
**B:** *Is it spelled M-o-n-d-a-y?*
**A:** *Yes, that's right.*

**Ask your classmates. Share the answers.**

1. What is your favourite day of the week? Why?
2. What is your busiest day of the week? Why?
3. What is your favourite season of the year? Why?

# Calendar Events

1. birthday

2. wedding

3. anniversary

4. appointment

5. parent-teacher conference

6. vacation

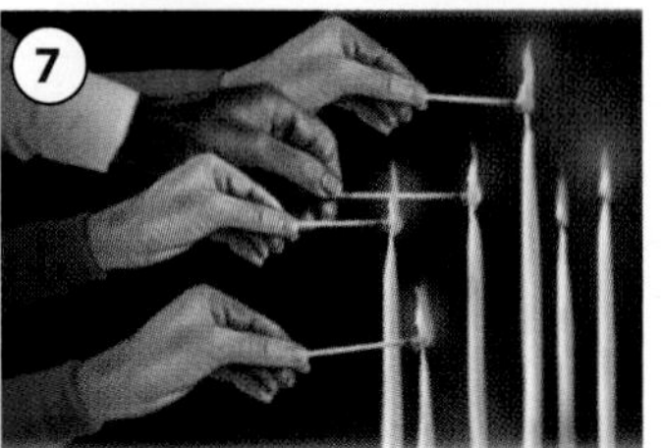
7. religious holiday

8. legal holiday

## Statutory Holidays

9. New Year's Day
10. Good Friday
11. Victoria Day
12. Canada Day
13. Labour Day
14. Thanksgiving
15. Remembrance Day
16. Christmas Day
17. Boxing Day

**Pair practice. Make new conversations.**

**A:** *When is your birthday?*
**B:** *It's on January 31st. How about you?*
**A:** *It's on December 22nd.*

**Ask your classmates. Share the answers.**

1. What are the legal holidays in your native country?
2. When is Labour Day in your native country?
3. When do you celebrate the New Year in your native country?

1. **little** hand
2. **big** hand

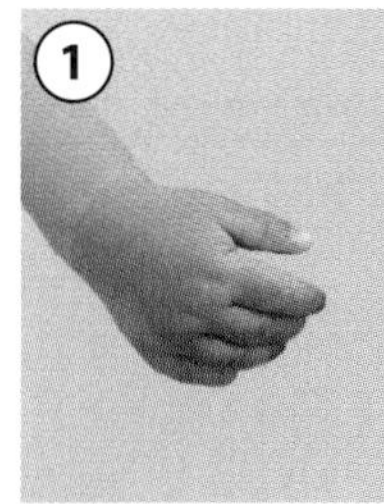

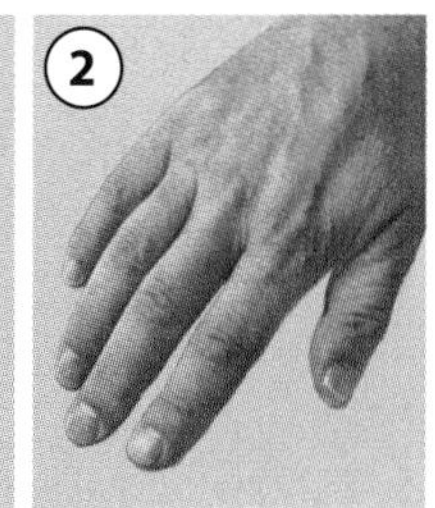

13. **heavy** box
14. **light** box

3. **fast** driver
4. **slow** driver

15. **same** colour
16. **different** colours

5. **hard** chair
6. **soft** chair

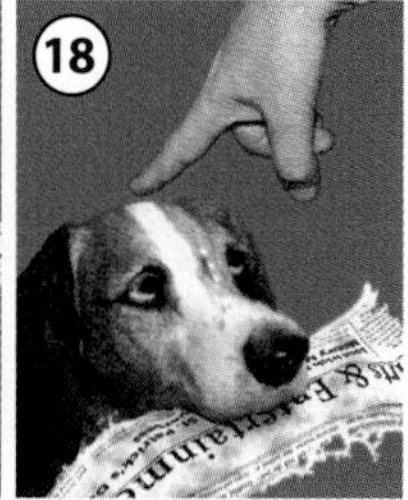


17. **good** dog
18. **bad** dog

7. **thick** book
8. **thin** book

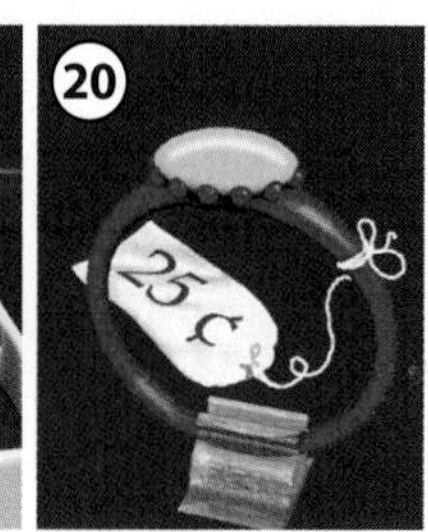


19. **expensive** ring
20. **cheap** ring

9. **full** glass
10. **empty** glass

21. **beautiful** view
22. **ugly** view

11. **noisy** children / **loud** children
12. **quiet** children

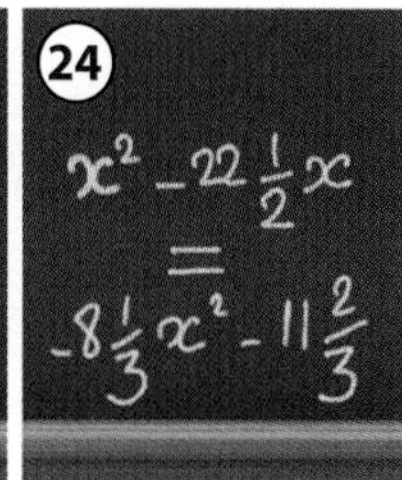


23. **easy** problem
24. **difficult** problem / **hard** problem

**Ask your classmates. Share the answers.**

1. Are you a slow driver or a fast driver?
2. Do you prefer a hard bed or a soft bed?
3. Do you like loud parties or quiet parties?

**Use the new words.**

Look at pages 150–151. Describe the things you see.

**A:** *<u>The street</u> is <u>hard</u>.*

**B:** *<u>The truck</u> is <u>heavy</u>.*

# Colours

**Basic Colours**

1. red
2. yellow
3. blue
4. orange
5. green
6. purple
7. pink
8. violet
9. turquoise
10. dark blue
11. light blue
12. bright blue

**Neutral Colours**

13. black
14. white
15. grey
16. cream / ivory
17. brown
18. beige / tan

**Ask your classmates. Share the answers.**

1. What colours are you wearing today?
2. What colours do you like?
3. Is there a colour you don't like? What is it?

**Use the new words. Look at pages 86–87.**
Take turns naming the colours you see.

**A:** *His shirt is blue.*
**B:** *Her shoes are white.*

1. The yellow sweaters are **on the left**.
2. The purple sweaters are **in the middle**.
3. The brown sweaters are **on the right**.
4. The red sweaters are **above** the blue sweaters.
5. The blue sweaters are **below** the red sweaters.
6. The turquoise sweater is **in** the box.
7. The white sweater is **in front of** the black sweater.
8. The black sweater is **behind** the white sweater.
9. The orange sweater is **on** the grey sweater.
10. The violet sweater is **next to** the grey sweater.
11. The grey sweater is **under** the orange sweater.
12. The green sweater is **between** the pink sweaters.

**More vocabulary**

**near:** in the same area
**far from:** not near

**Role play. Make new conversations.**

**A:** *Excuse me. Where are the red sweaters?*
**B:** *They're on the left, above the blue sweaters.*
**A:** *Thanks very much.*

# Money

## Coins

1. $.01 = 1¢
   a penny / 1 cent
2. $.05 = 5¢
   a nickel / 5 cents
3. $.10 = 10¢
   a dime / 10 cents
4. $.25 = 25¢
   a quarter / 25 cents
5. $1.00
   a loonie / a dollar
6. $2.00
   a toonie / two dollars

## Bills

7. $5.00
   five dollars

8. $10.00
   ten dollars

9. $20.00
   twenty dollars

10. $50.00
    fifty dollars

11. $100.00
    one hundred dollars

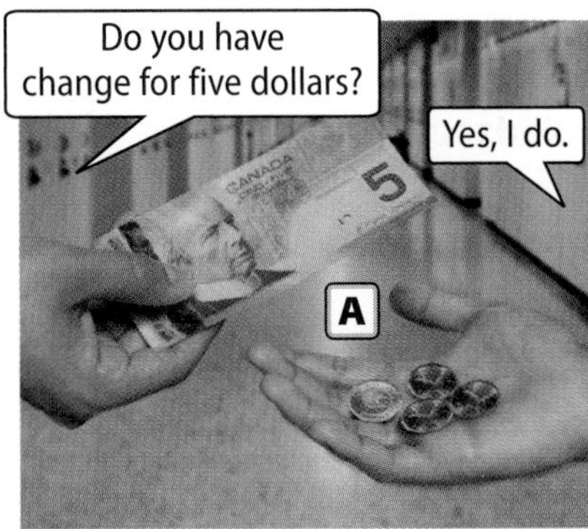


A. **Get** change.

B. **Borrow** money.

C. **Lend** money.

D. **Pay back** the money.

**Pair practice. Make new conversations.**

**A:** *Do you have change for <u>a dollar</u>?*
**B:** *Sure. How about <u>two quarters</u> and <u>five dimes</u>?*
**A:** *Perfect!*

**Think about it. Discuss.**

1. Is it a good idea to lend money to a friend? Why or why not?
2. Is it better to carry a dollar or four quarters? Why?

## Ways to Pay

A. **pay** cash

B. **use** a credit card

C. **use** a debit card

D. **write** a (personal) cheque

E. **use** a gift card

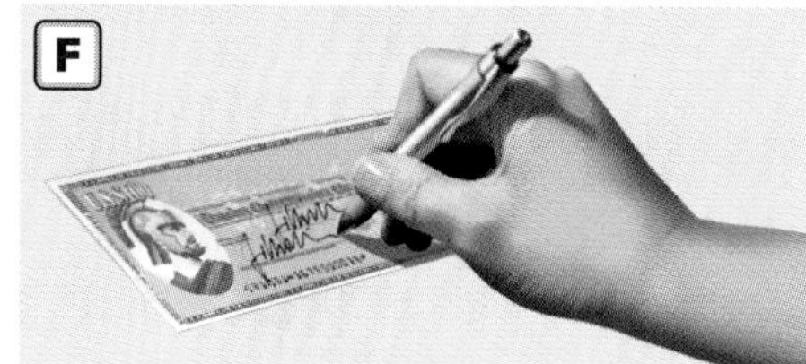

F. **cash** a traveller's cheque

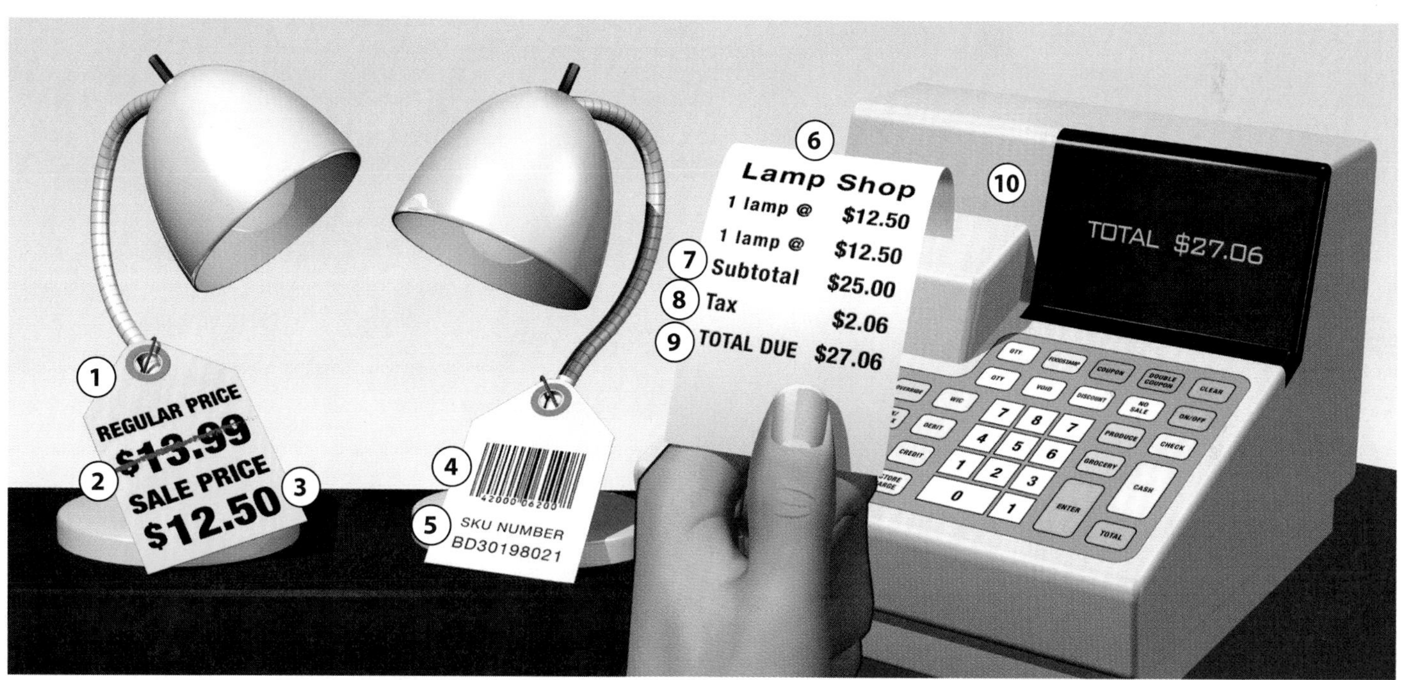


1. price tag
2. regular price
3. sale price
4. bar code
5. SKU number
6. receipt
7. price / cost
8. sales tax
9. total
10. cash register

G. **buy / pay for**

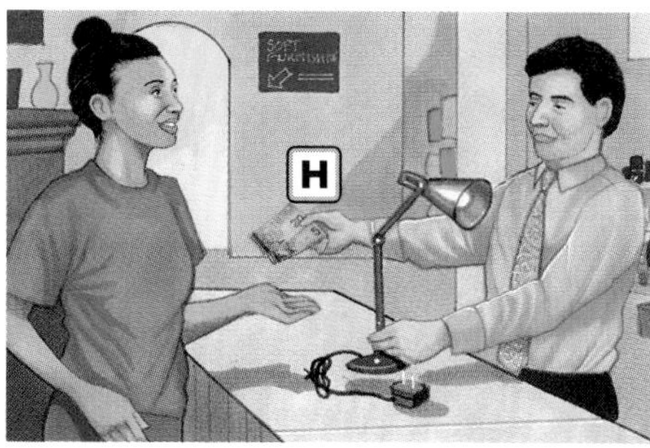

H. **return**

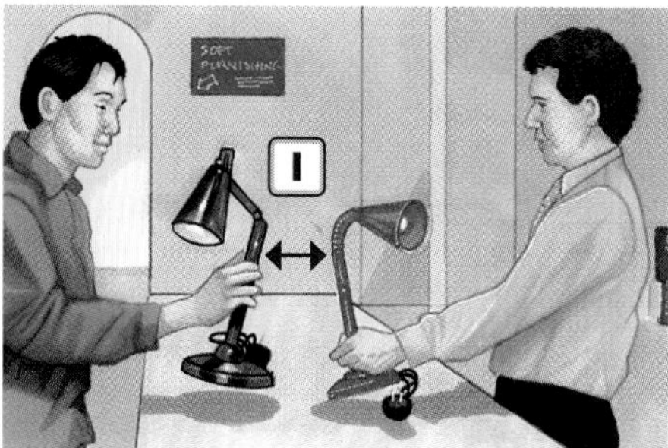

I. **exchange**

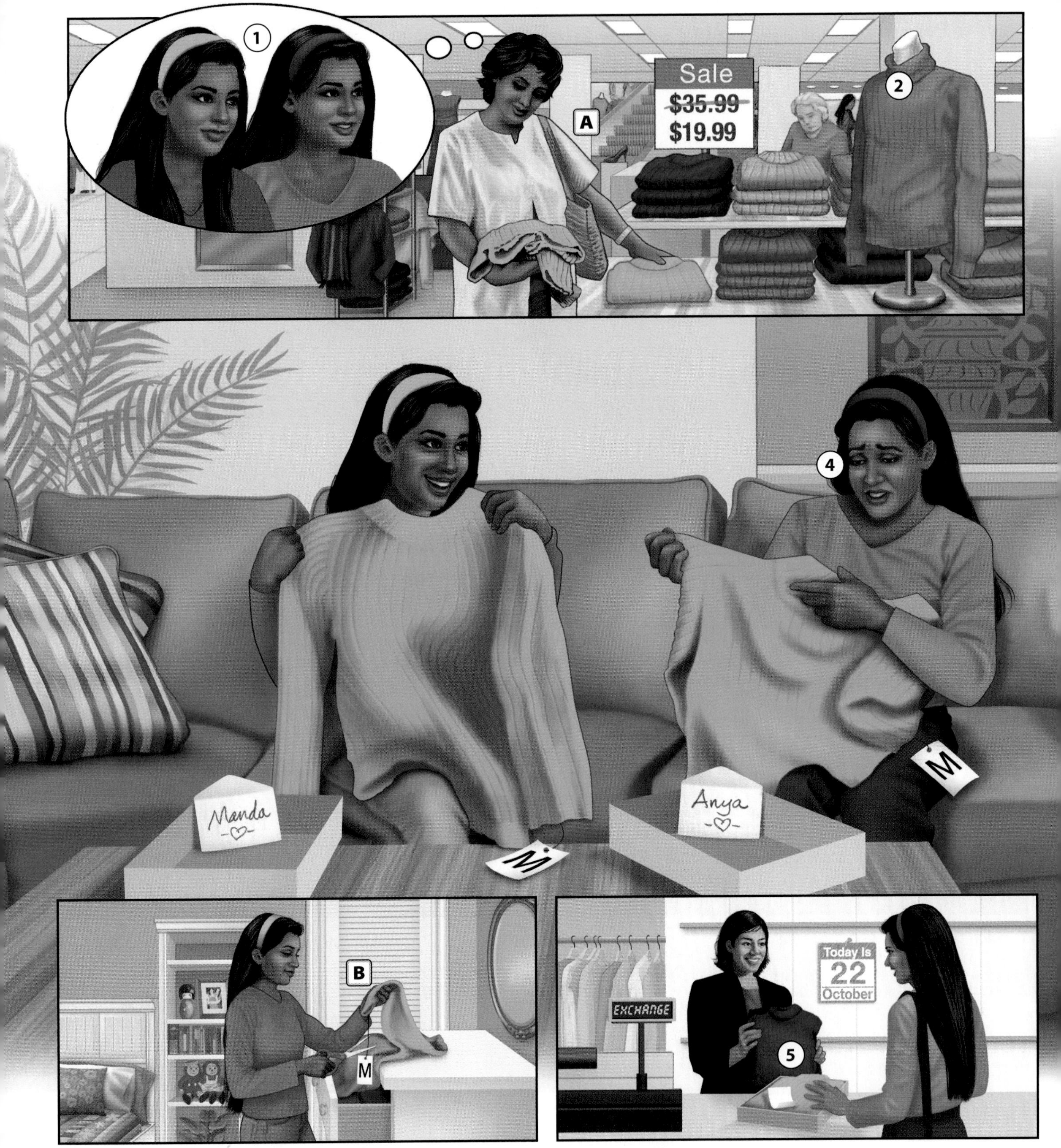

# Same and Different

1. twins
2. sweater
3. matching
4. disappointed
5. navy blue
6. happy

A. **shop**

B. **keep**

**Look at the pictures.**
**What do you see?**

**Answer the questions.**

1. Who is the woman shopping for?
2. Does she buy matching sweaters or different sweaters?
3. How does Anya feel about her green sweater? What does she do?
4. What does Manda do with her sweater?

 **Read the story.**

## Same and Different

Mrs. Kumar likes to shop for her twins. Today she's looking at sweaters. There are many different colours on sale. Mrs. Kumar chooses two matching green sweaters.

The next day, Manda and Anya open their gifts. Manda likes the green sweater, but Anya is disappointed. Mrs. Kumar understands the problem. Anya wants to be different.

Manda keeps her sweater. But Anya goes to the store. She exchanges her green sweater for a navy blue sweater. It's an easy answer to Anya's problem. Now the twins can be warm, happy, and different.

**Think about it.**

1. Do you like to shop for other people? Why or why not?
2. Imagine you are Anya. Would you keep the sweater or exchange it? Why?

1. man
2. woman
3. women
4. men
5. senior citizen

**Listen and point. Take turns.**

**A:** *Point to a woman.*
**B:** *Point to a senior citizen.*
**A:** *Point to an infant.*

**Dictate to your partner. Take turns.**

**A:** *Write woman.*
**B:** *Is that spelled w-o-m-a-n?*
**A:** *Yes, that's right, woman.*

**Ways to talk about age**

1 month – 3 months old = **infant**
18 months – 3 years old = **toddler**
3 years old – 12 years old = **child**
13 – 19 years old = **teenager**
18+ years old = **adult**
65+ years old = **senior citizen**

**Pair practice. Make new conversations.**

**A:** *How old is Sandra?*
**B:** *She's thirteen years old.*
**A:** *Wow, she's a teenager now!*

# Describing People

## Age

1. young
2. middle-aged
3. elderly

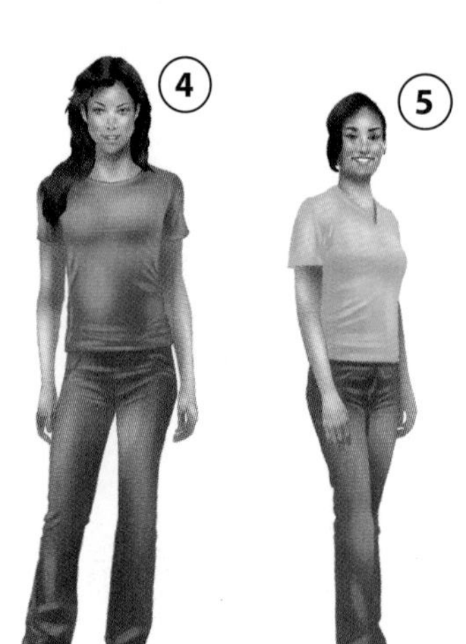

## Height

4. tall
5. average height
6. short

## Weight

7. heavy / fat
8. average weight
9. thin / slender

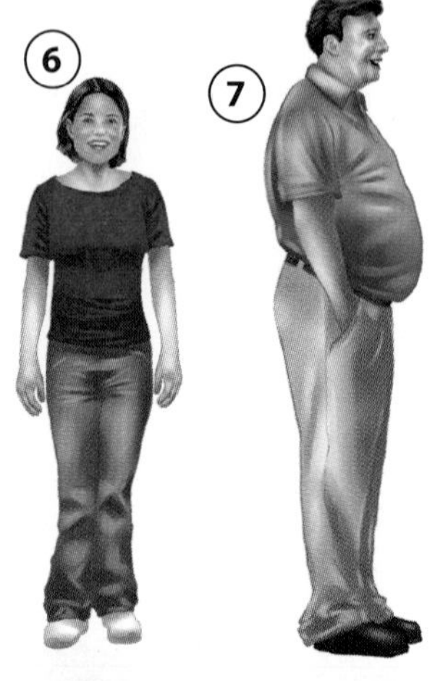

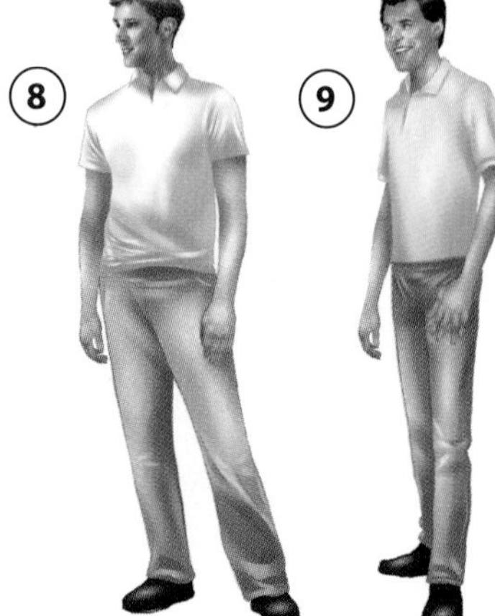

## Disabilities

10. physically challenged
11. visually impaired / blind
12. hearing-impaired / deaf

## Appearance

13. attractive 14. cute

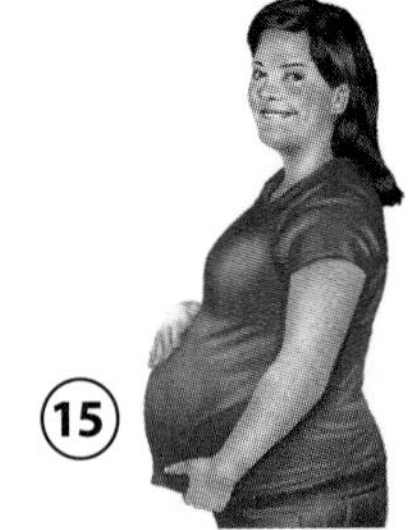

15. pregnant

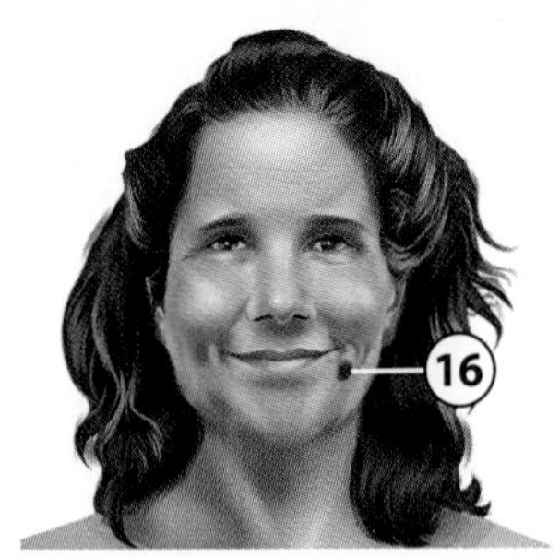

16. mole

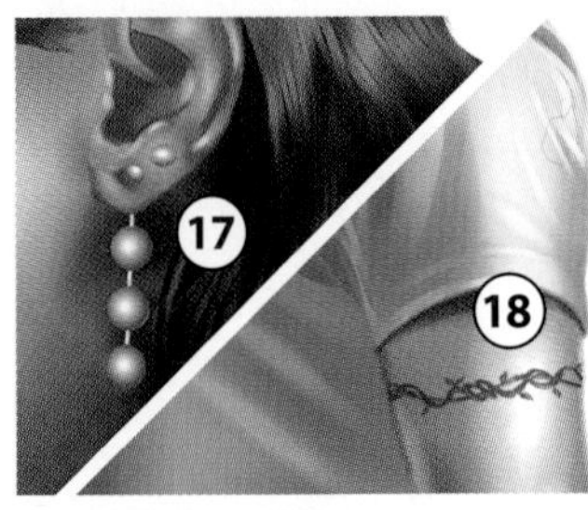

17. pierced ear

18. tattoo

**Ways to describe people**

*He's a heavy, young man.*
*She's a pregnant woman with a mole.*
*He's visually impaired.*

**Use the new words. Look at pages 2–3.**
Describe the people and point. Take turns.

**A:** *He's a tall, thin, middle-aged man.*
**B:** *She's a short, average-weight young woman.*

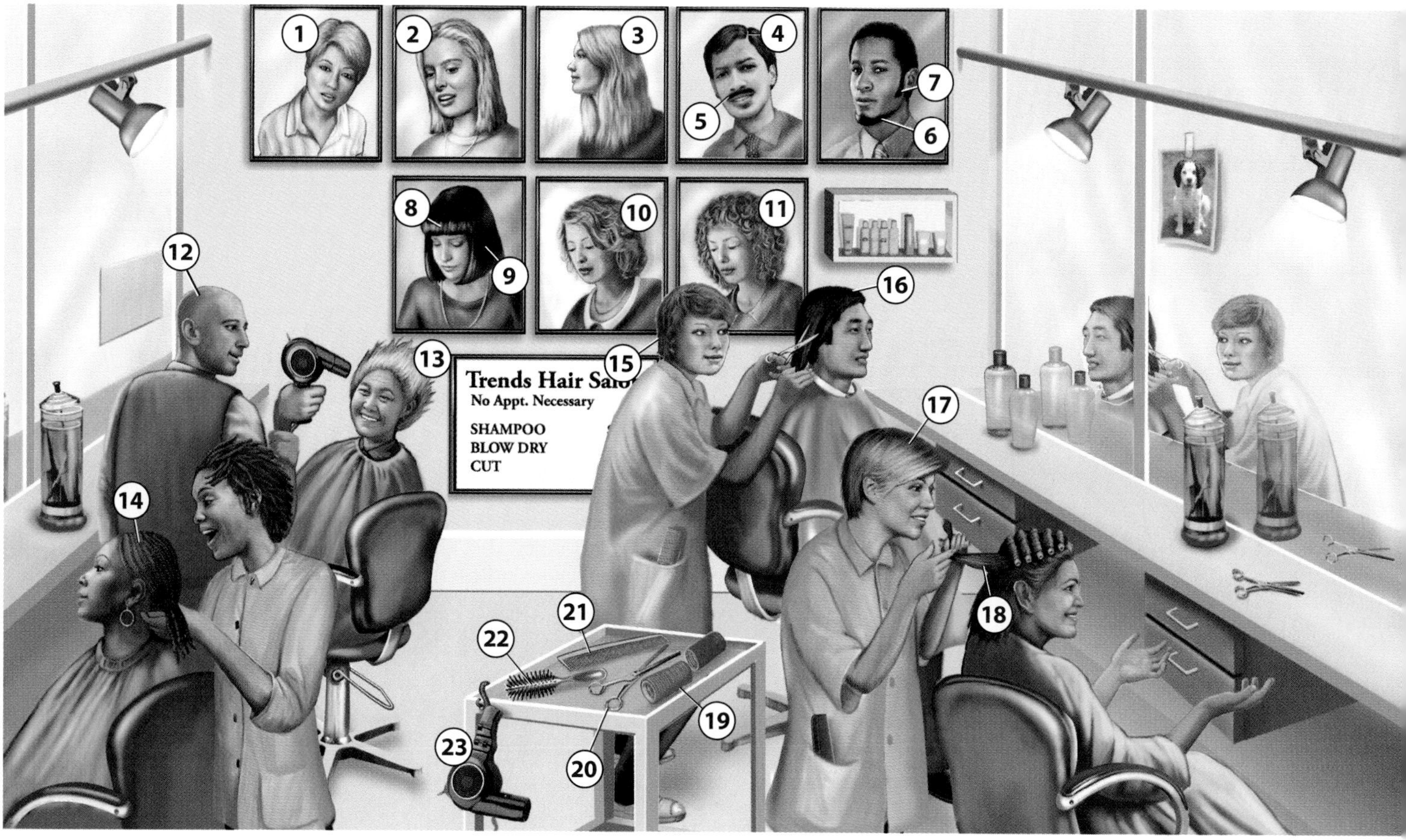

1. short hair
2. shoulder-length hair
3. long hair
4. part
5. moustache
6. beard
7. sideburns
8. bangs
9. straight hair
10. wavy hair
11. curly hair
12. bald
13. grey hair
14. cornrows
15. red hair
16. black hair
17. blond hair
18. brown hair
19. rollers
20. scissors
21. comb
22. brush
23. blow dryer

## Style Hair

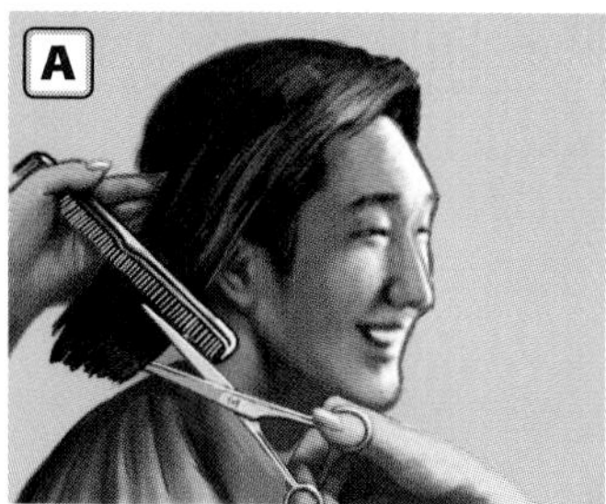

A. **cut** hair

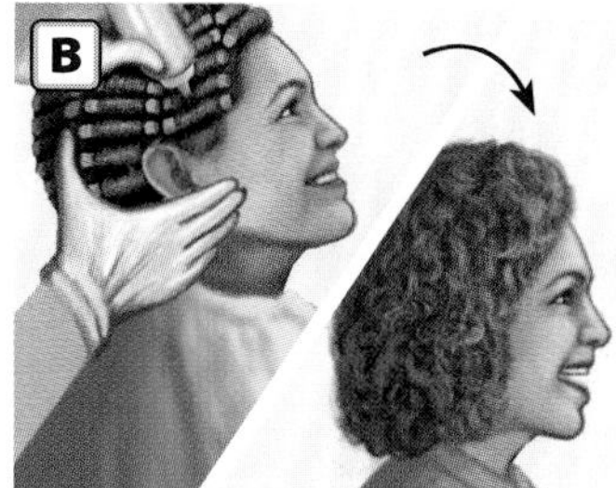

B. **perm** hair

C. **set** hair

D. **colour** hair / **dye** hair

**Ways to talk about hair**

Describe hair in this order: length, style, and then colour.
*She has long, straight, brown hair.*

**Role play. Talk to a stylist.**

**A:** *I need a new hairstyle.*
**B:** *How about short and straight?*
**A:** *Great. Do you think I should dye it?*

1. grandmother
2. grandfather
3. mother
4. father
5. sister
6. brother
7. aunt
8. uncle
9. cousin

10. mother-in-law
11. father-in-law
12. wife
13. husband
14. daughter
15. son
16. sister-in-law
17. brother-in-law
18. niece
19. nephew

**More vocabulary**

Tim is Min and Lu's **grandson**.
Lily and Emily are Min and Lu's **granddaughters**.
Alex is Min's youngest **grandchild**.

Ana is Tito's **wife**.
Ana is Eva and Sam's **daughter-in-law**.
Carlos is Eva and Sam's **son-in-law**.

20
21
22
23
Carol, Bruce, and Lisa
Lisa, Age 4

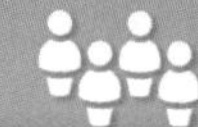

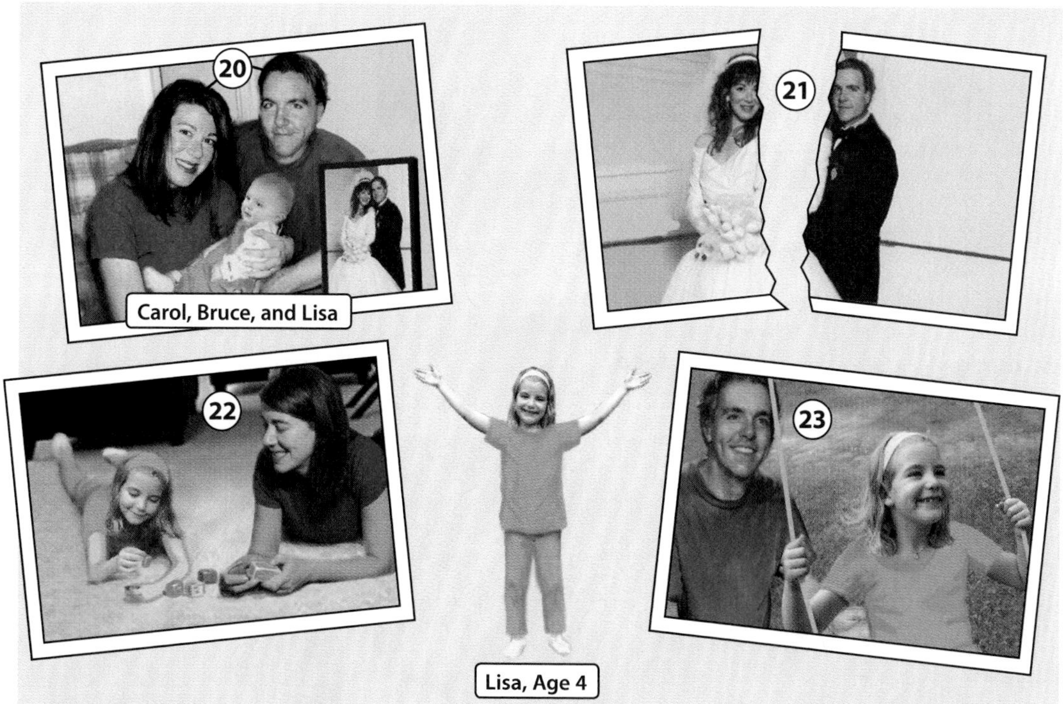

20. married couple

21. divorced couple

22. single mother

23. single father

## Lisa Green's Family

24
25
26
27
28
29
30
Lisa, Age 7
Rick
Carol
Bruce
Sue
Lisa, Today
Mary
David
Kim
Bill

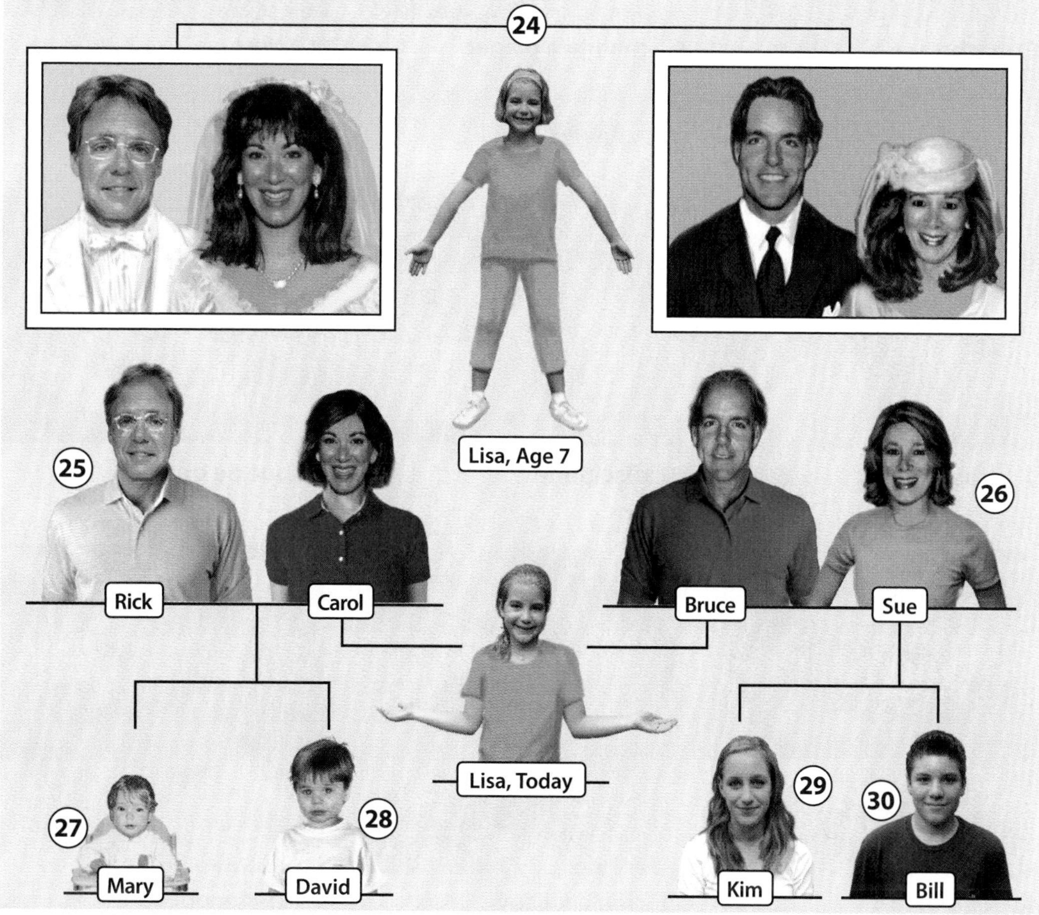

24. remarried

25. stepfather

26. stepmother

27. half sister

28. half brother

29. stepsister

30. stepbrother

**More vocabulary**

Bruce is Carol's **former husband** or **ex-husband.**
Carol is Bruce's **former wife** or **ex-wife.**
Lisa is the **stepdaughter** of both Rick and Sue.

**Look at the pictures.**
Name the people.

**A:** *Who is Lisa's half sister?*
**B:** *Mary is. Who is Lisa's stepsister?*

# Child Care and Parenting

A. **hold**

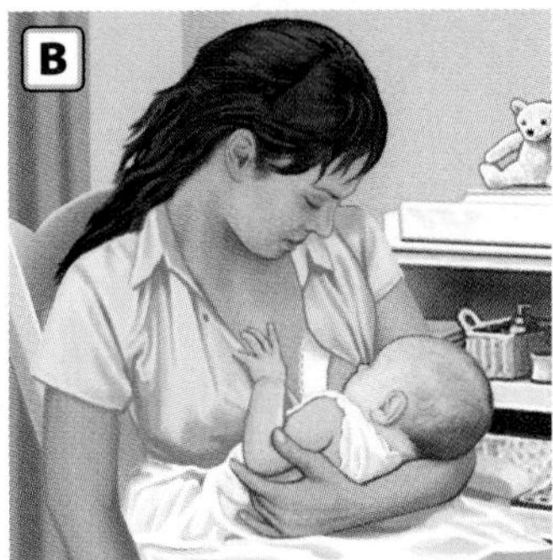

B. **nurse**

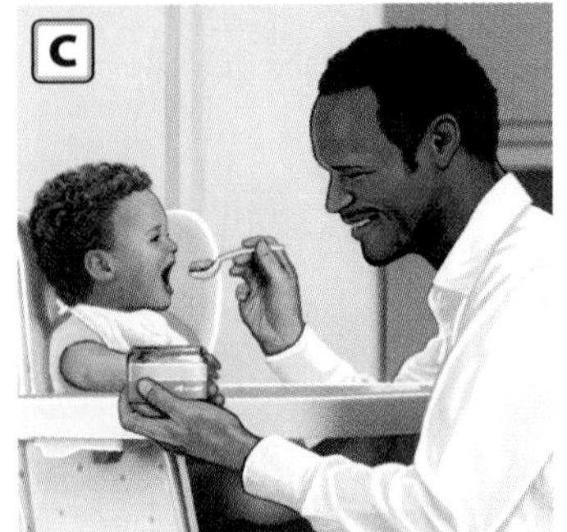

C. **feed**

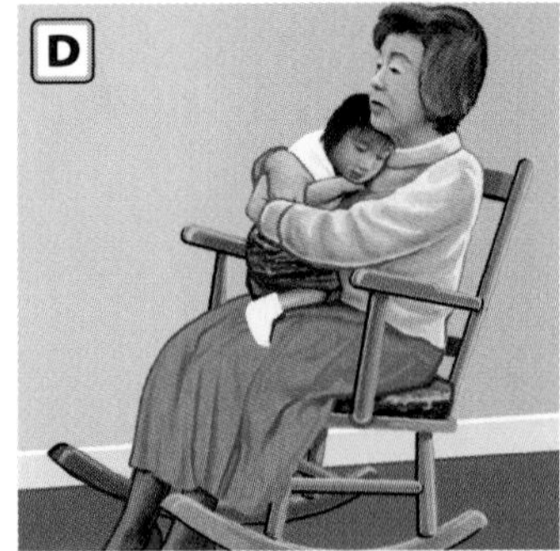

D. **rock**

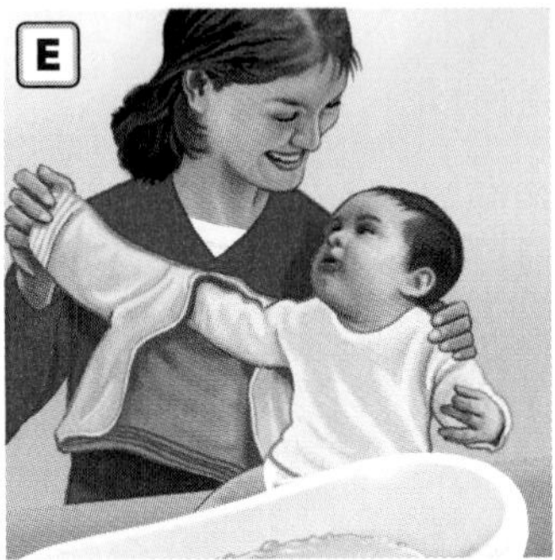

E. **undress**

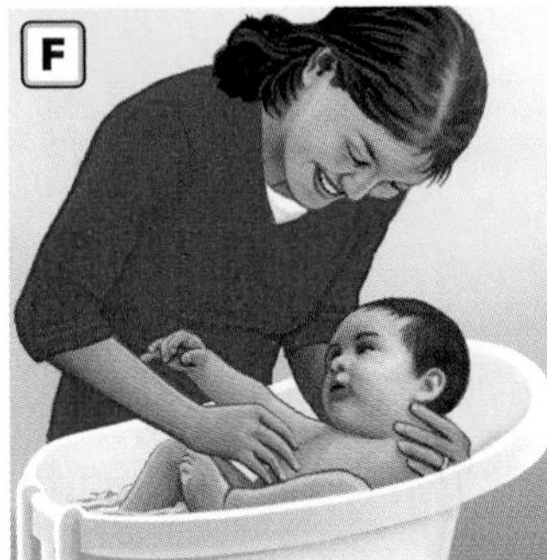

F. **bathe**

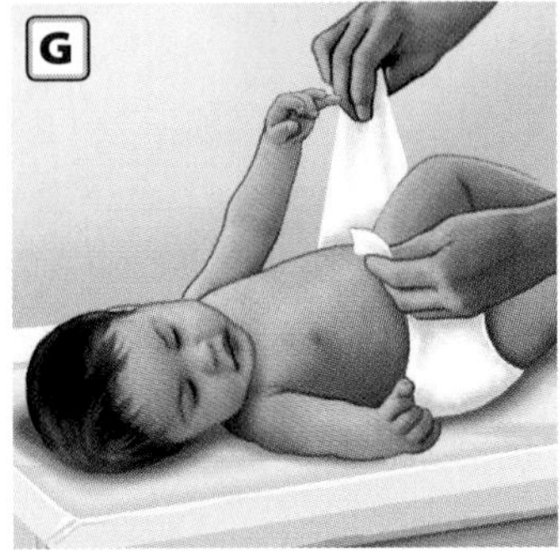

G. **change** a diaper

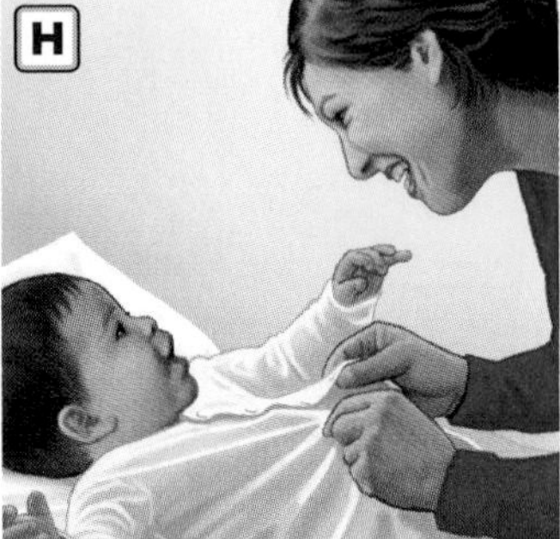

H. **dress**

I. **comfort**

J. **praise**

K. **discipline**

L. **buckle up**

M. **play** with

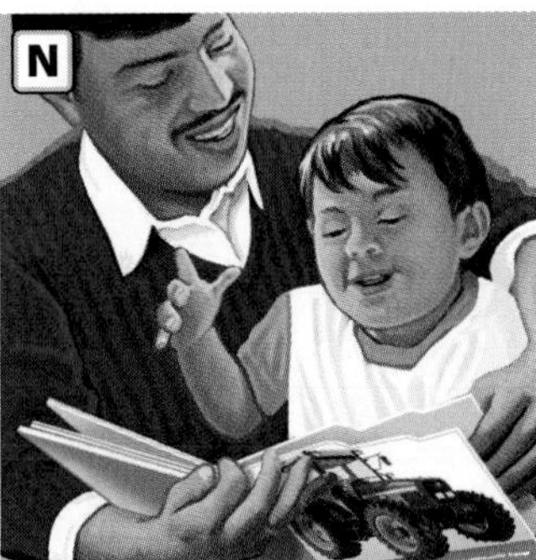

N. **read** to

O. **sing** a lullaby

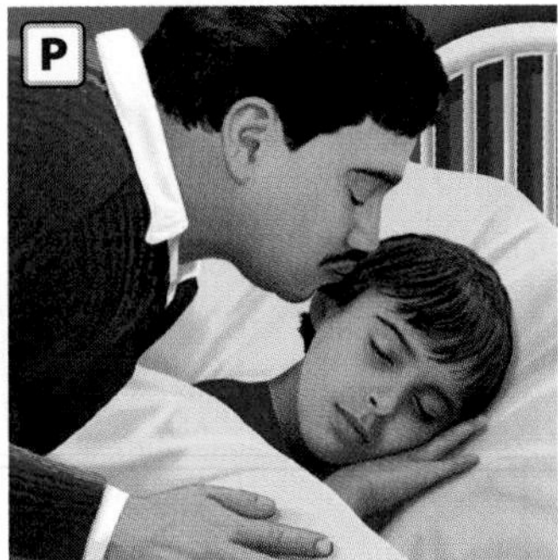

P. **kiss** good night

**Look at the pictures.**
Describe what is happening.

A: *She's changing her baby's diaper.*
B: *He's kissing his son good night.*

**Ask your classmates. Share the answers.**

1. Do you like to take care of children?
2. Do you prefer to read to children or play with them?
3. Can you sing a lullaby? Which one?

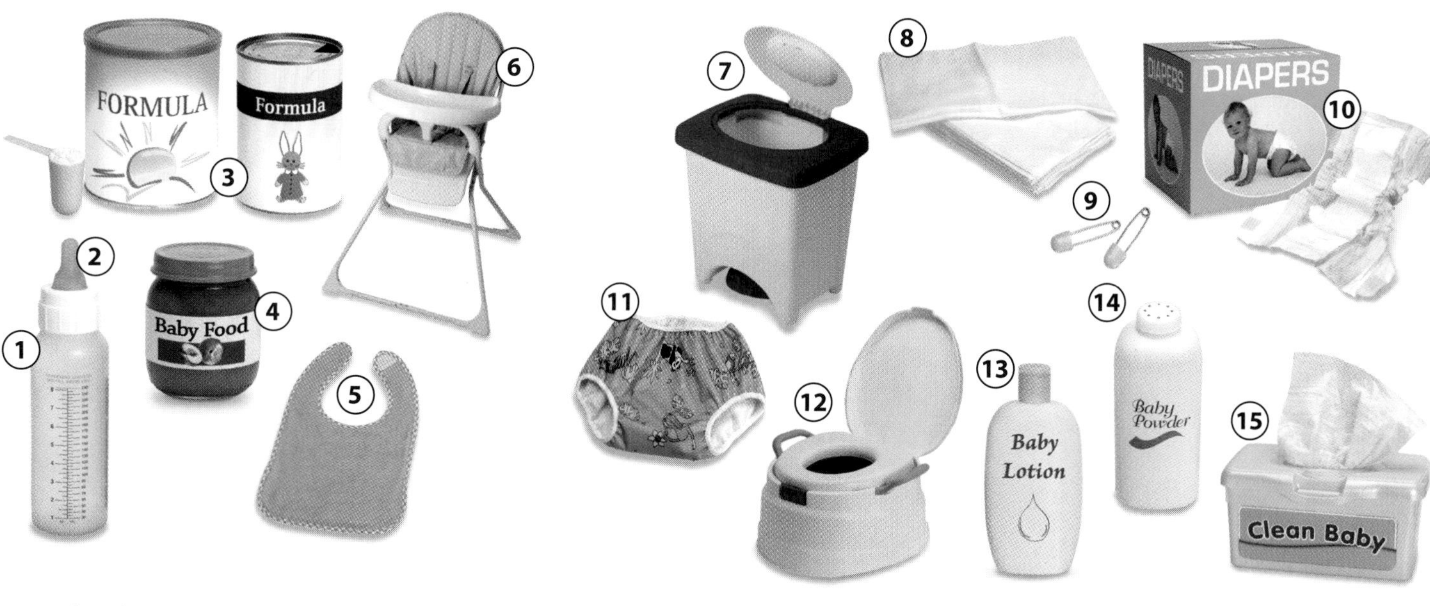


1. bottle
2. nipple
3. formula
4. baby food
5. bib
6. high chair
7. diaper pail
8. cloth diaper
9. safety pins
10. disposable diaper
11. training pants
12. potty seat
13. baby lotion
14. baby powder
15. wipes

16. baby bag
17. baby carrier
18. stroller
19. car safety seat
20. carriage
21. rocking chair
22. nursery rhymes
23. teddy bear
24. pacifier
25. teething ring
26. rattle
27. night light

**Dictate to your partner. Take turns.**

**A:** *Write pacifier.*
**B:** *Was that pacifier, p-a-c-i-f-i-e-r?*
**A:** *Yes, that's right.*

**Think about it. Discuss.**

1. How can parents discipline toddlers? teens?
2. What are some things you can say to praise a child?
3. Why are nursery rhymes important for young children?

# Daily Routines

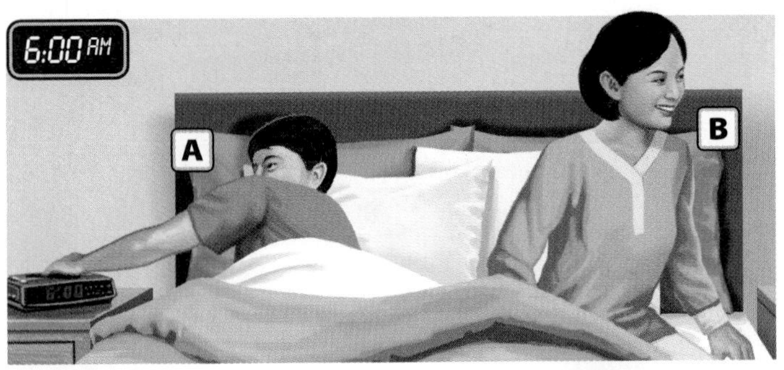


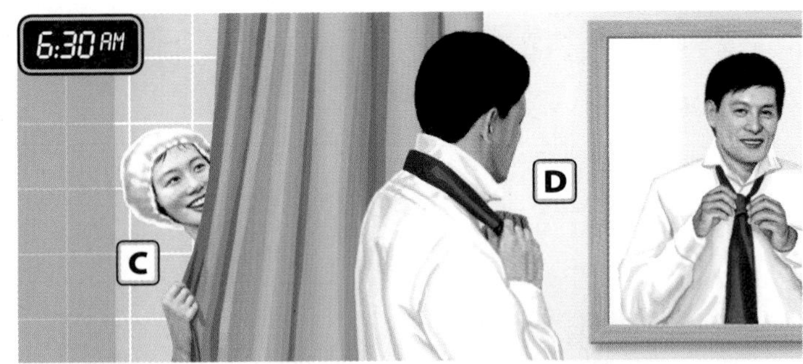

A. **wake up**

B. **get up**

C. **take** a shower

D. **get dressed**

E. **eat** breakfast

F. **make** lunch

G. **take** the children to school / **drop off** the kids

H. **take** the bus to school

I. **drive** to work / **go** to work

J. **go** to class

K. **work**

L. **go** to the grocery store

M. **pick up** the kids

N. **leave** work

**Grammar Point: third person singular**

For ***he*** and ***she***, add **-s** or **-es** to the verb:

| | |
|---|---|
| *He wake**s** up.* | *He watch**es** TV.* |
| *He get**s** up.* | *She go**es** to the store.* |

**These verbs are different (irregular):**

***Be:*** *She* ***is*** *in school at 10:00 a.m.*

***Have:*** *He* ***has*** *dinner at 6:30 p.m.*

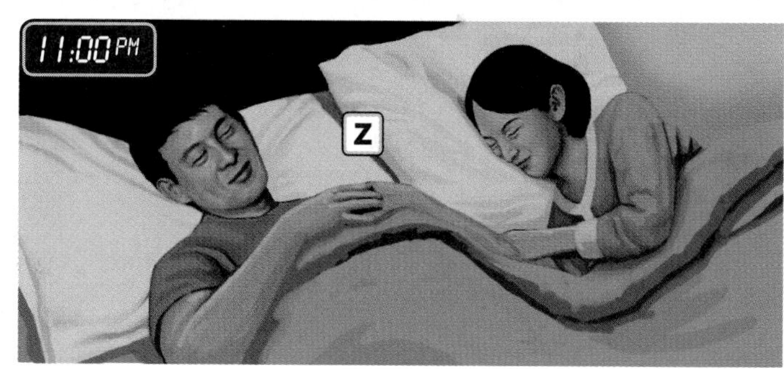


O. **clean** the house

P. **exercise**

Q. **cook** dinner / **make** dinner

R. **come** home / **get** home

S. **have** dinner / **eat** dinner

T. **do** homework

U. **relax**

V. **read** the paper

W. **check** email

X. **watch** TV

Y. **go** to bed

Z. **go** to sleep

**Pair practice. Make new conversations.**

**A:** *When does he go to work?*
**B:** *He goes to work at 8:00 a.m. When does she go to class?*
**A:** *She goes to class at 10:00 a.m.*

**Ask your classmates. Share the answers.**

1. Who cooks dinner in your family?
2. Who goes to the grocery store?
3. Who goes to work?

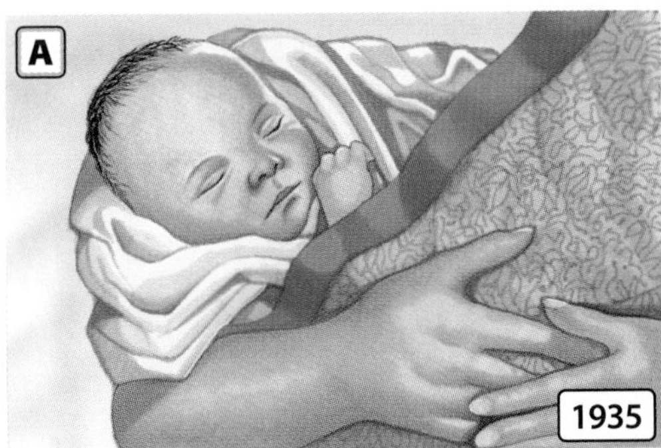


A. **be born**

B. **start** school

C. **immigrate**

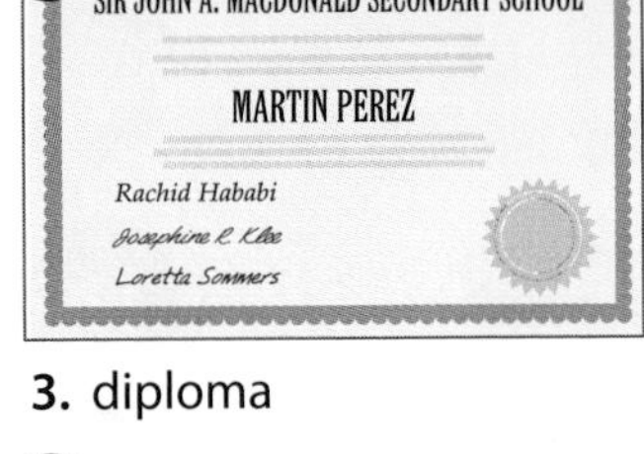

D. **graduate**

E. **learn** to drive

F. **get** a job

G. **become** a citizen

H. **fall in love**

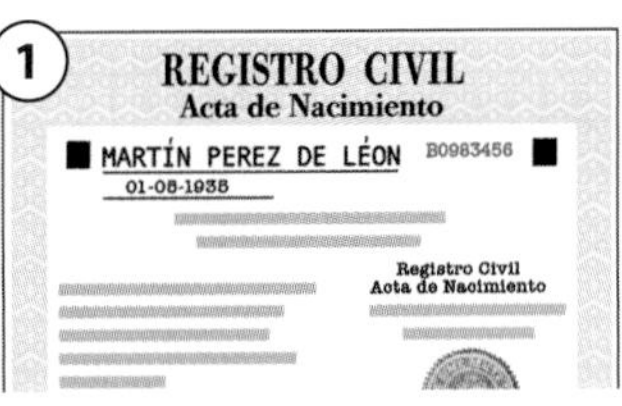


1. birth certificate

2. permanent resident card

3. diploma

4. driver's licence

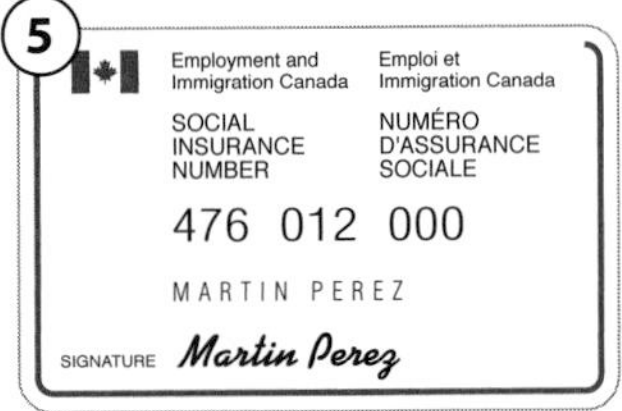

5
Employment and Immigration Canada
Emploi et Immigration Canada
SOCIAL INSURANCE NUMBER
NUMÉRO D'ASSURANCE SOCIALE
476 012 000
MARTIN PEREZ
SIGNATURE Martin Perez

5. social insurance number card

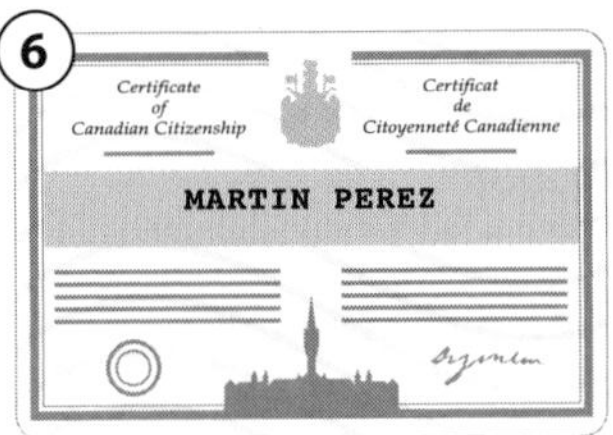

6
Certificate of Canadian Citizenship
Certificat de Citoyenneté Canadienne
MARTIN PEREZ


6. citizenship certificate

**Grammar Point: past tense**

start, learn, travel } +ed

immigrate, graduate, retire, die } +d

**These verbs are different (irregular):**

be – was
get – got
become – became
go – went
have – had
fall – fell
buy – bought

I. **go** to college

J. **get** engaged

CARLETON UNIVERSITY
Martin Perez
Bachelor of Arts
High Honours in English

7. university degree

K. **get** married

L. **have** a baby

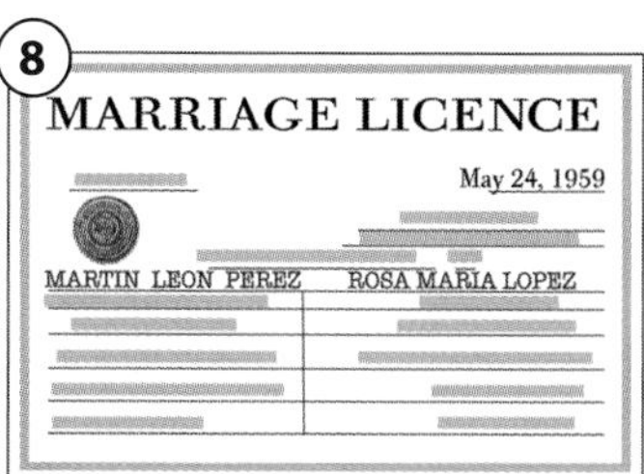
MARRIAGE LICENCE
May 24, 1959
MARTIN LEON PEREZ
ROSA MARIA LOPEZ

8. marriage licence

M. **buy** a home

N. **become** a grandparent

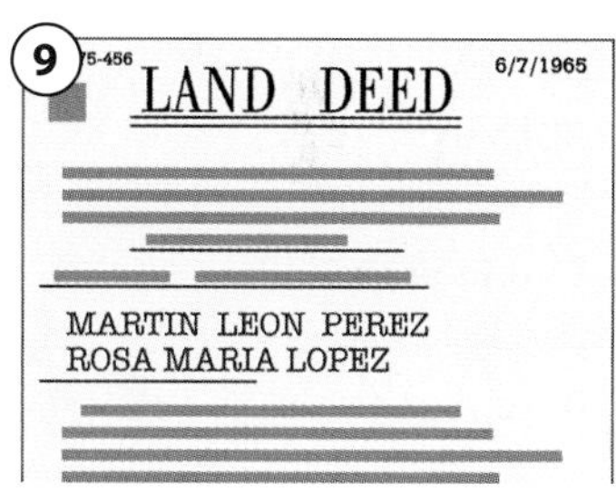
75-456
LAND DEED
6/7/1965
MARTIN LEON PEREZ
ROSA MARIA LOPEZ

9. deed

O. **retire**

P. **travel**

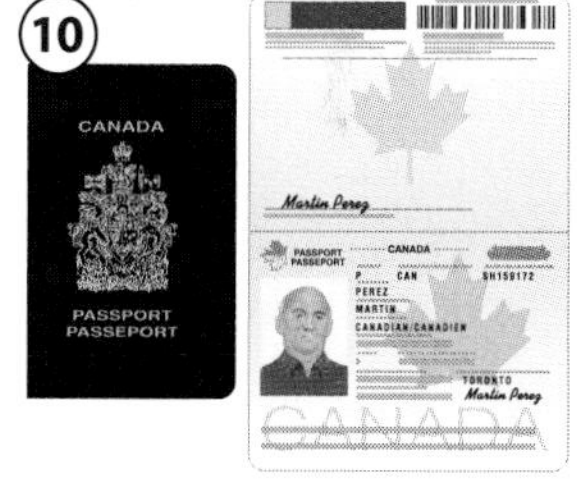

10. passport

Q. **volunteer**

R. **die**

CERTIFICATE OF DEATH
MARTIN LEON PEREZ
December 12th, 2009

11. death certificate

**More vocabulary**

When a husband dies, his wife becomes a **widow**.
When a wife dies, her husband becomes a **widower**.

**Ask your classmates. Share the answers.**

1. When did you start school?
2. When did you get your first job?
3. Do you want to travel?

1. hot
2. thirsty
3. sleepy
4. cold
5. hungry
6. full / satisfied

7. disgusted
8. calm
9. uncomfortable
10. nervous

11. in pain
12. sick
13. worried
14. well
15. relieved

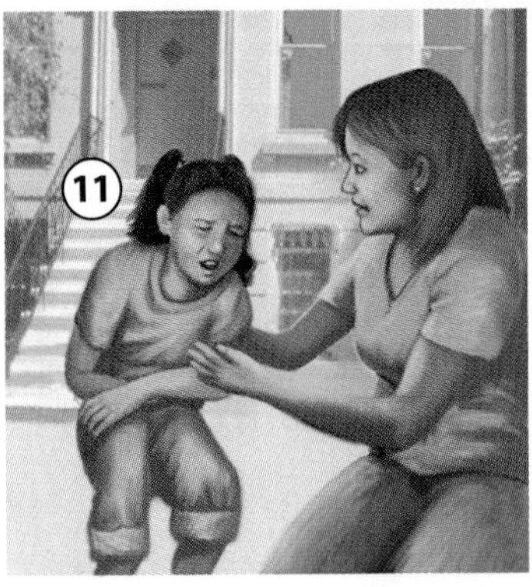

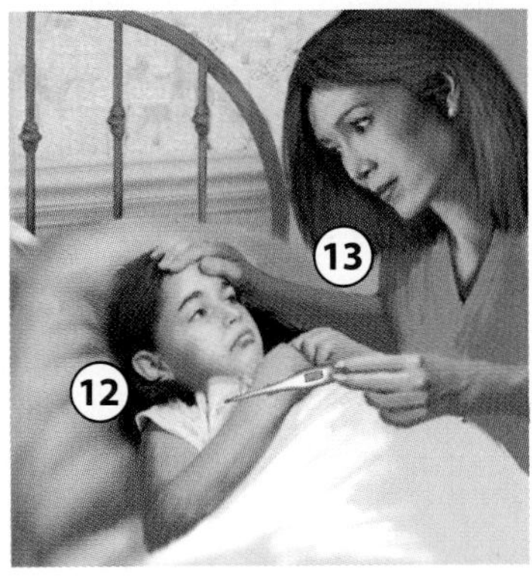

16. hurt
17. lonely
18. in love

**Pair practice. Make new conversations.**

**A:** *How are you doing?*
**B:** *I'm hungry. How about you?*
**A:** *I'm hungry and thirsty, too!*

**Use the new words.**
Look at pages 40–41. Describe what each person is feeling.

**A:** *Martin is excited.*
**B:** *Martin's mother is proud.*

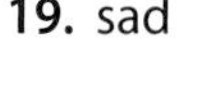

19. sad
20. homesick
21. proud

22. excited
23. scared / afraid
24. embarrassed

25. bored
26. confused
27. frustrated

28. upset
29. angry

30. surprised
31. happy
32. tired

**Ask your classmates. Share the answers.**

1. Do you ever feel homesick?
2. What makes you feel frustrated?
3. Describe a time when you were very happy.

**More vocabulary**

**exhausted:** very tired
**furious:** very angry
**humiliated:** very embarrassed
**overjoyed:** very happy
**starving:** very hungry
**terrified:** very scared

# A Family Reunion

| | | | |
|---|---|---|---|
| **1.** banner | **3.** opinion | **5.** glad | **A. laugh** |
| **2.** baseball game | **4.** balloons | **6.** relatives | **B. misbehave** |

**Look at the picture.**
**What do you see?**

**Answer the questions.**

1. How many relatives are there at this reunion?
2. How many children are there? Which children are misbehaving?
3. What are people doing at this reunion?

 **Read the story.**

## A Family Reunion

Ben Lu has a lot of relatives and they're all at his house. Today is the Lu family reunion.

There is a lot of good food. There are also balloons and a banner. And this year there are four new babies!

People are having a good time at the reunion. Ben's grandfather and his aunt are talking about the baseball game. His cousins are laughing. His mother-in-law is giving her opinion. And many of the children are misbehaving.

Ben looks at his family and smiles. He loves his relatives, but he's glad the reunion is once a year.

**Think about it.**

1. Do you like to have large parties? Why or why not?
2. Imagine you see a little girl at a party. She's misbehaving. What do you do? What do you say?

1. roof
2. bedroom
3. door
4. bathroom
5. kitchen
6. floor
7. dining area

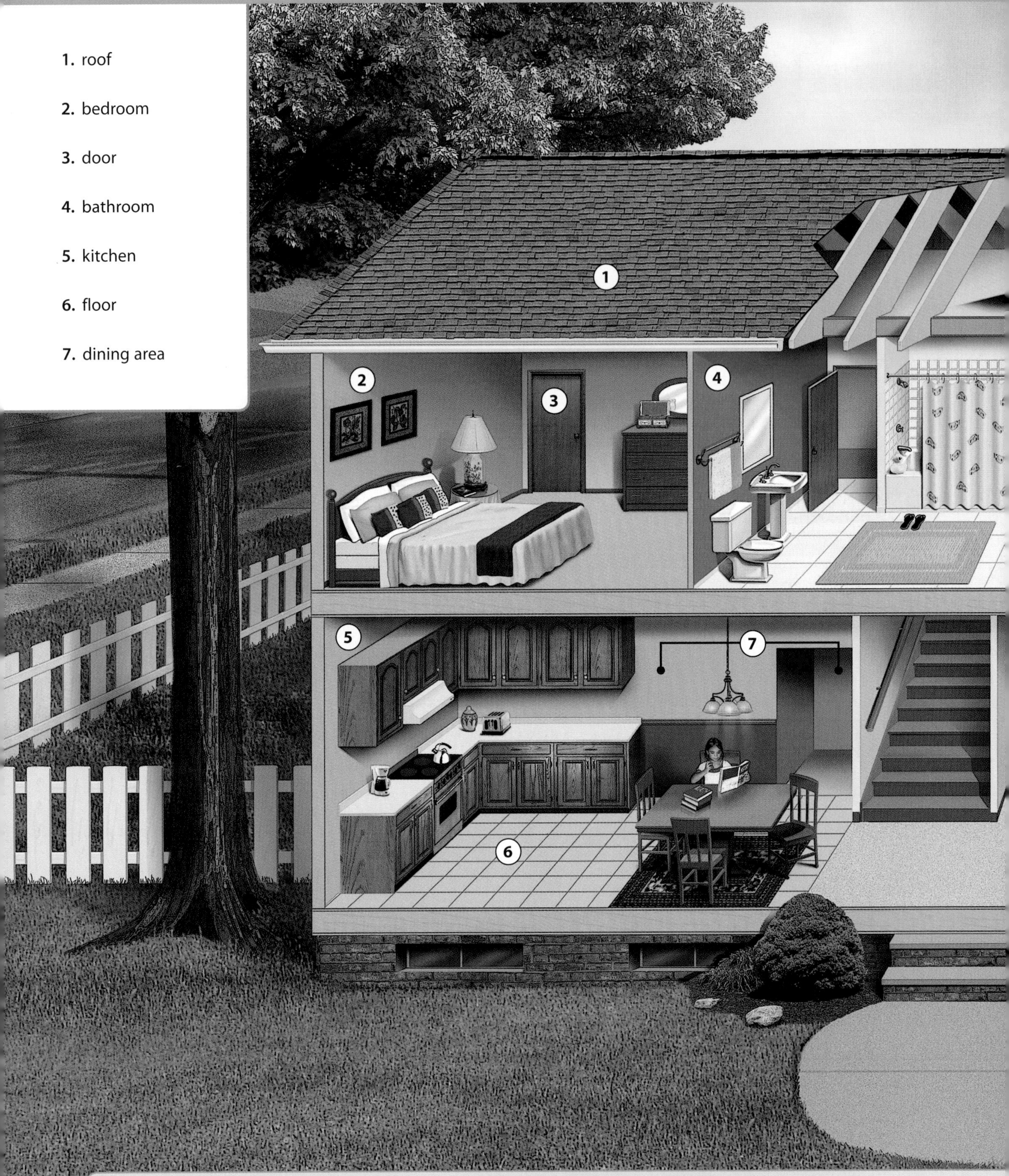

**Listen and point. Take turns.**

**A:** *Point to the kitchen.*

**B:** *Point to the living room.*

**A:** *Point to the basement.*

**Dictate to your partner. Take turns.**

**A:** *Write kitchen.*

**B:** *Was that k-i-t-c-h-e-n?*

**A:** *Yes, that's right, kitchen.*

8. attic
9. kids' bedroom
10. baby's room
11. window
12. living room
13. basement
14. garage

**Ways to give locations**

*I'm home.*
*I'm in the kitchen.*
*I'm on the roof.*

**Pair practice. Make new conversations.**

**A:** *Where's the man?*
**B:** *He's in the attic. Where's the teenager?*
**A:** *She's in the laundry room.*

1. Internet listing

2. classified ad

### Abbreviations

apt = apartment
bdrm = bedroom
ba = bathroom
kit = kitchen
yd = yard
util = utilities
incl = included
mo = month
furn = furnished
unfurn = unfurnished
mgr = manager
eves = evenings

3. furnished apartment

4. unfurnished apartment

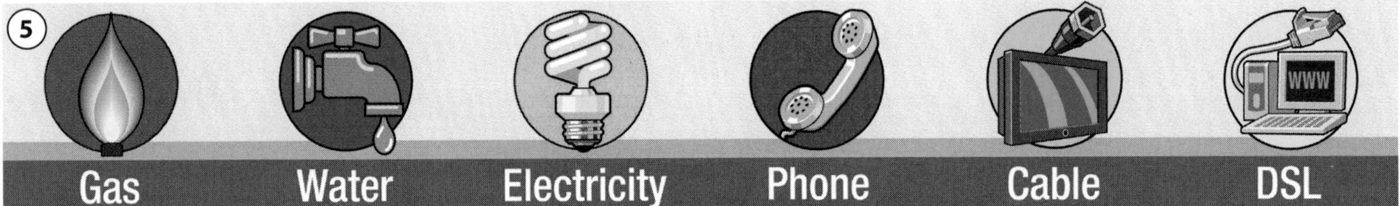


5. utilities

## Renting an Apartment

A. **Call** the manager.

B. **Ask** about the features.

Rental Application
Name: Khalidah Ali
Telephone number: 514-555-8907


C. **Submit** an application.

D. **Sign** the rental agreement.

E. **Pay** the first and last months' rent.

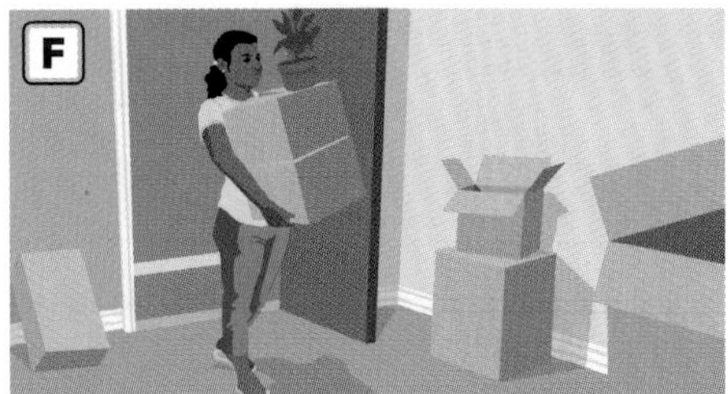

F. **Move in**.

**More vocabulary**

**lease:** a monthly or yearly rental agreement
**redecorate:** to change the paint and furniture in a home
**move out:** to pack and leave a home

**Ask your classmates. Share the answers.**

1. How did you find your home?
2. Do you like to paint or arrange furniture?
3. Does gas or electricity cost more for you?

## Buying a House

G. **Meet** with a realtor.

H. **Look** at houses.

I. **Make** an offer.

J. **Get** a loan.

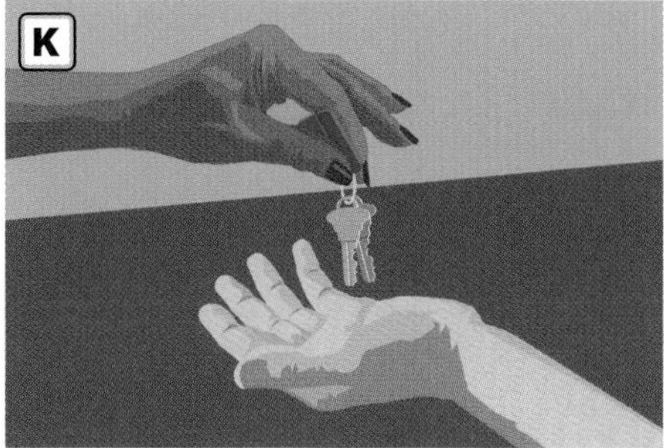
K. **Take** ownership.

L. **Make** a mortgage payment.

## Moving In

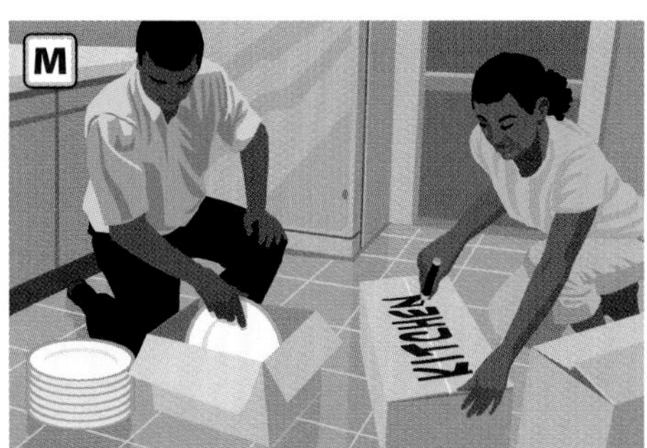

M. **Pack**.

N. **Unpack**.

O. **Put** the utilities in your name.

P. **Paint**.

Q. **Arrange** the furniture.

R. **Meet** the neighbours.

**Ways to ask about a home's features**

*Are utilities included?*
*Is the kitchen large and sunny?*
*Are the neighbours quiet?*

**Role play. Talk to an apartment manager.**

**A:** *Hi. I'm calling about the apartment.*
**B:** *OK. It's unfurnished and rent is $800 a month.*
**A:** *Are utilities included?*

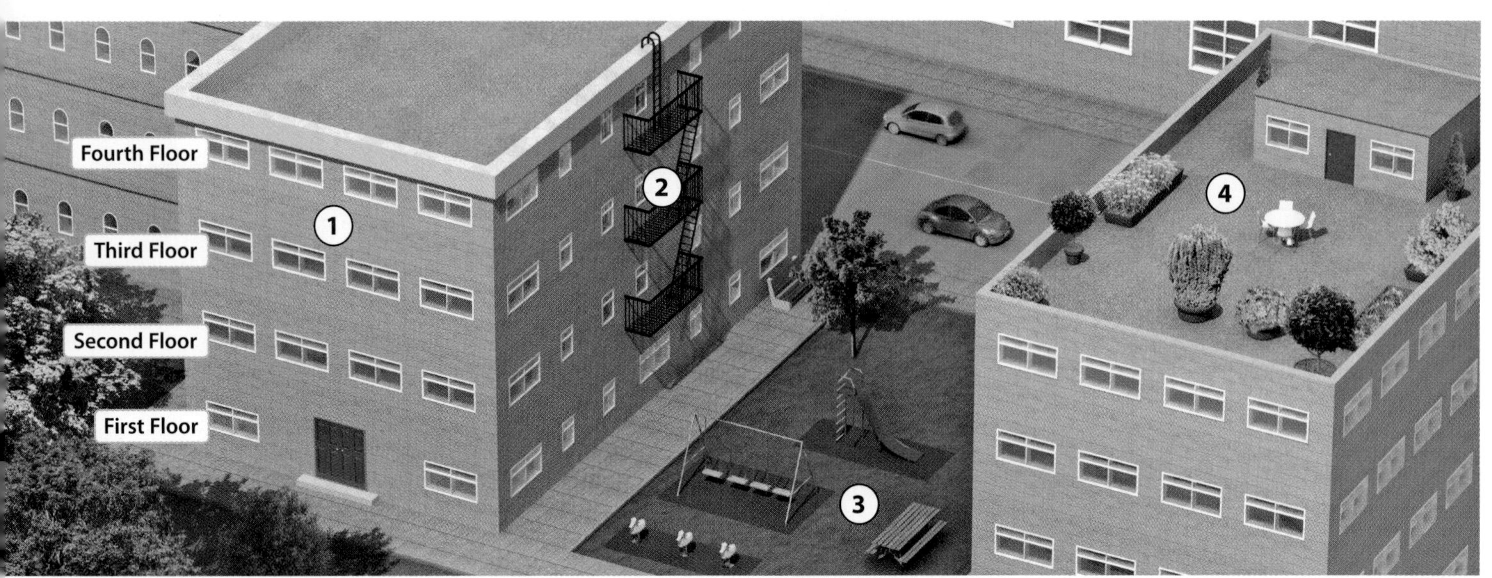


1. apartment building
2. fire escape
3. playground
4. roof garden

## Entrance

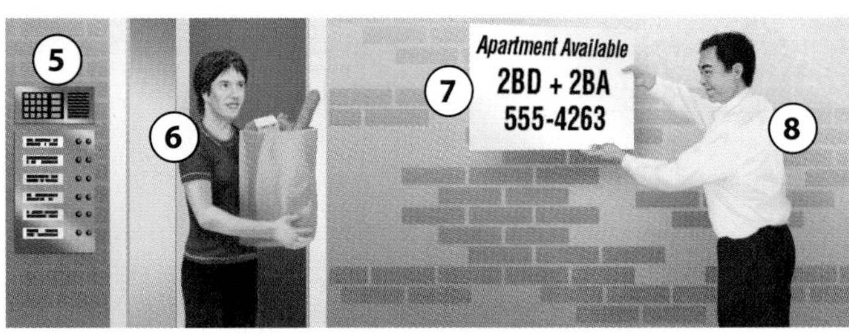


5. intercom / speaker
6. tenant
7. vacancy sign
8. manager / superintendent

## Lobby

9. elevator
10. stairs / stairway
11. mailboxes

## Basement

16
17
18
19
GARAGE

12. washer
13. dryer
14. big-screen TV
15. pool table
16. security gate
17. storage locker
18. parking space
19. security camera

**Grammar Point: *there is / there are***

**singular:** there is **plural:** there are

***There is*** *a recreation room in the basement.*

***There are*** *mailboxes in the lobby.*

**Look at the pictures.**

Describe the apartment building.

**A:** *There's a pool table in the recreation room.*

**B:** *There are parking spaces in the garage.*

20. balcony
21. courtyard
22. swimming pool
23. garbage bin
24. alley

## Hallway

25. emergency exit
26. garbage chute

## Rental Office

27. landlord
28. lease / rental agreement

## An Apartment Entranceway

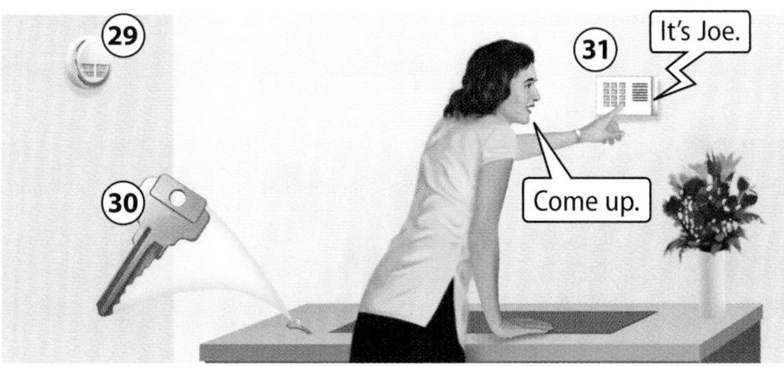


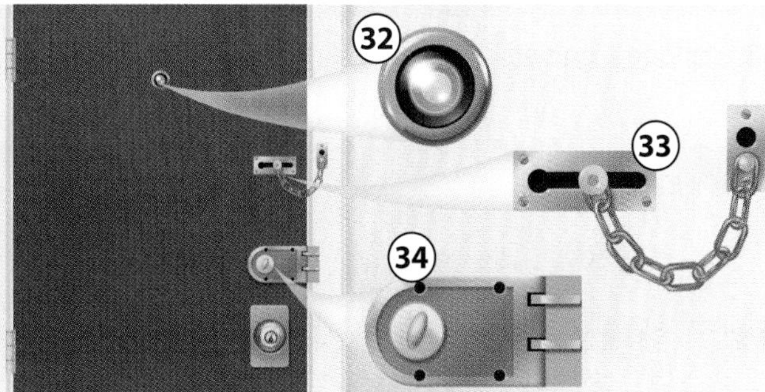


29. smoke detector
30. key
31. buzzer
32. peephole
33. door chain
34. dead bolt lock

**More vocabulary**

**upstairs:** the floor(s) above you
**downstairs:** the floor(s) below you
**fire exit:** another name for emergency exit

**Role play. Talk to a landlord.**

**A:** *Is there a swimming pool in this complex?*
**B:** *Yes, there is. It's near the courtyard.*
**A:** *Is there…?*

# Different Places to Live

1. the city / an urban area
2. the suburbs
3. a small town / a village
4. the country / a rural area

5. condominium / condo

6. townhouse

7. mobile home

8. college / university residence

9. farm

10. ranch

11. senior housing

12. nursing home

13. shelter

**More vocabulary**

**co-op:** an apartment building owned by residents
**duplex:** a house divided into two homes
**two-storey house:** a house with two floors

**Think about it. Discuss.**

1. What's good and bad about these places to live?
2. How are small towns different from cities?
3. How do shelters help people in need?

## Front Yard and House

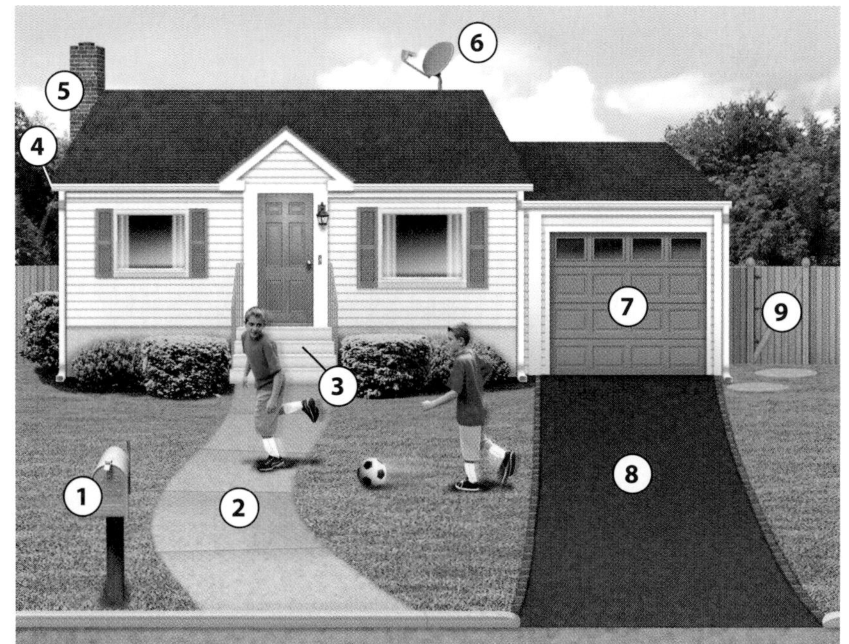

1. mailbox
2. front walk
3. steps
4. eavestrough
5. chimney
6. satellite dish
7. garage door
8. driveway
9. gate

## Front Porch

10. storm door
11. front door
12. doorknob
13. porch light
14. doorbell
15. screen door

## Backyard

16. patio
17. barbecue
18. sliding glass door
19. patio furniture
20. flower bed
21. hose
22. sprinkler
23. hammock
24. garbage can
25. compost pile
26. lawn
27. vegetable garden

A. **take** a nap

B. **garden**

1. cabinet
2. shelf
3. paper towels
4. sink
5. dish rack
6. toaster
7. garbage disposal
8. dishwasher
9. refrigerator
10. freezer
11. coffee maker
12. blender
13. microwave
14. electric can opener
15. toaster oven
16. pot
17. kettle
18. stove
19. burner
20. oven
21. broiler
22. counter
23. drawer
24. pan
25. electric mixer
26. food processor
27. cutting board
28. mixing bowl

**Ways to talk about location using *on* and *in***

Use ***on*** for the counter, shelf, burner, stove, and cutting board. *It's **on** the counter.* Use ***in*** for the dishwasher, oven, sink, and drawer. *Put it **in** the sink.*

**Pair practice. Make new conversations.**

**A:** *Please move the blender.*
**B:** *Sure. Do you want it in the cabinet?*
**A:** *No, put it on the counter.*

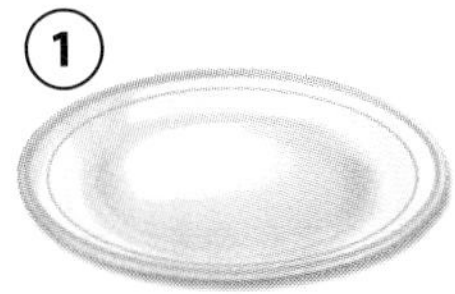

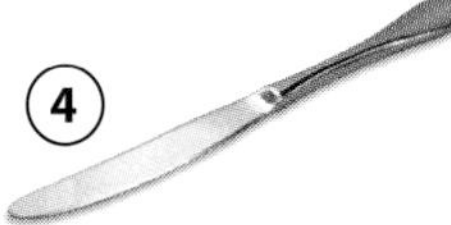

1. dish / plate
2. bowl
3. fork
4. knife
5. spoon
6. teacup
7. coffee mug
8. dining room chair
9. dining room table
10. napkin
11. placemat
12. tablecloth
13. salt and pepper shakers
14. sugar bowl
15. creamer
16. teapot
17. tray
18. light fixture
19. fan
20. platter
21. serving bowl
22. hutch
23. vase
24. buffet

**Ways to make requests at the table**

*May I have the sugar bowl?*
*Would you pass the creamer, please?*
*Could I have a coffee mug?*

**Role play. Request items at the table.**

**A:** *What do you need?*
**B:** *Could I have a coffee mug?*
**A:** *Certainly. And would you...*

1. loveseat
2. throw pillow
3. basket
4. houseplant
5. entertainment centre
6. TV (television)
7. DVD player
8. stereo system
9. painting
10. wall
11. mantle
12. fire screen
13. fireplace
14. end table
15. floor lamp
16. drapes
17. window
18. sofa / couch
19. coffee table
20. candle
21. candle holder
22. armchair / easy chair
23. magazine holder
24. carpet

**Use the new words.**
Look at pages 44–45. Name the things in the room.
**A:** *There's a TV.*
**B:** *There's a carpet.*

**More vocabulary**
**light bulb:** the light inside a lamp
**lampshade:** the part of the lamp that covers the light bulb
**sofa cushions:** the pillows that are part of the sofa

1. hamper
2. bathtub
3. soap dish
4. soap
5. rubber mat
6. washcloth
7. drain
8. faucet
9. hot water
10. cold water
11. grab bar
12. tile
13. shower head
14. shower curtain
15. towel rack
16. bath towel
17. hand towel
18. mirror
19. toilet paper
20. toilet brush
21. toilet
22. medicine cabinet
23. toothbrush
24. toothbrush holder
25. sink
26. wastebasket
27. scale
28. bath mat

**More vocabulary**

**stall shower:** a shower without a bathtub
**half bath:** a bathroom with no shower or tub
**linen closet:** a closet for towels and sheets

**Ask your classmates. Share the answers.**

1. Is your toothbrush on the sink or in the medicine cabinet?
2. Do you have a bathtub or a shower?
3. Do you have a shower curtain or a shower door?

# A Bedroom

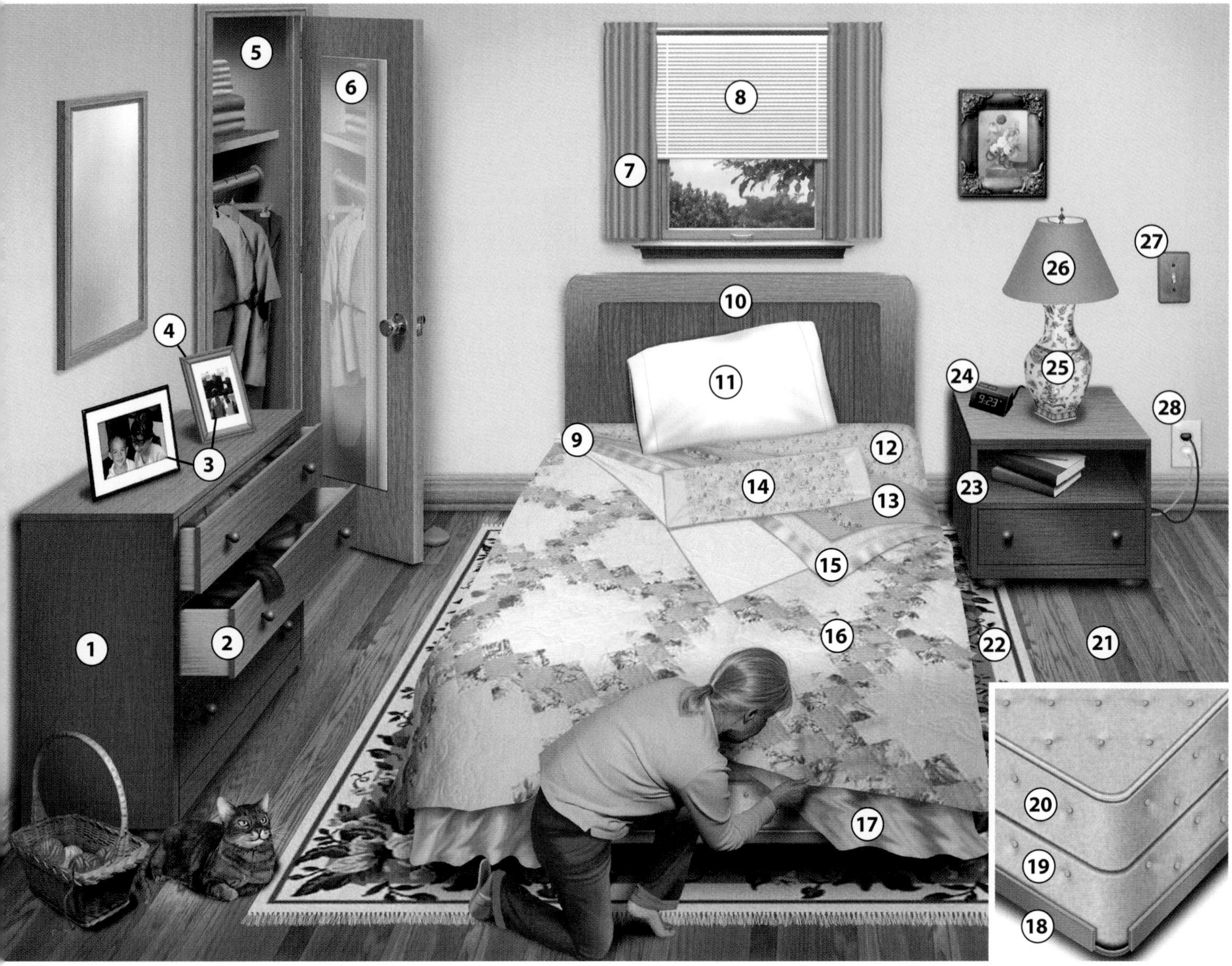

| | | | |
|---|---|---|---|
| **1.** dresser / bureau | **8.** mini-blinds | **15.** blanket | **22.** rug |
| **2.** drawer | **9.** bed | **16.** quilt | **23.** night table / nightstand |
| **3.** photos | **10.** headboard | **17.** dust ruffle | **24.** alarm clock |
| **4.** picture frame | **11.** pillow | **18.** bed frame | **25.** lamp |
| **5.** closet | **12.** fitted sheet | **19.** box spring | **26.** lampshade |
| **6.** full-length mirror | **13.** flat sheet | **20.** mattress | **27.** light switch |
| **7.** curtains | **14.** pillowcase | **21.** wood floor | **28.** outlet |

**Look at the pictures.**
Describe the bedroom.

**A:** *There's a lamp on the nightstand.*
**B:** *There's a mirror in the closet.*

**Ask your classmates. Share the answers.**

1. Do you prefer a hard or a soft mattress?
2. Do you prefer mini-blinds or curtains?
3. How many pillows do you like on your bed?

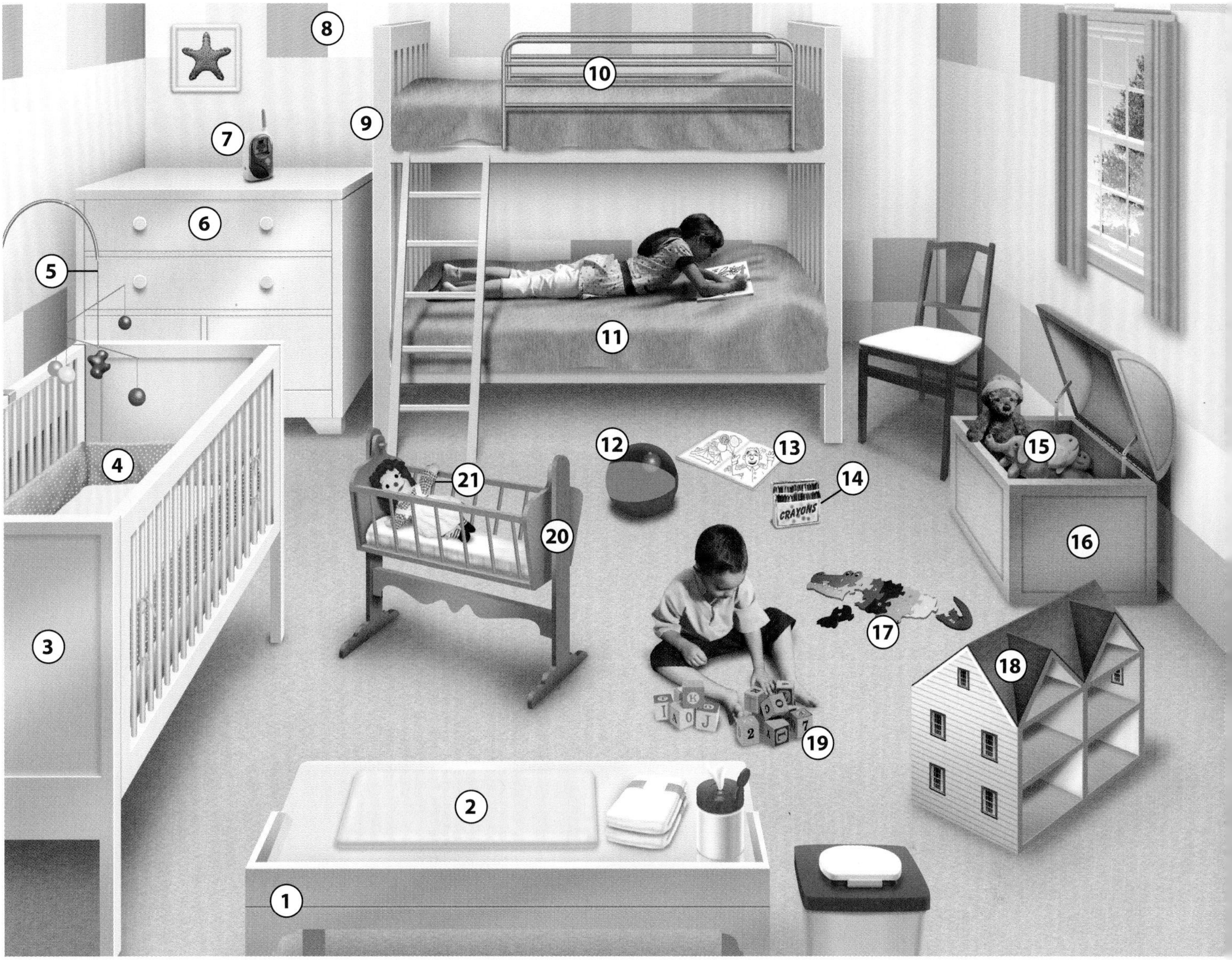

## Furniture and Accessories

1. changing table
2. changing pad
3. crib
4. bumper pad
5. mobile
6. chest of drawers
7. baby monitor
8. wallpaper
9. bunk beds
10. safety rail
11. bedspread

## Toys and Games

12. ball
13. colouring book
14. crayons
15. stuffed animals
16. toy chest
17. puzzle
18. dollhouse
19. blocks
20. cradle
21. doll

**Pair practice. Make conversations.**

**A:** *Where's the changing pad?*
**B:** *It's on the changing table.*

**Think about it. Discuss.**

1. Which toys help children learn? How?
2. Which toys are good for older and younger children?
3. What safety features does this room need? Why?

A. **dust** the furniture
B. **recycle** the newspapers
C. **clean** the oven
D. **mop** the floor
E. **polish** the furniture
F. **make** the bed
G. **put away** the toys
H. **vacuum** the carpet
I. **wash** the windows
J. **sweep** the floor
K. **scrub** the sink
L. **empty** the trash
M. **wash** the dishes
N. **dry** the dishes
O. **wipe** the counter
P. **change** the sheets
Q. **take out** the garbage

**Pair practice. Make new conversations.**

A: *Let's clean this place. First, I'll sweep the floor.*
B: *I'll mop the floor when you finish.*

**Ask your classmates. Share the answers.**

1. Who does the housework in your home?
2. How often do you wash the windows?
3. When should kids start to do housework?

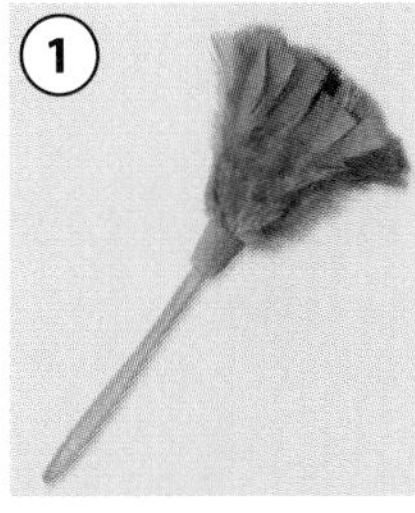

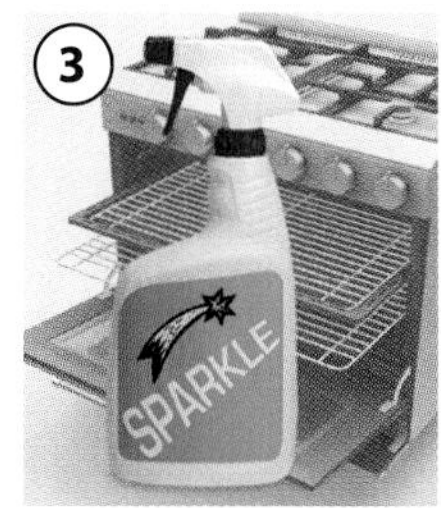


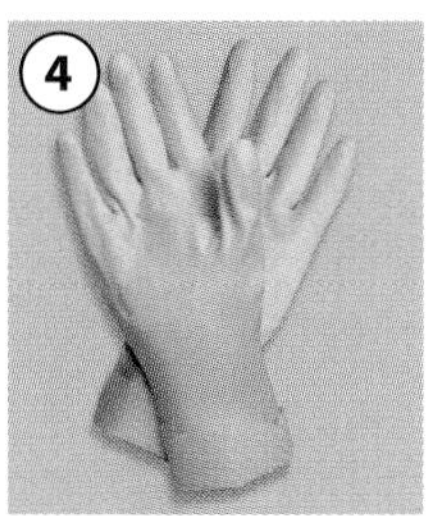

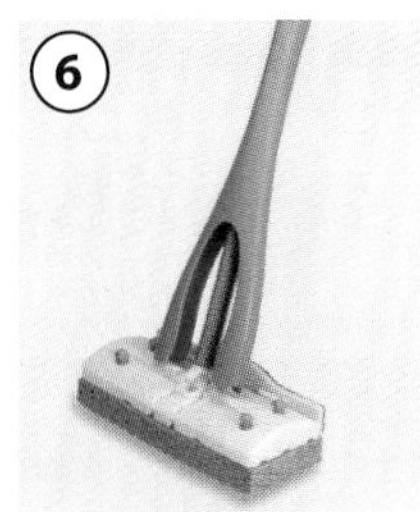

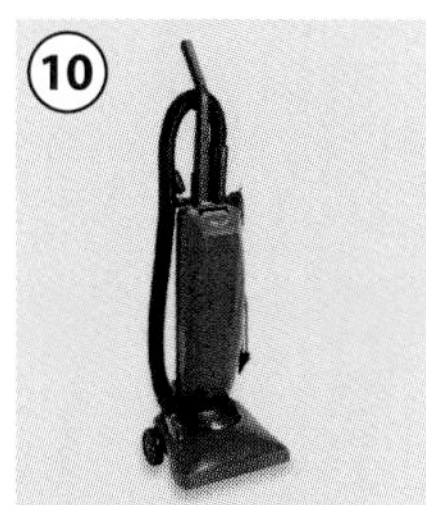

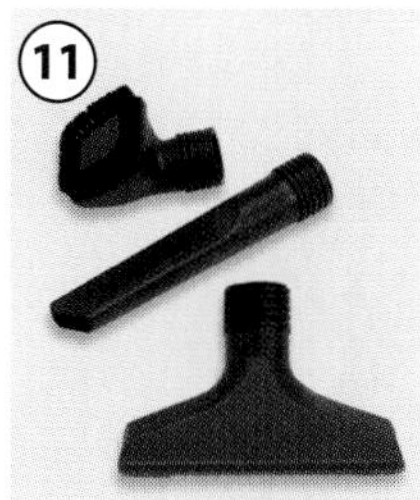

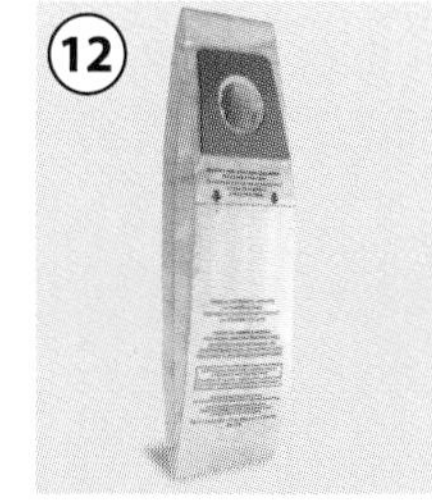

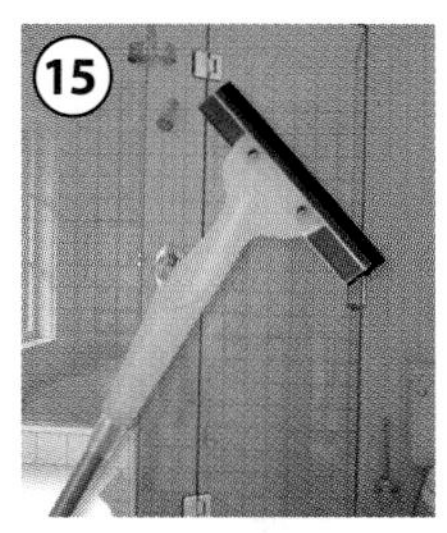

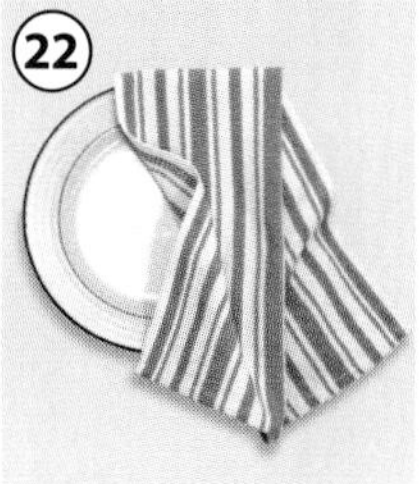

1. feather duster
2. recycling bin
3. oven cleaner
4. rubber gloves
5. steel-wool soap pads
6. sponge mop
7. bucket / pail
8. furniture polish
9. rags
10. vacuum cleaner
11. vacuum cleaner attachments
12. vacuum cleaner bag
13. stepladder
14. glass cleaner
15. squeegee
16. broom
17. dust pan
18. cleanser
19. sponge
20. scrub brush
21. dishwashing liquid
22. dish towel
23. disinfectant wipes
24. garbage bags

**Ways to ask for something**

*Please hand me the squeegee.*
*Can you get me the broom?*
*I need the sponge mop.*

**Pair practice. Make new conversations.**

**A:** *Please hand me the sponge mop.*
**B:** *Here you go. Do you need the bucket?*
**A:** *Yes, please. Can you get me the rubber gloves, too?*

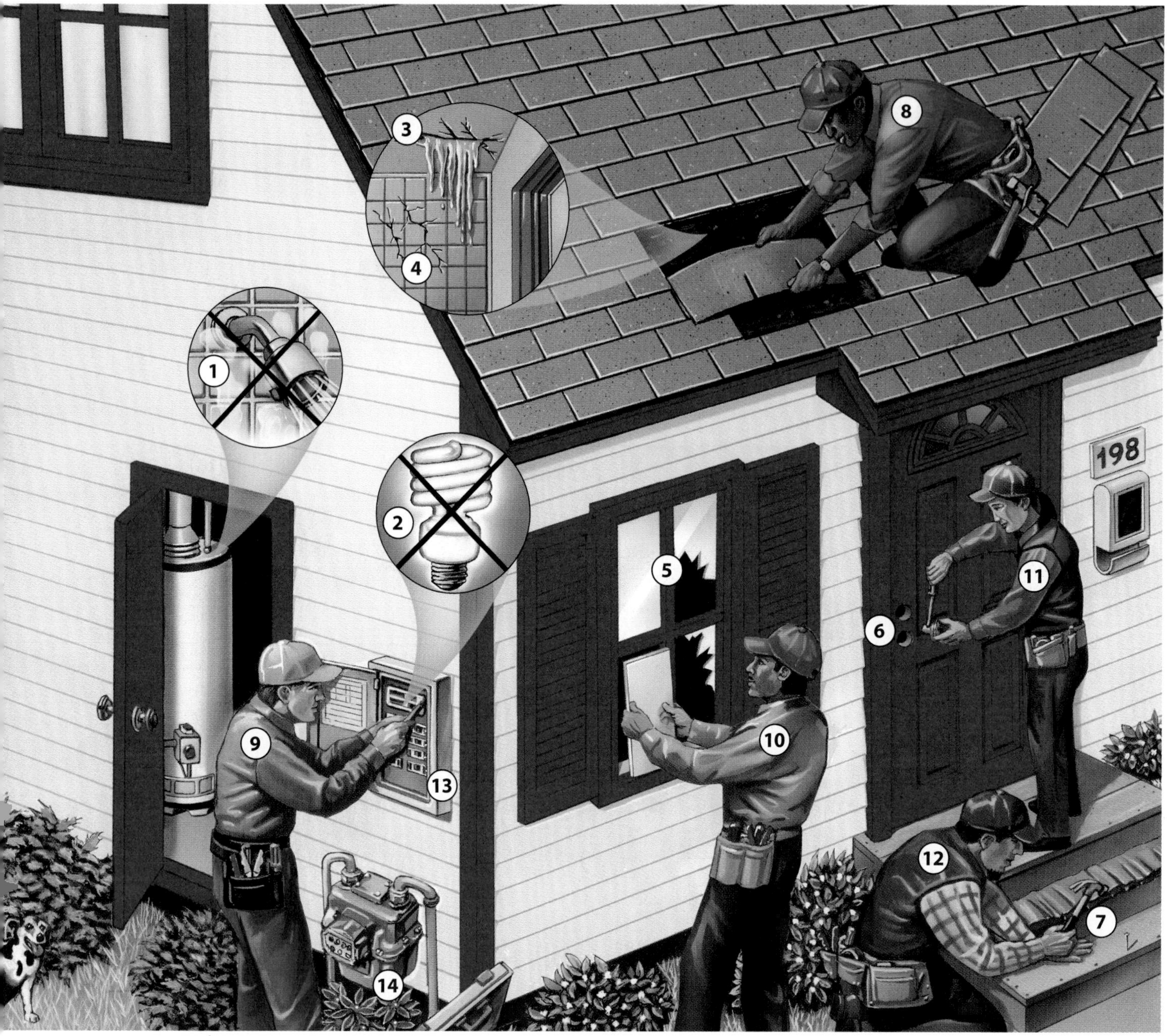

# Household Problems and Repairs

1. The water heater is **not working**.
2. The power is **out**.
3. The roof is **leaking**.
4. The tile is **cracked**.
5. The window is **broken**.
6. The lock is **broken**.
7. The steps are **broken**.
8. roofer
9. electrician
10. repair person
11. locksmith
12. carpenter
13. fuse box
14. gas meter

**More vocabulary**

**fix:** to repair something that is broken
**pests:** termites, fleas, rats, etc.
**exterminate:** to kill household pests

**Pair practice. Make new conversations.**

**A:** *The faucet is leaking.*
**B:** *Let's call the plumber. He can fix it.*

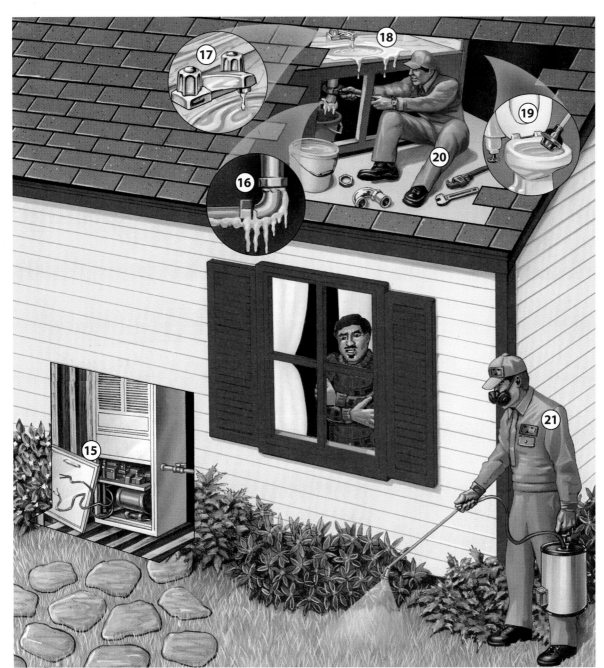


15. The furnace is **broken**.
16. The pipes are **frozen**.
17. The faucet is **dripping**.
18. The sink is **overflowing**.
19. The toilet is **stopped up**.
20. plumber
21. exterminator
22. termites
23. ants
24. bedbugs
25. fleas
26. cockroaches / roaches
27. rats
28. mice*

*__Note:__ one mouse, two mice

**Ways to ask about repairs**

*How much will this repair cost?*
*When can you begin?*
*How long will the repair take?*

**Role play. Talk to a repair person.**

**A:** *Can you fix the roof?*
**B:** *Yes, but it will take two weeks.*
**A:** *How much will the repair cost?*

| | | | | |
|---|---|---|---|---|
| **1.** roommates | **3.** music | **5.** noise | **7.** rules | **9.** invitation |
| **2.** party | **4.** DJ | **6.** irritated | **8.** mess | **A. dance** |

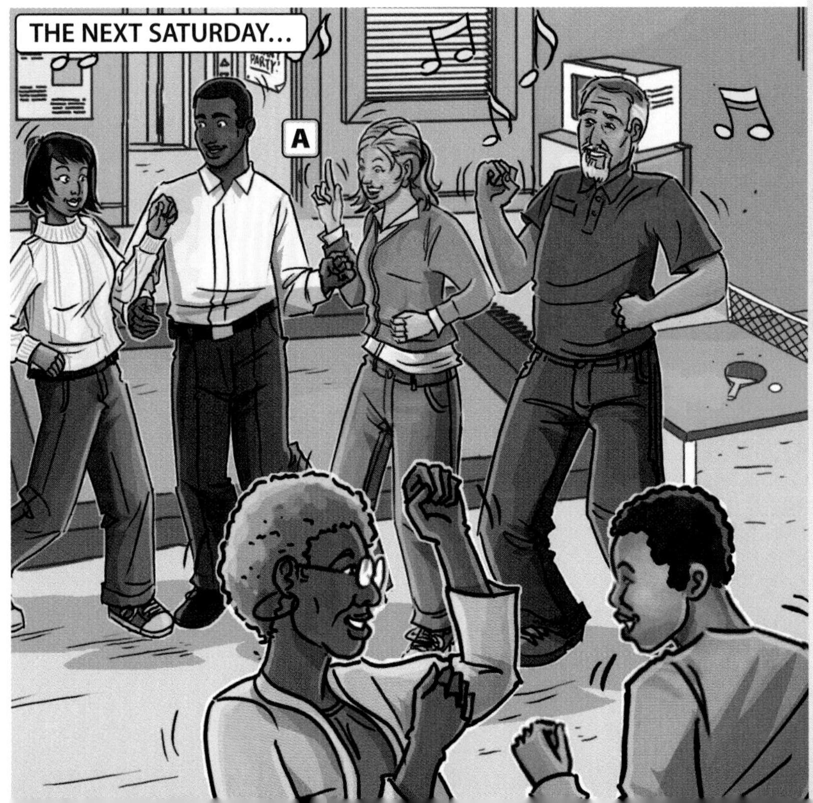


**Look at the pictures. What do you see?**

**Answer the questions.**

1. What happened in apartment 2B? How many people were there?
2. How did the neighbour feel? Why?
3. What rules were written at the tenant meeting?
4. What did the roommates do after the tenant meeting?

 **Read the story.**

## The Tenant Meeting

Sally Lopez and Tina Green are roommates. They live in apartment 2B. One night they had a big party with music and a DJ. There was a mess in the hallway. Their neighbours were very unhappy. Mr. Clark in 2A was very irritated. He hates noise!

The next day there was a tenant meeting. Everyone wanted rules about parties and loud music. The girls were very embarrassed.

After the meeting, the girls cleaned the mess in the hallway. Then they gave each neighbour an invitation to a new party. Everyone had a good time at the rec room party. Now the tenants have two new rules and a new place to dance.

**Think about it.**

1. What are the most important rules in an apartment building? Why?
2. Imagine you are the neighbour in 2A. What do you say to Tina and Sally?

# Back from the Market

1. fish
2. meat
3. chicken
4. cheese
5. milk
6. butter
7. eggs
8. vegetables

**Listen and point. Take turns.**

**A:** *Point to the* *<u>vegetables</u>.*
**B:** *Point to the* *<u>bread</u>.*
**A:** *Point to the* *<u>fruit</u>.*

**Pair Dictation**

**A:** *Write <u>vegetables</u>.*
**B:** *Please spell <u>vegetables</u> for me.*
**A:** *V-e-g-e-t-a-b-l-e-s.*

9. fruit
10. rice
11. bread
12. pasta
13. grocery bag
14. shopping list
15. coupons

**Ways to talk about food.**

*Do we need* eggs*?*
*Do we have any* pasta*?*
*We have some* vegetables*, but we need* fruit*.*

**Role play. Talk about your shopping list.**

**A:** *Do we need eggs?*
**B:** *No, we have some.*
**A:** *Do we have any...*

# Fruit

1. apples
2. bananas
3. grapes
4. pears
5. oranges
6. grapefruit
7. lemons
8. limes
9. tangerines
10. peaches
11. cherries
12. apricots
13. plums
14. strawberries
15. raspberries
16. blueberries
17. blackberries
18. watermelons
19. melons
20. papayas
21. mangoes
22. kiwi
23. pineapples
24. coconuts
25. raisins
26. prunes
27. figs
28. dates
29. a bunch of bananas
30. **ripe** banana
31. **unripe** banana
32. **rotten** banana

**Pair practice. Make new conversations.**

**A:** *What's your favourite fruit?*
**B:** *I like apples. Do you?*
**A:** *I prefer bananas.*

**Ask your classmates. Share the answers.**

1. Which fruit do you put in a fruit salad?
2. What kinds of fruit are common in your native country?
3. What kinds of fruit are in your kitchen right now?

1. lettuce
2. cabbage
3. carrots
4. radishes
5. beets
6. tomatoes
7. bell peppers
8. string beans
9. celery
10. cucumbers
11. spinach
12. corn
13. broccoli
14. cauliflower
15. bok choy
16. turnips
17. potatoes
18. sweet potatoes
19. onions
20. green onions / scallions
21. peas
22. artichokes
23. eggplants
24. squash
25. zucchini
26. asparagus
27. mushrooms
28. parsley
29. chili peppers
30. garlic
31. a **bag of** lettuce
32. a **head of** lettuce

**Pair practice. Make new conversations.**

**A:** *Do you eat broccoli?*
**B:** *Yes. I like most vegetables, but not peppers.*
**A:** *Really? Well, I don't like cauliflower.*

**Ask your classmates. Share the answers.**

1. Which vegetables do you eat raw? cooked?
2. Which vegetables do you put in a green salad?
3. Which vegetables are in your refrigerator right now?

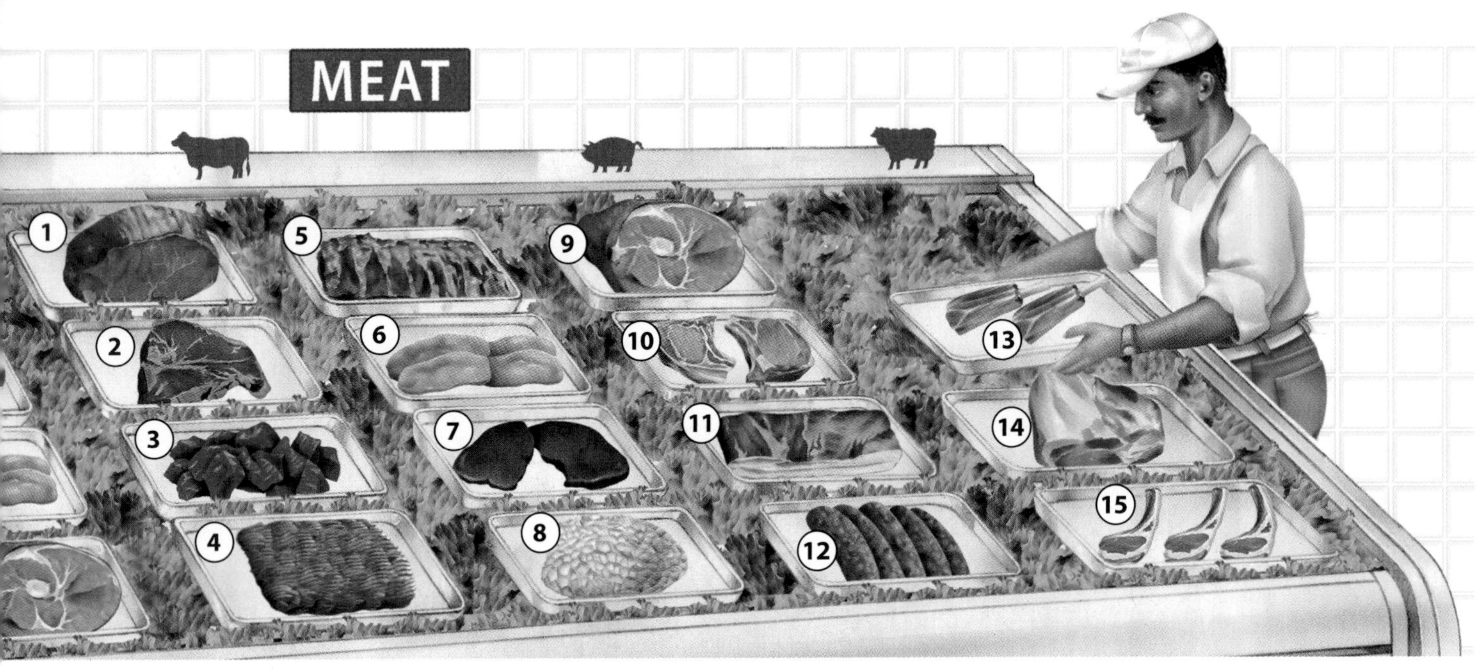


**Beef**

1. roast
2. steak
3. stewing beef
4. ground beef
5. beef ribs
6. veal cutlets
7. liver
8. tripe

**Pork**

9. ham
10. pork chops
11. bacon
12. sausage

**Lamb**

13. lamb shanks
14. leg of lamb
15. lamb chops

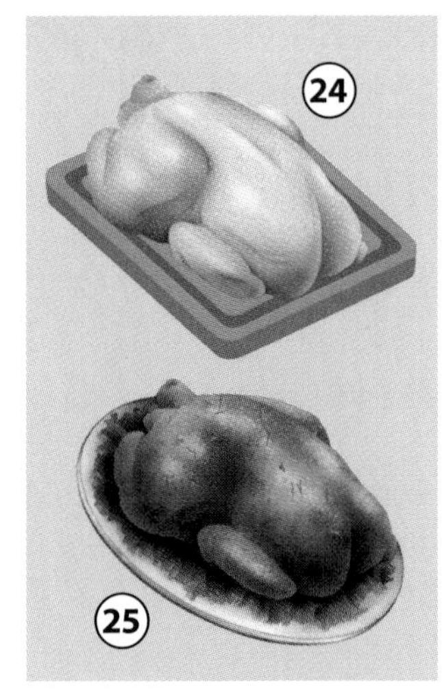

**Poultry**

16. chicken
17. turkey
18. duck
19. breasts
20. wings
21. legs
22. thighs
23. drumsticks
24. **raw** chicken
25. **cooked** chicken

**More vocabulary**

**vegetarian:** a person who doesn't eat meat
**boneless:** meat and poultry without bones
**skinless:** poultry without skin

**Ask your classmates. Share the answers.**

1. What kind of meat do you eat most often?
2. What kind of meat do you use in soups?
3. What part of the chicken do you like the most?

**Fish**

1. trout
2. catfish
3. whole salmon
4. salmon steak
5. swordfish
6. halibut steak
7. tuna
8. cod

**Shellfish**

9. crab
10. lobster
11. shrimp
12. scallops
13. mussels
14. oysters
15. clams
16. **fresh** fish
17. **frozen** fish

18. white bread
19. wheat bread
20. rye bread
21. roast beef
22. corned beef
23. pastrami
24. salami
25. smoked turkey
26. processed cheese
27. Swiss cheese
28. cheddar cheese
29. mozzarella cheese

**Ways to order at the counter**

*I'd like some roast beef.*
*I'll have a halibut steak and some shrimp.*
*Could I get some Swiss cheese?*

**Pair practice. Make new conversations.**

**A:** *What can I get for you?*
**B:** *I'd like some roast beef. How about a pound?*
**A:** *A pound of roast beef coming up!*

# A Grocery Store

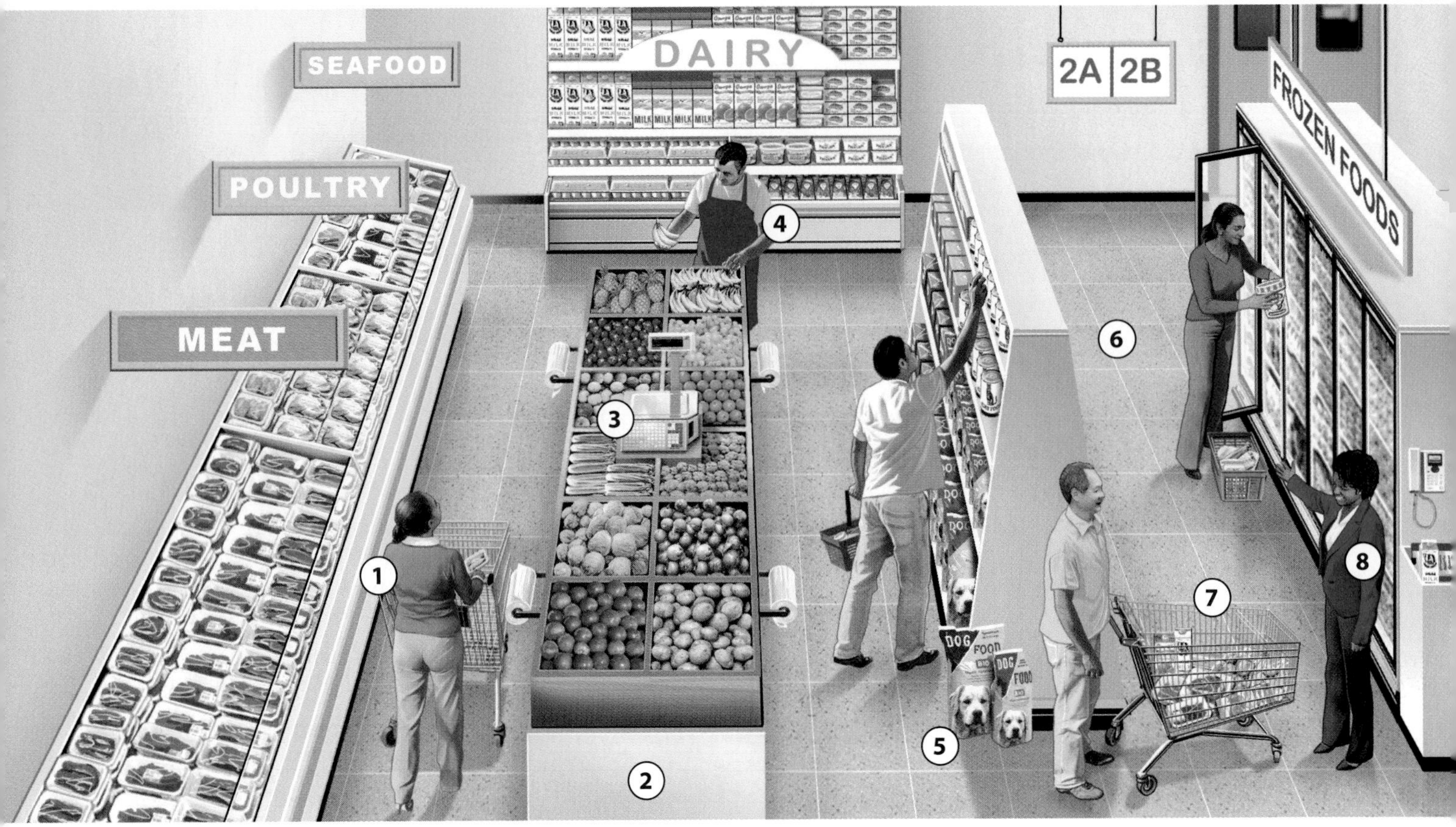

1. customer
2. produce section
3. scale
4. grocery clerk
5. pet food
6. aisle
7. cart
8. manager

### Canned Foods

17. beans
18. soup
19. tuna

### Dairy

20. margarine
21. sour cream
22. yogourt

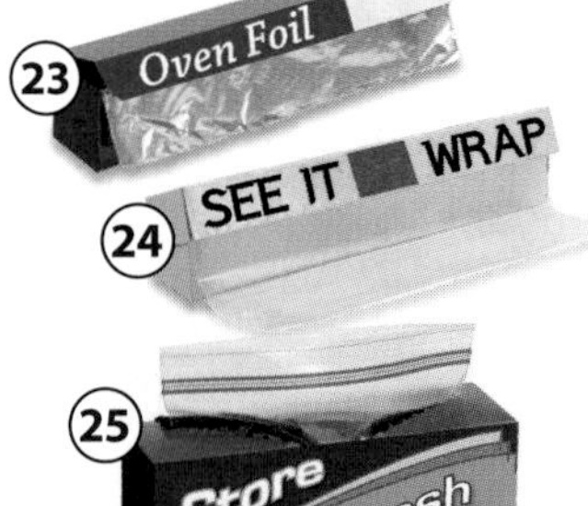


### Grocery Products

23. aluminum foil
24. plastic wrap
25. plastic storage bags

### Frozen Foods

26. ice cream
27. frozen vegetables
28. frozen dinner

**Ways to ask for information in a grocery store**

*Excuse me, where are the carrots?*
*Can you please tell me where to find the dog food?*
*Do you have any lamb chops today?*

**Pair practice. Make conversations.**

**A:** *Can you please tell me where to find the dog food?*
**B:** *Sure. It's in aisle 1B. Do you need anything else?*
**A:** *Yes, where are the carrots?*

9. shopping basket
10. self-checkout
11. line
12. checkout
13. cashier
14. bagger
15. cash register
16. bottle return

## Baking Products

29. flour
30. sugar
31. oil

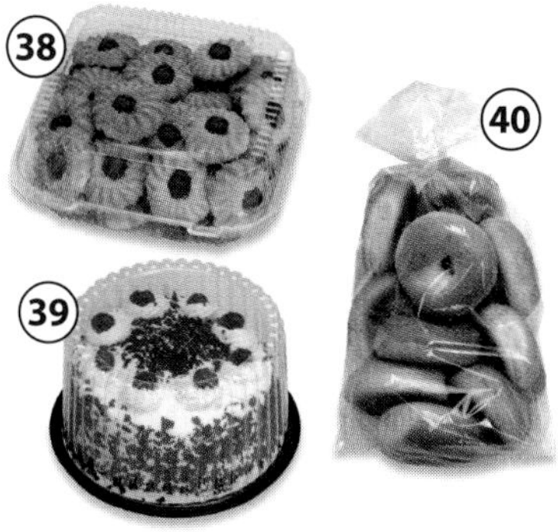

## Beverages

32. apple juice
33. coffee
34. pop

## Snack Foods

35. potato chips
36. nuts
37. chocolate bar

## Baked Goods

38. cookies
39. cake
40. bagels

**Ask your classmates. Share the answers.**

1. What is your favourite grocery store?
2. Do you prefer to shop alone or with friends?
3. Which foods from your country are hard to find?

**Think about it. Discuss.**

1. Is it better to shop every day or once a week? Why?
2. Why do grocery stores put snacks near the checkouts?
3. What's good and what's bad about small grocery stores?

# Containers and Packaging

1. bottles

2. jars

3. cans

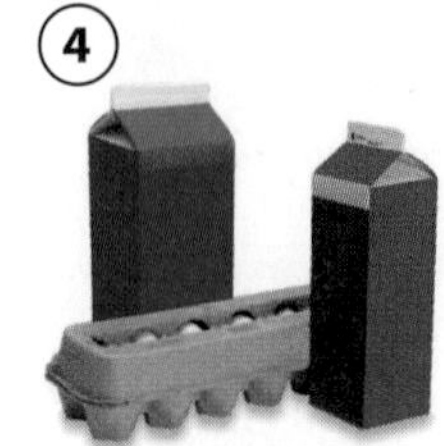
4. cartons

5. containers

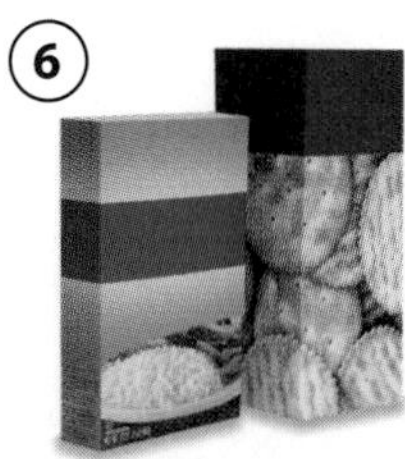
6. boxes

7. bags

8. packages

9. six-packs

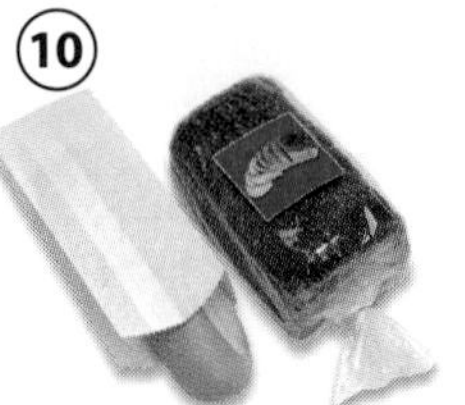
10. loaves

11. rolls

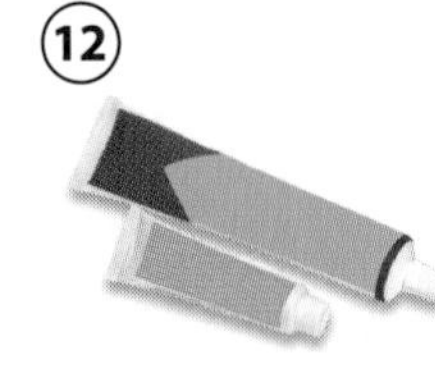
12. tubes

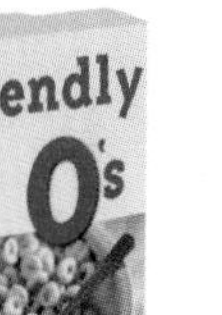

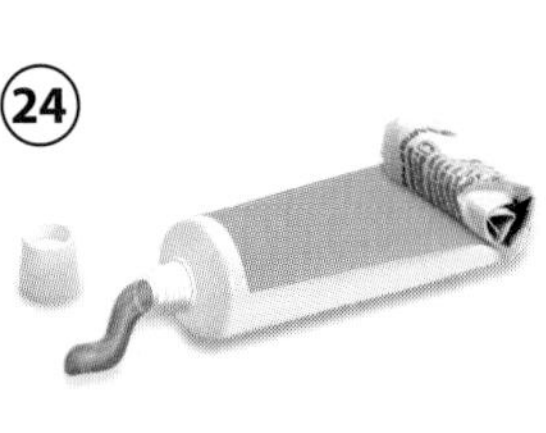

13. a bottle of water
14. a jar of jam
15. a can of beans
16. a carton of eggs
17. a container of cottage cheese
18. a box of cereal
19. a bag of flour
20. a package of cookies
21. a six-pack of pop
22. a loaf of bread
23. a roll of paper towels
24. a tube of toothpaste

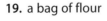

**Grammar Point: countable and non-countable**

Some foods can be counted: *an apple, two apples.*
Some foods can't be counted: *some rice, some water.*
For non-countable foods, count containers: *two bags of rice.*

**Pair practice. Make conversations.**

**A:** *How many boxes of cereal do we need?*
**B:** *We need two boxes.*

A. **Measure** the ingredients.

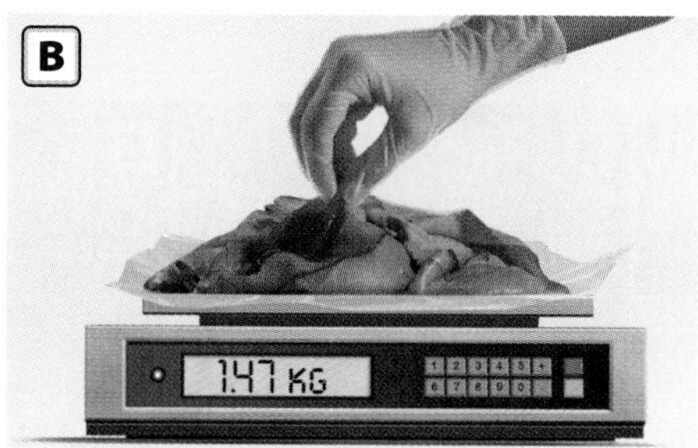


B. **Weigh** the food.

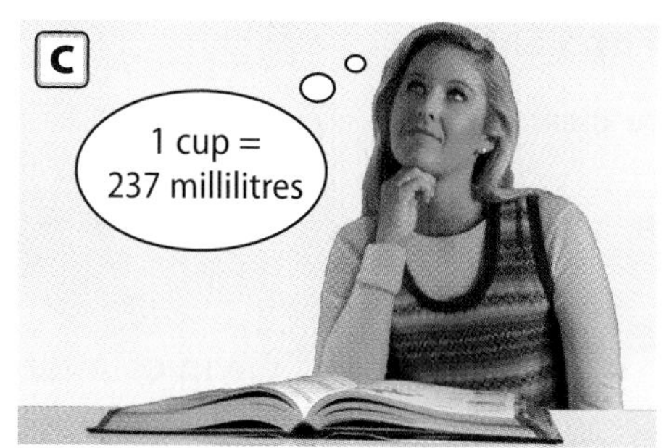


C. **Convert** the measurements.

## Liquid Measures

1 fl. oz.

1 c.

500 mL

1 L

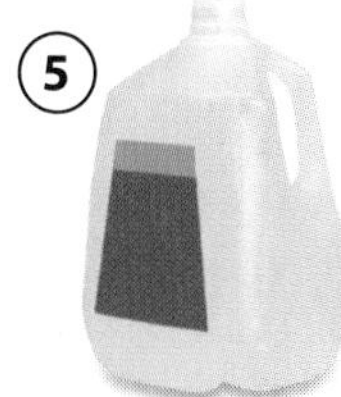


4 L / 1 gal.

## Dry Measures

5 mL / 1 tsp.

15 mL / 1 tbsp.

60 mL / 1/4 c.

118 mL / 1/2 c.

237 mL / 1 c.

## Weight

12
1 KG

1. a fluid ounce of milk
2. a cup of oil
3. 500 millilitres of frozen yogourt
4. a litre of milk
5. a 4-litre jug or a gallon of water
6. 5 millilitres or a teaspoon of salt
7. 15 millilitres or a tablespoon of sugar
8. 60 millilitres or a quarter cup of brown sugar
9. 118 millilitres or a half cup of raisins
10. 237 millilitres or a cup of flour
11. 500 grams of cheese
12. a kilogram of roast beef

| Equivalencies | |
|---|---|
| 3 tsp. = 1 tbsp. | 5 mL = 1 tsp. |
| 2 tbsp. = 1 fl. oz. | 15 mL = 1 tbsp. |
| 8 fl. oz. = 1 c. | |

| Volume |
|---|
| 1 fl. oz. = 30 mL |
| 1 c. = 237 mL |
| 1 L = 1000 mL |
| 1 gal. = 3.79 L |

| Weight |
|---|
| 1 oz. = 28.35 grams (g) |
| 1 lb. = 453.6 g |
| 2.205 lbs. = 1 kilogram (kg) |
| 1 lb. = 16 oz. |
| 1 kg = 1000 g |

## Food Safety

A. **clean**

B. **separate**

C. **cook**

D. **chill**

A
Clean counters!
20 SECONDS
Wash your hands!
B
Use separate cutting boards for vegetables and meat!
C
74
70
Cook to the right temperature!
D
Refrigerate leftovers quickly!

## Ways to Serve Meat and Poultry

Oil

1. fried chicken

2. barbecued / grilled ribs

3. broiled steak

4. roasted turkey

5. boiled ham

6. stir-fried beef

## Ways to Serve Eggs

7. scrambled eggs

8. hard-boiled eggs

9. poached eggs

10. eggs sunny side up

11. eggs over easy

12. omelette

**Role play. Make new conversations.**

A: *How do you like your eggs?*
B: *I like them scrambled. And you?*
A: *I like them hard-boiled.*

**Ask your classmates. Share the answers.**

1. Do you use separate cutting boards?
2. What is your favourite way to serve meat? poultry?
3. What are healthy ways of preparing meat? poultry?

## Cheesy Tofu Vegetable Casserole

A. **Preheat** the oven.

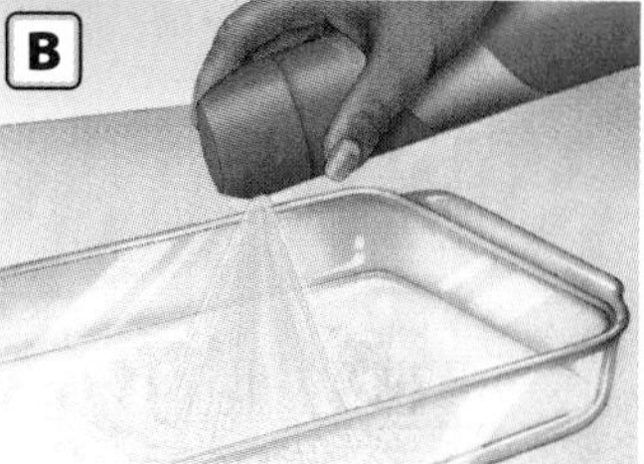


B. **Grease** a baking pan.

C. **Slice** the tofu.

D. **Steam** the broccoli.

E. **Sauté** the mushrooms.

F. **Spoon** sauce on top.

G. **Grate** the cheese.

H. **Bake**.

## Easy Chicken Soup

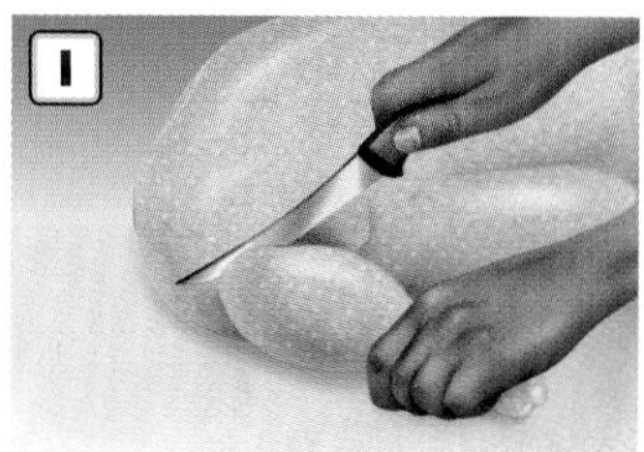


I. **Cut up** the chicken.

J. **Dice** the celery.

K. **Peel** the carrots.

L. **Chop** the onions.

M. **Boil** the chicken.

N. **Add** the vegetables.

O. **Stir**.

P. **Simmer**.

## Quick and Easy Cake

Q. **Break** 2 eggs into a microwave-safe bowl.

R. **Mix** the ingredients.

S. **Beat** the mixture.

T. **Microwave** for 5 minutes.

# Kitchen Utensils

1. can opener
2. grater
3. steamer
4. plastic storage container
5. frying pan
6. pot
7. ladle
8. double boiler
9. wooden spoon
10. casserole dish
11. garlic press
12. carving knife
13. roasting pan
14. roasting rack
15. vegetable peeler
16. paring knife
17. colander
18. kitchen timer
19. spatula
20. egg beater
21. whisk
22. strainer
23. tongs
24. lid
25. saucepan
26. cake pan
27. cookie sheet
28. pie pan
29. pot holders
30. rolling pin
31. mixing bowl

**Pair practice. Make new conversations.**

**A:** *Please hand me the whisk.*
**B:** *Here's the whisk. Do you need anything else?*
**A:** *Yes, pass me the casserole dish.*

**Use the new words.**
Look at page 77. Name the kitchen utensils you see.

**A:** *Here's a grater.*
**B:** *This is a mixing bowl.*

1. hamburger
2. french fries
3. cheeseburger
4. onion rings
5. chicken sandwich
6. hot dog
7. nachos
8. taco
9. burrito
10. pizza
11. pop
12. iced tea
13. ice cream cone
14. milkshake
15. doughnut / donut
16. muffin
17. counter person
18. straw
19. plastic utensils
20. sugar substitute
21. ketchup
22. mustard
23. mayonnaise
24. salad bar

**Grammar Point: yes/no questions *(do)***

***Do** you like hamburgers? Yes, I do.*
***Do** you like nachos? No, I don't.*

**Think about it. Discuss.**

1. Do you think that fast food is bad for people? Why or why not?
2. What fast foods do you have in your country?
3. Do you have a favourite fast-food restaurant? Which one?

# A Coffee Shop Menu

1. bacon
2. sausage
3. hash browns
4. toast
5. English muffin
6. biscuits
7. pancakes
8. waffles
9. hot cereal

10. grilled cheese sandwich
11. pickle
12. club sandwich
13. spinach salad
14. chef's salad
15. dinner salad
16. soup
17. rolls
18. coleslaw
19. potato salad
20. pasta salad
21. fruit salad

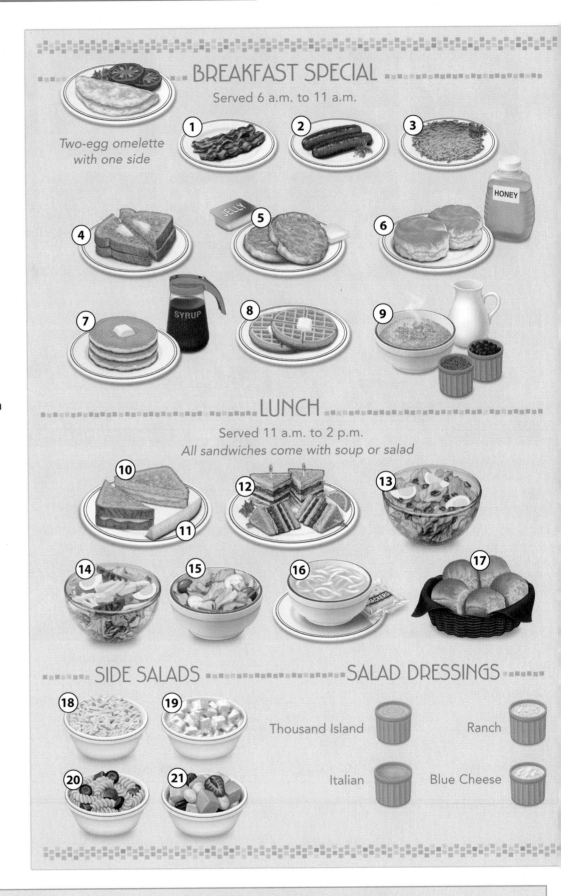

**Ways to order from a menu**

*I'd like a grilled cheese sandwich.*
*I'll have a bowl of tomato soup.*
*Could I get the chef's salad with ranch dressing?*

**Pair practice. Make conversations.**

**A:** *I'd like a grilled cheese sandwich, please.*
**B:** *Anything else for you?*
**A:** *Yes, I'll have a bowl of tomato soup with that.*

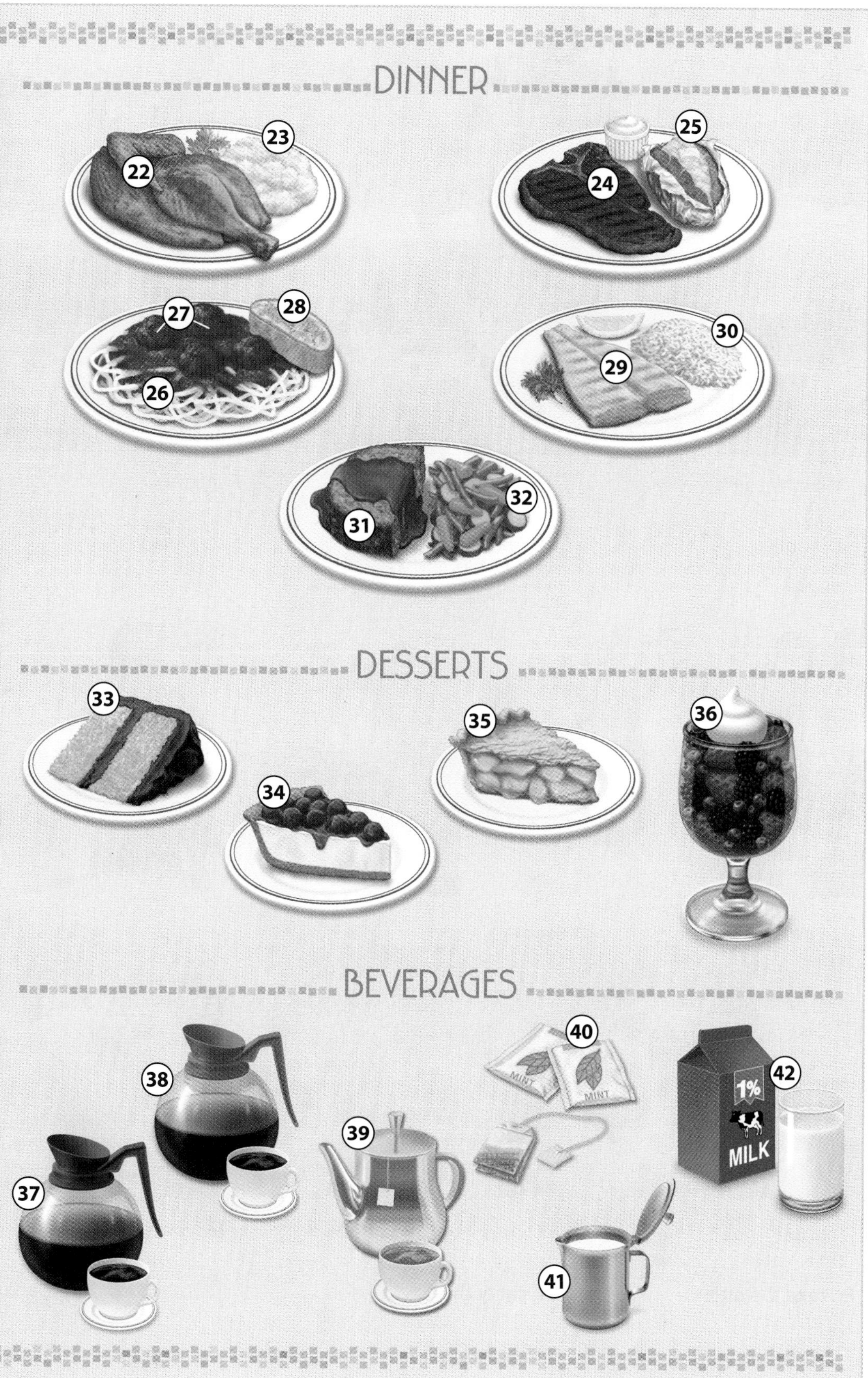


22. roast chicken
23. mashed potatoes
24. steak
25. baked potato
26. spaghetti
27. meatballs
28. garlic bread
29. grilled fish
30. rice
31. meatloaf
32. steamed vegetables

33. layer cake
34. cheesecake
35. pie
36. mixed berries

37. coffee
38. decaffeinated coffee
39. tea
40. herbal tea
41. cream
42. low-fat milk

**Ask your classmates. Share the answers.**

1. Do you prefer vegetable soup or chicken soup?
2. Do you prefer tea or coffee?
3. Which desserts on the menu do you like?

**Role play. Order a dinner from the menu.**

**A:** *Are you ready to order?*
**B:** *I think so. I'll have the roast chicken.*
**A:** *Would you also like…?*

1. dining room
2. hostess
3. high chair
4. booth
5. to-go box
6. patron / diner
7. menu
8. server / waiter

A. **set** the table
B. **seat** the customer
C. **pour** the water
D. **order** from the menu
E. **take** the order
F. **serve** the meal
G. **clear** / **bus** the dishes
H. **carry** the tray
I. **pay** the bill
J. **leave** a tip

**More vocabulary**

**eat out:** go to a restaurant to eat
**take out:** buy food at a restaurant and take it home to eat

**Look at the pictures.**
Describe what is happening.
**A:** *She's seating the customer.*
**B:** *He's taking the order.*

9. server / waitress
10. dessert tray
11. bread basket
12. busser
13. dish room
14. dishwasher
15. kitchen
16. chef

17. place setting
18. dinner plate
19. bread-and-butter plate
20. salad plate
21. soup bowl
22. water glass
23. wine glass
24. cup
25. saucer
26. napkin
27. salad fork
28. dinner fork
29. steak knife
30. knife
31. teaspoon
32. soup spoon

**Pair practice. Make new conversations.**

**A:** *Excuse me, this spoon is dirty.*
**B:** *I'm so sorry. I'll get you a clean spoon right away.*
**A:** *Thanks.*

**Role play. Talk to a new busser.**

**A:** *Do the salad forks go on the left?*
**B:** *Yes. They go next to the dinner forks.*
**A:** *What about the…?*

# The Farmers' Market

1. live music
2. organic
3. lemonade
4. sour
5. samples
6. avocados
7. vendors
8. sweets
9. herbs

A. **count**

**Look at the pictures.**
**What do you see?**

**Answer the questions.**

1. How many vendors are at the market today?
2. Which vegetables are organic?
3. What are the children eating?
4. What is the woman counting? Why?

 **Read the story.**

## The Farmers' Market

On Saturdays, the Novaks go to the farmers' market. They like to visit the vendors. Alex Novak always goes to the hot food stand for lunch. His children love to eat the fruit samples. Alex's father usually buys some sweets and lemonade. The lemonade is very sour.

Nina Novak likes to buy organic herbs and vegetables. Today, she is buying avocados. The market worker counts eight avocados. She gives Nina one more for free.

There are other things to do at the market. The Novaks like to listen to the live music. Sometimes they meet friends there. The farmers' market is a great place for families on a Saturday afternoon.

**Think about it.**

1. What's good or bad about shopping at a farmers' market?
2. Imagine you are at the farmers' market. What will you buy?

1. shirt
2. jeans
3. dress
4. T-shirt
5. baseball cap
6. socks
7. athletic shoes

A. **tie**

**Listen and point. Take turns.**

**A:** *Point to the dress.*
**B:** *Point to the T-shirt.*
**A:** *Point to the baseball cap.*

**Dictate to your partner. Take turns.**

**A:** *Write dress.*
**B:** *Is that spelled d-r-e-s-s?*
**A:** *Yes. That's right.*

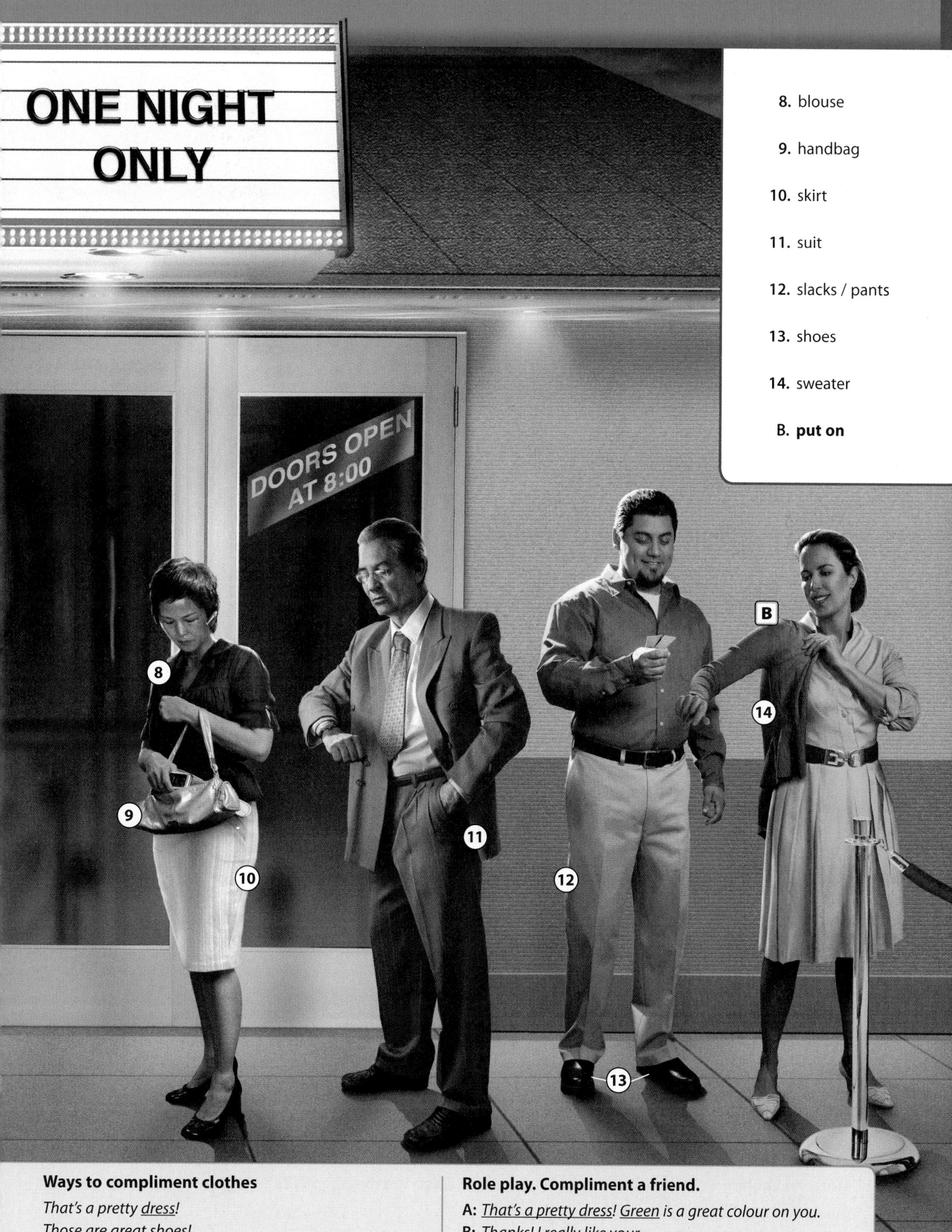


8. blouse
9. handbag
10. skirt
11. suit
12. slacks / pants
13. shoes
14. sweater

B. **put on**

**Ways to compliment clothes**

*That's a pretty dress!*

*Those are great shoes!*

*I really like your baseball cap!*

**Role play. Compliment a friend.**

**A:** *That's a pretty dress! Green is a great colour on you.*

**B:** *Thanks! I really like your…*

# Casual, Work, and Formal Clothes

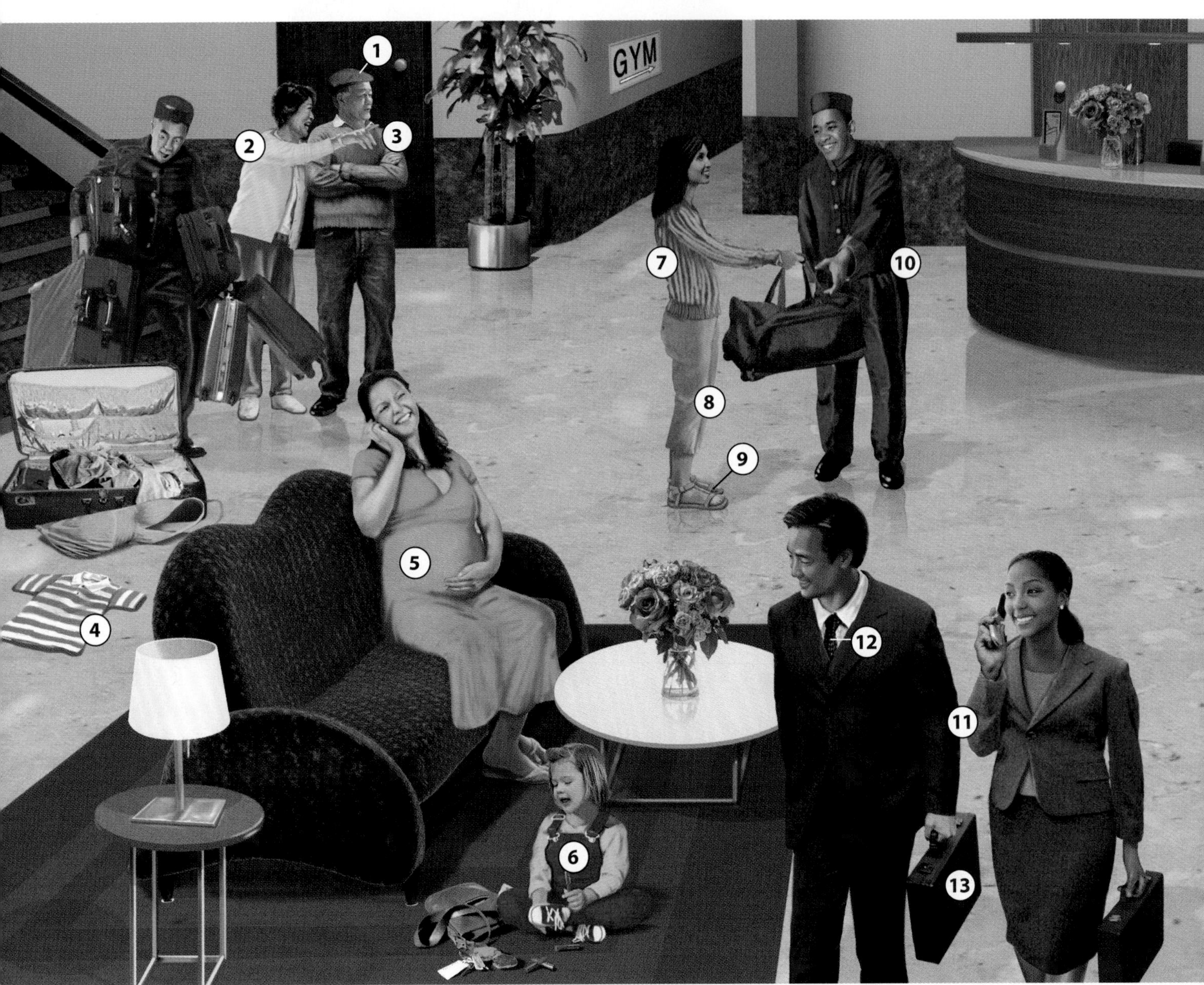


## Casual Clothes

1. cap
2. cardigan sweater
3. pullover sweater
4. sports shirt
5. maternity dress
6. overalls
7. knit top
8. capris
9. sandals

## Work Clothes

10. uniform
11. business suit
12. tie
13. briefcase

**More vocabulary**

**three-piece suit:** matching jacket, vest, and slacks
**outfit:** clothes that look nice together
**in fashion / in style:** clothes that are popular now

**Describe the people. Take turns.**

**A:** *She's wearing a maternity dress.*
**B:** *He's wearing a uniform.*

## Formal Clothes

14. sports jacket / sports coat
15. vest
16. bow tie
17. tuxedo
18. evening gown
19. clutch bag
20. cocktail dress
21. high heels

## Exercise Wear

22. sweatshirt / hoodie
23. sweatpants
24. tank top
25. shorts

**Ask your classmates. Share the answers.**

1. What's your favourite outfit?
2. Do you like to wear formal clothes? Why or why not?
3. Do you prefer to exercise in shorts or sweatpants?

**Think about it. Discuss.**

1. What jobs require formal clothes? Uniforms?
2. What's good and bad about wearing school uniforms?
3. What is your opinion of today's popular clothing?

# Seasonal Clothing

1. hat
2. (over)coat
3. headband
4. leather jacket
5. winter scarf
6. gloves
7. headwrap
8. jacket

9. parka
10. mittens
11. ski hat
12. leggings
13. earmuffs
14. down vest
15. ski mask
16. down jacket

17. umbrella
18. raincoat
19. poncho
20. rain boots
21. trench coat

22. swimming trunks
23. straw hat
24. windbreaker
25. cover-up
26. swimsuit / bathing suit
27. sunglasses

**Grammar Point: *should***

*It's raining. You* **should** *take an umbrella.*
*It's snowing. You* **should** *wear a scarf.*
*It's sunny. You* **should** *wear a straw hat.*

**Pair practice. Make new conversations.**

**A:** *It's snowing. You should wear a scarf.*
**B:** *Don't worry. I'm wearing my parka.*
**A:** *Good, and don't forget your mittens.*

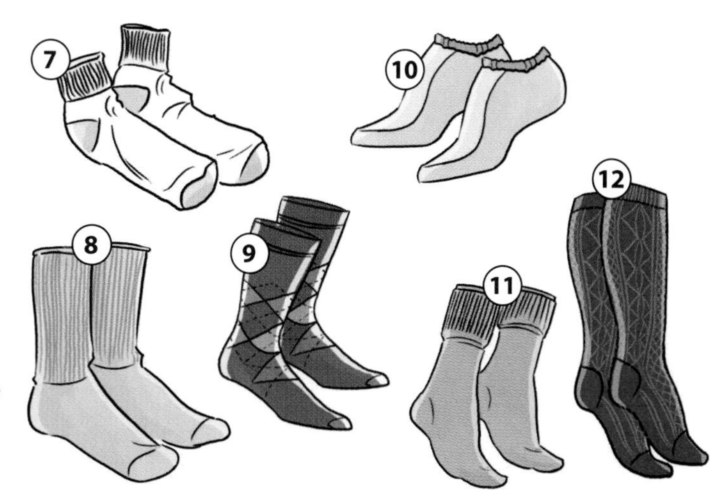


## Unisex Underwear

1. undershirt
2. thermal undershirt
3. long underwear

## Men's Underwear

4. boxer shorts
5. briefs
6. athletic supporter / jockstrap

## Unisex Socks

7. ankle socks
8. crew socks
9. dress socks

## Women's Socks

10. low-cut socks
11. anklets
12. knee-highs

## Women's Underwear

13. (bikini) panties
14. briefs / underpants
15. body shaper / girdle
16. garter belt
17. stockings
18. pantyhose
19. tights
20. bra
21. camisole
22. full slip
23. half slip

## Sleepwear

24. pyjamas
25. nightgown
26. slippers
27. blanket sleeper
28. nightshirt
29. robe

### More vocabulary

**lingerie:** underwear or sleepwear for women

**loungewear:** very casual clothing for relaxing around the home

### Ask your classmates. Share the answers.

1. What kind of socks are you wearing today?
2. What kind of sleepwear do you prefer?
3. Do you wear slippers at home?

# Workplace Clothing

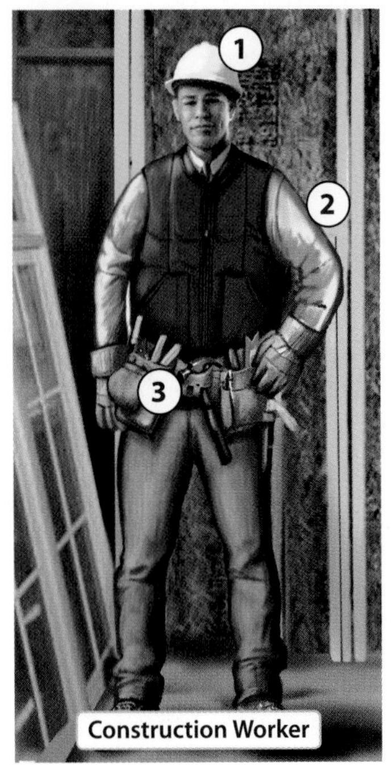


Construction Worker

1. hard hat
2. work shirt
3. tool belt

Road Worker

4. safety vest
5. work pants
6. steel toe boots

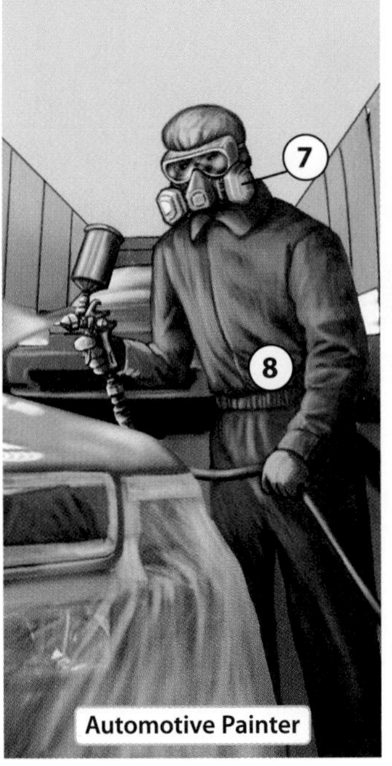


Automotive Painter

7. ventilation mask
8. coveralls

Food Processor

9. bump cap
10. safety glasses
11. apron

Manager

12. blazer
13. tie

Salesperson

14. polo shirt
15. name tag

Farmhand

16. bandana
17. work gloves

Ranch Hand

18. cowboy hat
19. jeans

**Pair practice. Make new conversations.**

**A:** *What do* *construction workers* *wear to work?*
**B:** *They wear* *hard hats* *and* *tool belts.*
**A:** *What do* *road workers* *wear to work?*

**Use the new words.**

Look at pages 166–169. Name the workplace clothing you see.

**A:** *He's wearing* *a hard hat.*
**B:** *She's wearing* *scrubs.*

20. security shirt
21. badge
22. security pants

23. helmet
24. jumpsuit

25. hairnet
26. smock
27. disposable gloves

28. chef's hat
29. chef's jacket
30. waist apron

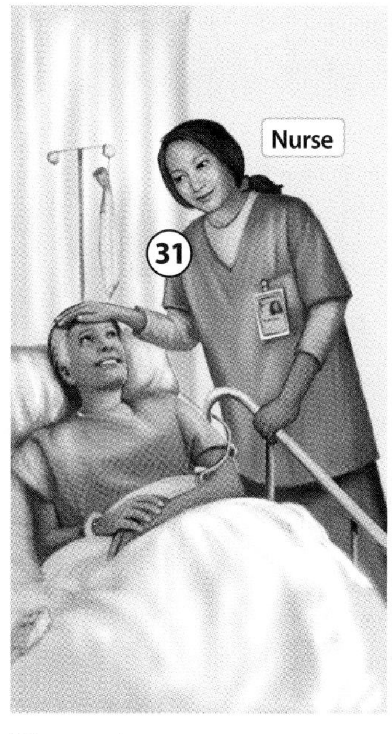


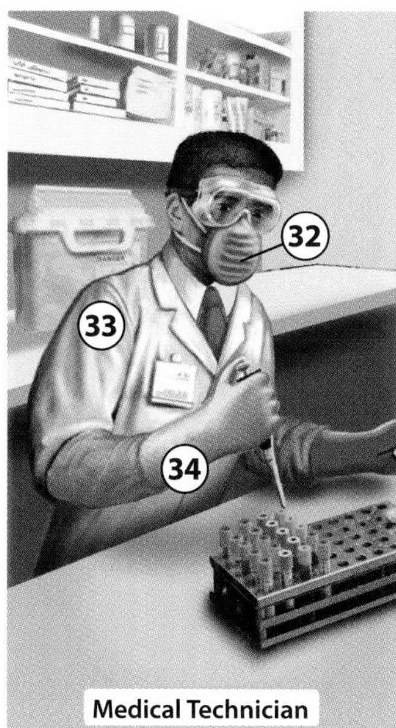


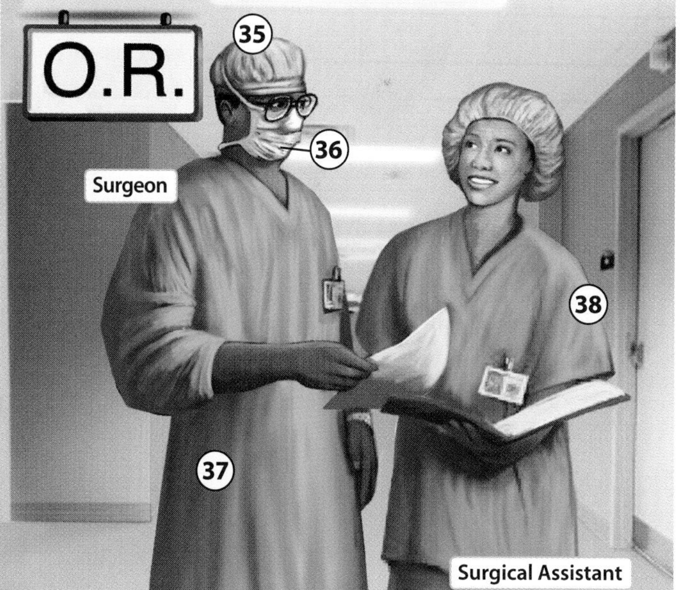


31. scrubs
32. face mask

33. lab coat
34. latex gloves

35. surgical scrub cap
36. surgical mask

37. surgical gown
38. surgical scrubs

**Ask your classmates. Share the answers.**

1. Which of these outfits would you like to wear?
2. Which of these items are in your closet?
3. Do you wear safety clothing at work? What kinds?

**Think about it. Discuss.**

1. What other jobs require helmets? disposable gloves?
2. Is it better to have a uniform or wear your own clothes at work? Why?

# Shoes and Accessories

A. **purchase**

B. **wait** in line

1. suspenders
2. purses / handbags
3. sales clerk
4. customer
5. display case
6. belts

13. wallet
14. change purse / coin purse
15. cellphone holder
16. (wrist)watch
17. shoulder bag
18. backpack
19. tote bag
20. belt buckle
21. sole
22. heel
23. toe
24. shoelaces

**More vocabulary**

**gift:** something you give or receive from friends or family for a special occasion

**present:** a gift

**Grammar Point: object pronouns**

*My **sister** loves jewellery. I'll buy **her** a necklace.*
*My **dad** likes belts. I'll buy **him** a belt buckle.*
*My **friends** love scarves. I'll buy **them** scarves.*

7. shoe department
8. jewellery department
9. bracelets
10. necklaces
11. hats
12. scarves
C. **try on** shoes
D. **assist** a customer

25. high heels
26. pumps
27. flats
28. boots
29. oxfords
30. loafers
31. hiking boots
32. tennis shoes
33. chain
34. beads
35. locket
36. pierced earrings
37. clip-on earrings
38. pin
39. string of pearls
40. ring

**Ways to talk about accessories**

*I need a hat to wear with this scarf.*
*I'd like earrings to go with the necklace.*
*Do you have a belt that would go with my shoes?*

**Role play. Talk to a salesperson.**

**A:** *Do you have boots that would go with this skirt?*
**B:** *Let me see. How about these brown ones?*
**A:** *Perfect. I also need…*

# Describing Clothes

## Sizes

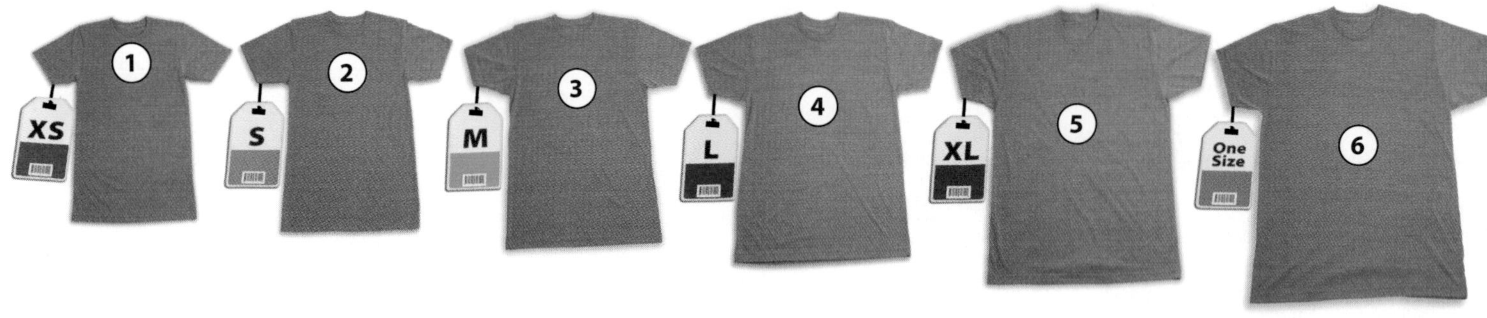


1. extra small
2. small
3. medium
4. large
5. extra large
6. one-size-fits-all

## Styles

7. **crewneck** sweater
8. **V-neck** sweater
9. **turtleneck** sweater
10. **scoop neck** sweater
11. **sleeveless** shirt
12. **short-sleeved** shirt
13. **3/4-sleeved** shirt
14. **long-sleeved** shirt
15. **mini** skirt
16. **short** skirt
17. **mid-length** / **calf-length** skirt
18. **long** skirt

## Patterns

19. solid
20. striped
21. polka-dotted
22. plaid
23. print
24. checked
25. floral
26. paisley

**Ask your classmates. Share the answers.**

1. Do you prefer crewneck or V-neck sweaters?
2. Do you prefer checked or striped shirts?
3. Do you prefer short-sleeved or sleeveless shirts?

**Role play. Talk to a salesperson.**

**A:** *Excuse me. I'm looking for this V-neck sweater in large.*
**B:** *Here's a large. It's on sale for $19.99.*
**A:** *Wonderful! I'll take it. I'm also looking for…*

## Comparing Clothing

27. **heavy** jacket
28. **light** jacket
29. **tight** pants
30. **loose** / **baggy** pants
31. **low** heels
32. **high** heels
33. **plain** blouse
34. **fancy** blouse
35. **narrow** tie
36. **wide** tie

## Clothing Problems

37. It's **too small**.

38. It's **too big**.

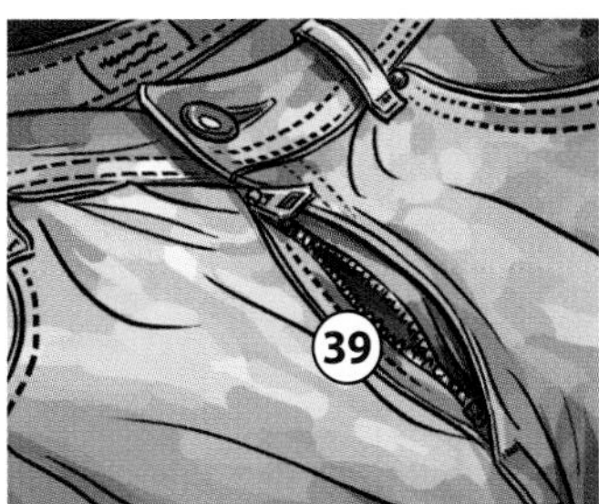

39. The zipper is **broken**.

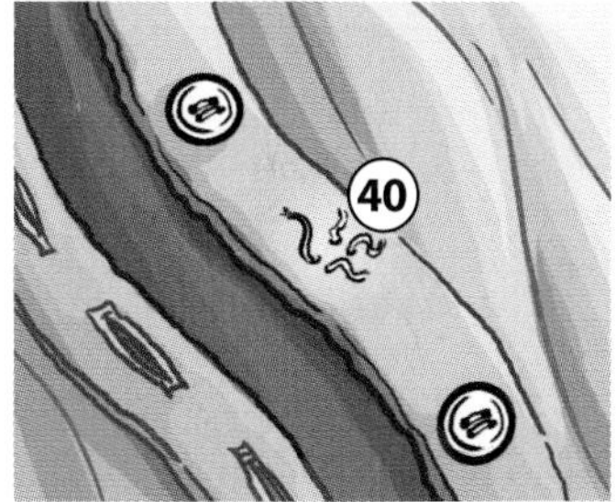

40. A button is **missing**.

41. It's **ripped** / **torn**.

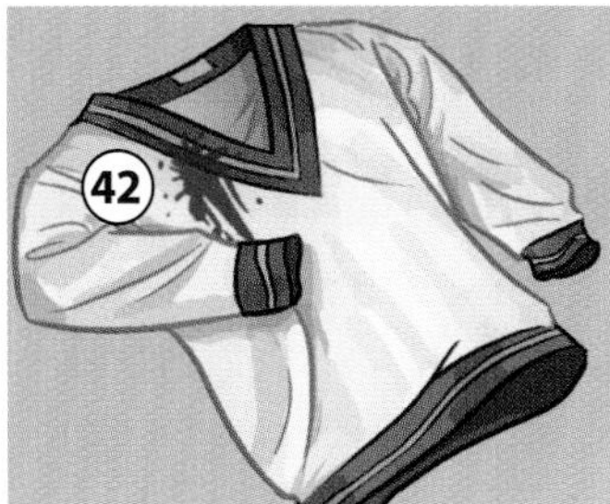

42. It's **stained**.

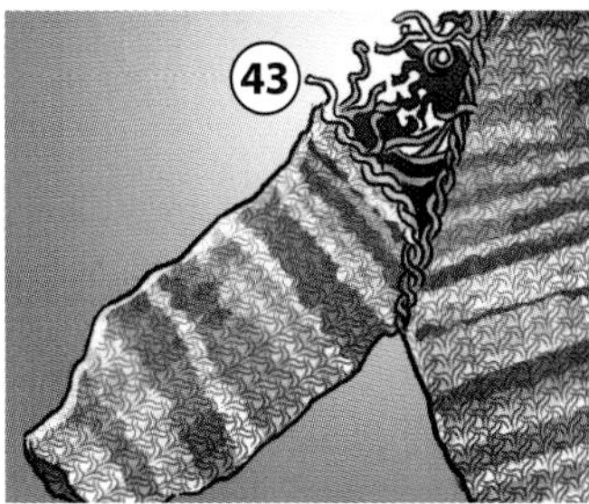

43. It's **unravelling**.

44. It's **too expensive**.

**More vocabulary**

**refund:** money you get back when you return an item to the store
**complaint:** a statement that something is not right
**customer service:** the place customers go with their complaints

**Role play. Return an item to a salesperson.**

**A:** *Welcome to Shopmart. How may I help you?*
**B:** *This sweater is new, but it's unravelling.*
**A:** *I'm sorry. Would you like a refund?*

# Making Clothes

## Types of Material

1. cotton

2. linen

3. wool

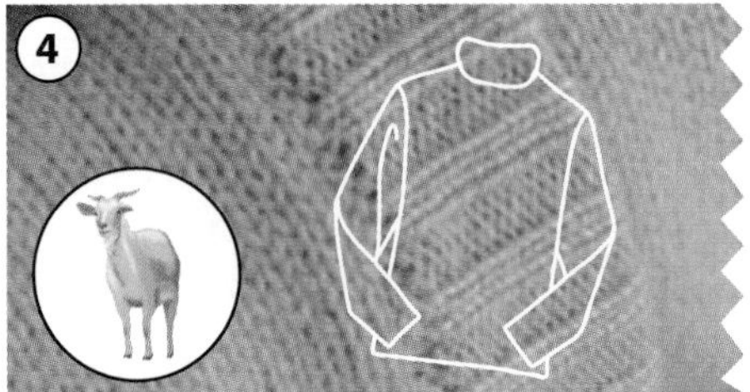


4. cashmere

5. silk

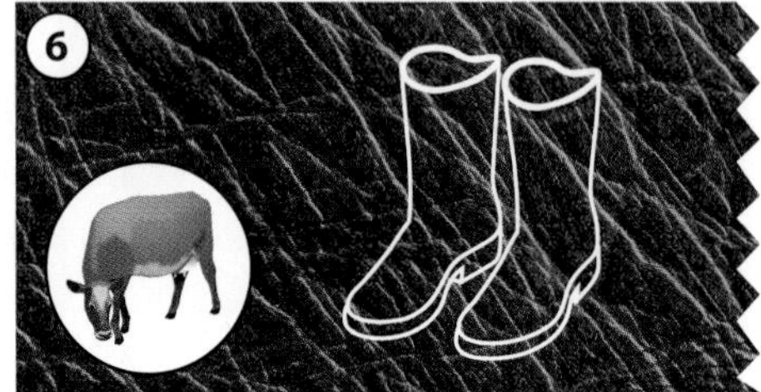


6. leather

## A Garment Factory

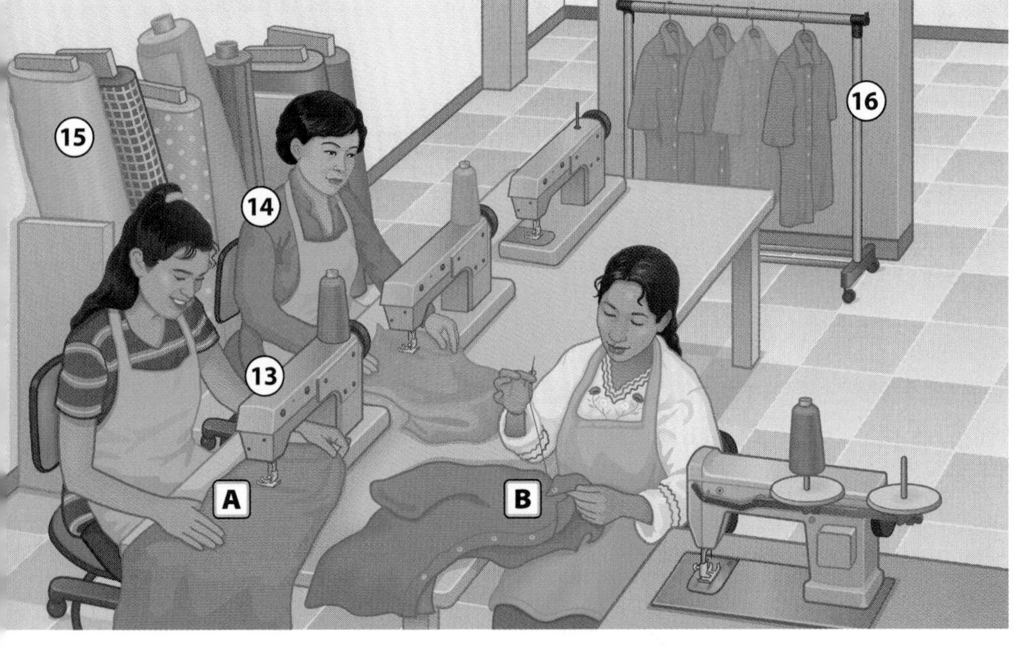


## Parts of a Sewing Machine

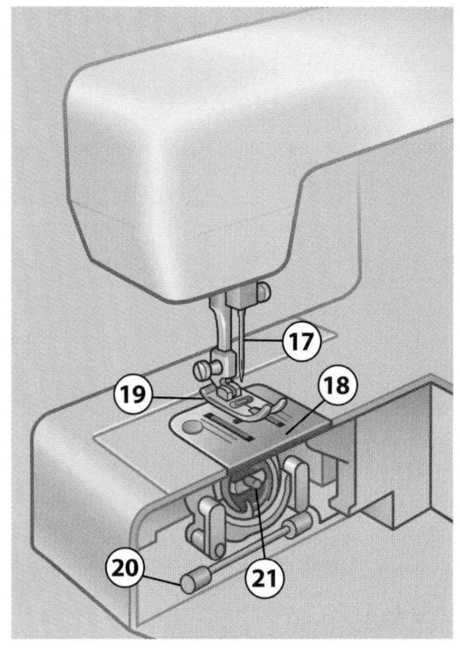


A. **sew** by machine

B. **sew** by hand

13. sewing machine

14. sewing machine operator

15. bolt of fabric

16. rack

17. needle

18. needle plate

19. presser foot

20. feed dog / feed bar

21. bobbin

**More vocabulary**

**fashion designer:** a person who makes original clothes
**natural materials:** cloth made from things that grow in nature
**synthetic materials:** cloth made by people, such as nylon

**Use the new words.**

Look at pages 86–87. Name the materials you see.

**A:** *That's denim.*
**B:** *That's leather.*

## Types of Material

7. denim

8. suede

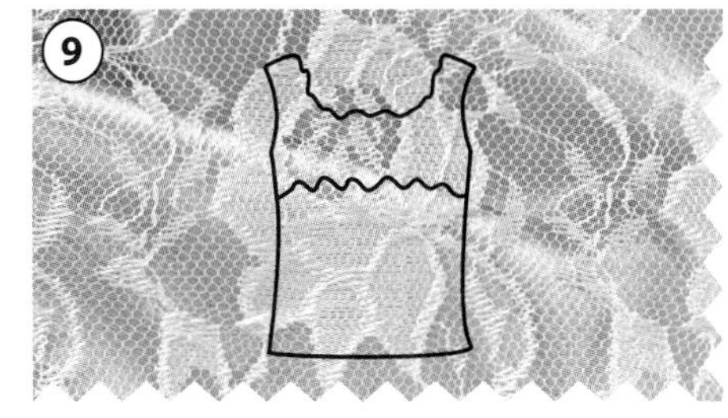
9. lace

10. velvet

11. corduroy

12. nylon

## A Fabric Store

## Closures

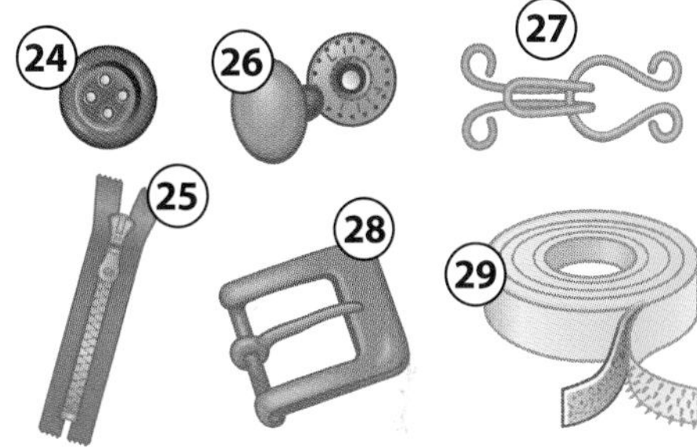

## Trim

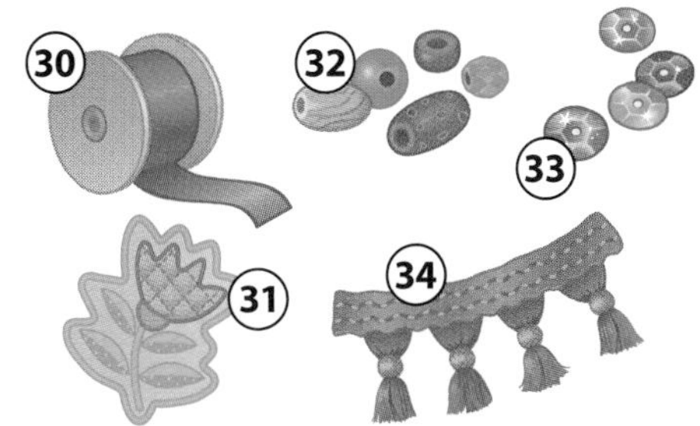

22. pattern
23. thread
24. button
25. zipper
26. snap
27. hook and eye
28. buckle
29. hook and loop fastener (velcro)
30. ribbon
31. appliqué
32. beads
33. sequins
34. fringe

**Ask your classmates. Share the answers.**

1. Can you sew?
2. What's your favourite type of material?
3. How many types of material are you wearing today?

**Think about it. Discuss.**

1. Do most people make or buy clothes in your country?
2. Is it better to make or buy clothes? Why?
3. Which materials are best for formal clothes?

# Making Alterations

## An Alterations Shop

1. dressmaker
2. dressmaker's dummy
3. tailor
4. collar
5. waistband
6. sleeve
7. pocket
8. hem
9. cuff

## Sewing Supplies

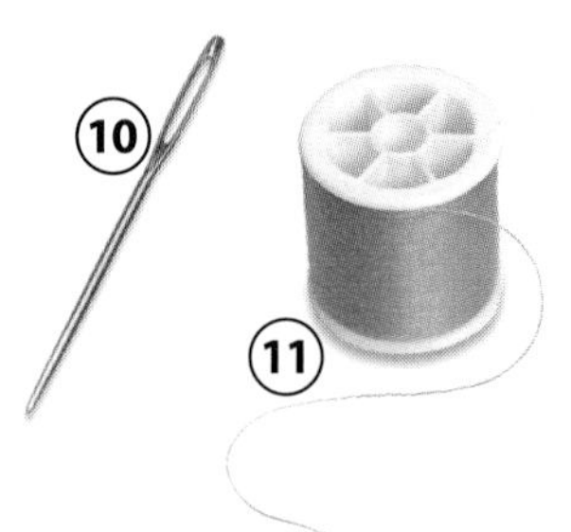

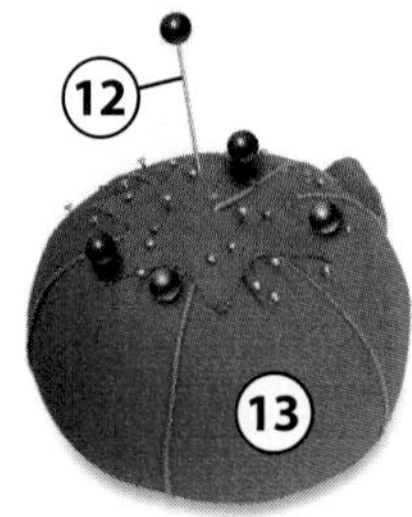

10. needle
11. thread
12. (straight) pin
13. pin cushion
14. safety pin
15. thimble
16. pair of scissors
17. tape measure
18. seam ripper

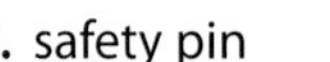

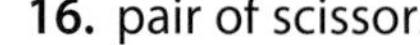

## Alterations

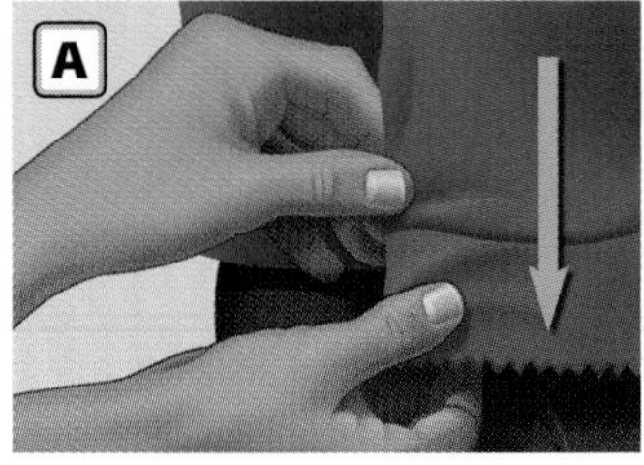

A. **Lengthen** the pants.

B. **Shorten** the pants.

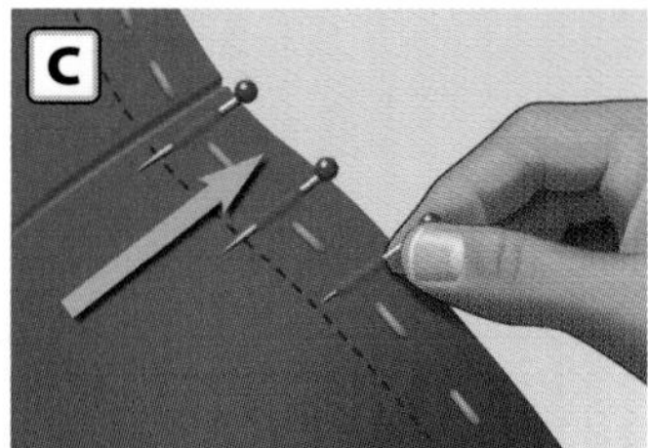

C. **Let out** the pants.

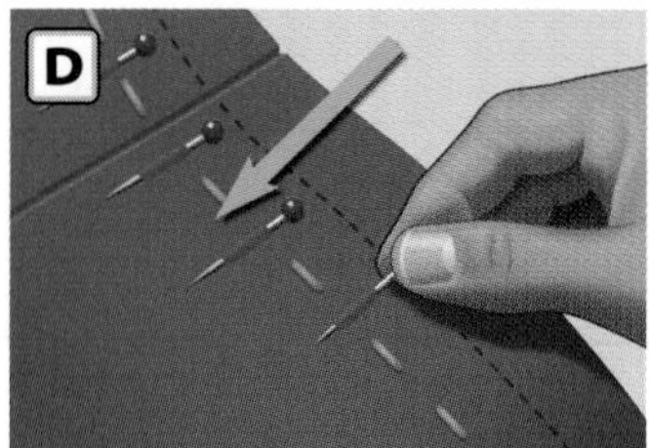

D. **Take in** the pants.

**Pair practice. Make new conversations.**

A: *Would you hand me the thread?*
B: *OK. What are you going to do?*
A: *I'm going to take in these pants.*

**Ask your classmates. Share the answers.**

1. Is there an alterations shop near your home?
2. Do you ever go to a tailor or a dressmaker?
3. What sewing supplies do you have at home?

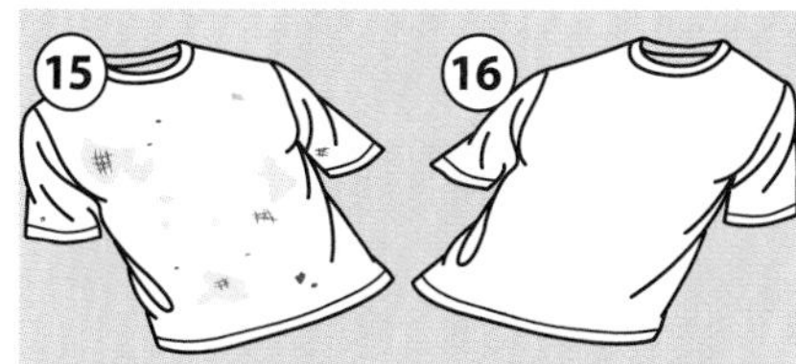

1. laundry
2. laundry basket
3. washer
4. dryer
5. dryer sheets
6. fabric softener
7. bleach
8. laundry detergent
9. clothesline
10. clothespin
11. hanger
12. spray starch
13. iron
14. ironing board
15. **dirty** T-shirt
16. **clean** T-shirt
17. **wet** shirt
18. **dry** shirt
19. **wrinkled** shirt
20. **ironed** shirt

A. **Sort** the laundry.

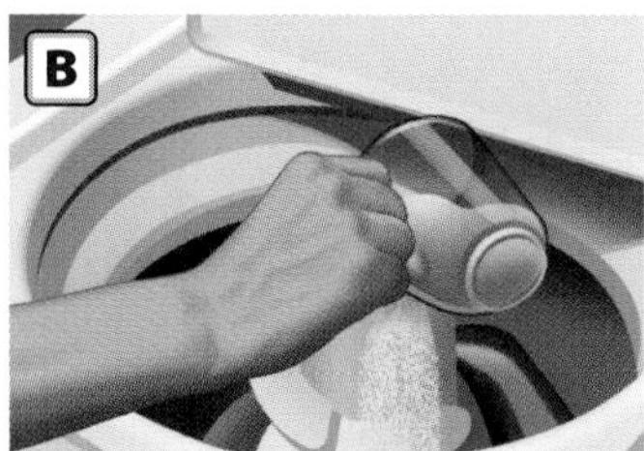

B. **Add** the detergent.

C. **Load** the washer.

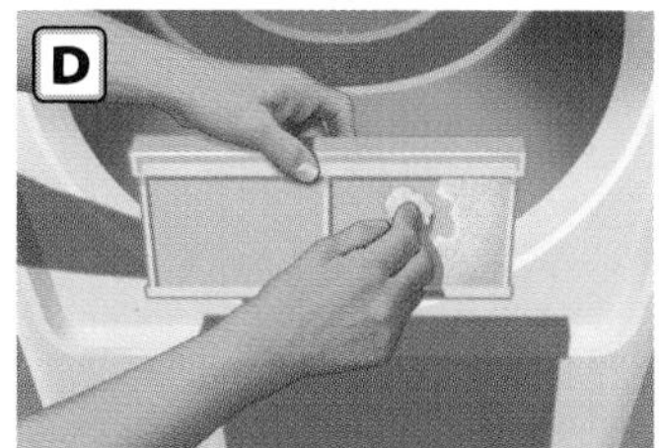

D. **Clean** the lint trap.

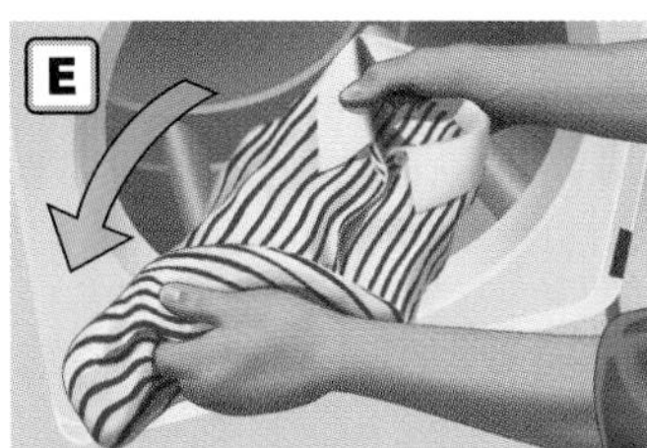

E. **Unload** the dryer.

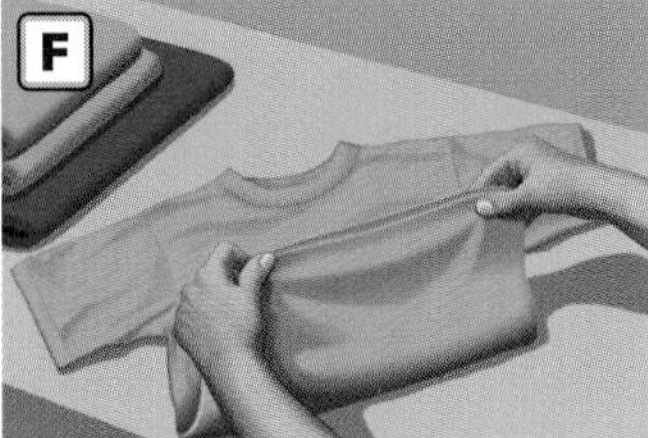

F. **Fold** the laundry.

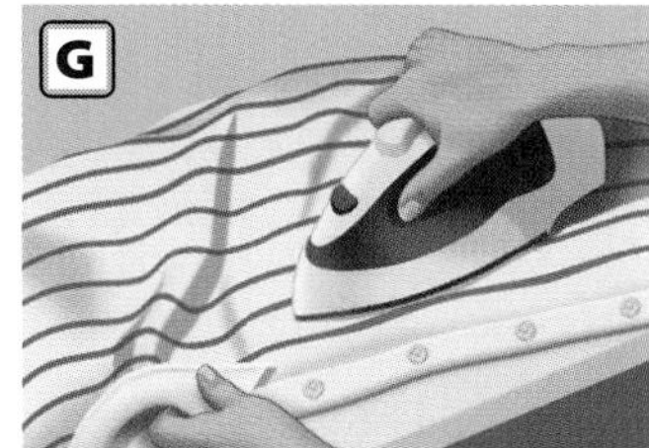

G. **Iron** the clothes.

H. **Hang up** the clothes.

 wash in cold water

 no bleach

 line dry

dry clean only, do not wash

**Pair practice. Make new conversations.**

A: *I have to sort the laundry. Can you help?*
B: *Sure. Here's the laundry basket.*
A: *Thanks a lot!*

# A Garage Sale

GARAGE SALE
TODAY 7-7
-CLOTHING
-SHOES
-ACCESSORIES
-ELECTRONICS

A Two dollars.

It's stained. I can give you seventy-five cents.

$.50 $5.00
$1.00 $10.00
$2.00 ASK ME

ALL PURSES $.75

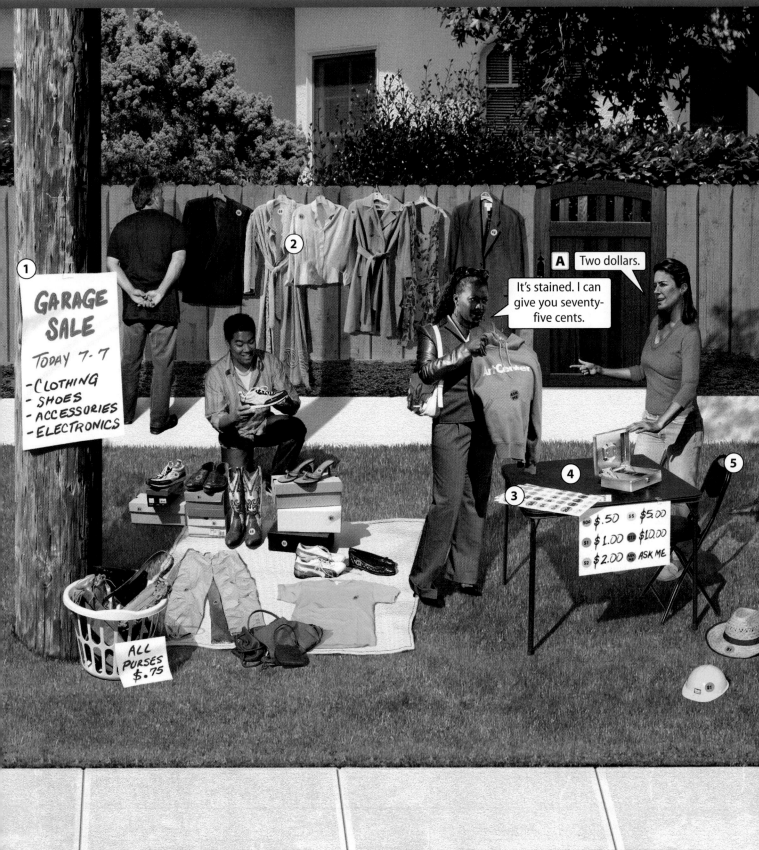

1. flyer
2. used clothing
3. sticker
4. folding card table
5. folding chair
6. clock radio
7. VCR

A. **bargain**
B. **browse**

**Look at the pictures.**
**What do you see?**

**Answer the questions.**

1. What kind of used clothing do you see?
2. What information is on the flyer?
3. Why are the stickers different colours?
4. How much is the clock radio? the VCR?

**Read the story.**

## A Garage Sale

Last Sunday, I had a garage sale. At 5:00 a.m., I put up flyers in my neighbourhood. Next, I put price stickers on my used clothing, my VCR, and some other old things. At 7:00 a.m., I opened my folding card table and folding chair. Then I waited.

At 7:05 a.m., my first customer arrived. She asked, "How much is the sweatshirt?"

"Two dollars," I said.

She said, "It's stained. I can give you seventy-five cents." We bargained for a minute and she paid $1.00.

All day people came to browse, bargain, and buy. At 7:00 p.m., I had $85.00.

Now I know two things: Garage sales are hard work and nobody wants to buy an old clock radio!

**Think about it.**

1. Do you like to buy things at garage sales? Why or why not?
2. Imagine you want the VCR. How will you bargain for it?

1. head
2. hair
3. neck
4. chest
5. back
6. nose
7. mouth
8. foot

**Listen and point. Take turns.**

**A:** *Point to the chest.*
**B:** *Point to the neck.*
**A:** *Point to the mouth.*

**Dictate to your partner. Take turns.**

**A:** *Write hair.*
**B:** *Did you say hair?*
**A:** *That's right, h-a-i-r.*

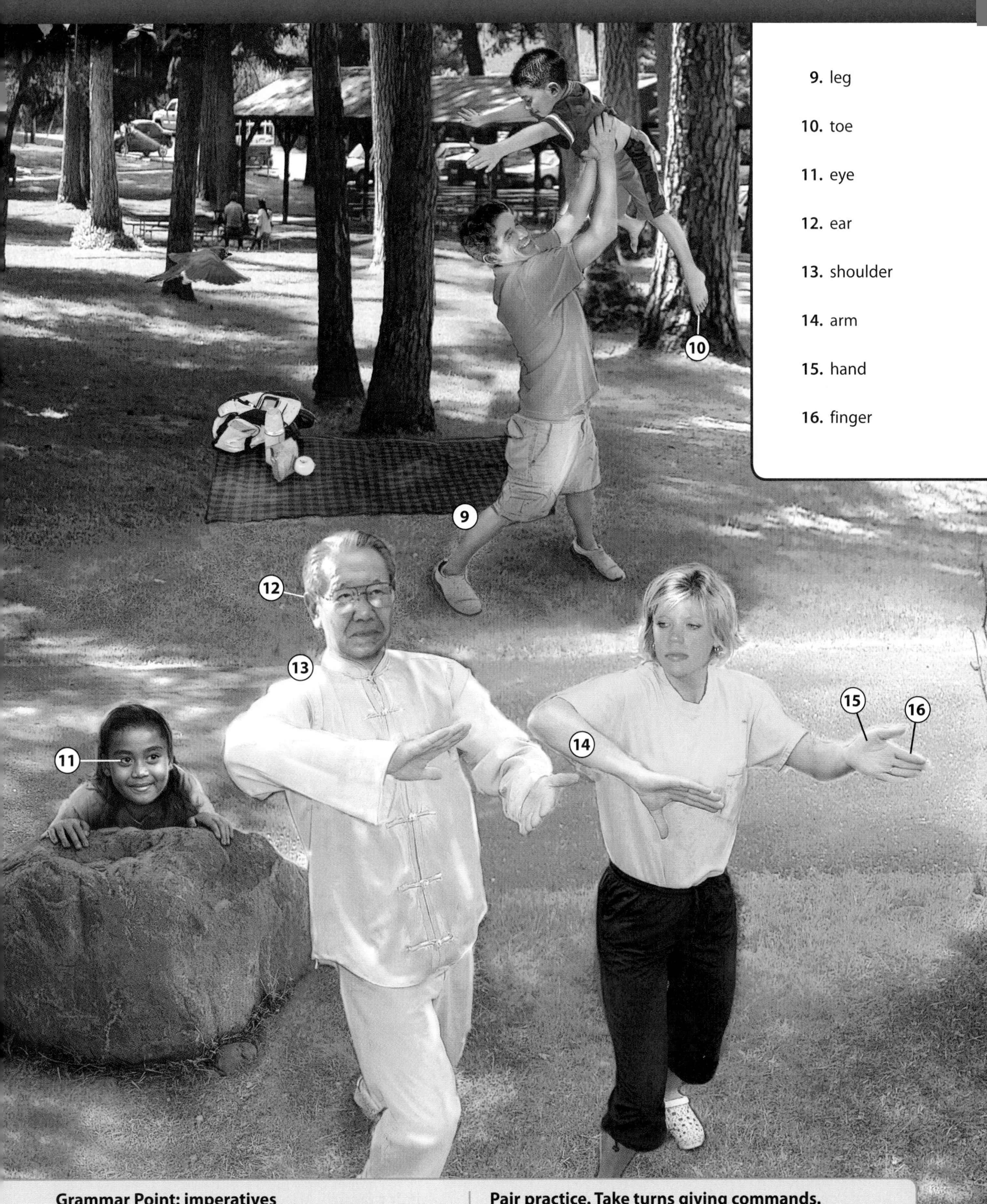


9. leg
10. toe
11. eye
12. ear
13. shoulder
14. arm
15. hand
16. finger

**Grammar Point: imperatives**

***Please touch*** *your right foot.*
***Put*** *your hands on your feet.*
***Don't*** *put your hands on your shoulders.*

**Pair practice. Take turns giving commands.**

**A:** *Raise your arms.*
**B:** *Touch your feet.*
**A:** *Put your hand on your shoulder.*

# Inside and Outside the Body

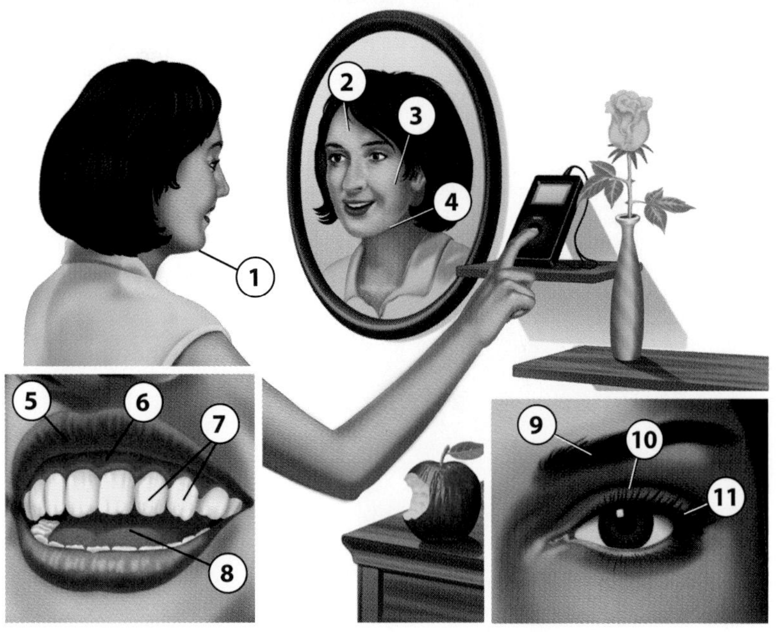


### The Face

1. chin
2. forehead
3. cheek
4. jaw

### The Mouth

5. lip
6. gums
7. teeth
8. tongue

### The Eye

9. eyebrow
10. eyelid
11. eyelashes

### The Senses

A. **see**
B. **hear**
C. **smell**
D. **taste**
E. **touch**

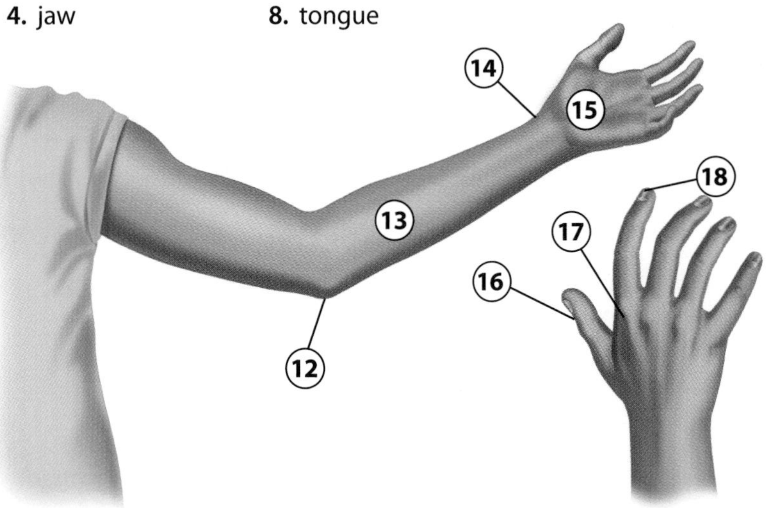


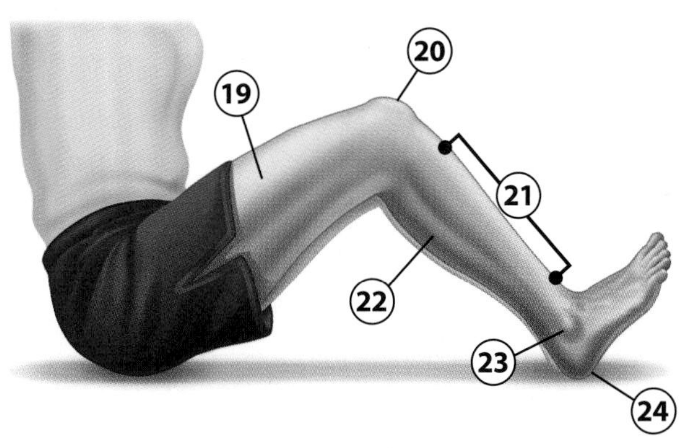


### The Arm, Hand, and Fingers

12. elbow
13. forearm
14. wrist
15. palm
16. thumb
17. knuckle
18. fingernail

### The Leg and Foot

19. thigh
20. knee
21. shin
22. calf
23. ankle
24. heel

**More vocabulary**

**torso:** the part of the body from the shoulders to the pelvis
**limbs:** arms and legs
**toenail:** the nail on your toe

**Pair practice. Make new conversations.**

A: *Is your arm OK?*
B: *Yes, but now my elbow hurts.*
A: *I'm sorry to hear that.*

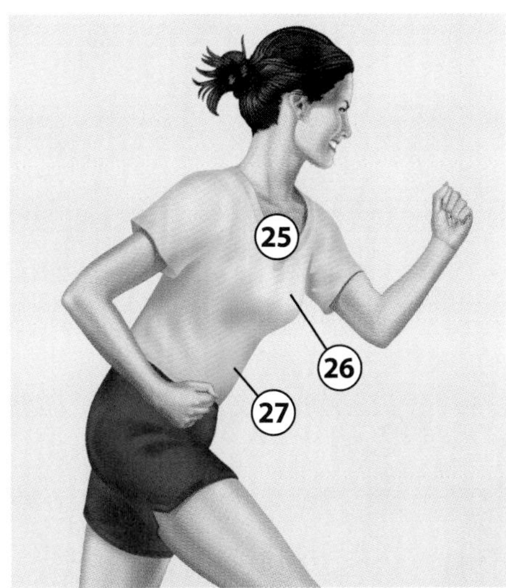

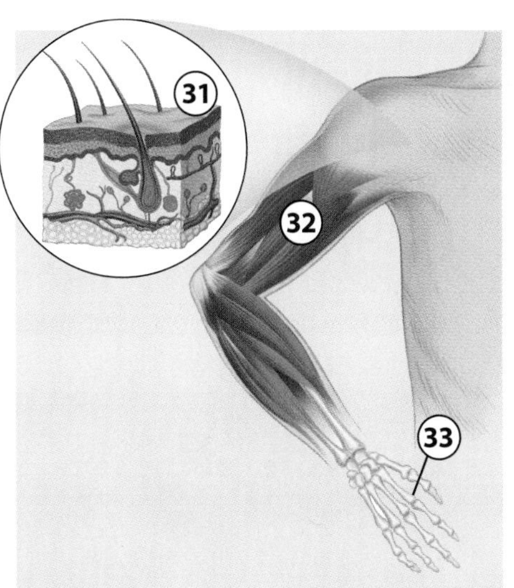

25. chest
26. breast
27. abdomen
28. shoulder blade
29. lower back
30. buttocks
31. skin
32. muscle
33. bone

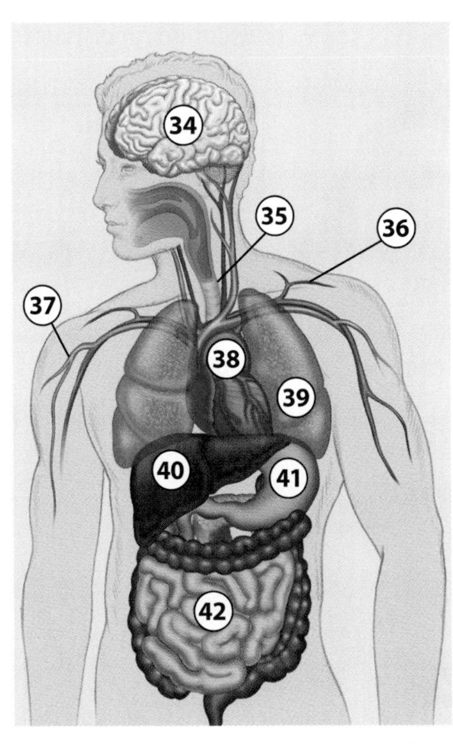


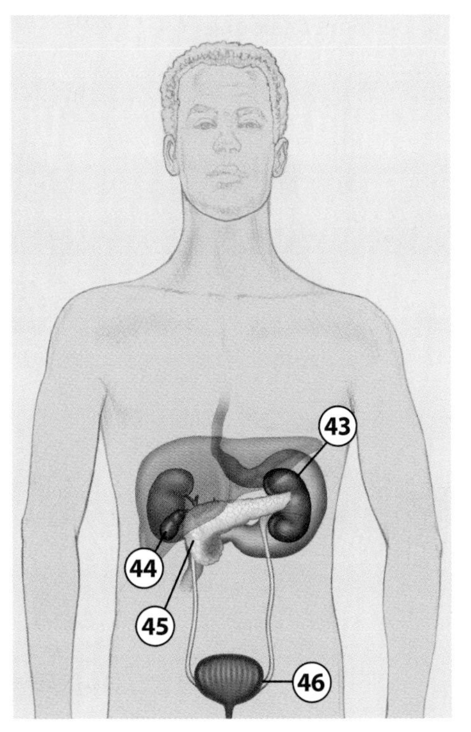


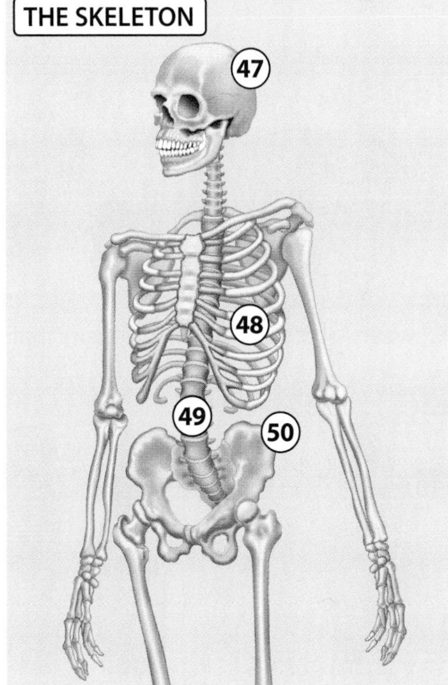


34. brain
35. throat
36. artery
37. vein
38. heart
39. lung
40. liver
41. stomach
42. intestines
43. kidney
44. gallbladder
45. pancreas
46. bladder
47. skull
48. rib cage
49. spinal column
50. pelvis

# Personal Hygiene

A. **take** a shower

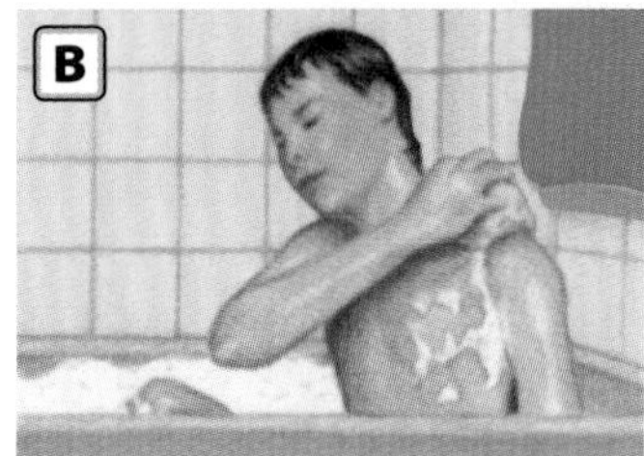
B. **take** a bath / **bathe**

C. **use** deodorant

D. **put on** sunscreen

1. shower cap
2. shower gel
3. soap
4. bath powder
5. deodorant / antiperspirant
6. perfume / cologne
7. sunscreen
8. sunblock
9. body lotion / moisturizer

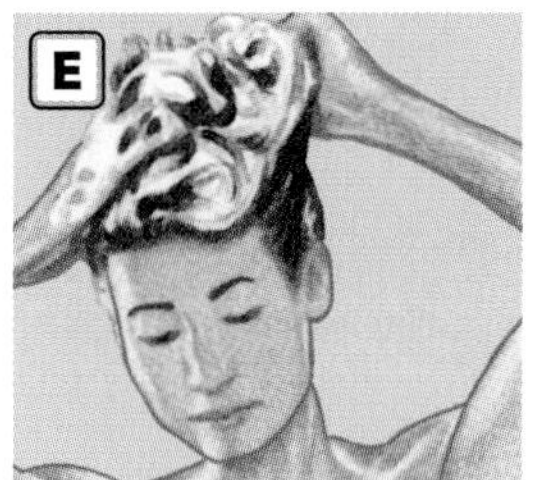
E. **wash**...hair

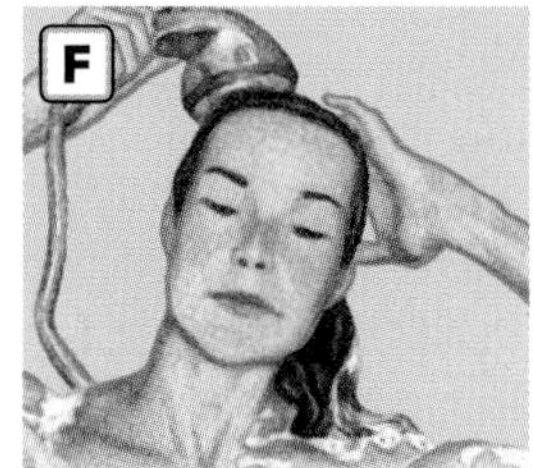
F. **rinse**...hair

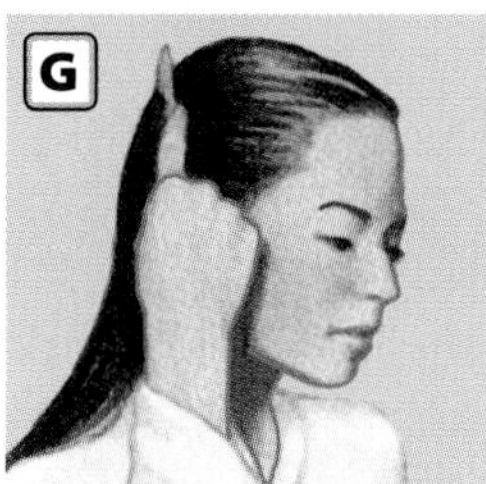
G. **comb**...hair

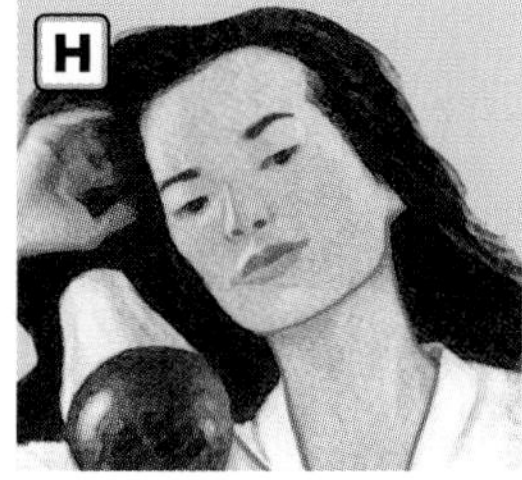
H. **dry**...hair

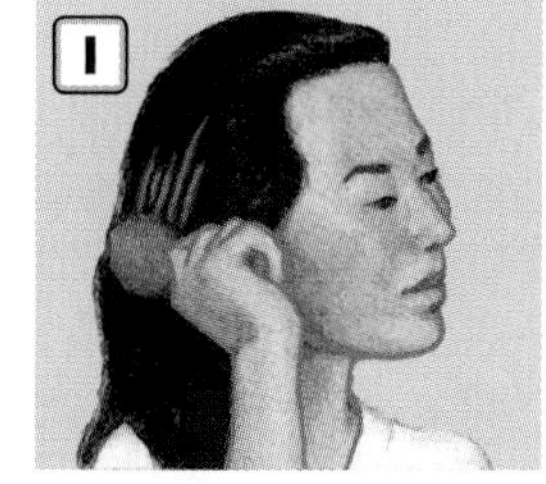
I. **brush**...hair

10. shampoo
11. conditioner
12. hairspray
13. comb
14. brush
15. pick
16. hair gel
17. curling iron
18. blow dryer
19. hair clip
20. barrette
21. bobby pins

**More vocabulary**

**unscented:** a product without perfume or scent

**hypoallergenic:** a product that is better for people with allergies

**Think about it. Discuss.**

1. Which personal hygiene products should someone use before a job interview?
2. What is the right age to start wearing makeup? Why?

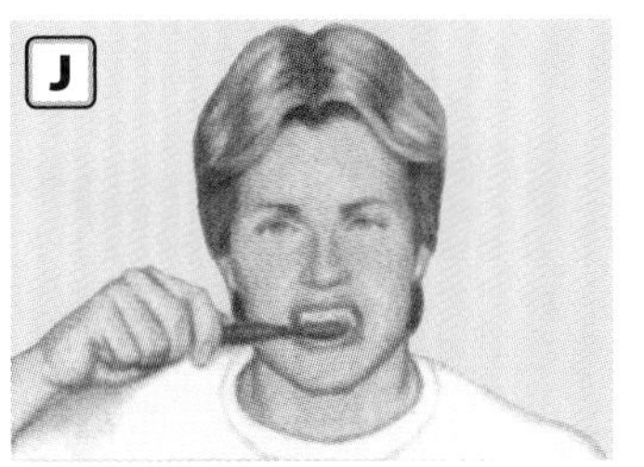

J. **brush**...teeth

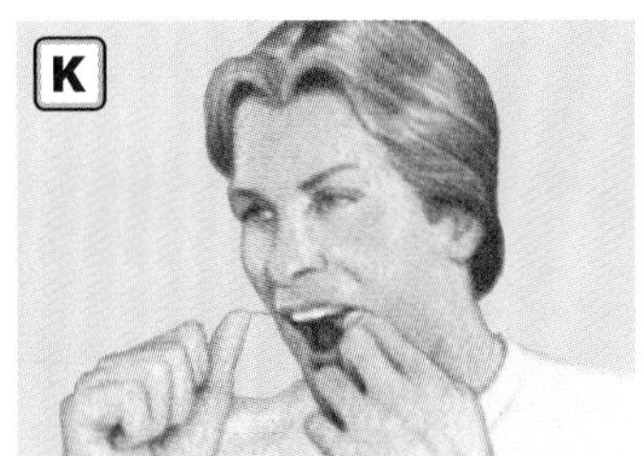

K. **floss**...teeth

L. **gargle**

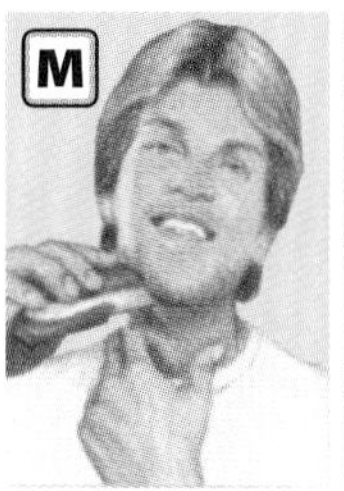

M. **shave**

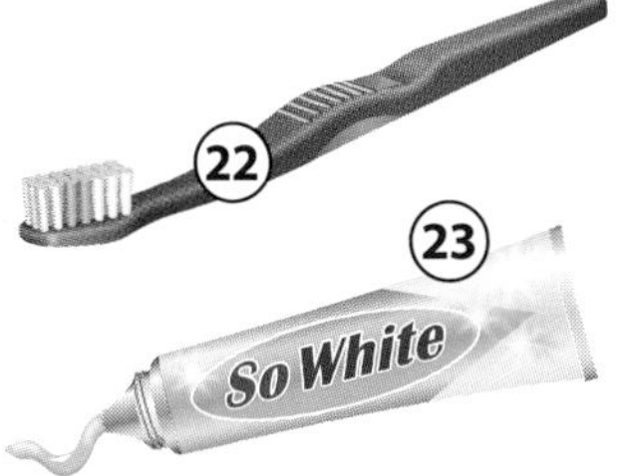

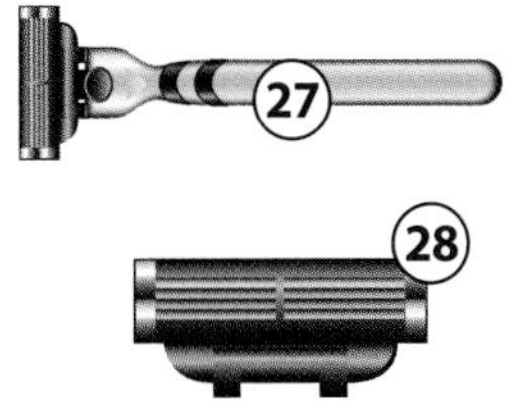

22. toothbrush
23. toothpaste
24. dental floss

25. mouthwash
26. electric shaver
27. razor
28. razor blade
29. shaving cream
30. aftershave

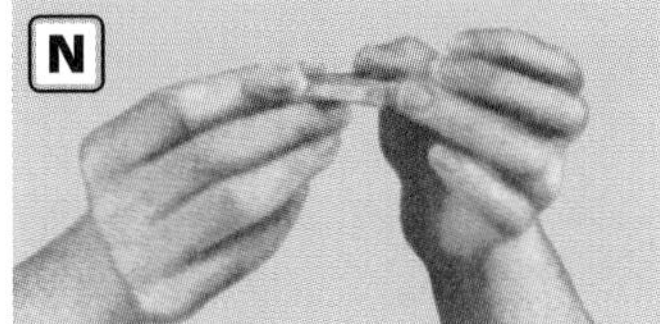

N. **cut**...nails

O. **polish**...nails

P. **put on / apply**

Q. **take off / remove**

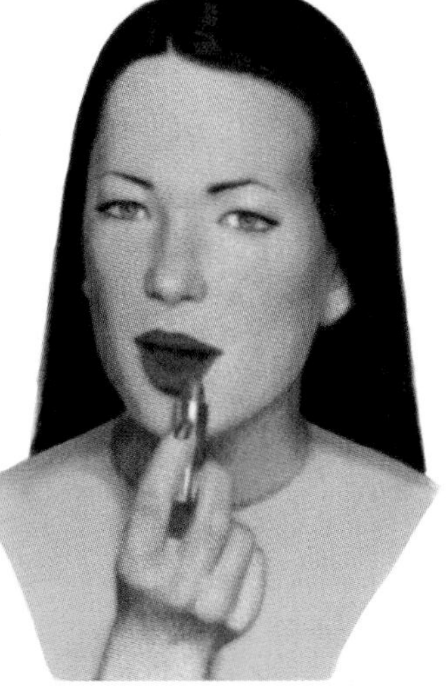

## Makeup

31. nail clipper

32. emery board
33. nail polish
34. eyebrow pencil

35. eyeshadow

36. eyeliner
37. blush
38. lipstick
39. mascara
40. foundation
41. face powder
42. makeup remover

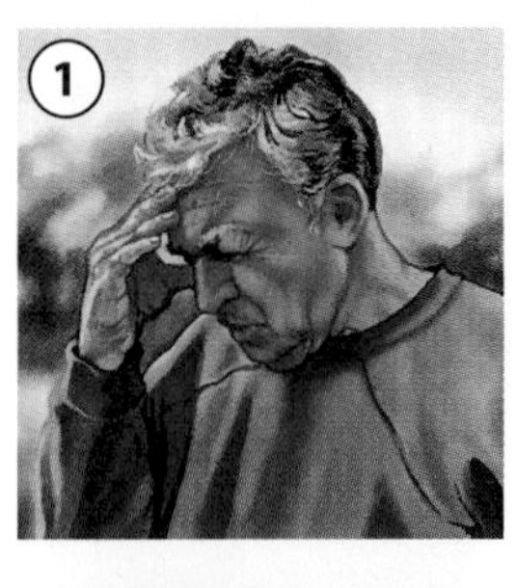

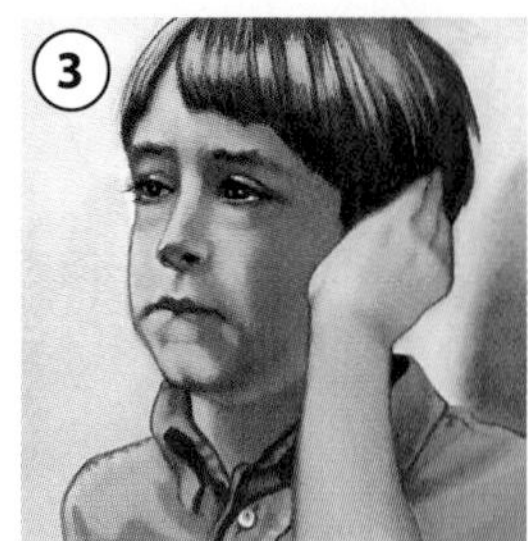

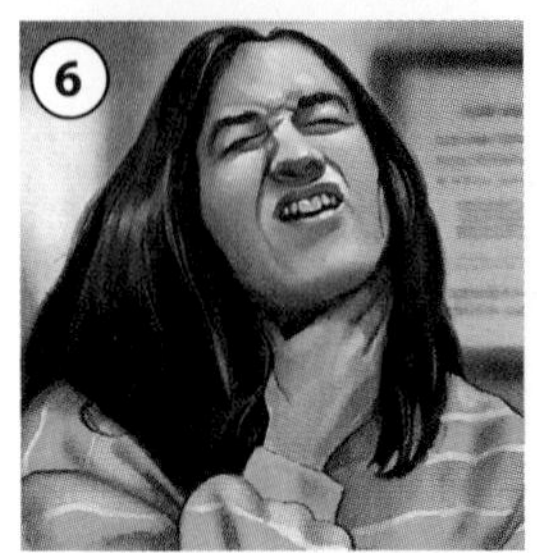
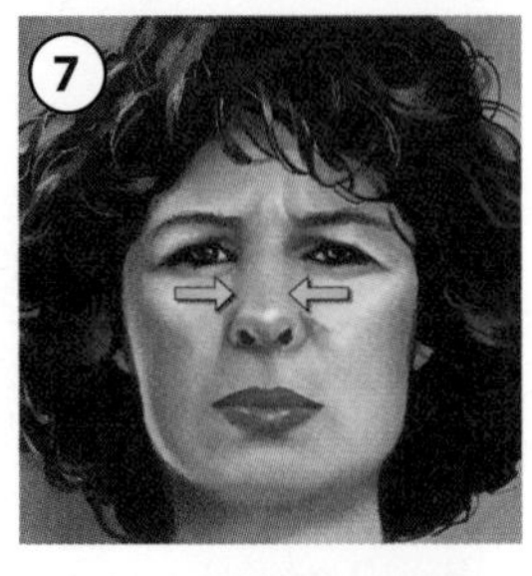
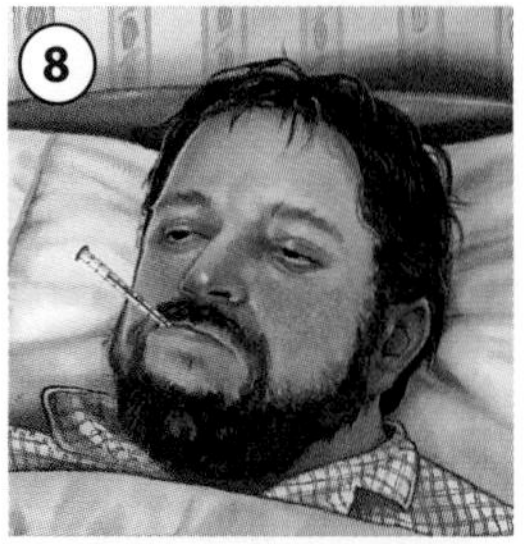
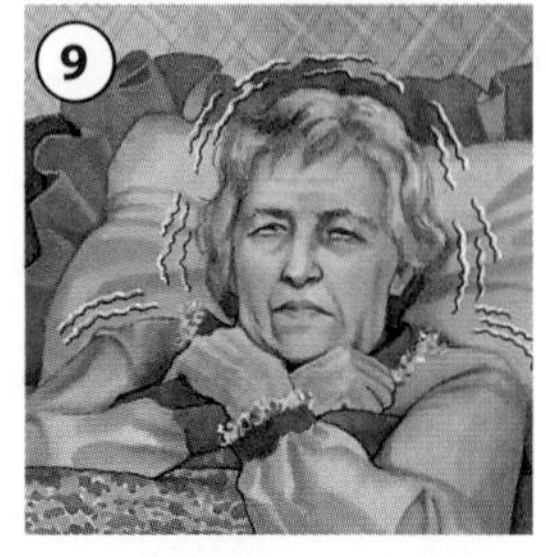
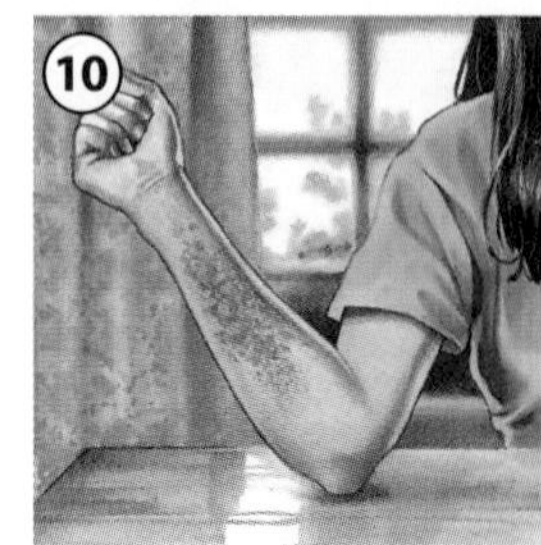
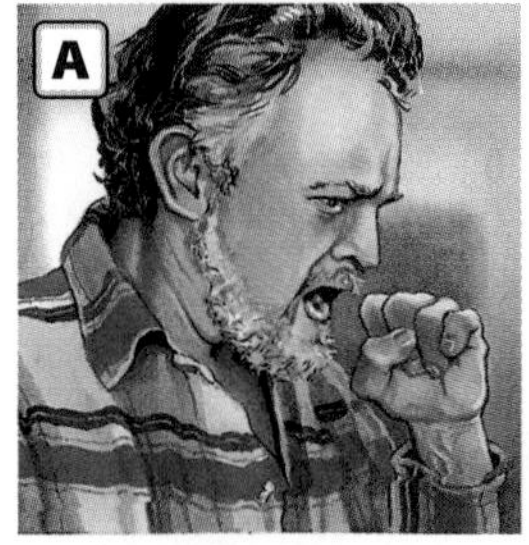
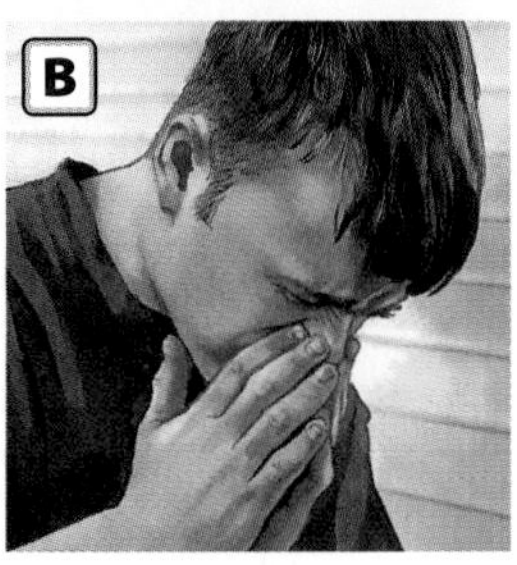

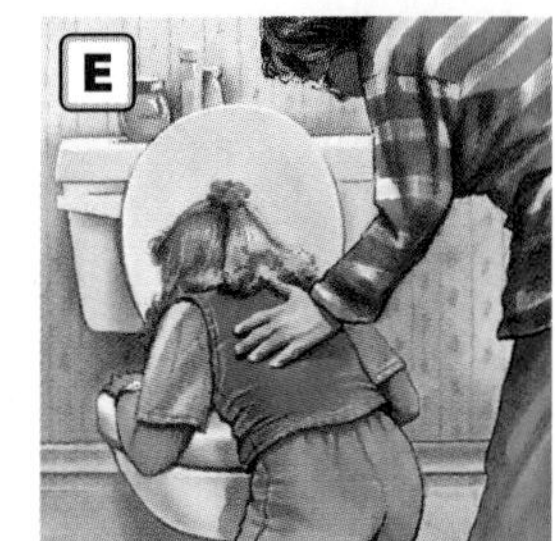

1. headache
2. toothache
3. earache
4. stomach ache
5. backache
6. sore throat
7. nasal congestion
8. fever / temperature
9. chills
10. rash

A. **cough**
B. **sneeze**
C. **feel** dizzy
D. **feel** nauseous
E. **throw up / vomit**

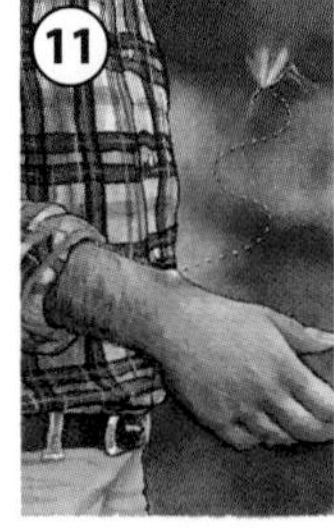
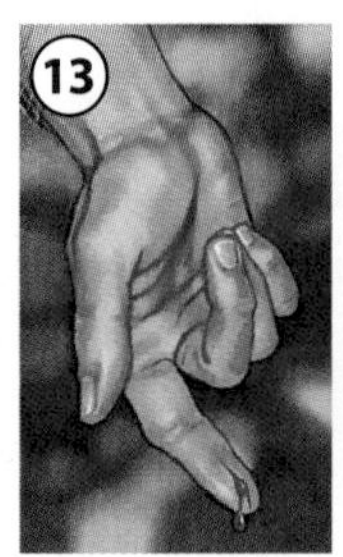

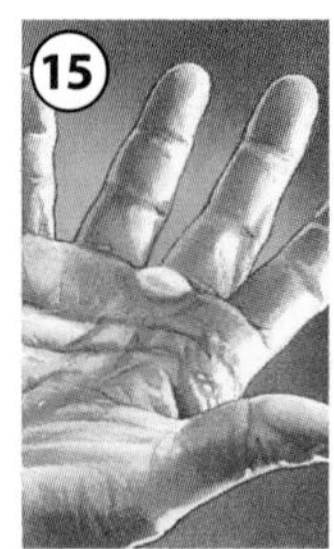
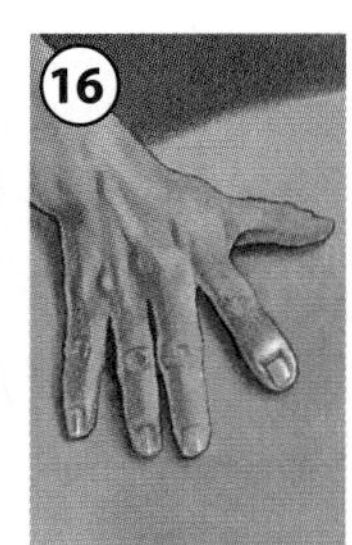
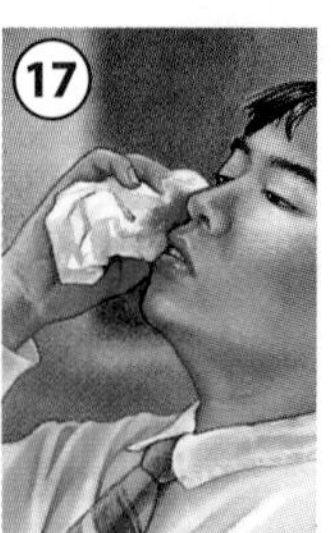
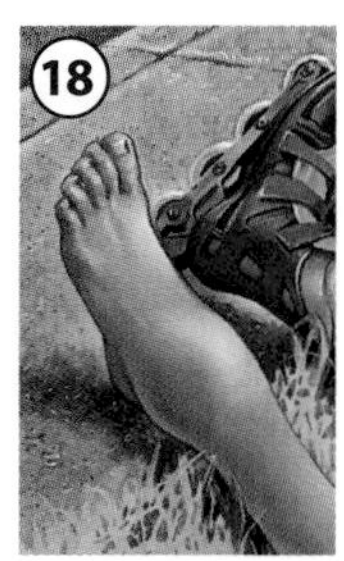

11. insect bite
12. bruise
13. cut
14. sunburn
15. blister
16. swollen finger
17. bloody nose
18. sprained ankle

**Look at the pictures.**
Describe the symptoms and injuries.

**A:** *He has a backache.*
**B:** *She has a toothache.*

**Think about it. Discuss.**

1. What are some common cold symptoms?
2. What do you recommend for a stomach ache?
3. What is the best way to stop a bloody nose?

## Common Illnesses and Childhood Diseases

1. cold

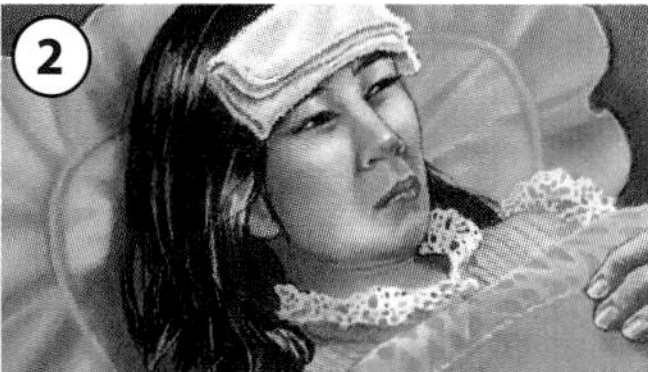

2. flu

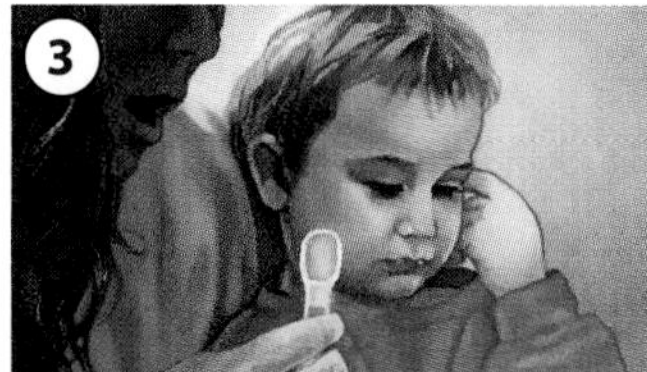

3. ear infection

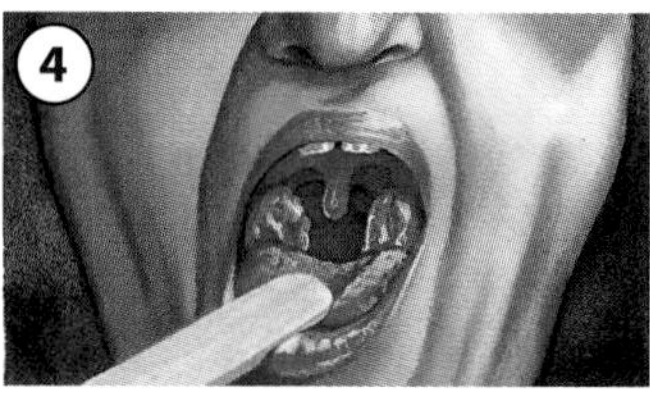

4. strep throat

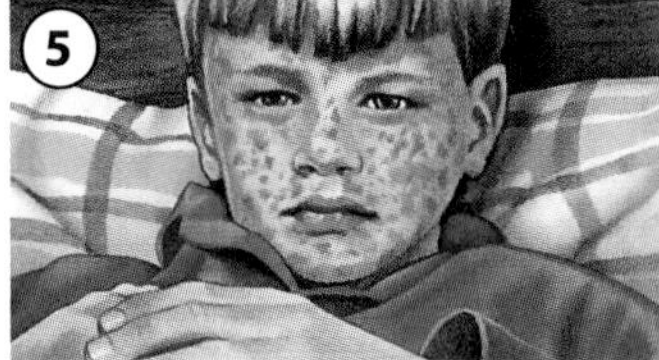

5. measles

6. chicken pox

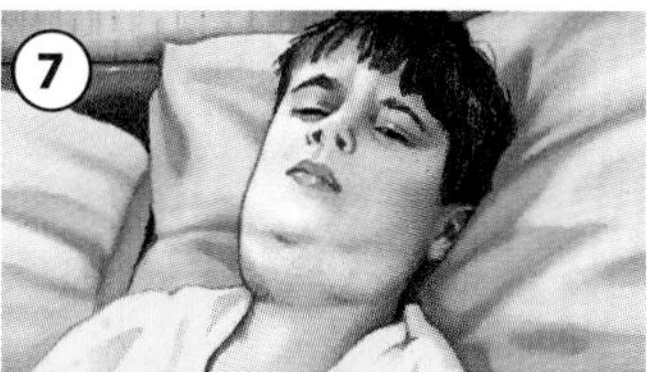

7. mumps

8. allergies

## Serious Medical Conditions and Diseases

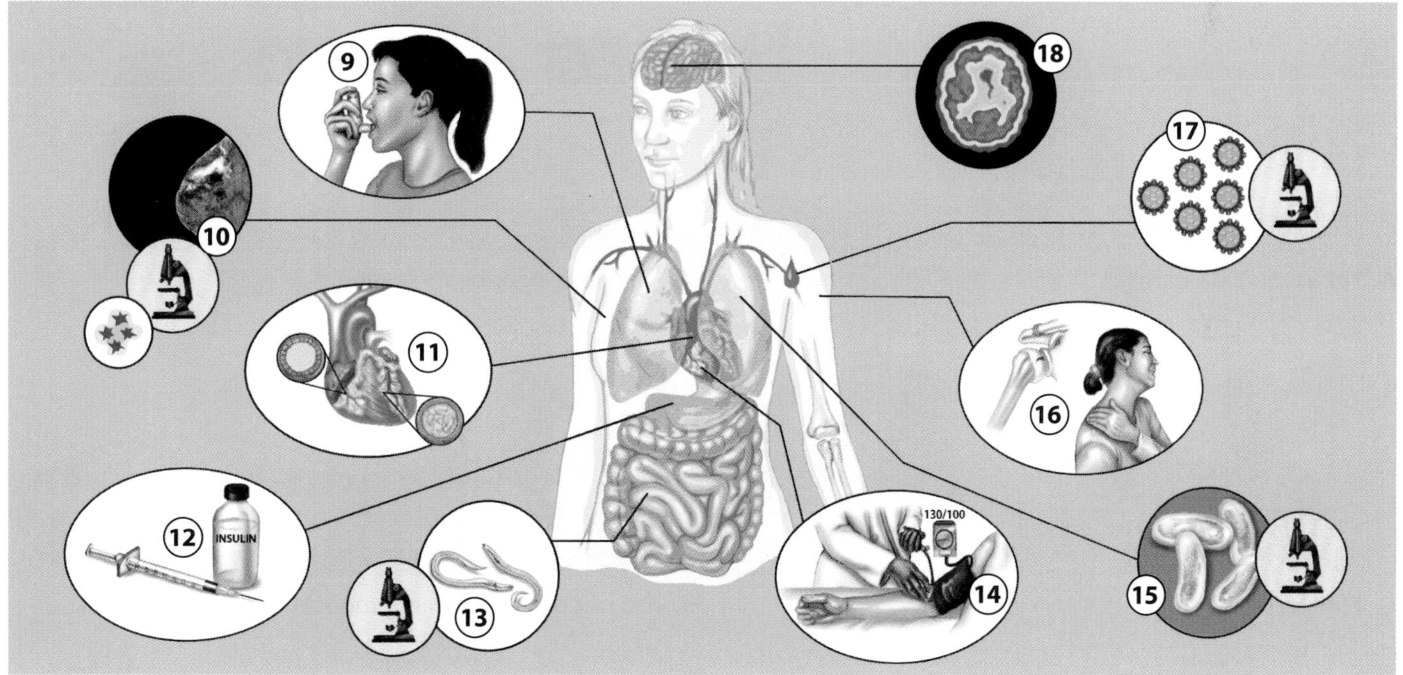


9. asthma
10. cancer
11. heart disease
12. diabetes
13. intestinal parasites
14. high blood pressure / hypertension
15. TB (tuberculosis)
16. arthritis
17. HIV (human immunodeficiency virus)
18. dementia

**More vocabulary**

**AIDS (acquired immune deficiency syndrome):** a medical condition that results from contracting the HIV virus

**Alzheimer's disease:** a disease that causes dementia

**coronary disease:** heart disease

**infectious disease:** a disease that is spread through air or water

**influenza:** flu

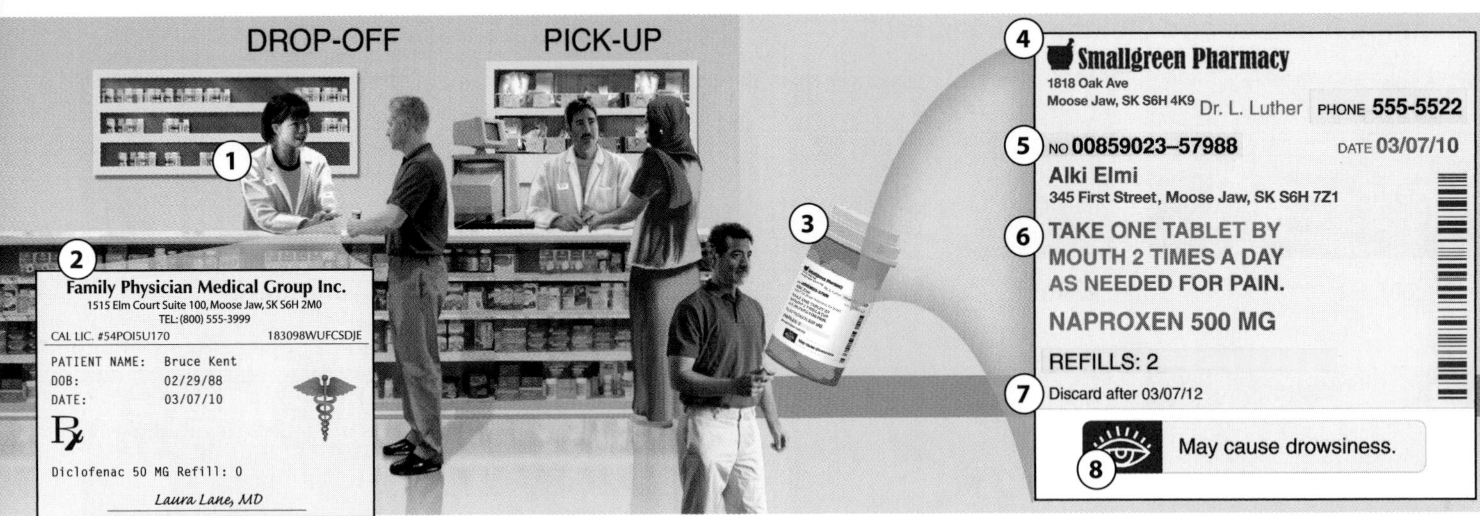

DROP-OFF
PICK-UP
Family Physician Medical Group Inc.
1515 Elm Court Suite 100, Moose Jaw, SK S6H 2M0
TEL: (800) 555-3999
CAL LIC. #54POI5U170
183098WUFCSDJE
PATIENT NAME: Bruce Kent
DOB: 02/29/88
DATE: 03/07/10
℞
Diclofenac 50 MG Refill: 0
Laura Lane, MD
Smallgreen Pharmacy
1818 Oak Ave
Moose Jaw, SK S6H 4K9
Dr. L. Luther
PHONE 555-5522
NO 00859023–57988
DATE 03/07/10
Alki Elmi
345 First Street, Moose Jaw, SK S6H 7Z1
TAKE ONE TABLET BY MOUTH 2 TIMES A DAY AS NEEDED FOR PAIN.
NAPROXEN 500 MG
REFILLS: 2
Discard after 03/07/12
May cause drowsiness.


1. pharmacist
2. prescription
3. prescription medication
4. prescription label
5. prescription number
6. dosage
7. expiration date
8. warning label

## Medical Warnings

A. **Take** with food or milk.

B. **Take** one hour before eating.

C. **Finish** all medication.

D. **Do not take** with dairy products.

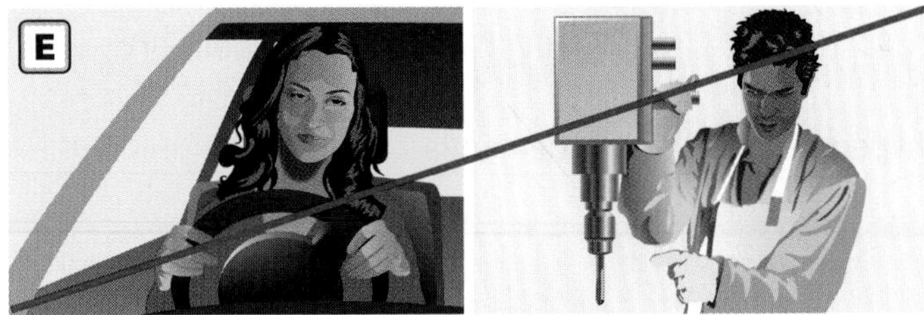

E. **Do not drive or operate** heavy machinery.

F. **Do not drink** alcohol.

### More vocabulary

**prescribe medication:** to write a prescription
**fill prescriptions:** to prepare medication for patients
**pick up a prescription:** to get prescription medication

### Role play. Talk to the pharmacist.

**A:** *Hi. I need to pick up a prescription for Jones.*
**B:** *Here's your medication, Mr. Jones. Take these once a day with milk or food.*

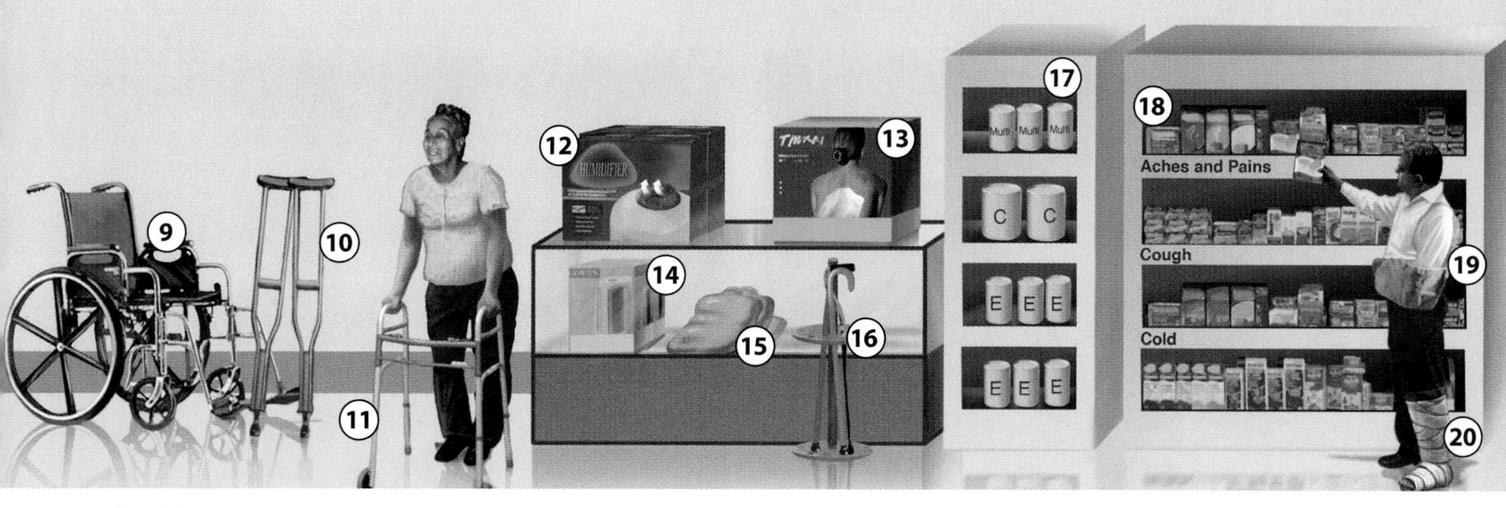


9. wheelchair
10. crutches
11. walker
12. humidifier
13. heating pad
14. air purifier
15. hot water bottle
16. cane
17. vitamins
18. over-the-counter medication
19. sling
20. cast

## Types of Medication

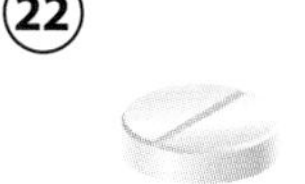
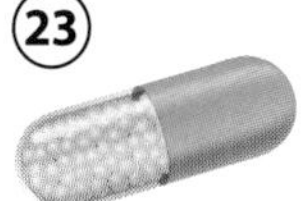

21. pill
22. tablet
23. capsule
24. ointment
25. cream

## Over-the-Counter Medication

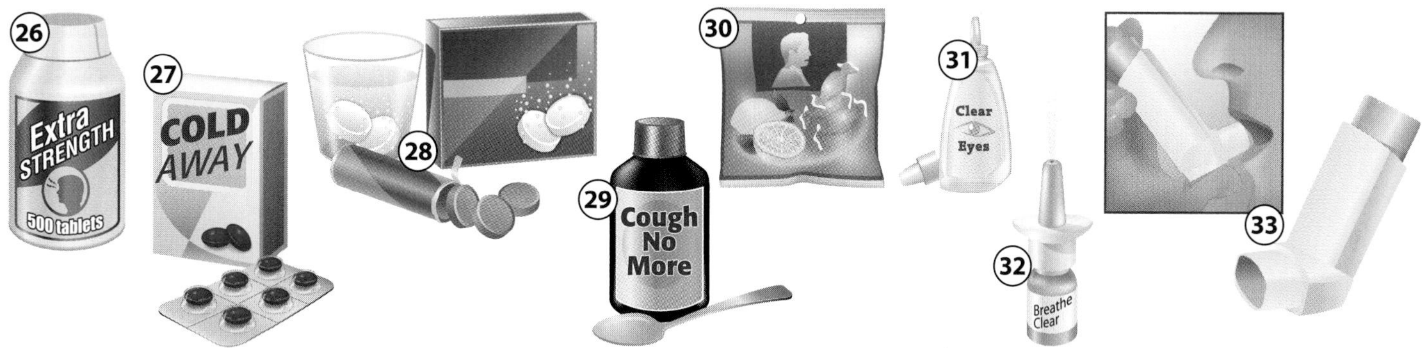


26. pain reliever
27. cold tablets
28. antacid
29. cough syrup
30. throat lozenges
31. eye drops
32. nasal spray
33. inhaler

**Ways to talk about medication**

Use *take* for pills, tablets, capsules, and cough syrup.
Use *apply* for ointments and creams.
Use *use* for drops, nasal sprays, and inhalers.

**Ask your classmates. Share the answers.**

1. What pharmacy do you go to?
2. Do you ever ask the pharmacist for advice?
3. Do you take any vitamins? Which ones?

# Taking Care of Your Health

## Ways to Get Well

A. **Seek** medical attention.

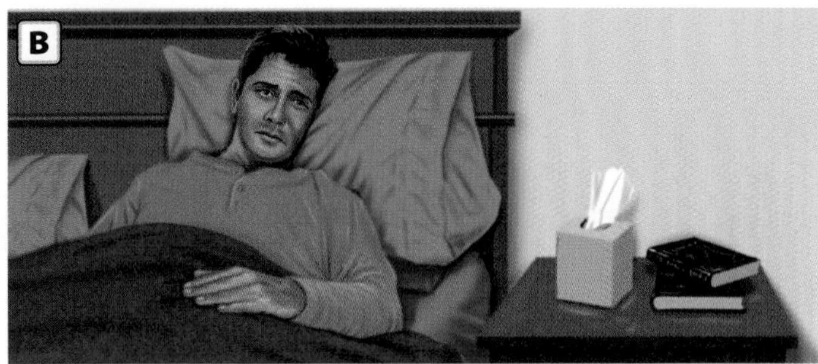


B. **Get** bed rest.

C. **Drink** fluids.

D. **Take** medicine.

## Ways to Stay Well

E. **Stay** fit.

F. **Eat** a healthy diet.

G. **Don't smoke**.

H. **Have** regular checkups.

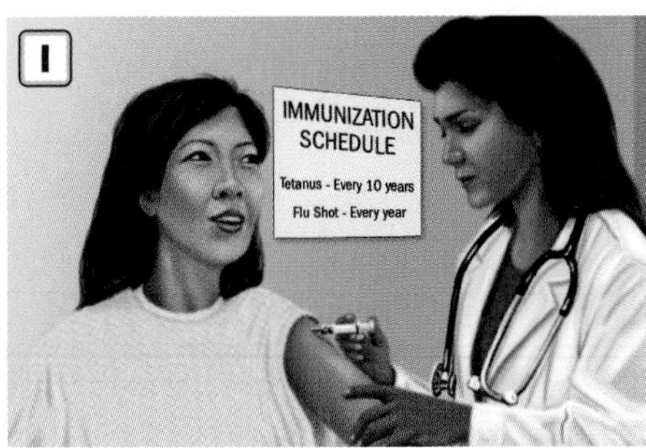


I. **Get** immunized.

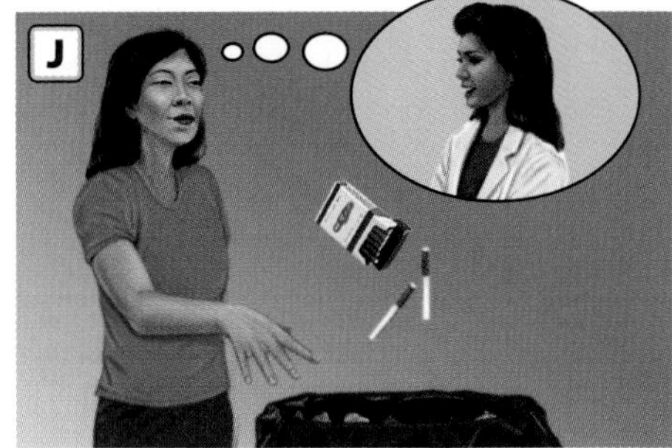


J. **Follow** medical advice.

**More vocabulary**

**injection:** medicine in a syringe that is put into the body

**immunization / vaccination:** an injection that stops serious diseases

**Ask your classmates. Share the answers.**

1. How do you stay fit?
2. What do you do when you're sick?
3. Which two foods are a part of your healthy diet?

## Types of Health Problems

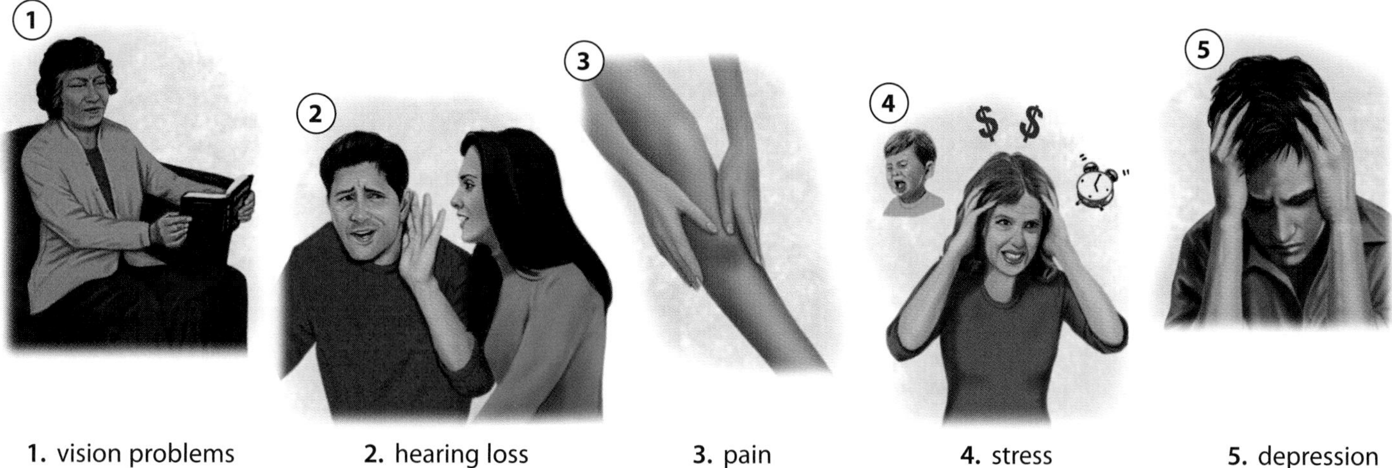

1. vision problems
2. hearing loss
3. pain
4. stress
5. depression

## Help with Health Problems

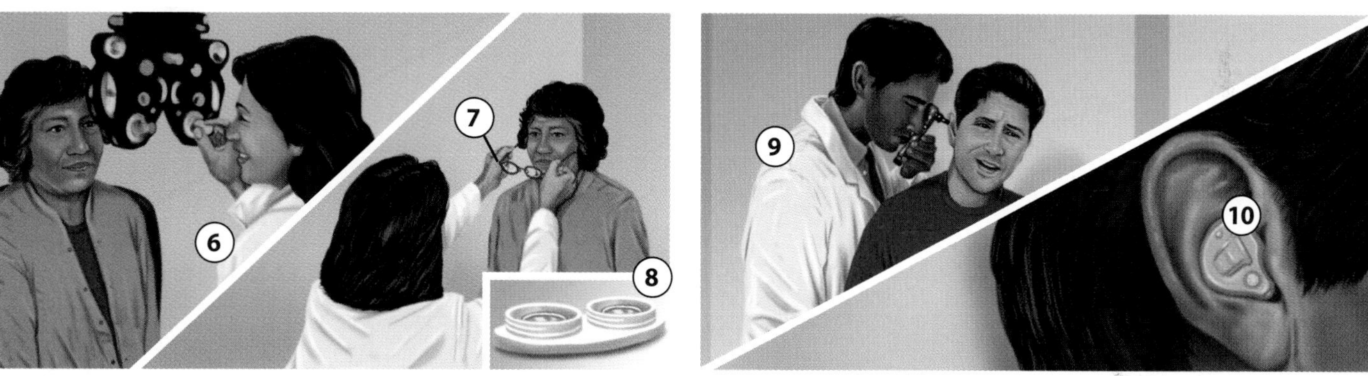

6. optometrist
7. glasses
8. contact lenses
9. audiologist
10. hearing aid

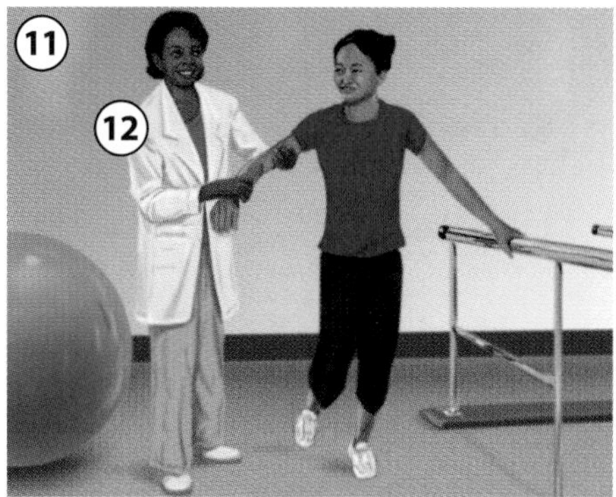

11. physical therapy
12. physical therapist

13. talk therapy
14. therapist

15. support group

**Ways to ask about health problems**

*Are you in pain?*
*Are you having vision problems?*
*Are you experiencing depression?*

**Pair practice. Make new conversations.**

**A:** *Do you know a good optometrist?*
**B:** *Why? Are you having vision problems?*
**A:** *Yes, I might need glasses.*

# Medical Emergencies

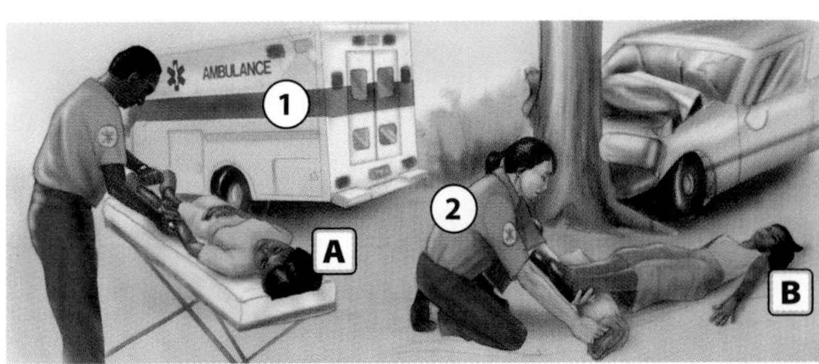

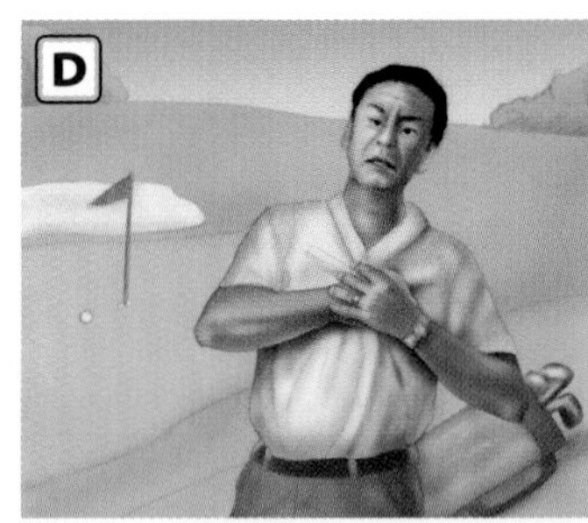


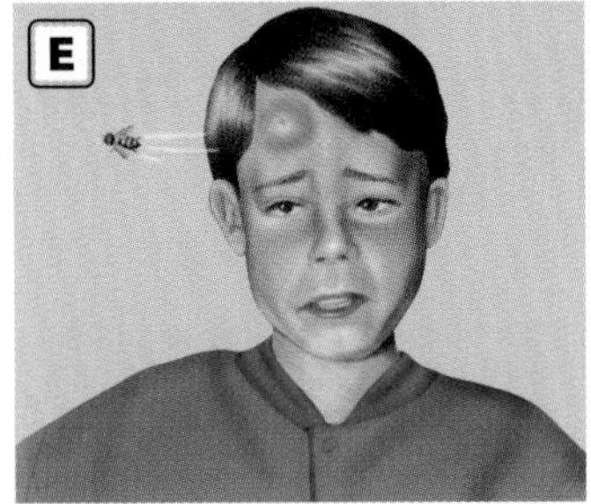


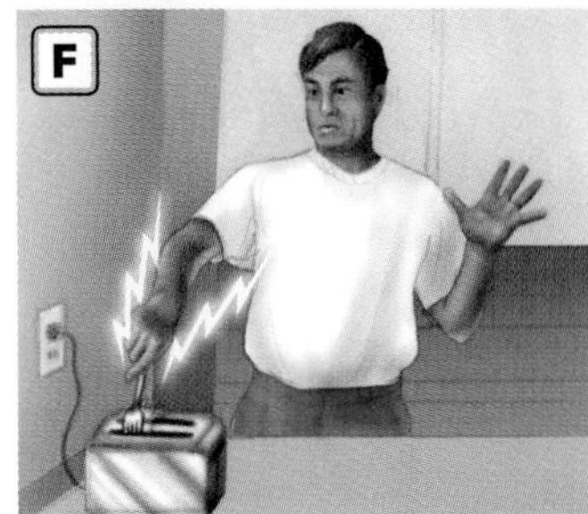

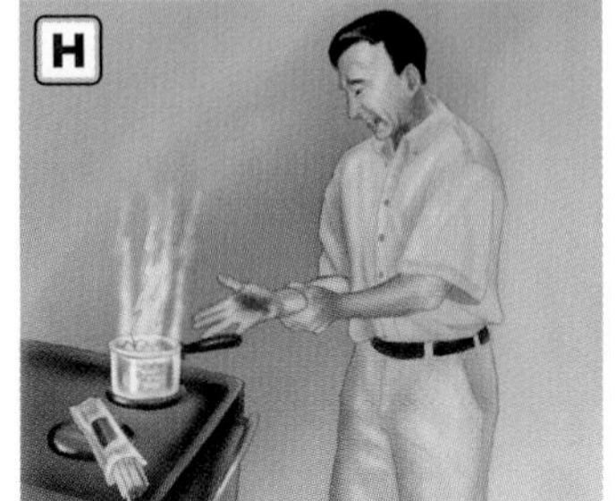

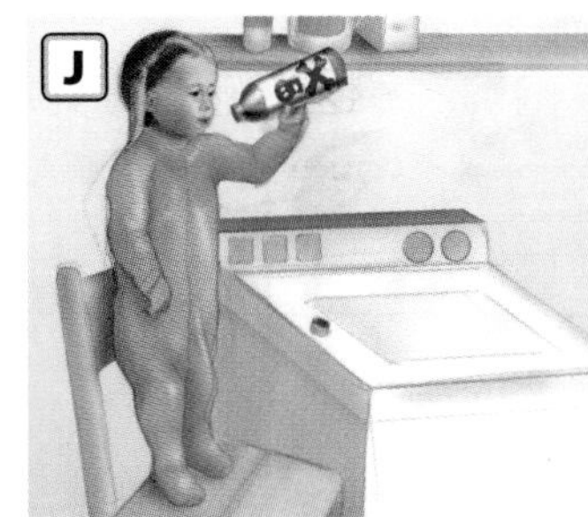


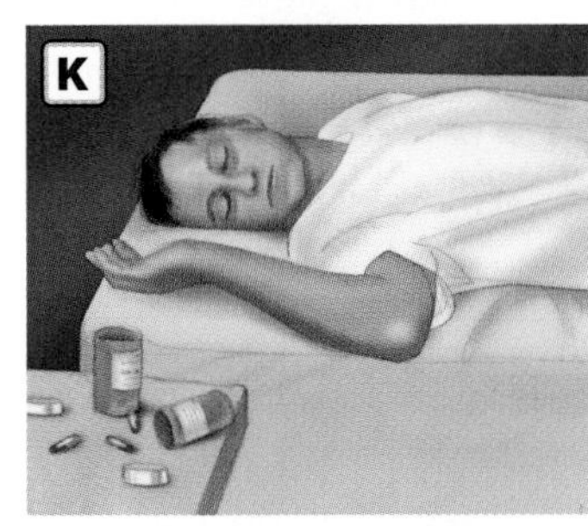


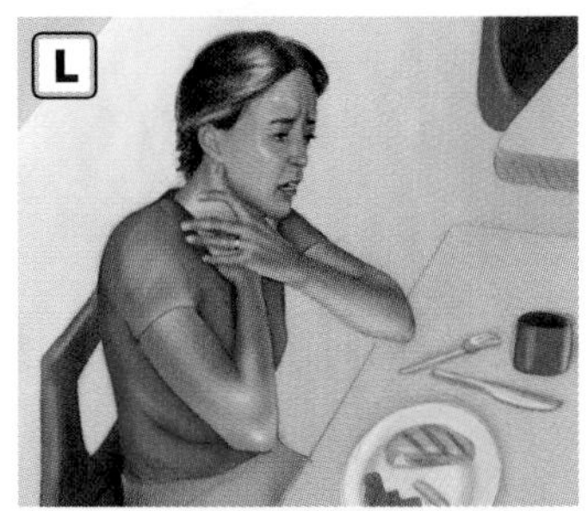


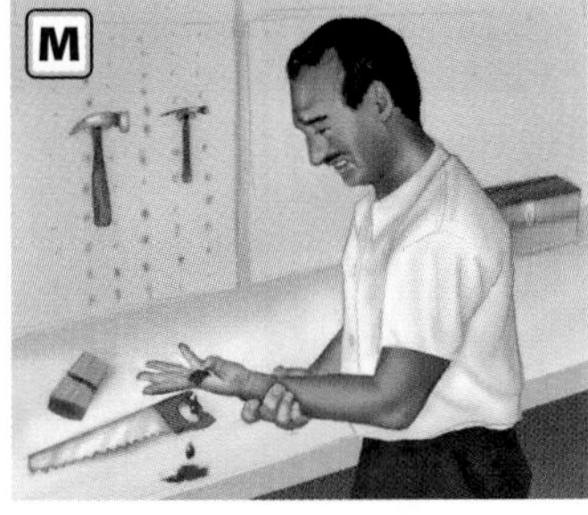

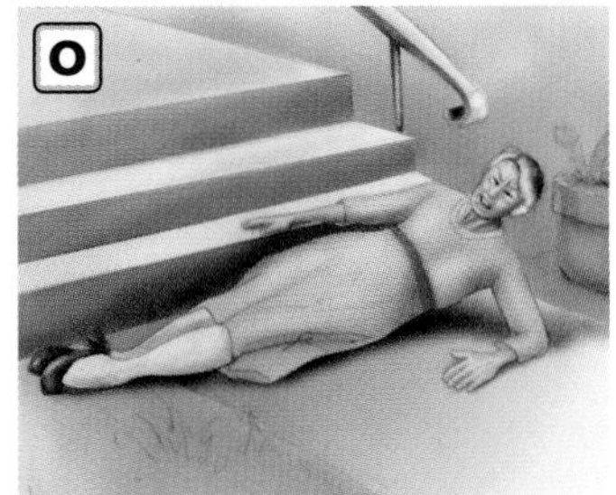


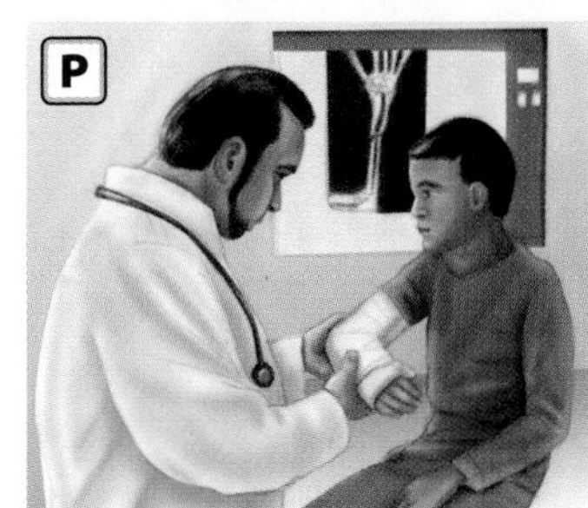


1. ambulance
2. paramedic

A. **be** unconscious
B. **be** in shock
C. **be** injured / **be** hurt
D. **have** a heart attack
E. **have** an allergic reaction
F. **get** an electric shock
G. **get** frostbite
H. **burn** (your)self
I. **drown**
J. **swallow** poison
K. **overdose** on drugs
L. **choke**
M. **bleed**
N. **be unable to breathe**
O. **fall**
P. **break** a bone

**Grammar Point: past tense**

For past tense add –ed:
burned, drowned, swallowed, overdosed, choked

**These verbs are different (irregular):**

be – was, were
have – had
get – got
bleed – bled
break – broke
fall – fell

## First Aid

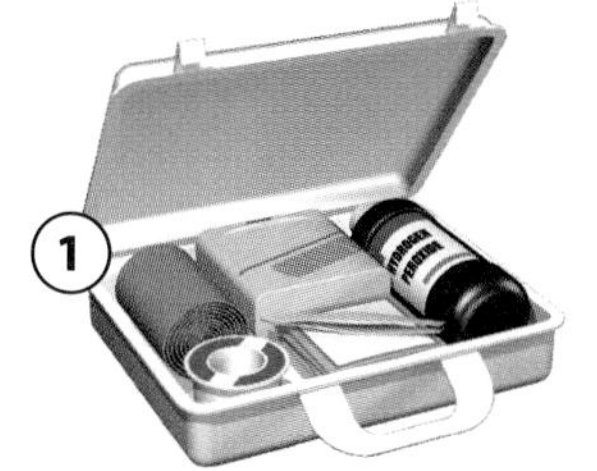


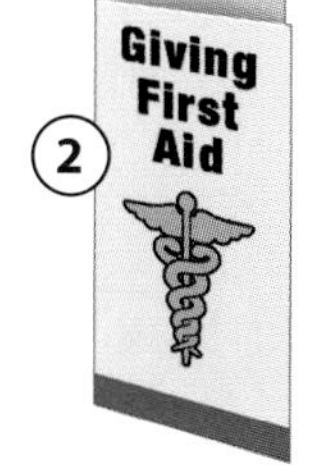


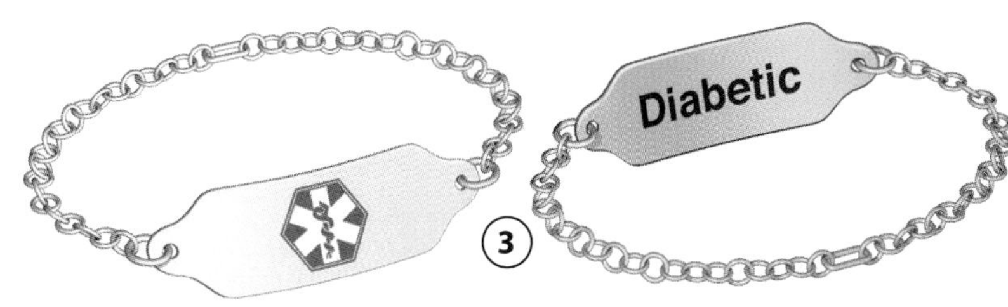


1. first aid kit
2. first aid manual
3. medical emergency bracelet

## Inside the Kit

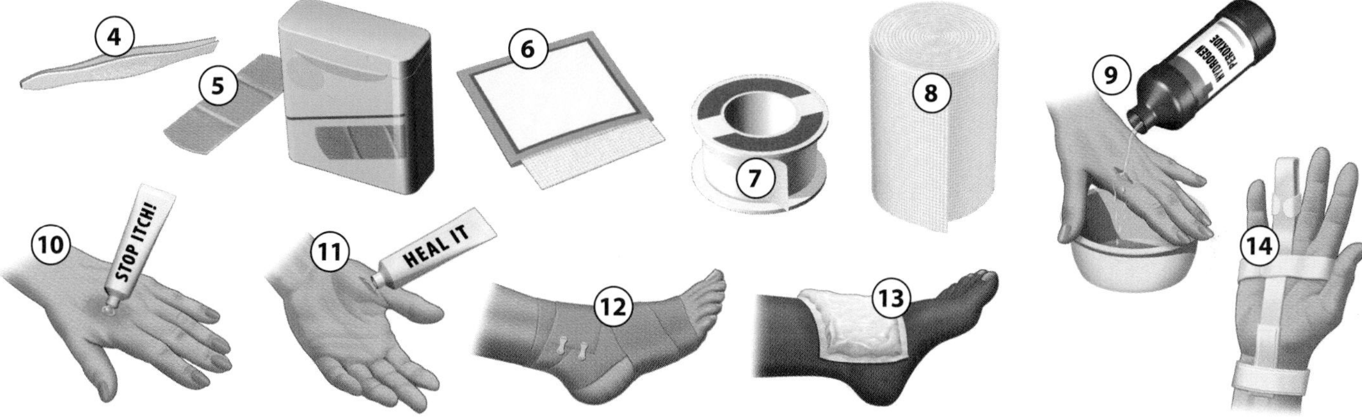


4. tweezers
5. adhesive bandage
6. sterile pad
7. sterile tape
8. gauze
9. hydrogen peroxide
10. antihistamine cream
11. antibacterial ointment
12. elastic bandage
13. ice pack
14. splint

## First Aid Procedures

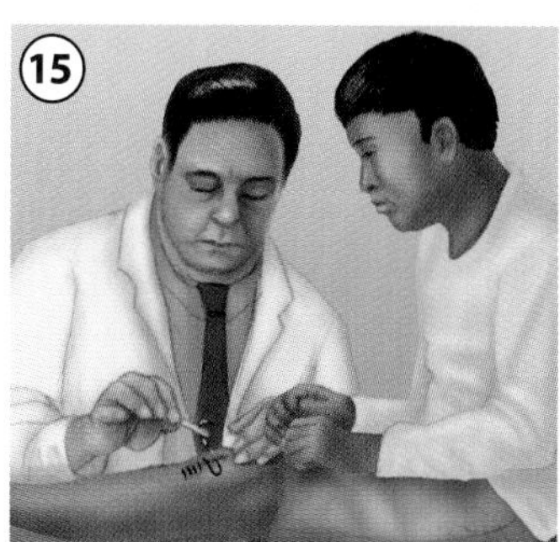


15. stitches

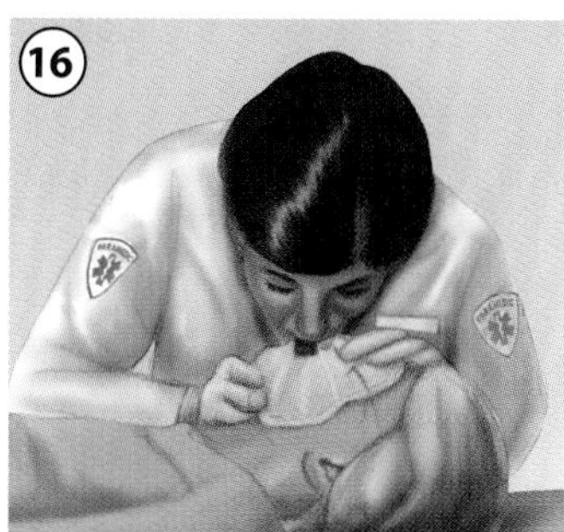


16. rescue breathing

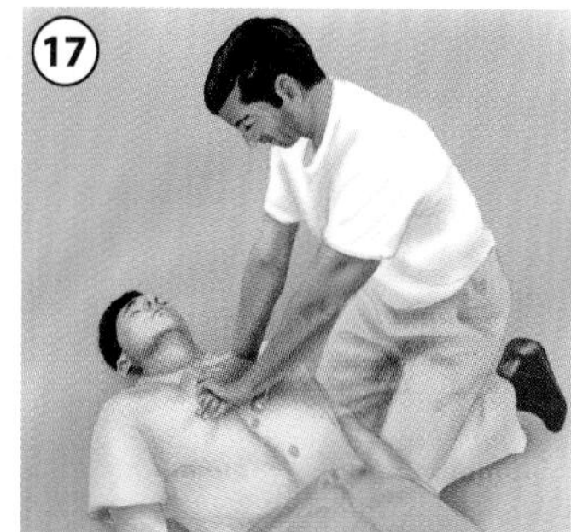


17. CPR (cardiopulmonary resuscitation)

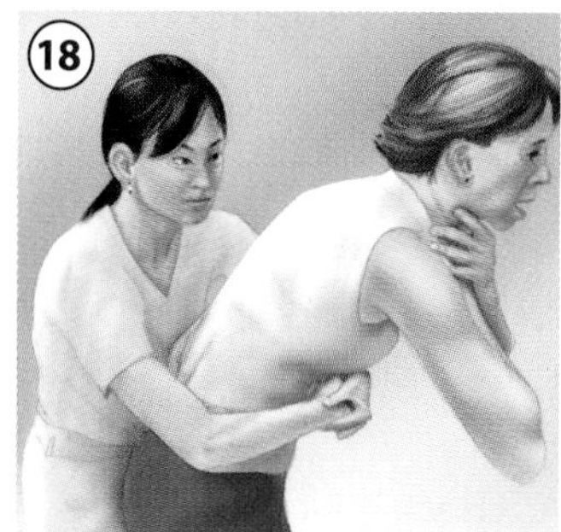


18. Heimlich manoeuvre

**Pair practice. Make new conversations.**

**A:** *What do we need in the first aid kit?*
**B:** *We need* tweezers *and* gauze.
**A:** *I think we need* sterile tape, *too.*

**Think about it. Discuss.**

1. What are the three most important first aid items? Why?
2. Which first aid procedures should everyone know? Why?
3. What are some good places to keep a first aid kit?

# Medical Care

## In the Waiting Room

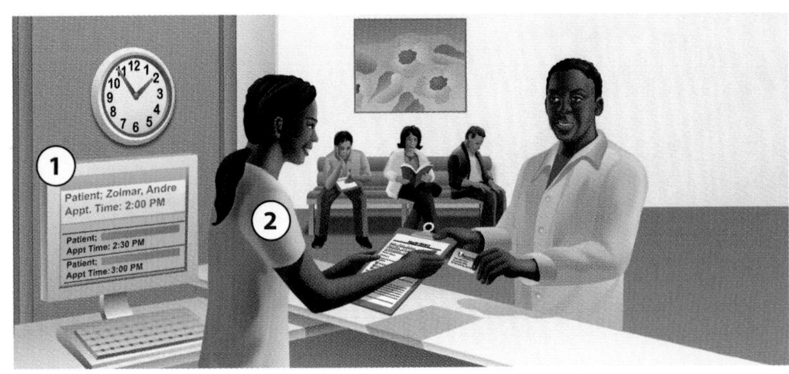

**Health Form**

**Name:** *Andre Zolmar*
**Date of birth:** *July 8, 1973*
**Current symptoms:** *stomach ache*

**Health History:**

**Childhood Diseases:**

- ☑ chicken pox
- ☑ diphtheria
- ☑ rubella
- ☑ measles
- ☐ mumps
- ☐ other

**Description of symptoms:**

1. appointment
2. receptionist
3. health card
4. health history form

## In the Examining Room

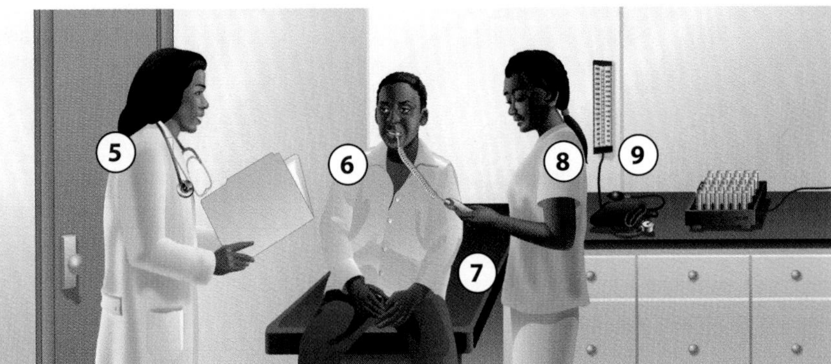

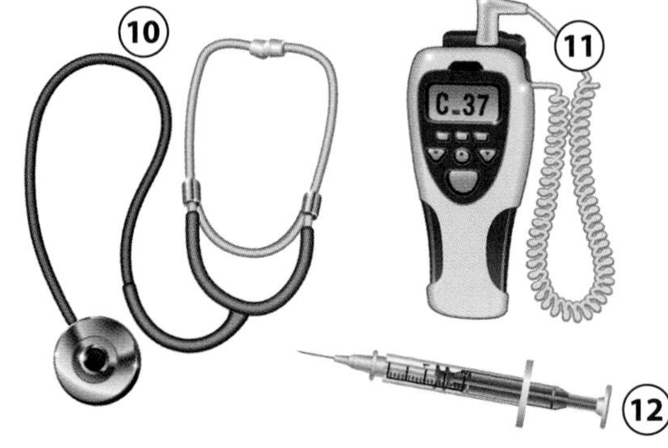


5. doctor
6. patient
7. examination table
8. nurse
9. blood pressure gauge
10. stethoscope
11. thermometer
12. syringe

## Medical Procedures

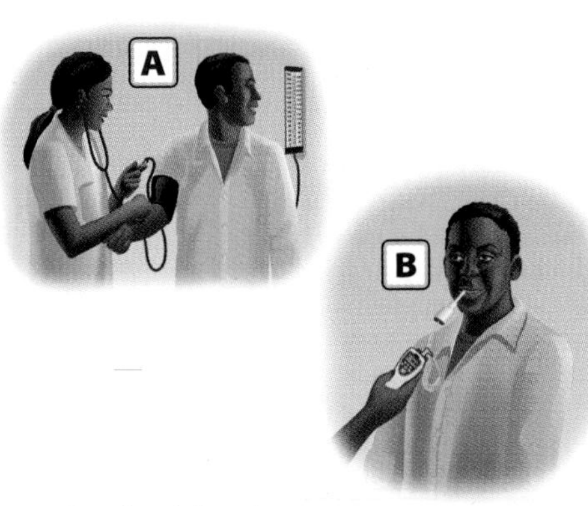

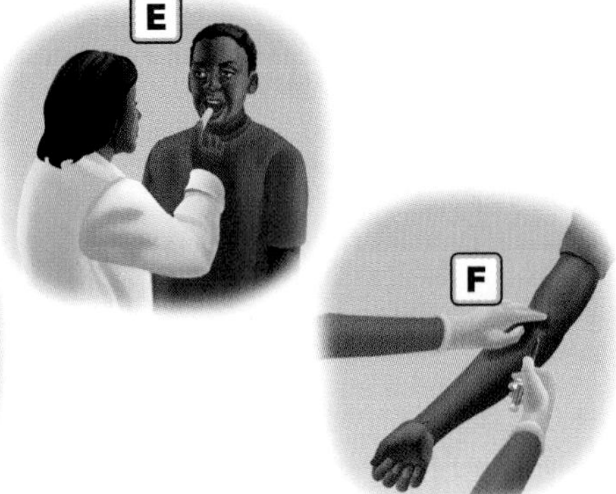

A. **check**...blood pressure

B. **take**...temperature

C. **listen** to...heart

D. **examine**...eyes

E. **examine**...throat

F. **draw**...blood

**Grammar Point: future tense with *will* + verb**

To show a future action, use **will** + verb.
The subject pronoun contraction of **will** is **-'ll.**
*She **will draw** your blood. = She**'ll draw** your blood.*

**Role play. Talk to a medical receptionist.**

**A:** *Will the nurse <u>examine my eyes</u>?*
**B:** *No, but she'll <u>draw your blood</u>.*
**A:** *What will the doctor do?*

# Dental Care 

## Dentistry

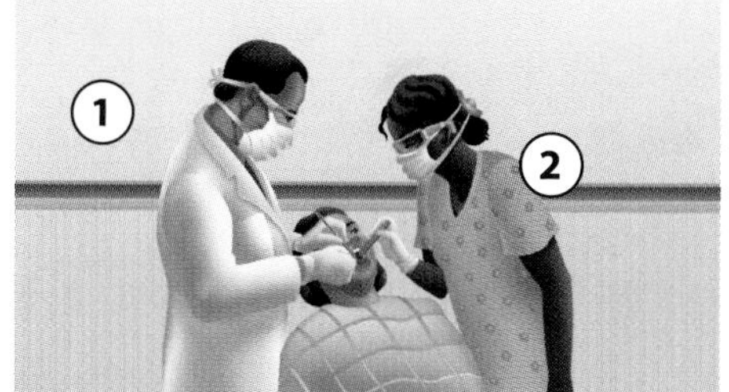


1. dentist
2. dental assistant

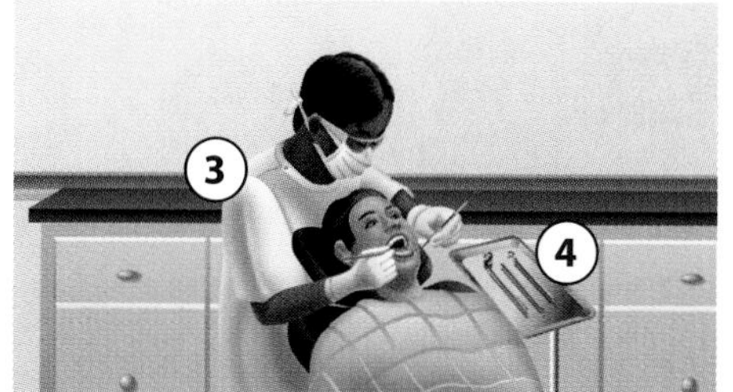


3. dental hygienist
4. dental instruments

## Orthodontics

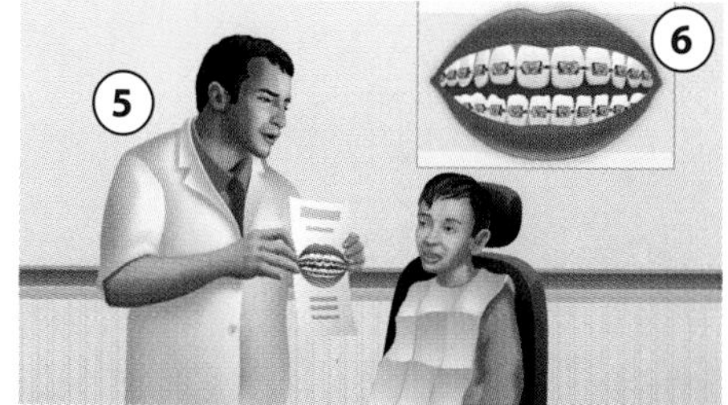


5. orthodontist
6. braces

## Dental Problems

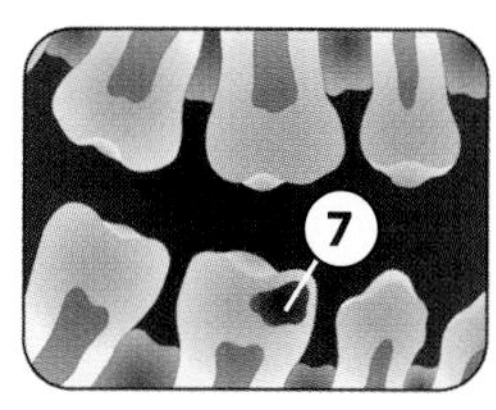


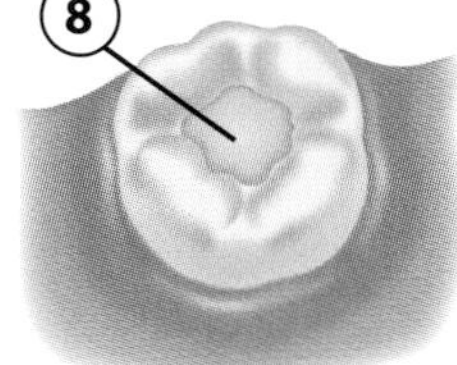


7. cavity / decay
8. filling

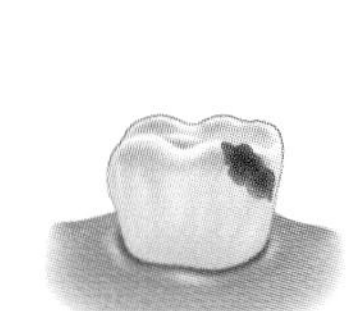

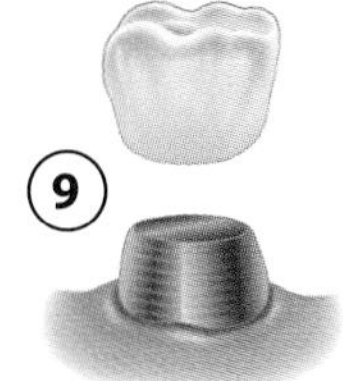


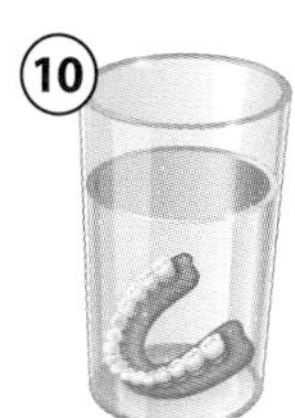


9. crown
10. dentures

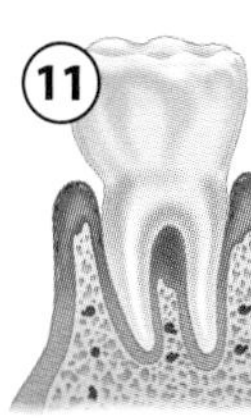


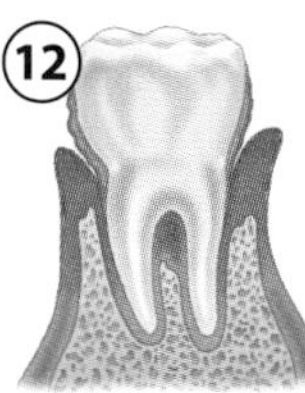


11. gum disease
12. plaque

## An Office Visit

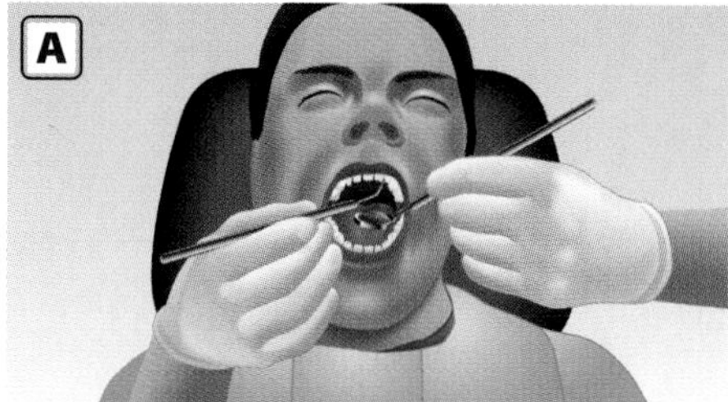


A. **clean**…teeth

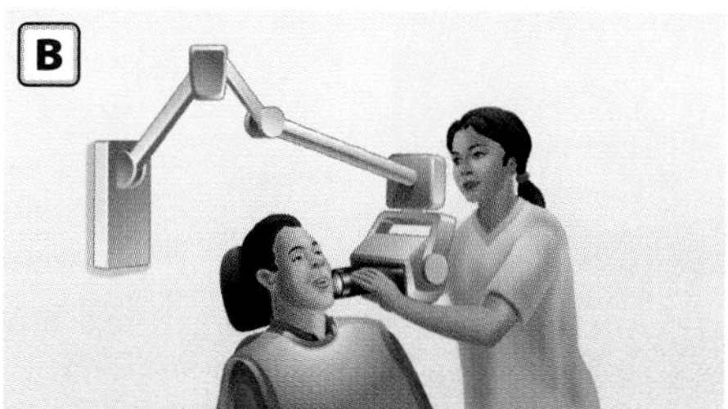


B. **take** X-rays

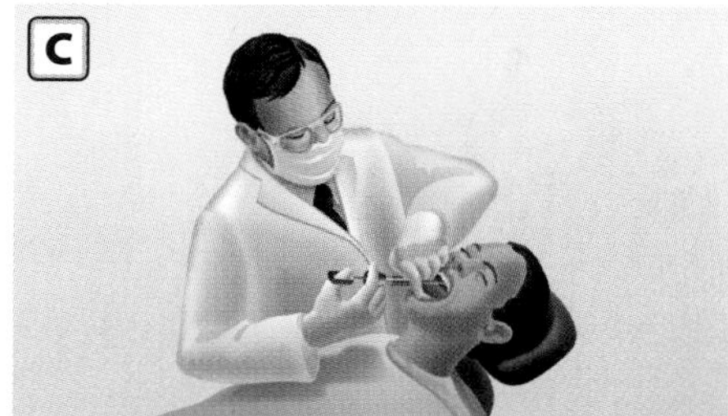


C. **numb** the mouth

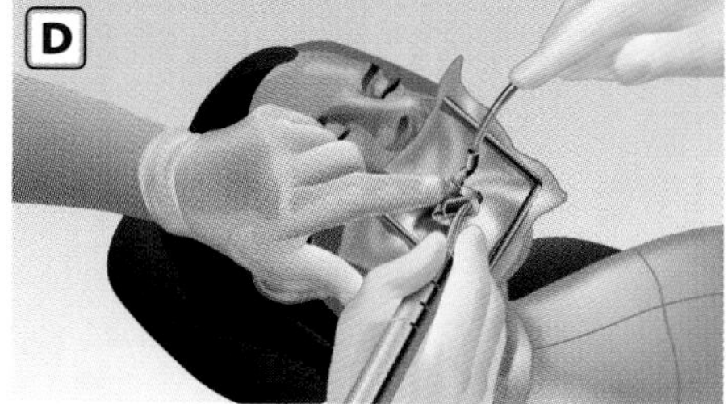


D. **drill** a tooth

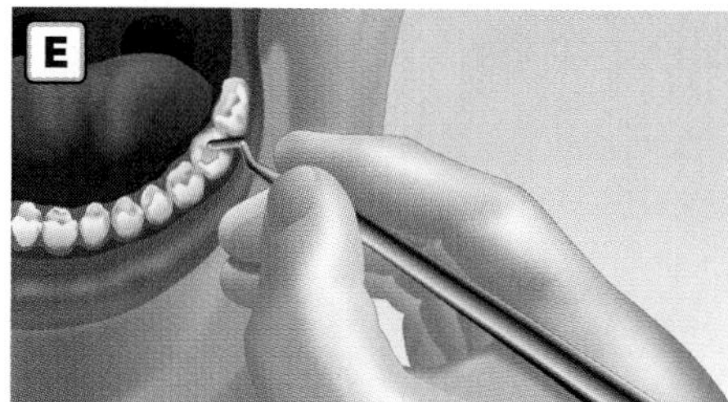


E. **fill** a cavity

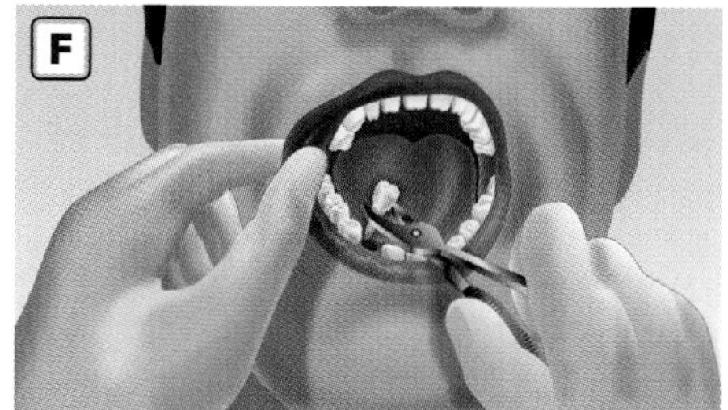


F. **pull** a tooth

**Ask your classmates. Share the answers.**

1. Do you know someone with braces? Who?
2. Do dentists make you nervous? Why or why not?
3. How often do you go to the dentist?

**Role play. Talk to a dentist.**

**A:** *I think I have a cavity.*
**B:** *Let me take a look.*
**A:** *Will I need a filling?*

## Medical Specialists

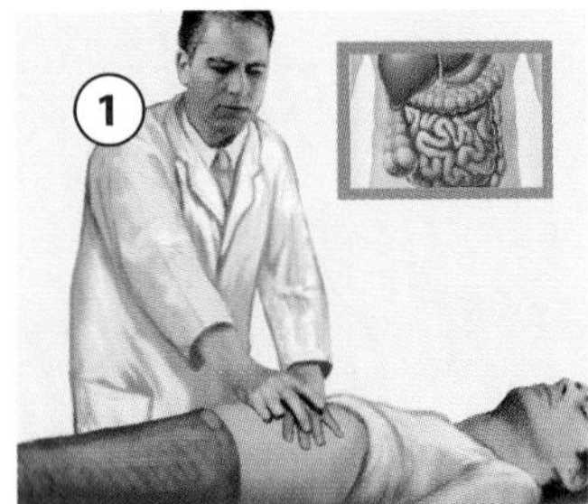

1. internist

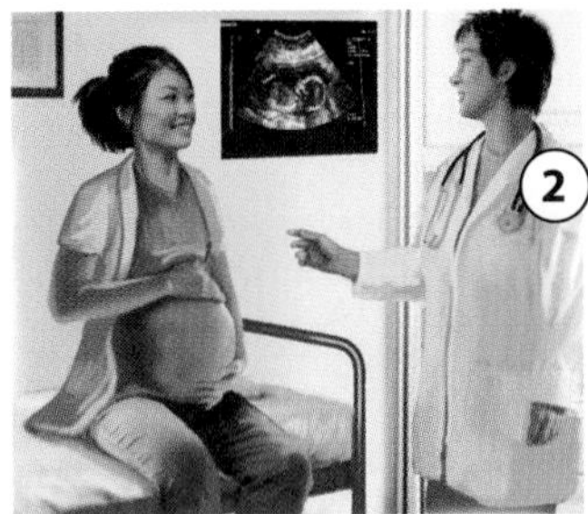

2. obstetrician

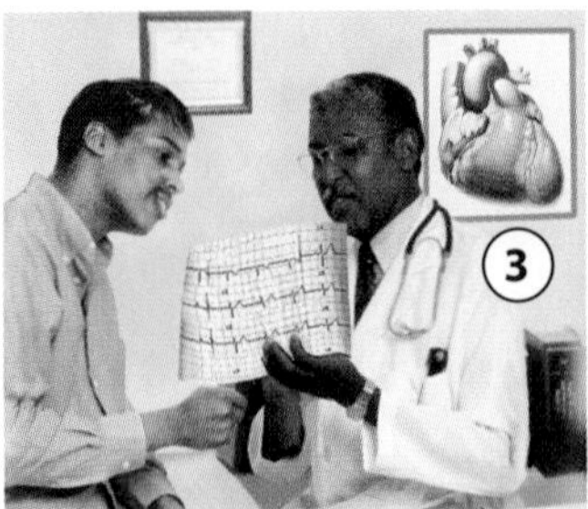

3. cardiologist

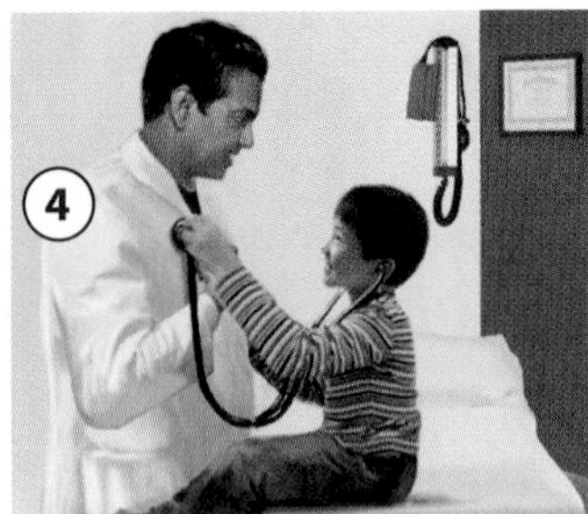

4. pediatrician

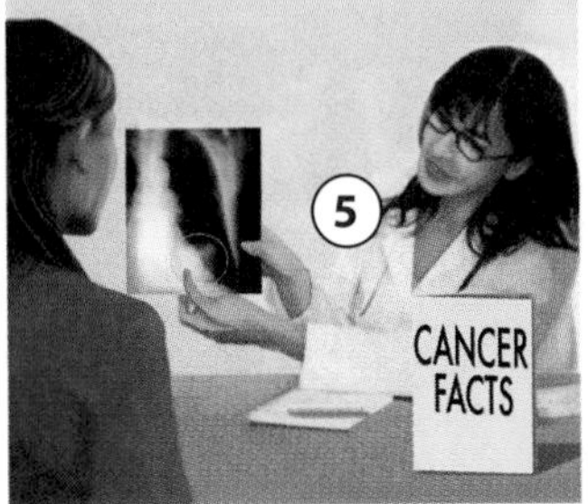


5. oncologist

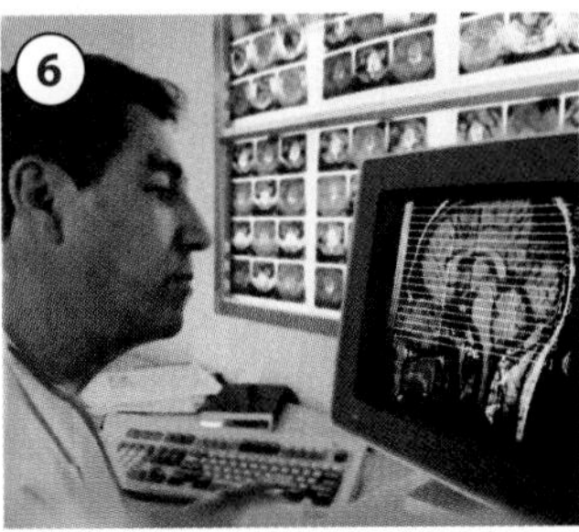

6. radiologist

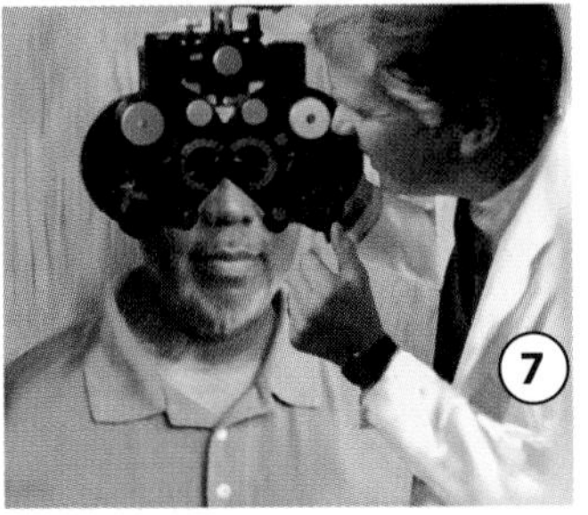

7. ophthalmologist

8. psychiatrist

## Nursing Staff

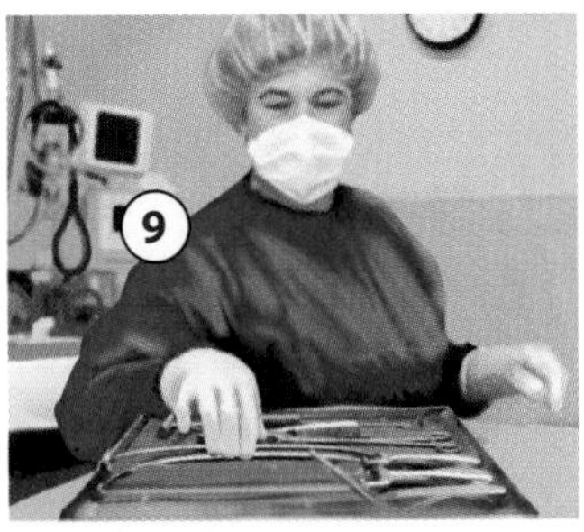

9. surgical nurse

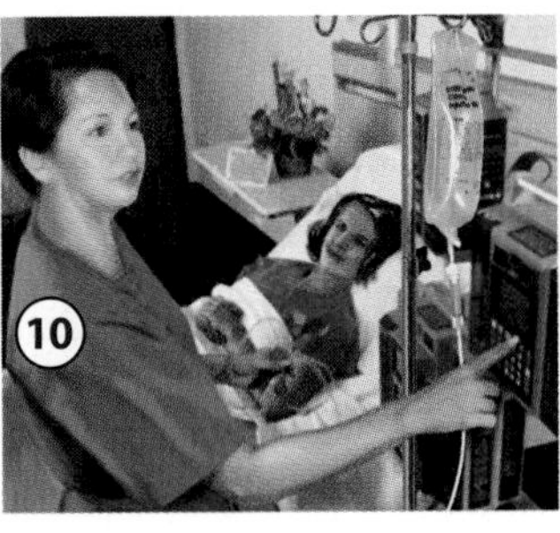

10. registered nurse (RN)

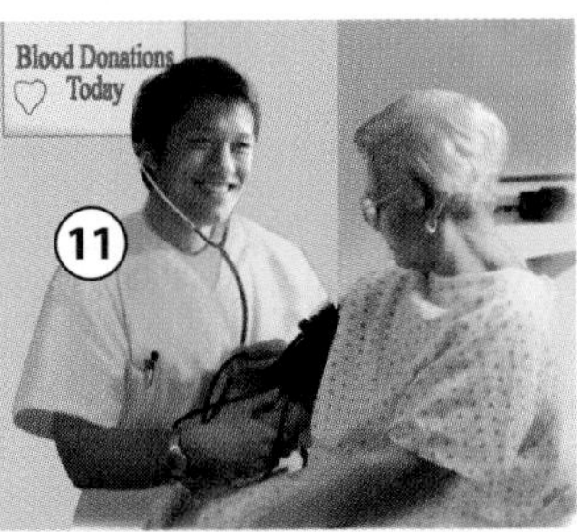


11. registered practical nurse (RPN)

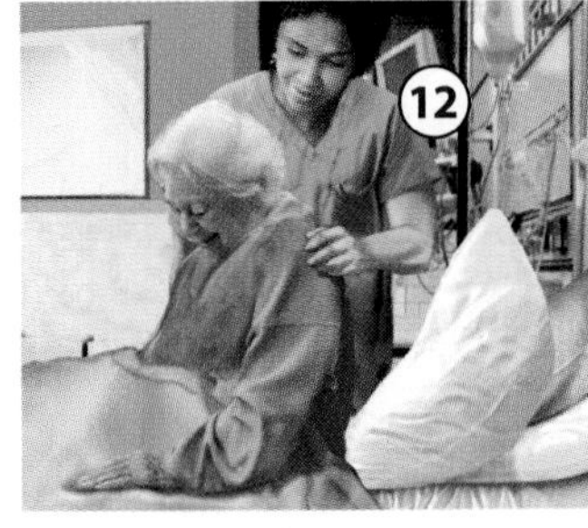

12. nursing assistant

## Hospital Staff

13. administrator

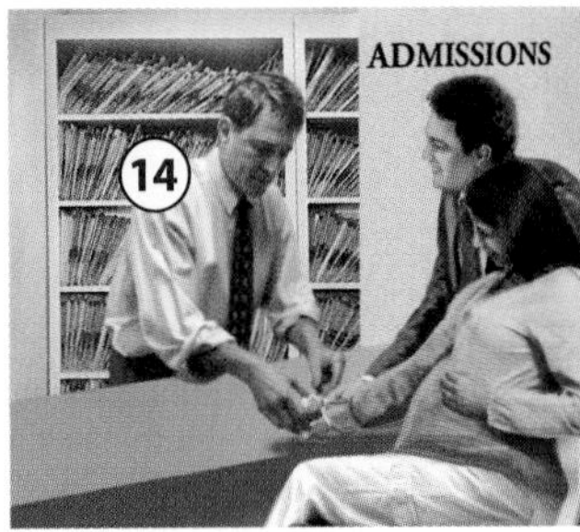


14. admissions clerk

15. dietician

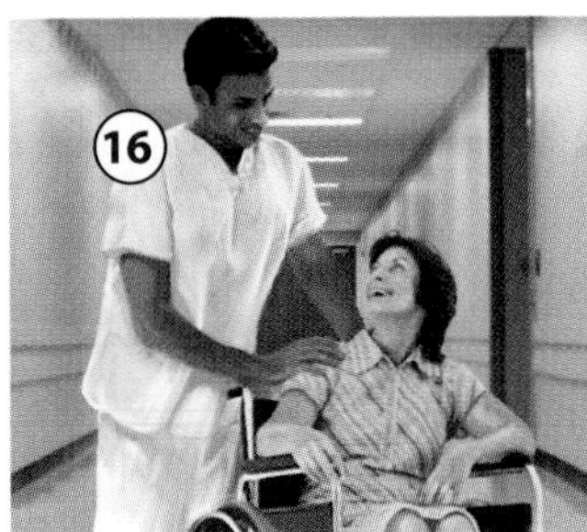

16. orderly

**More vocabulary**

**Gynecologists** examine and treat women.
**Nurse practitioners** can give medical exams.
**Midwives** deliver babies.
**Chiropractors** move the joints to improve health.
**Orthopaedists** treat bone, muscle, and joint problems.

## A Hospital Room

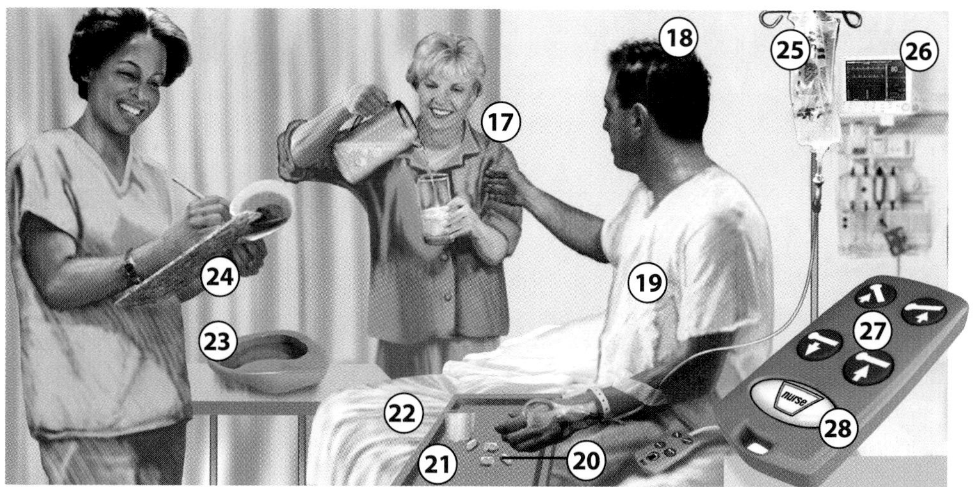


17. volunteer
18. patient
19. hospital gown
20. medication
21. over-bed table
22. hospital bed
23. bedpan
24. medical chart
25. IV (intravenous drip)
26. vital signs monitor
27. bed control
28. call button

## Lab

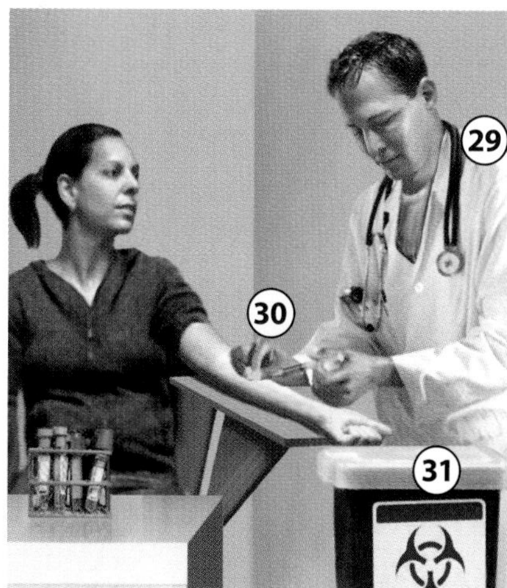

29. phlebotomist
30. blood work / blood test
31. medical waste disposal

## Emergency Room Entrance

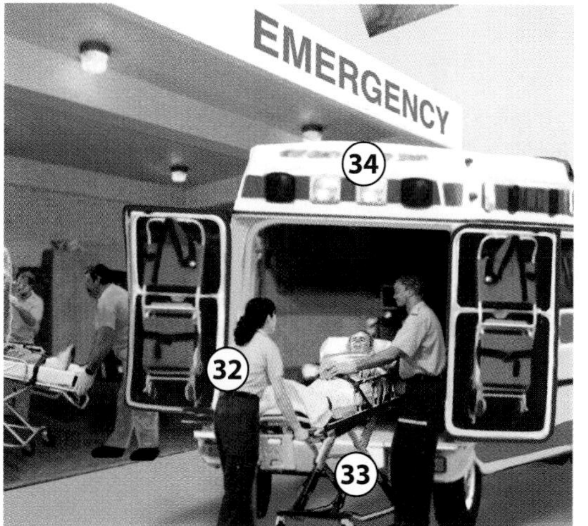


32. paramedic
33. stretcher / gurney
34. ambulance

## Operating Room

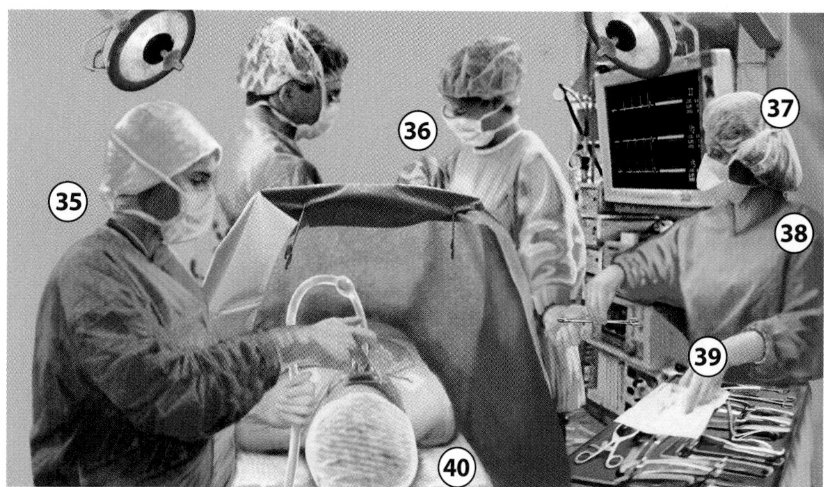

35. anesthesiologist
36. surgeon
37. surgical cap
38. surgical gown
39. surgical gloves
40. operating table

**Dictate to your partner. Take turns.**

**A:** *Write this sentence. She's a volunteer.*
**B:** *She's a what?*
**A:** *Volunteer. That's v-o-l-u-n-t-e-e-r.*

**Role play. Ask about a doctor.**

**A:** *I need to find a good surgeon.*
**B:** *Dr. Jones is a great surgeon. You should call him.*
**A:** *I will! Please give me his number.*

# A Health Fair

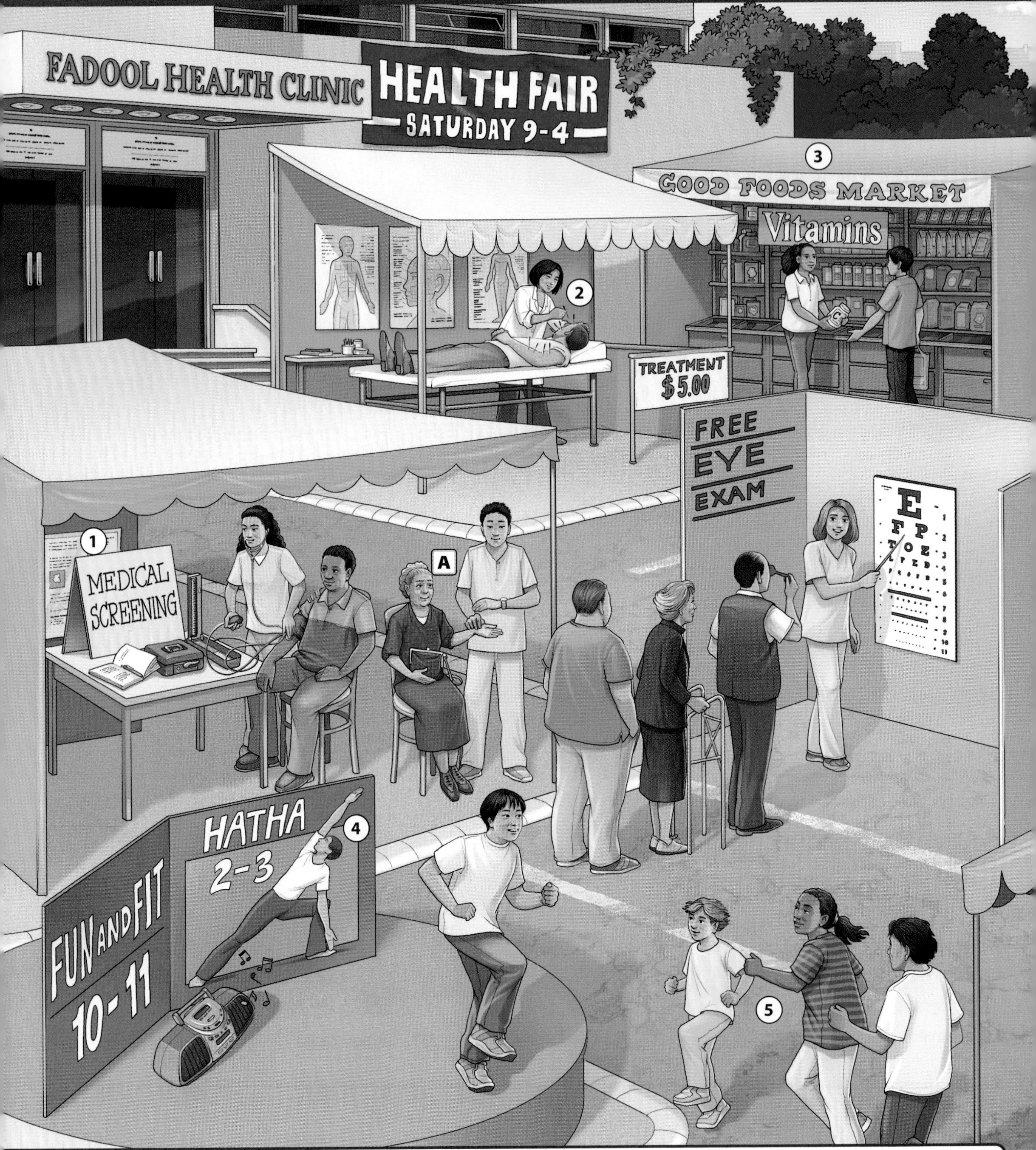

1. medical exam
2. acupuncture
3. booth
4. yoga
5. aerobic exercise
6. demonstration
7. sugar-free
8. nutrition label

A. **check** … pulse

B. **give** a lecture

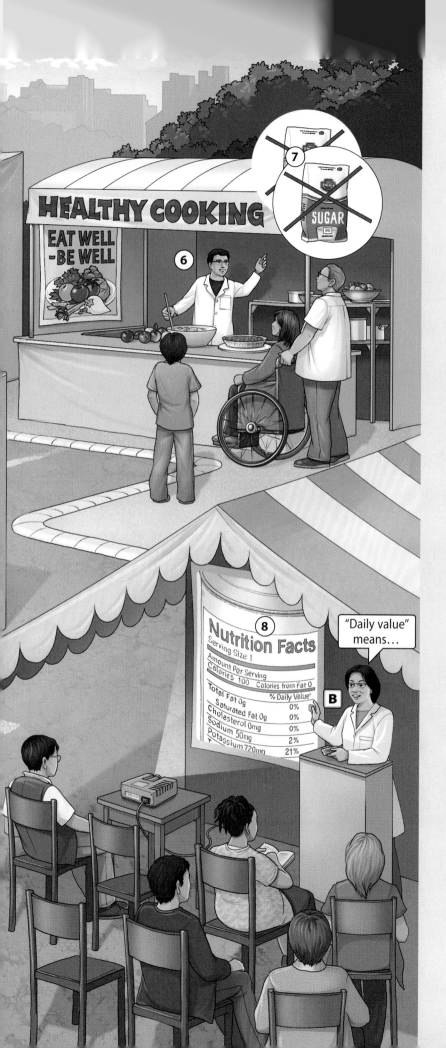

## Look at the picture. What do you see?

**Answer the questions.**

1. How many different booths are there at the health fair?
2. What kinds of exams and treatments can you get at the fair?
3. What kinds of lectures and demonstrations are there?
4. How much is an acupuncture treatment? an eye exam?

---

 **Read the story.**

### A Health Fair

Once a month the Fadool Health Clinic has a health fair. You can get a medical exam at one booth. The nurses check your blood pressure and check your pulse. At another booth you can get a free eye exam. And an acupuncture treatment is only $5.00.

You can learn a lot at the fair. This month a doctor is giving a lecture on nutrition labels. There is also a demonstration on sugar-free cooking. You can learn to do aerobic exercise and yoga, too.

Do you want to get healthy and stay healthy? Then come to the Fadool Clinic Health Fair!

---

## Think about it.

1. Which booths at this fair look interesting to you? Why?
2. Do you read nutrition labels? Why or why not?

1. parking garage
2. office building
3. hotel
4. driver licensing office
5. bank
6. police station
7. bus station
8. city hall

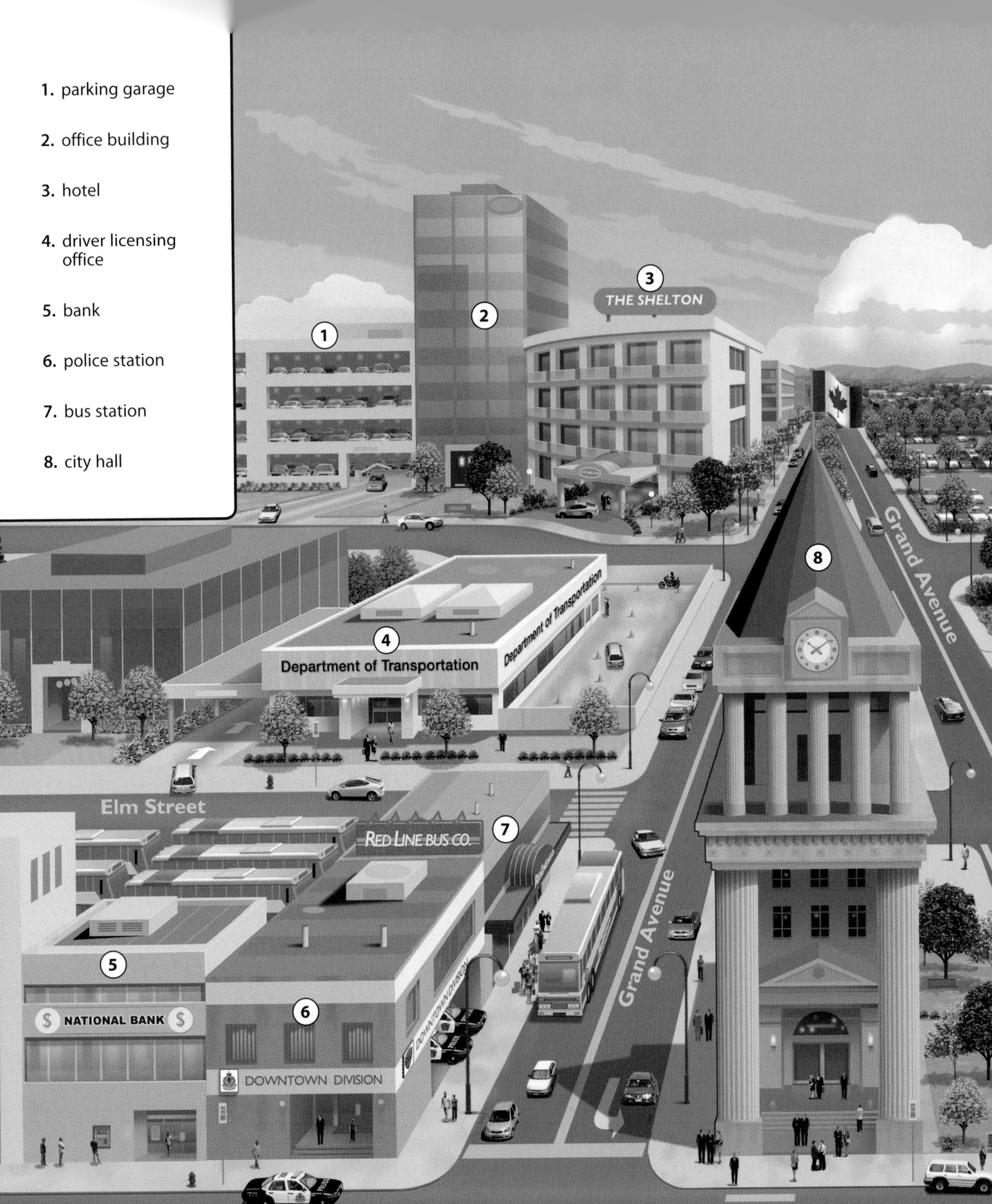


**Listen and point. Take turns.**

**A:** *Point to the bank.*
**B:** *Point to the hotel.*
**A:** *Point to the restaurant.*

**Dictate to your partner. Take turns.**

**A:** *Write bank.*
**B:** *Is that spelled b-a-n-k?*
**A:** *Yes, that's right.*

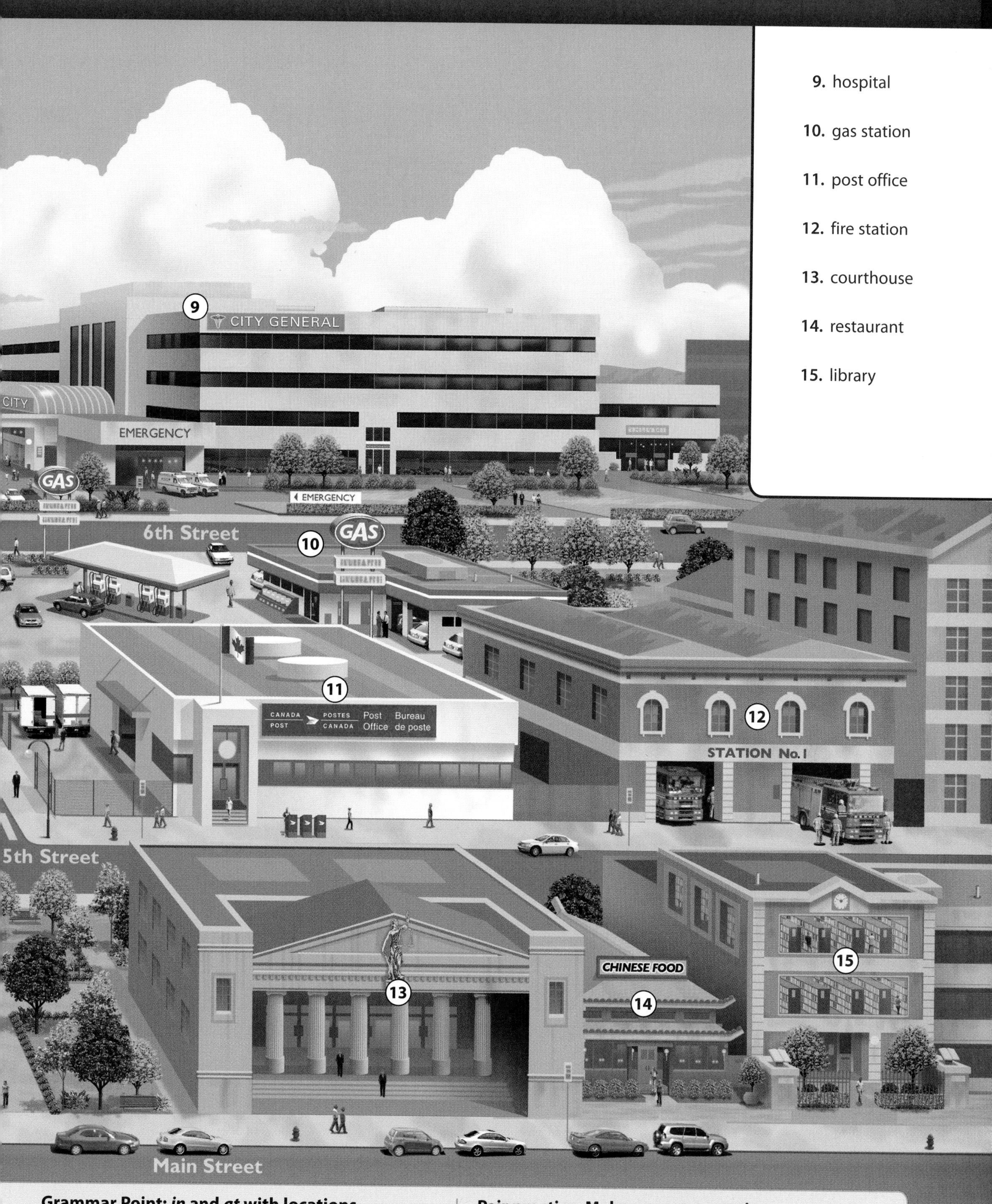


9. hospital
10. gas station
11. post office
12. fire station
13. courthouse
14. restaurant
15. library

**Grammar Point: *in* and *at* with locations**

Use ***in*** when you are inside the building. *I am* ***in*** *(inside) the bank.* Use ***at*** to describe your general location. *I am* ***at*** *the bank.*

**Pair practice. Make new conversations.**

**A:** *I'm in the* <u>*bank*</u>*. Where are you?*
**B:** *I'm at the* <u>*bank*</u>*, too, but I'm outside.*
**A:** *OK. I'll meet you there.*

1. stadium
2. construction site
3. factory
4. car dealership
5. mosque
6. movie theatre
7. shopping mall
8. furniture store
9. school
10. gym
11. coffee shop
12. motel

**Ways to state your destination using *to* and *to the***

Use ***to*** for schools, churches, and synagogues.
*I'm going **to** school.*
Use ***to the*** for all other locations. *I have to go **to the** bakery.*

**Pair practice. Make new conversations.**

**A:** *Where are you going today?*
**B:** *I'm going to school. How about you?*
**A:** *I have to go to the bakery.*

**13.** skyscraper / high-rise

**14.** church

**15.** cemetery

**16.** synagogue

**17.** (community) college

**18.** supermarket / grocery store

**19.** bakery

**20.** home improvement store

**21.** office supply store

**22.** garbage truck

**23.** theatre

**24.** convention centre

**Ways to give locations**

*The mall is on 2nd Street.*
*The mall is on the corner of 2nd and Elm.*
*The mall is next to the movie theatre.*

**Ask your classmates. Share the answers.**

1. Where's your favourite coffee shop?
2. Where's your favourite supermarket?
3. Where's your favourite movie theatre?

# An Intersection

1. laundromat
2. dry cleaners
3. convenience store
4. pharmacy
5. parking space
6. handicapped parking
7. corner
8. traffic light
9. bus
10. fast-food restaurant
11. drive-through window
12. newsstand
13. mailbox
14. pedestrian
15. crosswalk

A. **cross** the street

B. **wait for** the light

C. **jaywalk**

**Pair practice. Make new conversations.**

**A:** *I have a lot of errands to do today.*

**B:** *Me, too. First, I'm going to the laundromat.*

**A:** *I'll see you there after I stop at the copy centre.*

**Think about it. Discuss.**

1. Which businesses are good to have in a neighbourhood? Why?
2. Would you like to own a small business? If yes, what kind? If no, why not?

**16.** bus stop

**17.** doughnut shop

**18.** copy centre

**19.** barbershop

**20.** video store

**21.** curb

**22.** bike

**23.** pay phone

**24.** sidewalk

**25.** parking meter

**26.** street sign

**27.** fire hydrant

**28.** cart

**29.** street vendor

**30.** childcare centre

**D.** **ride** a bike

**E.** **park** the car

**F.** **walk** a dog

**More vocabulary**

**neighbourhood:** the area close to your home

**do errands:** to make a short trip from your home to buy or pick up things

**Ask your classmates. Share the answers.**

1. What errands do you do every week?
2. What stores do you go to in your neighbourhood?
3. What things can you buy from a street vendor?

1. music store
2. jewellery store
3. nail salon
4. bookstore
5. toy store
6. pet store
7. card store
8. florist
9. optician
10. shoe store
11. play area
12. guest services

**More vocabulary**

**beauty shop:** hair salon
**men's store:** men's clothing store
**gift shop:** a store that sells T-shirts, mugs, and other small gifts

**Pair practice. Make new conversations.**

**A:** *Where is the florist?*
**B:** *It's on the first floor, next to the optician.*

| | | |
|---|---|---|
| **13.** department store | **17.** candy store | **21.** elevator |
| **14.** travel agency | **18.** hair salon | **22.** cellphone kiosk |
| **15.** food court | **19.** maternity store | **23.** escalator |
| **16.** ice cream shop | **20.** electronics store | **24.** directory |

**Ways to talk about plans**

*Let's go to the card store.*
*I have to go to the card store.*
*I want to go to the card store.*

**Role play. Talk to a friend at the mall.**

**A:** *Let's go to the card store. I need to buy a card for Maggie's birthday.*
**B:** *OK, but can we go to the shoe store next?*

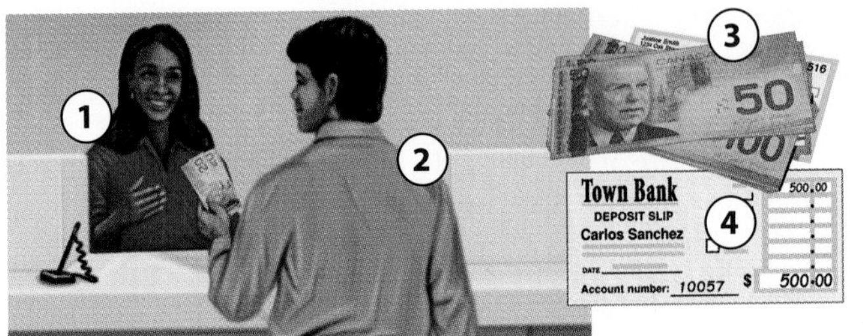


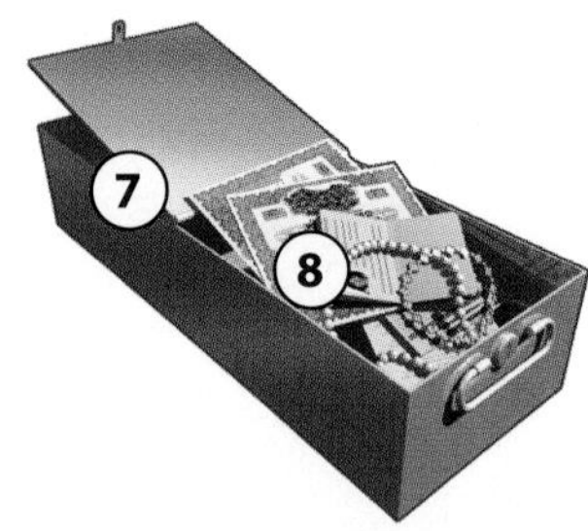


1. teller
2. customer
3. deposit
4. deposit slip
5. security guard
6. vault
7. safety deposit box
8. valuables

## Opening an Account

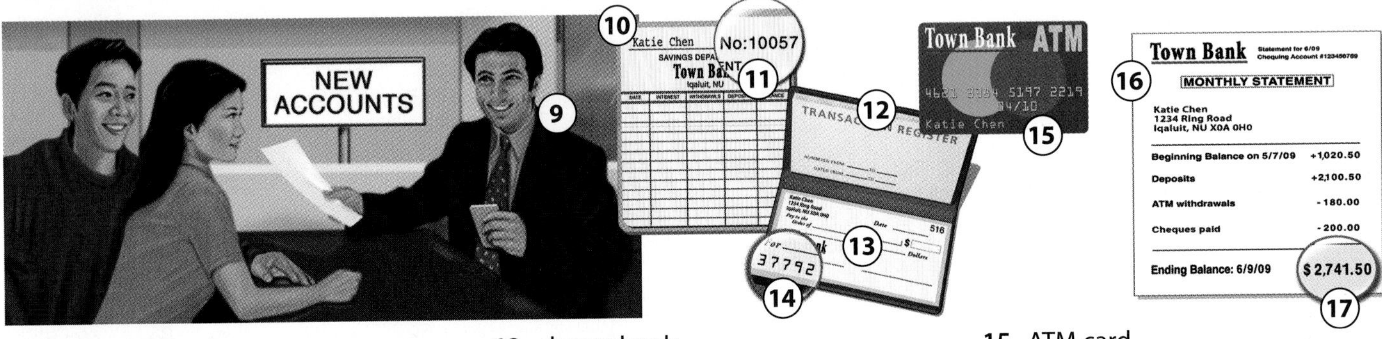


9. account manager
10. passbook
11. savings account number
12. chequebook
13. cheque
14. chequing account number
15. ATM card
16. bank statement
17. balance

A. **Cash** a cheque.

B. **Make** a deposit.

C. **Bank** online.

## The ATM (Automated Teller Machine)

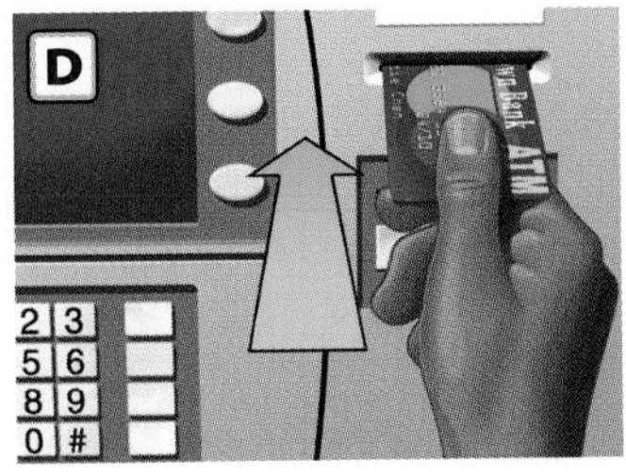


D. **Insert** your ATM card.

E. **Enter** your PIN.*

F. **Withdraw** cash.

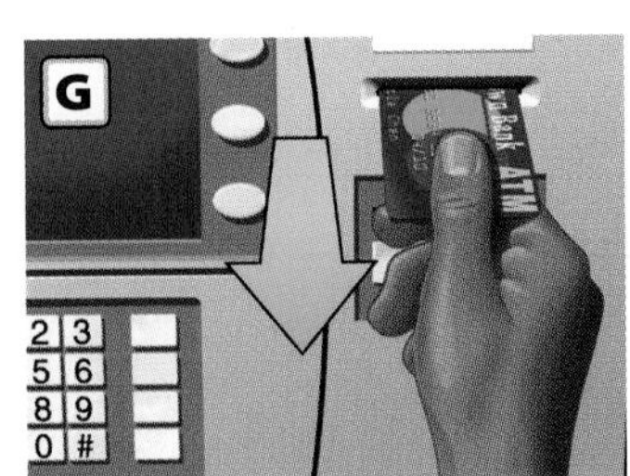


G. **Remove** your card.

***PIN** = personal identification number

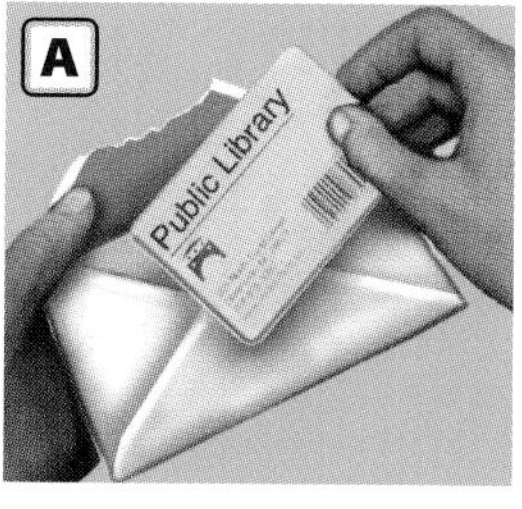

A. **get** a library card

B. **look for** a book

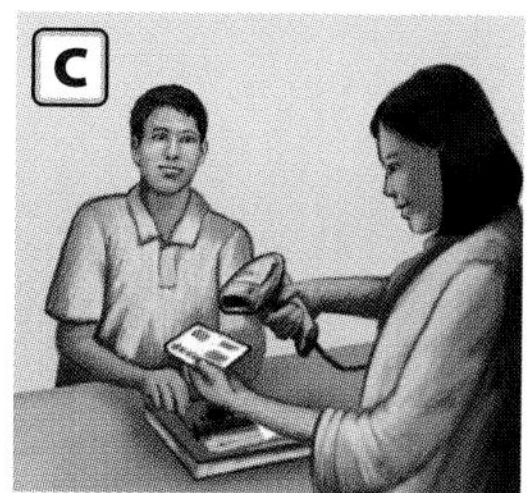


C. **check out** a book

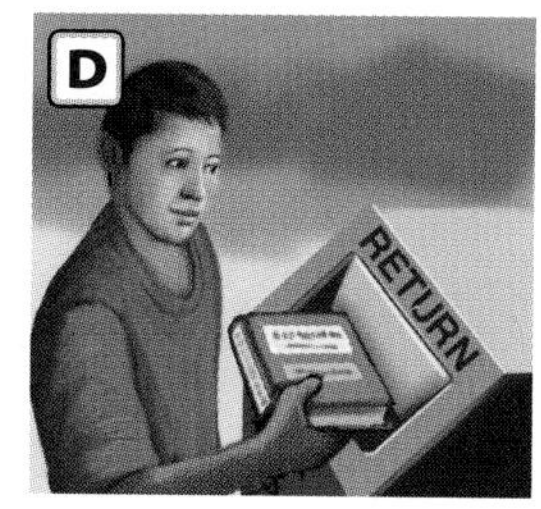


D. **return** a book

E. **pay** a late fine

1. library clerk
2. circulation desk
3. library patron
4. periodicals
5. magazine
6. newspaper
7. headline
8. atlas
9. reference librarian
10. self-checkout
11. online catalogue
12. picture book

13. biography
14. title
15. author
16. novel
17. audio book
18. video cassette
19. DVD

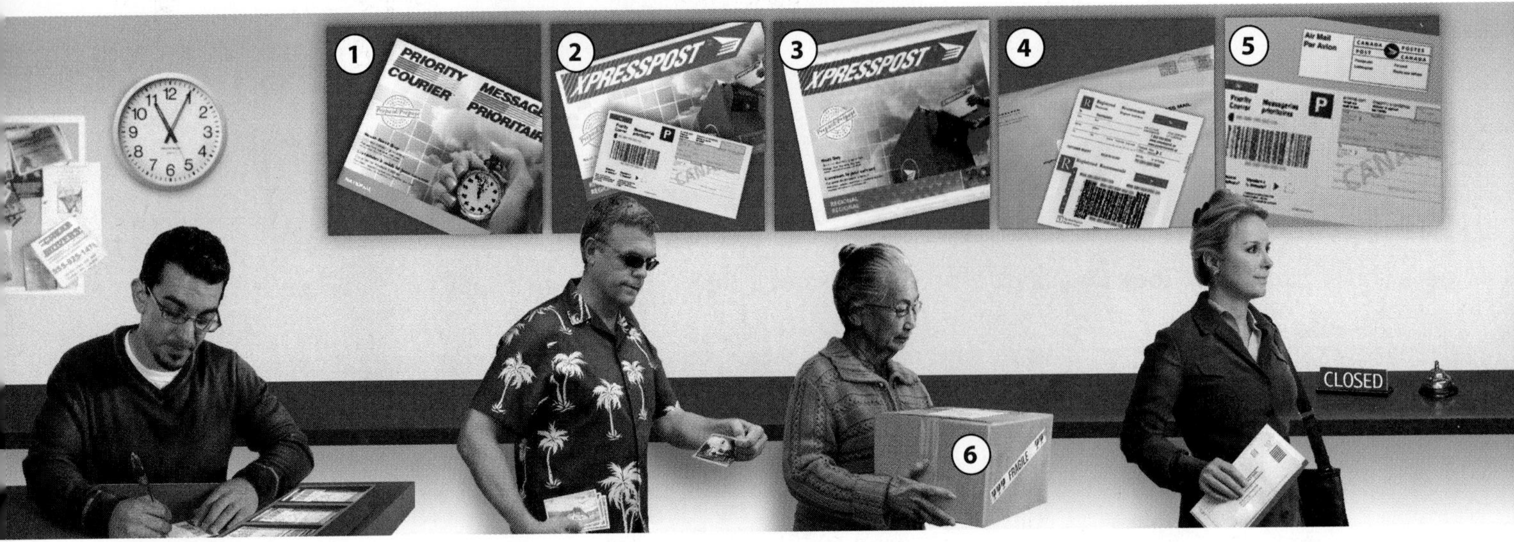


1. Priority Courier™
2. Xpresspost™
3. Xpresspost™ bubble envelope
4. registered mail
5. air mail
6. surface mail / parcel post

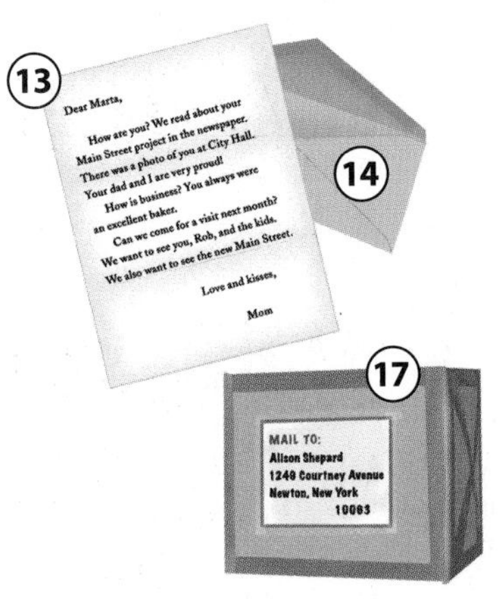

13. letter
14. envelope
15. greeting card
16. postcard
17. package
18. book of stamps
19. postal forms
20. letter carrier

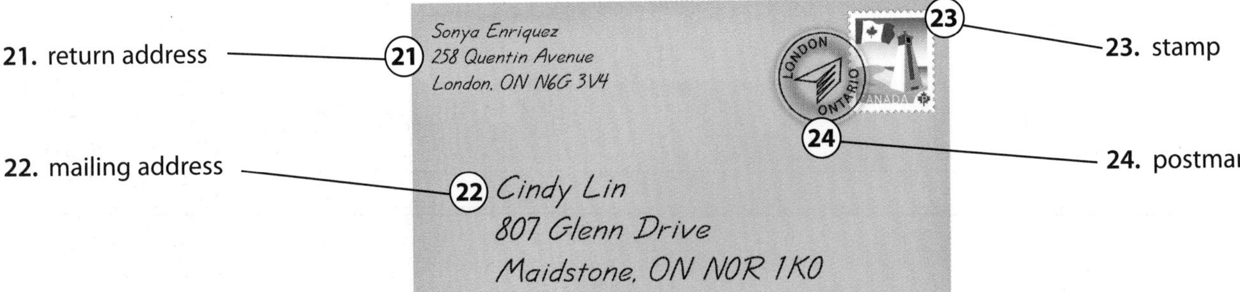

Sonya Enriquez
258 Quentin Avenue
London, ON N6G 3V4
LONDON ONTARIO
CANADA
Cindy Lin
807 Glenn Drive
Maidstone, ON N0R 1K0


21. return address
22. mailing address
23. stamp
24. postmark

**Ways to talk about sending mail**

*This letter has to get there tomorrow.* **(Xpresspost™)**
*This letter has to arrive in two days.* **(Priority Courier™)**
*This letter can go in regular mail.* **(Lettermail™)**

**Pair practice. Make new conversations.**

**A:** *Hi. This letter has to get there tomorrow.*
**B:** *You can send it by Xpresspost™* service.
**A:** *OK. I need a book of stamps, too.*

7. postal clerk
8. scale
9. post office box (PO box)
10. mailbox
11. online shipping

## Sending a Card

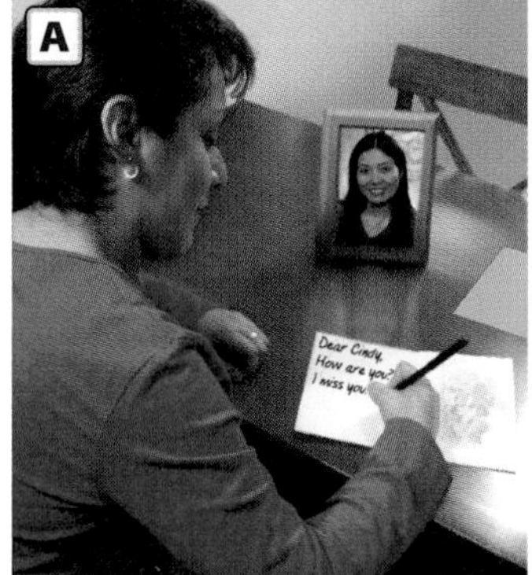


A. **Write** a note in a card.

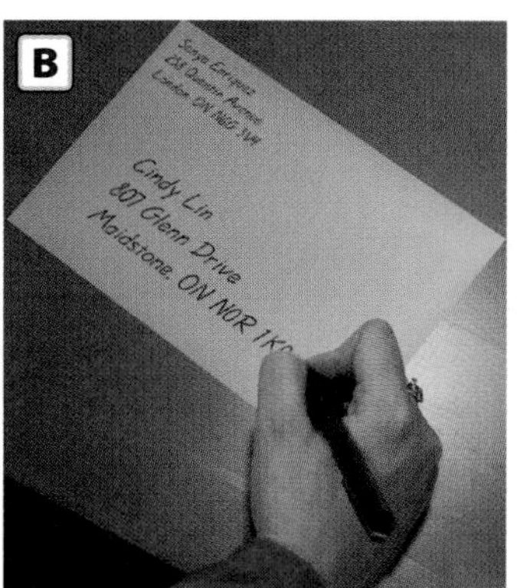


B. **Address** the envelope.

C. **Put on** a stamp.

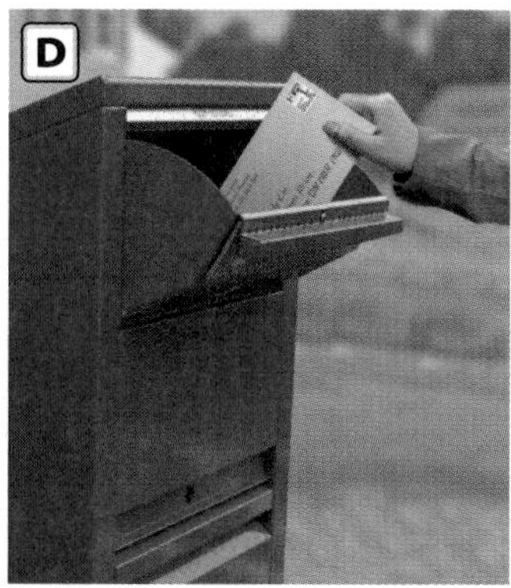


D. **Mail** the card.

E. **Deliver** the card.

F. **Receive** the card.

G. **Read** the card.

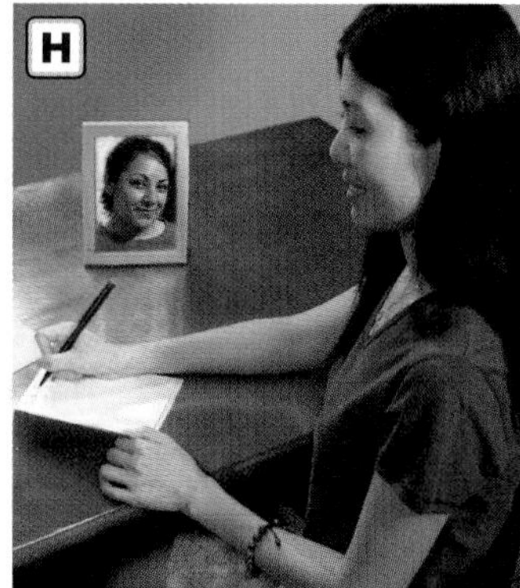


H. **Write** back.

**More vocabulary**

**overnight / next day mail:** Xpresspost™
**postage:** the cost to send mail
**junk mail:** mail you don't want

**Think about it. Discuss.**

1. What kind of mail do you send overnight?
2. Do you want to be a letter carrier? Why or why not?
3. Do you get junk mail? What do you do with it?

# Driver Licensing Office

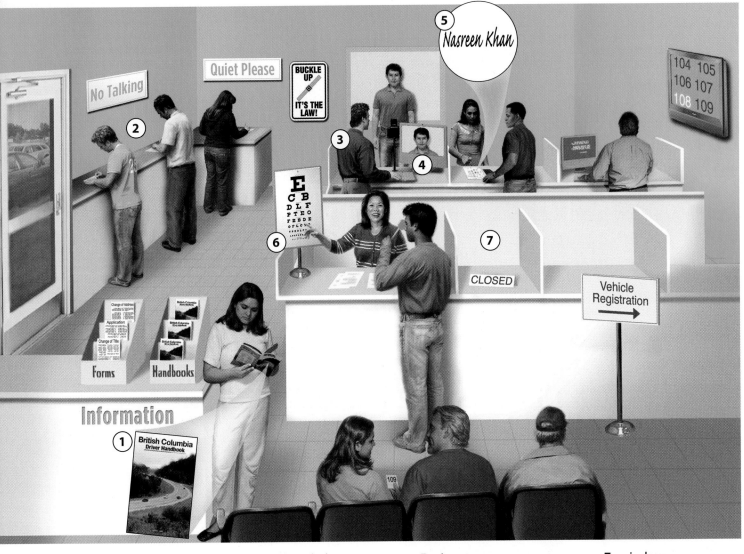

1. driving handbook
2. testing area
3. licensing clerk
4. photo
5. signature
6. vision exam
7. window

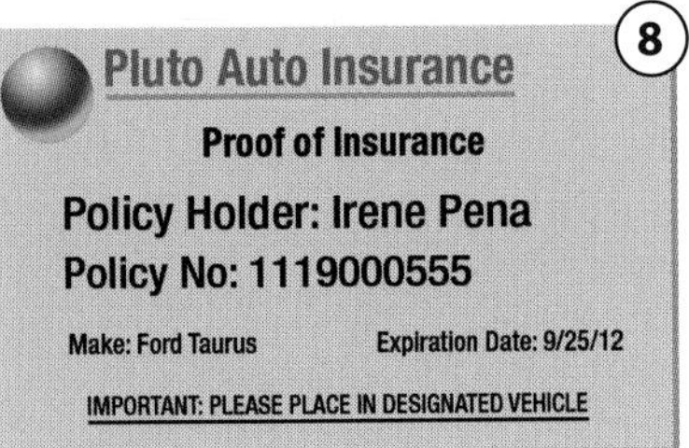

Pluto Auto Insurance

Proof of Insurance

Policy Holder: Irene Pena

Policy No: 1119000555

Make: Ford Taurus Expiration Date: 9/25/12

IMPORTANT: PLEASE PLACE IN DESIGNATED VEHICLE

8. proof of insurance
9. driver's licence
10. expiration date
11. driver's licence number
12. licence plate
13. registration sticker / tag

**More vocabulary**

**expire:** a licence is no good, or **expires**, after the expiration date

**renew a licence:** to apply to keep a licence before it expires

**vanity plate:** a more expensive, personalized licence plate

**Ask your classmates. Share the answers.**

1. How far is the driver licensing office from your home?
2. Do you have a driver's licence? If yes, when does it expire? If not, do you want one?

## Getting Your First Licence

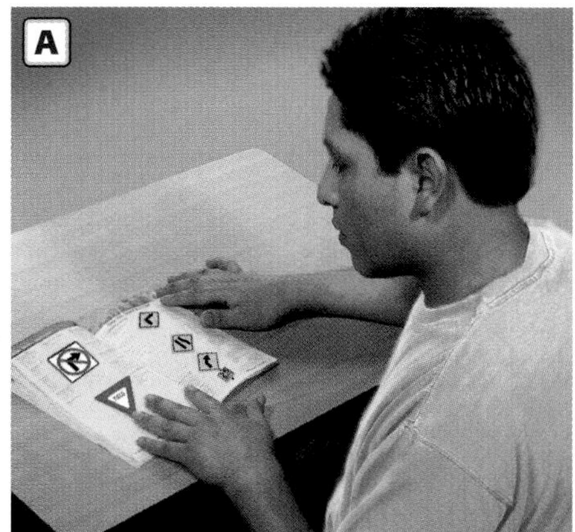

A. **Study** the handbook.

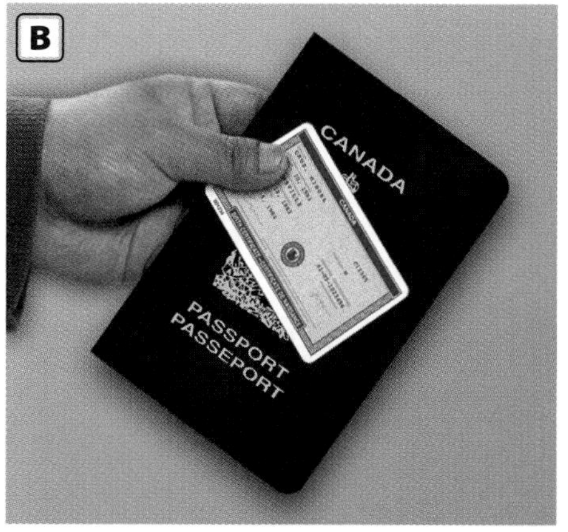


B. **Show** your identification.

C. **Pay** the application fee.

D. **Take** a written test.

E. **Get** a beginner's / learner's permit.

F. **Take** a driver education and training course.

G. **Pass** a driving test.

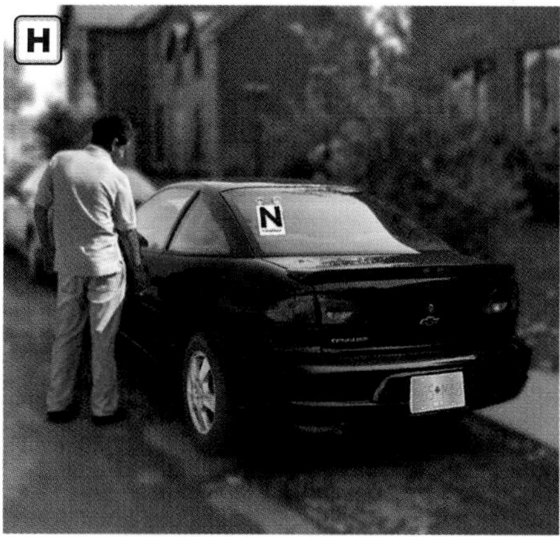


H. **Get** your licence.

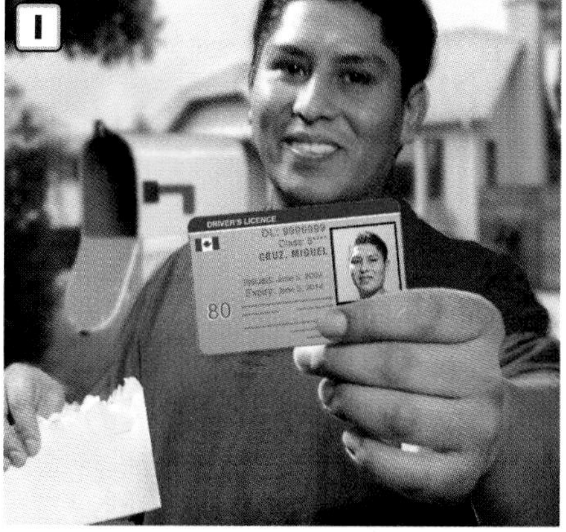


I. **Get** your unrestricted licence.*

*__Note:__ This process will vary by province.

### Ways to request more information

*What do I do next?*
*What's the next step?*
*Where do I go from here?*

### Role play. Talk to a DMV clerk.

**A:** *I want to apply for a driver's licence.*
**B:** *Did you study the handbook?*
**A:** *Yes, I did. What do I do next?*

# Government and Military Service

## Federal Government

1. sovereign
2. Governor General
3. prime minister
4. cabinet
5. minister
6. Parliament of Canada
7. House of Commons
8. Senate
9. member of parliament
10. senator

Head of State →

Sovereign's Representative →

Head of Government

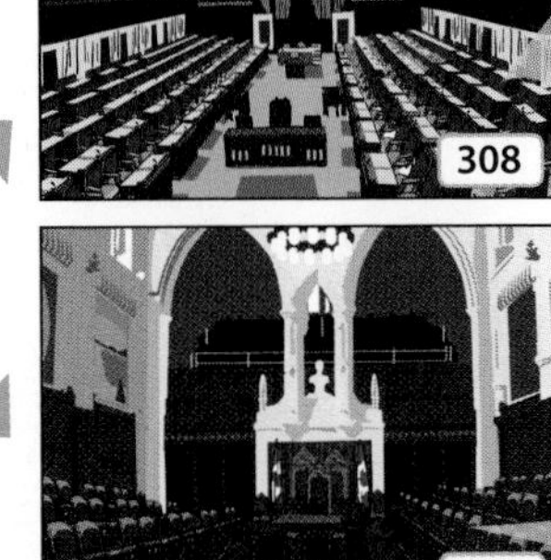

11. Supreme Court of Canada
12. judges
13. chief justice

## The Military

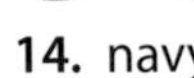

14. navy

15. army

16. air force

## Provincial Government

17. premier
18. lieutenant governor
19. provincial capital
20. Legislative Assembly / House of Assembly / National Assembly
21. member of legislative assembly

## City Government

22. mayor
23. city council
24. city councillors

## An Election

A. **run for** office

25. political campaign

B. **debate**

26. opponent

C. **get elected**

27. election results

D. **serve**

28. elected official

### More vocabulary

**term:** the period of time an elected official serves
**political party:** a group of people with the same political goals

### Think about it. Discuss.

1. Should everyone have to serve in the military? Why or why not?
2. Would you prefer to run for city council or mayor? Why?

# Civic Rights and Responsibilities

## Responsibilities

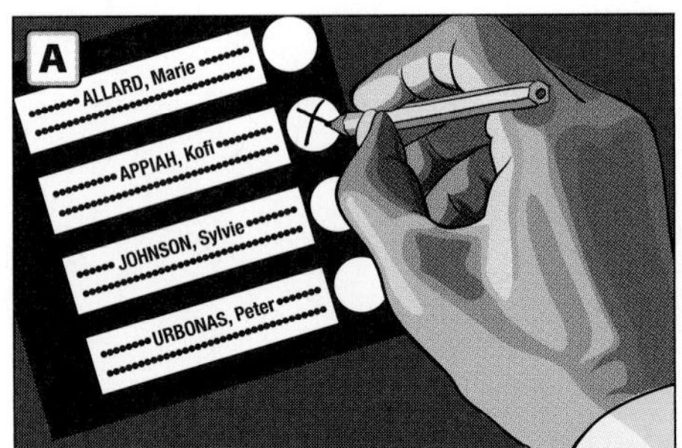


A. **vote** in elections

B. **help** others in the community

C. **care for** and **protect** our heritage and environment

D. **obey** Canada's laws

E. **express** opinions freely while respecting the rights and freedoms of others

F. **eliminate** discrimination and injustice

## Citizenship Requirements

G. **be** 18 or older

H. **live** in Canada for 3 of the last 4 years

I. **take** a citizenship test

## Rights (Fundamental Freedoms)

1. freedom of conscience and religion

2. freedom of thought, belief, opinion, and expression

3. peaceful assembly

4. freedom of association

A. **arrest** a suspect

1. police officer
2. handcuffs

B. **hire** a lawyer / **hire** an attorney

3. guard
4. defence lawyer

C. **appear** in court

5. defendant
6. judge

D. **stand** trial

7. courtroom
8. jury
9. evidence
10. Crown counsel
11. witness
12. court reporter
13. bailiff

E. **convict** the defendant

14. verdict*

F. **sentence** the defendant

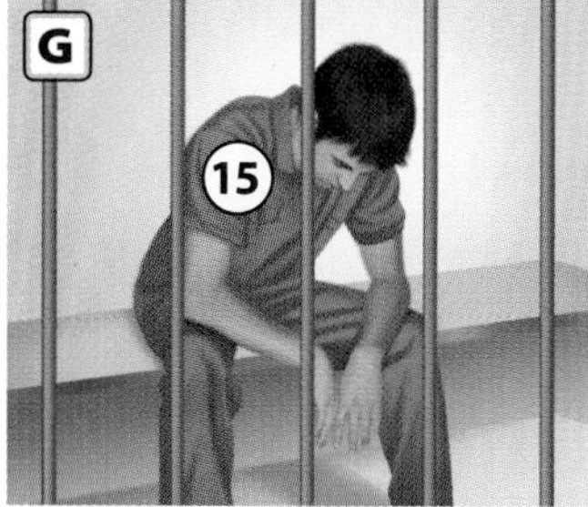


G. **go** to jail / **go** to prison

15. convict / prisoner

H. **be** released

*__Note:__ There are two possible verdicts, "guilty" and "not guilty."

**Look at the pictures.**
Describe what happened.

**A:** *The police officer arrested a suspect.*
**B:** *He put handcuffs on him.*

**Think about it. Discuss.**

1. Would you want to serve on a jury? Why or why not?
2. Look at the crimes on page 142. What sentence would you give for each crime? Why?

1. vandalism
2. burglary

3. assault
4. gang violence

5. drunk driving
6. illegal drugs

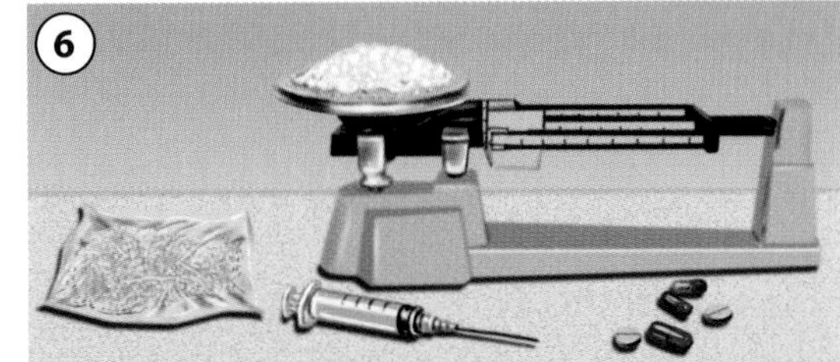


7. arson
8. shoplifting

9. identity theft
10. victim

11. mugging
12. murder
13. gun

**More vocabulary**

**steal:** to take money or things from someone illegally
**commit a crime:** to do something illegal
**criminal:** someone who does something illegal

**Think about it. Discuss.**

1. Is there too much crime on TV or in the movies? Explain.
2. How can communities help stop crime?

A. **Walk** with a friend.

B. **Stay** on well-lit streets.

C. **Conceal** your PIN number.

D. **Protect** your purse or wallet.

E. **Lock** your doors.

F. Don't **open** your door to strangers.

G. Don't **drink** and **drive**.

H. **Shop** on secure websites.

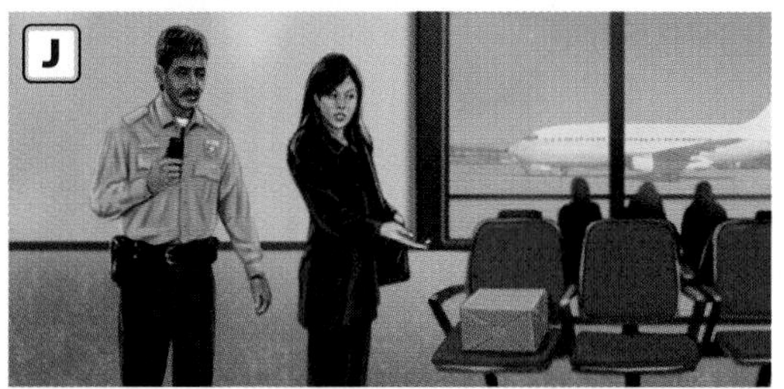

I. **Be** aware of your surroundings.

J. **Report** suspicious packages.

K. **Report** crimes to the police.

L. **Join** a neighbourhood watch.

**More vocabulary**

**sober:** not drunk

**designated drivers:** sober drivers who drive drunk people home safely

**Ask your classmates. Share the answers.**

1. Do you feel safe in your neighbourhood?
2. Look at the pictures. Which of these things do you do?
3. What other things do you do to stay safe?

# Emergencies and Natural Disasters

1. lost child
2. car accident
3. airplane crash
4. explosion
5. earthquake
6. mudslide
7. forest fire
8. fire
9. firefighter
10. fire truck

**Ways to report an emergency**

First, give your name. *My name is* <u>*Tim Johnson*</u>*.*
Then, state the emergency and give the address.
*There was* <u>*a car accident*</u> *at* <u>*219 Elm Street*</u>*.*

**Role play. Call 911.**

**A:** *911 Emergency Operator.*

**B:** *My name is* <u>*Lisa Diaz*</u>*. There is* <u>*a fire*</u> *at* <u>*323 Oak Street*</u>*. Please hurry!*

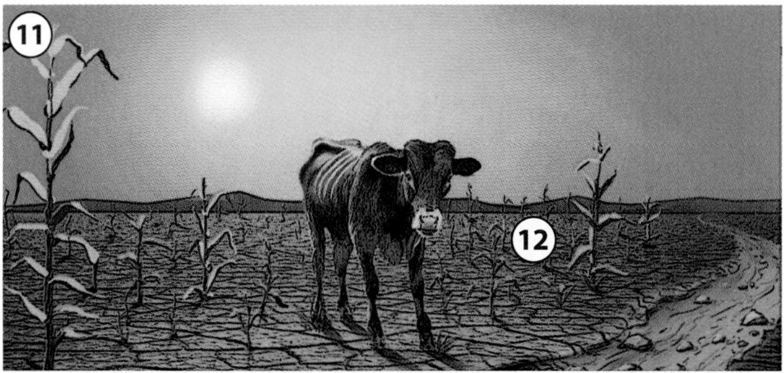

11. drought
12. famine
13. blizzard
14. hurricane
15. tornado
16. volcanic eruption
17. tidal wave / tsunami
18. avalanche
19. flood
20. search and rescue team

**Ask your classmates. Share the answers.**

1. Which natural disaster worries you the most?
2. Which natural disaster worries you the least?
3. Which disasters are common in your local area?

**Think about it. Discuss.**

1. What organizations can help you in an emergency?
2. What are some ways to prepare for natural disasters?
3. Where would you go in an emergency?

# Emergency Procedures

## Before an Emergency

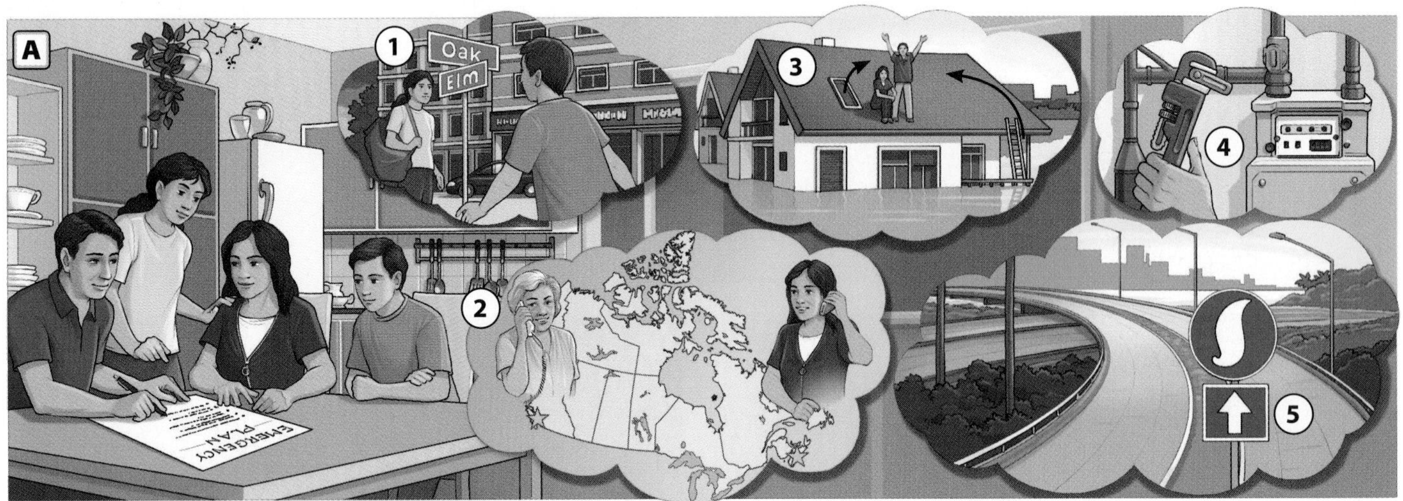


A. **Plan** for an emergency.
1. meeting place
2. out-of-town contact
3. escape route
4. gas shut-off valve
5. evacuation route

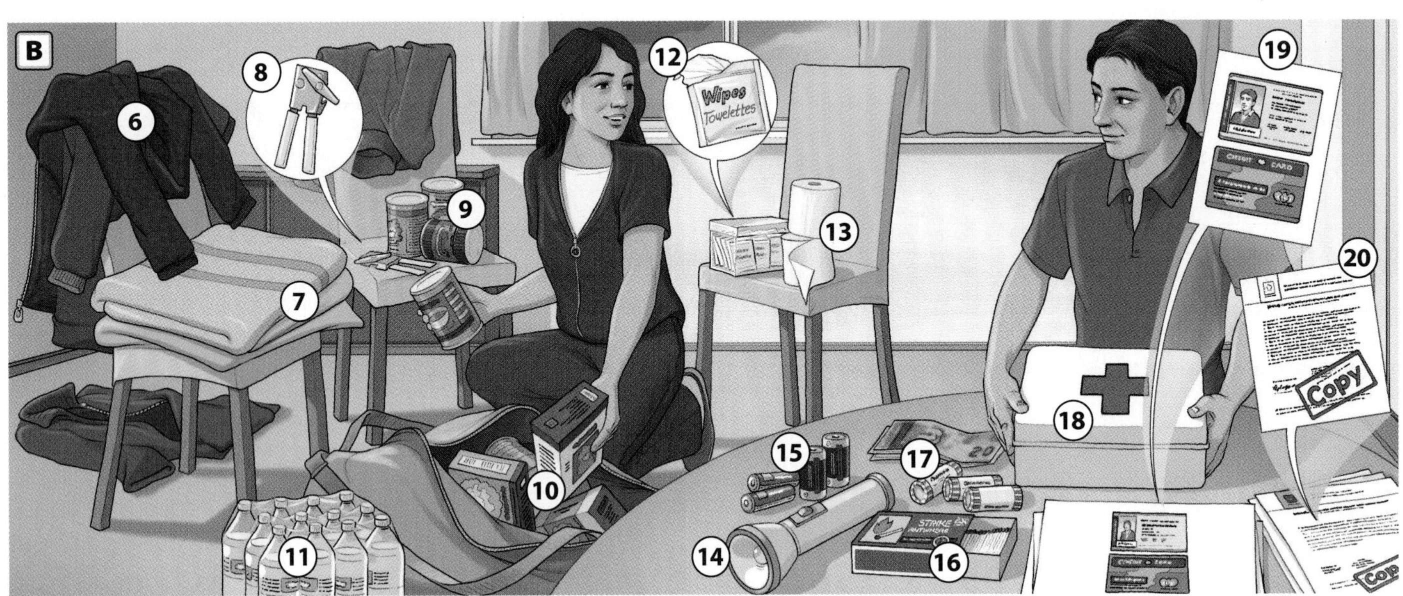


B. **Make** a disaster kit.
6. warm clothes
7. blankets
8. can opener
9. canned food
10. packaged food
11. bottled water
12. moist towelettes
13. toilet paper
14. flashlight
15. batteries
16. matches
17. cash and coins
18. first aid kit
19. copies of ID and credit cards
20. copies of important papers

**Pair practice. Make new conversations.**

**A:** *What do we need for our disaster kit?*
**B:** *We need* *__blankets__* *and* *__matches__*.
**A:** *I think we also need* *__batteries__*.

**Ask your classmates. Share the answers.**

1. Who would you call first after an emergency?
2. Do you have escape and evacuation routes planned?
3. Are you a calm person in case of an emergency?

## During an Emergency

C. **Watch** the weather.

D. **Pay attention** to warnings.

E. **Remain** calm.

F. **Follow** directions.

G. **Help** people with disabilities.

H. **Seek** shelter.

I. **Stay away** from windows.

J. **Take** cover.

## After an Emergency

K. **Call** out-of-town contacts.

L. **Clean up** debris.

M. **Inspect** utilities.

**Ways to say you're OK**

*I'm fine.*
*We're OK here.*
*Everything's under control.*

**Ways to say you need help**

*We need help.*
*Someone is hurt.*
*I'm injured. Please get help.*

**Role play. Prepare for an emergency.**

**A:** *They just issued a tornado warning.*
**B:** *OK. We need to stay calm and follow directions.*
**A:** *What do we need to do first?*

1. graffiti
2. litter
3. streetlight
4. hardware store
5. **petition**
A. **give** a speech
B. **applaud**
C. **change**

**Look at the pictures.**
**What do you see?**

**Answer the questions.**

1. What were the problems on Main Street?
2. What was the petition for?
3. Why did the city council applaud?
4. How did the people change the street?

**Read the story.**

## Community Cleanup

Marta Lopez has a doughnut shop on Main Street. One day she looked at her street and was very upset. She saw graffiti on her doughnut shop and the other stores. Litter was everywhere. All the streetlights were broken. Marta wanted to fix the lights and clean up the street.

Marta started a petition about the streetlights. Five hundred people signed it. Then she gave a speech to the city council. The councillors voted to repair the streetlights. Everyone applauded. Marta was happy, but her work wasn't finished.

Next, Marta asked for volunteers to clean up Main Street. The hardware store manager gave the volunteers free paint. Marta gave them free doughnuts and coffee. The volunteers painted and cleaned. They changed Main Street. Now Main Street is beautiful and Marta is proud.

**Think about it.**

1. What are some problems in your community? How can people help?
2. Imagine you are Marta. What do you say in your speech to the city council?

1. car
2. passenger
3. taxi
4. motorcycle
5. street
6. truck
7. train
8. (air)plane

**Listen and point. Take turns.**

**A:** *Point to <u>the motorcycle</u>.*
**B:** *Point to <u>the truck</u>.*
**A:** *Point to <u>the train</u>.*

**Dictate to your partner. Take turns.**

**A:** *Write <u>motorcycle</u>.*
**B:** *Could you repeat that for me?*
**A:** *<u>Motorcycle</u>. <u>M-o-t-o-r-c-y-c-l-e</u>.*

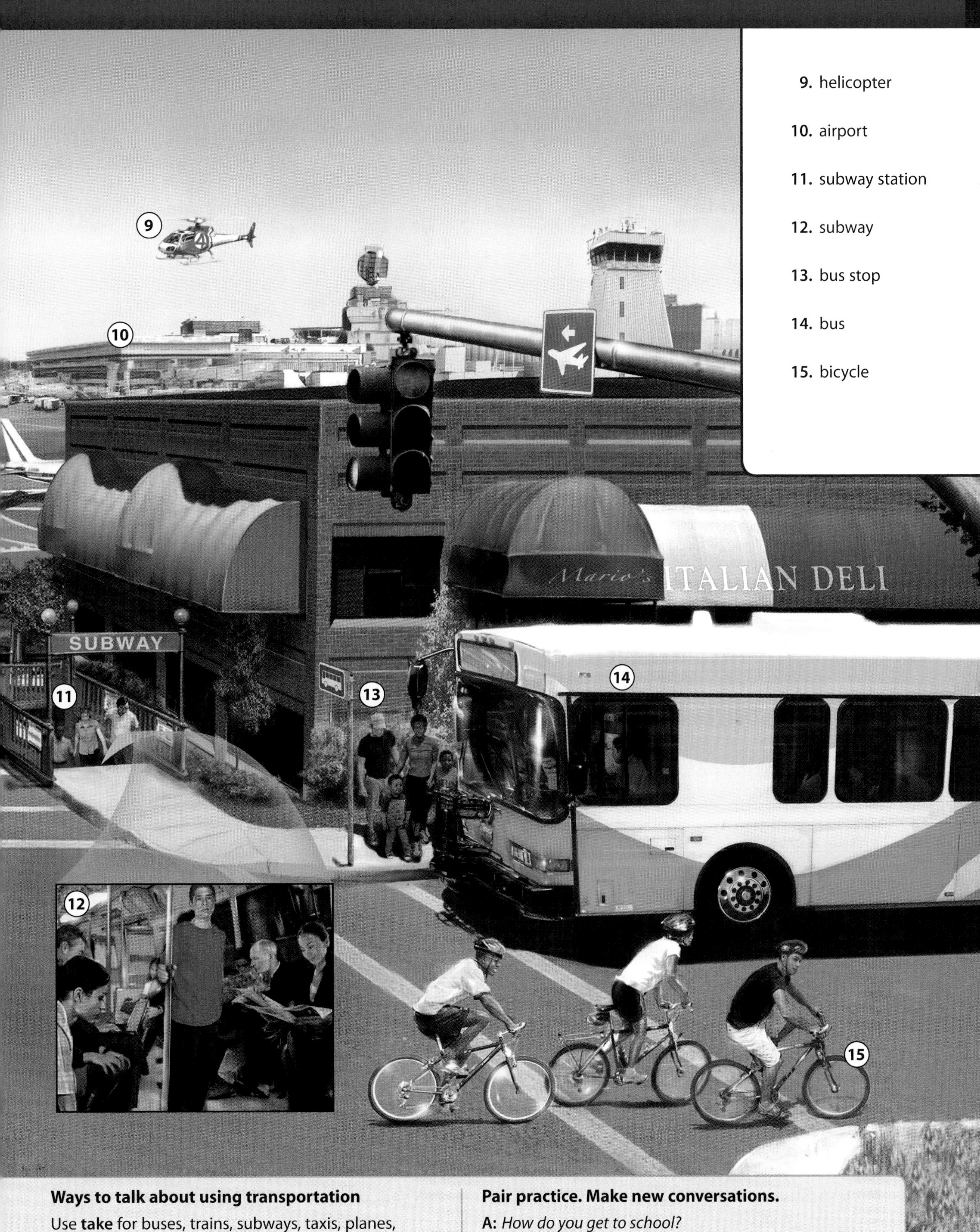


9. helicopter
10. airport
11. subway station
12. subway
13. bus stop
14. bus
15. bicycle

**Ways to talk about using transportation**

Use **take** for buses, trains, subways, taxis, planes, and helicopters. Use **drive** for cars and trucks. Use **ride** for bicycles and motorcycles.

**Pair practice. Make new conversations.**

**A:** *How do you get to school?*
**B:** *I take the bus. How about you?*
**A:** *I ride a bicycle to school.*

## A Bus Stop

4

BUS 10 Northbound

| Main | Elm | Oak |
|---|---|---|
| 6:00 | 6:10 | 6:13 |
| 6:30 | 6:40 | 6:43 |
| 7:00 | 7:10 | 7:13 |
| 7:30 | 7:40 | 7:43 |

5
512 ST CLAIR
SUN
SEP 7
212
Thanks for Riding the Rocket!
010101
This Transfer Expires at:
SUN SEP 7


1. bus route
2. fare
3. rider
4. schedule
5. transfer

## A Subway Station

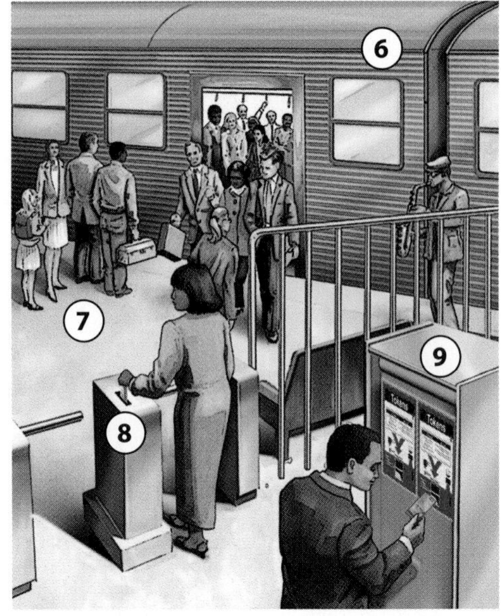

11
Ride the Rocket.
THE BETTER WAY
A
ADULT
METROPASS


6. subway car
7. platform
8. turnstile
9. vending machine
10. token
11. fare card

## A Train Station

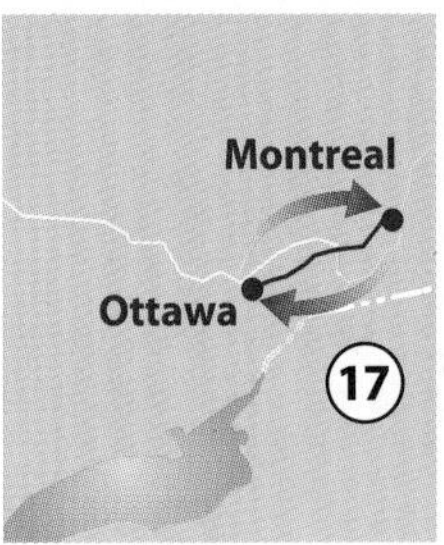

12. ticket window
13. conductor
14. track
15. ticket
16. one-way trip
17. round trip

## Airport Transportation

18. taxi stand
19. shuttle
20. town car
21. taxi driver
22. taxi licence
23. meter

### More vocabulary

**hail a taxi:** to raise your hand to get a taxi

**miss the bus:** to get to the bus stop after the bus leaves

### Ask your classmates. Share the answers.

1. Is there a subway system in your city?
2. Do you ever take taxis? When?
3. Do you ever take the bus? Where?

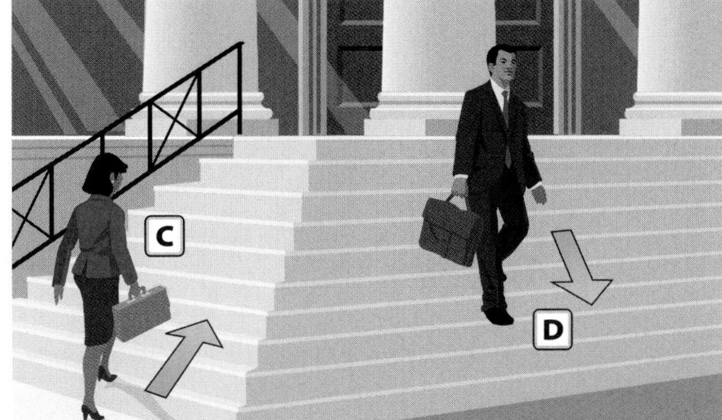


A. **go under** the bridge
B. **go over** the bridge
C. **walk up** the steps
D. **walk down** the steps

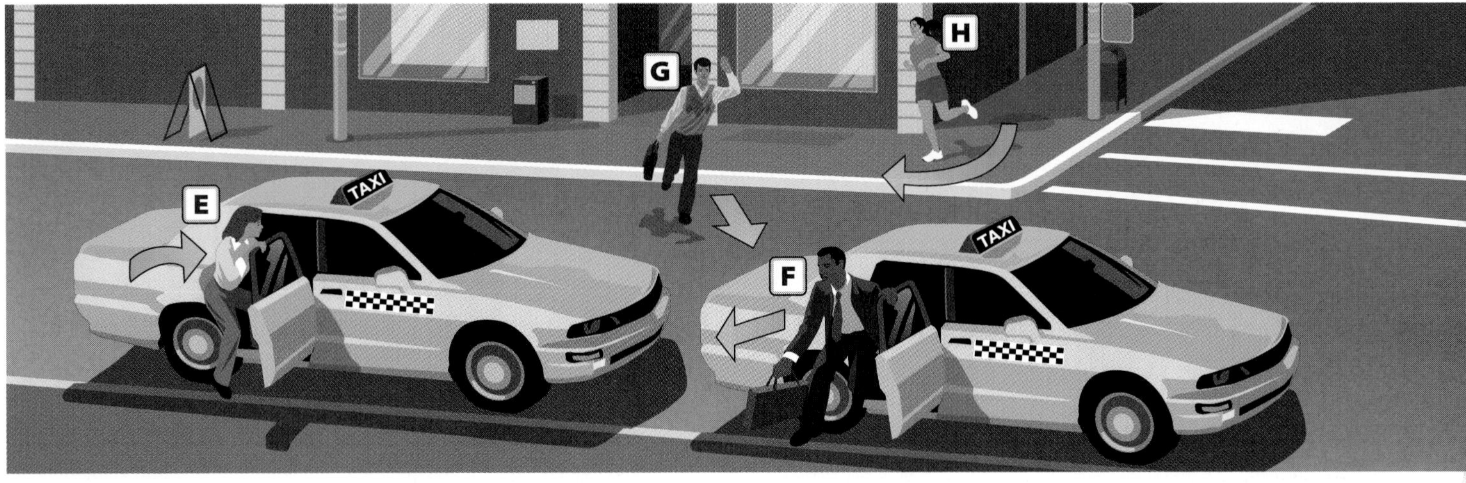


E. **get into** the taxi
F. **get out of** the taxi
G. **run across** the street
H. **run around** the corner

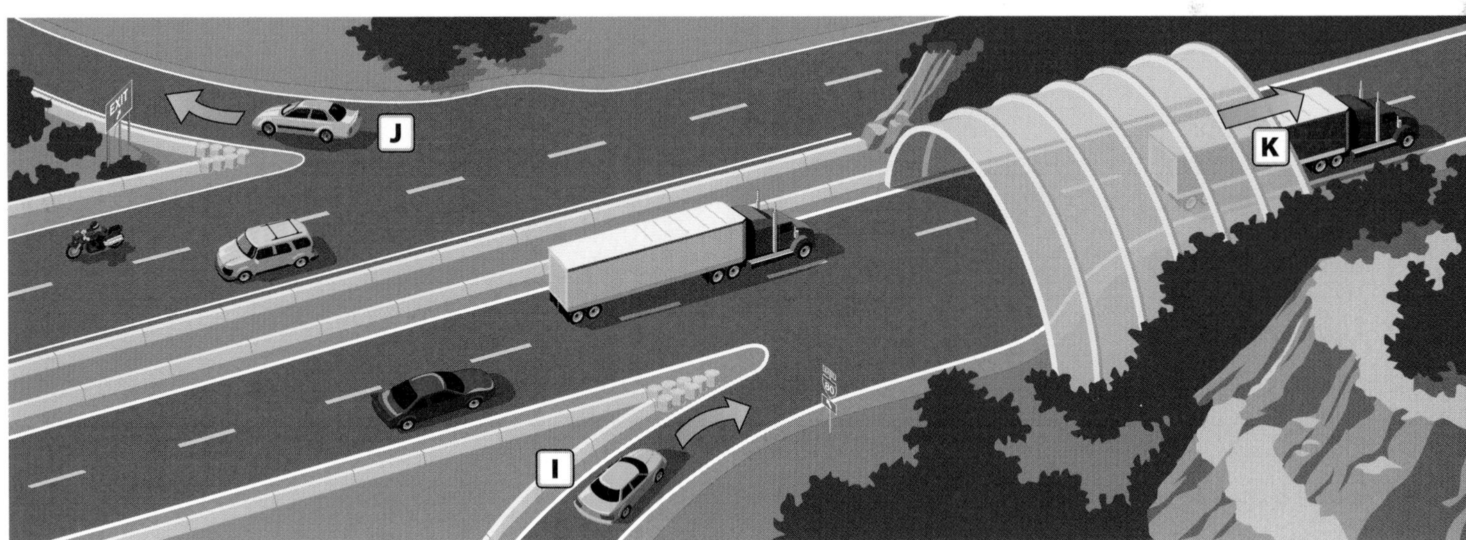


I. **get on** the highway
J. **get off** the highway
K. **drive through** the tunnel

**Grammar Point: *into, out of, on, off***

Use ***get into*** for taxis and cars.
Use ***get on*** for buses, trains, planes, and highways.

Use ***get out of*** for taxis and cars.
Use ***get off*** for buses, trains, planes, and highways.

# Traffic Signs

1. stop

2. do not enter / wrong way
3. one way

4. speed limit

5. U-turn OK

6. no exit / dead end

7. right turn only

8. no left turn

9. yield

10. merge

11. no parking

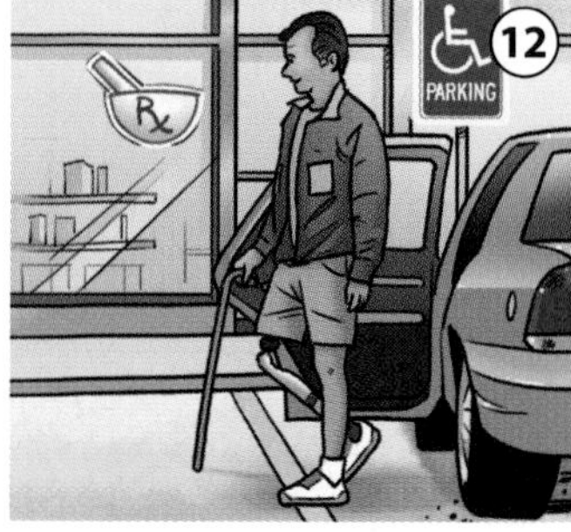


12. handicapped parking

13. pedestrian crossing
14. railroad crossing
15. school crossing
16. road work
17. highway marker
18. hospital

**Pair practice. Make new conversations.**

**A:** *Watch out! The sign says no left turn.*
**B:** *Sorry, I was looking at the stop sign.*
**A:** *That's OK. Just be careful!*

**Ask your classmates. Share the answers.**

1. How many traffic signs are on your street?
2. What's the speed limit on your street?
3. What traffic signs are the same in your native country?

## Directions

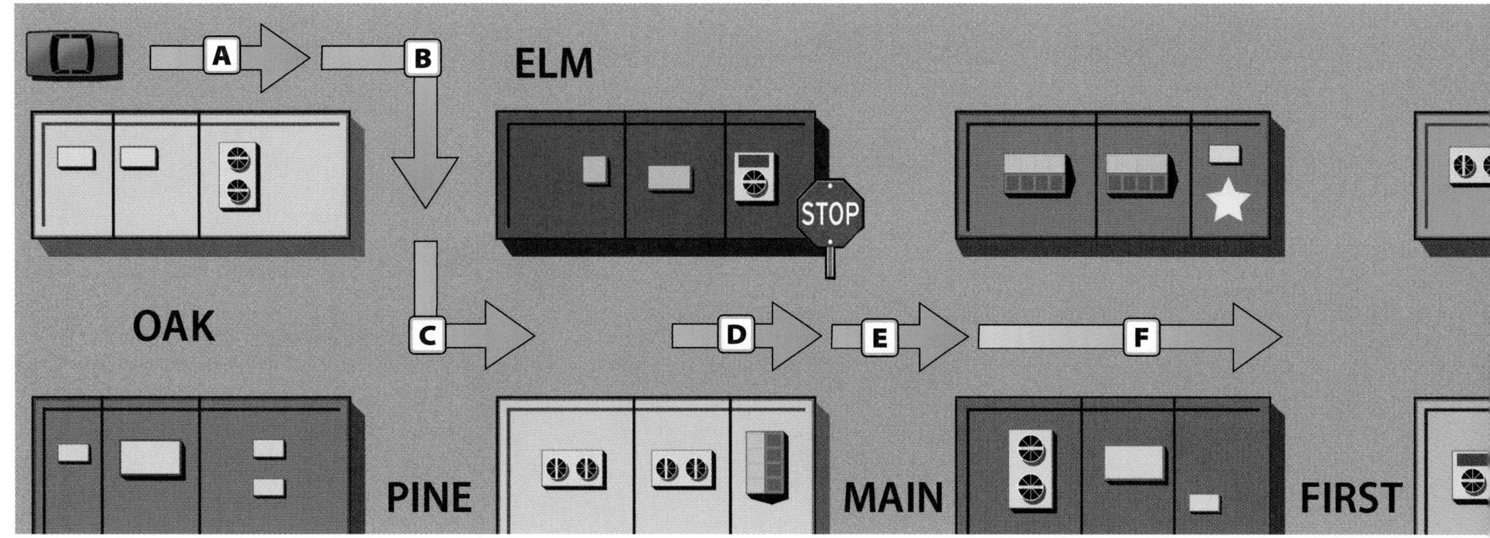


A. **Go straight** on Elm Street.

B. **Turn right** on Pine Street.

C. **Turn left** on Oak Street.

D. **Stop** at the corner.

E. **Go** past Main Street.

F. **Go** one block to First Street.

## Maps

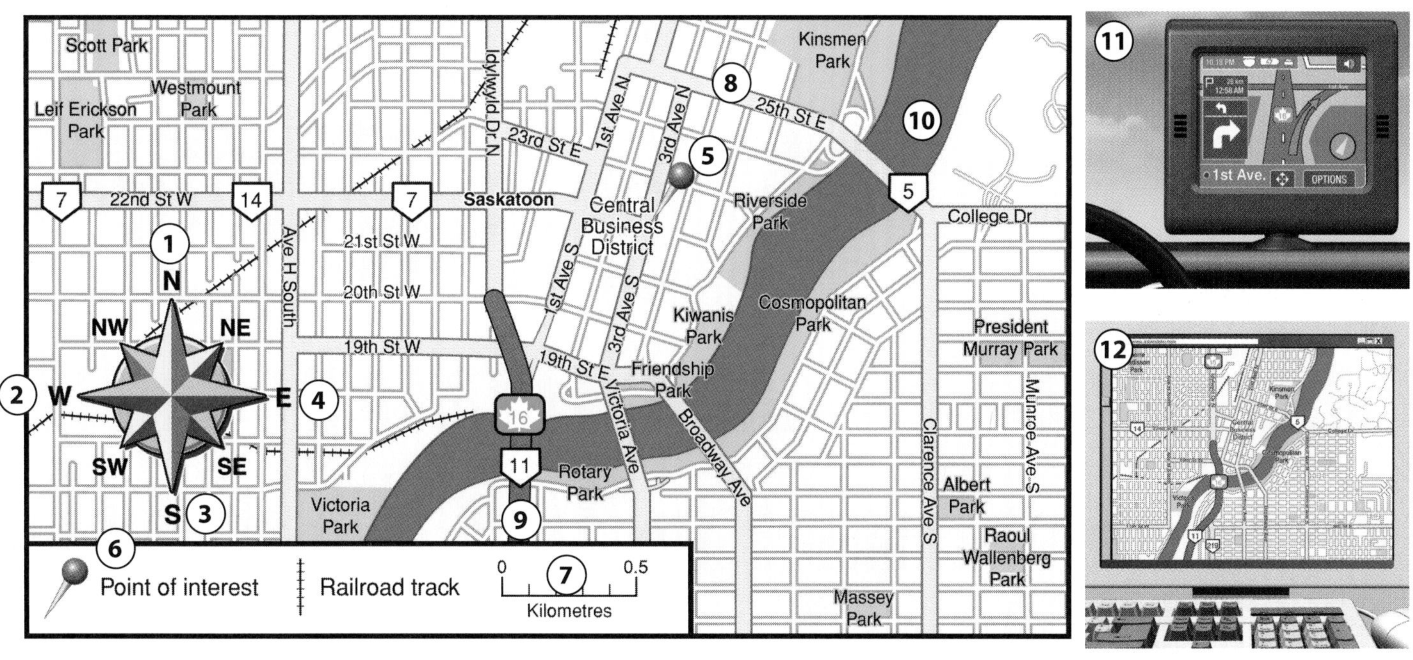


1. north
2. west
3. south
4. east
5. symbol
6. key
7. scale
8. street
9. highway
10. river
11. GPS (global positioning system)
12. Internet map

**Role play. Ask for directions.**

**A:** *I'm lost. I need to get to Elm and Pine.*
**B:** *Go straight on Oak and make a right on Pine.*
**A:** *Thanks so much.*

**Ask your classmates. Share the answers.**

1. How often do you use Internet maps? GPS? paper maps?
2. What was the last map you used? Why?

# Cars and Trucks

1. 4-door car / sedan
2. 2-door car / coupe
3. hybrid
4. sports car
5. convertible
6. station wagon
7. SUV (sport–utility vehicle)
8. minivan
9. camper
10. RV (recreational vehicle)
11. limousine / limo

12. pickup truck
13. cargo van
14. tow truck
15. tractor trailer / semi
16. cab
17. trailer
18. moving van
19. dump truck
20. tanker
21. school bus

**Pair practice. Make new conversations.**

**A:** *I have a new car!*
**B:** *Did you get a hybrid?*
**A:** *Yes, but I really wanted a sports car.*

**More vocabulary**

**make:** the name of the company that makes the car
**model:** the style of the car

## Buying a Used Car

A. **Look at** car ads.

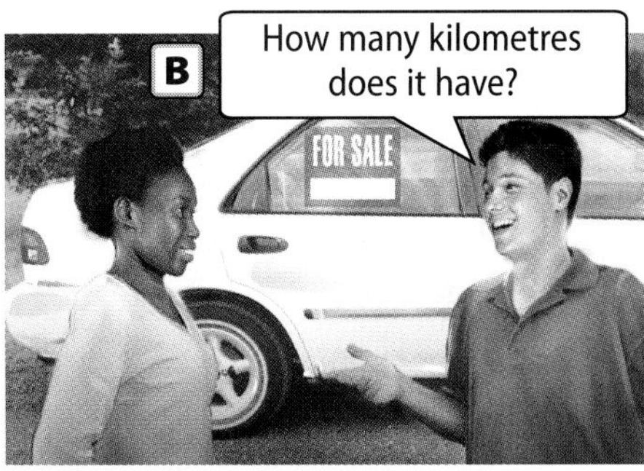


B. **Ask** the seller about the car.

C. **Take** the car to a mechanic.

D. **Negotiate** a price.

E. **Get** the title from the seller.

F. **Register** the car.

## Taking Care of Your Car

G. **Fill** the tank with gas.

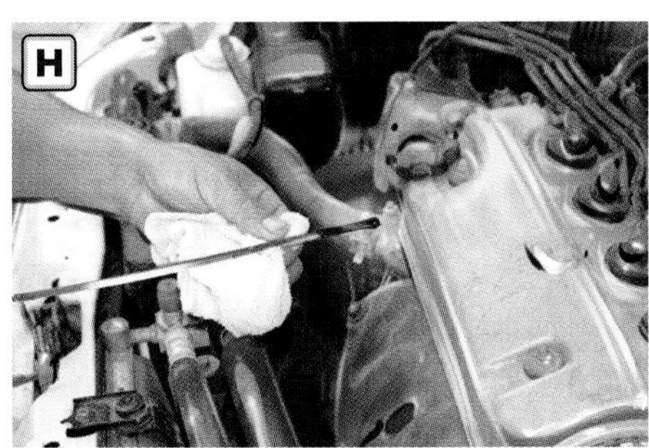


H. **Check** the oil.

I. **Put in** coolant.

J. **Go** for an emissions test.

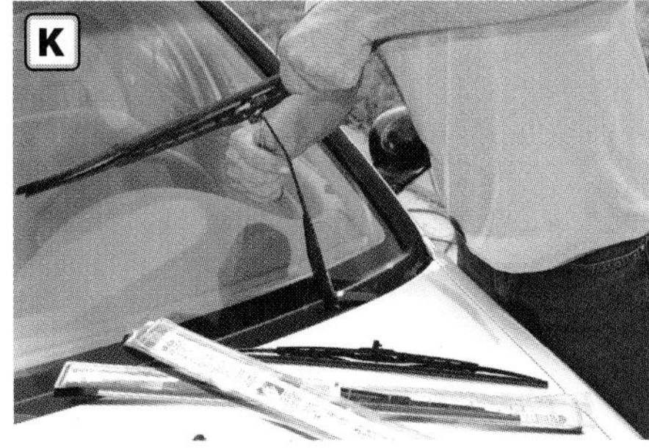


K. **Replace** the windshield wipers.

L. **Fill** the tires with air.

**Ways to request service**

*Please check the oil.*
*Could you fill the tank?*
*Put in coolant, please.*

**Think about it. Discuss.**

1. What's good and bad about a used car?
2. Do you like to negotiate car prices? Why?
3. Do you know any good mechanics? Why are they good?

## At the Dealer

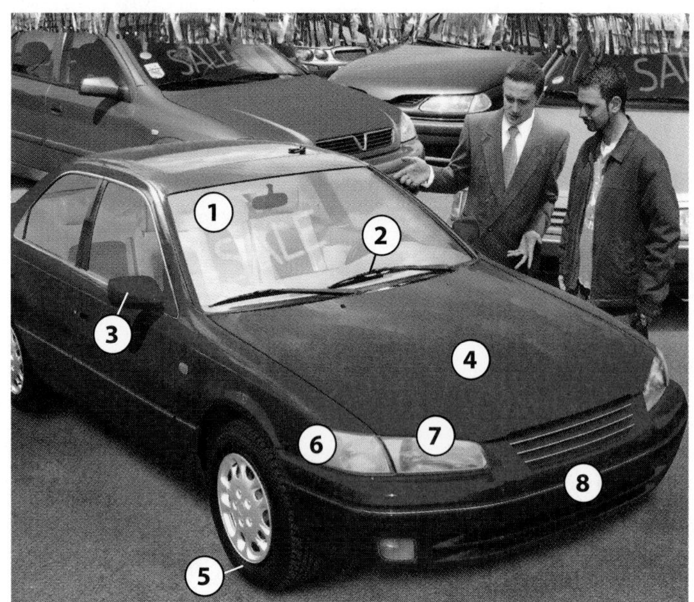


1. windshield
2. windshield wipers
3. side-view mirror
4. hood
5. tire
6. turn signal
7. headlight
8. bumper

## At the Mechanic

9. hubcap / wheel cover
10. gas tank
11. trunk
12. licence plate
13. tail light
14. brake light
15. tailpipe
16. muffler

## Under the Hood

17. fuel injection system
18. engine
19. radiator
20. battery

## Inside the Trunk

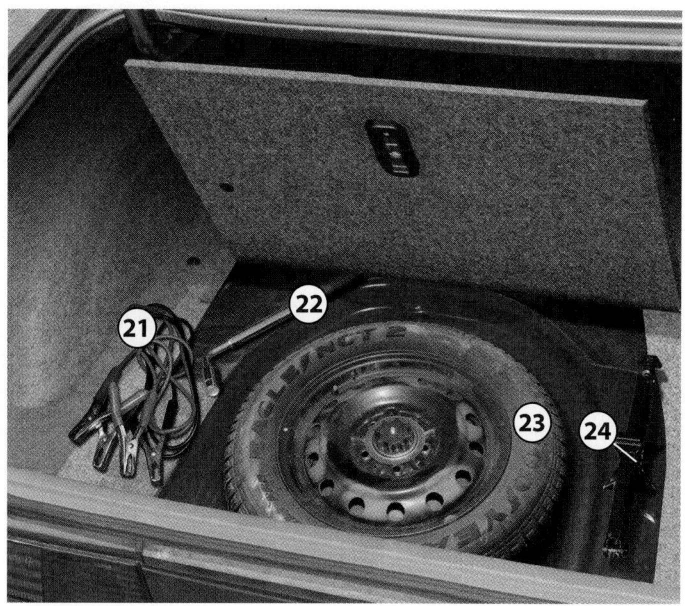


21. jumper cables
22. lug wrench
23. spare tire
24. jack

## The Dashboard and Instrument Panel

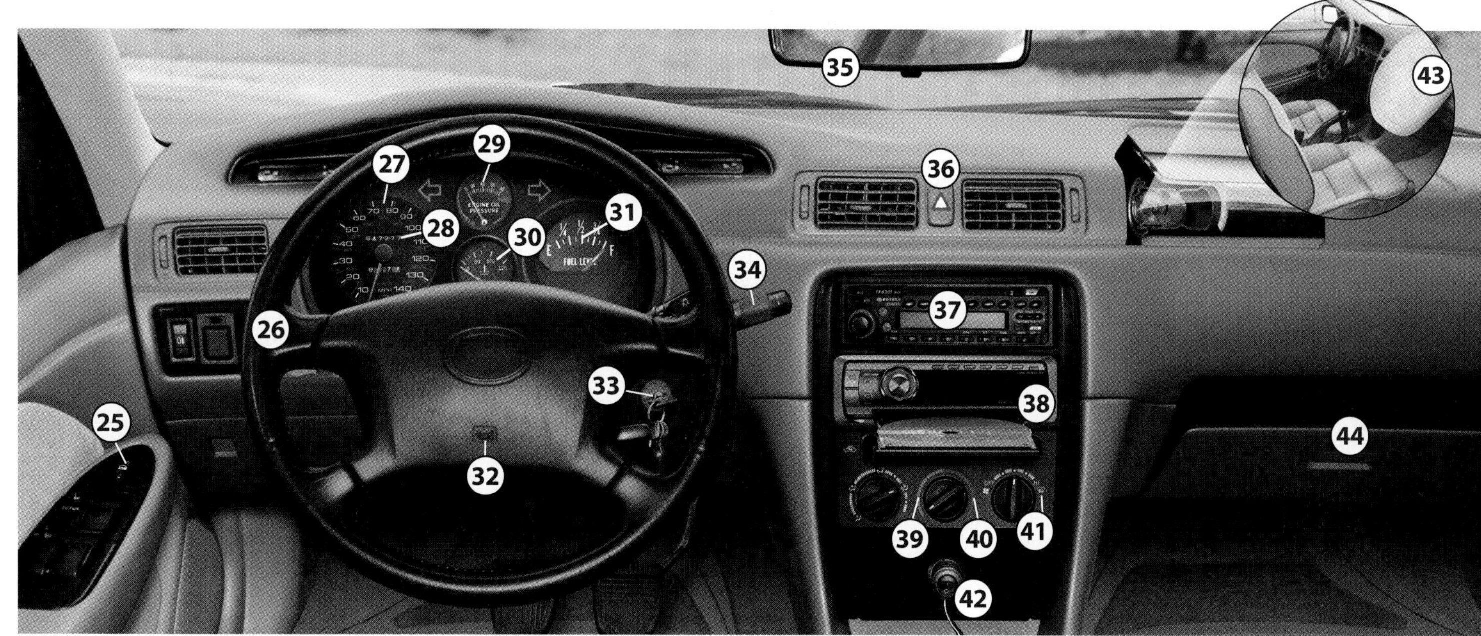

25. door lock
26. steering wheel
27. speedometer
28. odometer
29. oil gauge
30. temperature gauge
31. gas gauge
32. horn
33. ignition
34. turn signal
35. rear-view mirror
36. hazard lights
37. radio
38. CD player
39. air conditioner
40. heater
41. defroster
42. power outlet
43. airbag
44. glove compartment

## An Automatic Transmission

45. brake pedal
46. gas pedal / accelerator
47. gearshift
48. hand brake

## A Manual Transmission

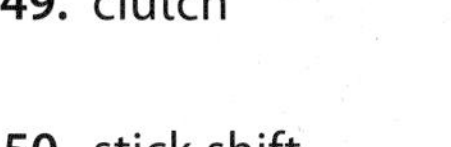

49. clutch
50. stick shift

## Inside the Car

51. front seat
52. seat belt
53. child safety seat
54. back seat

## In the Airline Terminal

## At the Security Checkpoint

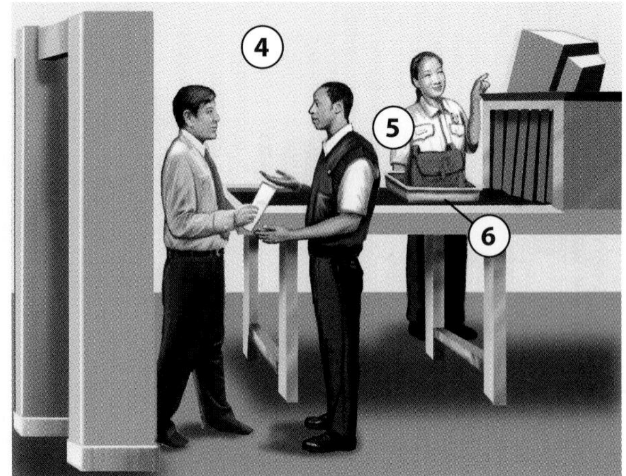


1. porter
2. check-in kiosk
3. ticket agent
4. screening area
5. security screener
6. bin

## Taking a Flight

A. **Check in** electronically.

B. **Check** your bags.

C. **Show** your boarding pass and ID.

D. **Go through** security.

E. **Board** the plane.

F. **Find** your seat.

G. **Stow** your carry-on bag.

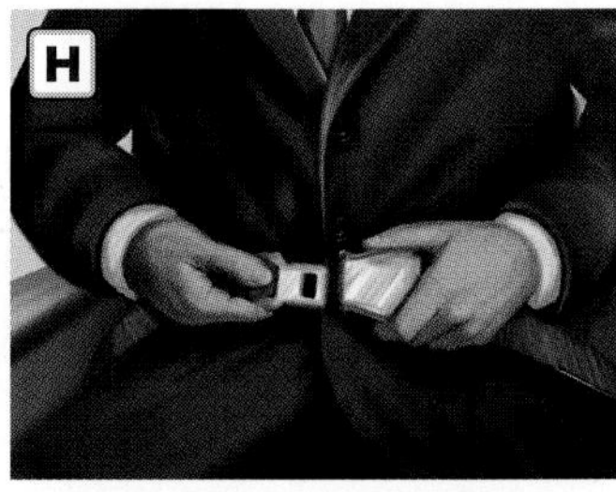


H. **Fasten** your seat belt.

I. **Turn off** your cellphone.

J. **Take off**. / **Leave**.

K. **Land**. / **Arrive**.

L. **Claim** your baggage.

## At the Gate

## On the Airplane

## At Customs

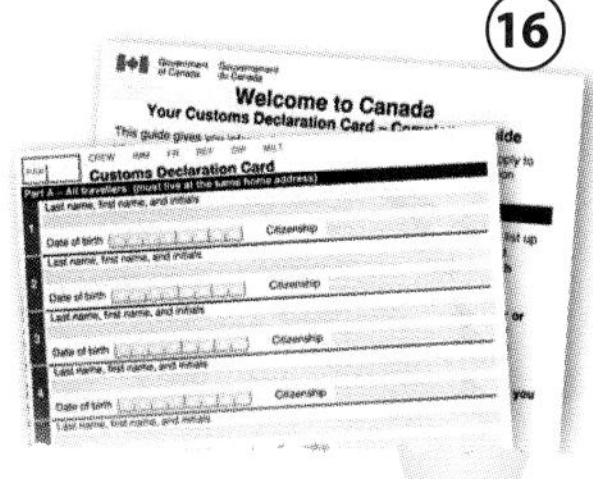

7. arrival and departure monitors
8. gate
9. boarding area
10. cockpit
11. pilot
12. flight attendant
13. overhead compartment
14. emergency exit
15. passenger
16. declaration form
17. customs officer
18. luggage / bag

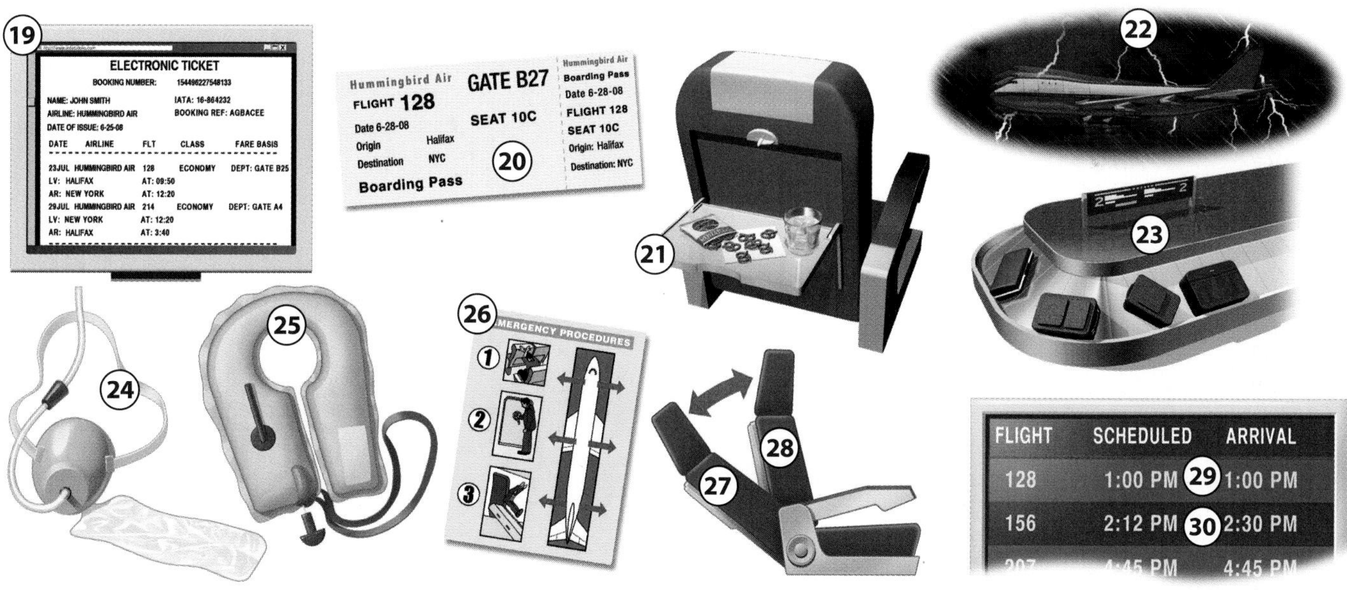


19. e-ticket
20. boarding pass
21. tray table
22. turbulence
23. baggage carousel
24. oxygen mask
25. life vest
26. emergency card
27. reclined seat
28. upright seat
29. on-time
30. delayed flight

**More vocabulary**

**departure time:** the time the plane takes off
**arrival time:** the time the plane lands
**direct flight:** a trip with no stops

**Pair practice. Make new conversations.**

A: *Excuse me. Where do I check in?*
B: *At the check-in kiosk.*
A: *Thanks.*

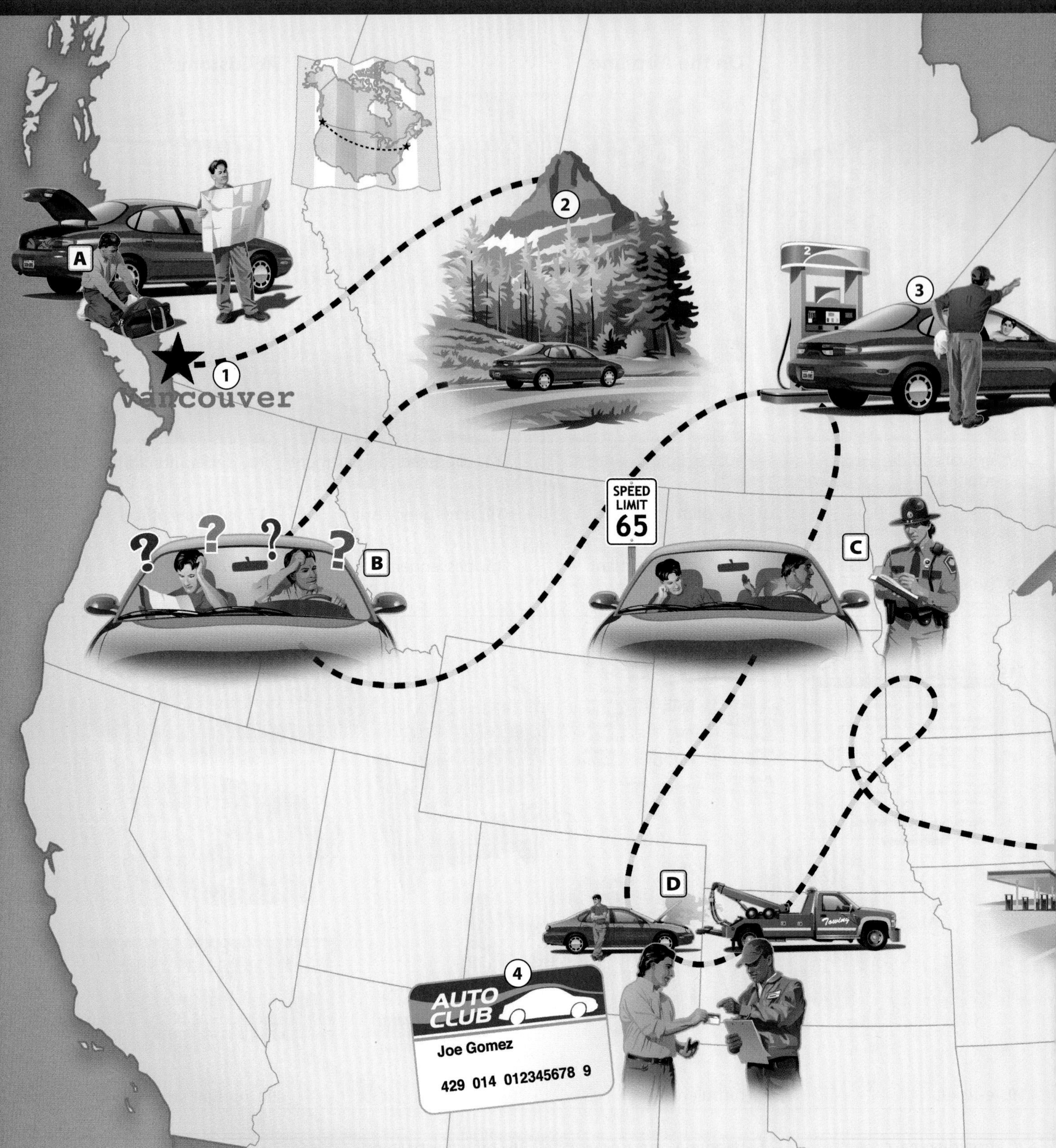


1. starting point
2. scenery
3. gas station attendant
4. auto club card
5. destination

A. **pack**
B. **get** lost
C. **get** a speeding ticket
D. **break down**
E. **run out** of gas
F. **have** a flat tire

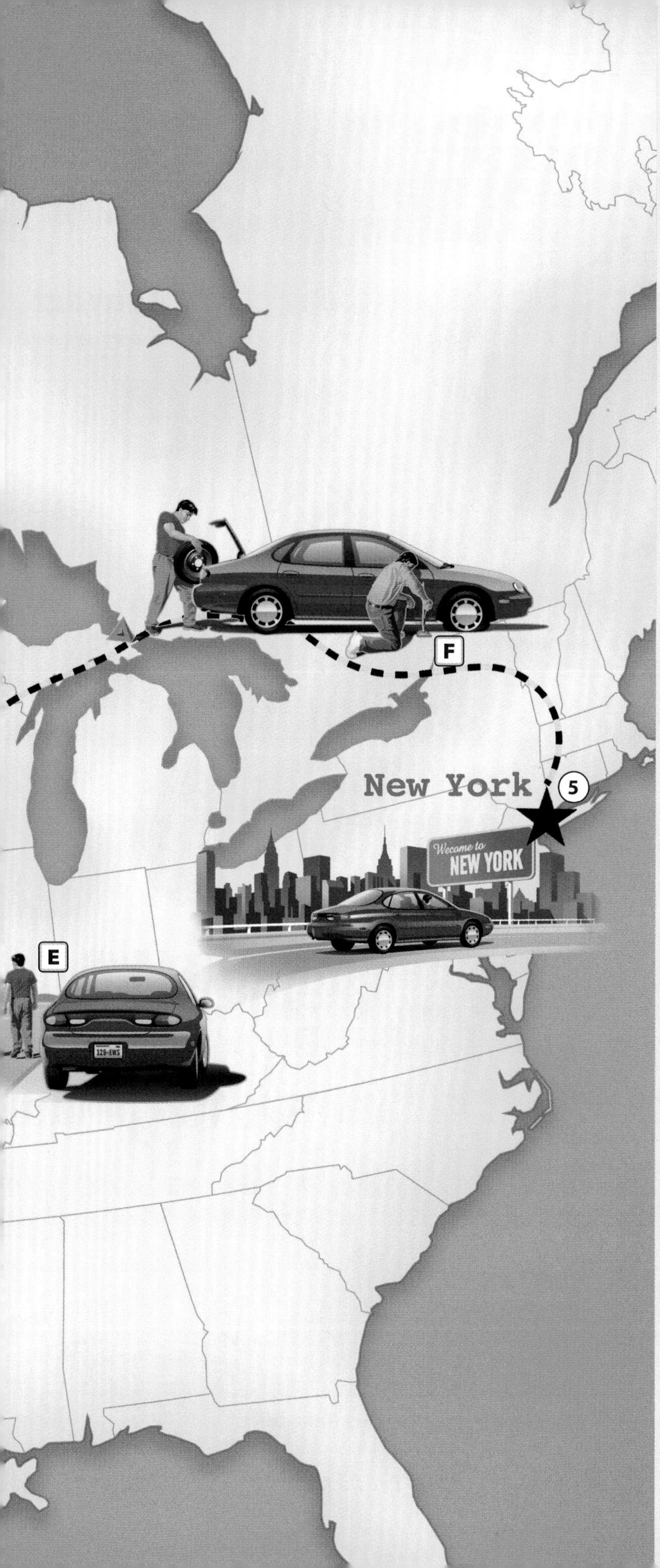

**Look at the pictures.**
**What do you see?**

**Answer the questions.**

1. What are the young men's starting point and destination?
2. What do they see on their trip?
3. What kinds of problems do they have?

---

 **Read the story.**

## A Road Trip

On July 7th Joe and Rob packed their bags for a road trip. Their starting point was Vancouver. Their destination was New York City.

The young men saw beautiful scenery on their trip. But there were also problems. They got lost. Then, a gas station attendant gave them bad directions. Next, they got a speeding ticket. Joe was very upset. After that, their car broke down. Joe called a tow truck and used his auto club card.

The end of their trip was difficult, too. They ran out of gas and then they had a flat tire.

After 7,000 kilometres of problems, Joe and Rob arrived in New York City. They were happy, but tired. Next time, they're going to take the train.

---

**Think about it.**

1. What is the best way to travel across North America? by car? by plane? by train? Why?
2. Imagine your car breaks down on the road. Who can you call? What can you do?

1. entrance
2. customer
3. office
4. employer / boss
5. receptionist
6. safety regulations

**Listen and point. Take turns.**

**A:** Point to the front entrance.
**B:** Point to the receptionist.
**A:** Point to the time clock.

**Dictate to your partner. Take turns.**

**A:** *Can you spell employer?*
**B:** *I'm not sure. Is it e-m-p-l-o-y-e-r?*
**A:** *Yes, that's right.*

**Ways to talk about wages**

*I* ***earn*** *$250 a week.*
*He* ***makes*** *$9 an hour.*
*I'm* ***paid*** *$1,000 a month.*

**Role play. Talk to an employer.**

**A:** *Is everything correct on your paycheque?*
**B:** *No, it isn't. I make $250 a week, not $200.*
**A:** *Let's talk to the payroll clerk. Where is she?*

# Jobs and Occupations A–C

1. accountant

2. actor

3. administrative assistant

4. appliance repair person

5. architect

6. artist

7. assembler

8. auto mechanic

9. babysitter

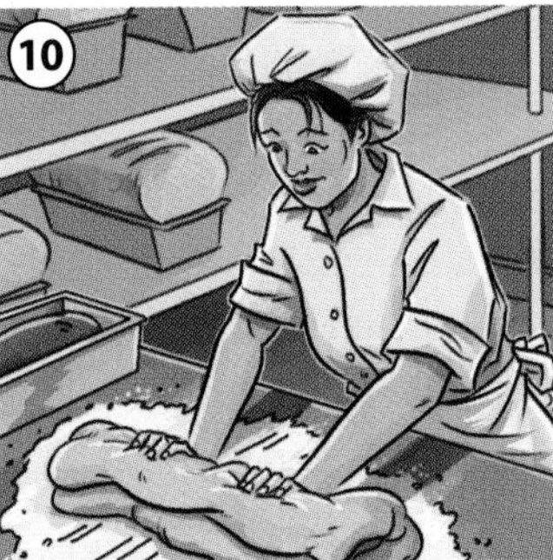

10. baker

11. business owner

12. businessperson

13. butcher

14. carpenter

15. cashier

16. childcare worker

**Ways to ask about someone's job**

*What's her job?*
*What does he do?*
*What kind of work do they do?*

**Pair practice. Make new conversations.**

**A:** *What kind of work does she do?*
**B:** *She's an accountant. What do they do?*
**A:** *They're actors.*

17. commercial fisher

18. computer software engineer

19. computer technician

We have that shirt in red.
20. customer service representative

21. delivery person

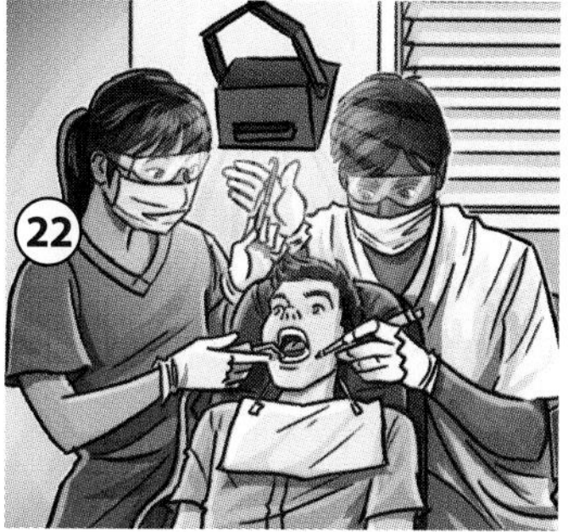
22. dental assistant

23. dockworker

TOM'S TV
24. electronics repair person

25. engineer

26. firefighter

27. florist

28. gardener

29. garment worker

STAR
30. graphic designer

31. hairdresser / hair stylist

32. home health care aide

**Ways to talk about jobs and occupations**

*Sue's a garment worker. She works* ***in*** *a factory.*
*Tom's an engineer. He works* ***for*** *a large company.*
*Ann's a dental assistant. She works* ***with*** *a dentist.*

**Role play. Talk about a friend's new job.**

**A:** *Does your friend like his new job?*
**B:** *Yes, he does. He's a graphic designer.*
**A:** *Does he work in an office?*

# Jobs and Occupations H–P

33. homemaker

34. housekeeper

35. interpreter / translator

36. lawyer

37. machine operator

38. manicurist

39. medical records technician

40. messenger / courier

41. model

42. mover

43. musician

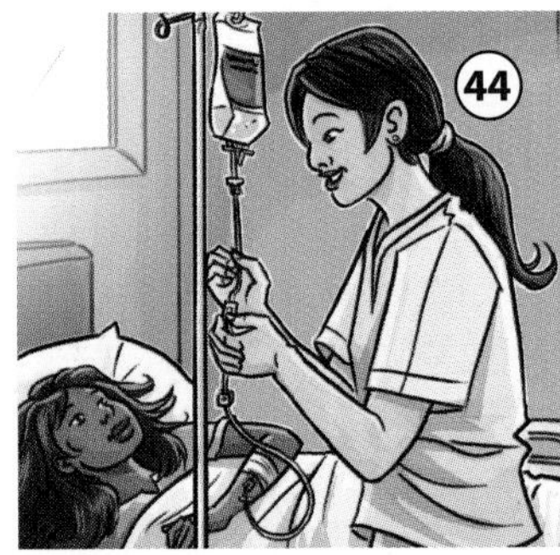
44. nurse

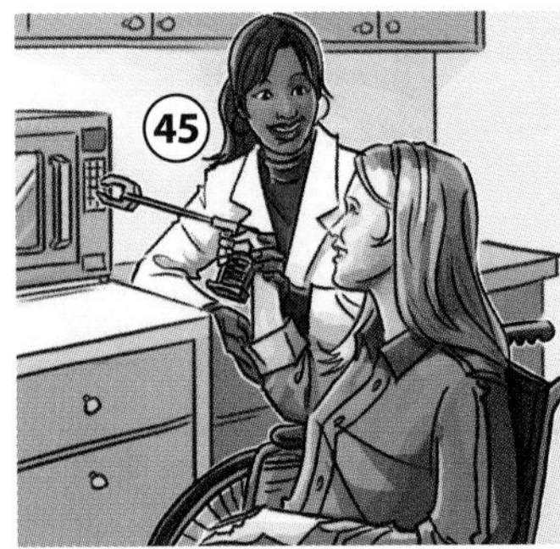
45. occupational therapist

46. (house) painter

47. physician assistant

48. police officer

**Grammar Point: past tense of *be***

*I **was** a machine operator for 5 years.*
*She **was** a nurse for a year.*
*They **were** movers from 2003–2007.*

**Pair practice. Make new conversations.**

**A:** *What was your first job?*
**B:** *I was a musician. How about you?*
**A:** *I was a messenger for a small company.*

49. postal worker

50. printer

51. receptionist

52. reporter

53. retail clerk

54. sanitation worker

55. security guard

56. server

57
Here are some programs that will help you.
HELPING
HEART
AGENCY

57. social worker

58. soldier

59. stock clerk

60
Hello. I'm calling with a very special offer.

60. telemarketer

61. truck driver

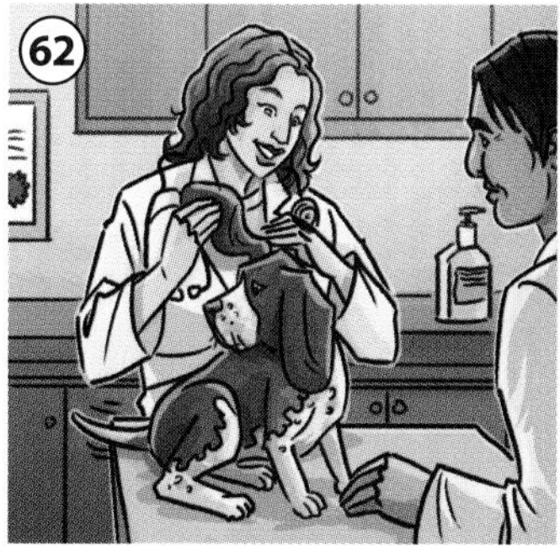

62. veterinarian

63. welder

64. writer / author

**Ask your classmates. Share the answers.**

1. Which of these jobs could you do now?
2. What is one job you don't want to have?
3. Which jobs do you want to have?

**Think about it. Discuss.**

1. Which jobs need special training?
2. What kind of person makes a good interpreter? A good nurse? A good reporter? Why?

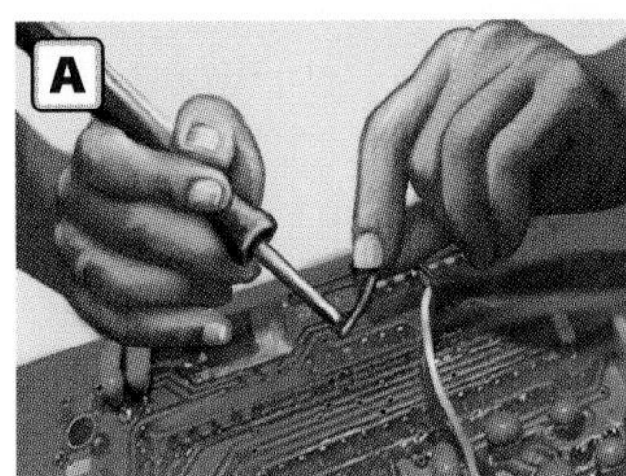
A. **assemble** components

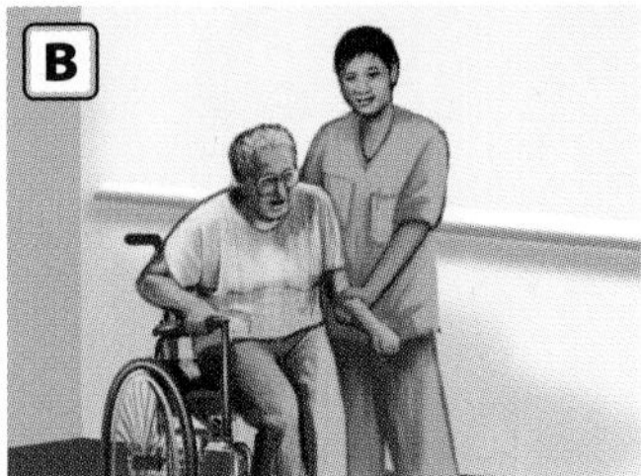
B. **assist** medical patients

C. **cook**

D. **do** manual labour

E. **drive** a truck

F. **fly** a plane

G. **make** furniture

H. **operate** heavy machinery

I. **program** computers

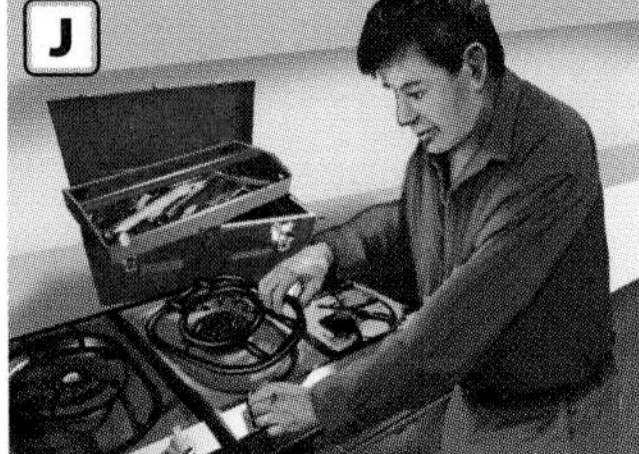
J. **repair** appliances

K. **sell** cars

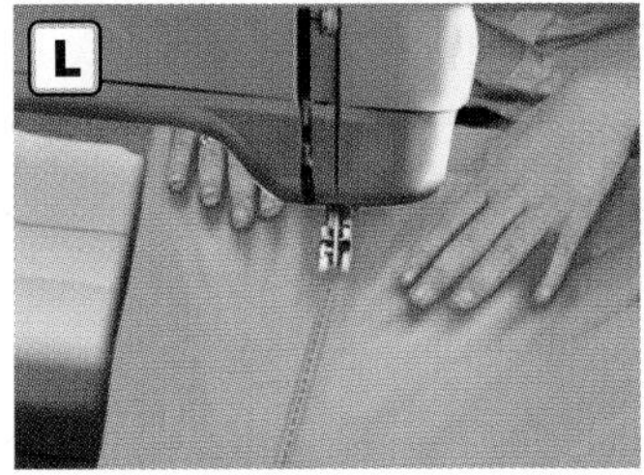
L. **sew** clothes

M. **solve** math problems

N. **speak** another language

O. **supervise** people

P. **take** care of children

Q. **teach**

R. **type**

S. **use** a cash register

T. **wait on** customers

**Grammar Point: *can, can't***

*I am a chef. I* ***can*** *cook.*
*I'm not a pilot. I* ***can't*** *fly a plane.*
*I* ***can't*** *speak French, but I* ***can*** *speak Spanish.*

**Role play. Talk to a job counselor.**

**A:** *Tell me about your skills. Can you type?*
**B:** *No, I can't, but I can use a cash register.*
**A:** *OK. What other skills do you have?*

better service…

## Office Skills

A. **type** a letter

B. **enter** data

C. **transcribe** notes

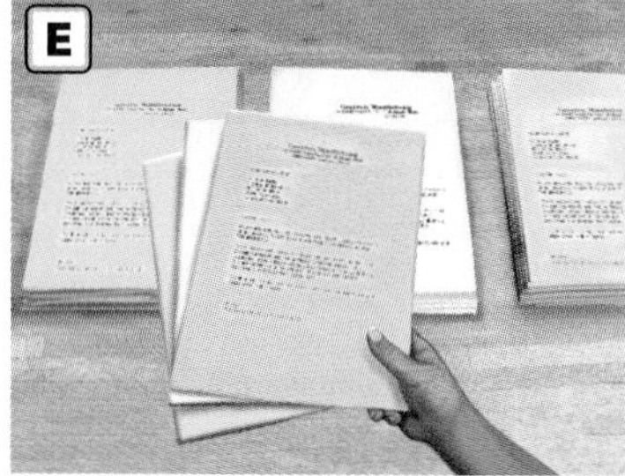

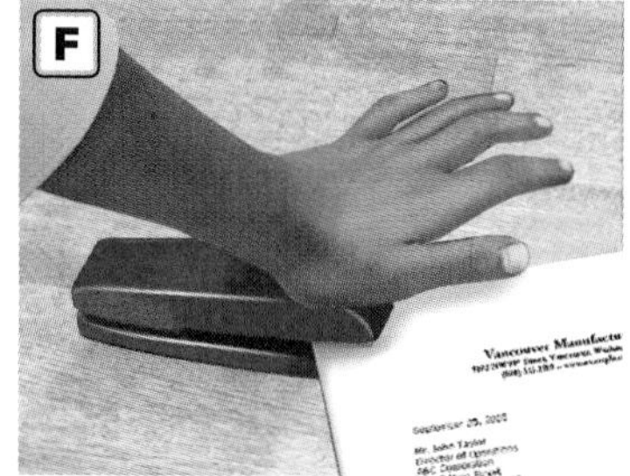

D. **make** copies

E. **collate** papers

F. **staple**

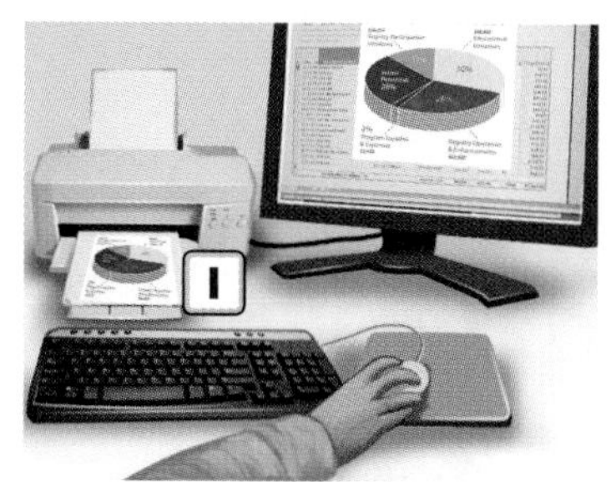

G. **fax** a document

H. **scan** a document

I. **print** a document

Let's meet

Dear Mr. Smith…

J. **schedule** a meeting

K. **take** dictation

L. **organize** materials

Hello. ABC

Please hold.

Mr. Hebert, I'm
transferring you.


## Telephone Skills

M. **greet** the caller

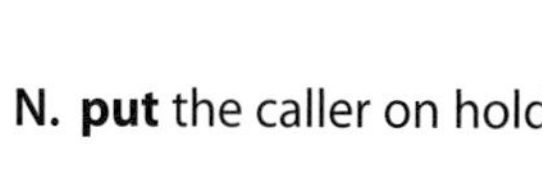

N. **put** the caller on hold

O. **transfer** the call

Hello. This is Sue
Jones. Please call me.

Message Pad
Call From: Ana Puerta
Tel: 555-1234
Message:
Please Call

This is Lee Tran.
Please call me back.


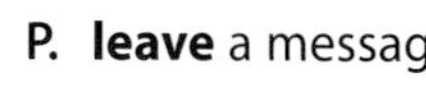

P. **leave** a message

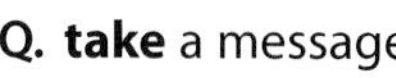

Q. **take** a message

R. **check** messages

# Career Planning

## Career Path

1. entry-level job
2. training
3. new job
4. promotion

## Types of Job Training

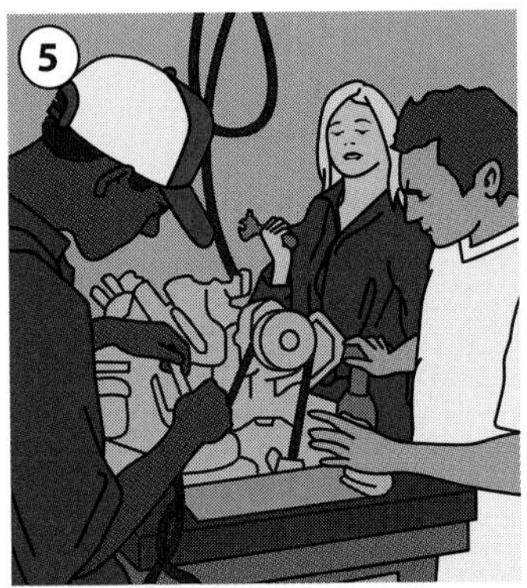

5. vocational training

6. internship

7. on-the-job training

8. online course

## Planning a Career

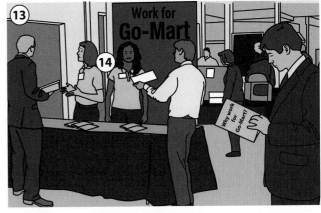


9. resource centre
10. career counsellor
11. interest inventory
12. skill inventory
13. job fair
14. recruiter

**Ways to talk about job training**

*I'm looking into an online course.*
*I'm interested in on-the-job training.*
*I want to sign up for an internship.*

**Ask your classmates. Share the answers.**

1. What kind of job training are you interested in?
2. Would your rather learn English in an online course or in a classroom?

A. **talk** to friends / **network**

B. **look in** the classifieds

C. **look for** help wanted signs

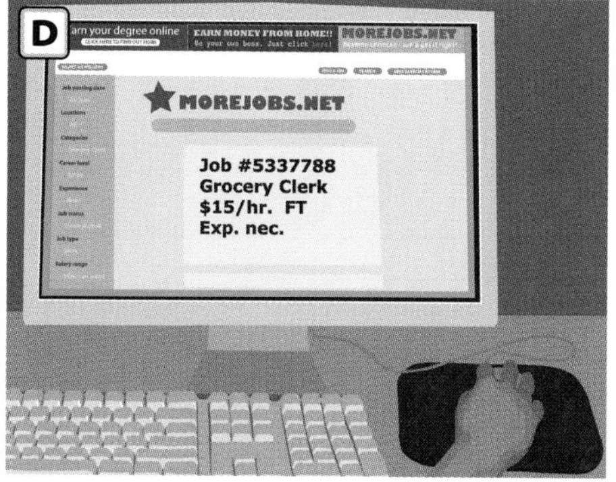

D. **check** Internet job sites

E. **go** to an employment agency

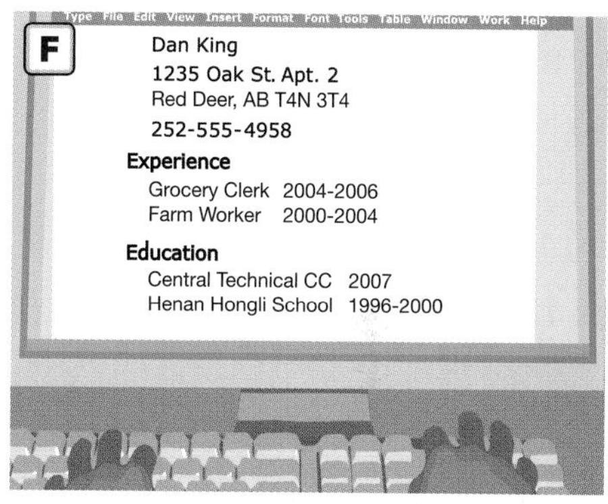

F. **write** a resume

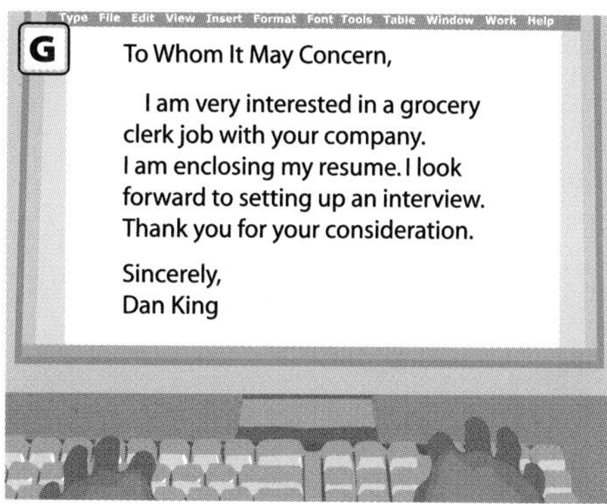

G. **write** a cover letter

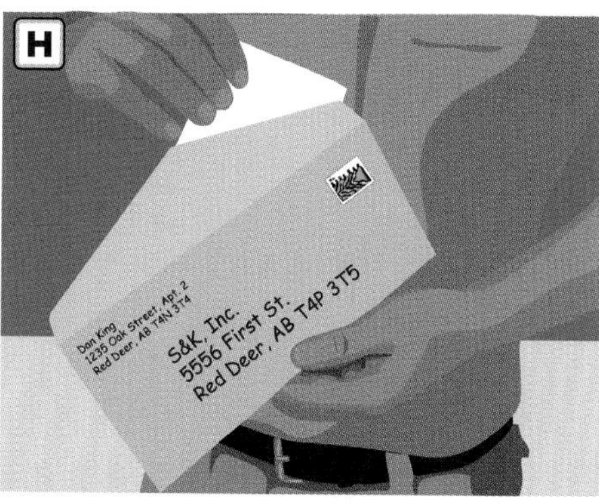

H. **send in** your resume and cover letter

I. **set up** an interview

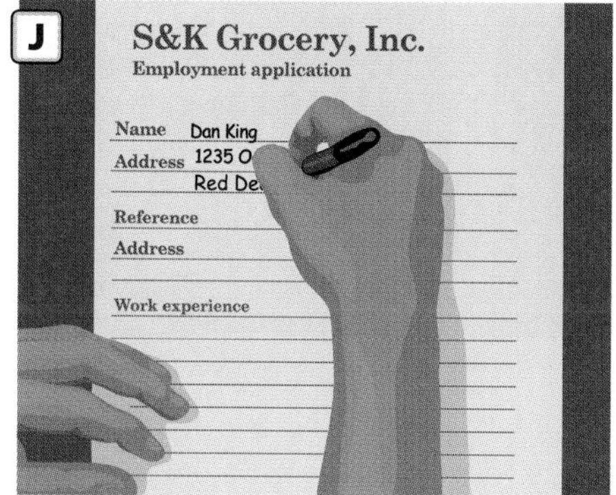

J. **fill out** an application

K. **go on** an interview

L. **get** hired

A. **Prepare** for the interview.

B. **Dress** appropriately.

C. **Be** neat.

Interview at
GBG- 9a.m.
GBG
Facts About GBG Inc.

D. **Bring** your resume and ID.

E. **Don't be** late.

F. **Be** on time.

Aazam Shirazi
6623 Queens Blvd.
Kingston, ON K7L 4V1
Work Experience:
Al's Computers 3 years.

9:05 AM
GBG

8:50 AM

G. **Turn off** your cellphone.

H. **Greet** the interviewer.

I. **Shake** hands.

Hello, I'm Aazam Shirazi.
Hello, Mr. Shirazi. I'm Mrs. Perez.

J. **Make** eye contact.

K. **Listen** carefully.

L. **Talk** about your experience.

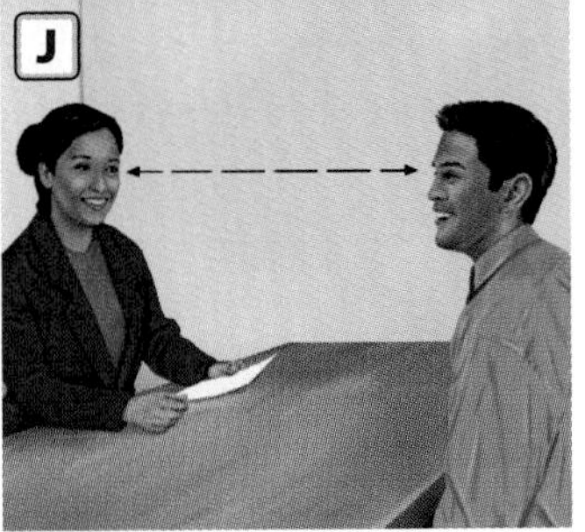

Computer skills are important.
I have those skills.

I worked with computers on my last job.

M. **Ask** questions.

N. **Thank** the interviewer.

O. **Write** a thank-you note.

Do you offer training?

Thank you for your time.

Dear Mrs. Perez,
Thank you for the opportunity to meet with you.

**More vocabulary**

**benefits:** health insurance, vacation pay, or other things the employer can offer an employee

**inquire about benefits:** ask about benefits

**Think about it. Discuss.**

1. How can you prepare for an interview?
2. Why is it important to make eye contact?
3. What kinds of questions should you ask?

# A Factory

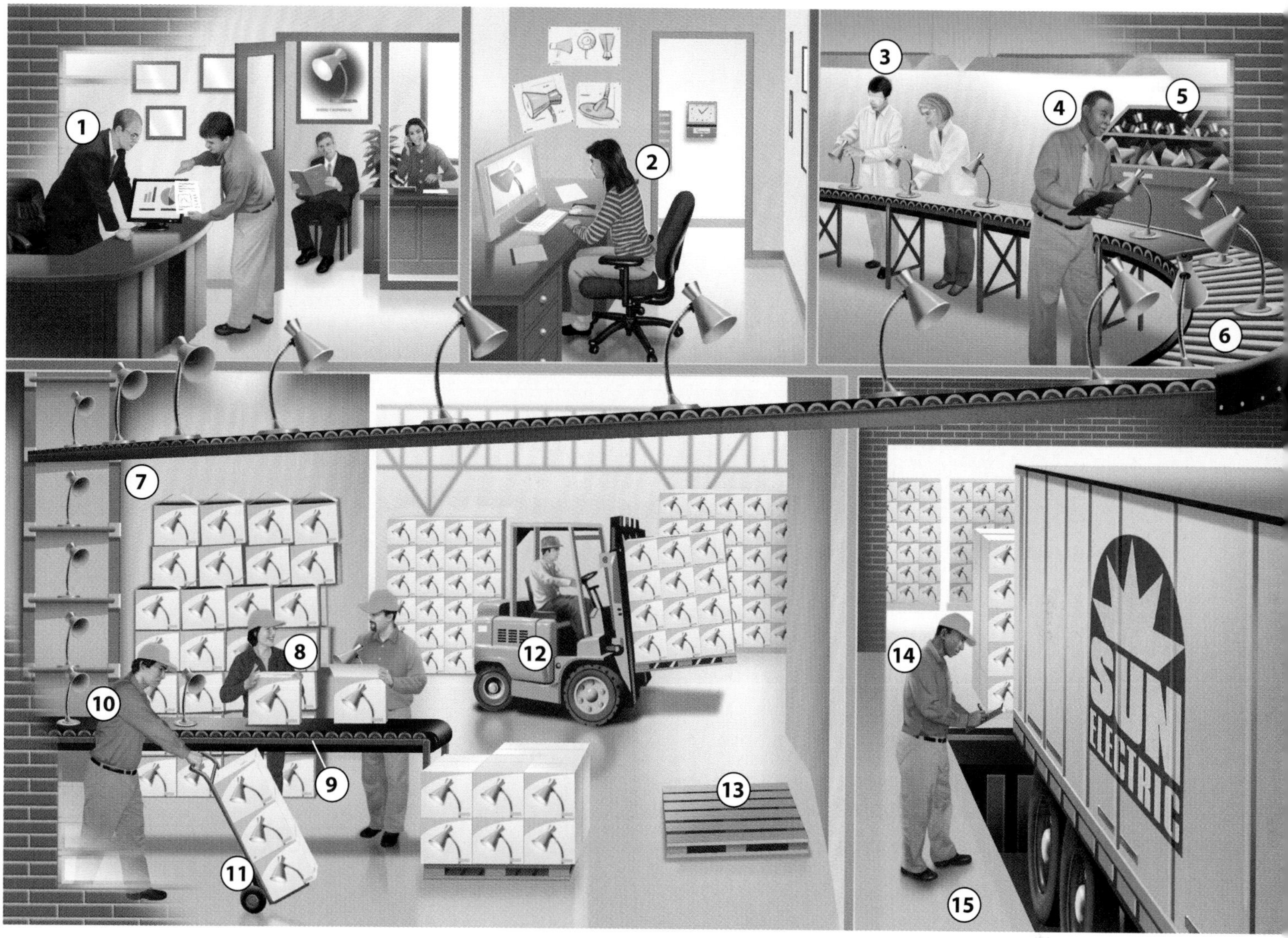

1. factory owner
2. designer
3. factory worker
4. line supervisor
5. parts
6. assembly line
7. warehouse
8. packer
9. conveyor belt
10. order picker
11. hand truck
12. forklift
13. pallet
14. shipping clerk
15. loading dock

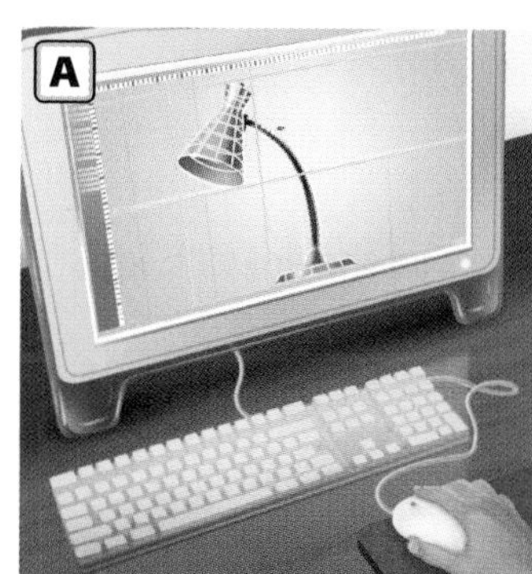


A. **design**

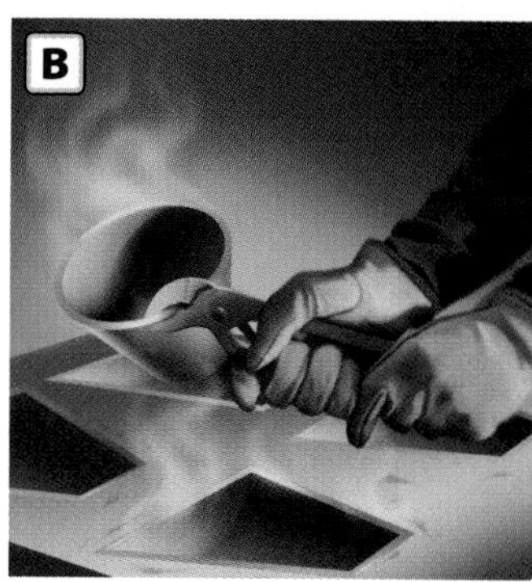


B. **manufacture**

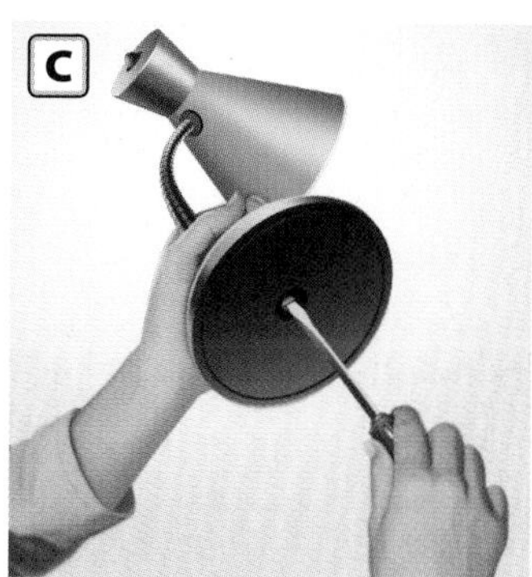


C. **assemble**

D. **ship**

# Landscaping and Gardening

1. gardening crew
2. leaf blower
3. wheelbarrow
4. gardening crew leader
5. landscape designer
6. lawn mower
7. shovel
8. rake
9. pruning shears
10. trowel
11. hedge clippers
12. weed whacker

A. **mow** the lawn
B. **trim** the hedges
C. **rake** the leaves
D. **fertilize** / **feed** the plants
E. **plant** a tree
F. **water** the plants
G. **weed** the flower beds
H. **install** a sprinkler system

**Use the new words.**

Look at page 53. Name what you can do in the yard.

A: *I can* *mow the lawn*.

B: *I can* *weed the flower bed*.

**Ask your classmates. Share the answers.**

1. Do you know someone who does landscaping? Who?
2. Do you enjoy gardening? Why or why not?
3. Which gardening activity is the hardest to do? Why?

## Crops

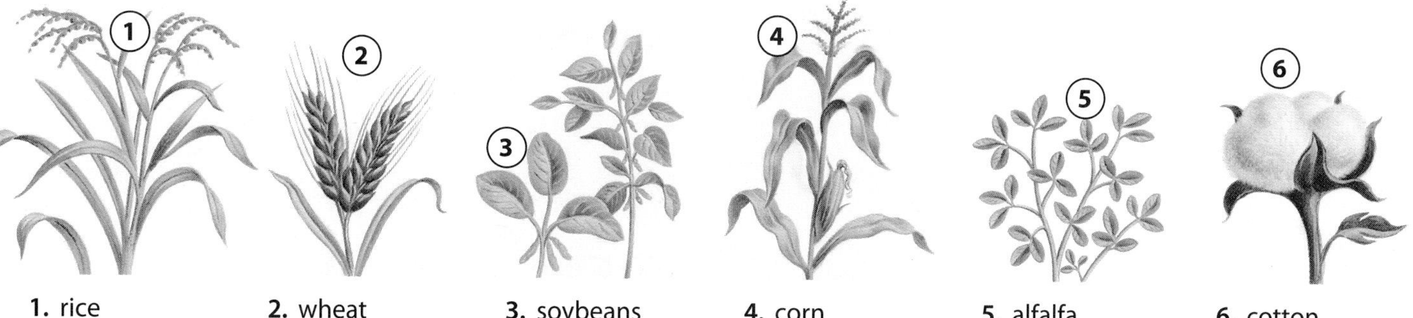


1. rice
2. wheat
3. soybeans
4. corn
5. alfalfa
6. cotton

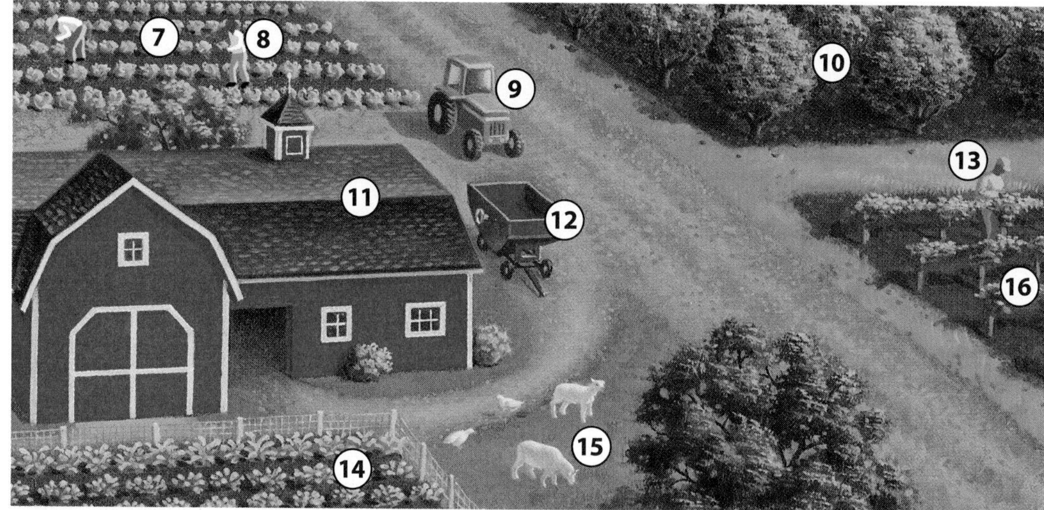

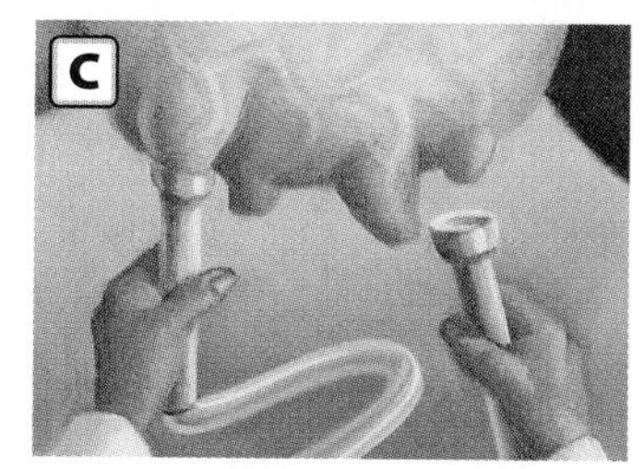

7. field
8. farmhand
9. tractor
10. orchard
11. barn
12. farm equipment
13. farmer / grower
14. vegetable garden
15. livestock
16. vineyard
17. corral
18. hay
19. fence
20. hired hand
21. cattle
22. rancher

A. **plant**
B. **harvest**
C. **milk**
D. **feed**

# Construction

1. construction worker
2. ladder
3. I-beam/girder
4. scaffolding
5. cherry picker
6. bulldozer
7. crane
8. backhoe
9. jackhammer / pneumatic drill

10. concrete
11. tile
12. bricks
13. trowel
14. insulation
15. stucco
16. window pane
17. wood / lumber
18. plywood
19. drywall
20. shingles
21. pickaxe
22. shovel
23. sledgehammer

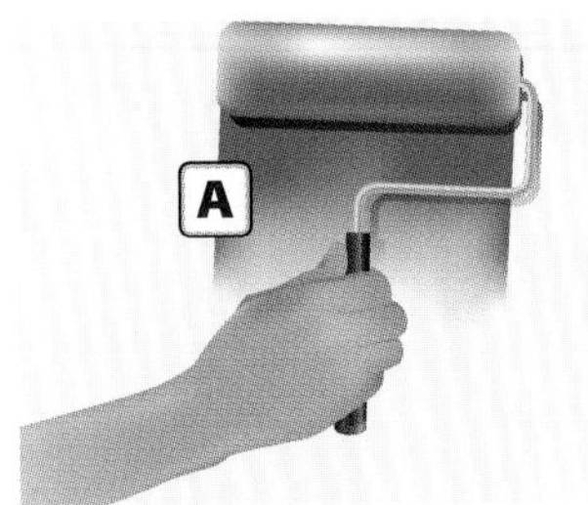


A. **paint**

B. **lay** bricks

C. **install** tile

D. **hammer**

## Safety Hazards and Hazardous Materials

1. careless worker
2. careful worker
3. poisonous fumes
4. broken equipment
5. frayed cord
6. slippery floor
7. radioactive materials
8. flammable liquids

## Safety Equipment

9. hard hat
10. safety glasses
11. safety goggles
12. safety visor
13. respirator
14. particle mask
15. ear plugs
16. earmuffs
17. work gloves
18. back support belt
19. knee pads
20. safety boots
21. fire extinguisher
22. two-way radio

# Tools and Building Supplies

1. hammer
2. mallet
3. axe
4. handsaw
5. hacksaw
6. C-clamp
7. pliers
8. electric drill
9. circular saw
10. jigsaw
11. power sander
12. router

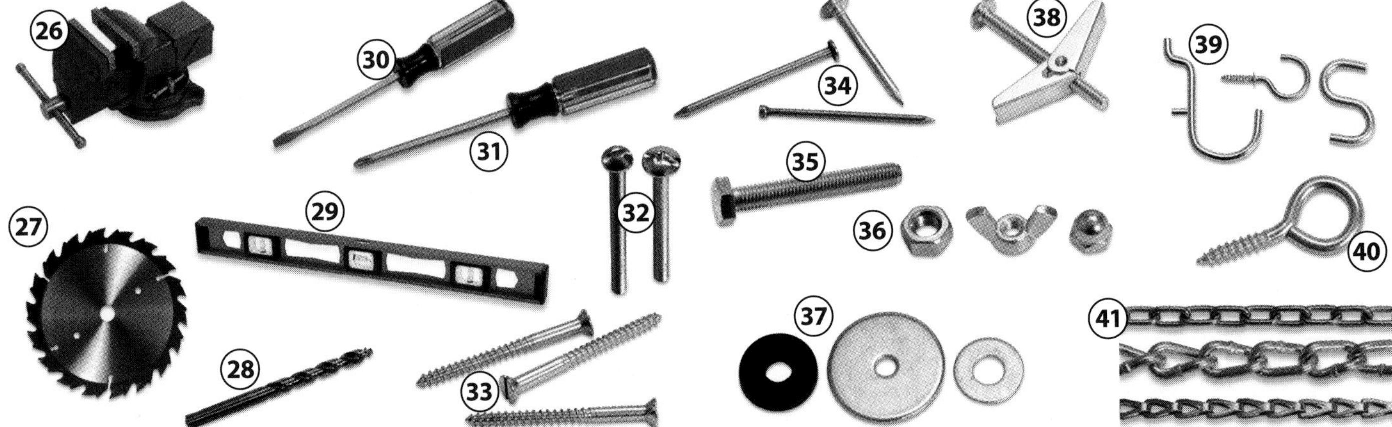

26. vise
27. blade
28. drill bit
29. level
30. screwdriver
31. Phillips screwdriver
32. machine screw
33. wood screw
34. nail
35. bolt
36. nut
37. washer
38. toggle bolt
39. hook
40. eye hook
41. chain

**Use the new words.**
Look at pages 62–63. Name the tools you see.

A: *There's a hammer.*
B: *There's a pipe wrench.*

**Ask your classmates. Share the answers.**

1. Are you good with tools?
2. Which tools do you have at home?
3. Where can you shop for building supplies?

13. wire
14. extension cord
15. bungee cord
16. metre stick / yardstick
17. pipe
18. fittings
19. 2 x 4 (two by four)
20. particle board
21. spray gun
22. paintbrush
23. paint roller
24. wood stain
25. paint

42. wire stripper
43. electrical tape
44. work light
45. tape measure
46. outlet cover
47. pipe wrench
48. adjustable wrench
49. duct tape
50. plunger
51. paint tray
52. scraper
53. masking tape
54. drop cloth
55. chisel
56. sandpaper
57. plane

**Role play. Find an item in a building supply store.**

A: *Where can I find particle board?*
B: *It's on the back wall, in the lumber section.*
A: *Great. And where are the nails?*

**Think about it. Discuss.**

1. Which tools are the most important to have? Why?
2. Which tools can be dangerous? Why?
3. Do you borrow tools from friends? Why or why not?

# An Office

1. supply cabinet
2. clerk
3. janitor
4. conference room
5. executive
6. presentation
7. cubicle
8. office manager
9. desk
10. file clerk
11. file cabinet
12. computer technician
13. PBX (private branch exchange)
14. receptionist
15. reception area
16. waiting area

**Ways to greet a receptionist**

*I'm here for a job interview.*
*I have a 9:00 a.m. appointment with Mr. Lee.*
*I'd like to leave a message for Mr. Lee.*

**Role play. Talk to a receptionist.**

**A:** *Hello. How can I help you?*
**B:** *I'm here for a job interview with Mr. Lee.*
**A:** *OK. What is your name?*

## Office Equipment

17. computer
18. inkjet printer
19. laser printer
20. scanner
21. fax machine
22. paper cutter
23. photocopier
24. paper shredder
25. calculator
26. electric pencil sharpener
27. postal scale

## Office Supplies

28. stapler
29. staples
30. clear tape
31. paper clip
32. packing tape
33. glue
34. rubber band
35. pushpin
36. correction fluid
37. correction tape
38. legal pad
39. sticky notes
40. mailer
41. mailing label
42. letterhead / stationery
43. envelope
44. rotary card file
45. ink cartridge
46. ink pad
47. stamp
48. appointment book
49. organizer
50. file folder

# A Hotel

1. doorman
2. revolving door
3. parking attendant
4. concierge
5. gift shop
6. bell captain
7. bellhop
8. luggage cart
9. elevator
10. guest
11. desk clerk
12. front desk

13. guest room
14. double bed
15. king-size bed
16. suite
17. room service
18. hallway
19. housekeeping cart
20. housekeeper

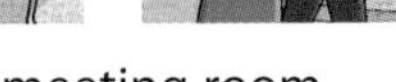

21. pool service
22. pool
23. maintenance
24. gym
25. meeting room
26. ballroom

## A Restaurant Kitchen

1. short-order cook
2. dishwasher
3. walk-in freezer
4. food preparation worker
5. storeroom
6. sous chef
7. head chef / executive chef

## Restaurant Dining

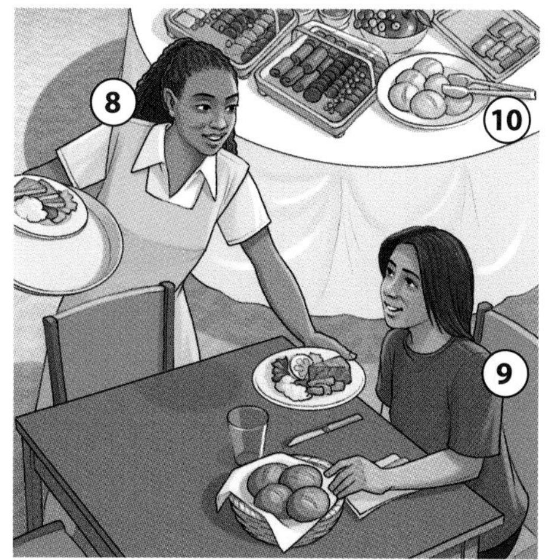

8. server
9. diner
10. buffet
11. maitre d'
12. head waiter
13. bus person
14. banquet room
15. runner
16. caterer

**More vocabulary**

**line cook:** short-order cook
**wait staff:** servers, head waiters, and runners

**Ask your classmates. Share the answers.**

1. Have you ever worked in a hotel? What did you do?
2. What is the hardest job in a hotel?
3. Would you prefer to stay at a hotel in the city or in the country?

1. dangerous
2. clinic
3. budget
4. floor plan
5. contractor
6. electrical hazard
7. wiring
8. bricklayer

A. **call in** sick

## Look at the picture.
## What do you see?

### Answer the questions.

1. How many workers are there? How many are working?
2. Why did two workers call in sick?
3. What is dangerous at the construction site?

---

 **Read the story.**

### A Bad Day at Work

Sam Lopez is the contractor for a new building. He makes the schedule and supervises the budget. He also solves problems. Today there are a lot of problems.

Two bricklayers called in sick this morning. Now Sam has only one bricklayer at work. One hour later, a construction worker fell. Now he has to go to the clinic. Sam always tells his workers to be careful. Construction work is dangerous. Sam's also worried because the new wiring is an electrical hazard.

Right now, the building owner is in Sam's office. Her new floor plan has 25 more offices. Sam has a headache. Maybe he needs to call in sick tomorrow.

---

### Think about it.

1. What do you say when you can't come in to work? to school?
2. Imagine you are Sam. What do you tell the building owner? Why?

# Schools and Subjects

1. preschool / nursery school
2. elementary school / grade school
3. middle school / junior high school
4. high school
5. vocational school / technical school
6. college / CEGEP
7. university
8. adult school

**Listen and point. Take turns.**

**A:** *Point to the preschool.*
**B:** *Point to the high school.*
**A:** *Point to the adult school.*

**Dictate to your partner. Take turns.**

**A:** *Write preschool.*
**B:** *Is that p-r-e-s-c-h-o-o-l?*
**A:** *Yes. That's right.*

9. language arts
10. math
11. science
12. history
13. world languages
14. ESL
15. arts
16. music
17. physical education

13

15

**More vocabulary**

**core course:** a subject students have to take. Math is a core course.

**elective:** a subject students choose to take. Art is an elective.

**Pair practice. Make new conversations.**

**A:** *I go to college.*
**B:** *What subjects are you taking?*
**A:** *I'm taking history and science.*

① factory

② I worked in a factory.

③ Little by little, work and success came to me. My first job wasn't good. I worked in a small factory. Now, I help manage two factories.

④

1. word
2. sentence
3. paragraph
4. essay

## Parts of an Essay

5. title
6. introduction
7. body
8. conclusion
9. quotation
10. footnote

Erdem Koca
Eng. Comp.
10/21/10

⑤ Success in Canada

⑥ I came to Calgary from Turkey in 2006. I had no job, no friends, and no family here. I was homesick and scared, but I did not go home. I took English classes (always at night) and I studied hard. I believed in my future success!

⑦ More than 200,000 new immigrants come to Canada every year.[1] Most of us need to find work. During my first year here, my routine was the same: get up; look for work; go to class; go to bed. I had to take jobs with long hours and low pay. Often I had two or three jobs.

Little by little, work and success came to me. My first job wasn't good. I worked in a small factory. Now, I help manage two factories.

⑧ Hard work makes success possible. Henry David Thoreau said, ⑨ "Men are born to succeed, not fail." My story shows that he was right.

⑩ [1] Citizenship and Immigration Canada

## Punctuation

| | |
|---|---|
| . | 11. period |
| ? | 12. question mark |
| ! | 13. exclamation mark |
| , | 14. comma |
| " " | 15. quotation marks |
| ' | 16. apostrophe |
| : | 17. colon |
| ; | 18. semicolon |
| ( ) | 19. parentheses |
| - | 20. hyphen |

## Writing Rules

**A** Erdem Turkey Calgary

**B** Hard work makes success possible.

**C** I was homesick and scared, but I did not go home.

**D** I came to Calgary from Turkey in 2006. I had no job, no friends, and no family here. I was homesick and scared, but I did not go home. I took English classes (always at night) and I studied hard. I believed in my future success!

A. **Capitalize** names.

B. **Capitalize** the first letter in a sentence.

C. **Use** punctuation.

D. **Indent** the first sentence in a paragraph.

**Ways to ask for suggestions on your compositions**

*What do you think of this* _title_*?*
*Is this* _paragraph_ *OK? Is the* _punctuation_ *correct?*
*Do you have any suggestions for the* _conclusion_*?*

**Pair practice. Make new conversations.**

**A:** What do you think of this _title_?
**B:** *I think you need to* _revise_ *it.*
**A:** *Thanks. Do you have any more suggestions?*

## The Writing Process

### PREWRITING

E. **Think about** the assignment.

F. **Brainstorm** ideas.

G. **Organize** your ideas.

### WRITING AND REVISING

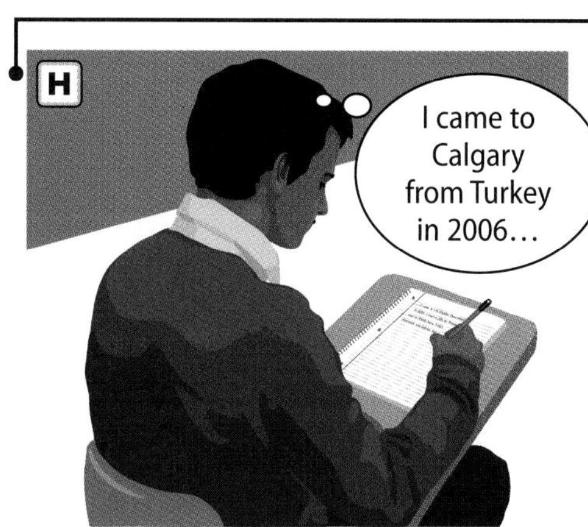


H. **Write** a first draft.

I. **Edit**. / **Proofread**.

J. **Revise**. / **Rewrite**.

### SHARING AND RESPONDING

K. **Get** feedback.

L. **Write** a final draft.

M. **Turn in** your paper.

**Ask your classmates. Share the answers.**

1. Do you like to write essays?
2. Which part of the writing process do you like best? least?

**Think about it. Discuss.**

1. In which jobs are writing skills important?
2. What tools can help you edit your writing?
3. What are some good subjects for essays?

## Integers

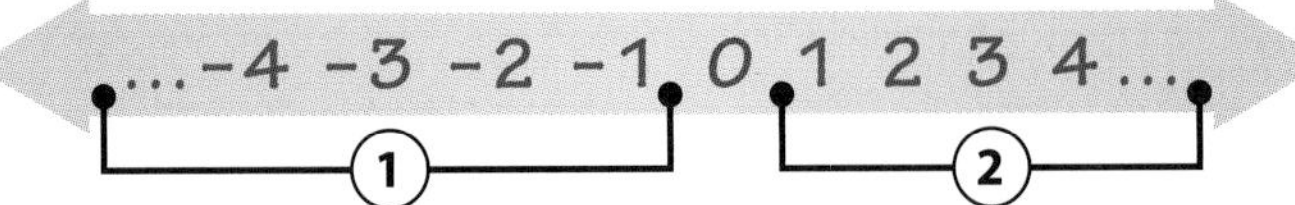


1. negative integers
2. positive integers

3. odd numbers
4. even numbers

## Fractions

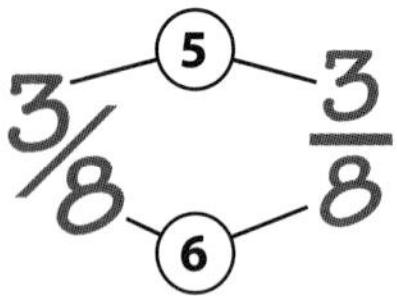


3 1, 3, 5, 7, 9, 11...

4 2, 4, 6, 8, 10...

5. numerator
6. denominator

## Math Operations

A. **add**
B. **subtract**
C. **multiply**
D. **divide**

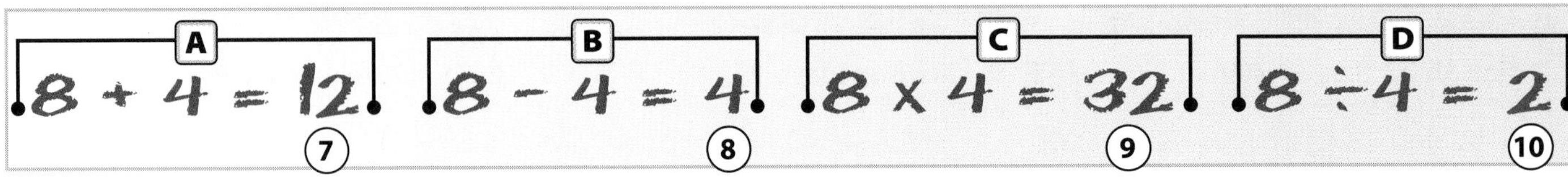


7. sum
8. difference
9. product
10. quotient

## A Math Problem

11 Tom is 10 years older than Kim. Next year he will be twice as old as Kim. How old is Tom this year?

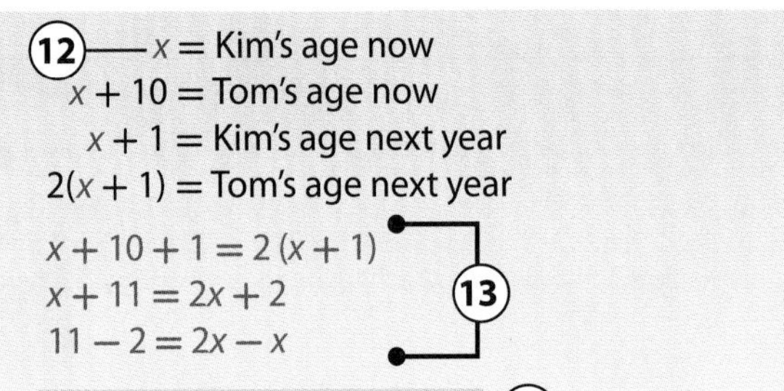


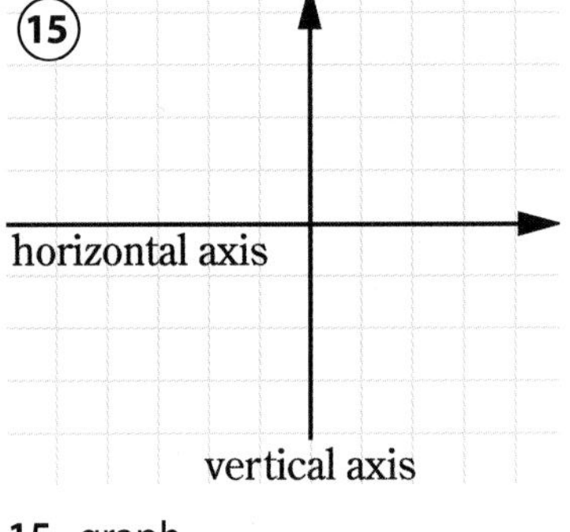


11. word problem
12. variable
13. equation
14. solution
15. graph

## Types of Math

x = the sale price
x = 79.00 - .40 (79.00)
x = $47.40

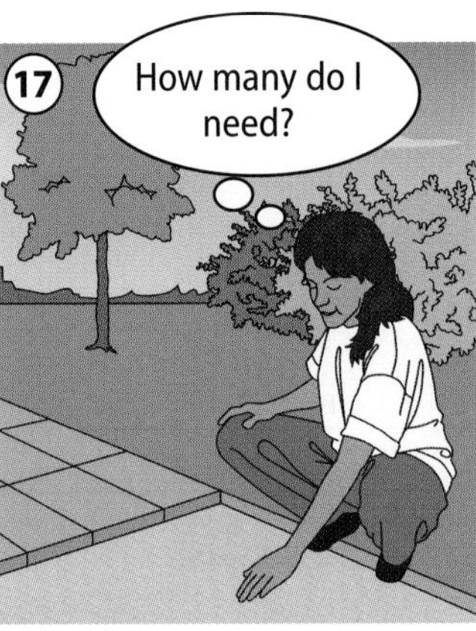


area of path = 6 square metres
area of brick = 0.5 square metres
6/0.5 = 12 bricks

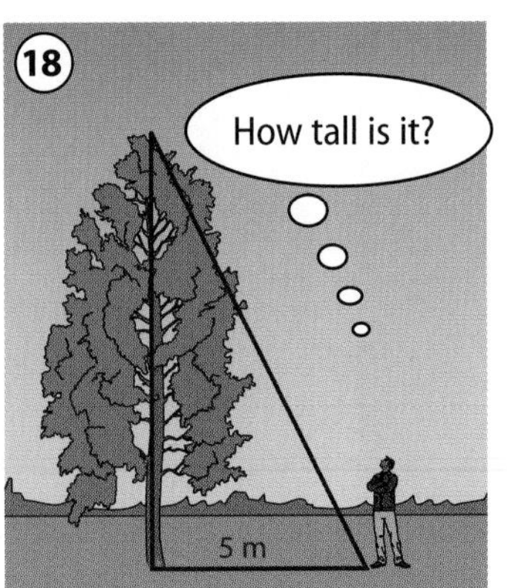


tan 63° = height / 5 metres
height = 5 metres (tan 63°)
height ≃ 9.81 metres

$s(t) = -½ gt^2 + V_0 t + h$
$s^{I}(t) = -gt + V_0 = 0$
$t = V_0 / g$

16. algebra
17. geometry
18. trigonometry
19. calculus

## Lines

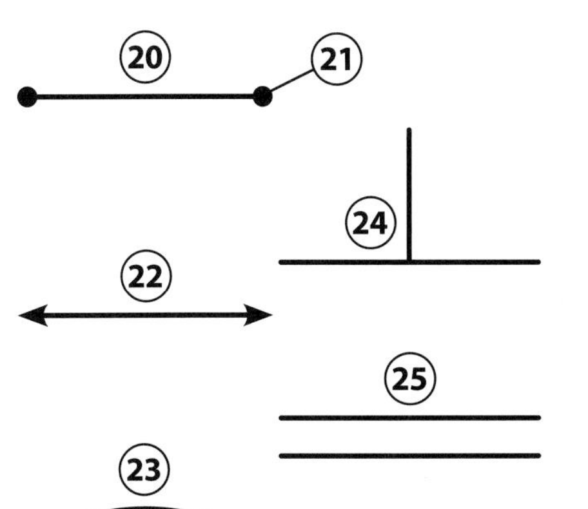


## Angles

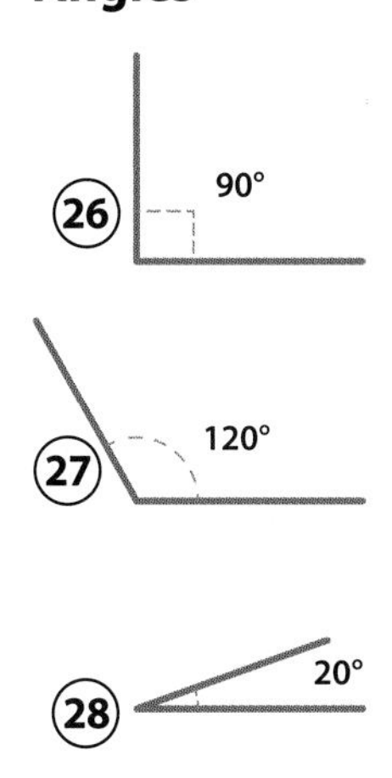


## Shapes

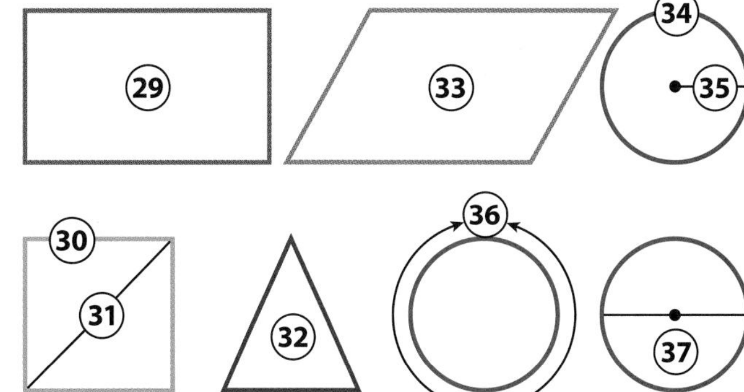


**20.** line segment
**21.** endpoint
**22.** straight line
**23.** curved line
**24.** perpendicular lines

**25.** parallel lines
**26.** right angle / 90° angle
**27.** obtuse angle
**28.** acute angle

**29.** rectangle
**30.** square
**31.** diagonal
**32.** triangle
**33.** parallelogram

**34.** circle
**35.** radius
**36.** circumference
**37.** diameter

## Geometric Solids

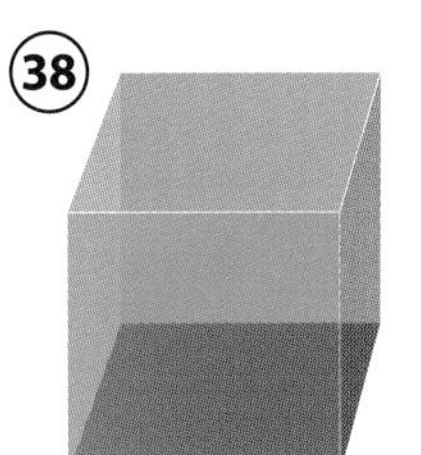


**38.** cube

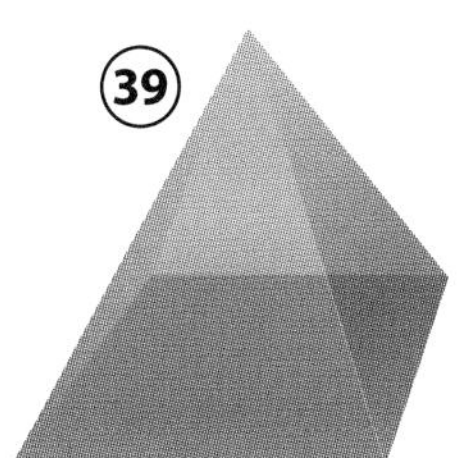


**39.** pyramid

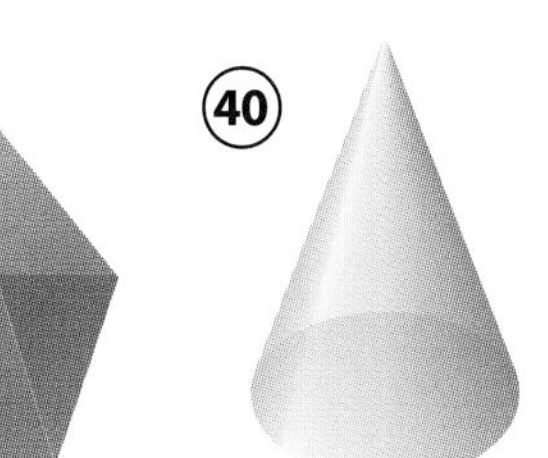


**40.** cone

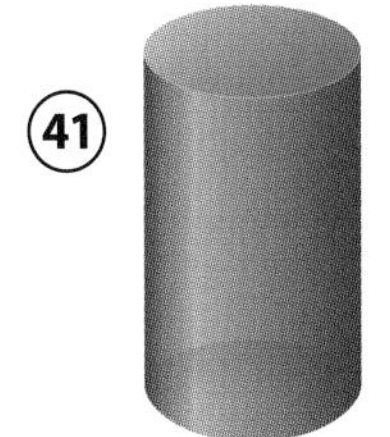


**41.** cylinder

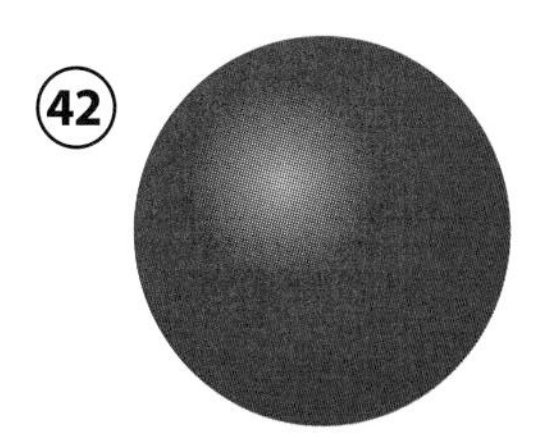

**42.** sphere

## Measuring Area and Volume

$\ell \times w =$ area

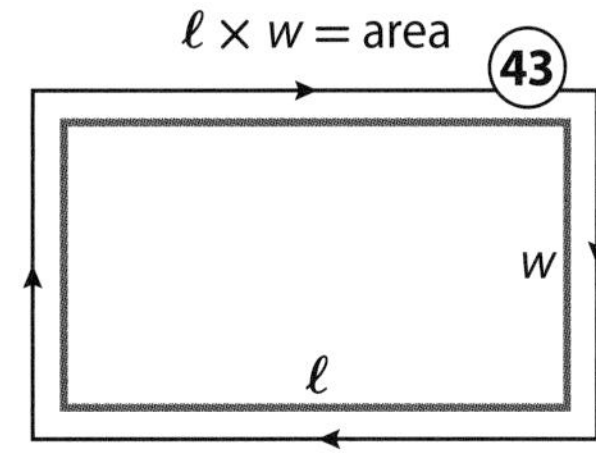


**43.** perimeter

$6 \times f =$ surface area

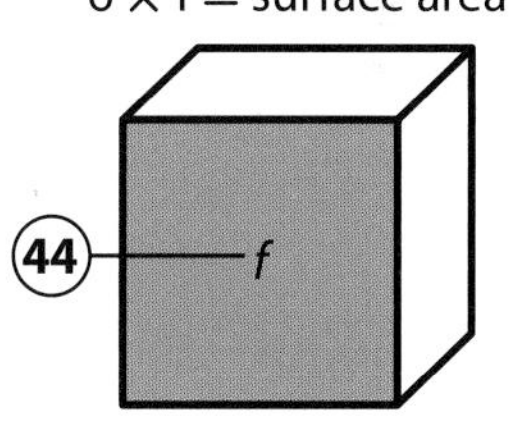


**44.** face

$\pi \times r^2 \times h =$ volume

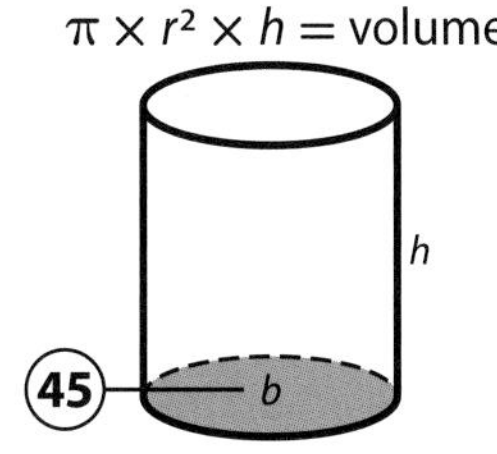
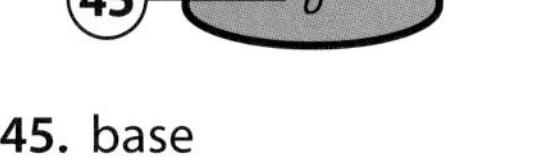


**45.** base

$\frac{4}{3} \times \pi \times r^3 =$ volume

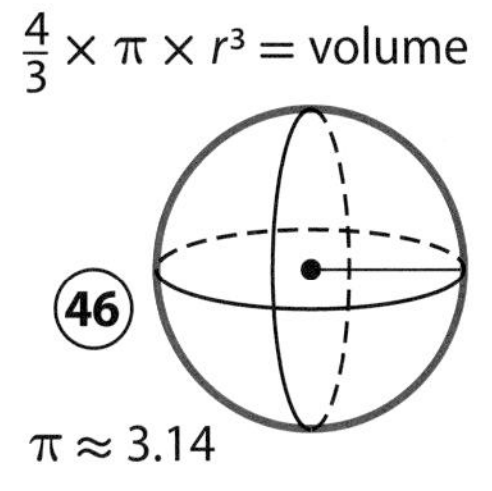


$\pi \approx 3.14$

**46.** pi

**Ask your classmates. Share the answers.**

1. Are you good at math?
2. Which types of math are easy for you?
3. Which types of math are difficult for you?

**Think about it. Discuss.**

1. What's the best way to learn mathematics?
2. How can you find the area of your classroom?
3. Which jobs use math? Which don't?

## Biology

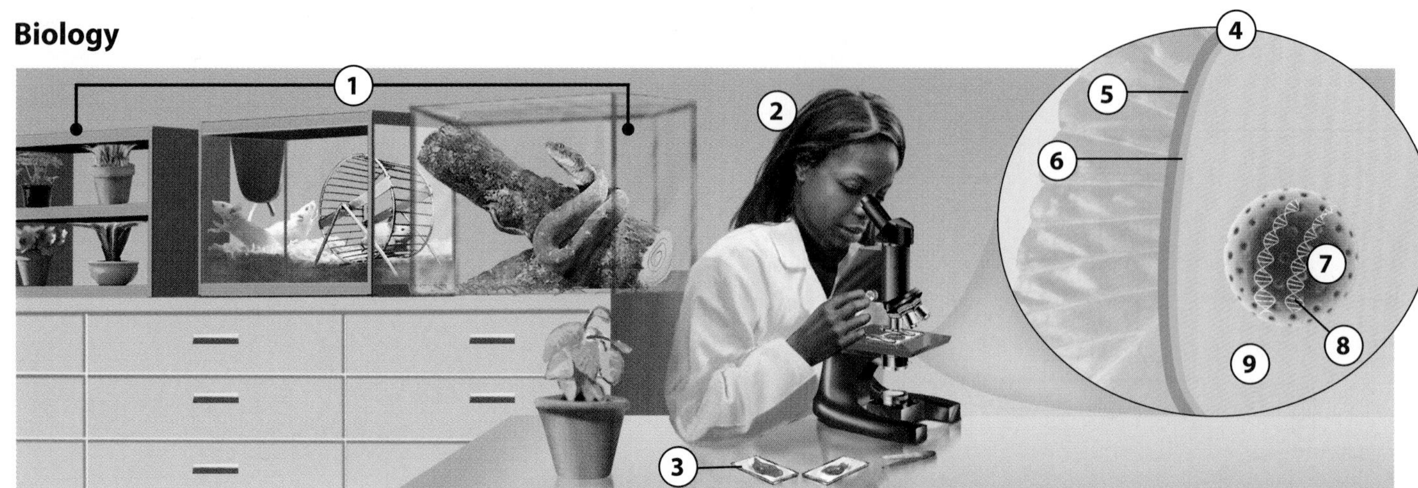

1. organisms
2. biologist
3. slide
4. cell
5. cell wall
6. cell membrane
7. nucleus
8. chromosome
9. cytoplasm

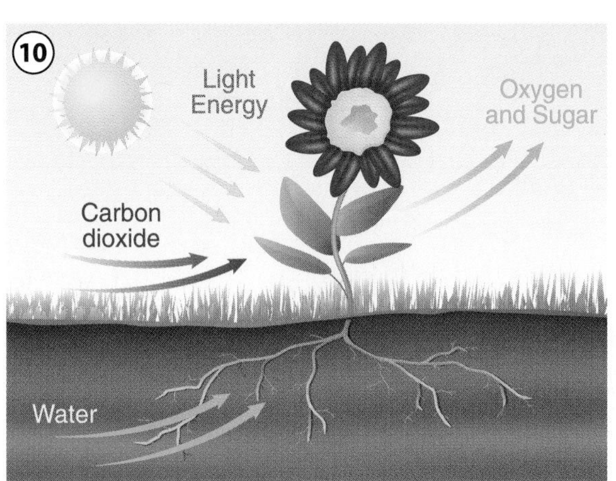
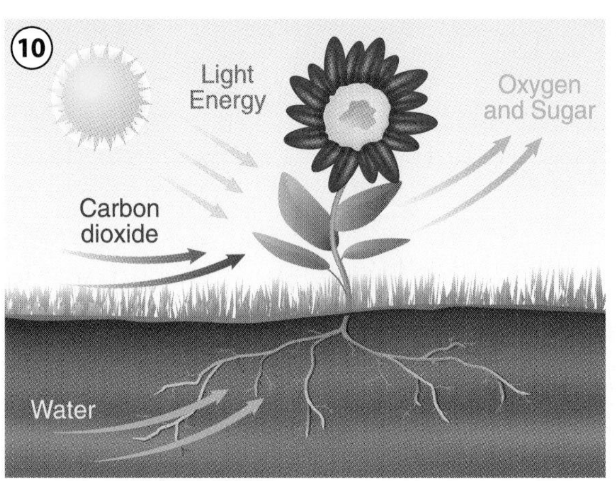

10. photosynthesis
11. habitat
12. vertebrates
13. invertebrates

## A Microscope

14. eyepiece
15. revolving nosepiece
16. objective
17. stage
18. diaphragm
19. light source
20. base
21. stage clips
22. fine adjustment knob
23. arm
24. coarse adjustment knob

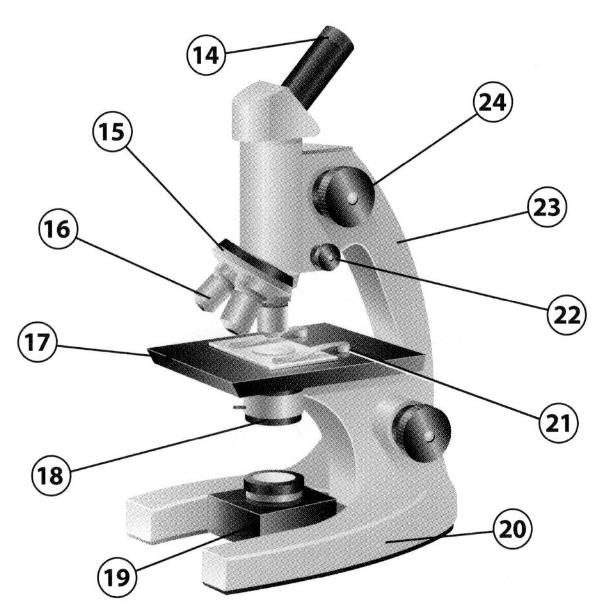

## Chemistry

## Physics

25. chemist
26. periodic table
27. molecule
28. atom
29. nucleus
30. electron
31. proton
32. neutron
33. physicist
34. formula
35. prism
36. magnet

## A Science Lab

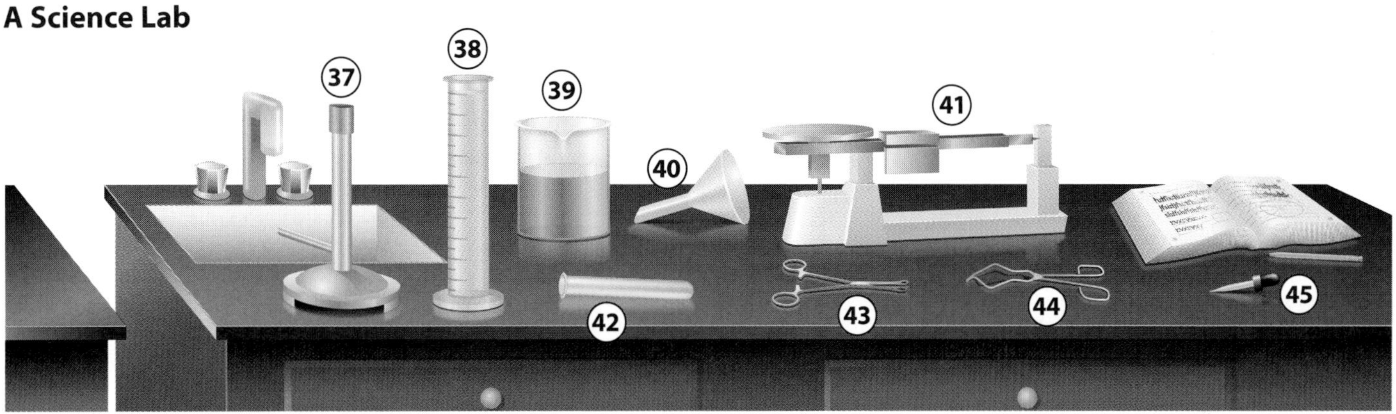

37. Bunsen burner
38. graduated cylinder
39. beaker
40. funnel
41. balance / scale
42. test tube
43. forceps
44. crucible tongs
45. dropper

## An Experiment

A
Salt and sugar crystals will grow the same way.


A. **State** a hypothesis.

B. **Do** an experiment.

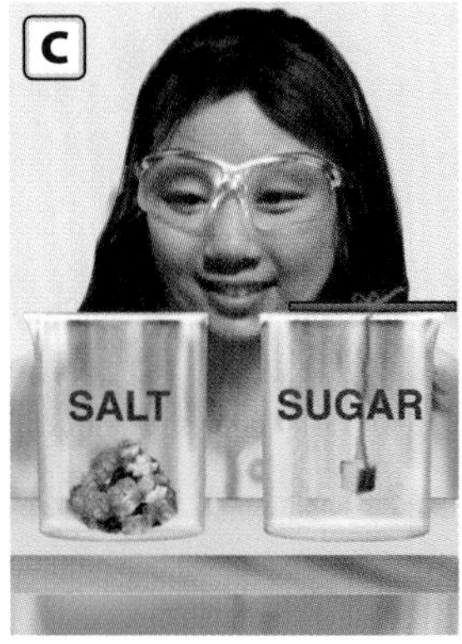


C. **Observe.**

D. **Record** the results.

E. **Draw** a conclusion.

# Computers

## Desktop Computer

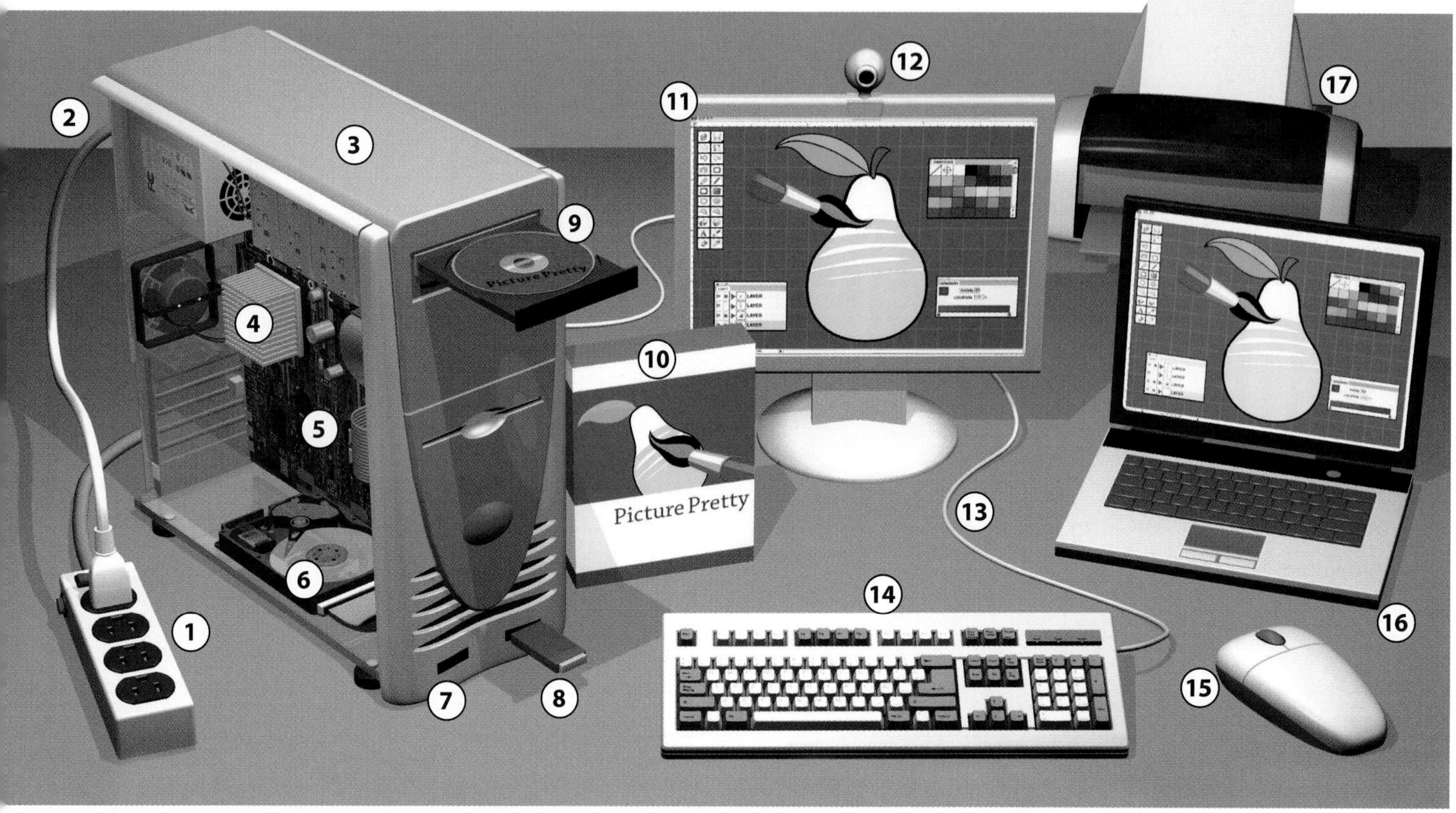

1. surge protector
2. power cord
3. tower
4. microprocessor / CPU
5. motherboard
6. hard drive
7. USB port
8. flash drive
9. DVD and CD-ROM drive
10. software
11. monitor /screen
12. webcam
13. cable
14. keyboard
15. mouse
16. laptop
17. printer

## Keyboarding

A. **type**

B. **select**

C. **delete**

D. **go to** the next line

## Navigating a Webpage

1. menu bar
2. back button
3. forward button
4. URL / website address
5. search box
6. search engine
7. tab
8. drop-down menu
9. pop-up ad
10. links
11. video player
12. pointer
13. text box
14. cursor
15. scroll bar

## Logging on and Sending Email

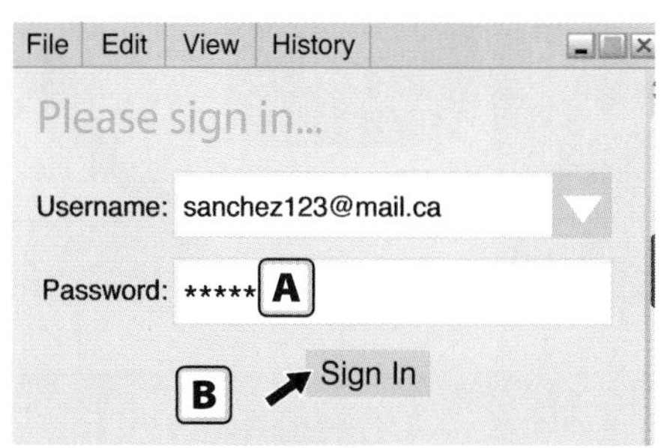


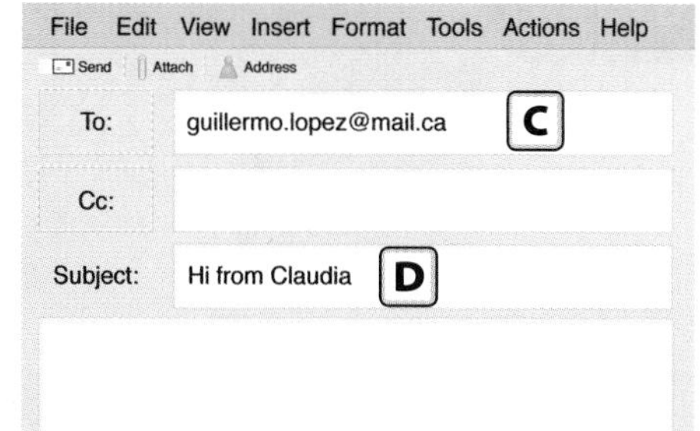


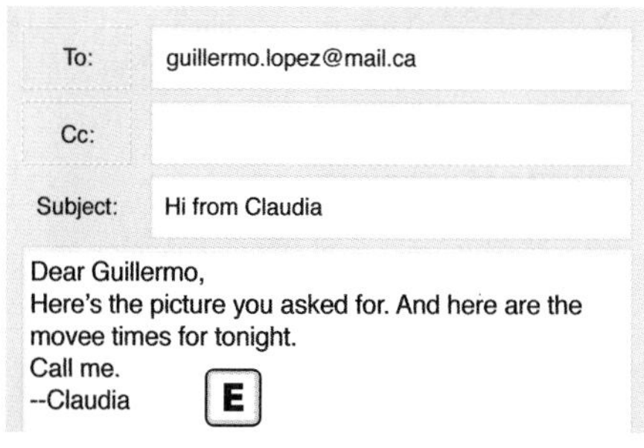


A. **type** your password

B. **click** "sign in"

C. **address** the email

D. **type** the subject

E. **type** the message

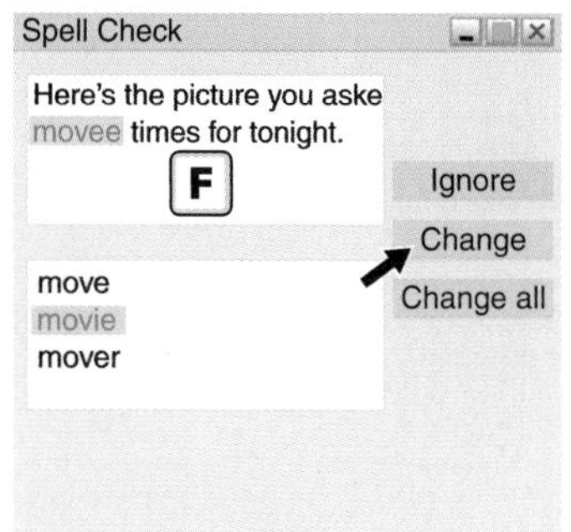


F. **check** your spelling

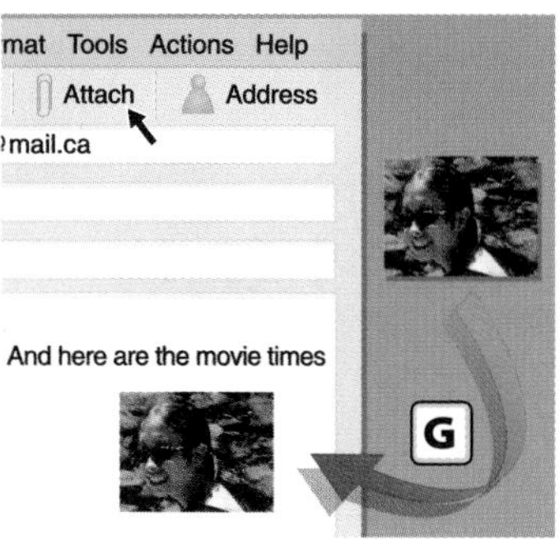


G. **attach** a picture

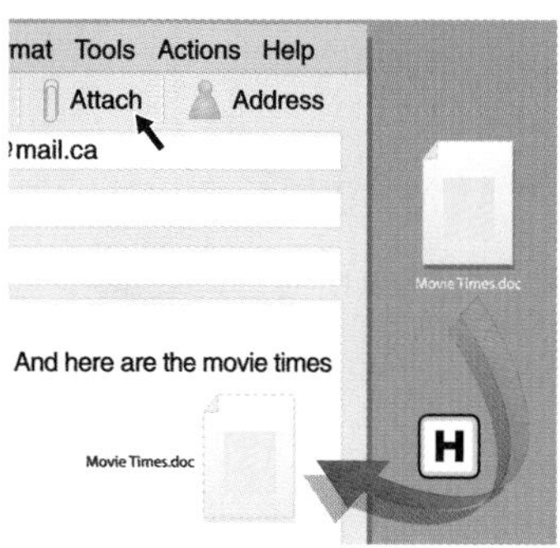


H. **attach** a file

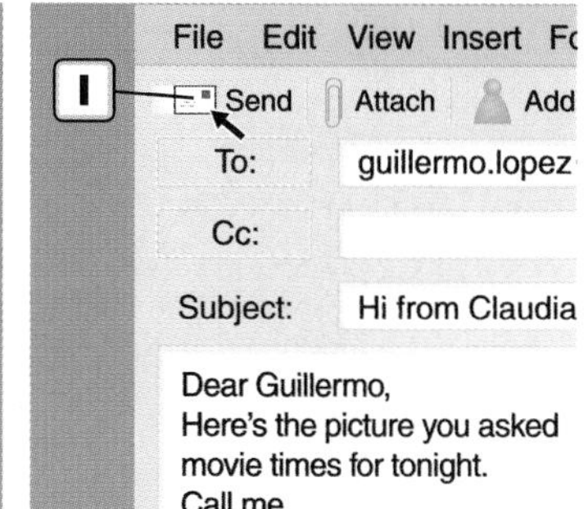


I. **send** the email

# Canadian History

## Confederation

1. provinces
2. settlers
3. British North America Act
4. First Nations
5. Fathers of Confederation
6. Inuit
7. first prime minister

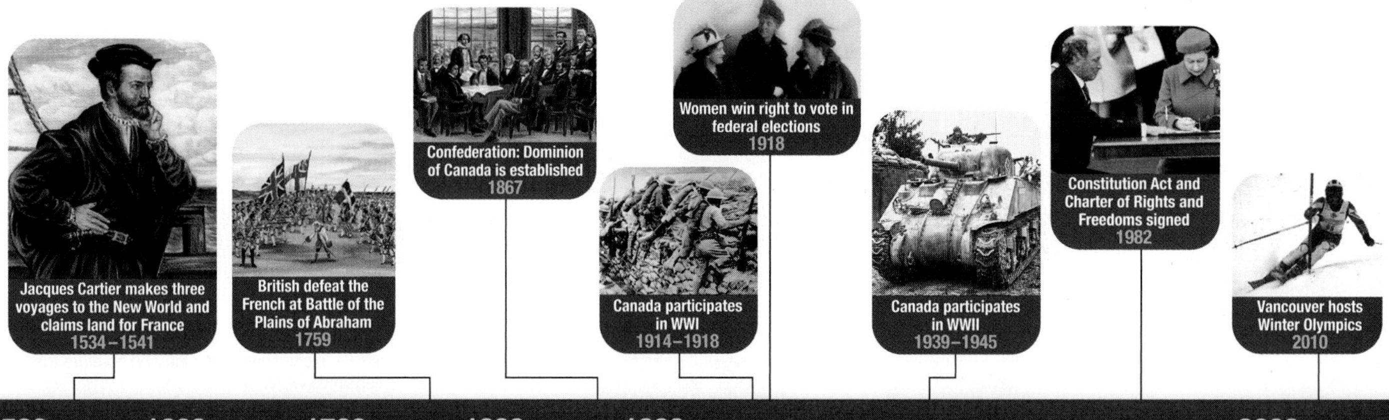


1500 1600 1700 1800 1900 2000 →

## Civilizations

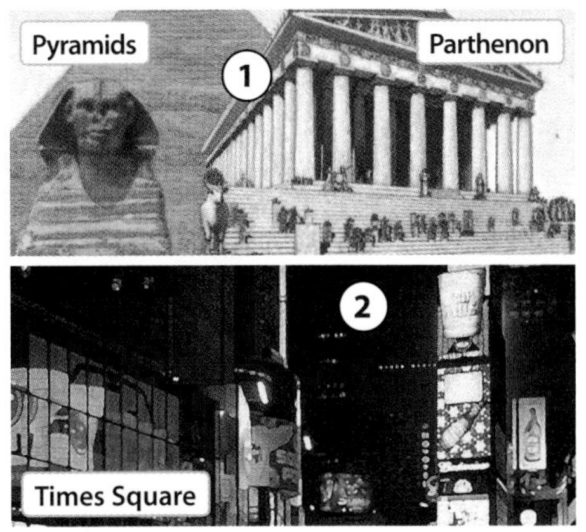

1. ancient
2. modern
3. emperor
4. monarch
5. president
6. dictator
7. prime minister

## Historical Terms

8. exploration
9. explorer
10. war
11. army
12. immigration
13. immigrant

14. composer
15. composition
16. political movement
17. activist
18. inventor
19. invention

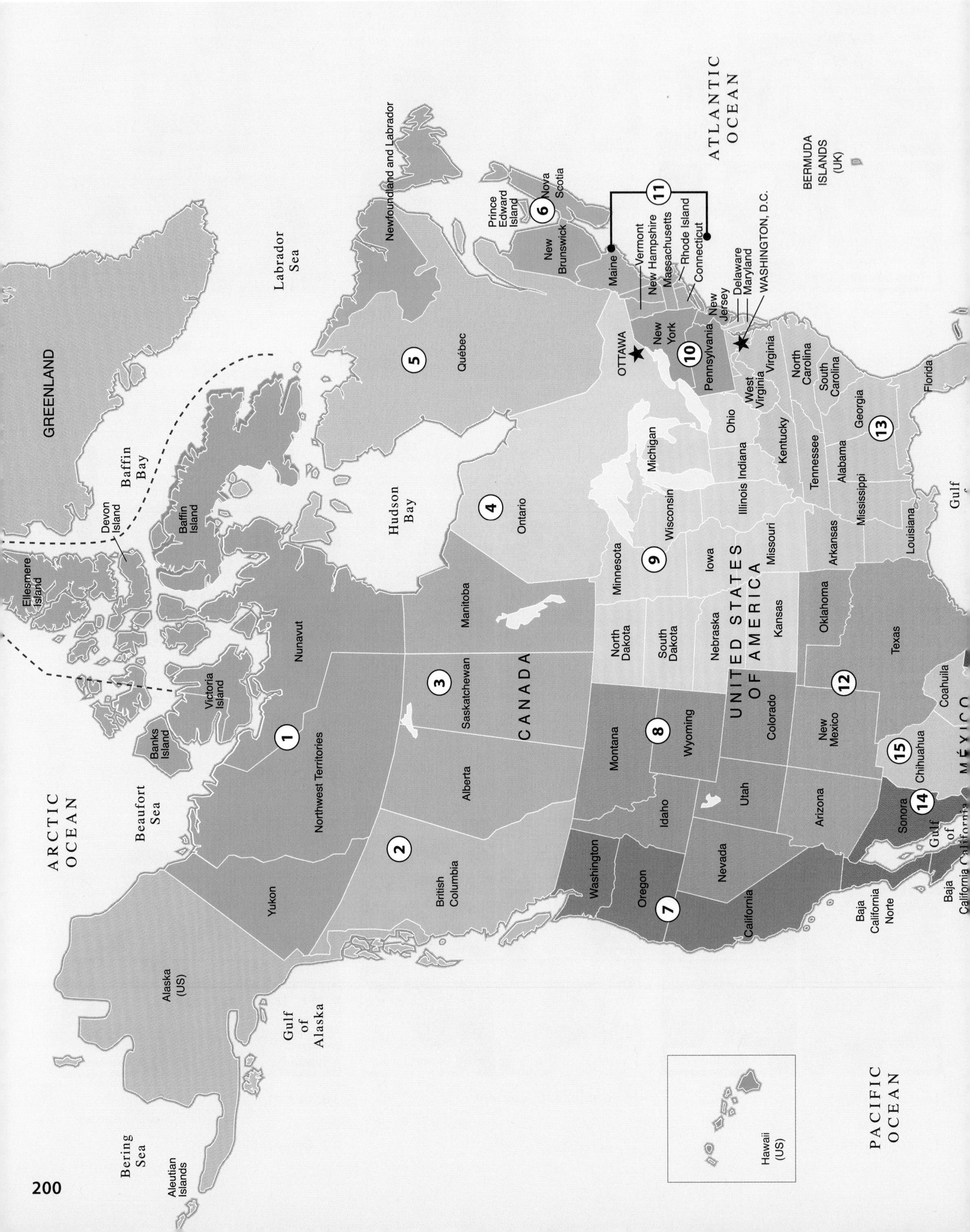

# North America and Central America

ARCTIC OCEAN
Beaufort Sea
Bering Sea
Aleutian Islands
Gulf of Alaska
Alaska (US)
Yukon
Northwest Territories
Nunavut
Banks Island
Victoria Island
Ellesmere Island
Devon Island
Baffin Island
Baffin Bay
GREENLAND
Labrador Sea
Hudson Bay
British Columbia
Alberta
Saskatchewan
Manitoba
Ontario
Québec
Newfoundland and Labrador
New Brunswick
Prince Edward Island
Nova Scotia
CANADA
OTTAWA
1
2
3
4
5
6
7
8
9
10
11
12
13
14
15
Maine
Vermont
New Hampshire
Massachusetts
Rhode Island
Connecticut
New York
New Jersey
Pennsylvania
Delaware
Maryland
WASHINGTON, D.C.
Virginia
West Virginia
North Carolina
South Carolina
Georgia
Florida
Ohio
Michigan
Indiana
Illinois
Kentucky
Tennessee
Alabama
Mississippi
Wisconsin
Minnesota
Iowa
Missouri
Arkansas
Louisiana
North Dakota
South Dakota
Nebraska
Kansas
Oklahoma
Texas
Montana
Wyoming
Colorado
New Mexico
Idaho
Utah
Arizona
Washington
Oregon
Nevada
California
UNITED STATES OF AMERICA
Hawaii (US)
ATLANTIC OCEAN
BERMUDA ISLANDS (UK)
PACIFIC OCEAN
Gulf
MÉXICO
Coahuila
Chihuahua
Sonora
Gulf of California
Baja California Norte
Baja California

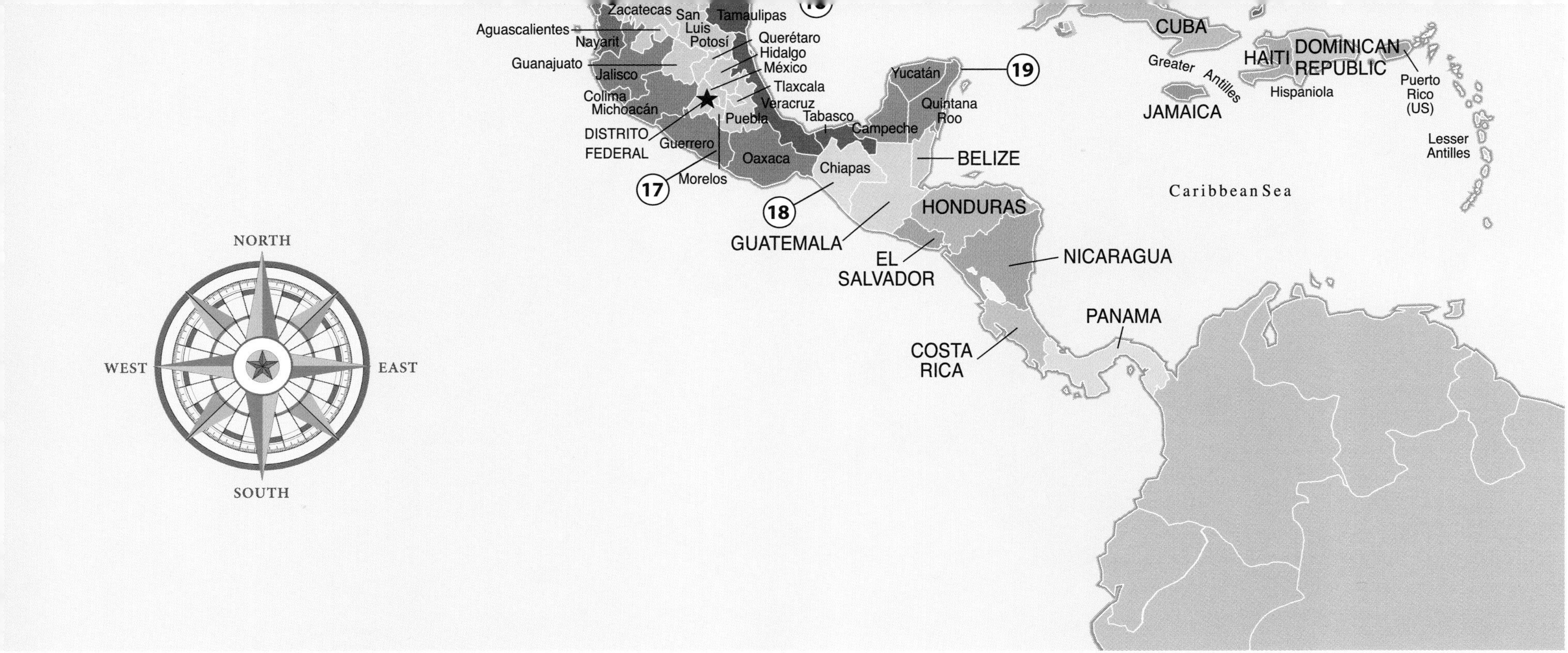

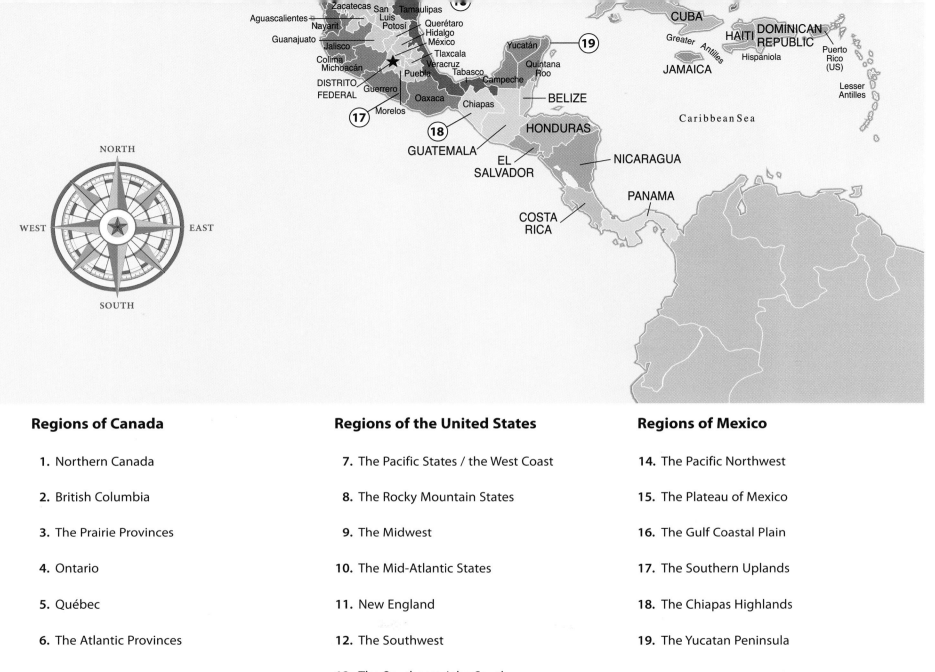

## Regions of Canada

1. Northern Canada
2. British Columbia
3. The Prairie Provinces
4. Ontario
5. Québec
6. The Atlantic Provinces

## Regions of the United States

7. The Pacific States / the West Coast
8. The Rocky Mountain States
9. The Midwest
10. The Mid-Atlantic States
11. New England
12. The Southwest
13. The Southeast / the South

## Regions of Mexico

14. The Pacific Northwest
15. The Plateau of Mexico
16. The Gulf Coastal Plain
17. The Southern Uplands
18. The Chiapas Highlands
19. The Yucatan Peninsula

# World Map

## Continents

1. North America
2. South America
3. Europe
4. Asia
5. Africa
6. Australia
7. Antarctica

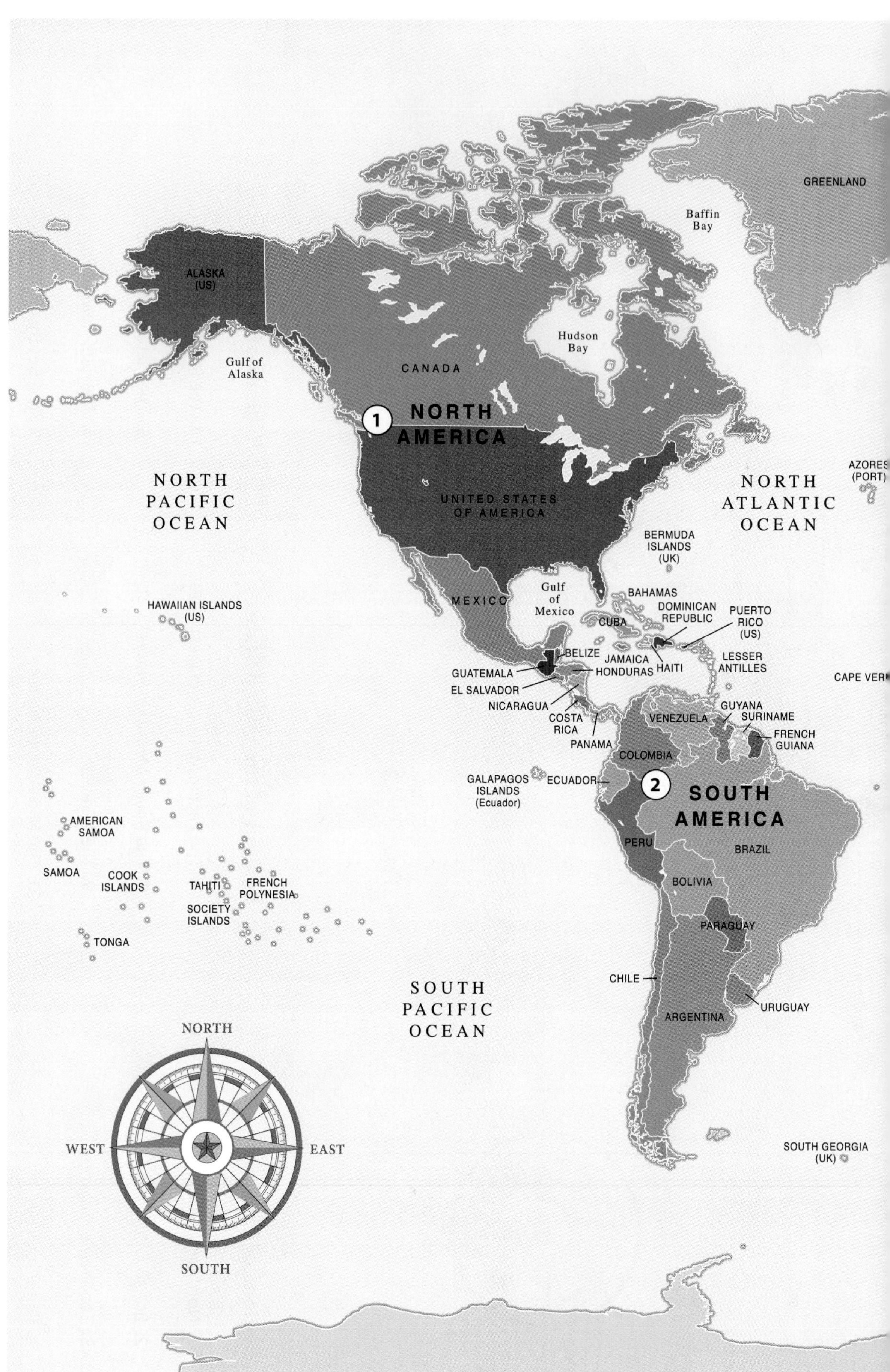

ARCTIC OCEAN
SVALBARD (NORWAY)
FRANZ JOSEF LAND (RUSSIA)
ICELAND
RUSSIA
4
ALEUTIAN ISLANDS (US)
EUROPE
3
KAZAKHSTAN
ASIA
MONGOLIA
Caspian Sea
Black Sea
GEORGIA
AZERBAIJAN
ARMENIA
UZBEKISTAN
KYRGYZSTAN
TURKMENISTAN
TAJIKISTAN
TURKEY
NORTH KOREA
SOUTH KOREA
JAPAN
NORTH PACIFIC OCEAN
DEIRA
LANDS
ORT)
TUNISIA
CYPRUS
SYRIA
Mediterranean Sea
LEBANON
ISRAEL
IRAQ
IRAN
AFGHANISTAN
CHINA
MOROCCO
NARY
ANDS
SP)
ALGERIA
LIBYA
EGYPT
JORDAN
KUWAIT
BAHRAIN
QATAR
PAKISTAN
NEPAL
BHUTAN
STERN
HARA
SAUDI ARABIA
UNITED ARAB EMIRATES
Red Sea
INDIA
BANGLADESH
Taiwan
5
Hong Kong
OMAN
MYANMAR
LAOS
MAURITANIA
MALI
NIGER
CHAD
ERITREA
YEMEN
ANDAMAN ISLANDS (INDIA)
THAILAND
PHILIPPINES
NORTHERN MARIANA ISLANDS (US)
WAKE ISLAND (US)
NEGAL
GAMBIA
BURKINA FASO
AFRICA
SUDAN
DJIBOUTI
VIETNAM
CAMBODIA
Philippine Sea
GUAM (US)
MARSHALL ISLANDS
GUINEA
BENIN
SOMALIA
NEA-SAU
IVORY COAST
NIGERIA
CENTRAL AFRICAN REPUBLIC
ETHIOPIA
BRUNEI
PALAU
FEDERATED STATES OF MICRONESIA
IERRA
LEONE
GHANA
TOGO
CAMEROON
MALDIVES
SRI LANKA
MALAYSIA
SINGAPORE
LIBERIA
UGANDA
KENYA
EQUATORIAL GUINEA
CONGO
GABON
KIRIBATI
DEMOCRATIC REPUBLIC OF THE CONGO
RWANDA
BURUNDI
TANZANIA
ZANZIBAR
SEYCHELLES
INDONESIA
PAPUA NEW GUINEA
SOLOMON ISLANDS
COMOROS
ANGOLA
ZAMBIA
MALAWI
INDIAN OCEAN
Coral Sea
VANUATU
MOZAMBIQUE
NAMIBIA
ZIMBABWE
MAURITIUS
MADAGASCAR
6
FIJI
BOTSWANA
SOUTH ATLANTIC OCEAN
AUSTRALIA
NEW CALEDONIA
SWAZILAND
LESOTHO
SOUTH AFRICA
SOUTH PACIFIC OCEAN
TASMANIA (AUSTRALIA)
NEW ZEALAND
SOUTHERN OCEAN
ANTARCTICA
7

ICELAND
FINLAND
NORWAY
SWEDEN
North Sea
ESTONIA
Baltic Sea
LATVIA
RUSSIA
DENMARK
NETHERLANDS
LITHUANIA
IRELAND
UNITED KINGDOM
GERMANY
POLAND
BELARUS
BELGIUM
LUXEMBOURG
CZECH REPUBLIC
SLOVAKIA
UKRAINE
SWITZERLAND
AUSTRIA
HUNGARY
MOLDOVA
SLOVENIA
CROATIA
ROMANIA
FRANCE
CORSICA (FR)
BOSNIA
SERBIA
MONTENEGRO
BULGARIA
Black Sea
SPAIN
MONACO
ITALY
MACEDONIA
ALBANIA
PORTUGAL
GREECE
TURKEY
MALTA
TUNISIA
CYPRUS
SYRIA
MOROCCO
ALGERIA
LIBYA
Mediterranean Sea
LEBANON

# Geography and Habitats

1. rainforest
2. waterfall
3. river
4. desert
5. sand dune
6. ocean
7. peninsula
8. island
9. bay
10. beach
11. forest
12. shore
13. lake
14. mountain peak
15. mountain range
16. hills
17. canyon
18. valley
19. plains
20. meadow
21. pond

**More vocabulary**

**a body of water:** a river, lake, or ocean
**stream / creek:** a very small river

**Ask your classmates. Share the answers.**

1. Would you rather live near a river or a lake?
2. Would you rather travel through a forest or a desert?
3. How often do you go to the beach or the shore?

## The Solar System and the Planets

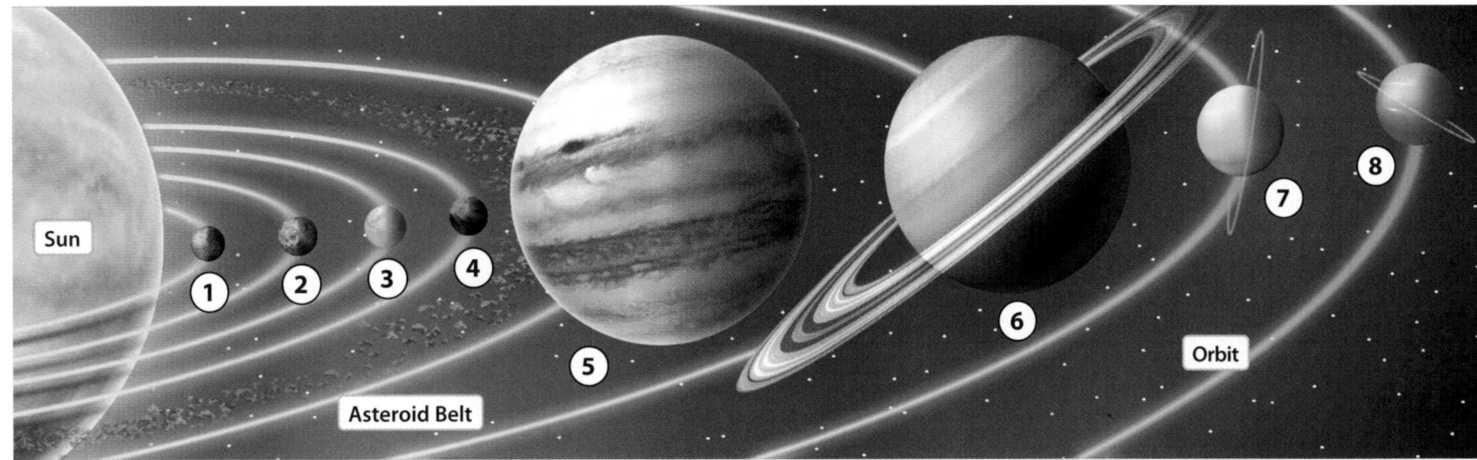


1. Mercury
2. Venus
3. Earth
4. Mars
5. Jupiter
6. Saturn
7. Uranus
8. Neptune

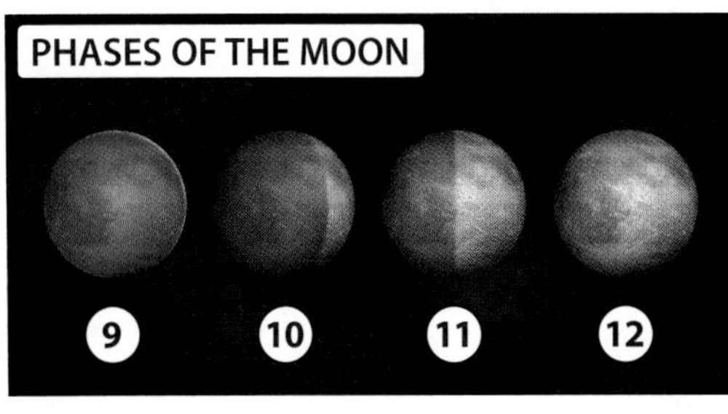

9. new moon
10. crescent moon
11. quarter moon
12. full moon
13. star
14. constellation
15. galaxy
16. solar eclipse

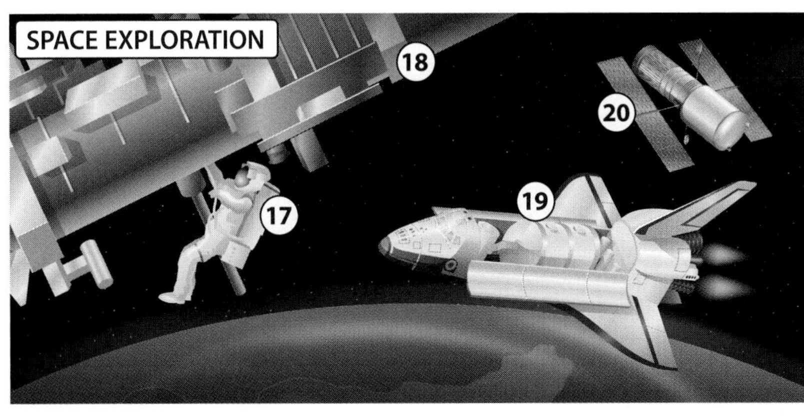


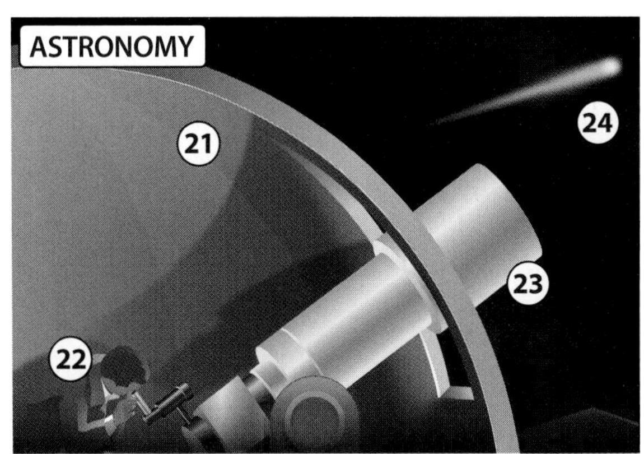


17. astronaut
18. space station
19. space shuttle
20. satellite
21. observatory
22. astronomer
23. telescope
24. comet

**More vocabulary**

**solar eclipse:** when the moon is between the earth and the sun
**Big Dipper:** a famous part of the constellation Ursa Major
**Sirius:** the brightest star in the night sky

**Ask your classmates. Share the answers.**

1. How do you feel when you look at the night sky?
2. Can you name one or more constellations?
3. Do you want to travel in space?

# A Graduation

MySpot.Edu | Help | SignOut

Home | Search | Invite | Mail |

All Adelia's photos

I loved Art History.

My last economics lesson

Marching Band is great!

The photographer was upset.

We look good!

I get my diploma.

Dad and his digital camera

1. photographer
2. funny photo
3. serious photo
4. guest speaker
5. podium
6. ceremony
7. cap
8. gown

A. **take** a picture
B. **cry**
C. **celebrate**

MySpot en Français | International

Videos | Music | Classifieds |

| People | Comments | |
|---|---|---|
| Sara | June 29th 8:19 p.m. Great pictures! What a day! | Delete |
| Zannie baby | June 30th 10 a.m. Love the funny photo. | Delete |

I'm behind the mayor.

We're all very happy.

**Look at the pictures. What do you see?**

**Answer the questions.**

1. How many people are wearing caps and gowns?
2. How many people are being funny? How many are being serious?
3. Who is standing at the podium?
4. Why are the graduates throwing their caps in the air?

 **Read the story.**

## A Graduation

Look at these great photos on my web page! The first three are from my favourite classes, but the other pictures are from graduation day.

There are two pictures of my classmates in caps and gowns. In the first picture, we're laughing and the photographer is upset. In the second photo, we're serious. I like the serious photo, but I love the funny photo!

There's also a picture of our guest speaker, the mayor. She is standing at the podium. Next, you can see me at the graduation ceremony. My dad wanted to take a picture of me with my diploma. That's my mom next to him. She cries when she's happy.

After the ceremony, everyone was happy, but no one cried. We wanted to celebrate and we did!

**Think about it.**

1. What kinds of ceremonies are important for children? for teens? for adults?
2. Imagine you are the guest speaker at a graduation. What will you say to the graduates?

1. trees
2. soil
3. path
4. bird
5. plants
6. rock
7. flowers

**Listen and point. Take turns.**

**A:** *Point to the trees.*
**B:** *Point to a bird.*
**A:** *Point to the flowers.*

**Dictate to your partner. Take turns.**

**A:** *Write it's a tree.*
**B:** *Let me check that. I-t-'s -a- t-r-e-e?*
**A:** *Yes, that's right.*

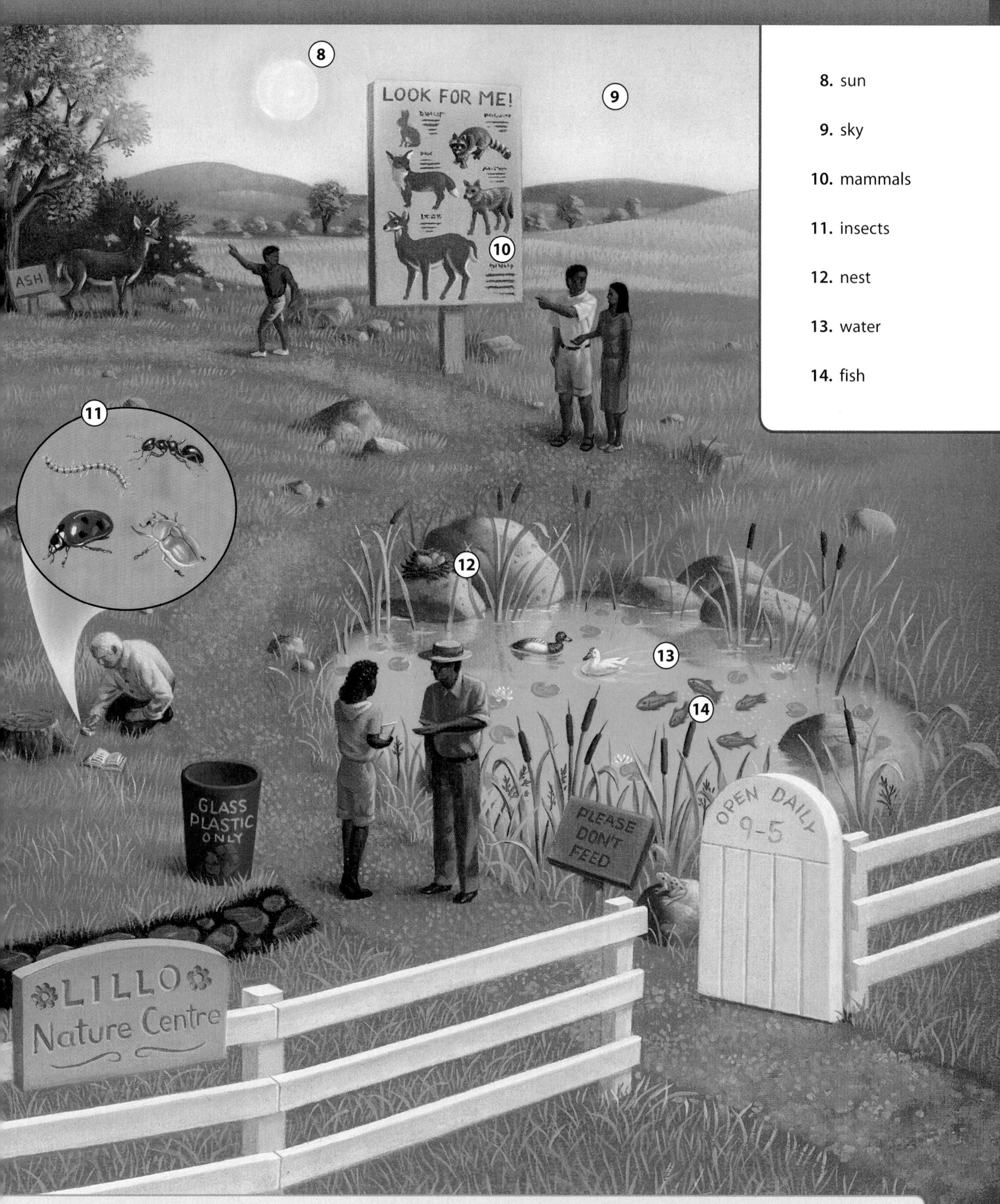


8. sun
9. sky
10. mammals
11. insects
12. nest
13. water
14. fish

**Ways to talk about nature**

*Look at the sky! Isn't it beautiful?*
*Did you see the fish / insects?*
*It's / They're so interesting.*

**Pair practice. Make new conversations.**

**A:** *Do you know the name of that yellow flower?*
**B:** *I think it's a sunflower.*
**A:** *Oh, and what about that blue bird?*

# Trees and Plants

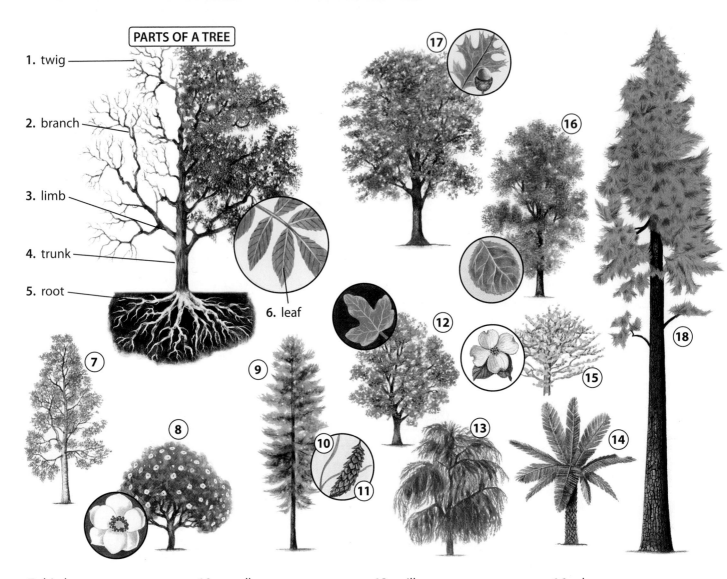

PARTS OF A TREE

1. twig
2. branch
3. limb
4. trunk
5. root
6. leaf

7. birch
8. magnolia
9. pine
10. needle
11. pine cone
12. maple
13. willow
14. palm
15. dogwood
16. elm
17. oak
18. redwood

## Plants

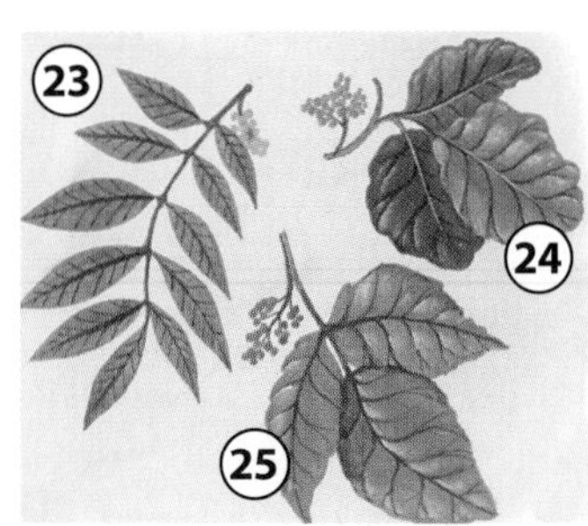

19. holly
20. berries
21. cactus
22. vine
23. poison sumac
24. poison oak
25. poison ivy

## Parts of a Flower

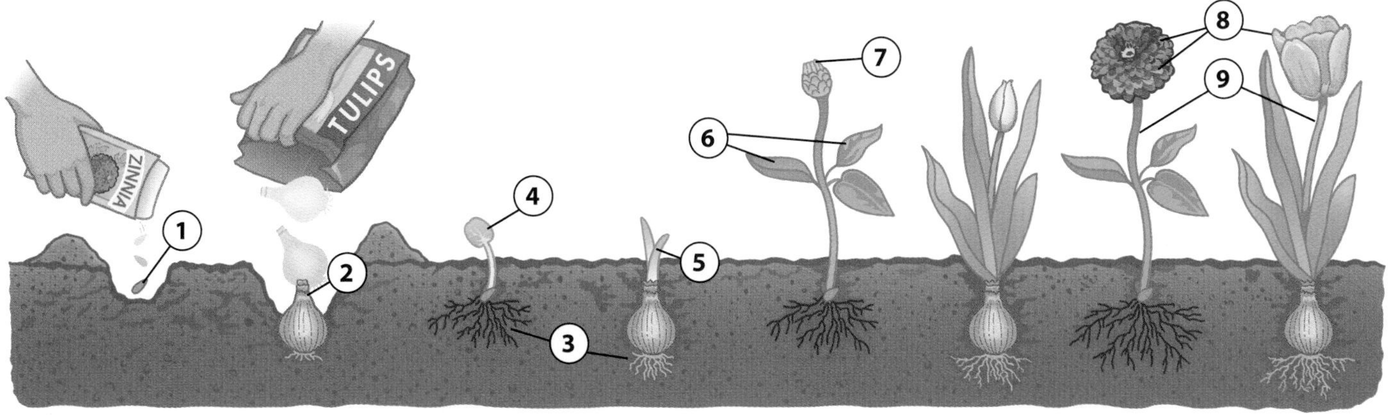


1. seed
2. bulb
3. roots
4. seedling
5. shoot
6. leaves
7. bud
8. petals
9. stems

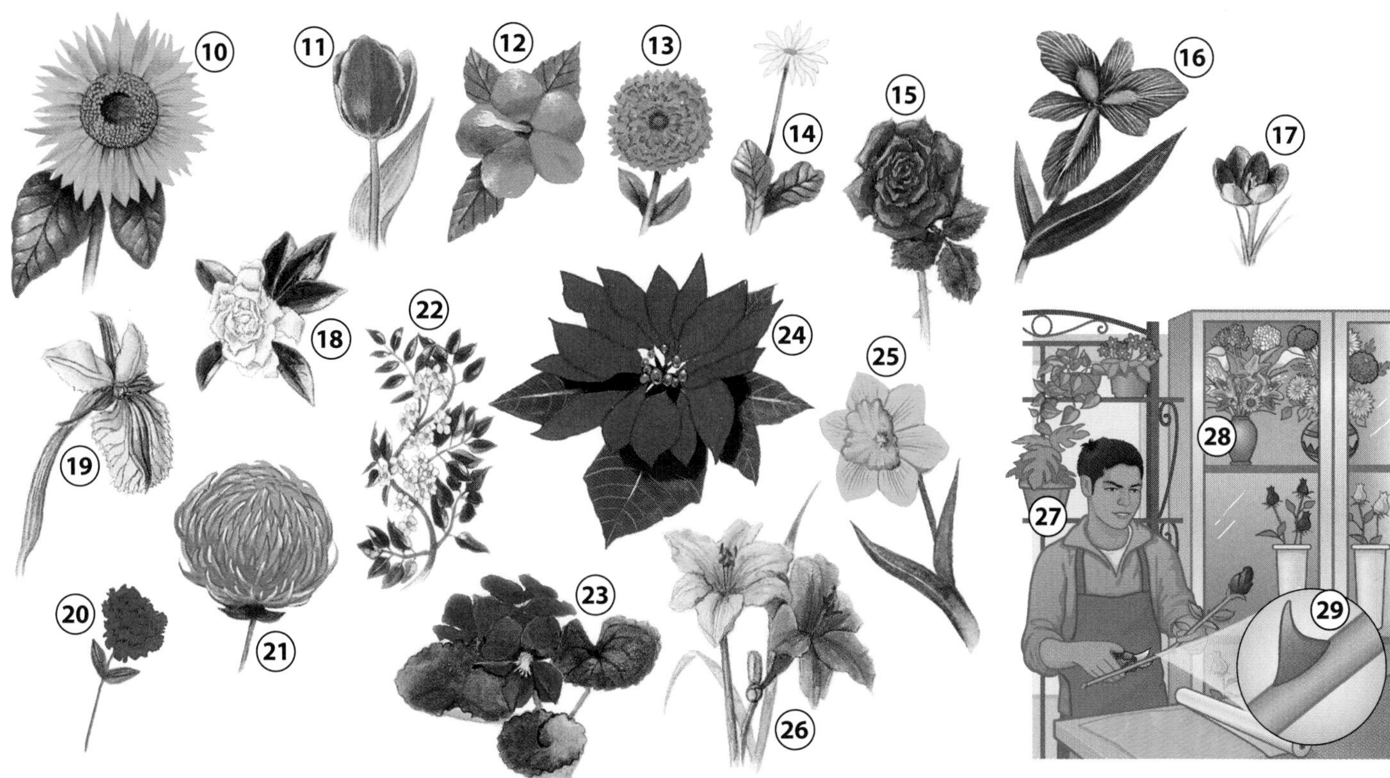

10. sunflower
11. tulip
12. hibiscus
13. marigold
14. daisy
15. rose
16. iris
17. crocus
18. gardenia
19. orchid
20. carnation
21. chrysanthemum
22. jasmine
23. violet
24. poinsettia
25. daffodil
26. lily
27. houseplant
28. bouquet
29. thorn

## Sea Animals

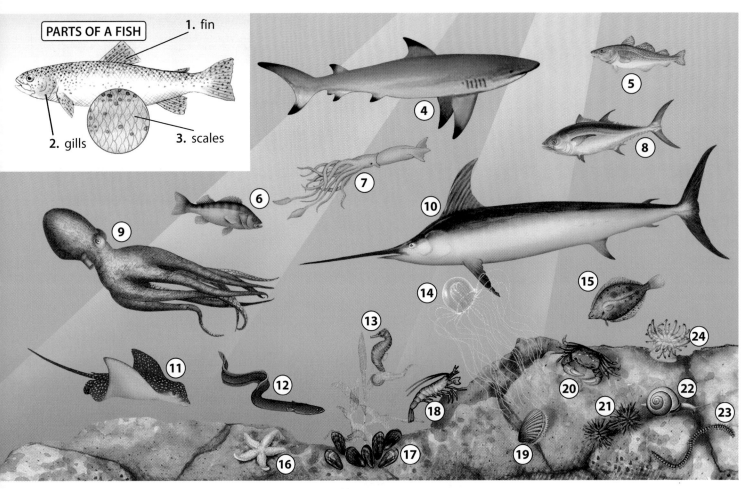

PARTS OF A FISH

1. fin
2. gills
3. scales

4. shark
5. cod
6. bass
7. squid
8. tuna
9. octopus
10. swordfish
11. ray
12. eel
13. sea horse
14. jellyfish
15. flounder
16. starfish
17. mussel
18. shrimp
19. scallop
20. crab
21. sea urchin
22. snail
23. worm
24. sea anemone

## Amphibians

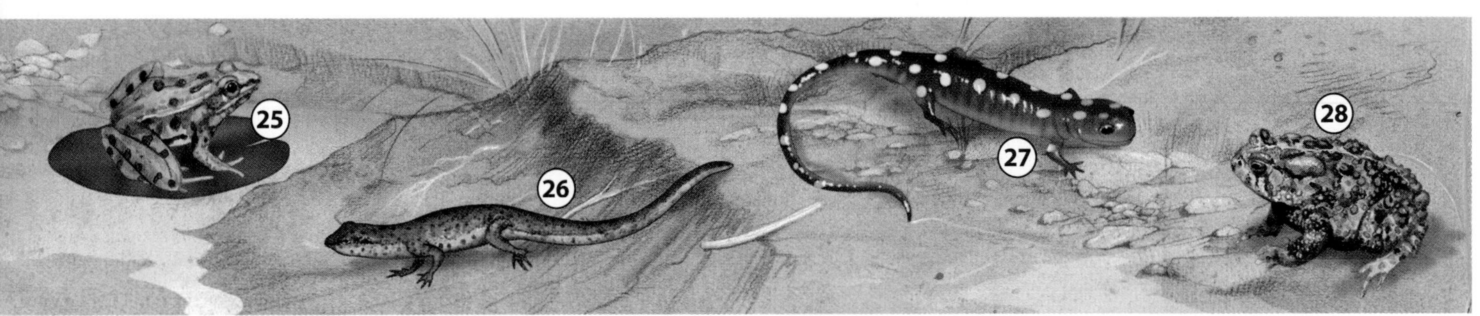

25. frog
26. newt
27. salamander
28. toad

### Sea Mammals

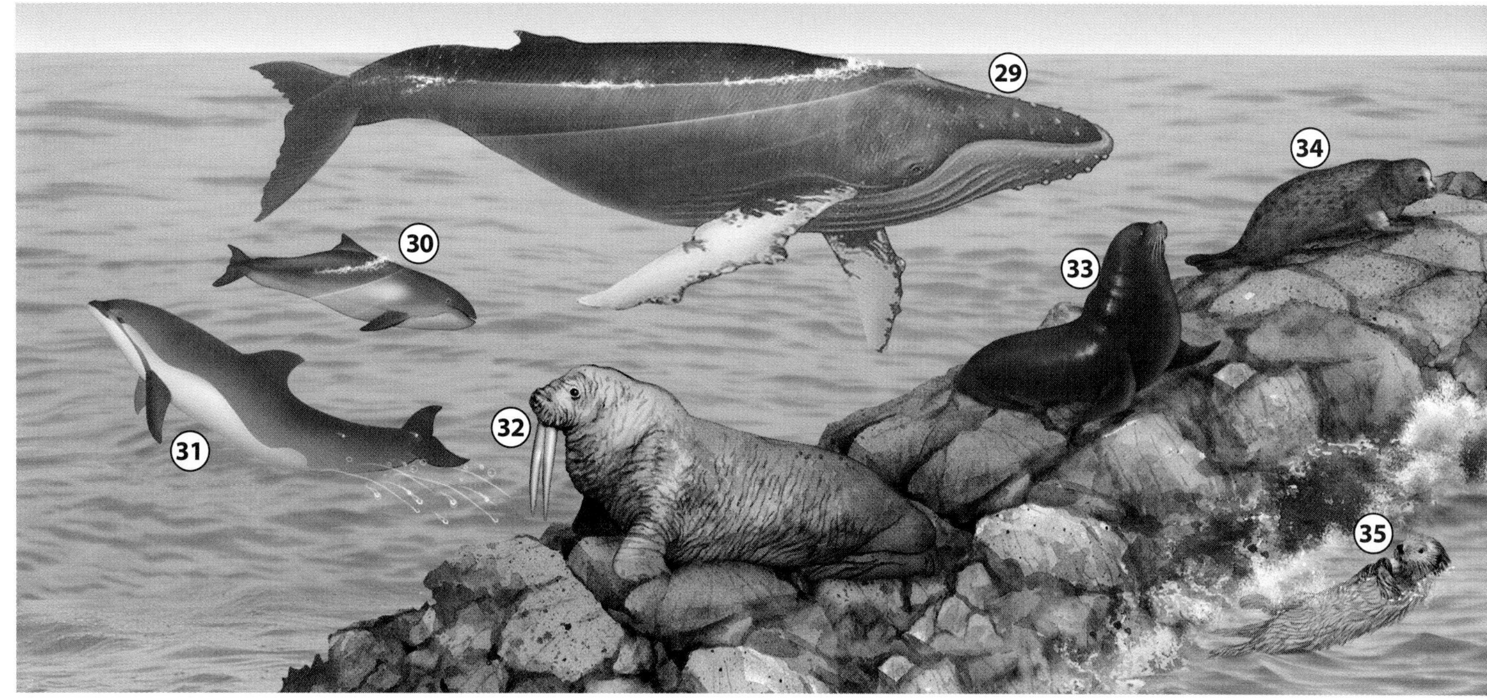


**29.** whale

**30.** porpoise

**31.** dolphin

**32.** walrus

**33.** sea lion

**34.** seal

**35.** sea otter

### Reptiles

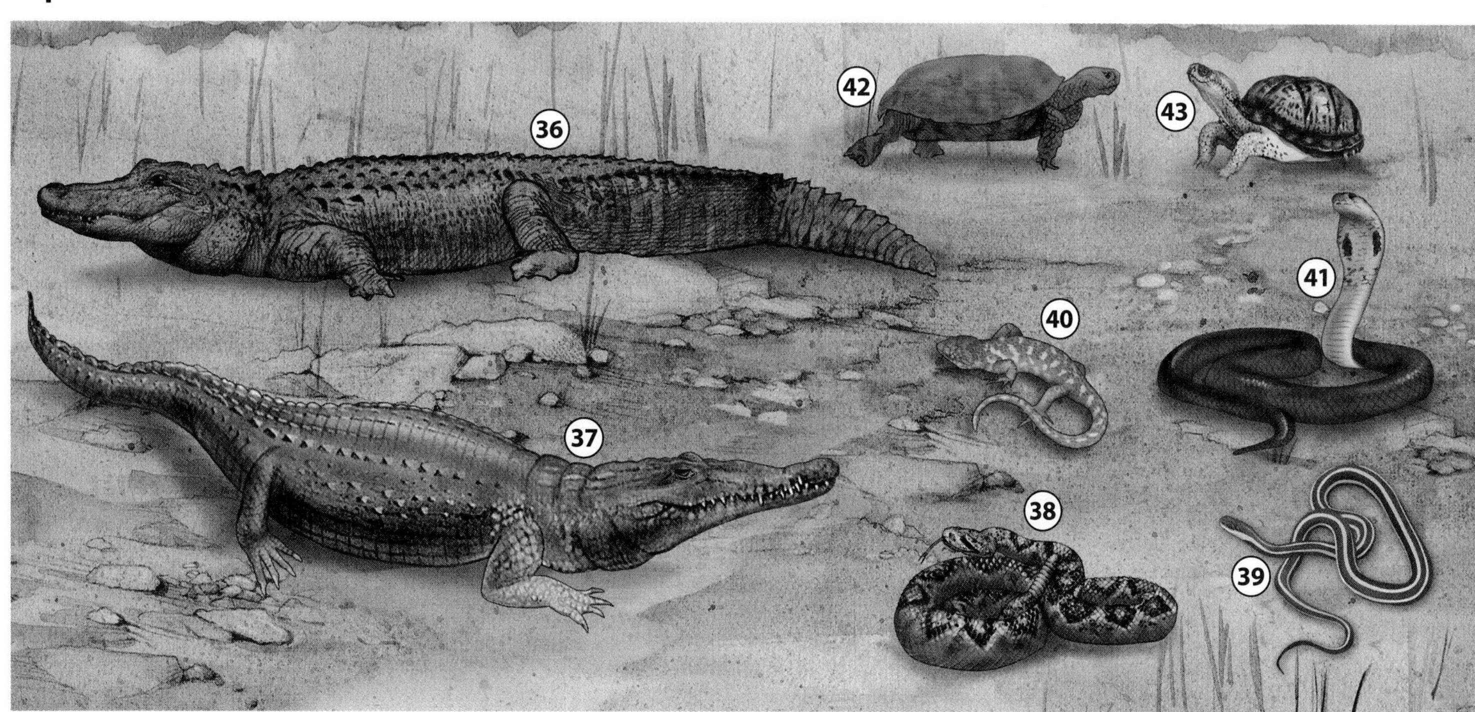


**36.** alligator

**37.** crocodile

**38.** rattlesnake

**39.** garter snake

**40.** lizard

**41.** cobra

**42.** tortoise

**43.** turtle

# Birds, Insects, and Arachnids

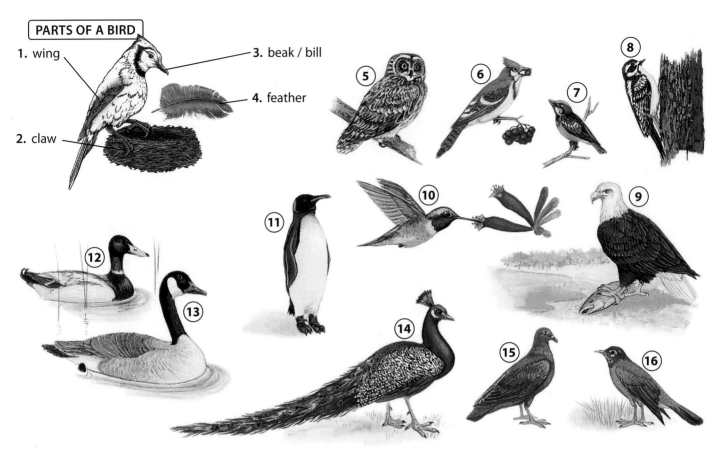

PARTS OF A BIRD

1. wing
2. claw
3. beak / bill
4. feather

5. owl
6. blue jay
7. sparrow
8. woodpecker
9. eagle
10. hummingbird
11. penguin
12. duck
13. goose
14. peacock
15. pigeon
16. robin

## Insects and Arachnids

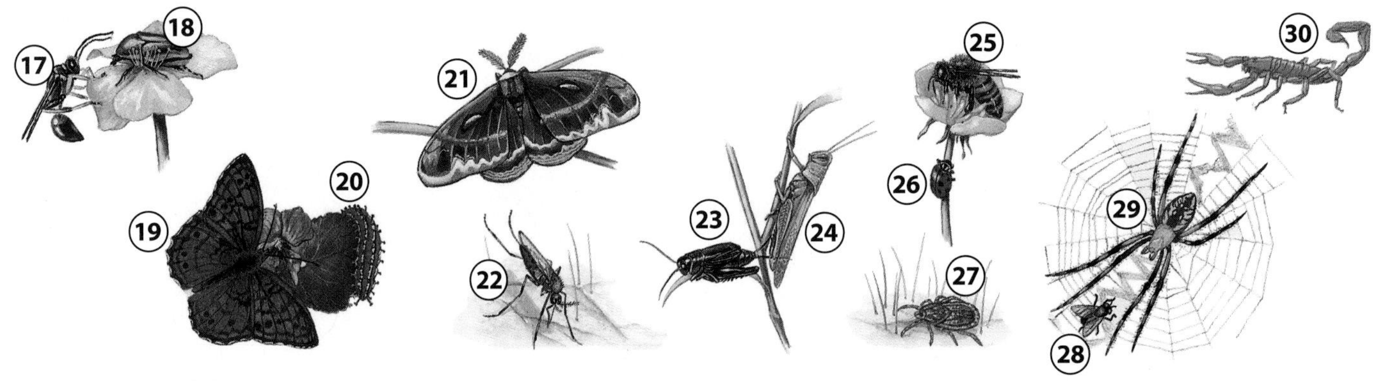

17. wasp
18. beetle
19. butterfly
20. caterpillar
21. moth
22. mosquito
23. cricket
24. grasshopper
25. honeybee
26. ladybug
27. tick
28. fly
29. spider
30. scorpion

## Farm Animals

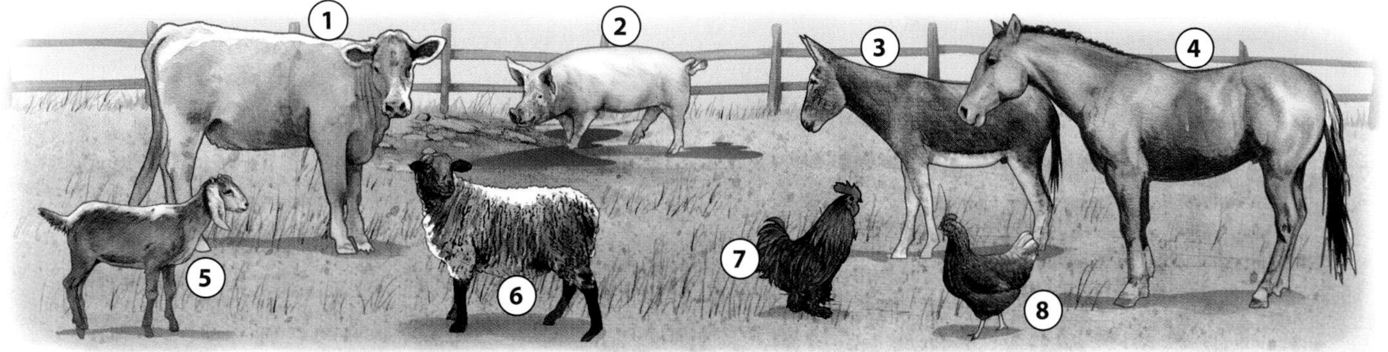

1. cow
2. pig
3. donkey
4. horse
5. goat
6. sheep
7. rooster
8. hen

## Pets

9. cat
10. kitten
11. dog
12. puppy
13. rabbit
14. guinea pig
15. parakeet
16. goldfish

## Rodents

17. rat
18. mouse
19. gopher
20. chipmunk
21. squirrel
22. prairie dog

**More vocabulary**

**domesticated:** animals that work for and / or live with people

**wild:** animals that live away from people

**Ask your classmates. Share the answers.**

1. Have you worked with farm animals? Which ones?
2. Are you afraid of rodents? Which ones?
3. Do you have a pet? What kind?

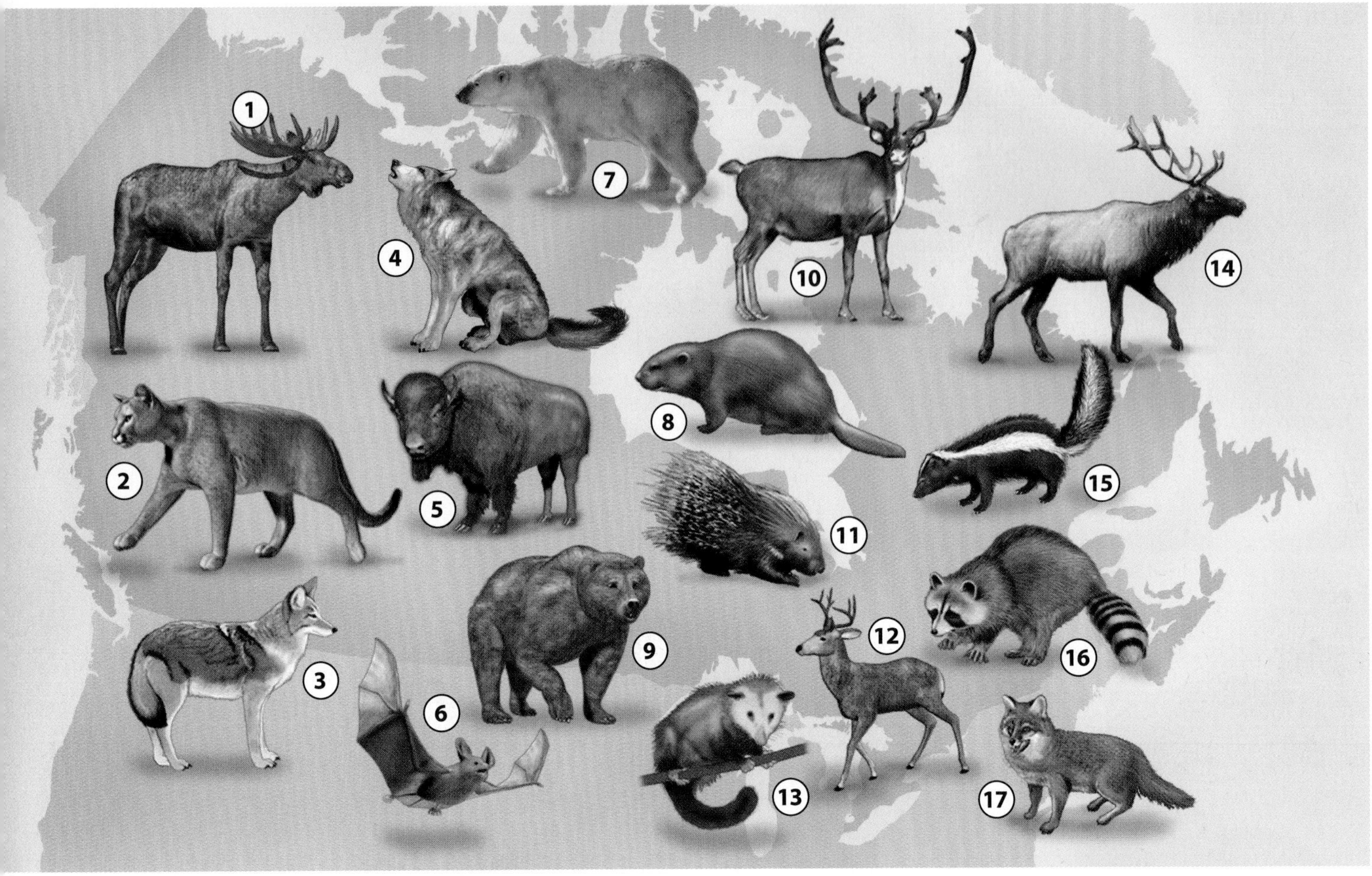

1. moose
2. mountain lion
3. coyote
4. wolf
5. buffalo / bison
6. bat
7. polar bear
8. beaver
9. bear
10. caribou
11. porcupine
12. deer
13. opossum
14. elk
15. skunk
16. raccoon
17. fox

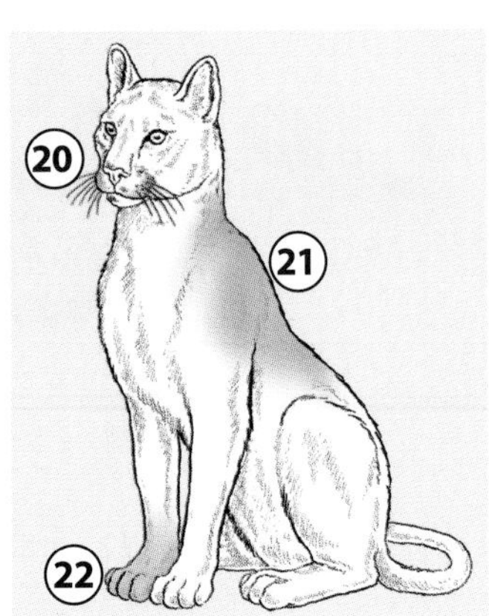

18. antlers
19. hooves
20. whiskers
21. coat / fur
22. paw
23. horn
24. tail
25. quill

26. anteater
27. llama
28. monkey
29. chimpanzee
30. rhinoceros
31. gorilla
32. hyena
33. baboon
34. giraffe
35. zebra
36. leopard
37. antelope
38. lion
39. tiger
40. camel
41. orangutan
42. panther
43. panda
44. elephant
45. hippopotamus
46. kangaroo
47. koala
48. platypus

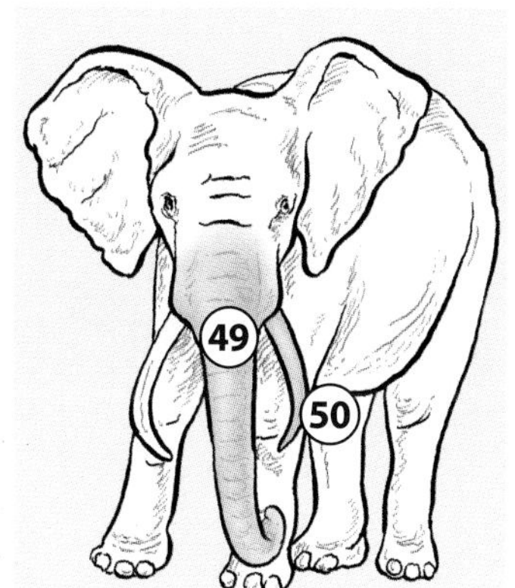


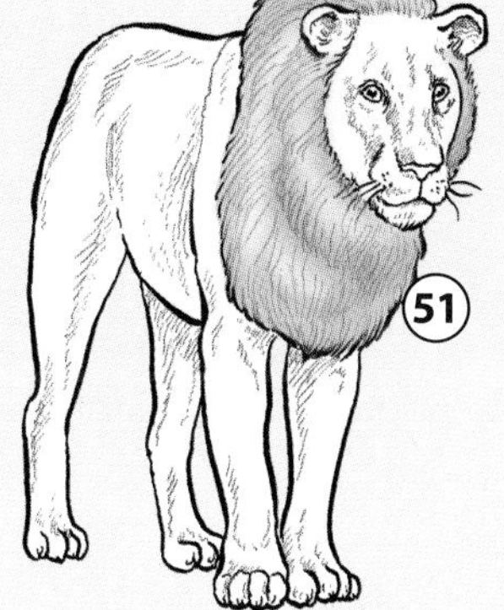

49. trunk
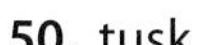
50. tusk
51. mane
52. pouch
53. hump

# Energy and Conservation

## Energy Sources

1. solar energy

2. wind power

3. natural gas

4. coal

5. hydroelectric power

6. oil / petroleum

7. geothermal energy

8. nuclear energy

9. biomass / bioenergy

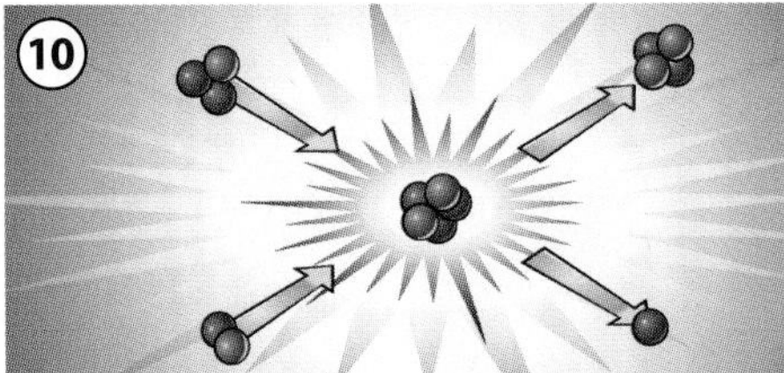

10. fusion

## Pollution

11. air pollution / smog

12. hazardous waste

13. acid rain

14. water pollution

15. radiation

16. pesticide poisoning

17. oil spill

**Ask your classmates. Share the answers.**

1. What types of things do you recycle?
2. What types of energy sources are in your area?
3. What types of pollution do you worry about?

**Think about it. Discuss.**

1. How can you save energy in the summer? winter?
2. What are some other ways that people can conserve energy or prevent pollution?

## Ways to Conserve Energy and Resources

A. **reduce** trash

B. **reuse** shopping bags

C. **recycle**

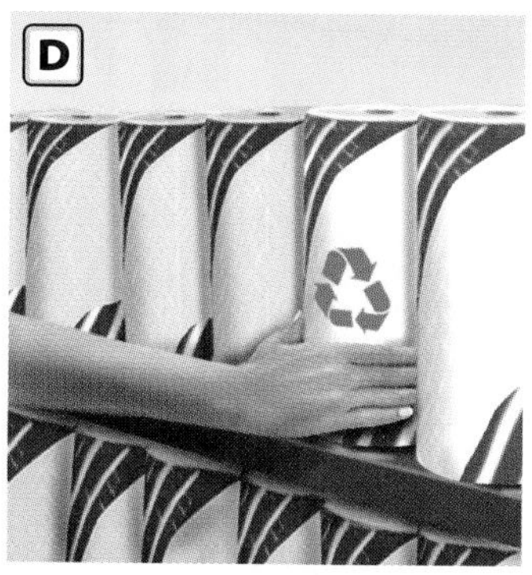

D. **buy** recycled products

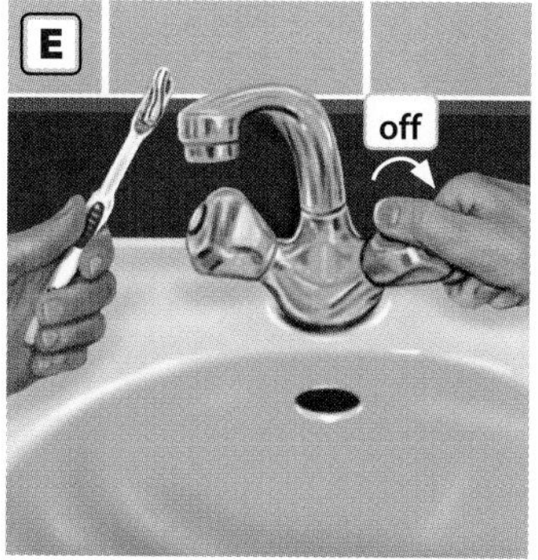


E. **save** water

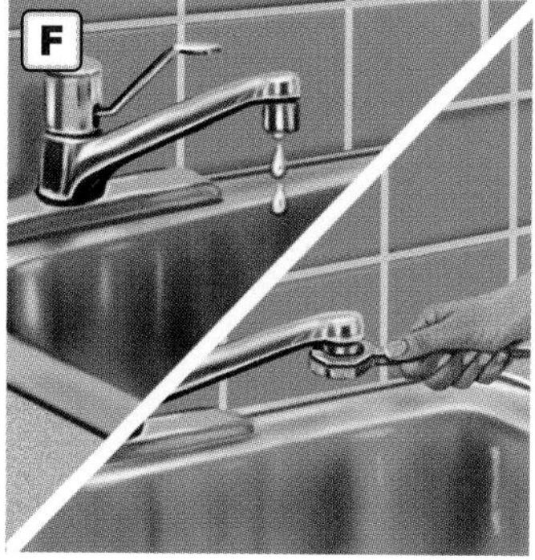

F. **fix** leaky faucets

G. **turn off** lights

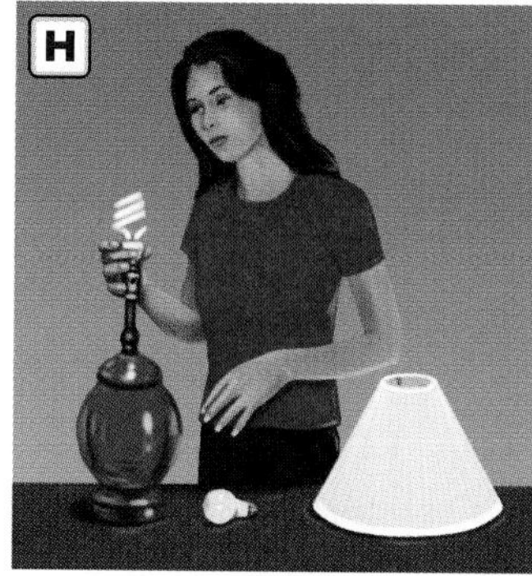

H. **use** energy-efficient bulbs

I. **carpool**

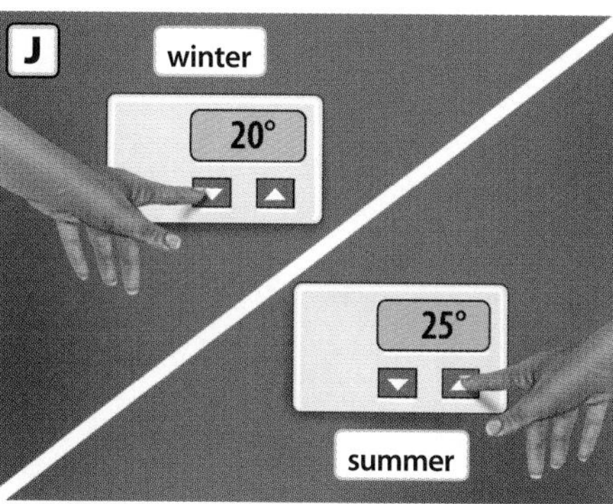


J. **adjust** the thermostat

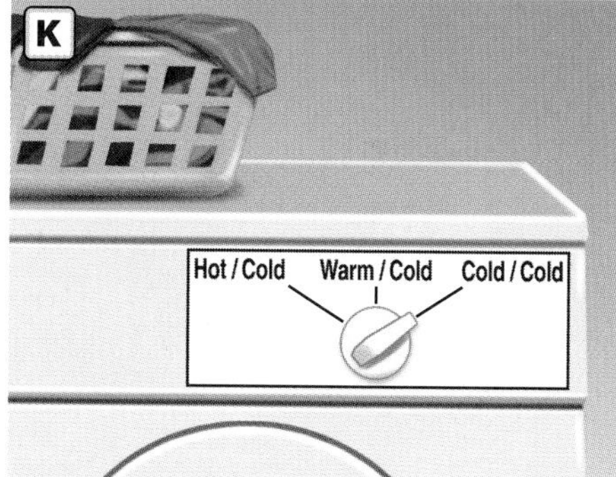


K. **wash** clothes in cold water

L. **don't litter**

M. **compost** food scraps

N. **plant** a tree

| | | | |
|---|---|---|---|
| 1. landscape | 3. landmarks | 5. park ranger | A. **take a tour** |
| 2. wildlife | 4. cave | 6. ferry | |

WAPUSK
NATIONAL PARK

A

**Look at the pictures.**
**What do you see?**

**Answer these questions.**

1. How many Canadian landmarks are in the pictures?
2. What kinds of wildlife do you see?
3. What can you do at Wapusk National Park?

 **Read the story.**

## Canadian National Parks

Canada's national parks protect the country's natural landscapes and they are home to a variety of wildlife. Some parks also have well-known landmarks that people enjoy visiting. Each park is unique, and each one is beautiful.

At Glacier National Park, in British Columbia, you can see mountain goats, mountain caribou, and grizzly bears. If you are adventurous, you can explore the Nakimu Caves.

Gros Morne, in Newfoundland and Labrador, is a great place to cross-country ski or learn about the area from a park ranger. Many people get to this park on a ferry.

A lot of polar bears live in Wapusk National Park, Manitoba. If you take a tour of the park, you might get to see one!

There are national parks in every province and territory. Go online for information about a park near you.

**Think about it.**

1. Why are national parks important?
2. Imagine you are a park ranger at a national park. Give your classmates a tour of the landmarks and wildlife.

1. zoo
2. movies
3. botanical garden
4. bowling alley
5. rock concert
6. swap meet / flea market
7. aquarium

File Edit View History Bookmarks Tools

# Places to Go in Our City

**Listen and point. Take turns.**

**A:** *Point to* *<u>the zoo</u>*.

**B:** *Point to* *<u>the flea market</u>*.

**A:** *Point to* *<u>the rock concert</u>*.

**Dictate to your partner. Take turns.**

**A:** *Write these words:* *<u>zoo, movies, aquarium</u>*.

**B:** *<u>Zoo, movies</u>, and what?*

**A:** *<u>Aquarium</u>*.

8. play
9. art gallery
10. amusement park
11. opera
12. nightclub
13. county fair
14. classical concert

**Ways to make plans using *Let's go***

***Let's go*** *to* *the amusement park* *tomorrow.*
***Let's go*** *to* *the opera* *on Saturday.*
***Let's go*** *to* *the movies* *tonight.*

**Pair practice. Make new conversations.**

**A:** *Let's go to the zoo this afternoon.*
**B:** *OK. And let's go to the movies tonight.*
**A:** *That sounds like a good plan.*

# The Park and Playground

1. ball field
2. cyclist
3. bike path
4. jump rope
5. fountain
6. tennis court
7. skateboard
8. picnic table
9. water fountain
10. bench
11. swings
12. tricycle
13. slide
14. jungle gym
15. sandbox
16. see-saw

A. **pull** the wagon

B. **push** the swing

C. **climb** the bars

D. **picnic / have** a picnic

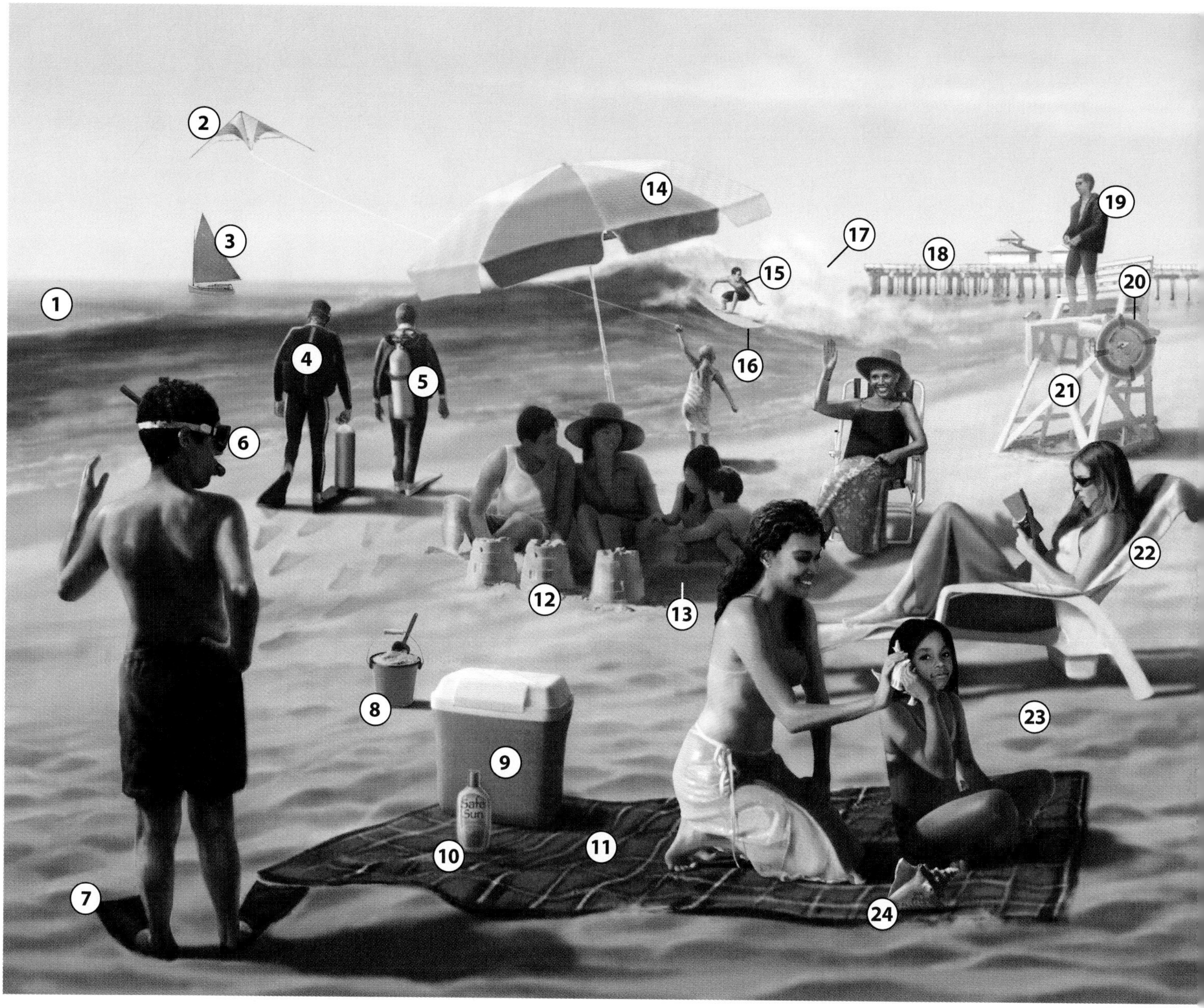

1. ocean / water
2. kite
3. sailboat
4. wetsuit
5. scuba tank
6. diving mask
7. fins
8. pail / bucket
9. cooler
10. sunscreen / sunblock
11. blanket
12. sandcastle
13. shade
14. beach umbrella
15. surfer
16. surfboard
17. wave
18. pier
19. lifeguard
20. life preserver
21. lifeguard station
22. beach chair
23. sand
24. seashell

**More vocabulary**

**seaweed:** a plant that grows in the ocean

**tide:** the level of the ocean. The tide goes in and out every 12 hours.

**Ask your classmates. Share the answers.**

1. Do you like to go to the beach?
2. Are there famous beaches in your native country?
3. Do you prefer to be on the sand or in the water?

# Outdoor Recreation

1. boating
2. rafting
3. canoeing
4. fishing
5. camping
6. backpacking
7. hiking
8. mountain biking
9. horseback riding

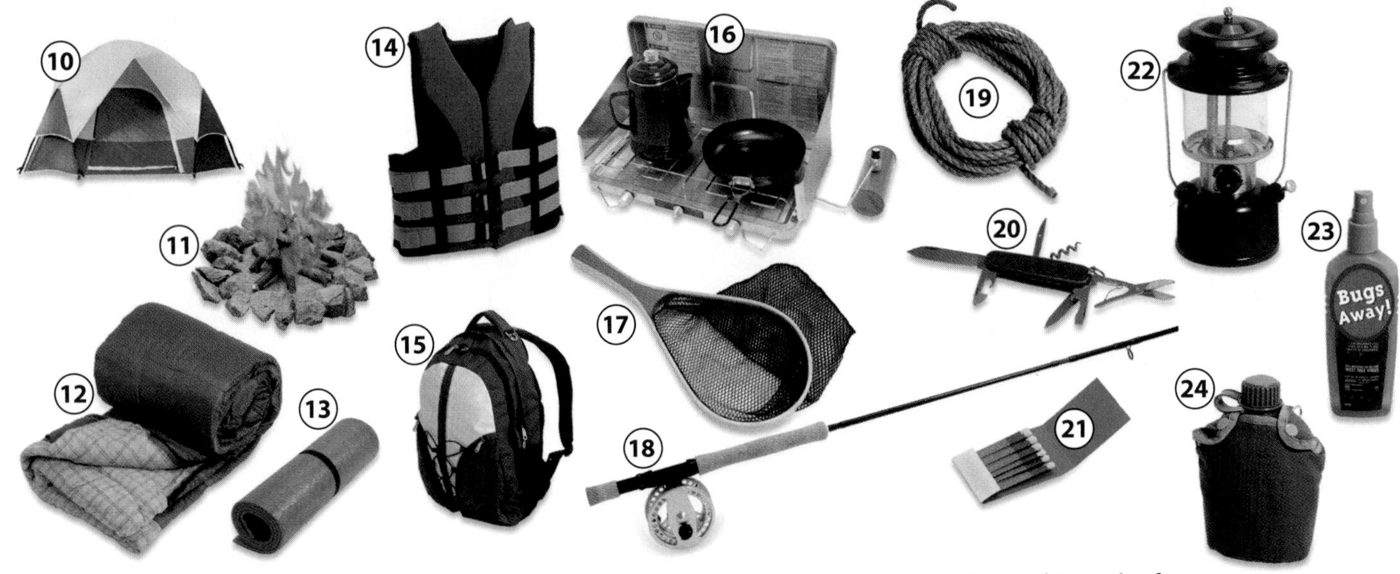


10. tent
11. campfire
12. sleeping bag
13. foam pad
14. life vest
15. backpack
16. camping stove
17. fishing net
18. fishing pole
19. rope
20. multi-use knife
21. matches
22. lantern
23. insect repellent
24. canteen

1. downhill skiing

2. snowboarding

3. cross-country skiing

4. ice skating

5. figure skating

6. sledding

7. water skiing

8. sailing

9. surfing

10. windsurfing

11. snorkelling

12. scuba diving

**More vocabulary**

**speed skating:** racing while ice skating
**windsurfing:** sailboarding

**Ask your classmates. Share the answers.**

1. Which of these sports do you like?
2. Which of these sports would you like to learn?
3. Which of these sports is the most fun to watch?

# Individual Sports

1. archery

2. billiards / pool

3. bowling

4. boxing

5. cycling / biking

6. badminton

7. fencing

8. golf

9. gymnastics

10. inline skating

11. martial arts

12. racquetball

13. skateboarding

14. table tennis

15. tennis

16. weightlifting

17. wrestling

18. track and field

19. horse racing

**Pair practice. Make new conversations.**

**A:** *What sports do you like?*
**B:** *I like bowling. What do you like?*
**A:** *I like gymnastics.*

**Think about it. Discuss.**

1. Why do people like to watch sports?
2. Which sports can be dangerous?
3. Why do people play dangerous sports?

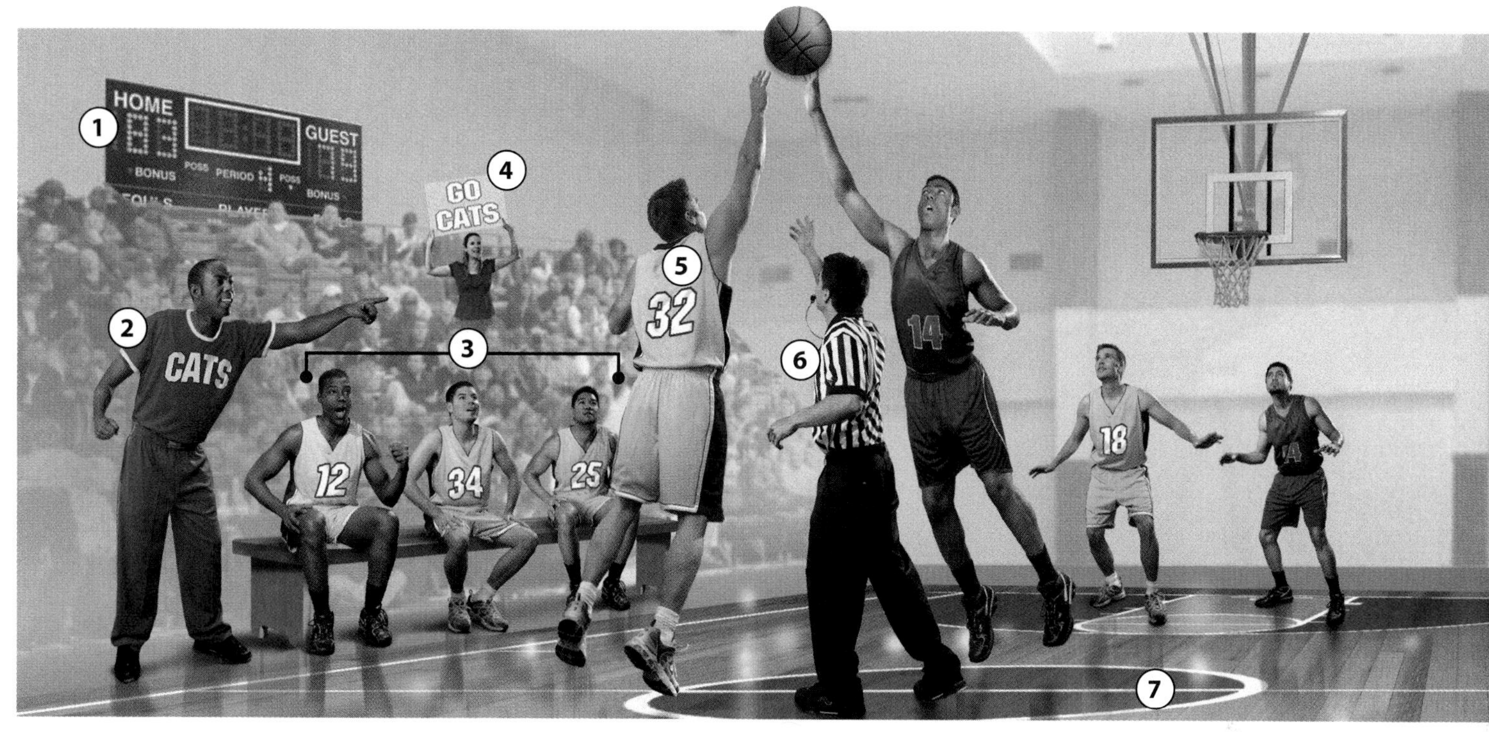


1. score
2. coach
3. team
4. fan
5. player
6. official / referee
7. basketball court

8. basketball

9. baseball

10. softball

11. football

12. soccer

13. hockey

14. volleyball

15. water polo

**More Vocabulary**

**win:** to have the best score
**lose:** the opposite of win
**tie:** to have the same score
**captain:** the team leader
**umpire:** the name of the referee in baseball
**Little League:** a baseball and softball program for children

# Sports Verbs

A. pitch
B. hit
C. throw
D. catch
E. kick
F. tackle
G. pass
H. shoot
I. jump
J. dribble
K. dive
L. swim
M. stretch
N. exercise / work out
O. bend
P. serve
Q. swing
R. start
S. race
T. finish
U. skate
V. ski

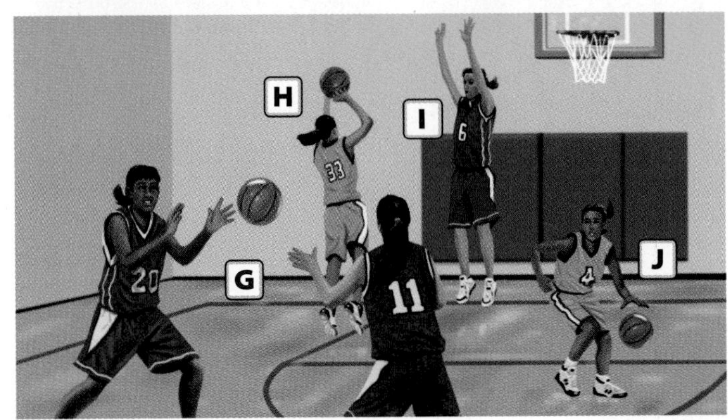

**Use the new words.**
Look on page 229. Name the actions you see.

**A:** *He's throwing.*
**B:** *She's jumping.*

**Ways to talk about your sports skills**

*I can throw, but I can't catch.*
*I swim well, but I don't dive well.*
*I'm good at skating, but I'm terrible at skiing.*

1. golf club
2. tennis racquet
3. volleyball
4. basketball
5. bowling ball
6. bow
7. target
8. arrow
9. ice skates
10. inline skates
11. hockey stick
12. soccer ball
13. shin guards
14. baseball bat
15. catcher's mask
16. uniform
17. glove
18. baseball
19. football helmet
20. shoulder pads
21. football
22. weights
23. snowboard
24. skis
25. ski poles
26. ski boots
27. flying disc*

* **Note:** one brand is Frisbee®, of Wham-O, Inc.

**Use the new words.**

Look at pages 228–229. Name the sports equipment you see.

**A:** *Those are ice skates.*

**B:** *That's a football.*

**Ask your classmates. Share the answers.**

1. Do you own any sports equipment? What kind?
2. What do you want to buy at this store?
3. Where is the best place to buy sports equipment?

# Hobbies and Games

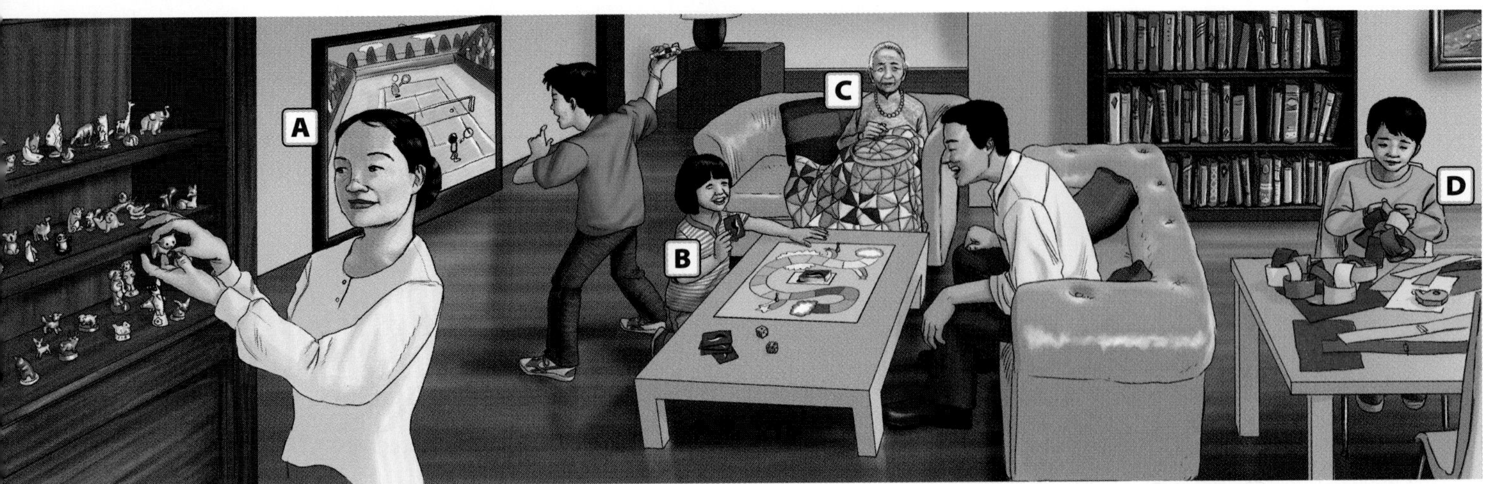


A. **collect** things

B. **play** games

C. **quilt**

D. **do** crafts

1. figurine
2. baseball cards
3. video game console
4. video game controller
5. board game
6. dice
7. checkers
8. chess
9. model kit
10. acrylic paint
11. glue stick
12. construction paper
13. doll-making kit
14. woodworking kit
15. quilt block
16. rotary cutter

**Grammar Point:** *How often do you play cards?*

*I play **all the time.** (every day)*
*I play **sometimes.** (once a month)*
*I **never** play. (0 times)*

**Pair practice. Make new conversations.**

**A:** *How often do you do your hobbies?*
**B:** *I play games all the time. I love chess.*
**A:** *Really? I never play chess.*

E. **paint**

F. **knit**

G. **pretend**

H. **play** cards

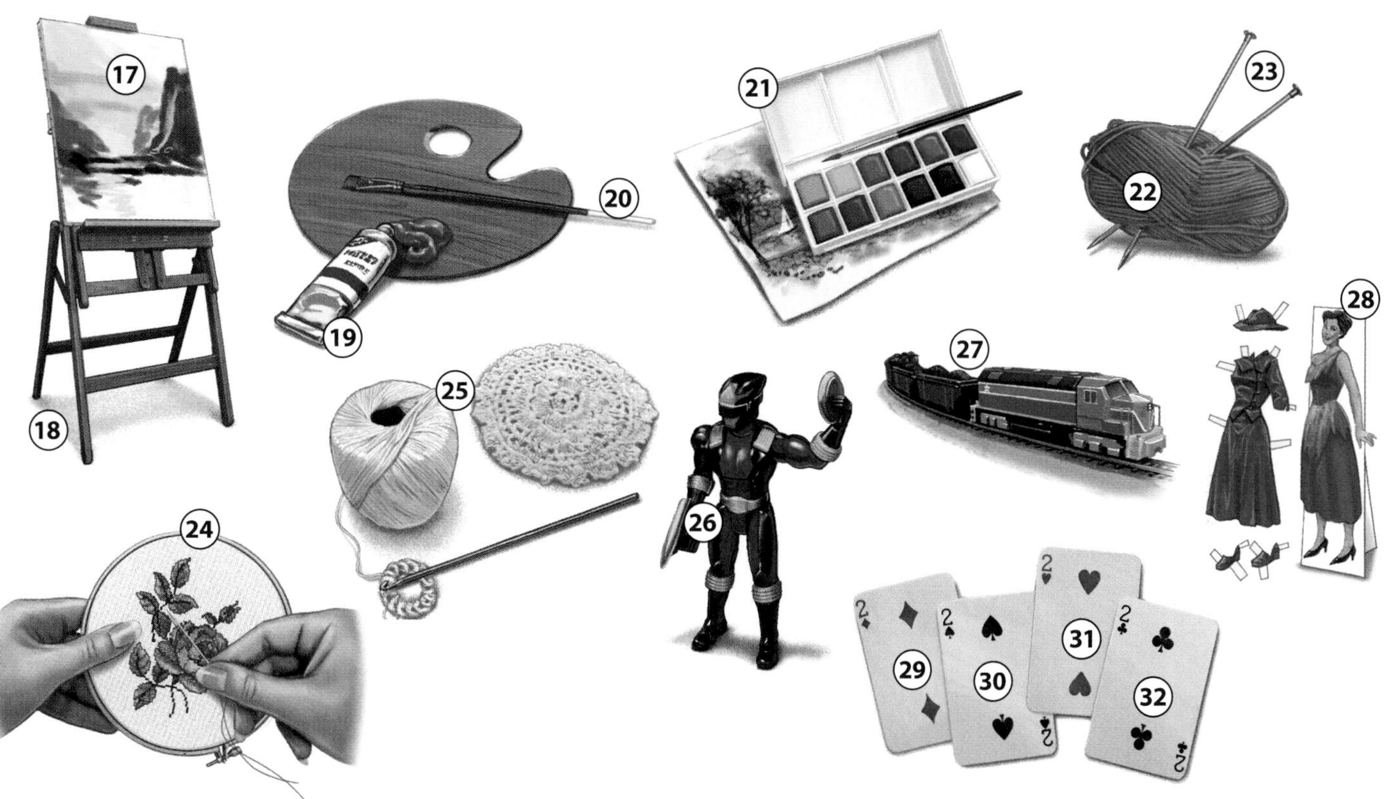


17. canvas
18. easel
19. oil paint
20. paintbrush
21. watercolour
22. yarn
23. knitting needles
24. embroidery
25. crochetting
26. action figure
27. model trains
28. paper dolls
29. diamonds
30. spades
31. hearts
32. clubs

**Ways to talk about hobbies and games**

*This board game is **interesting**. It makes me think.*
*That video game is **boring**. Nothing happens.*
*I love to play cards. It's **fun** to play with my friends.*

**Ask your classmates. Share the answers.**

1. Do you collect anything? What?
2. Which games do you like to play?
3. What hobbies did you have as a child?

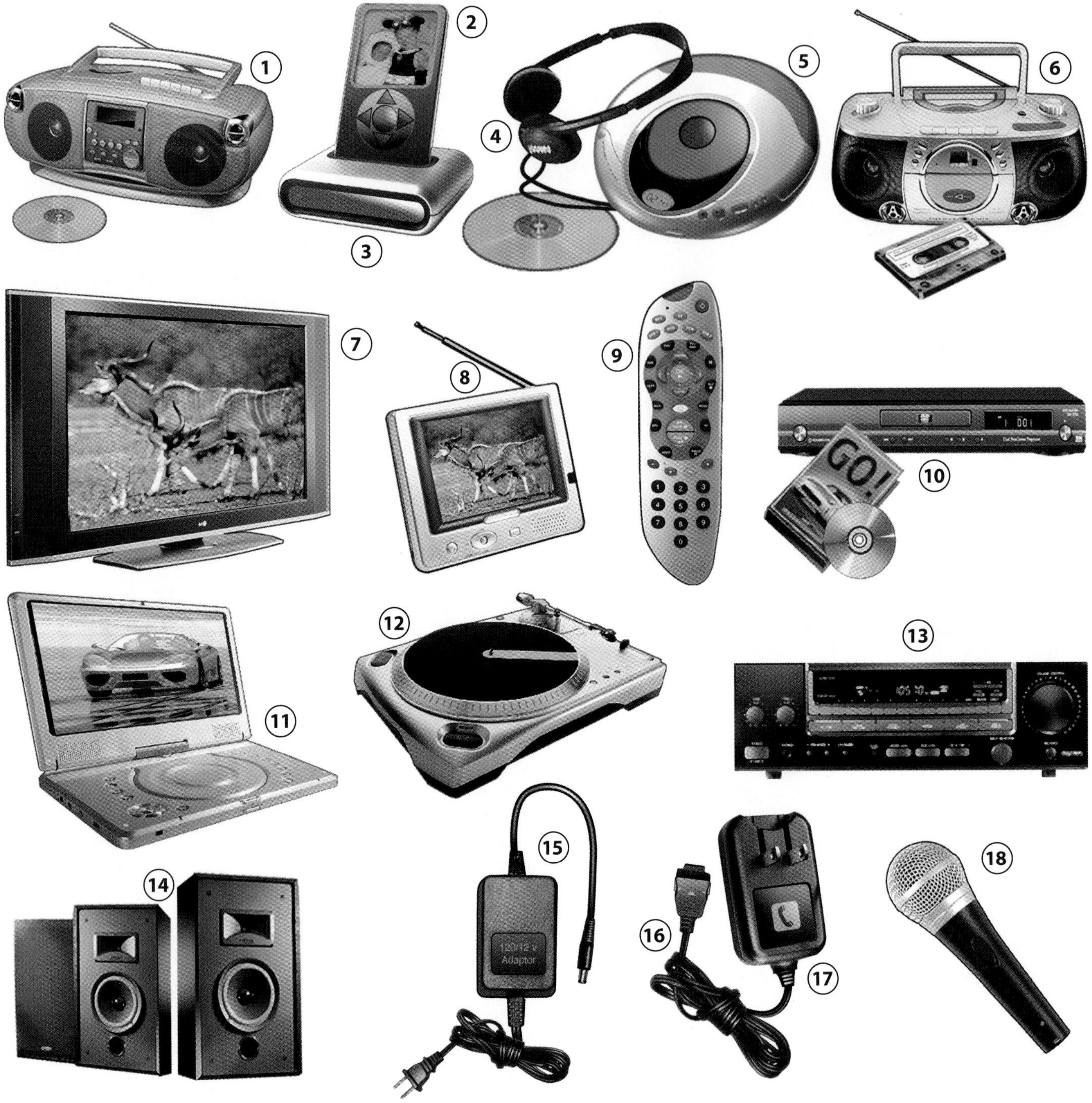

# Electronics and Photography

1. CD boom box
2. MP3 player
3. dock
4. headphones
5. personal CD player
6. portable cassette player
7. flat screen TV / flat panel TV
8. portable TV
9. universal remote
10. DVD player
11. portable DVD player
12. turntable
13. tuner
14. speakers
15. adapter
16. plug
17. charger
18. microphone

19. digital camera
20. memory card
21. film camera / 35mm camera
22. film
23. zoom lens
24. camcorder
25. tripod
26. battery pack
27. battery charger
28. camera case
29. LCD projector
30. screen

31. photo album
32. digital photo album
33. out of focus
34. overexposed
35. underexposed

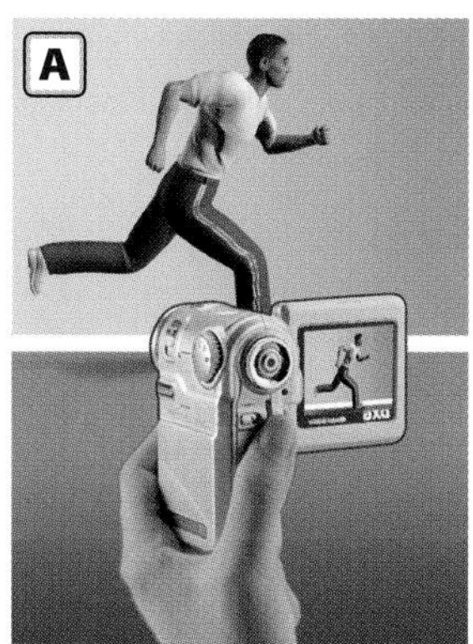

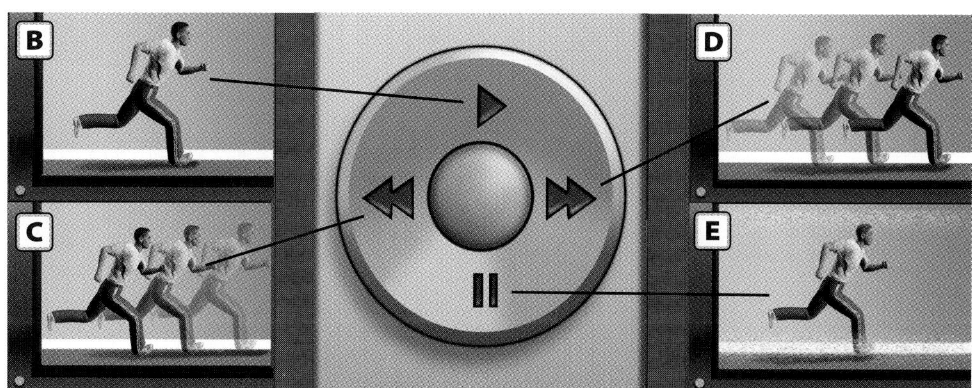

A. **record**

B. **play**

C. **rewind**

D. **fast forward**

E. **pause**

## Types of TV Programs

1. news program

2. sitcom (situation comedy)

3. cartoon

4. talk show

5. soap opera

6. reality show

7. nature program

8. game show

9. children's program

10. shopping program

11. sports program

12. drama

## Types of Movies

13. comedy

14. tragedy

15. western

16. romance

17. horror story

18. science fiction story

19. action story / adventure story

20. mystery / suspense

## Types of Music

21. classical

22. blues

23. rock

24. jazz

25. pop

26. hip hop

27. country

28. R&B / soul

29. folk

30. gospel

31. reggae

32. world music

A. **play** an instrument

B. **sing** a song

C. **conduct** an orchestra

D. **be** in a rock band

**Woodwinds**

1. flute
2. clarinet
3. oboe
4. bassoon
5. saxophone

**Strings**

6. violin
7. cello
8. bass
9. guitar

**Brass**

10. trombone
11. trumpet / horn
12. tuba
13. French horn

**Percussion**

14. piano
15. xylophone
16. drums
17. tambourine

**Other Instruments**

18. electric keyboard
19. accordion
20. organ
21. harmonica

1. parade
2. float
3. confetti
4. couple
5. card
6. heart
7. fireworks
8. flag
9. feast
10. turkey
11. mask
12. jack-o'-lantern
13. costume
14. candy
15. ornament
16. Christmas tree
17. candy cane
18. string lights

*Thanksgiving is on the second Monday in October.

1. decorations
2. deck
3. present / gift

A. **videotape**
B. **make** a wish
C. **blow out**
D. **hide**
E. **bring**
F. **wrap**

## Look at the picture. What do you see?

## Answer the questions.

1. What kinds of decorations do you see?
2. What are people doing at this birthday party?
3. What wish did the teenager make?
4. How many presents did people bring?

## Read the story.

### A Birthday Party

Today is Lou and Gani Bombata's birthday barbecue. There are decorations around the backyard, and food and drinks on the deck. There are also presents. Everyone in the Bombata family likes to bring presents.

Right now, it's time for cake. Gani is blowing out the candles, and Lou is making a wish. Lou's mom wants to videotape everyone, but she can't find Lou's brother, Todd. Todd hates to sing, so he always hides for the birthday song.

Lou's sister, Amaka, has to wrap some gifts. She doesn't want Lou to see. Amaka isn't worried. She knows her family loves to sing. She can put her gifts on the present table before they finish the first song.

## Think about it.

1. What wish do you think Gani made?
2. What kinds of presents do you give to relatives? What kinds of presents can you give to friends or co-workers?

# Verb Guide

Verbs in English are either regular or irregular in the past tense and past participle forms.

**Regular Verbs**

The regular verbs below are marked 1, 2, 3, or 4 according to four different spelling patterns. (See page 244 for the irregular verbs which do not follow any of these patterns.)

| *Spelling Patterns for the Past and the Past Participle* | *Example* | |
|---|---|---|
| 1. Add -ed to the end of the verb. | **ASK** | **ASKED** |
| 2. Add -d to the end of the verb. | **LIVE** | **LIVED** |
| 3. Double the final consonant and add -ed to the end of the verb. | **DROP** | **DROPPED** |
| 4. Drop the final y and add -ied to the end of the verb. | **CRY** | **CRIED** |

## The Oxford Picture Dictionary List of Regular Verbs

accept (1)
add (1)
address (1)
adjust (1)
agree (2)
answer (1)
apologize (2)
appear (1)
applaud (1)
apply (4)
arrange (2)
arrest (1)
arrive (2)
ask (1)
assemble (2)
assist (1)
attach (1)
bake (2)
bank (1)
bargain (1)
bathe (2)
board (1)
boil (1)
borrow (1)
bow (1)
brainstorm (1)
breathe (2)
browse (2)
brush (1)
bubble (2)
buckle (2)
burn (1)
bus (1)
calculate (2)
call (1)
capitalize (2)
carpool (1)
carry (4)
cash (1)
celebrate (2)
change (2)
check (1)
chill (1)
choke (2)
chop (3)
circle (2)
claim (1)
clean (1)
clear (1)
click (1)
climb (1)
close (2)
collate (2)
collect (1)
colour (1)
comb (1)
comfort (1)
commit (3)
compliment (1)
compost (1)
conceal (1)
conduct (1)
convert (1)
convict (1)
cook (1)
copy (4)
correct (1)
cough (1)
count (1)
cross (1)
cry (4)
dance (2)
debate (2)
decline (2)
delete (2)
deliver (1)
design (1)
dial (1)
dice (2)
dictate (2)
die (2)
disagree (2)
discipline (2)
discuss (1)
dive (2)
divide (2)
dress (1)
dribble (2)
drill (1)
drop (3)
drown (1)
dry (4)
dust (1)
dye (2)
edit (1)
empty (4)
enter (1)
erase (2)
evacuate (2)
examine (2)
exchange (2)
exercise (2)
expire (2)
explain (1)
exterminate (2)
fasten (1)
fast forward (1)
fax (1)
fertilize (2)
fill (1)
finish (1)
fix (1)
floss (1)
fold (1)
follow (1)
garden (1)
gargle (2)
graduate (2)
grate (2)
grease (2)
greet (1)
hail (1)
hammer (1)
hand (1)
harvest (1)
help (1)
hire (2)
hug (3)
immigrate (2)
indent (1)
inquire (2)
insert (1)
inspect (1)
install (1)
introduce (2)
invite (2)
iron (1)
jaywalk (1)
join (1)
jump (1)
kick (1)
kiss (1)
knit (3)
label (1)
land (1)
laugh (1)
learn (1)
lengthen (1)

lift (1)
listen (1)
litter (1)
live (2)
load (1)
lock (1)
look (1)
mail (1)
manufacture (2)
match (1)
measure (2)
microwave (2)
milk (1)
misbehave (2)
miss (1)
mix (1)
mop (3)
move (2)
mow (1)
multiply (4)
negotiate (2)
network (1)
numb (1)
nurse (2)
obey (1)
observe (2)
offer (1)
open (1)
operate (2)
order (1)
organize (2)
overdose (2)
pack (1)
paint (1)
park (1)
participate (2)
pass (1)
pause (2)
peel (1)
perm (1)
pick (1)
pitch (1)
plan (3)
plant (1)
play (1)
polish (1)
pour (1)
praise (2)
preheat (1)
prepare (2)
prescribe (2)
press (1)
pretend (1)
print (1)
program (3)
protect (1)
pull (1)
purchase (2)
push (1)
quilt (1)
race (2)
raise (2)
rake (2)
receive (2)
record (1)
recycle (2)
redecorate (2)
reduce (2)
register (1)
relax (1)
remain (1)
remove (2)
renew (1)
repair (1)
replace (2)
report (1)
request (1)
retire (2)
return (1)
reuse (2)
revise (2)
rinse (2)
rock (1)
sauté (1)
save (2)
scan (3)
schedule (2)
scrub (3)
seat (1)
select (1)
sentence (2)
separate (2)
serve (2)
share (2)
shave (2)
ship (3)
shop (3)
shorten (1)
sign (1)
simmer (1)
skate (2)
ski (1)
slice (2)
smell (1)
smile (2)
smoke (2)
sneeze (2)
solve (2)
sort (1)
spell (1)
spoon (1)
staple (2)
start (1)
state (2)
stay (1)
steam (1)
stir (3)
stop (3)
stow (1)
stretch (1)
study (4)
submit (3)
subtract (1)
supervise (2)
swallow (1)
tackle (2)
talk (1)
taste (2)
thank (1)
tie (2)
touch (1)
transcribe (2)
transfer (3)
translate (2)
travel (1)
trim (3)
try (4)
turn (1)
type (2)
underline (2)
undress (1)
unload (1)
unpack (1)
unscramble (2)
use (2)
vacuum (1)
videotape (2)
volunteer (1)
vomit (1)
vote (2)
wait (1)
walk (1)
wash (1)
watch (1)
water (1)
wave (2)
weed (1)
weigh (1)
wipe (2)
work (1)
wrap (3)

### Irregular Verbs

These verbs have irregular endings in the past and/or the past participle.

## The Oxford Picture Dictionary List of Irregular Verbs

| simple | past | past participle |
|---|---|---|
| be | was | been |
| beat | beat | beaten |
| become | became | become |
| bend | bent | bent |
| bleed | bled | bled |
| blow | blew | blown |
| break | broke | broken |
| bring | brought | brought |
| buy | bought | bought |
| catch | caught | caught |
| choose | chose | chosen |
| come | came | come |
| cut | cut | cut |
| do | did | done |
| draw | drew | drawn |
| drink | drank | drunk |
| drive | drove | driven |
| eat | ate | eaten |
| fall | fell | fallen |
| feed | fed | fed |
| feel | felt | felt |
| find | found | found |
| fly | flew | flown |
| get | got | gotten |
| give | gave | given |
| go | went | gone |
| hang | hung | hung |
| have | had | had |
| hear | heard | heard |
| hide | hid | hidden |
| hit | hit | hit |
| hold | held | held |
| keep | kept | kept |
| lay | laid | laid |
| leave | left | left |
| lend | lent | lent |
| let | let | let |

| simple | past | past participle |
|---|---|---|
| make | made | made |
| meet | met | met |
| pay | paid | paid |
| picnic | picnicked | picnicked |
| proofread | proofread | proofread |
| put | put | put |
| read | read | read |
| rewind | rewound | rewound |
| rewrite | rewrote | rewritten |
| ride | rode | ridden |
| run | ran | run |
| say | said | said |
| see | saw | seen |
| seek | sought | sought |
| sell | sold | sold |
| send | sent | sent |
| set | set | set |
| sew | sewed | sewn |
| shake | shook | shaken |
| shoot | shot | shot |
| show | showed | shown |
| sing | sang | sung |
| sit | sat | sat |
| speak | spoke | spoken |
| stand | stood | stood |
| steal | stole | stolen |
| sweep | swept | swept |
| swim | swam | swum |
| swing | swung | swung |
| take | took | taken |
| teach | taught | taught |
| think | thought | thought |
| throw | threw | thrown |
| wake | woke | woken |
| withdraw | withdrew | withdrawn |
| write | wrote | written |

# Index

## Index Key

### *Font*

**bold** type = verbs or verb phrases (example: **catch**)
ordinary type = all other parts of speech (example: baseball)
ALL CAPS = unit titles (example: MATHEMATICS)
Initial caps = subunit titles (example: Equivalencies)

### *Symbols*

✦ = word found in exercise band at bottom of page

### *Numbers/Letters*

first number in **bold** type = page on which word appears
second number, or letter, following number in **bold** type = item number on page
(examples: cool [ko͞ol] **13**-5 means that the word *cool* is item number 5 on page 13;
across [ə krŏs′] **153**–G means that the word *across* is item G on page 153).

## Pronunciation Guide

The index includes a pronunciation guide for all the words and phrases illustrated in the book. This guide uses symbols commonly found in dictionaries for native speakers. These symbols, unlike those used in pronunciation systems such as the International Phonetic Alphabet, tend to use English spelling patterns and so should help you to become more aware of the connections between written English and spoken English.

### *Consonants*

[b] as in back [băk]
[ch] as in cheek [chēk]
[d] as in date [dāt]
[dh] as in this [dhĭs]
[f] as in face [fās]
[g] as in gas [găs]
[h] as in half [hăf]
[j] as in jam [jăm]
[k] as in key [kē]
[l] as in leaf [lēf]
[m] as in match [măch]
[n] as in neck [nĕk]
[ng] as in ring [rĭng]
[p] as in park [pärk]
[r] as in rice [rīs]
[s] as in sand [sănd]
[sh] as in shoe [sho͞o]
[t] as in tape [tāp]
[th] as in three [thrē]
[v] as in vine [vīn]
[w] as in wait [wāt]
[y] as in yams [yămz]
[z] as in zoo [zo͞o]
[zh] as in measure [mĕzh′ər]

### *Vowels*

[ā] as in bake [bāk]
[ă] as in back [băk]
[ä] as in car [kär]
[ē] as in beat [bēt]
[ĕ] as in bed [bĕd]
[ë] as in bear [bër]
[ī] as in line [līn]
[ĭ] as in lip [lĭp]
[ï] as in near [nïr]
[ō] as in cold [kōld]
[ŏ] as in box [bŏks]
[ö] as in short [shört]
[o͞o] as in cool [ko͞ol]
[o͝o] as in cook [ko͝ok]
[ow] as in cow [kow]
[oy] as in boy [boy]
[ŭ] as in cut [kŭt]
[ü] as in curb [kürb]
[ə] as in above [ə bŭv′]

All the pronunciation symbols used are alphabetical except for the schwa [ə]. The schwa is the most frequent vowel sound in English. If you use the schwa appropriately in unstressed syllables, your pronunciation will sound more natural.

Vowels before [r] are shown with the symbol [ ¨ ] to call attention to the special quality that vowels have before [r]. You should listen carefully to native speakers to discover how these vowels actually sound.

### *Stress*

This index follows the system for marking stress used in many dictionaries for native speakers.

**1.** Stress is not marked if a word consisting of a single syllable occurs by itself.
**2.** Where stress is marked, two levels are distinguished:
a bold accent [**′**] is placed after each syllable with primary (or strong) stress, a light accent [′] is placed after each syllable with secondary (or weaker) stress. In phrases and other combinations of words, stress is indicated for each word as it would be pronounced within the whole phrase.

### *Syllable Boundaries*

Syllable boundaries are indicated by a single space or by a stress mark.

**Note:** The pronunciations shown in this index are based on patterns of Canadian English. There has been no attempt to represent all of the varieties of Canadian English. Students should listen to native speakers to hear how the language actually sounds in a particular region.

Abbreviations [ə brē/vē ā/shənz] **48**
abdomen [ăb/də mən] **107**–27
about [ə bowt/] **48**–B, **174**–L, **191**–E
above [ə bŭv/] **25**–4
accelerator [ək sĕl/ə rā/tər] **159**–46
**accept** [ək sĕpt/] **12**–G, **12**–I, **12** ✦
access number [ăk/sĕs/ nŭm/bər] **14**–16
Accessories [ək sĕs/ə rēz] **59, 94–95**
accident [ăk/sə dənt] **144**–2
accordion [ə kör/dē ən] **238**–19
account [ə kownt/] **132**–11, **132**–14
  account manager [ə kownt/ măn/ə jər] **132**–9
Account [ə kownt/] **132**
accountant [ə kown/tənt] **166**–1
ache [āk]
  backache [băk/āk/] **110**–5
  earache [ïr/āk/] **110**–3
  headache [hĕd/āk/] **110**–1
  stomach ache [stŭm/ək/ āk] **110**–4
  toothache [tōōth/āk/] **110**–2
acid rain [ăs/əd rān/] **218**–13
across [ə krŏs] **153**–G
acrylic paint [ə krĭl/ĭk pānt] **232**–10
action [ăk/shən]
  action figure [ăk/shən fĭg/yər] **233**–26
  action story [ăk/shən stör/ē] **237**–19
activist [ăk/tə vĭst] **199**–17
actor [ăk/tər] **166**–2
acupuncture [ăk/yə pŭngk/chər] **122**–2
acute angle [ə kyōōt/ ăng/gəl] **193**–28
ad [ăd] **48**–2, **197**–9
adapter [ə dăp/tər] **234**–15
**add** [ăd] **77**–N, **101**–B, **192**–A
address [ə drĕs/, ă/drĕs] **4**–5
  mailing address [mā/lĭng ə drĕs/, –ă/drĕs] **134**–22
  return address [rĭ türn/ ə drĕs/, –ă/drĕs] **134**–21
  website address [wĕb/sīt ə drĕs/, –ă/drĕs] **197**–4
**address** [ə drĕs/] **135**–B, **197**–C
adhesive bandage [əd hē/sĭv băn/dĭj] **117**–5
**adjust** [ə jŭst/] **219**–J
  adjustable wrench [ə jŭs/tə bəl rĕnch/] **181**–48
  adjustment [ə jŭst/mənt] **194**–22, **194**–24
administrative assistant
  [əd mĭn/ə strā/tĭv ə sĭs/tənt] **166**–3
administrator [əd mĭn/ə strā/tər] **120**–13
Administrators [əd mĭn/ə strā/tərz] **5**
admissions clerk [əd mĭ/shənz klürk/] **120**–14
ADULTS AND CHILDREN [ə dŭlts/ en chĭl/ drən, ăd/ŭlt–] **30–31**
adult school [ə dŭlt/ skōōl/, ăd/ŭlt–] **188**–8
adventure story [əd vĕn/chər stör/ē] **237**–19
aerobic exercise [ə rō/bĭk ĕk/sər sīz/] **122**–5
afraid [ə frād/] **43**–23
after [ăf/tər]
  afternoon [ăf/tər nōōn/] **18**–17
  aftershave [ăf/tər shāv/] **109**–30
  five after one [fīv/ ăf/tər wŭn/] **18**–7
  quarter after one [kwör/tər ăf/tər wŭn/] **18**–9
  ten after one [tĕn/ ăf/tər wŭn/] **18**–8
  twenty after one [twĕn/tē ăf/tər wŭn/] **18**–10
After an Emergency [ăf/tər ən ĭ mür/jən sē] **147**
Age [āj] **32**
agency [ā/jən sē] **131**–14
agent [ā/jənt] **160**–3
**agree** [ə grē/] **12**–K
agreement [ə grē/mənt] **51**–28
aid [ād]
  first aid kit [fürst/ ād/ kĭt/] **117**–1, **146**–18
  first aid manual [fürst/ ād/ măn/yōō əl] **117**–2
  hearing aid [hïr/ĭng ād/] **115**–10
aide [ād] **167**–32
AIDS (acquired immune deficiency syndrome) [ādz] / [ə kwī/rd ĭ myōōn/ də fĭ/shən sē sĭn/drōm] **111** ✦
air [ër]
  airbag [ër/ băg/] **159**–43
  air conditioner [ër/ kən dĭsh/ə nər] **159**–39
  air force [ër/ förs/] **138**–16
  air mail [ër/māl/] **134**–5
  airplane [ër/plān/] **150**–8
  airplane crash [ër/plān/ krăsh/] **144**–3
  air pollution [ër/ pə lōō/shən] **218**–11
  airport [ër/pört/] **151**–10
  air purifier [ër/ pyōōr/ə fī ər] **113**–14
Airline Terminal [ër/līn/ tür/mə nəl] **160**
Airplane [ër/plān/] **161**
AIRPORT [ër/pört/] **160–161**
Airport Transportation
  [ër/pört/ trăns/pər tā/shən] **152**
aisle [īl] **72**–6
alarm clock [ə lärm/ klŏk/] **58**–24
Alaska time [ə lăs/kə tīm/] **19**–28
album [ăl/bəm] **235**–31, **235**–32
alfalfa [ăl făl/fə] **177**–5
algebra [al/jə brə] **192**–16
allergic reaction [ə lür/jĭk rē ăk/shən] **116**–E
allergies [ăl/ər jēz] **111**–8
alley [ăl/ē] **51**–24, **222**–4
alligator [ăl/ə gā/tər] **213**–36
alphabet [ăl/fə bĕt/] **7**–13
Alterations [öl/tə rā/shənz] **100**
ALTERATIONS [öl/tə rā/shənz] **100**
Alteration Shop [öl/tə rā/shən shŏp/] **100**
aluminum foil [ə lōō/mə nəm foyl/] **72**–23
Alzheimer's disease [älts/hī mərz dĭ zēz/] **111** ✦
a.m. [ā/ĕm/] **18**–4
ambulance [ăm/byə ləns] **116**–1, **121**–34
AMERICA [ə mĕr/ə kə] **200–201**
Amphibians [ăm fĭb/ē ənz] **212**
AMPHIBIANS [ăm fĭb/ē ənz] **212–213**
amusement park [ə myōōz/mənt pärk/] **223**–10
ancient [ān/shənt] **199**–1
anemone [ə nĕ/mə nē] **212**–24
anesthesiologist [ă/nəs thē/zē ŏ/lə jĭst] **121**–35
angle [ăng/gəl] **193**–26, **193**–27, **193**–28
Angles [ăng/gəlz] **193**
angry [ăng/grē] **43**–29
animals [ăn/ə məlz] **59**–15
Animals [ăn/ə məlz] **212, 215**
ANIMALS [ăn/ə məlz] **215**
ankle [ăng/kəl] **106**–23, **110**–18
  ankle socks [ăng/kəl sŏks/] **91**–7
anklets [ăngk/ləts/] **91**–11
anniversary [ăn/ə vür/sə rē] **22**–3
**answer** [ăn/sər] **8**–L
answering machine [ăn/sə rĭng mə shēn/] **14**–17
answer sheet [ăn/sər shēt/] **10**–2
antacid [ănt ăs/əd] **113**–28
anteater [ănt/ē/tər] **217**–26
antelope [ăn/tə lōp/] **217**–37
antenna [ăn tĕ/nə, ŭn–] **14**–9
antibacterial ointment
  [ăn/tē băk tïr/ē əl oynt/mənt] **117**–11
antihistamine cream [ăn/tĭ hĭs/tə mēn krēm/] **117**–10
antiperspirant [ăn/tē pürs/pə rənt] **108**–5
antlers [ănt/lərz] **216**–18
ants [ănts] **63**–23
apartment [ə pärt/mənt] **48**–3, **48**–4
  apartment building [ə pärt/mənt bĭl/dĭng] **50**–1
  apartment number [ə pärt/mənt nŭm/bər] **4**–6
Apartment [ə pärt/mənt] **48**
Apartment Complex [ə pärt/mənt kŏm/plĕx] **51**
Apartment Entranceway [ə pärt/mənt ĕn/trəns wā/] **51**
APARTMENTS [ə pärt/məntz] **50–51**
**apologize** [ə pŏl/ə jīz/] **12**–F
apostrophe [ə pŏs/trə fē] **190**–16
**appear** [ə pïr/] **141**–C
Appearance [ə pïr/əns] **32**
**applaud** [ə plŏd/] **148**–B
apples [ăp/əlz] **68**–1
  apple juice [ăp/əl jōōs/] **73**–32
appliance repair person
  [ə plī/əns rĭ për/ pür/sən] **166**–4
appliqué [ăp/lē kā/] **99**–31
**apply** [ə plī/] **109**–P
appointment [ə poynt/mənt] **22**–4, **118**–1
  appointment book [ə poynt/mənt bŏŏk/] **183**–48
apricots [ăp/rə kŏts/] **68**–12
April [ā/prəl] **21**–28
apron [ā/prən] **92**–11, **93**–30
aquarium [ə kwër/ē əm] **222**–7
Arachnids [ə răk/nĭdz/] **214**
ARACHNIDS [ə răk/nĭdz/] **214**
archery [är/chə rē] **228**–1
architect [är/kə tĕkt/] **166**–5
area [ër/ē ə]
  area code [ër/ē ə kōd/] **4**–10, **15**–29
  boarding area [bör/dĭng ër/ē ə] **161**–9
  dining area [dī/nĭng ër/ē ə] **46**–7
  play area [plā/ ër/ē ə] **130**–11
  reception area [rĭ sĕp/shən ër/ē ə] **182**–15
  rural area [rōōr/əl ër/ē ə] **52**–4
  screening area [skrē/nĭng ër/ē ə] **160**–4
  testing area [tĕs/tĭng ër/ē ə] **136**–2
  urban area [ür/bən ër/ē ə] **52**–1
AREA [ër/ē ə] **55**
Area and Volume [ër/ē ə ən vŏl/yōōm] **193**
arm [ärm] **105**–14, **194**–23
  armchair [ärm/ chër/] **56**–22
Arm, Hand, and Fingers [ärm/ hănd/ ən fĭng/gərz] **106**
army [är/mē] **138**–15, **199**–11
around [ə rownd/] **153**–H
Around Campus [ə rownd/ kăm/pəs] **5**
**arrange** [ə rānj/] **49**–Q
**arrest** [ə rĕst/] **141**–A
arrival [ə rī/vəl] **161**–7, **161** ✦
**arrive** [ə rīv/] **160**–K

arrow [ër/ō] **231**–8
arson [är/sən] **142**–7
artery [är/tə rē] **107**–36
arthritis [är thrī/təs] **111**–16
artichokes [är/tə chōks/] **69**–22
artist [är/tĭst] **166**–6
arts [ärts] **189**–9, **189**–15, **228**–11
art gallery [ärt/ găl/ərē] **223**–9
**ask** [ăsk] **2**–B
**ask** about [ăsk/ ə bowt/] **48**–B, **157**–B
**ask** for [ăsk/ för/] **10**–F
**ask** questions [ăsk/ kwĕs/chənz] **8**–K, **174**–M
asparagus [ə spër/ə gəs] **69**–26
assault [ə sült/] **142**–3
**assemble** [ə sĕm/bəl] **170**–A, **175**–C
assembler [ə sĕm/blər] **166**–7
assembly [ə sĕm/blē/] **139**–24, **140**–3
assembly line [ə sĕm/blē līn/] **175**–6
**assist** [ə sĭst/] **95**–D, **170**–B
assistance [ə sĭs/tĕns] **14**–22
assistant [ə sĭs/tĕnt]
administrative assistant [əd mĭn/ ə strā/ tĭv ə sĭs/tĕnt] **166**–3
dental assistant [dĕn/təl ə sĭs/tĕnt] **119**–2, **167**–22
nursing assistant [nür/sĭng ə sĭs/tĕnt] **120**–12
physician assistant [fĭ zĭ/shən ə sĭs/tĕnt] **168**–47
Assistant [ə sĭs/tĕnt] **93**
asthma [ăz/mə] **111**–9
astronaut [ăs/trə nöt/] **205**–17
astronomer [ə strö/nə mər] **205**–22
Astronomy [ə strö/nə mē] **205**
At Customs [ăt/ kŭs/təmz] **161**
athletic [ăth lĕt/ĭk]
athletic shoes [ăth lĕt/ĭk shōōz/] **86**–7
athletic supporter [ăth lĕt/ĭk sə pör/tər] **91**–6
Atlantic time [ət lăn/tĭk tīm/] **19**–33
atlas [ăt/ləs] **133**–8
ATM (Automated Teller Machine) [ā/tē/ĕm/] / [ö/tə māt ĭd tĕ/lər mə shēn/] **132**
ATM card [ā/tē/ĕm/ kärd/] **132**–15
atom [ăt/əm] **195**–28
**attach** [ə tăch/] **197**–G, **197**–H
attachments [ə tăch/mənts] **61**–11
attack [ə tăk/] **116**–D
attendant [ə tĕn/dənt] **161**–12, **162**–3, **184**–3
At the Dealer [ăt/ dhə dē/lər] **158**
At the Gate [ăt/ dhə gāt/] **161**
At the Mechanic [ăt/ dhə mə kăn/ĭk] **158**
At the Security Checkpoint [ăt/ dhə sə kyōō/ rə tē/ chĕk/ poynt/] **160**
attic [ăt/ək] **47**–8
attractive [ə trăk/tĭv] **32**–13
audiobook [ö/dē ō bŏŏk/] **133**–17
audiologist [ö dē ö/lə jĭst] **115**–9
auditorium [ö/də tör/ē əm] **5**–18
August [ö/gəst] **21**–32
aunt [ănt] **34**–7
author [ö/thər] **133**–15, **169**–64
auto [ö/tō]
auto club card [ö/tō klŭb/ kärd/] **162**–4
auto mechanic [ö/tō mə kăn/ĭk] **166**–8
automated [ö/tə māt ĭd]
automated phone system [ö/tə māt ĭd fōn/ sĭs/təm] **14**–23
Automated Teller Machine [ö/tə māt ĭd tĕl/ər mə shēn/] **132**
Automatic Transmission [ö tə măt/ĭk trănz mĭ/shən] **159**
Automotive Painter [ö tə mōt/ĭv pān/tər] **92**
autumn [ö/təm] **21**–39
avalanche [ăv/ə lănch/] **145**–18
average [ăv/rĭj]
average height [ăv/rĭj hīt/] **32**–5
average weight [ăv/rĭj wāt/] **32**–8
avocados [ä/və kō/dōz, ăv/ə–] **84**–6
axe [ăks] **180**–3
baboon [bă bōōn/] **217**–33
baby [bā/bē] **31**–7
baby bag [bā/bē băg/] **37**–16
baby carrier [bā/bē kë/rē/ər] **37**–17
baby food [bā/bē fōōd/] **37**–4
baby lotion [bā/bē lō/shən] **37**–13
baby monitor [bā/bē mön/ə tər] **59**–7
baby powder [bā/bē pow/dər] **37**–14
babysitter [bā/bē sĭt/ər] **166**–9
baby's room [bā/bēz/ rōōm/] **47**–10
back [băk] **104**–5
backache [băk/āk/] **110**–5
back button [băk/ bŭt/n] **197**–2
backhoe [băk/hō/] **178**–8
backpack [băk/păk/] **94**–18, **226**–15
backpacking [băk/păk/ĭng] **226**–6
back seat [băk/sēt/] **159**–54
back support belt [băk/ sə pört/ bĕlt/] **179**–18
**go** back [ gō/ băk/] **11**–M
horseback riding [hörs/băk/ rī/dĭng] **226**–9
lower back [lō/ər băk/] **107**–29
**pay back** [pā/ băk/] **26**–D
Backyard [băk/yärd/] **53**
BACK FROM THE MARKET [băk/ frəm dhə mär/kət] **66–67**
bacon [bā/kən] **70**–11, **80**–1
bad [băd] **23**–18
BAD DAY AT WORK [băd/ dā/ ăt würk/] **186–187**
badge [băj] **93**–21
badminton [băd/mĭn tən] **228**–6
bag [băg] **69**–31, **74**–7, **74**–19, **161**–18
airbag [ër/ băg/] **159**–43
baby bag [bā/bē băg/] **37**–16
clutch bag [klŭch/băg/] **89**–19
garbage bags [gär/bĭj băgz] **61**–24
grocery bag [grōs/rē băg/] **67**–13
handbag [hănd/băg/] **87**–9, **94**–2
plastic storage bags [plăs/tĭk stör/ĭj băgz/] **72**–25
shoulder bag [shōl/dər băg/] **94**–17
sleeping bag [slē/pĭng băg/] **226**–12
tote bag [tōt/ băg/] **94**–19
vacuum cleaner bag [văk/yōōm klē/nər băg/] **61**–12
bagels [bā/gəlz] **73**–40
baggage [băg/ĭj]
baggage carousel [băg/ĭj kăr/ə sĕl/] **161**–23
bagger [băg/ər] **73**–14
baggy [băg/ē] **97**–30
bailiff [bā/lĭf] **141**–13
**bake** [bāk] **77**–H
Baked Goods [bākt/ gŏŏdz/] **73**
baked potato [bākt/ pə tā/tō] **81**–25
baker [bā/kər] **166**–10
bakery [bā/kə rē] **127**–19
Baking Products [bā/kĭng prŏd/ŭkts] **73**
balance [băl/əns] **132**–17, **195**–41
balcony [băl/kə nē] **51**–20
bald [böld] **33**–12
ball [böl] **59**–12, **231**–5, **231**–12
ball field [böl/ fēld/] **224**–1
ballroom [böl/rōōm/] **184**–26
baseball [bās/böl/] **231**–18, **231**–14
basketball [băs/kət böl/] **229**–8, **231**–4
basketball court [băs/kət böl/ kört/] **229**–7
football [fŏŏt/böl/] **229**–11, **231**–21
meatballs [mēt/bölz/] **81**–27
racquetball [răk/ət böl/] **228**–12
softball [söft/böl/] **229**–10
volleyball [völ/ē böl/] **229**–14, **231**–3
balloons [bə lōōnz/] **44**–4
bananas [bə năn/əz] **68**–2
band [bănd] **183**–34
headband [hĕd/bănd/] **90**–3
waistband [wāst/bănd/] **100**–5
bandage [băn/dĭj] **117**–5, **117**–12
bandana [băn dă/nə] **92**–16
bangs [băngz] **33**–8
bank [băngk] **124**–5
bank statement [băngk/ stāt/mənt] **132**–16
**bank** online [băngk/ ön līn/] **132**–C
BANK [băngk] **132**
banner [băn/ər] **44**–1
banquet room [băng/kwət rōōm/] **185**–14
bar [bär]
bar code [bär/ kōd/] **27**–4
chocolate bar [chŏk/lət bär/] **73**–37
grab bar [grăb/ bär/] **57**–11
menu bar [mĕn/yōō bär/] **197**–1
salad bar [săl/əd bär/] **79**–24
scroll bar [skrōl/ bär/] **197**–15
barbecue [bär/bĭ kyōō/] **53**–17
barbecued ribs [bär/bĭ kyōō/d rĭbz/] **76**–2
barbershop [bär/bər shŏp/] **129**–19
**bargain** [bär/gən] **102**–A
barn [bärn] **177**–11
barrette [bə rĕt/] **108**–20
base [bās] **193**–45, **194**–20
baseball [bās/böl/] **229**–9, **231**–18
baseball bat [bās/böl/ băt/] **231**–14
baseball cap [bās/böl/ kăp/] **86**–5
baseball cards [bās/böl/ kärds/] **232**–2
baseball game [bās/böl/ gām/] **44**–2
basement [bās/mənt] **47**–13
Basement [bās/mənt] **50**
Basic Colours [bā/sĭk kŭ/lərz] **24**
BASIC TRANSPORTATION [bā/sĭk trănz/pər tā/shən] **150–151**
basket [băs/kət] **56**–3
basketball [băs/kət böl/] **229**–8, **231**–4
basketball court [băs/kət böl kört/] **229**–7

bread basket [brĕd/ băs/kət] **83**–11
laundry basket [lön/drē băs/kət] **101**–2
shopping basket [shŏp/ĭng băs/kət] **73**–9
wastebasket [wāst/băs/kət] **57**–26
bass [băs] **212**–6, [bās] **238**–8
bassoon [bə so͞on/] **238**–4
bat [băt] **216**–6, **231**–14
bath [băth]
bath mat [băth/ măt/] **57**–28
bath powder [băth/ pow/dər] **108**–4
bathroom [băth/ro͞om/] **46**–4
bath towel [băth/ tow/əl] **57**–16
bathtub [băth/tŭb/] **57**–2
half bath [hăf/ băth/] **57** ✦
**bathe** [bādh] **36**–F, **108**–B
bathing suit [bā/dhĭng so͞ot/] **90**–26
BATHROOM [băth/ro͞om/] **57**
battery / batteries [băt/ə rē] / [băt/ə rēz]
**146**–15, **158**–20
battery charger [băt/ə rē chär/jər] **235**–27
battery pack [băt/ə rē păk/] **235**–26
bay [bā] **204**–9
**be** [bē]
**be** aware [bē ə wër/] **143**–I
**be** born [bē börn/] **40**–A
**be** 18 or older [bē ā/tēn/ ör ōld/ər] **140**–G
**be** hurt [bē hürt/] **116**–C
**be** in a rock band [bē ĭn ə rŏk/ bănd/] **238**–D
**be** injured [bē ĭn/jərd] **116**–C
**be** in shock [bē ĭn shŏk/] **116**–B
**be** neat [bē nēt/] **174**–C
**be** on time [bē ŏn tīm/] **174**–F
**be** released [bē rĭ lēst/] **141**–H
**be** unable to breathe [bē ŭnā/bəl to͞o brēdh/] **116**–N
**be** unconscious [bē ŭn kŏn/shəs] **116**–A
**don't be** late [dōnt/ bē lāt/] **174**–E
beach [bēch] **204**–10
beach chair [bēch/ chër/] **225**–22
beach umbrella [bēch/ ŭm brĕl/ə] **225**–14
BEACH [bēch] **225**
beads [bēdz] **95**–34, **99**–32
beak [bēk] **214**–3
beaker [bē/kər] **195**–39
beam [bēm] **178**–3
beans [bēnz] **69**–8, **72**–17
soybeans [soy/bēnz/] **177**–3
bear [bër] **37**–23, **216**–9
polar bear [pōlär bër] **216**–7
beard [bërd] **33**–6
**beat** [bēt] **77**–S
beater [bē/tər]
egg beater [ĕg/bē/tər] **78**–20
beautiful [byo͞o/tə fəl] **23**–21
beauty shop [byo͞o/tē shŏp/] **130** ✦
beaver [bē/vər] **216**–8
**become** [bē kŭm/] **40**–G, **41**–N
bed [bĕd] **58**–9
bedbugs [bĕd/bŭgz/] **63**–24
bed control [bĕd/ kən trōl/] **121**–27
bed frame [bĕd/ frām/] **58**–18
bedpan [bĕd/ păn/] **121**–23
bedroom [bĕd/ro͞om/] **46**–2
bedspread [bĕd/sprĕd/] **59**–11
bunk beds [bŭnk/ bĕdz/] **59**–9
double bed [dŭb/əl bĕd/] **184**–14
flower bed [flow/ər bĕd/] **53**–20
hospital bed [hŏs/pĭ tl bĕd/] **121**–22
kids' bedroom [kĭdz/ bĕd/ro͞om/] **47**–9
king-size bed [kĭng/sīz/ bĕd/] **184**–15
BEDROOM [bĕd/ro͞om/] **58, 59**
bee [bē]
honeybee [hŭn/ē bē/] **214**–25
beef [bēf]
beef ribs [bēf/ rĭbz/] **70**–5
corned beef [körnd/ bēf/] **71**–22
ground beef [grownd/ bēf/] **70**–4
roast beef [rōst/ bēf/] **71**–21
stewing beef [sto͞o/ĭng bēf/] **70**–3
stir-fried beef [stür/frīd/ bēf/] **76**–6
Beef [bēf] **70**
beetle [bēt/l] **214**–18
beets [bēts] **69**–5
Before an Emergency [bĭ för/ ən ĭ mür/ jən sē] **146**
behind [bĭ hīnd/] **25**–8
beige [bāzh] **24**–18
bell [bĕl]
bell captain [bĕl/ kăp/tən] **184**–6
bellhop [bĕl/hŏp/] **184**–7
bell peppers [bĕl/pĕp/ərz] **69**–7
doorbell [dör/bĕl/] **53**–14
below [bĭ lō/] **25**–5
belts [bĕlts] **94**–6
back support belt [băk/ sə pört/ bĕlt/] **179**–18
belt buckle [bĕlt/ bŭk/əl] **94**–20
conveyor belt [kən vā/ər bĕlt/] **175**–9
garter belt [gär/tər bĕlt/] **91**–16
seat belt [sēt/ bĕlt/] **159**–52
tool belt [to͞ol/ bĕlt/] **92**–3
bench [bĕnch] **224**–10
**bend** [bĕnd] **230**–O
benefits [bĕn/ə fĭts] **174** ✦
berries [bĕr/ēz] **210**–20
blackberries [blăk/bĕr/ēz] **68**–17
blueberries [blo͞o/bĕr/ēz] **68**–16
mixed berries [mĭkst/ bĕr/ēz] **81**–36
raspberries [răz/bĕr/ēz] **68**–15
strawberries [strö/bĕr/ēz] **68**–14
between [bĭ twēn/] **25**–12
Beverages [bĕv/rə jəz] **73, 81**
bib [bĭb] **37**–5
bicycle / bike [bī/sĭ kəl] / [bīk] **129**–22, **151**–15
big [bĭg] **23**–2, **97**–38
Big Dipper [bĭg/ dĭ/pər] **205** ✦
big-screen TV [bĭg/skrēn/ tē/vē/] **50**–14
bike / bicycle [bīk] / [bī/sĭ kəl] **129**–22, **151**–15
bike path [bīk/ păth/] **224**–3
biking [bī/kĭng] **226**–8, **228**–5
bikini panties [bə kē/nē păn/tēz] **91**–13
bill [bĭl] **214**–3
Bill [bĭl] **15**
billiards [bĭl/yərdz] **228**–2
Bills [bĭlz] **26**
bin [bĭn] **51**–23, **61**–2, **160**–6
bioenergy [bī/ō ĕn/ər jē] **218**–9
biography [bī ŏ/grə fē] **133**–13
biologist [bī ŏ/lə jĭst] **194**–2
Biology [bī ŏ/lə jē] **194**
biomass [bī/ō măs/] **218**–9
birch [bürch] **210**–7
bird [bürd] **208**–4
Bird [bürd] **214**
BIRDS, INSECTS, AND ARACHNIDS
[bürdz/ ĭn/sĕkts ən ə răk/nĭdz] **214**
birth [bürth]
birth certificate [bürth/ sər tĭf/ə kət] **40**–1
birthday [bürth/dā/] **22**–1
BIRTHDAY PARTY [bürth/dā/ pär/tē] **240–241**
biscuits [bĭs/kəts] **80**–6
bison [bī/sən, bī/zən] **216**–5
bit [bĭt] **180**–28
bite [bīt] **110**–11
black [blăk] **24**–13
blackberries [blăk/bĕr/ēz] **68**–17
black hair [blăk/ hër/] **33**–16
bladder [blăd/ər] **107**–46
blade [blād] **107**–28, **109**–28, **180**–27
blankets [blăng/kəts] **58**–15, **146**–7, **225**–11
blanket sleeper [blăng/kət slē/pər] **91**–27
blazer [blā/zər] **92**–12
bleach [blēch] **101**–7
bleachers [blē/chərz] **5**–3
**bleed** [blēd] **116**–M
blender [blĕn/dər] **54**–12
blind [blīnd] **32**–11
blister [blĭs/tər] **110**–15
blizzard [blĭz/ərd] **13**–23, **145**–13
blocks [blŏks] **59**–19
quilt block [kwĭlt/ blŏk/] **232**–15
sunblock [sŭn/blŏk/] **108**–8, **225**–10
blond hair [blŏnd/ hër/] **33**–17
blood [blŭd] **111**–14
blood pressure gauge [blŭd/ prĕsh/ər gāj/] **118**–9
blood test [blŭd/ tĕst/] **121**–30
blood work [blŭd/ würk/] **121**–30
bloody nose [blŭd/ē nōz/] **110**–17
blouse [blows] **87**–8
blow dryer [blō/ drī/ər] **33**–23, **108**–18
blower [blō/ər] **176**–2
**blow out** [blō/ owt/] **240**–C
blue [blo͞o] **24**–3
blueberries [blo͞o/bĕr/ēz] **68**–16
blue jay [blo͞o/ jā/] **214**–6
bright blue [brīt/ blo͞o/] **24**–12
dark blue [därk/ blo͞o/] **24**–10
light blue [līt/ blo͞o/] **24**–11
navy blue [nā/vē blo͞o/] **28**–5
blues [blo͞oz] **237**–22
blush [blŭsh] **109**–37
board [börd]
board game [börd/ gām/] **232**–5
bulletin board [bo͝ol/ə tn börd/] **7**–14
chalkboard [chök/börd/] **6**–1
cutting board [kŭt/ĭng börd/] **54**–27
emery board [ĕm/ə rē börd/, ĕm/rē–] **109**–32
headboard [hĕd/börd/] **58**–10
ironing board [ī/ər nĭng börd/] **101**–14
motherboard [mŭdh/ər börd/] **196**–5
particle board [pär/tə kəl börd/] **181**–20
skateboard [skāt/börd/] **224**–7

snowboard [snō/börd/] **231**–23
surfboard [sürf/börd/] **225**–16
whiteboard [wīt/börd/] **6**–3
**board** [börd] **160**–E
boarding [bör/dĭng]
boarding area [bör/dĭng ër/ē ə] **161**–9
boarding pass [bör/dĭng păs/] **161**–20
sailboarding [sāl/bör/dĭng] **227** ✦
skateboarding [skāt/bör/dĭng] **228**–13
snowboarding [snō/bör/dĭng] **227**–2
boat [bōt]
sailboat [sāl/bōt/] **225**–3
boating [bō/tĭng] **226**–1
bobbin [bŏ/bĭn] **98**–21
bobby pins [bŏb/ē pĭnz/]**108**–21
body [bŏd/ē] **190**–7
body lotion [bŏd/ē lō/shən] **108**–9
body of water [bŏd/ē əv wö/tär] **204** ✦
body shaper [bŏd/ē/ shā/pər] **91**–15
BODY [bŏd/ē] **104–105, 106–107**
**boil** [boyl] **77**–M
boiled ham [boyld/ hăm/] **76**–5
boiler [boy/lər] **78**–8
bok choy [bŏk/ choy/] **69**–15
bolt [bōlt] **51**–34, **180**–35, **180**–38
bolt of fabric [bōlt/ əv făb/rĭk] **98**–15
bone [bōn] **107**–33, **116**–P
boneless [bōn/ləs] **70** ✦
book [bo͝ok]
appointment book [ə poynt/mənt bo͝ok/] **183**–48
audio book [ö/dē ō bo͝ok/] **133**–17
book of stamps [bo͝ok/ əv stămps/] **134**–18
bookcase [bo͝ok/ kās/] **7**–10
bookstore [bo͝ok/ stör/] **130**–4
cheque book [chĕk/ bo͝ok/] **132**–12
coloring book [kŭl/ə rĭng bo͝ok/] **59**–13
notebook [nōt/bo͝ok/] **7**–27
passbook [păs/bo͝ok/] **132**–10
picture book [pĭk/chər bo͝ok/] **133**–12
spiral notebook [spī/rəl nōt/bo͝ok/] **7**–29
test booklet [tĕst/ bo͝ok/lət] **10**–1
textbook [tĕkst/bo͝ok/, tĕks/–] **7**–25
workbook [würk/bo͝ok/] **7**–26
boom box [bo͞om/bŏks/] **234**–1
booth [bo͞oth] **82**–4, **122**–3
boots [bo͞ots] **95**–28
hiking boots [hī/kĭng bo͞ots/] **95**–31
rain boots [ rān/ bo͞ots/] **90**–20
safety boots [sāf/tē bo͞ots/] **179**–20
ski boots [skē/ bo͞ots/] **231**–26
steel toe boots [stēl/ tō/ bo͞ots/] **92**–6
bored [börd] **43**–25
**borrow** [bŏr/ō] **26**–B
boss [bŏs] **164**–4
botanical garden [bə tăn/ĭ kəl gär/dn] **222**–3
bottle [bŏt/l] **37**–1, **74**–1, **74**–13
bottle return [bŏt/l rĭ türn/] **73**–16
hot water bottle [hŏt/ wö/tər bŏt/l] **113**–15
bottled water [bŏt/ld wö/tər] **146**–11
bouquet [bō kā/, bo͞o–] **211**–28
bow [bō] **231**–6
bow tie [bō/ tī/] **89**–16
**bow** [bow] **3**–H
bowl [bōl] **55**–2
mixing bowl [mĭks/ĭng bōl/] **54**–28, **78**–31
serving bowl [sürv/ĭng bōl/] **55**–21
soup bowl [so͞op/ bōl/] **83**–21
sugar bowl [sho͝og/ər bōl/] **55**–14
bowling [bō/lĭng] **228**–3
bowling alley [bō/lĭng ăl/ē] **222**–4
bowling ball [bō/lĭng bŏl/] **231**–5
box / boxes [bŏks/, bŏks/ĭz] **74**–6, **74**–18
box spring [bŏks/ sprĭng/] **58**–19
CD boom box [sē/dē/ bo͞om/bŏks/] **234**–1
fuse box [fyo͞oz/ bŏks/] **62**–13
mailboxes [māl/bŏk/səz] **50**–11, **128**–13
post office box (PO box)
[pōst/ ö/fəs bŏks/] / [pē/ō bŏks/] **135**–9
safety deposit box [sāf/tē dĭ pŏz/ət bŏks/] **132**–7
sandbox [sănd/bŏks/] **224**–15
search box [sürch/ bŏks/] **197**–5
text box [tĕkst/ bŏks/] **197**–13
to-go box [tə gō/ bŏks/] **82**–5
boxer shorts [bŏk/sər shörts/] **91**–4
boxing [bŏks/ĭng] **228**–4
Boxing Day [bŏks/ĭng dā] **22**–17
boy [boy] **31**–9
bra [brä] **91**–20
bracelets [brās/ləts] **95**–9, **117**–3
braces [brā/səz] **119**–6
brain [brān] **107**–34
**brainstorm** [brān/störm/] **8**–H, **191**–F
brake [brāk] **159**–48
brake light [brāk/ līt/] **158**–14
brake pedal [brāk/ pĕd/l] **159**–45
branch [brănch] **210**–2
Brass [brăs] **238**
bread [brĕd] **67**–11
bread-and-butter plate [brĕd/ n bŭt/ər plāt/] **83**–19
bread basket [brĕd/ băs/kət] **83**–11
garlic bread [gär/lĭk brĕd/] **81**–28
rye bread [rī/ brĕd/] **71**–20
wheat bread [wēt/ brĕd/] **71**–19
white bread [wīt/ brĕd] **71**–18
**break** [brāk] **77**–Q, **116**–P
**break down** [brāk/ down/] **162**–D
Breakfast Special [brĕk/fəst spĕ/shəl] **80**
breasts [brĕsts] **70**–19, **107**–26
**breathe** [brēdh] **116**–N
breathing [brē/dhĭng] **117**–16
bricklayer [brĭk/lā/ər] **186**–8
bricks [brĭks] **178**–12, **178**–B
briefcase [brēf/kās/] **88**–13
briefs [brēfs] **91**–5, **91**–14
bright blue [brīt/ blo͞o/] **24**–12
**bring** [brĭng] **174**–D, **240**–E
British North America Act [brĭt/ĭsh nörth ə mër/ə kə ăkt] **198**–3
broccoli [brŏk/ə lē] **69**–13
broiled steak [broyld/ stāk/] **76**–3
broiler [broy/lər] **54**–21
broken [brō/kən] **62**–5, **62**–6, **62**–7, **63**–15, **97**–39
broken equipment [brō/kən ĭ kwĭp/mənt] **179**–4
broom [bro͞om] **61**–16
brother [brŭdh/ər] **34**–6, **35**–28
brother-in-law [brŭdh/ər ĭn lö/] **34**–17
stepbrother [stĕp/brŭdh/ər] **35**–30
brown [brown] **24**–17
brown hair [brown/ hër/] **33**–18
hash browns [hăsh/ brownz/] **80**–3
**browse** [browz] **102**–B
bruise [bro͞oz] **110**–12
brush [brŭsh] **33**–22, **108**–14
paintbrush [pānt/brŭsh/] **181**–22, **233**–20
scrub brush [skrŭb/ brŭsh/] **61**–20
toilet brush [toy/lət brŭsh/] **57**–20
toothbrush [to͞oth/brŭsh/] **109**–22
**brush** [brŭsh] **108**–I, **109**–J
bubble envelope [bŭbəl ĕn/və lōp] **134**–3
bucket [bŭk/ət] **61**–7, **225**–8
buckle [bŭk/əl] **94**–20, **99**–28
**buckle up** [bŭk/əl ŭp/] **36**–L
bud [bŭd] **211**–7
budget [bŭ jĭt/] **186**–3
buffalo [bŭf/ə lō] **216**–5
buffet [bə fā/] **55**–24, **185**–10
bugs [bŭgz]
bedbugs [bĕd/bŭgz/] **63**–24
building [bĭl/dĭng] **50**–1, **124**–2
BUILDING SUPPLIES [bĭl/dĭng sə plīz/] **180–181**
bulb [bŭlb] **56** ✦, **211**–2
bulldozer [bo͝ol/dō/zər] **178**–6
bulletin board [bo͝ol/ə tn börd/] **7**–14
bump cap [bŭmp/ kăp/] **92**–9
bumper [bŭm/pər] **158**–8
bumper pad [bŭm/pər păd/] **59**–4
bunch [bŭnch] **68**–29
bunk beds [bŭngk/ bĕdz/] **59**–9
Bunsen burner [bŭn/sən bür/nər] **195**–37
bureau [byo͝or/ō] **58**–1
burger [bür/gər]
cheeseburger [chēz/bür/gər] **79**–3
hamburger [hăm/bür/gər] **79**–1
burglary [bür/glə rē] **142**–2
burn [bürn]
sunburn [sŭn/bürn/] **110**–14
**burn** [bürn] **116**–H
burner [bür/nər] **54**–19, **195**–37
burrito [bə rē/tō] **79**–9
bus [bŭs] **128**–9, **151**–14
bus person [bŭs/ pür/sən] **185**–13
bus route [bŭs/ ro͞ot/, –rowt/] **152**–1
bus station [bŭs/ stā/shən] **124**–7
bus stop [bŭs/ stŏp/] **129**–16, **151**–13
**miss** the bus [mĭs/ dhə bŭs/] **152** ✦
**bus** [bŭs] **82**–G
business [bĭz/nəs]
business owner [bĭz/nəs ō/nər] **166**–11
businessperson [bĭz/nəs pür/sən] **166**–12
business suit [bĭz/nəs so͞ot/] **88**–11
busser [bŭ/sər] **83**–12
Bus Stop [bŭs/ stŏp/] **152**
butcher [bo͝och/ər] **166**–13
butter [bŭt/ər] **66**–6, **83**–19
butterfly [bŭt/ər flī/] **214**–19
buttocks [bŭt/əks] **107**–30
button [bŭt/n] **99**–24
back button [băk/ bŭt/n] **197**–2
call button [köl/ bŭt/n] **121**–28

forward button [för/wərd bŭt/n] **197**–3
**buy** [bī] **27**–G
**buy** a home [bī/ ə hōm/] **41**–M
**buy** a snack [bī/ ə snăk/] **11**–K
**buy** recycled products
[bī/ rē sī/kəld prŏd/ŭkts] **219**–D
Buying a House [bī/ĭng ə hows/] **49**
BUYING AND MAINTAINING A CAR
[bī/ĭng ən mān tā/nĭng ə kär/] **157**
Buying a Used Car [bī/ĭng ə yo͞ozd/ kär/] **157**
buzzer [bŭz/ər] **51**–31
cab [kăb] **156**–16
cabbage [kăb/ĭj] **69**–2
cabinet [kăb/ə nət] **138**–4
cabinet [kăb/ə nət] **54**–1
file cabinet [fīl/ kăb/ə nət] **182**–11
medicine cabinet [mĕd/ə sən kăb/ə nət] **57**–22
supply cabinet [sə plī/ kăb/ə nət] **182**–1
cables [kā/bəlz] **158**–21, **196**–13
cactus [kăk/təs] **210**–21
cafeteria [kăf/ə tïr/ē ə] **5**–14
cage [kāj] **107**–48
cake [kāk] **73**–39, **81**–33
cake pan [kāk/ păn/] **78**–26
cheesecake [chēz/kāk/] **81**–34
pancakes [păn/kāks/] **80**–7
Cake [kāk] **77**
**calculate** [kăl/kyə lāt/] **17**–B
calculator [kăl/kyə lā/tər] **17**–6, **183**–25
calculus [kăl/kyə ləs] **192**–19
CALENDAR [kăl/ən dər] **20–21**
CALENDAR EVENTS [kăl/ən dər ĭ vĕnts/] **22**
calf [kăf] **106**–22
calf-length [kăf/ lĕngkth/] **96**–17
call [köl]
call button [köl/ bŭt/n] **121**–28
international call [ĭn/tər năsh/ə nəl köl/] **15**–35
Internet phone call [ĭn/tər nĕt/ fōn/ köl/] **14**–20
local call [lō/kəl köl/] **15**–31
long distance call [lŏng/ dĭs/təns köl/] **15**–32
**call** [köl] **48**–A, **147**–K
**call in** [köl/ ĭn/] **186**–A
calling card [kö/lĭng kärd/] **14**–15
calm [kŏm] **42**–8
camcorder [kăm/kör dər] **235**–24
camel [kăm/əl] **217**–40
camera [kăm/rə]
camera case [kăm/rə kās/] **235**–28
digital camera [dĭ/jə təl kăm/rə] **235**–19
film camera [fĭlm/ kăm/rə] **235**–21
security camera [sĭ kyo͝or/ə tē kăm/rə] **50**–19
35mm camera
[thür/tē fīv/ mĭl/ə mē/tər kăm/rə] **235**–21
camisole [kăm/ə sōl/] **91**–21
campaign [kăm pān/] **139**–29
camper [kăm/pər] **156**–9
campfire [kămp/fīr/] **226**–11
camping [kăm/pĭng] **226**–5
camping stove [kăm/pĭng stōv/] **226**–16
Campus [kăm/pəs] **5**
can [kăn] **74**–3, **74**–15
can opener [kăn/ ō/pə nər] **78**–1, **146**–8
electric can opener [ĭ lĕk/trĭk/ kăn/ ō/pə nər] **54**–14
garbage can [gär/bĭj kăn/] **53**–24
Canada Day [kăn/ə də dā] **22**–12
CANDIAN NATIONAL PARKS [kənā/dēən năsh/ənəl pärks] **220**
cancer [kăn/sər] **111**–10
candle [kăn/dl] **56**–20
candle holder [kăn/dl hōl/dər] **56**–21
candy [kăn/dē] **239**–14
candy cane [kăn/dē kān/] **239**–17
candy store [kăn/dē stör/] **131**–17
cane [kān] **113**–16, **239**–17
canned food [kănd/ fo͞od/] **146**–9
Canned Foods [kănd/ fo͞odz/] **72**
canoeing [kə no͞o/ĭng] **226**–3
canteen [kăn tēn/] **226**–24
canvas [kăn/vəs] **233**–17
canyon [kăn/yən] **204**–17
cap [kăp] **88**–1, **206**–7
baseball cap [bās/böl/ kăp/] **86**–5
bump cap [bŭmp/ kăp/] **92**–9
shower cap [show/ər kăp/] **108**–1
surgical cap [sür/jĭ kəl kăp/] **121**–37
surgical scrub cap [sür/jĭ kəl skrŭb/ kăp/] **93**–35
capital [kă/pət əl] **139**–22
**capitalize** [kă/pət əl īz/] **190**–A, **190**–B
capris [kə prēz] **88**–8
capsule [kăp/səl] **113**–23
car [kär] **150**–1
car accident [kär/ ăk/sə dənt] **144**–2
car dealership [kär/ dē/lər shĭp/] **126**–4
car safety seat [kär/ sāf/tē sēt/] **37**–19
4-door car [för/dör/ kär/] **156**–1
sports car [spörts/kär/] **156**–4
subway car [sŭb/wā/ kär/] **152**–6
town car [town/ kär/] **152**–20
2-door car [to͞o/dör/ kär/] **156**–2
Car [kär] **157, 159**
CAR [kär] **156, 157, 158–159**
card [kärd] **239**–5
ATM card [ā/tē/ĕm/ kärd/] **132**–15
auto club card [ö tō/ klŭb/ kärd/] **162**–4
baseball cards [bās/böl/ kärdz/] **232**–2
card store [kärd/ stör/] **130**–7
copies of ID and credit cards
[kŏp/ēz əv ī/dē/ ən krĕd/ət/ kärdz/] **146**–19
emergency card [ĭ mür/jən sē/ kärd/] **161**–26
fare card [fër/ kärd/] **152**–11
folding card table [fōl/dĭng/ kärd/ tā/bəl] **102**–4
greeting card [grē/tĭng kärd/] **134**–15
health card [hĕlth/ kärd/] **118**–3
memory card [mĕm/ə rē kärd/] **235**–20
permanent resident card [pür/mə nənt rez/ĭdənt kärd] **40**–2
postcard [pōst/ kärd/] **134**–16
rotary card file [rō/tə rē kärd/ fīl/] **183**–44
Social Insurance Number card
[sō/shəl in sho͝or/əns nŭm/ bar kärd/] **40**–5
Card [kärd] **135**
cardigan sweater [kär/də gən swĕt/ər] **88**–2
Cardinal Numbers [kärd/nəl nŭm/bərz] **16**
cardiologist [kär/dē ŏl/ə jĭst] **120**–3
cardiopulmonary resuscitation (CPR)
[kär/dē ō pŭl mə nër/ē rĭ sŭs/ə tā/shən] /
[sē/pē/är/] **117**–17
care [kër] **167**–32
careful worker [kër/fəl wür/kər] **179**–2
careless worker [kër/ləs wür/kər] **179**–1
childcare worker [chīld/kër wür/kər] **166**–16
CARE [kër] **114–115, 118, 119**
**care for** [kër för] **140**–C
career counsellor [kə rēr/ kown/slər] **172**–10
Career Path [kə rēr/ păth/] **172**
CAREER PLANNING [kə rēr/ plăn/ĭng] **172**
cargo van [kär/gō văn/] **156**–13
caribou [kër/ə bo͞o] **216**–10
carnation [kër nā/shən] **211**–20
carousel [kër/ə sĕl/] **161**–23
carpenter [kär/pən tər] **62**–12, **166**–14
carpet [kär/pət] **56**–24
**carpool** [kär/po͞ol/] **219**–I
carriage [kër/ĭj] **37**–20
carrier [kër/ē ər] **37**–17, **134**–20
carrots [kër/əts] **69**–3
**carry** [kër/ē] **11**–F, **82**–H
CARS AND TRUCKS [kärz/ ən trŭks/] **156**
cart [kärt] **72**–7, **129**–28
housekeeping cart [hows/kē/pĭng kärt/] **184**–19
luggage cart [lŭg/ĭj/ kärt/] **184**–8
carton [kär/tn] **74**–4, **74**–16
cartoon [kär/to͞on] **236**–3
cartridge [kär/trĭj] **183**–45
carving knife [kär/vĭng nīf/] **78**–12
case [kās] **94**–5, **235**–28
cash [kăsh]
cash and coins [kăsh/ ən koynz/] **146**–17
cash register [kăsh/ rĕj/ə stər] **27**–10, **73**–15
**cash** [kăsh] **27**–F, **132**–A
cashier [kă shïr/] **73**–13, **166**–15
cashmere [kăzh/mïr/] **98**–4
Casserole [kăs/ə rōl] **77**
casserole dish [kăs/ə rōl dĭsh/] **78**–10
cassette [kə sĕt/] **234**–6
videocassette [vĭ/dē ō kə sĕt/] **133**–18
cast [kăst] **113**–20
castle [kă/səl] **225**–12
Casual Clothes [kăzh/o͞o əl klōz/] **88**
CASUAL, WORK, AND FORMAL CLOTHES
[kăzh/o͞o əl würk/ ən för/məl klōz/] **88–89**
cat [kăt] **215**–9
catfish [kăt/fĭsh/] **71**–2
catalogue [kăt ə /lŏg] **133**–11
**catch** [kăch] **230**–D
catcher's mask [kăch/ərz măsk/] **231**–15
caterer [kā/tər ər] **185**–16
caterpillar [kăt/ər pĭl/ər] **214**–20
cattle [kăt/l] **177**–21
cauliflower [kŏ/lĭ flow/ər] **69**–14
cave [kāv] **220**–4
cavity [kăv/ə tē] **119**–7
C-clamp [sē/klămp/] **180**–6
CD [sē/dē/] **196**–9, **234**–5
CD boom box [sē/dē/ bo͞om/bŏks/] **234**–1
CD player [sē/dē/ plā/ər] **159**–38

CEGEP [sē/ē/jē/ē/pē/] **188**–6
**celebrate** [sĕl/ə brāt] **206**–C
celery [sĕl/ə rē] **69**–9
cell [sĕl] **194**–4
cell membrane [sĕl/ mĕm/brān] **194**–6
cellphone holder [sĕl/ fōn/ hōl/dər] **94**–15
cellphone kiosk [sĕl/ fōn/ kē/ösk] **131**–22
cellphone number [sĕl/ fōn/ nŭm/bər] **4**–12
cell wall [sĕl/ wöl/] **194**–5
cello [chĕl/ō] **238**–7
cellular phone [sĕl/yə lər fōn/] **14**–8
Celsius [sĕl/sē əs] **13**–2
cemetery [sĕ/mə tĕr/ē] **127**–15
cent [sĕnt] **26**–1, **26**–2, **26**–3, **26**–4
centre [sĕn/tər]
childcare centre [chīld/kër/ sĕn/tər] **129**–30
convention centre [kən vĕn/shən sĕn/tər] **127**–24
copy centre [kŏp/ē sĕn/tər] **129**–18
entertainment centre [ĕn/tər tān/mənt sĕn/tər] **56**–5
resource centre [rē/sörs sĕn/tər] **172**–9
CENTRE [sĕn/tər] **208–209**
centimetre [cm] [sĕn/tə mē/tər] **17**–15
CENTRAL AMERICA [sĕn/trəl ə mĕr/ə kə] **200–201**
Central time [sĕn/trəl tīm/] **19**–31
cereal [sïr/ē əl] **80**–9
ceremony [sĕr/ə mō/nē] **206**–6
certificate [sər tĭf/ə kət] **40**–1, **41**–11
Citizenship Certificate [sĭt/ə zən shĭp sər tĭf/ə kət] **40**–6
chain [chān] **51**–33, **95**–33, **180**–41
chair [chër] **7**–11
armchair [ärm/chër] **56**–22
beach chair [bēch/ chër/] **225**–22
dining room chair [dī/nĭng ro͞om/chër/] **55**–8
easy chair [ē/zē/ chër] **56**–22
folding chair [fōld/ĭng chër/] **102**–5
high chair [hī/ chër/] **37**–6, **82**–3
rocking chair [rŏk/ĭng chër/] **37**–21
wheelchair [wēl/chër/] **113**–9
chalk [chök] **7**–18
chalkboard [chök/börd/] **6**–1
challenged [chăl/ənjd] **32**–10
**change** [chānj] **36**–G, **60**–P, **148**–C
change purse [chānj/ pürs/] **94**–14
changing [chān/jĭng]
changing pad [chān/jĭng păd/] **59**–2
changing table [chān/jĭng tā/bəl] **59**–1
charger [chär/jər] **14**–10, **234**–17, **235**–27
chart [chärt] **121**–24
cheap [chēp] **23**–20
check [chĕk]
check-in kiosk [chĕk/ĭn/ kē/ösk] **160**–2
checkout [chĕk/owt] **73**–12
**check** [chĕk]
**check** blood pressure [chĕk/ blŭd/ prĕsh/ər] **118**–A
**check** email [chĕk/ ē/ māl/] **39**–W
**check in** [chĕk/ ĭn/] **160**–A
**check** Internet job sites [chĕk/ ĭn/tər nĕt/ jŏb/ sīts/] **173**–D
**check** messages [chĕk/ mĕs/ə jĭz] **171**–R
**check out** [chĕk/ owt/] **133**–C
**check** the correct boxes [chĕk/ dhə kə rĕkt/ bŏk/səz] **9**–U
**check** the oil [chĕk/ dhə oyl/] **157**–H
**check** the pronunciation [chĕk/ dhe prə nən sē ā/ shən] **8**–D
**check** your bags [chĕk/ yər băgz/] **160**–B
**check** pulse [chĕk/ pŭls/] **122**–A
**check** your spelling [chĕk/ yər spĕl/ĭng] **197**–F
**check** your understanding [chĕk/ yər ŭn/dər stănd/ĭng] **12**–N
**check** your work [chĕk/ yər würk/] **10**–L
checked [chĕkt] **96**–24
checkers [chĕk/ərz] **232**–7
checkout [chĕk/owt/] **133**–10
Checkpoint [chĕk/poynt/] **160**
cheddar cheese [chĕd/ər chēz/] **71**–28
cheek [chēk] **106**–3
cheese [chēz] **66**–4
cheddar cheese [chĕd/ər chēz/] **71**–28
cheeseburger [chēz/bür/gər] **79**–3
cheesecake [chēz/kāk/] **81**–34
grilled cheese sandwich [grĭld/ chēz/ săn/wĭch, –sănd/–] **80**–10
processed cheese [prō/ sĕst chēz/] **71**–26
Swiss cheese [swĭs/ chēz/] **71**–27
Cheesy Tofu Vegetable Casserole [chē/zē tō/fo͞o vĕj/tə bəl kăs/ə rōl] **77**
chef [shĕf] **83**–16
chef's hat [shĕfs/ hăt/] **93**–28
chef's jacket [shĕfs/ jăk/ət] **93**–29
chef's salad [shĕfs/ săl/ əd] **80**–14
executive chef [ĭg zĕk/yə tĭv shĕf/] **185**–7
head chef [hĕd/ shĕf/] **185**–7
sous chef [so͞o/ shĕf/] **185**–6
Chef [shĕf] **93**
chemist [kĕm/ĭst] **195**–25
Chemistry [kĕm/ə strē] **195**
cheque [chĕk/] **132**–13
chequebook [chĕk/ bo͝ok] **132**–12
paycheque [pā/ chĕk/] **165**–14
chequing account number [chĕk/ing ə kownt/ nŭm/bər] **132**–14
cherries [chĕr/ēz] **68**–11
cherry picker [chĕr/ē pĭk/ər] **178**–5
chess [chĕs] **232**–8
chest [chĕst] **59**–16, **104**–4, **107**–25
chest of drawers [chĕst/ əv drörz/] **59**–6
chicken [chĭk/ən] **66**–3, **70**–16
chicken pox [chĭk/ən pŏks/] **111**–6
chicken sandwich [chĭk/ən săn/wĭch, –sănd–] **79**–5
fried chicken [frīd/ chĭk/ən] **76**–1
roast chicken [rōst/ chĭk/ən] **81**–22
Chicken [chĭk/ən] **77**
chief justice [chēf/ jŭs/təs] **138**–13
CHILD CARE AND PARENTING [chīld/ kër ən për/ən tĭng] **36–37**
child / children [chīld] / [chĭl/ drən]
childcare centre [chīld/kër sĕn/tər] **129**–30
childcare worker [chīld/kër wür/kər] **166**–16
children's program [chĭl/drənz prō/grăm] **236**–9
child safety seat [chīld/ sāf/tē sēt/] **159**–53
grandchild [grăn/chīld/, grănd/–] **34** ✦
lost child [löst/ chīld/] **144**–1
Childhood Diseases [chīld/ho͝od dĭ zē/zəz] **111**
chili peppers [chĭl/ē pĕp/ərz] **69**–29
**chill** [chĭl] **76**–D
chills [chĭlz] **110**–9
chimney [chĭm/nē] **53**–5
chimpanzee [chĭm/păn zē/] **217**–29
chin [chĭn] **106**–1
chipmunk [chĭp/mŭngk] **215**–20
chips [chĭps] **73**–35
chiropractors [kī/rō prăk/tərz] **120** ✦
chisel [chĭz/əl] **181**–55
chocolate bar [chŏk/lət bär] **73**–37
**choke** [chōk] **116**–L
**choose** [cho͞oz] **9**–P
**chop** [chŏp] **77**–L
chops [chŏps] **70**–10, **70**–15
Christmas Day [krĭs/məs dā] **22**–16
Christmas tree [krĭs/məs trē/] **239**–16
chromosome [krō/mə zōm/] **194**–8
chrysanthemum [krĭ săn/thə məm] **211**–21
church [chürch] **127**–14
chute [sho͞ot] **51**–26
circle [sür/ kəl] **193**–34
**circle** [sür/ kəl] **9**–Q
circular saw [sür/kyə lər sö/] **180**–9
circulation desk [sür/kyə lā/shən dĕsk/] **133**–2
circumference [sər kŭm/frəns] **193**–36
citizen [sĭt/ə zən] **30**–5
Citizenship Certificate [sĭt/ə zən shĭp sər tĭf/ə kət] **40**–6
Citizenship Requirements [sĭt/ə zən shĭp/ rĭ kwīr/mənts] **140**
city [sĭt/ē] **4**–7, **52**–1
city code [sĭt/ē kōd/] **15**–34
city council [sĭt/ē kown/səl] **139**–23
city councillor [sĭt/ē kown/slər] **139**–24
city hall [sĭt/ē höl/] **124**–8
City Government [sĭt/ē gŭv/ər mənt] **139**
CITY STREETS [sĭt/ē strēts/] **126–127**
CIVIC RIGHTS AND RESPONSIBILITIES [sĭ/vĭk rīts n rĭ spŏn/sə bĭl/ə tēz] **140**
Civilizations [sĭ/və lə zā/shenz] **199**
**claim** [klām] **160**–L
clamp [klămp] **180**–6
clams [klămz] **71**–15
clarinet [klăr/ə nĕt/] **238**–2
classical [klă/sĭ kəl] **237**–21
classical concert [kla/sĭ kəl kŏn/sərt] **223**–14
classified ad [klăs/e fīd ăd] **48**–2
Classmates [klăs/māts/] **8**
classroom [klăs/ro͞om/] **5**–7
CLASSROOM [klăs/ro͞om/] **6–7**
claw [klö] **214**–2
clean [klēn] **101**–16
**clean** [klēn] **76**–A
**clean** teeth [klēn/ tēth/] **119**–A
**clean** the house [klēn/ dhə hows/] **39**–O
**clean** the lint trap [klēn/ dhə lĭnt/ trăp/] **101**–D
**clean** the oven [klēn/ dhə ŭv/ən] **60**–C
**clean up** [klēn/ ŭp/] **147**–L
cleaner [klēn/ər]
dry cleaners [drī/ klēn/ərz] **128**–2
glass cleaner [glăs/ klēn/ər] **61**–14

# Index

oven cleaner [ŭv/ən klēn/ər] 61–3
vacuum cleaner [văk/yo͞om klēn/ər] 61–10
vacuum cleaner attachments
[văk/yo͞om klēn/ər ə tăch/mənts] 61–11
vacuum cleaner bag [văk/yo͞om klēn/ər băg/] 61–12
CLEANING SUPPLIES [klē/nĭng sə plīz/] 61
cleanser [klĕn/zər] 61–18
CLEANUP [klēn/ŭp/] 148–149
clear [klïr] 13–9
clear tape [klïr/tāp/] 183–30
**clear** [klïr] 82–G
**clear off** [klïr/ ŏf/] 10–I
clerk [klürk] 5–13, 182–2
admissions clerk [əd mĭsh/ənz klürk/] 120–14
desk clerk [dĕsk/ klürk/] 184–11
file clerk [fīl/ klürk/] 182–10
grocery clerk [grōs/rē klürk/, grō/sə–] 72–4
library clerk [lī/brër ē klürk/] 133–1
licensing clerk [lī/səns ing klürk/] 136–3
payroll clerk [pā/rōl/ klürk/] 165–10
postal clerk [pō/stəl klürk/] 135–7
retail clerk [rē/tāl/ klürk/] 169–53
sales clerk [sālz/klürk/] 94–3
shipping clerk [shĭp/ĭng klürk/] 175–14
stock clerk [stŏk/ klürk/] 169–59
**click** [klĭk] 197–B
**climb** [klīm] 224–C
clinic [klĭn/ĭk] 186–2
clip-on earrings [klĭp/ŏn ïr/ĭngz] 95–37
clipper [klĭp/ər] 109–31, 176–11
clips [klĭps] 108–19, 183–31, 194–21
clock [klŏk] 7–9, 58–24, 165–7
clock radio [klŏk/ rā/dē ō] 102–6
**close** [klōz] 6–H
closet [klŏz/ət] 57 ✦, 58–5
Closures [klō/zhərz] 99
cloth [klŏth] 181–54
cloth diaper [klŏth/ dī/pər] 37–8
tablecloth [tā/bəl klŏth/] 55–12
washcloth [wŏsh/klŏth/] 57–6
clothes [klōz] 146–6
clothesline [klōz/līn/] 101–9
clothespin [klōz/pĭn/] 101–10
CLOTHES [klōz] 86–87, 88–89, 96–97, 98–99
clothing [klō/dhĭng] 102–2
CLOTHING [klō/dhĭng] 90, 92–93
Clothing Problems [klō/dhĭng prŏb/ləmz] 97
cloudy [klow/dē] 13–10
club [klŭb] 162–4, 223–12, 231–1
club sandwich [klŭb săn/wĭch/, –sănd–] 80–12
clubs [klŭbz] 233–32
clutch [klŭch] 159–49
clutch bag [klŭch/ băg/] 89–19
coach [kōch] 5–20, 229–2
coal [kōl] 218–4
coarse adjustment knob
[körs/ ə jŭst/mənt nŏb/] 194–24
coat [kōt] 90–2, 216–21
lab coat [lăb/ kōt/] 93–33
raincoat [rān/ kōt/] 90–18
sports coat [spörts/ kōt/] 89–14
trench coat [trĕnch/ kōt/] 90–21
cobra [kō/brə] 213–41
cockpit [kŏk/pĭt/] 161–10
cockroaches [kŏk/rō/chəz] 63–26
cocktail dress [kŏk/tāl/ drĕs/] 89–20
coconuts [kō/kə nŭts/] 68–24
cod [kŏd] 71–8, 212–5
code [kōd]
area code [ër/ē ə kōd/] 15–29
bar code [bär/ kōd/] 27–4
city code [sĭt/ē kōd/] 15–34
country code [kŭn/trē kōd/] 15–33
coffee [kŏ/fē] 73–33, 81–37, 81–38
coffee maker [kŏ/fē mā/kər] 54–11
coffee mug [kŏ/fē mŭg/] 55–7
coffee shop [kŏ/fē shŏp/] 126–11
coffee table [kŏ/fē tā/bəl] 56–19
COFFEE SHOP MENU [kŏ/fē shŏp/ mĕn/yo͞o] 80–81
coins [koynz] 146–17
coin purse [koyn/ pürs/] 94–14
Coins [koynz] 26
colander [kŏl/ən dər] 78–17
cold [kōld] 13–6, 42–4, 111–1
cold tablets [kōld tăb/ləts] 113–27
cold water [kōld wŏ/tər] 57–10
coleslaw [kōl/slä/] 80–18
collar [kŏl/ər] 100–4
**collate** [kō/lāt/, kə lāt/] 171–E
**collect** [kə lĕkt/] 232–A
college [kŏl/ĭj] 127–17, 188–6
college residence [kŏl/ĭj rĕz/ə dəns] 52–8
cologne [kə lōn/] 108–6
colon [kō/lən] 190–17
colour [kŭl/ər]
watercolour [wŏ/tər kŭl/ər] 233–21
**colour** [kŭl/ər] 33–D
colouring book [kŭl/ə rĭng bo͝ok/] 59–13
Colours [kŭl/ərs] 24
COLOURS [kŭl/ərs] 24
column [kŏl/ŭm] 107–49
comb [kōm] 33–21, 108–13
**comb** [kōm] 108–G
**come** [kŭm] 39–R
comedy [kŏm/ə dē] 236–2, 237–13
comet [kŏm/ət] 205–24
**comfort** [kŭm/fərt] 36–I
comma [kŏm/ə] 190–14
commercial fisher [kə mür/shəl fĭsh/ər] 167–17
**commit** a crime [kə mĭt/ ə krīm/] 142 ✦
Common Illnesses and Childhood Diseases
[kŏm/ən ĭl/nə səz ən child/ho͝od-dĭ zē/zəz] 111
COMMUNITY CLEANUP
[kə myo͞o/nə tē klēn/ŭp] 148–149
(community) college
[kə myo͞o/nə tē kŏl/ĭj] 127–17
Comparing Clothing [kəm për/ĭng klō/dhĭng] 97
compartment [kəm pärt/mənt] 159–44, 161–13
complaint [kəm plānt/] 97 ✦
Complex [kŏm/plĕks/] 51
compliment [kŏm/plə mĕnt/] 12 ✦
**compliment** [kŏm/plə mĕnt/] 12–C
composer [kəm pō/zər] 199–14
composition [kŏm/pə zĭsh/ən] 199–15
**compost** [kŏm/pōst/] 219–M
compost pile [kŏm/pōst pīl/] 53–25
computer [kəm pyo͞o/tər] 7–15, 183–17
computer lab [kəm pyo͞o/tər lăb/] 5–15
computer software engineer
[kəm pyo͞o/tər sŏft/wër/ ĕn/jə nïr/] 167–18
computer technician [kəm pyo͞o/tər tĕk nĭsh/ən]
167–19, 182–12
Computer [kəm pyo͞o/tər] 196
COMPUTERS [kəm pyo͞o/tərz] 196
**conceal** [kən sēl/] 143–C
concert [kŏn/sərt] 222–5, 223–14
concierge [kŏn/sē ërzh/] 184–4
conclusion [kən klo͞o/zhən] 190–8
concrete [kŏng/krēt, kŏn krēt/] 178–10
conditioner [kən dĭsh/ə nər] 108–11, 159–39
Conditions [kən dĭsh/ənz] 13, 111
CONDITIONS [kən dĭsh/ənz] 111
condominium [kŏn/də mĭn/ē əm] 52–5
**conduct** [kən dŭkt/] 238–C
conductor [kən dŭk/tər] 152–13
cone [kōn] 79–13, 193–40
pine cone [pīn/kōn] 210–11
Confederation [kən fĕd ə rā/shŭn] 198–5
conference room [kŏn/frəns ro͞om/] 182–4
confetti [kən fĕt/ē] 239–3
confused [kən fyo͞ozd/] 43–26
congestion [kən jĕs/chən] 110–7
CONSERVATION [kŏn/sər vā/shən] 218–219
Conserve Energy and Resources
[kən sürv/ ĕn/ər jē ən rē/sörs/əz] 219
console [kən/sōl] 232–3
constellation [kŏn/stə lā/shən] 205–14
construction [kən strŭk/shən]
construction paper [kən strŭk/shən pā/pər] 232–12
construction site [kən strŭk/shən sīt/] 126–2
construction worker
[kən strŭk/shən wür/kər] 178–1
CONSTRUCTION [kən strŭk/shən] 178
Construction Worker [kən strŭk/shən wür/kər] 92
contact [kŏn/tăkt] 146–2
contact lenses [kŏn/tăkt lĕn/zəz] 115–8
container [kən tā/nər] 74–5, 74–17, 78–4
CONTAINERS AND PACKAGING
[kən tā/nərz ən păk/ĭ jĭng] 74
contractor [kŏn/trăk tər] 186–5
control [kən trōl/] 121–27
controller [kən/ trōl ər] 232–4
convenience store [kən vēn/yəns stör/] 128–3
convention centre [kən vĕn/shən sĕn/tər] 127–24
**convert** [kən vürt/] 17–D, 75–C
convertible [kən vür/tə bəl] 156–5
conveyor belt [kən vā/ər bĕlt/] 175–9
convict [kŏn/vĭkt/] 141–15
**convict** [kən vĭkt/] 141–E
cook [ko͝ok] 185–1, 185 ✦
**cook** [ko͝ok] 39–Q, 76–C, 170–C
cooked [ko͝okt] 70–25
cookies [ko͝ok/ēz] 73–38
cookie sheet [ko͝ok/ē shēt/] 78–27
cool [ko͞ol] 13–5
cooler [ko͞o/lər] 225–9

co-op [kō/ŏp/] **52** ✦
copier [kŏ/pē ər]
photocopier [fō/tō kŏ/pē ər] **183**–23
copies / copy [kŏ/pēz] / [kŏ/pē]
copies of ID and credit cards [kŏp/ēz əv ī/dē ən krĕd/ət kärdz/] **146**–19
copies of important papers [kŏp/ēz əv ĭm pört/ənt pā/pərz] **146**–20
copy centre [kŏp/ē sĕn/tər] **129**–18
**copy** [kŏp/ē] **8**–E
cord [körd] **14**–2
bungee cord [bŭn/jē körd/] **181**–15
cordless phone [körd/ləs fōn/] **15**–24
extension cord [ĕk stĕn/shən körd/] **181**–14
frayed cord [frād/ körd/] **179**–5
power cord [pow/ər körd/] **196**–2
corduroy [kör/də roy/] **99**–11
core course [kör/ körs/] **189** ✦
corn [körn] **69**–12, **177**–4
cornrows [körn/ rōz/] **33**–14
corned beef [körnd/ bēf/] **71**–22
corner [kör/nər] **128**–7
coronary disease [kör/ə nĕ/rē dĭ zēz/] **111** ✦
corral [kə răl/] **177**–17
**correct** [kə rĕkt/] **10**–N
correction [kə rĕk/shən]
correction fluid [kə rĕk/shən flōō/əd] **183**–36
correction tape [kə rĕk/shən tāp/] **183**–37
cost [kŏst] **27**–7
costume [kŏs/tōōm] **239**–13
cotton [kŏt/n] **98**–1, **177**–6
couch [kowch] **56**–18
**cough** [kŏf] **110**–A
cough syrup [kŏf/ sĭr/əp] **113**–29
council [kown/səl] **139**–26
councillor [kown/slər] **139**–27
counsellor [kown/slər] **5**–6, **172**–10
**count** [kownt] **84**–A
counter [kown/tər] **54**–22, **113**–18
counter person [kown/tər pür/sən] **79**–17
country [kŭn/trē] **52**–4, **227**–3, **237**–27
country code [kŭn/trē kōd/] **15**–33
county fair [kown/tē fër/] **223**–13
coupe [kōōp] **156**–2
couple [kŭ/pəl] **35**–20, **35**–21, **239**–4
coupons [kōō/pŏnz/] **67**–15
courier [kür/ē ər, kōōr/–] **168**–40
course [körs] **172**–8, **189** ✦
court [kört]
basketball court [băs/kət böl/ kört/] **229**–7
courthouse [kört/hows/] **125**–13
courtroom [kört/rōōm/] **141**–7
court reporter [kört/ rĭ pör/tər] **141**–12
courtyard [kört/yärd/] **5**–1, **51**–21
food court [fōōd/ kört/] **131**–15
Supreme Court [sə prēm/ kört/] **138**–11
tennis court [tĕ/nəs kört/] **224**–6
cousin [kŭz/ən] **34**–9
cover [kŭv/ər] **158**–9, **181**–46
coveralls [kŭv/ər ölz/] **92**–8
cover-up [kŭv/ər ŭp/] **90**–25
cow [kow] **215**–1
cowboy hat [kow/boy/ hăt/] **92**–18
coyote [kī ō/tē, kī/ōt/] **216**–3
CPR (cardiopulmonary resuscitation) [sē/pē/är/] / [kär/dē ō pŭl/mə nër/ē-rē sŭs/ə tā/shən] **117**–17
CPU [sē/pē/yōō/] **196**–4
crab [krăb] **71**–9, **212**–20
cracked [krăkt] **62**–4
cradle [krād/l] **59**–20
crane [krān] **178**–7
crash [krăsh] **144**–3
crayons [krā/ŏnz] **59**–14
cream [krēm] **24**–16, **81**–41, **113**–25
antihistamine cream [ăn/tĭ hĭs/tə mēn krēm/] **117**–11
ice-cream [īs/ krēm/] **72**–26
ice-cream cone [īs/ krēm kōn/] **79**–13
ice cream shop [īs/ krēm shŏp/] **131**–16
shaving cream [shā/vĭng krēm/] **109**–29
sour cream [sow/ər krēm/] **72**–21
creamer [krē/mər] **55**–15
credit [krĕd/ət] **146**–19
creek [krēk] **204** ✦
crescent moon [krĕs/ənt mōōn/] **205**–10
crew [krōō] **176**–1, **176**–4
crewneck [krōō/nĕk] **96**–7
crew socks [krōō/sŏks/] **91**–8
crib [krĭb] **59**–3
cricket [krĭk/ət] **214**–23
crime [krīm] **142** ✦
CRIME [krīm] **142**
criminal [krĭm/ə nəl] **142** ✦
crochetting [krō shā/ĭng] **233**–25
crocodile [krŏk/ə dīl/] **213**–37
crocus [krō/kəs] **211**–17
Crops [krŏps] **177**
cross [krŏs]
cross-country skiing [krŏs/kŭn/trē skē/ĭng] **227**–3
crosswalk [krŏs/wök/] **128**–15
**cross** [krŏs] **128**–A
**cross out** [krŏs/ owt/] **9**–R
crossing [krŏ/sĭng] **154**–13, **154**–14, **154**–15
crown [krown] **119**–9
crown counsel [krown kown/səl] **141**–10
crucible tongs [krōō/sə bəl tŏngz/] **195**–44
crutches [krŭch/əz] **113**–10
**cry** [krī] **206**–B
cube [kyōōb] **193**–38
cubicle [kyōōb/ə kəl] **182**–7
cucumbers [kyōō/kŭm bərz] **69**–10
cuff [kŭf] **100**–9
cup [kŭp] **75**–2, **75**–10, **83**–24
1/2 cup [hăf/ kŭp/] **75**–9
1/4 cup [kwör/tər kŭp/] **75**–8
teacup [tē/kŭp/] **55**–6
curb [kürb] **129**–21
curling iron [kür/lĭng ī/ərn] **108**–17
curly hair [kür/lē hër/] **33**–11
cursor [kür/sər] **197**–14
curtains [kür/tnz] **57**–14, **58**–7
curved line [kürvd/ līn/] **193**–23
cushion [kōō/shən] **56** ✦, **100**–13
customer [kŭs/tə mər] **72**–1, **94**–4, **132**–2, **164**–2
customer service [kŭs/tə mər sür/vəs] **97** ✦
customer service representative [kŭs/tə mər sür/vəs rĕ/prə zĕn/tə tĭv] **167**–20
Customs [kŭs/təmz] **161**
customs officer [kŭs/təmz ŏ/fə sər] **161**–17
cut [kŭt] **91**–10, **110**–13
**cut** [kŭt] **33**–A, **109**–N
**cut up** [kŭt/ ŭp/] **77**–I
cute [kyōōt] **32**–14
cutlets [kŭt/ləts] **70**–6
cutter [kŭt/ər] **183**–22, **232**–16
cutting board [kŭt/ĭng börd/] **54**–27
cycling [sī/klĭng] **228**–5
cyclist [sī/klĭst] **224**–2
cylinder [sĭl/ən dər] **193**–41, **195**–38
cytoplasm [sī/tə plăzm] **194**–9
daffodil [dăf/ə dĭl/] **211**–25
daily [dā/lē] **20**–21
DAILY ROUTINES [dā/lē rōō tēnz/] **38–39**
Dairy [dër/ē] **72**
daisy [dā/zē] **211**–14
**dance** [dăns] **64**–A
dangerous [dān/jər əs] **186**–1
dark blue [därk/ blōō/] **24**–10
Dashboard and Instrument Panel [dăsh/börd/ ən ĭn/strə mənt păn/əl] **159**
dates [dāts] **20**–1, **68**–28
date of birth [dāt əv bürth/] **4**–13
expiration date [ĕk/spə rā/shən dāt/] **112**–7, **136**–10
daughter [dö/tər] **34**–14
daughter-in-law [dö/tər ĭn lö/] **34** ✦
granddaughters [grăn/dö/tərz] **34** ✦
stepdaughter [stĕp/dö/tər] **35** ✦
day [dā] **20**–2
birthday [bürth/dā/] **22**–1
Boxing Day [bŏks/ĭng dā] **22**–17
Canada Day [kăn/ə də dā] **22**–12
Christmas Day [krĭs/məs dā] **22**–16
daylight saving time [dā/līt/ sā/vĭng tīm/] **19**–25
every day [ĕv/rē dā/] **20**–21
Labour Day [lā/bər dā/] **22**–13
New Year's Day [nōō/ yïrz/ dā/] **22**–9
Victoria Day [vĭk/tö/rĭ/ə dā] **22**–11
Day [dā] **18**
DAY AT SCHOOL [dā/ ăt skōōl/] **11**
DAY AT WORK [dā/ ăt würk/] **186–187**
Days of the Week [dāz/ əv dhə wēk/] **20**
dead [dĕd]
dead bolt lock [dĕd/bōlt/ lŏk/] **51**–34
dead end [dĕd/ĕnd/] **154**–6
deaf [dĕf] **32**–12
Dealer [dē/lər] **158**
dealership [dē/lər shĭp/] **126**–4
death certificate [dĕth/ sər tĭf/ə kət] **41**–11
**debate** [də bāt/] **139**–B
decaffeinated coffee [dē/kăf/ə nāt əd kö/fē] **81**–38
decay [də kā/] **119**–7
December [dĭ sĕm/bər] **21**–36
decimal point [dĕ/sə məl poynt/] **17**–7
Decimals [dĕ/sə məlz] **17**
deck [dĕk] **240**–2

declaration [dĕk/lə rā/shən]
  declaration form [dĕk/lə rā/shən förm/] **161**–16
**decline** [dĭ klīn/] **12**–J
decorations [dĕk/ə rā/shənz] **240**–1
deductions [dĭ dŭk/shənz] **165**–13
deed [dēd] **41**–9
deer [dïr] **216**–12
defence lawyer [dĭ fĕns/ loy/ər] **141**–4
defendant [dĭ fĕn/dənt] **141**–5
defroster [dĭ frös/tər] **159**–41
degrees [də grēz/] **13**–8, **193**–26
delayed flight [də lād/ flīt/] **161**–30
**delete** [də lēt/] **196**–C
DELI [dĕl/ē] **71**
**deliver** [də lĭv/ər] **11**–G, **135**–E
delivery person [də lĭv/ə rē pür/sən] **167**–21
dementia [də mĕn/shə] **111**–18
demonstration [dĕ/mən strā/shən] **122**–6
denim [dĕ/nəm] **99**–7
denominator [də nŏmə nā/tər] **192**–6
dental [dĕn/təl]
  dental assistant [dĕn/təl ə sĭs/tənt] **119**–2, **167**–22
  dental floss [dĕn/təl flös/] **109**–24
  dental hygienist [dĕn/təl hī jē/nĭst, –jĕ/nĭst] **119**–3
  dental instruments [dĕn/təl ĭn/strə mənts] **119**–4
DENTAL CARE [dĕn/təl kër/] **119**
Dental Problems [dĕn/təl prŏb/ləmz] **119**
dentist [dĕn/tĭst] **119**–1
Dentistry [dĕn/təs trē/] **119**
dentures [dĕn/chərz] **119**–10
deodorant [dē ō/dər ənt] **108**–5
department [dĭ pärt/mənt] **95**–7, **95**–8
  department store [dĭ pärt/mənt stör/] **131**–13
departure [dĭ pär/chər] **161** ✦, **161**–7
deposit [dĭ pŏz/ət] **132**–3, **132**–7
  deposit slip [dĭ pŏz/ət slĭp/] **132**–4
depression [də prĕ/shən] **115**–5
depth [dĕpth] **17**–19
DESCRIBING CLOTHES [dĭ skrī/bĭng klōz/] **96–97**
DESCRIBING HAIR [dĭ skrī/bĭng hër/] **33**
DESCRIBING PEOPLE [dĭ skrī/bĭng pē/pəl] **32**
DESCRIBING THINGS [dĭ skrī/bĭng thĭngz/] **23**
desert [dĕz/ərt] **204**–4
**design** [dĭ zīn/] **175**–A
designated drivers [dĕz/ĭg nā/təd drī/vərz] **143** ✦
designer [dĭ zī/nər] **98** ✦, **167**–30, **175**–2, **176**–5
desk [dĕsk] **6**–7, **182**–9
  circulation desk [sür/kyə lā/shən dĕsk/] **133**–2
  desk clerk [dĕsk klürk/] **184**–11
  front desk [frŭnt/ dĕsk/] **184**–12
Desktop Computer [dĕsk/tŏp/ kəm pyo͞o/tər] **196**
Desserts [dĭ zürts] **81**
dessert tray [dĭ zürt/ trā/] **83**–10
destination [dĕs/tə nā/shən] **162**–5
detector [dĭ tĕk/tər] **51**–29
detergent [dĭ tür/jənt] **101**–8
diabetes [dī/ə bē/tēz, –təs] **111**–12
diagonal [dī ăg/ə nəl, –ăg/nəl] **193**–31
**dial** [dī/əl] **15**–A, **15**–E
diameter [dī ăm/ə tər] **193**–37
diamonds [dī/məndz] **233**–29
diaper [dī/pər] **37**–8, **37**–10
  diaper pail [dī/pər pāl/] **37**–7
diaphragm [dī/ə frăm] **194**–18
dice [dīs] **232**–6
**dice** [dīs] **77**–J
**dictate** [dĭk/tāt] **8**–N
dictator [dĭk/tā/tər] **199**–6
dictionary [dĭk/shə nër/ē] **7**–30, **7**–31
**die** [dī] **41**–R
dietician [dī/ə tĭsh/ən] **120**–15
difference [dĭf/rəns] **192**–8
different [dĭ/frənt, dĭ/fə rənt] **23**–16
DIFFERENT [dĭ/frənt, dĭ/fə rənt] **28–29**
DIFFERENT PLACES TO LIVE
  [dĭ/frənt plā/səz tə lĭv/, dĭ/fə rənt] **52**
difficult [dĭf/ĭ kŭlt/] **23**–24
digital [dĭ/jə təl]
  digital camera [dĭ/jə təl kăm/rə] **235**–19
  digital photo album [dĭ/jə təl fō/tō ăl/bəm] **235**–32
dime [dīm] **26**–3
Dimensions [də mĕn/shənz] **17**
diner [dī/nər] **82**–6, **185**–9
dining [dī/nĭng]
  dining area [dī/nĭng ër/ē ə] **46**–7
  dining room [dī/nĭng ro͞om/] **82**–1
  dining room chair [dī/nĭng ro͞om/ chër/] **55**–8
  dining room table [dī/nĭng ro͞om/tā/bəl] **55**–9
Dining [dī/nĭng] **185**
DINING AREA [dī/nĭng ër/ē ə] **55**
dinner [dĭn/ər] **72**–28
  dinner fork [dĭn/ər förk/] **83**–28
  dinner plate [dĭn/ər plāt/] **83**–18
  dinner salad [dĭn/ər săl/əd] **80**–15
Dinner [dĭn/ər] **81**
diploma [də plō/mə] **40**–3
direct flight [də rĕkt/ flīt/, dī–] **161** ✦
Directions [də rĕk/shənz, dī–] **9, 155**
DIRECTIONS AND MAPS
  [də rĕk/shənz ən măps/, dī–] **155**
directory [də rĕk/tə rē, dī–] **131**–24
  directory assistance
    [də rĕk/tə rē ə sĭs/təns, dī–] **14**–22
dirty [dür/tē] **101**–15
Disabilities [dĭ/sə bĭ/lə tēz] **32**
**disagree** [dĭ/sə grē/] **12**–L
disappointed [dĭ/sə poyn/təd] **28**–4
DISASTERS [dĭ/zăs tərz] **144–145**
disc [dĭsk] **231**–27
**discipline** [dĭs/ə plən] **36**–K
**discuss** [dĭ skŭs/] **8**–G
disease [dĭ zēz/] **111**–11, **111** ✦, **119**–11
Diseases [dĭ zē/zəz] **111**
disgusted [dĭ skŭs/təd] **42**–7
dish [dĭsh] **55**–1
  casserole dish [kăs/ə rōl dĭsh/] **78**–10
  dish rack [dĭsh/ răk/] **54**–5
  dish room [dĭsh/ ro͞om/] **83**–13
  dish towel [dĭsh/ tow/əl] **61**–22
  dishwasher [dĭsh/wö/shər] **54**–8, **83**–14, **185**–2
  dishwashing liquid [dĭsh/wö/shĭng lĭk/wəd] **61**–21
  satellite dish [să/tə līt dĭsh/] **53**–6
  soap dish [sōp/ dĭsh/] **57**–3
disinfectant wipes [dĭs/ən fĕk/tənt wīps/] **61**–23
display case [dĭ splā/ kās/] **94**–5
disposable [dĭ spō/zə bəl]
  disposable diaper [dĭ spō/zə bəl dī/pər] **37**–10
  disposable gloves [dĭ spō/zə bəl glŭvz/] **93**–27
disposal [dĭ spō/zəl] **54**–7, **121**–31
**dive** [dīv] **230**–K
**divide** [dĭ vīd/] **17**–A, **192**–D
diving [dī/vĭng] **227**–12
  diving mask [dī/vĭng măsk/] **225**–6
divorced couple [də vörst/ kŭ/pəl] **35**–21
DJ [dē/jā/] **64**–4
**do** [do͞o]
  **do** an experiment [do͞o ən ĭk spĕr/ə mənt] **195**–B
  **do** crafts [do͞o krăfts/] **232**–D
  **do** errands [do͞o ĕr/əndz] **128** ✦
  **do** manual labour [do͞o măn/yo͞o əl lā/bər] **170**–D
  **do not drink** [do͞o nŏt drĭnk/] **112**–F
  **do not enter** [do͞o nŏt/ ĕn/tər] **154**–2
  **do not operate** [do͞o nŏt/ ŏp/ə rāt/] **112**–E
  **do not take** [do͞o nŏt/ tāk/] **112**–D
  **don't be** late [dōnt/ bē/ lāt/] **174**–E
  **don't litter** [dōnt/ lĭ/tər] **219**–L
  **don't smoke** [dōnt/smōk/] **114**–G
dock [dŏk] **175**–15, **234**–3
  dockworker [dŏk/wür/kər] **167**–23
doctor [dŏk/tər] **118**–5
DOCUMENTS [dŏ/kyə mənts] **40–41**
dog [dög] **79**–6, **215**–11, **215**–22
dogwood [dög/wo͝od/] **210**–15
DOING THE LAUNDRY [do͞o/ĭng dhə lön/drē] **101**
doll [dŏl] **59**–21, **233**–28
  dollhouse [dŏl/hows/] **59**–18
  doll-making kit [dŏl/ mā/kĭng kĭt/] **232**–13
dollar [dŏl/ər] **26**–5
  fifty dollars [fĭf/tē dŏl/ərz] **26**–10
  five dollars [fīv/ dŏl/ərz] **26**–7
  one hundred dollars
    [wŭn/ hŭn/drəd dŏl/ərz] **26**–11
  ten dollars [tĕn/ dŏl/ərz] **26**–8
  twenty dollars [twĕn/tē dŏl/ərz] **26**–9
  two dollars [to͞o dŏl/ərz] **26**–6
dolphin [dŏl/fən] **213**–31
domesticated [də mĕs/tə kā/təd] **215** ✦
DOMESTIC ANIMALS AND RODENTS
  [də mĕs/tĭk ăn/ə məlz ən rōd/nts] **215**
donkey [dŏng/kē] **215**–3
donut [dō/nŭt] **79**–15
door [dör] **46**–3
  doorbell [dör/bĕl/] **53**–14
  door chain [dör/ chān/] **51**–33
  doorknob [dör/nŏb/] **53**–12
  door lock [dör/ lŏk] **159**–25
  doorman [dör/măn/] **184**–1
  4-door car [för/dör kär/] **156**–1
  front door [frŭnt/ dör/] **53**–11
  garage door [gə rŏj/ dör/] **53**–7
  revolving door [rĭ vŏl/vĭng dör/] **184**–2
  screen door [skrēn/ dör/] **53**–15
  sliding glass door [slī/dĭng glăs/dör] **53**–18
  storm door [störm/ dör/] **53**–10
  2-door car [to͞o/dör kär/] **156**–2
dosage [dō/sĭj] **112**–6

double [dŭb/əl]
- double bed [dŭb/əl bĕd/] **184**–14
- double boiler [dŭb/əl boy/lər] **78**–8

doughnut [dō/ nŭt] **79**–15
- doughnut shop [dō/ nŭt shŏp] **129**–17

down [down]
- **break down** [brāk/ down/] **162**–D
- downhill skiing [down/hĭl/ skē/ĭng] **227**–1
- down jacket [down jăk/ət] **90**–16
- down vest [down vĕst/] **90**–14
- drop-down menu [drŏp/ down/ mĕn/yōō/] **197**–8
- **put down** [pŏŏt/ down/] **6**–J
- **sit down** [sĭt down/] **6**–F
- **walk** down [wŏk down/] **153**–D

downstairs [down/stërz/] **51** ✦

DOWNTOWN [down/town/] **124–125**

drain [drān] **57**–7

drama [drŏ/mə, drə̆/mə] **236**–12

drapes [drāps] **56**–16

**draw** [drŏ] **8**–F, **118**–F, **195**–E

drawer [drör] **54**–23, **58**–2, **59**–6

dress [drĕs] **86**–3, **88**–5, **89**–20
- dressmaker [drĕs/mā/kər] **100**–1
- dressmaker's dummy [drĕs/mā/kərz dŭ/mē] **100**–2
- dress socks [drĕs/ sŏks/] **91**–9

**dress** [drĕs] **36**–H, **174**–B

dressed [drĕst] **38**–D

dresser [drĕs/ər] **58**–1

Dressings [drĕs/ĭngz] **80**

**dribble** [drĭb/əl] **230**–J

drill [drĭl] **178**–9, **180**–8
- drill bit [drĭl bĭt] **180**–28

**drill** [drĭl] **119**–D

**drink** [drĭnk] **11**–J
- **do not drink** alcohol [dōō/ nŏt/ drĭnk/ ăl/kə hŏl/] **112**–F
- **don't drink** and **drive** [dōnt/ drĭnk ən drīv/] **143**–G
- **drink** fluids [drĭnk flōō/ədz] **114**–C

drip [drĭp] **121**–25

dripping [drĭp/ĭng] **63**–17

drive [drīv] **196**–6, **196**–8, **196**–9
- drive-through window [drīv/thrōō/ wĭn/dō] **128**–11
- driveway [drīv/wā/] **53**–8

**drive** [drīv]
- **don't drink** and **drive** [dōnt/drĭnk ən drīv/] **143**–G
- **drive** a truck [drīv ə trŭk] **170**–E
- **drive** through [drīv/ thrōō] **153**–K
- **drive** to work [drīv/ tə würk/] **38**–I

driver [drī/vər] **152**–21, **169**–61
- designated drivers [dĕz/ĭg nā/təd drī/vərz] **143** ✦
- driver's licence [drī/vərz lī/səns] **40**–4, **136**–9
- driver's licence number [drī/vərz lī/səns nŭm/bər] **136**–11
- Phillips screwdriver [fĭl/ĭps skrōō/drī/vər] **180**–31
- screwdriver [skrōō/drī/vər] **180**–30

driver licensing office [drī/vər lī sən sĭng ŏf/əs] **124**–4

DRIVER LICENSING OFFICE [drī/vər lī sən sĭng ŏf/əs] **136–137**

driving [drī/vĭng] **142**–5

driving handbook [drī/vĭng hănd/bŏŏk] **136**–1

drop [drŏp]
- drop cloth [drŏp/ klŏth/] **181**–54
- drop-down menu [drŏp/ down/ mĕn/yōō/] **197**–8

**drop off** [drŏp/ ŏf/] **38**–G

dropper [drŏp/ər] **195**–45

drops [drŏps] **113**–31

drought [drowt] **145**–11

**drown** [drown] **116**–I

drugs [drŭgz] **116**–K, **142**–6

drums [drŭmz] **238**–16

drumsticks [drŭm/stĭks/] **70**–23

drunk driving [drŭngk/ drī/vĭng] **142**–5

dry [drī] **101**–18
- dry cleaners [drī/ klē/nərz] **128**–2
- dry-erase marker [drī/ ĭ rās/ mär/kər] **7**–17
- drywall [drī/wŏl/] **178**–19

**dry** [drī] **60**–N, **108**–H

dryer [drī/ər] **50**–13, **101**–4
- blow dryer [blō/ drī/ər] **33**–23, **108**–18
- dryer sheets [drī/ər shēts/] **101**–5

Dry Measures [drī/ mĕzh/ərz] **75**

duck [dŭk] **70**–18, **214**–12

duct tape [dŭkt/ tāp/] **181**–49

dummy [dŭ/mē] **100**–2

dump truck [dŭmp/ trŭk/] **156**–19

dune [dōōn, dyōōn] **204**–5

duplex [dōō/plĕks/] **52** ✦

During an Emergency [dōō/rĭng ən ĭ mür/jən sē] **147**

dust [dŭst]
- dust pan [dŭst/păn/] **61**–17
- dust ruffle [dŭst/ rŭf/əl] **58**–17
- dust storm [dŭst/ störm/] **13**–19

**dust** [dŭst] **60**–A

duster [dŭs/tər] **61**–1

DVD [dē/vē/dē/] **133**–19, **234**–11
- DVD and CD-ROM drive [dē/vē/dē/ ən sē/dē/rŏm/ drīv/] **196**–9
- DVD player [dē/vē/dē/ plā/ ər] **56**–7, **234**–10

**dye** [dī] **33**–D

eagle [ē/gəl] **214**–9

ear [ïr] **32**–17, **105**–12
- earache [ïr/āk/] **110**–3
- ear infection [ïr/ ĭn fĕk/shən] **111**–3
- earmuffs [ïr/mŭfs/] **90**–13, **179**–16
- ear plugs [ïr/ plŭgz/] **179**–15
- pierced earrings [pïrst/ ïr/ĭngz] **95**–36

early [ür/lē] **19**–22

Earth [ürth] **205**–3

earthquake [ürth/kwāk/] **144**–5

easel [ē/zəl] **233**–18

east [ēst] **155**–4

Eastern time [ē/stərn tīm/] **19**–32

easy [ē/zē] **23**–23, **76**–11
- easy chair [ē/zē chër/] **56**–22

Easy Chicken Soup [ē/zē chĭk/ən sōōp/] **77**

**eat** [ēt] **11**–I
- **eat** a healthy diet [ēt ə hĕl/thē dī/ət] **114**–F
- **eat** breakfast [ēt brĕk/fəst] **38**–E
- **eat** dinner [ēt dĭn/ər] **39**–S
- **eat** out [ēt/ owt/] **82** ✦

eavestrough [ēvz/trŏf] **53**–4

eclipse [ĭ klĭps/] **205**–16, **205** ✦

**edit** [ĕd/ət] **191**–I

education [ĕ jyōō/ kā/shən] **189**–17

eel [ēl] **212**–12

eggplants [ĕg/plănts/] **69**–23

eggs [ĕgz] **66**–7
- egg beater [ĕg/bē/tər] **78**–20
- eggs over easy [ĕgz ō/vər ē/zē] **76**–11
- eggs sunny side up [ĕgz sŭn/ē sīd/ ŭp/] **76**–10
- hard-boiled eggs [härd/ boyld/ ĕgz/] **76**–8
- poached eggs [pōcht/ ĕgz/] **76**–9
- scrambled eggs [skrăm/bəld ĕgz/] **76**–7

Eggs [ĕgz] **76**

eight [āt] **16**

eighteen [ā/tēn/] **16**

eighteenth [ā/tēnth/] **16**

eighth [ātth, āth] **16**

eightieth [ā/tē/əth] **16**

eighty [ā/tē] **16**

elastic bandage [ĭ lăs/tĭk băn/dĭj] **117**–12

elbow [ĕl/bō] **106**–12

elderly [ĕl/dər lē] **32**–3

elected [ĭ lĕk/təd] **139**–C
- elected official [ĭ lĕk/təd ə fĭ/shəl] **139**–28

Election [ĭ lĕk/shən] **139**

election results [ĭ lĕk/shən rĭ zŭltz/] **139**–27

elective [ĭ lĕk/tĭv] **189** ✦

electric [ĭ lĕk/trĭk] **116**–F
- electric can opener [ĭ lĕk/trĭk kăn/ ō/pə nər] **54**–14
- electric drill [ĭ lĕk/trĭk drĭl/] **180**–8
- electric keyboard [ĭ lĕk/trĭk kē/börd/] **238**–18
- electric mixer [ĭ lĕk/trĭk mĭk/sər] **54**–25
- electric pencil sharpener [ĭ lĕk/trĭk pĕn/səl shär/pə nər] **183**–26
- electric shaver [ĭ lĕk/trĭk shā/vər] **109**–26

electrical [ĕ lĕk/trĭ kəl]
- electrical hazard [ĕ lĕk/trĭ kəl hăz/ərd] **186**–6
- electrical tape [ĕ lĕk/trĭ kəl tāp/] **181**–43

electrician [ĕ lĕk trĭsh/ən] **62**–9

electron [ĕ lĕk/trŏn] **195**–30

electronics [ĕ lĕk trŏn/ĭks]
- electronics repair person [ĕ lĕk trŏn/ĭks rĭ pĕr/ pür/sən] **167**–24
- electronics store [ĕ lĕk trŏn/ĭks stör/] **131**–20

ELECTRONICS AND PHOTOGRAPHY [ĕ lĕk trŏn/ĭks ən fə tŏg/rə fē] **234–235**

elementary school [ĕl/ə mĕn/trē skōōl/] **188**–2

elephant [ĕl/ə fənt] **217**–44

elevator [ĕl/ə vā/tər] **50**–9, **131**–21, **184**–9

eleven [ĭ lĕv/ən] **16**

eleventh [ĭ lĕv/ənth] **16**

**eliminate** [ĭ lĭ mĭ nāt] **140**–F

elk [ĕlk] **216**–14

elm [ĕlm] **210**–16

Email [ē/māl/] **197**

embarrassed [ĭm băr/əst] **43**–24

embroidery [ĭm broy/də rē] **233**–24

EMERGENCIES [ĭ mür/jən sēz] **116**

EMERGENCIES AND NATURAL DISASTERS [ĭ mür/jən sēz ən năch/rəl dĭ zăs/tərz,–năch/ə rəl–] **144–145**

emergency [ĭ mür/jən sē] **117**–3
- emergency card [ĭ mür/jən sē kärd/] **161**–26
- emergency exit [ĭ mür/jən sē ĕg/zət,–ĕk/sət] **51**–25, **161**–14

Emergency [ĭ mür′jən sē] **146–147**
Emergency Call [ĭ mür′jən sē köl′] **15**
EMERGENCY PROCEDURES
[ĭ mür′jən sē prə sē′jərz] **146–147**
Emergency Room Entrance
[ĭ mür′jən sē ro͞om′ ĕn′trəns] **121**
Emergency Worker [ĭ mür′jən sē wür′kər] **93**
emery board [ĕm′ə rē börd′, ĕm′rē-] **109**–32
emperor [ĕm′pər ər] **199**–3
employee [ĕm ploy′ē] **165**–9
employer [ĕm ploy′ər] **164**–4
empty [ĕmp′tē] **23**–10
**empty** [ĕmp′tē] **60**–L
end [ĕnd] **154**–6
endpoint [ĕnd′poynt′] **193**–21
end table [ĕnd′ tā′bəl] **56**–14
energy [ĕn′ər jē] **218**–1, **218**–7, **218**–8
bioenergy [bī′ō ĕn′ər jē] **218**–9
ENERGY AND CONSERVATION
[ĕn′ər jē ən kŏn′sər vā′shən] **218–219**
Energy and Resources [ĕn′ər jē ən rē′sör′səz] **219**
Energy Sources [ĕn′ər jē sör′səz] **218**
engine [ĕn′jən] **158**–18, **197**–6
engineer [ĕn′jə nïr′] **167**–18, **167**–25
ENGLISH COMPOSITION
[ĭng′glĭsh kŏm′pə zĭsh′ən] **190–191**
English muffin [ĭng′glĭsh mŭf′ən] **80**–5
**enter** [ ĕn′tər]
**do not enter** [do͞o′ nŏt′ ĕn′tər] **154**–2
**enter** data [ĕn′tər dā′tə] **171**–B
**enter** the room [ĕn′tər dhe ro͞om′] **11**–A
**enter** your PIN [ĕn′tər yər pĭn′] **132**–E
ENTERTAINMENT [ĕn′tər tān′mənt] **236–237**
entertainment centre [ĕn′tər tān′mənt sĕn′tər] **56**–5
entrance [ĕn′trəns] **164**–1
Entrance [ĕn′trəns] **50, 121**
entry-level job [ĕn′trē lĕv′əl jŏb′] **172**–1
envelope [ĕn′və lōp′] **134**–3, **134**–14, **183**–43
equation [ĭ kwā′zhən] **192**–13
equipment [ĭ kwĭp′mənt] **177**–12, **179**–4
Equipment [ĭ kwĭp′mənt] **179, 183**
EQUIPMENT [ĭ kwĭp′mənt] **231**
Equivalencies [ĭ kwĭ′və lən sēz′] **17, 75**
**erase** [ĭ rās′] **10**–M
eraser [ĭ rā′sər] **7**–19, **7**–21
errands [ĕr′əndz] **128** ✦
eruption [ĭ rŭp′shən] **145**–16
escalator [ĕs′kə lā′tər] **131**–23
escape [ĭs kāp′] **50**–2
escape route [ĭs kāp′ ro͞ot′, rowt′] **146**–3
ESL [ē′ĕs′ĕl′] **189**–14
essay [ĕs′ā] **190**–4
Essay [ĕs′ā] **190**
e-ticket [ē′tĭ kət] **161**–19
evacuation route [ĭ văk′yo͞o′ā shən ro͞ot′, rowt′] **146**–5
evening [ēv′nĭng] **18**–19
evening gown [ēv′nĭng gown′] **89**–18
even numbers [ē′vən nŭm′bərz] **192**–4
EVENTS [ĭ vĕnts′] **22, 40–41**
every day [ĕv′rē dā′] **20**–21
EVERYDAY CLOTHES [ĕv′rē dā′ klōz] **86–87**
EVERDAY CONVERSATION
[ĕv′rē dā′ kŏn′vər sā′shən] **12**
evidence [ĕv′ĭ dəns′] **141**–9
exam [ĭg zăm′] **122**–1, **136**–6
examination table [ĭg zăm′ə nā′shən tā′bəl] **118**–7
**examine** [ĭg zăm′ən] **118**–D, **118**–E
Examining Room [ĭg zăm′ə nĭng ro͞om′] **118**
**exchange** [ĭks chānj′] **27**–I
excited [ĭk sī′təd] **43**–22
exclamation mark [ĕk′sklə mā′shən märk′] **190**–13
executive [ĭg zĕk′yə tĭv] **182**–5
executive chef [ĭg zĕk′yə tĭv shĕf′] **185**–7
exercise [ĕk′sər sīz′] **122**–5
**exercise** [ĕk′sər sīz′] **39**–P, **230**–N
Exercise Wear [ĕk′sər sīz′wër] **89**
exhausted [ĭg zö′stəd] **43** ✦
ex-husband [ĕks′ hŭz′bənd] **35** ✦
exit [ĕg′zət, ĕk′sət] **51**–25, **51** ✦, **161**–14
expensive [ĭk spĕn′sĭv] **23**–19, **97**–44
Experiment [ĕk spĕr′ə mənt] **195**
expiration date [ĕk′spə rā′shən dāt′] **112**–7, **136**–10
**expire** [ĕk′spīr′] **136** ✦
**explain** [ĕk splān′] **12**–M
exploration [ĕk′splə rā′shən] **199**–8
explorer [ĕk splör′ər] **199**–9
explosion [ĕk splō′zhən] **144**–4
exposed [ĭk spōzd′]
overexposed [ō′vər ĭk spōzd′] **235**–34
underexposed [ŭn′dər ĭk spōzd′] **235**–35
**express** [ĕk sprĕs′] **140**–E
expression [ĕk sprĕ shŭn] **140**–2
Extended Family [ĕk stĕn′dəd făm′lē, făm′ə lē] **34**
extension cord [ĕk stĕn′shən körd′] **181**–14
**exterminate** [ĕk stür′mə nāt′] **62** ✦
exterminator [ĕk stür′mə nā′tər] **63**–21
extinguisher [ĕk stĭn′gwə shər] **179**–21
extra [ĕk′strə]
extra large [ĕk′strə lärj′] **96**–5
extra small [ĕk′strə smöl′] **96**–1
ex-wife [ĕks′ wīf′] **35** ✦
eye [ī] **99**–27, **105**–11
eyebrow [ī′brow′] **106**–9
eyebrow pencil [ī′brow′ pĕn′səl] **109**–34
eye drops [ī′drŏps′] **113**–31
eye hook [ī′ho͝ok′] **180**–40
eyelashes [ī′lăsh′əz] **106**–11
eyelid [ī′lĭd′] **106**–10
eyeliner [ī′lī′nər] **109**–36
eyepiece [ī′pēs′] **194**–14
eyeshadow [ī′shă′dō] **109**–35
Eye [ī] **106**
fabric [făb′rĭk] **98**–15
fabric softener [făb′rĭk sö′fə nər] **101**–6
Fabric Store [făb′rĭk stör′] **99**
face [fās] **193**–44
face mask [fās măsk′] **93**–32
face powder [fās′ pow′dər] **109**–41
Face [fās] **106**
factory [făk′tə rē, –trē] **126**–3
factory owner [făk′tə rē ō′nər, –trē] **175**–1
factory worker [făk′tə rē wür′kər, –trē] **175**–3
Factory [făk′tə rē, –trē] **98**
FACTORY [făk′tə rē, –trē] **175**
Fahrenheit [făr′ən hīt′] **13**–1
fair [fër] **172**–13, **223**–13
FAIR [fër] **122–123**
fall [föl] **21**–39
**fall** [föl] **40**–H, **116**–O
FAMILIES [făm′lēz, făm′ə lēz] **34–35**
Family [făm′lē, făm′ə lē ] **34**
FAMILY REUNION
[făm′lē rē yo͞on′yən, făm′ə lē] **44–45**
famine [fā′mĭn] **145**–12
fan [făn] **55**–19, **229**–4
fancy [făn′sē] **97**–34
far from [făr′ frŭm′, –frəm′] **25** ✦
fare [fër] **152**–2
fare card [fër kärd′] **152**–11
farm [färm] **52**–9
farm equipment [färm ĭ kwĭp′mənt] **177**–12
farmhand [färm′ hănd] **177**–8
Farm Animals [färm′ ăn′ə məlz] **215**
farmer [făr′mər] **177**–13
FARMERS' MARKET [făr′mərz mär′kət] **84–85**
Farmhand [färm′ hănd] **92**
FARMING AND RANCHING
[făr′mĭng ən răn′chĭng] **177**
fashion [făsh′ən] **88** ✦
fashion designer [făsh′ən dĭ zī′nər] **98** ✦
fast [făst] **23**–3
fast-food restaurant [făst′ fo͞od′ rĕs′tə rŏnt] **128**–10
**fasten** [făs′ən] **160**–H
fastener [făs′nər] **99**–29
FAST-FOOD RESTAURANT
[făst′ fo͞od′ rĕs′tə rŏnt] **79**
**fast forward** [făst′ för′wərd] **235**–D
fat [făt] **32**–7
father [fö′dhər] **34**–4, **35**–23
father-in-law [fö′dhər ĭn lö′] **34**–11
Fathers of Confederation [fö′dhərz əv kən fĕd ə rā′shŭn] **198**–5
grandfather [grăn′fö′dhər, grănd′–] **34**–2
stepfather [stĕp′födhər] **35**–25
faucet [fö′sət] **57**–8
**fax** [făks] **171**–G
fax machine [făks′ mə shēn′] **183**–21
feast [fēst] **239**–9
feather [fĕdh′ər] **214**–4
feather duster [fĕdh′ər dŭs′tər] **61**–1
February [fĕb′yo͞o ër′ē, fĕb′ro͞o–] **21**–26
Federal Government
[fĕ′də rəl gŭ′vərn mənt, fĕ′drəl] **138**
**feed** [fēd] **36**–C, **176**–D, **177**–D
feed dog / feed bar [fēd′dŏg′ / fēd′ bär′] **98**–20
**feel** [fēl] **110**–C, **110**–D
FEELINGS [fē′lĭngz] **42-43**
female [fē′māl′] **4**–18
fence [fĕns] **177**–19
fencing [fĕn′sĭng] **228**–7
ferry [fër′ē] **220**–6
**fertilize** [fürt′ əl īz′] **176**–D
fever [fē′vər] **110**–8
fiction [fĭk′shən] **237**–18
field [fēld] **5**–2, **177**–7

ball field [böl/ fēld/] **224**–1
track and field [trăk/ ən fēld/] **228**–18
fifteen [fĭf/tēn/] **16**
fifteenth [fĭf/tēnth/] **16**
fifth [fĭfth] **16**
fiftieth [fĭf/tē əth] **16**
fifty [fĭf/tē] **16**
fifty dollars [fĭf/tē dŏl/ərz] **26**–10
50 percent [fĭf/tē pər sĕnt/] **17**–10
fighter [fī/tər]
firefighter [fīr/fī/tər] **144**–9, **167**–26
figs [fĭgz] **68**–27
figure [fĭg/yər] **233**–26
figure skating [fĭg/yər skā/tĭng] **227**–5
figurine [fĭg/yə rēn/] **232**–1
file [fīl] **183**–44
file cabinet [fīl kăb/ə nət] **182**–11
file clerk [fīl klürk/] **182**–10
file folder [fīl fōl/dər] **183**–50
**fill** [fĭl]
**fill** a cavity [fĭl/ ə kăv/ə tē] **119**–E
**fill** prescriptions [fĭl/ prĭ skrĭp/shənz] **112** ✦
**fill in** [fĭl/ ĭn], **9**–O, **10**–K
**fill out** [fĭl/ owt/] **173**–J
**fill** the tank [fĭl/ dhe tănk/] **157**–G
**fill** the tires [fĭl/ dhe tīrz/] **157**–L
filling [fĭl/ĭng] **119**–8
Filling Out a Form [fĭl/ĭng owt ə förm/] **4**
film [fĭlm] **235**–22
film camera [fĭlm kăm/rə] **235**–21
**find** [fīnd] **160**–F
FINDING A HOME [fīn/dĭng ə hōm/] **48–49**
fine adjustment knob [fīn/ ə jŭst/mənt nŏb/] **194**–22
fingers [fĭng/gərz] **105**–16, **110**–16
fingernail [fĭng/gər nāl/] **106**–18
Fingers [fĭng/gərz] **106**
**finish** [fĭn/ĭsh] **112**–C, **230**–T
fins [fĭnz] **212**–1, **225**–7
fire [fīr] **144**–7, **144**–8
campfire [kămp/fīr/] **226**–11
fire escape [fīr ĭ skāp/] **50**–2
fire exit [fīr/ ĕg/zət, –ĕk/sət] **51** ✦
fire extinguisher [fīr ĭk stĭng/gwĭ shər] **179**–21
firefighter [fīr/fī/tər] **144**–9, **167**–26
fire hydrant [fīr hī/drənt] **129**–27
fireplace [fīr/plās/] **56**–13
fire screen [fīr skrēn/] **56**–12
fire station [fīr stā/shən] **125**–12
fire truck [fīr trŭk/] **144**–10
fireworks [fīr/würks/] **239**–7
first [fürst] **16**
first aid kit [fürst/ ād/ kĭt/] **117**–1, **146**–18
first aid manual [fürst/ ād/ măn/yōō əl] **117**–2
first name [fürst/ nām/] **4**–2
First Nations [fürst/ nā shənz] **198**–4
first prime minister [fürst/ prīm/mĭn/ə stər] **198**–7
First Aid [fürst/ ād/] **117**
FIRST AID [fürst/ ād/] **117**
First Aid Procedures [fürst/ ād/ prə sē/ jərz] **117**
First Floor [fürst/ flör/] **50**
First License [fürst/ lī/səns] **137**
fish [fĭsh] **66**–1, **81**–29, **209**–14
catfish [kăt/fĭsh/] **71**–2
goldfish [gōld/fĭsh/] **215**–16
jellyfish [jĕ/lē fĭsh/] **212**–14
starfish [stär/fĭsh/] **212**–16
swordfish [sörd/fĭsh/] **71**–5
Fish [fĭsh] **71, 212**
fisher [fĭsh/ər] **167**–17
fishing [fĭsh/ĭng] **226**–4
fishing net [fĭsh/ĭng nĕt/] **226**–17
fishing pole [fĭsh/ĭng pōl/] **226**–18
fitted sheet [fĭt/əd shēt/] **58**–12
fittings [fĭt/ĭngz] **181**–18
five [fīv] **16**
five after one [fīv ăf/tər wŭn/] **18**–7
five dollars [fīv dŏl/ərz] **26**–7
**fix** [fĭks] **62** ✦, **219**–F
fixture [fĭks/chər] **55**–18
flag [flăg] **239**–8
flammable liquids [flăm/ə bəl lĭk/wədz] **179**–8
flashlight [flăsh/līt/] **146**–14
flat [flăt]
flat panel TV [flăt/ păn/əl tē/vē/] **234**–7
flat screen TV [flăt/ skrēn/ tē/vē/] **234**–7
flat sheet [flăt/ shēt] **58**–13
**have** a flat tire [hăv/ ə flăt/ tīr/] **162**–F
flats [flăts] **95**–27
fleas [flēz] **63**–25
flea market [flē/ mär/kət] **222**–6
flight [flīt] **161**–30, **161** ✦
flight attendant [flīt/ ə tĕn/dənt] **161**–12
Flight [flīt] **160**
float [flōt/] **239**–2
flood [flŭd] **145**–19
floor [flör] **46**–6, **58**–21, **179**–6
floor lamp [flör lămp/] **56**–15
floor plan [flör plăn/] **186**–4
Floor [flör] **50**
floral [flör/əl] **96**–25
florist [flör/ĭst] **130**–8, **167**–27
floss [flös] **109**–24
**floss** [flös] **109**–K
flounder [flown/dər] **212**–15
flour [flow/ər] **73**–29
Flower [flow/ər] **211**
flowers [flow/ərz] **208**–7
flower bed [flow/ər bĕd/] **53**–20
FLOWERS [flow/ərz] **211**
flu [flōō] **111**–2
fluid [flōō/əd] **183**–36
fluid ounce [flōō/əd owns/] **75**–1
flute [flōōt] **238**–1
fly [flī] **214**–28
**fly** [flī] **170**–F
flyer [flī/ər] **102**–1
flying disc [flī/ĭng dĭsk/] **231**–27
foam pad [fōm/ păd/] **226**–13
focus [fō/kəs] **235**–33
foggy [fö/gē] **13**–20
foil [foyl] **72**–23
**fold** [fōld] **101**–F
folder [fōl/dər] **183**–50
folding [fōl/dĭng]
folding card table [fōl/dĭng kärd/ tā/bəl] **102**–4
folding chair [fōl/dĭng chër/] **102**–5
folk [fōk] **237**–29
**follow** [fŏl/ō] **114**–J, **147**–F
Following Directions [fŏl/ō ĭng də rek/shənz, –dī–] **9**
food [fōōd]
baby food [bā/bē fōōd/] **37**–4
canned food [kănd/ fōōd] **146**–9
fast-food restaurant [făst/ fōōd/ rĕs/tə rönt] **128**–10
food court [fōōd/kört] **131**–15
food preparation worker [fōōd/ prē/pə rā/shən wür/kər] **185**–4
food processor [fōōd/ prö/sĕ sər] **54**–26
packaged food [păk/ĭjd fōōd/] **146**–10
pet food [pĕt/ fōōd/] **72**–5
FOOD [fōōd] **79**
FOOD PREPARATION AND SAFETY [fōōd/ prē/pə rā/shən ən sāf/tē] **76–77**
Food Processor [fōōd/ prö/sĕ sər] **92**
Foods [fōōdz] **72, 73**
Food Safety [fōōd/ sāf/tē] **76**
FOOD SERVICE [fōōd/sür/vəs] **185**
foot [fŏŏt] **104**–8
football [fŏŏt/böl/] **229**–11, **231**–21
football helmet [fŏŏt/böl/ hĕl/mət] **231**–19
footnote [fŏŏt/nōt/] **190**–10
Foot [fŏŏt] **106**
for [för] **128**–B, **173**–C
forceps [för/səps, –sĕps] **195**–43
forearm [för/ärm/] **106**–13
forehead [för/hĕd/] **106**–2
forest [för/əst] **204**–1, **204**–11
forest fire [för/əst fīr/] **144**–7
rainforest [rān för/əst] **204**–1
fork [förk] **55**–3, **83**–27, **83**–28
forklift [förk/lĭft/] **175**–12
Form [förm] **4**
Formal Clothes [förm/əl klōz/] **89**
former husband [för/mər hŭz/bənd] **35** ✦
former wife [för/mər wīf/] **35** ✦
forms [förmz] **118**–4, **134**–19, **161**–16
formula [för/myə lə] **37**–3, **195**–34
fortieth [för/tē əth] **16**
forty [för/tē] **16**
forward [för/wərd] **235**–D
forward button [för/wərd bŭt/n] **197**–3
foundation [fown dā/shən] **109**–40
fountain [fown/tn] **224**–5, **224**–9
four [för] **16**
4-door car [för/dör kär/] **156**–1
2 x 4 (two by four) [tōō/ bī för/] **181**–19
fourteen [för/tēn/] **16**
fourteenth [för/tēnth/] **16**
fourth [förth] **16**
Fourth Floor [förth flör/] **50**
fox [fŏks] **216**–17
Fractions [frăk/shənz] **192**
Fractions and Decimals [frăk/shənz ən dĕ/sə məlz] **17**
frame [frām] **58**–4, **58**–18
frayed cord [frād/ körd/] **179**–5
free [frē] **122**–7
freedom [frē/dəm] **140**–1, **140**–2, **140**–4

freezer [frē′zər] **54**–10, **185**–3
freezing [frē′zĭng] **13**–7
French [frĕnch]
  french fries [frĕnch′ frīz′] **79**–2
  French horn [frĕnch′ hörn′] **238**–13
Frequency [frē′kwən sē′] **20**
fresh [frĕsh] **71**–16
Friday [frī′dā] **20**–13
fried [frīd] **76**–6
  fried chicken [frīd′ chĭk′ən] **76**–1
fringe [frĭnj] **99**–34
frog [frŏg] **212**–25
front [frŭnt] **25**–7
  front desk [frŭnt′ dĕsk′] **184**–12
  front door [frŭnt′ dör′] **53**–11
  front seat [frŭnt′ sēt′] **159**–51
  front walk [frŭnt′ wök′] **53**–2
Front Porch [frŭnt′ pörch′] **53**
Font Yard and House [frŭnt′ yärd′ en hows′] **53**
frostbite [frŏst′bīt′] **116**–G
frozen [frō′zən] **63**–16, **71**–17
  frozen dinner [frō′zən dĭn′ər] **72**–28
  frozen vegetables [frō′zən vĕj′tə bəlz] **72**–27
Frozen Foods [frō′zən fo͝odz′] **72**
fruit [fro͞ot] **67**–9
  fruit salad [fro͞ot săl′əd] **80**–21
FRUIT [fro͞ot] **68**
frustrated [frŭs′trā′təd] **43**–27
frying pan [frī′ĭng păn′] **78**–5
fuel injection system
  [fyo͞o′əl ĭn jĕk′shən sĭs′təm] **158**–17
full [fo͝ol] **23**–9, **42**–6
  full-length mirror [fo͝ol′lĕnth′ mĭr′ər] **58**–6
  full moon [fo͝ol′ mo͞on′] **205**–12
  full slip [fo͝ol′ slĭp′] **91**–22
fumes [fyo͞omz] **179**–3
Fundamental Freedoms [fŭn də mĕn təl frē′dəmz] **140**
funnel [fŭn′əl] **195**–40
funny photo [fŭn′ē fō′tō] **206**–2
fur [für] **216**–21
furious [fyo͝or′ē əs] **43** ✦
furnished apartment [für′nĭsht ə pärt′mənt] **48**–3
furniture [für′nĭ chər] **53**–19
  furniture polish [für′nĭ chər pŏl′ĭsh] **61**–8
  furniture store [für′nĭ chər stör′] **126**–8
Furniture and Accessories
  [für′nĭ chər ən ək sĕs′ə rēz] **59**
fuse box [fyo͞oz′ bŏks′] **62**–13
fusion [fyo͞o′zhən] **218**–10
galaxy [găl′ək sē] **205**–15
gallbladder [göl′blăd′ər] **107**–44
gallon [găl′ən] **75**–5
game [gām]
  baseball game [bās′böl gām′] **44**–2
  board game [börd′ gām′] **232**–5
  game show [gām′ shō′] **236**–8
  video game console [vĭd′ē ō gām′ kŏn′sōl] **232**–3
  video game controller [vĭd′ē ō gām kən trōl′ər] **232**–4
Games [gāmz] **59**
GAMES [gāmz] **232–233**
gang violence [găng′ vī′ə ləns] **142**–4
garage [gə rözh′, –rŏj′] **47**–14, **124**–1
  garage door [gə rözh′ dör′] **53**–7
Garage [gə rözh′, –rŏj′] **50**
GARAGE SALE [gə rözh′ sāl′] **102–103**
garbage [gär′bĭj]
  garbage bags [gär′bĭj băgz] **61**–24
  garbage bin [gär′bĭj bĭn] **51**–23
  garbage can [gär′bĭj kăn′] **53**–24
  garbage chute [gär′bĭj sho͞ot] **51**–26
  garbage disposal [gär′bĭj dĭ spō′zəl] **54**–7
  garbage truck [gär′bĭj trŭk′] **127**–22
garden [gär′dn]
  botanical garden [bə tăn′ə kəl gär′dn] **222**–3
  roof garden [ro͞of′gär′dn] **50**–4
  vegetable garden [vĕj′tə bəl gär′dn] **53**–27, **177**–14
**garden** [gär′dn] **53**–B
gardener [gär′dn er, gärd′nər] **167**–28
gardenia [gär dēn′yə] **211**–18
gardening [gärd′nĭng]
  gardening crew [gärd′nĭng kro͞o′] **176**–1
  gardening crew leader
    [gärd′nĭng kro͞o lēd′ər] **176**–4
GARDENING [gärd′nĭng] **176**
**gargle** [gär′gəl] **109**–L
garlic [gär′lĭk] **69**–30
  garlic bread [gär′lĭk brĕd′] **81**–28
  garlic press [gär′lĭk prĕs′] **78**–11
Garment Factory [gär′mənt făk′tə rē, făk′trē] **98**
garment worker [gär′mənt wür′kər] **167**–29
garter [gär′tər]
  garter belt [gär′tər bĕlt′] **91**–16
  garter snake [gär′tər snāk′] **213**–39
gas [găs] **218**–3
  gas gauge [găs′gāj′] **159**–31
  gas meter [găs mē′tər] **62**–14
  gas pedal [găs pĕd′l] **159**–46
  gas shut-off valve [găs′ shŭt′ŏf vălv′] **146**–4
  gas station [găs stā′shən] **125**–10
  gas station attendant
    [găs stā′shən ə tĕn′dənt] **162**–3
  gas tank [găs tăngk′] **158**–10
gate [gāt] **50**–16, **53**–9, **161**–8
Gate [gāt] **161**
gauge [gāj]
  blood pressure gauge [blŭd′ prĕsh′ər gāj′] **118**–9
  gas gauge [găs′gāj′] **159**–31
  oil gauge [oyl′gāj′] **159**–29
  temperature gauge [tĕm′prə chər gāj′] **159**–30
gauze [göz] **117**–8
gearshift [gïr′ shĭft′] **159**–47
gel [jĕl] **108**–2, **108**–16
GEOGRAPHY AND HABITATS
  [jē ŏg′rə fē ən hă′bə tăts′] **204**
Geometric Solids [jē′ə mĕ′trĭk sŏl′ədz] **193**
geometry [jē ŏm′ə trē] **192**–17
geothermal energy [jē′ō thür′məl ĕn′ər jē] **218**–7
**get** [gĕt]
  **get** a job [gĕt′ ə jŏb′] **40**–F
  **get** a beginner's / learner's permit
    [gĕt′ ə bĭ′gĭ nürs lürn′ərz pür′mĭt] **137**–E
  **get** a library card [gĕt′ ə lī′brër ē kärd′] **133**–A
  **get** a loan [gĕt′ ə lōn′] **49**–J
  **get** an electric shock [gĕt′ ən ĭ lĕk′trĭk shŏk′] **116**–F
  **get** a speeding ticket [gĕt′ ə spē′dĭng tĭk′ət] **162**–C
  **get** bed rest [gĕt′ bĕd′ rĕst′] **114**–B
  **get** change [gĕt′ chānj′] **26**–A
  **get** dressed [gĕt′ drĕst′] **38**–D
  **get** elected [gĕt′ ĭ lĕk′təd] **139**–C
  **get** engaged [gĕt′ ĭn gājd′] **41**–J
  **get** feedback [gĕt′ fēd′băk′] **191**–K
  **get** frostbite [gĕt′ frŏst′bīt′] **116**–G
  **get** good grades [gĕt′ go͝od′ grādz′] **10**–H
  **get** hired [gĕt′ hīrd′] **173**–L
  **get** home [gĕt′ hōm′] **39**–R
  **get** immunized [gĕt′ ĭm′yə nīzd] **114**–I
  **get** into [gĕt′ ĭn′to͞o] **153**–E
  **get** lost [gĕt′ löst′] **162**–B
  **get** married [gĕt′ măr′ēd] **41**–K
  **get** off [gĕt′ ŏf′] **153**–J
  **get** on [gĕt′ ŏn′] **153**–I
  **get** out of [gĕt′ owt′ əv] **153**–F
  **get** the title [gĕt′ dhə tīt′l] **157**–E
  **get up** [gĕt′ ŭp′] **38**–B
  **get** your license [gĕt′ yər lī′səns] **137**–H
  **get** your unrestricted licence
    [gĕt′ yər ŭn rə′strĭc tĕd lī′səns] **137**–I
Getting Your First Licence
  [gĕt′ĭng yər fürst′ lī′səns] **137**
Get Well [gĕt′ wĕl′] **114**
gift [gĭft] **94** ✦, **240**–3
gift shop [gĭft′ shŏp′] **130** ✦, **184**–5
gills [gĭlz] **212**–2
giraffe [jə răf′] **217**–34
girder [gür′dər] **178**–3
girdle [gür′dl] **91**–15
girl [gürl] **31**–10
**give** [gĭv] **15**–F, **122**–B, **148**–A,
glad [glăd] **44**–5
glass [glăs] **53**–18, **83**–22, **83**–23
  glass cleaner [glăs klē′nər] **61**–14
glasses [glăs′əz] **92**–10, **115**–7, **179**–10
  sunglasses [sŭn′glăs′əz] **90**–27
global positioning system (GPS) [glō′bəl
  pə zĭ′shə nĭng sĭs′təm] / [jē′pē′ĕs′] **155**–11
gloves [glŭvz] **90**–6, **231**–17
  disposable gloves [dĭ spō′ zə bəl glŭvz′] **93**–27
  glove compartment [glŭv′ kəm pärt′mənt] **159**–44
  latex gloves [lā′tĕks glŭvz′] **93**–34
  rubber gloves [rŭb′ər glŭvz′] **61**–4
  surgical gloves [sür′jĭ kəl glŭvz′] **121**–39
  work gloves [würk′ glŭvz′] **92**–17, **179**–17
glue [glo͞o] **183**–33
  glue stick [glo͞o′ stĭk] **232**–11
**go** [gō]
  **go** back [gō′ băk′] **11**–M
  **go** for [gō′ fər] **157**–J
  **go** on [gō′ ŏn] **173**–K
  **go** over [gō′ ō′vər] **153**–B
  **go** past [gō′ păst′] **155**–E
  **go** straight [gō′ strāt′] **155**–A
  **go** through [gō′ thro͞o′] **160**–D
  **go** to an employment agency
    [gō′ tə ən ĭm ploy′mənt ā′jən sē] **173**–E
  **go** to bed [gō′ tə bĕd′] **39**–Y
  **go** to college [gō′ tə kŏl′ĭj] **41**–I

**go** to jail [gō/ tə jāl/] **141**–G
**go** to prison [gō/ tə prĭz/ən] **141**–G
**go** to school [gō/ tə skōōl] **38**–J
**go** to sleep [gō/ tə slēp/] **39**–Z
**go** to the grocery store
[gō/ tə dhə grōs/rē stör/] **38**–L
**go** to the next line [gō/ tə dhə nĕkst/ līn] **196**–D
**go** to work [gō/ tə würk/] **38**–I
**go** under [gō/ ŭn/dər] **153**–A
to-go box [tə gō/ bŏks/] **82**–5
GO [gō] **222–223**
goat [gōt] **215**–5
goggles [gŏg/əlz] **179**–11
goldfish [gōld/fĭsh/] **215**–16
golf [gŏlf] **228**–8
golf club [gŏlf/ klŭb/] **231**–1
good [gŏŏd] **23**–17
Good Friday [gŏŏd frī/dā] **22**–10
Goods [gŏŏdz] **73**
goose [gōōs] **214**–13
gopher [gō/fər] **215**–19
gorilla [gə rĭl/ə] **217**–31
gospel [gŏs/pəl] **237**–30
Government [gŭ/ vərn mənt] **138–139**
GOVERNMENT AND MILITARY SERVICE
[gŭ/ vərn mənt ən mĭ/ lə tër ē sür/vəs]**138–139**
Governor General [gŭ/ vər nər jĕ/nə/rŭl] **138**–2
governor [gŭ/ vər nər] **139**–21
gown [gown] **206**–8
evening gown [ēv/nĭng gown/] **89**–18
hospital gown [hŏs/pĭ tl gown/] **121**–19
nightgown [nīt/gown/] **91**–25
surgical gown [sür/jə kəl gown/] **93**–37, **121**–38
GPS (global positioning system) [jē/pē/ĕs/] /
[glō/bəl pə zĭ/shə nĭng sĭs/təm] **155**–11
grab bar [grăb/ bär/] **57**–11
grade school [grād/ skōōl] **188**–2
grades [grādz] **10**–4
**graduate** [grăj/ōō āt/] **40**–D
graduated cylinder [grăj/ōō ā/təd sĭl/ən dər] **195**–38
GRADUATION [grăj/ōō ā/shən] **206–207**
graffiti [grə fē/tē] **148**–1
grams [grămz] **75**
grandchild [grăn/chīld/, grănd/–] **34** ✦
granddaughters [grăn/dö/tərz] **34** ✦
grandfather [grăn/fö/dhər, grănd/–] **34**–2
grandmother [grăn/mŭdh/ər, grănd/–] **34**–1
Grandparents [grăn/për/ənts, grănd/–] **34**
grandson [grăn/sŭn/, grănd/–] **34** ✦
grapefruit [grāp/frōōt/] **68**–6
grapes [grāps] **68**–3
graph [grăf] **192**–15
graphic designer [grăf/ĭk dĭ zī/nər] **167**–30
grasshopper [grăs/hŏp/ər] **214**–24
**grate** [grāt] **77**–G
grater [grā/tər] **78**–2
**grease** [grēs] **77**–B
green [grēn] **24**–5
green onions [grēn/ ŭn/yənz] **69**–20
**greet** [grēt] **3**–G, **171**–M, **174**–H
GREETING [grē/tĭng] **2–3**
greeting card [grē/tĭng kärd/] **134**–15
grey [grā] **24**–15
grey hair [grā hër/] **33**–13
grilled [grĭld/]
grilled cheese sandwich
[grĭld/ chēz/ săn/wĭch, –sănd/–] **80**–10
grilled fish [grĭld/ fĭsh/] **81**–29
grilled ribs [grĭld/ rĭbz/] **76**–2
grocery [grōs/rē]
grocery bag [grōs/rē băg/] **67**–13
grocery clerk [grōs/rē klürk/] **72**–4
Grocery Products [grōs/rē prŏd/ŭkts] **72**
GROCERY STORE [grōs/ rē stör/] **72–73, 127**–18
ground [grownd]
ground beef [grownd/ bēf/] **70**–4
playground [plā/grownd/] **50**–3
group [grōōp] **115**–15
grower [grō/ər] **177**–13
guard [gärd] **141**–3
lifeguard [līf/gärd/] **225**–19
lifeguard station [līf/gärd/ stā/shən] **225**–21
security guard [sĭ kyōōr/ə tē gärd/] **132**–5, **169**–55
shin guards [shĭn/ gärdz/] **231**–13
guest [gĕst] **184**–10
guest room [gĕst/ rōōm] **184**–13
guest services [gĕst/ sür/vəs əs] **130**–12
guest speaker [gĕst/ spē/kər] **206**–4
guinea pig [gĭn/ē pĭg/] **215**–14
guitar [gĭ tär/] **238**–9
gums [gŭmz] **106**–6
gum disease [gŭm/ dĭ zēz/] **119**–11
gun [gŭn] **142**–13, **181**–21
gurney [gür/nē] **121**–33
gym [jĭm] **5**–19, **126**–10, **184**–24
gymnastics [jĭm năs/tĭks] **228**–9
gynecologists [gī/nə kŏl/ə jĭsts] **120** ✦
habitat [hă/bə tăt/] **194**–11
HABITATS [hă/bə tăts/] **204**
hacksaw [hăk/sö/] **180**–5
**hail** a taxi [hāl/ ə tăx/ē/] **152** ✦
hailstorm [hāl/störm/] **13**–21
hair [hër] **104**–2
black hair [blăk/ hër/] **33**–16
blond hair [blŏnd/ hër/] **33**–17
brown hair [brown/ hër/] **33**–18
curly hair [kür/lē hër/] **33**–11
grey hair [grā/ hër] **33**–13
hair clip [hër klĭp/] **108**–19
hairdresser [hër/drĕs/ər] **167**–31
hair gel [hër jĕl/] **108**–16
hairnet [hër nĕt/] **93**–25
hair salon [hër sə lŏn/] **131**–18
hairspray [hër sprā/] **108**–12
hair stylist [hër stī/lĭst] **167**–31
long hair [lŏng/ hër/] **33**–3
red hair [rĕd/ hër/] **33**–15
short hair [shört/hër/] **33**–1
shoulder-length hair [shōl/dər lĕnth/ hër/] **33**–2
straight hair [strāt/ hër/] **33**–9
wavy hair [wā/vē hër/] **33**–10
HAIR [hër] **33**
half [hăf]
half bath [hăf/ băth/] **57** ✦
half brother [hăf/ brŭdh/ər] **35**–28
1/2 cup [hăf/ kŭp/] **75**–9
half past one [hăf/ păst/ wŭn/] **18**–11
half sister [hăf/ sĭs/tər] **35**–27
half slip [hăf/ slĭp/] **91**–23
halibut steak [hăl/ə bət stāk/] **71**–6
hall [höl] **124**–8
hallway [höl/wā/] **5**–10, **184**–18
Hallway [höl/wā/] **51**
ham [hăm] **70**–9, **76**–5
hamburger [hăm/bür/gər] **79**–1
hammer [hăm/ər] **180**–1
jackhammer [jăk/hăm/ər] **178**–9
sledgehammer [slĕj/ hăm/ər] **178**–23
**hammer** [hăm/ər] **178**–D
hammock [hăm/ək] **53**–23
hamper [hăm/pər] **57**–1
hand [hănd] **105**–15, **177**–20
driving handbook [drī/vĭng hănd/bŏŏk] **136**–1
farmhand [färm/hănd] **177**–8
handbag [hănd/băg/] **87**–9, **94**–2
handbrake [hănd/ brāk/] **159**–48
handcuffs [hănd/kŭfs/] **141**–2
handsaw [hănd/sö/] **180**–4
handset [hănd/sĕt] **14**–1
hand towel [hănd tow/əl] **57**–17
hand truck [hănd trŭk/] **175**–11
Hand [hănd] **106**
handicapped parking [hăn/dē kăpt pär/kĭng]
**128**–6, **154**–12
**hand in** [hănd/ ĭn/] **10**–O
hanger [hăng/gər] **101**–11
**hang up** [hăng/ ŭp/] **15**–D, **101**–H
happy [hăp/ē] **28**–6, **43**–31
hard [härd] **23**–5, **23**–24
hard-boiled eggs [härd/boyld/ ĕgz/] **76**–8
hard drive [härd/ drīv/] **196**–6
hard hat [härd/ hăt/] **92**–1, **179**–9
hardware store [härd/wër/stör/] **148**–4
harmonica [här mŏ/ nĭ kə] **238**–21
**harvest** [här/vəst] **177**–B
hash browns [hăsh/ brownz/] **80**–3
hats [hăts] **90**–1, **95**–11
chef's hat [shĕfs/ hăt/] **93**–28
cowboy hat [kow/boy/ hăt/] **92**–18
hard hat [härd/ hăt/] **92**–1, **179**–9
ski hat [skē/ hăt/] **90**–11
straw hat [strö/ hăt/] **90**–23
**have** [hăv]
**have** a baby [hăv/ ə bā/bē] **41**–L
**have** a conversation [hăv/ ə kŏn/vər sā/shən] **11**–L
**have** a heart attack [hăv/ ə härt/ ə tăk/] **116**–D
**have** an allergic reaction
[hăv/ ən ə lür/jĭk rē ăk/shən] **116**–E
**have** a picnic [hăv/ ə pĭk/nĭk] **224**–D
**have** dinner [hăv/ dĭn/ər] **39**–S
**have** regular checkups
[hăv/ rĕg/yə lər chĕk/ups] **114**–H
Hawaii-Aleutian time [hə wī/ē ə lōō/shən tīm/] **19**–27
hay [hā] **177**–18
hazard [hăz/ərd] **186**–6
hazard lights [hăz/ərd līts/] **159**–36

Hazardous Materials [hăz/ər dəs mə tïr/ē əlz] **179**
hazardous waste [hăz/ər dəs wāst/] **218**–12
Hazards [hăz/ərdz] **179**
head [hĕd] **69**–32, **104**–1
headache [hĕd/āk/] **110**–1
headband [hĕd/bănd/] **90**–3
headboard [hĕd/börd/] **58**–10
head chef [hĕd/ shĕf/] **185**–7
headlight [hĕd/līt/] **158**–7
headline [hĕd/līn] **133**–7
headphones [hĕd/fōnz/] **6**–8, **234**–4
headset [hĕd/sĕt] **14**–13
head waiter [hĕd/wā/tər] **185**–12
headwrap [hĕd/răp/] **90**–7
letterhead [lĕt/ər hĕd] **183**–42
overhead compartment [ō/vər hĕd/ kəm pärt/mənt] **161**–13
overhead projector [ō/vər hĕd/prə jĕk/tər] **7**–16
wireless headset [wīr/ləs hĕd/sĕt] **14**–14
health [hĕlth] **167**–32
health card [hĕlth/ kärd/] **118**–3
health history form [hĕlth/ hĭs/tə rē förm/] **118**–4
HEALTH [hĕlth] **114–115**
HEALTH FAIR [hĕlth/ fër/] **122–123**
Health Problems [hĕlth/ prŏb/ləmz] **115**
**hear** [hïr] **106**–B
hearing [hïr/ĭng]
hearing aid [hïr/ĭng ād/] **115**–10
hearing-impaired [hïr/ĭng ĭm përd/] **32**–12
hearing loss [hïr/ĭng lös/] **115**–2
heart [härt] **107**–38, **116**–D, **239**–6
heart disease [härt/ dĭ zēz/] **111**–11
hearts [härts] **233**–31
heater [hē/tər] **159**–40
heating pad [hē/tĭng păd/] **113**–13
heat wave [hēt/ wāv/] **13**–13
heavy [hĕv/ē] **23**–13, **32**–7, **97**–27
hedge clippers [hĕj/ klĭp/ərz] **176**–11
heel [hēl] **94**–22, **106**–24
high heels [hī/ hēlz/] **89**–21, **95**–25
height [hīt] **17**–17, **32**–5
Height [hīt] **32**
Heimlich manoeuvre [hīm/lĭk mə nōō/vər] **117**–18
helicopter [hĕl/ə kŏp/tər] **151**–9
helmet [hĕl/mət] **93**–23, **231**–19
**help** [hĕlp] **8**–J, **140**–B, **147**–G
Help with Health Problems [hĕlp/ wĭth/ hĕlth/ prŏb/ləmz] **115**
hem [hĕm] **100**–8
hen [hĕn] **215**–8
herbal tea [ür/bəl tē/, hür/bəl–] **81**–40
herbs [ürbz, hürbz] **84**–9
hibiscus [hī bĭs/kəs, hĭ–] **211**–12
**hide** [hīd] **240**–D
high [hī] **91**–12, **97**–32, **188**–3
high blood pressure [hī/ blŭd/ prĕsh/ər] **111**–14
high chair [hī/ chër/] **37**–6, **82**–3
high heels [hī/ hēlz/] **89**–21, **95**–25
high-rise [hī/ rīz/] **127**–13
high school [hī/ skōōl] **188**–4
highway [hī/wā] **155**–9
highway marker [hī/wā mär/kər] **154**–17
hiking [hī/kĭng] **226**–7
hiking boots [hī/kĭng bōōts/] **95**–31
hills [hĭlz] **204**–16
downhill skiing [down/hĭl/ skē/ĭng] **227**–1
hip hop [hĭp/hŏp] **237**–26
hippopotamus [hĭp/ə pŏt/ə məs] **217**–45
**hire** [hīr] **141**–B
hired hand [hīrd/ hănd/] **177**–20
Historical Terms [hĭs/tör/ə kəl türmz/] **199**
history [hĭs/tə rē] **118**–4, **189**–12
HISTORY [hĭs/tə rē] **198–199**
**hit** [hĭt] **230**–B
HIV (human immunodeficiency virus) [āch/ī/vē/] / [hyōō/mən ĭm/yə nō dĭ fĭsh/ən sē vī/rəs] **111**–17
HOBBIES AND GAMES [hŏb/ēz ən gāmz/] **232–233**
hockey [hŏk/ē] **229**–13
hockey stick [hŏk/ē stĭk/] **231**–11
**hold** [hōld] **36**–A
holder [hōl/dər]
candle holder [kăn/dl hōl/dər] **56**–21
cell phone holder [sĕl/ fōn/ hōld/ər] **94**–15
magazine holder [măg/ə zēn/ hōld/ər] **56**–23
pot holders [pŏt/ hōl/dərz] **78**–29
toothbrush holder [tōōth/brŭsh/ hōld/ər] **57**–24
holiday [hŏl/ə dā/] **22**–7, **22**–8
Holidays [hŏl/ə dāz/] **22**
HOLIDAYS [hŏl/ə dāz/] **239**
holly [hŏl/ē] **210**–19
home [hōm] **52**–7, **52**–12
home health care aide [hōm/ hĕlth/ kër ād] **167**–32
home improvement store [hōm/ ĭm prōōv/mənt stör/] **127**–20
homemaker [hōm/mā/kər] **168**–33
homesick [hōm/sĭk/] **43**–20
HOME [hōm] **46–47, 48–49**
honeybee [hŭn/ē bē/] **214**–25
hood [hŏŏd] **158**–4
Hood [hŏŏd] **158**
hoof / hooves [hŏŏf] / [hŏŏvz, hōōvz] **216**–19
hook [hŏŏk] **180**–39, **180**–40
hook and eye [hŏŏk/ ən ī/] **99**–27
hook and loop fastener [hŏŏk/ ən lōōp/ făs/sən ər] **99**–29
horn [hörn] **159**–32, **216**–23, **238**–11
French horn [frĕnch/ hörn] **238**–13
horror story [hör/ər stör/ē] **237**–17
horse [hörs] **215**–4
horseback riding [hörs/băk rī/dĭng] **226**–9
horse racing [hörs/ rā/sĭng] **228**–19
sea horse [sē/hörs/] **212**–13
hose [hōz] **53**–21, **91**–18
hospital [hŏs/pĭ tl] **125**–9, **154**–18
hospital bed [hŏs/pĭ tl bĕd/] **121**–22
hospital gown [hŏs/pĭ tl gown/] **121**–19
HOSPITAL [hŏs/pĭ tl] **120–121**
Hospital Room [hŏs/pĭ tl rōōm/] **121**
Hospital Staff [hŏs/pĭ tl stăf/] **120**
hostess [hō/stəs] **82**–2
hot [hŏt] **13**–3, **42**–1
hot cereal [hŏt sïr/ē əl] **80**–9
hot dog [hŏt/ dŏg/] **79**–6
hot water [hŏt/ wŏ/tər] **57**–9
hot water bottle [hŏt/ wŏ/tər bŏt/l] **113**–15
hotel [hō tĕl/] **124**–3
A HOTEL [hō tĕl/] **184**
hour [ow/ər] **18**–1
house [hows]
courthouse [kört/hows/] **125**–13
dollhouse [dŏl/hows/] **59**–18
housekeeper [hows/kē/pər] **168**–34, **184**–20
housekeeping cart [hows/kē/pĭng kärt/] **184**–19
House of Assembly [hows/ əv əsĕm/blĭ] **139**–20
House of Commons [hows/ əv kŏ/məns] **138**–7
house painter [hows/ pān/tər] **168**–46
houseplant [hows/plănt/] **56**–4, **211**–27
townhouse [town/hows/] **52**–6
two-storey house [tōō/stör/ē hows/] **52** ✦
warehouse [wër/hows/] **175**–7
House [hows] **49, 53**
A HOUSE AND YARD [hows/ən yärd/] **53**
HOUSEHOLD PROBLEMS AND REPAIRS [hows/hōld/ prŏb/ləmz ən rĭ përz/] **62–63**
HOUSEWORK [hows/würk/] **60**
housing [how/zĭng] **52**–11
hubcap [hŭb/kăp/] **158**–9
**hug** [hŭg] **2**–E
human immunodeficiency virus (HIV) [hyōō/mən ĭm/yə nō dĭ fĭsh/ən sē vī/rəs] / [āch/ī/vē/] **111**–17
humid [hyōō/məd] **13**–15
humidifier [hyōō mĭd/ə fī/ər] **113**–12
humiliated [hyōō mĭl/ē ā/təd] **43** ✦
hummingbird [hŭm/ĭng bürd/] **214**–10
hump [hŭmp] **217**–53
hungry [hŭng/grē] **42**–5
hurricane [hür/ə kān/] **145**–14
hurt [hürt] **42**–16, **116**–C
husband [hŭz/bənd] **34**–13
ex-husband [ĕks/ hŭz/bənd] **35** ✦
former husband [för/mər hŭz/bənd] **35** ✦
hutch [hŭch] **55**–22
hybrid [hy/brĭd] **156**–3
hydrant [hī/drənt] **129**–27
hydroelectric power [hī/drō ĭ lĕk/trĭk pow/ər] **218**–5
hydrogen peroxide [hī/drə jən pə rŏk/sīd] **117**–9
hyena [hī ē/nə] **217**–32
HYGIENE [hy/jēn] **108–109**
hygienist [hī jē/nĭst, –jĕn/ĭst] **119**–3
hypertension [hī/pər tĕn/shən] **111**–14
hyphen [hy/fən] **190**–20
hypoallergenic [hī/pō ăl/ər jĕn/ĭk] **108** ✦
I-beam [ī/ bēm/] **178**–3
ice [īs]
ice cream [īs/ krēm/] **72**–26
ice cream cone [īs/ krēm/ kōn] **79**–13
ice cream shop [īs/ krēm/ shŏp] **131**–16
ice pack [īs/ păk/] **117**–13
ice skates [īs/ skāts/] **231**–9
ice skating [īs/ skā/tĭng] **227**–4
iced tea [īst/ tē/] **79**–12
icy [ī/sē] **13**–22
ID [ī/dē/] **146**–19
identity theft [ī dĕn/tə tē thĕft/] **142**–9

ignition [ĭg nĭsh/ən] 159–33
illegal drugs [ĭ lē/gəl drŭgz/] 142–6
Illnesses and Childhood Diseases
[ĭl/nə səz ən chīld/ho͝od dĭ zēz/ əz] 111
ILLNESSES AND MEDICAL CONDITIONS
[ĭl/nə səz ən mĕd/ĭ kəl kən dĭsh/ənz] 111
Immediate Family [ĭ mē/ dē ət făm/lē, –fă/mə lē] 34
immigrant [ĭm/ə grənt] 199–13
**immigrate** [ĭm/ə grāt/] 40–C
immigration [ĭm/ə grā/shən] 199–12
immunization [ĭm/yə nə zā/shən] 114 ✦
immunodeficiency [ĭm/yə nō dĭ fĭsh/ən sē] 111–17
impaired [ĭm pĕrd/] 32–11, 32–12
important [ĭm pört/ənt] 146–20
improvement [ĭm pro͞ov/mənt] 127–20
in [ĭn] 25–6
**be** in shock [bē/ ĭn shŏk/] 116–B
**call in** [köl/ ĭn/] 186–A
**check in** [chĕk/ ĭn/] 160–A
check-in kiosk [chĕk/ĭn kē/ösk/] 160–2
**fall** in love [föl/ ĭn lŭv/] 40–H
**fill in** [fĭl/ ĭn/] 9–O, 10–K
**hand in** [hănd/ ĭn/] 10–O
in fashion [ĭn făsh/ən] 88 ✦
in front of [ĭn frŭnt/ əv] 25–7
in love [ĭn lŭv/] 42–18
in pain [ĭn pān/] 42–11
in style [ĭn stīl/] 88 ✦
in the middle [ĭn dhə mĭd/l] 25–2
**look** in [lo͝ok/ ĭn] 173–B
**move in** [mo͞ov/ ĭn/] 48–F
**send in** [sĕnd/ ĭn/] 173–H
**take in** [tāk/ ĭn/] 100–D
**turn in** [türn/ ĭn/] 191–M
walk-in freezer [wök/ĭn frē/zər] 185–3
inch [ĭnch] 17–16
**indent** [ĭn dĕnt/] 190–D
INDIVIDUAL SPORTS [ĭn/də vĭj/o͞o əl spörts/] 228
infant [ĭn/fənt] 31–6
infection [ĭn fĕk/shən] 111–3
infectious disease [ĭn fĕk/shəs dĭ zēz/] 111 ✦
influenza [ĭn/flo͞o ĕn/zə] 111 ✦
INFORMATION [ĭn/fər mā/shən] 4
inhaler [ĭn hā/lər] 113–33
injection [ĭn jĕk/shən] 114 ✦, 158–17
injured [ĭn/ jərd] 116–C
INJURIES [ĭn/jə rēz] 110
ink [ĭnk]
ink cartridge [ĭnk/ kär/trĭj] 183–45
inkjet printer [ĭnk/jĕt prĭn/tər] 183–18
ink pad [ĭnk/ păd/] 183–46
inline [ĭn/līn/]
inline skates [ĭn/līn/ skāts/] 231–10
inline skating [ĭn/līn/ skā/tĭng] 228–10
**inquire** about benefits
[ĭn kwīr/ ə bowt/bĕn/ə fĭts] 174 ✦
insects [ĭn/sĕkts] 209–11
insect bite [ĭn/sĕkt bīt/] 110–11
insect repellent [ĭn/sĕkt rĭ pĕl/ənt] 226–23
Insects [ĭn/sĕkts] 214
INSECTS [ĭn/sĕkts] 214
**insert** [ĭn sürt/] 132–D
INSIDE AND OUTSIDE THE BODY
[ĭn/sīd/ ən owt/sīd/ dhə bŏd/ē] 106–107
Inside the Car [ĭn/sīd/ dhə kär/] 159
Inside the Kit [ĭn/sīd/ dhə kĭt/] 117
Inside the Trunk [ĭn/sīd/ dhə trŭnk/] 158
**inspect** [ĭn spĕkt/] 147–M
**install** [ĭn stöl/] 176–H, 178–C
instructor [ĭn strŭk/tər] 6–4
Instrument Panel [ĭn/strə mənt păn/əl] 159
instruments [ĭn/strə mənts] 119–4, 238
insulation [ĭn/sə lā/shən] 178–14
insurance [ĭn sho͝or/əns] 136–8
integers [ĭn/tə jərz] 192–1, 192–2
Integers [ĭn/tə jərz] 192
intercom [ĭn/tər kŏm/] 50–5
interest inventory [ĭn/trəst ĭn/vən tör/ ē] 172–11
international call [ĭn/tər năsh/ə nəl köl/] 15–35
Internet [ĭn/tər nĕt/]
Internet listing [ĭn/tər nĕt/ lĭst/ĭng] 48–1
Internet map [ĭn/tər nĕt/ măp] 155–12
Internet phone call [ĭn/tər nĕt/ fōn/ köl] 14–20
INTERNET [ĭn/tər nĕt/] 197
internist [ĭn/tür/nĭst] 120–1
internship [ĭn/türn shĭp/] 172–6
interpreter [ĭn tür/prə tər] 168–35
INTERSECTION [ĭn/tər sĕk/shən] 128–129
INTERVIEW SKILLS [ĭn/tər vyo͞o/ skĭlz/] 174
intestinal parasites [ĭn tĕs/tə nəl păr/ə sīts/] 111–13
intestines [ĭn tĕs/tənz] 107–42
In the Airline Terminal [ĭn dhə ër/līn tür/mə nəl] 160
In the Examining Room [ĭn dhə ĭg zăm/ə nĭng ro͞om/] 118
In the Waiting Room [ĭn dhə wā/tĭng ro͞om/] 118
into [ĭn/to͞o, –tə] 153–E
intravenous drip (IV)
[ĭn/trə vē/nəs drĭp/] / [ī/vē/] 121–25
**introduce** [ĭn/trə do͞os/] 2–C, 3–I
introduction [ĭn/trə dŭk/shən] 190–6
Inuit [ĭn/o͞o ĭt] 198–6
invention [ĭn vĕn/shən] 199–19
inventor [ĭn vĕn/tər] 199–18
inventory [ĭn/vən tör/ ē] 172–11, 172–12
invertebrates [ĭn vür/ tə brəts/] 194–13
invitation [ĭn və tā/shən] 12–I, 12–J, 64–9
**invite** [ĭn vīt/] 12–H
iris [ī/rəs] 211–16
iron [ī/ərn] 101–13, 108–17
**iron** [ī/ərn] 101–G
ironed [ī/ərnd] 101–20
ironing board [ī/ər nĭng börd/] 101–14
irritated [ĭr/ə tā/təd] 64–6
island [ī/lənd] 204–8
IV (intravenous drip)
[ī/vē/] / [ĭn/trə vē/nəs drĭp/] 121–25
ivory [ī/vər ē] 24–16
ivy [ī/vē] 210–25
jack [jăk] 158–24
jacket [jăk/ət] 90–8
chef's jacket [shĕfs/ jăk/ət] 93–29
down jacket [down/ jăk/ət] 90–16
leather jacket [lĕdh/ər jăk/ət] 90–4
sports jacket [spörts/ jăk/ət] 89–14
jackhammer [jăk/ hăm/ər] 178–9
jack-o'-lantern [jăk/ə lăn/tərn] 239–12
janitor [jăn/ĭ tər] 182–3
January [jăn/yo͞o ër/ē] 21–25
jar [jär] 74–2, 74–14
jasmine [jăz/mən] 211–22
jaw [jö] 106–4
jay [jā] 214–6
**jaywalk** [jā/wök] 128–C
jazz [jăz] 237–24
jeans [jēnz] 86–2, 92–19
jellyfish [jĕl/ē fĭsh/] 212–14
jewellery [jo͞o/lə rē, jo͞o/əl rē]
jewellery department
[jo͞o/lə rē, jo͞o/əl rē dĭ pärt/mənt] 95–8
jewellery store [jo͞o/lə rē, jo͞o/əl rē stör/] 130–2
jigsaw [jĭg/sö/] 180–10
job [jŏb] 172–1, 172–3, 172–7
job fair [jŏb/ fër] 172–13
JOB SAFETY [jŏb/ sāf/tē] 179
JOBS AND OCCUPATIONS
[jŏbz/ ən ŏk/yə pā/shənz] 166–169
JOB SEARCH [jŏb/ sürch/] 173
JOB SKILLS [jŏb/ skĭlz/] 170
Job Training [jŏb/ trā/nĭng] 172
jockstrap [jŏk/străp/] 91–6
**join** [joyn] 143–L
judge [jŭj] 138–12, 141–6
Judiciary [jo͞o dĭ/shē ër ē] 138
juice [jo͞os] 73–32
July [jo͞o lī/] 21–31
**jump** [jŭmp] 230–I
jumper cables [jŭm/pər kā/bəlz] 158–21
jump rope [jŭmp/ rōp/] 224–4
jumpsuit [jŭmp/so͞ot/] 93–24
June [jo͞on] 21–30
jungle gym [jŭn/gəl jĭm] 224–14
junior high school [jo͞on/yər hī/ sko͞ol] 188–3
junk mail [jŭnk/ māl/] 135 ✦
Jupiter [jo͞o/pə tər] 205–5
jury [jür/ē] 141–8
kangaroo [kăng/gə ro͞o/] 217–46
**keep** [kēp] 28–B
ketchup [kĕch/əp, kăch/–] 79–21
kettle [kĕt/l] 54–17
key [kē] 51–30, 155–6
key pad [kē/ păd/] 14–5
pound key [pownd/ kē/] 14–7
star key [stär/ kē/] 14–6
keyboard [kē/börd/] 196–14, 238–18
Keyboarding [kē/börd/ĭng] 196
**kick** [kĭk] 230–E
kidney [kĭd/nē] 107–43
kids' bedroom [kĭdz/ bĕd/ro͞om/] 47–9
KIDS' BEDROOM [kĭdz/ bĕd/ro͞om/] 59
kilogram [kĭl/əgrăm] 75
king-size bed [kĭng/sīz/ bĕd/] 184–15
kiosk [kē/ösk/] 131–22, 160–2
**kiss** [kĭs] 3–K, 36–P
kit [kĭt]
doll-making kit [dŏl/ mā/kĭng kĭt/] 232–13
first aid kit [fürst/ ād/ kĭt/] 117–1, 146–18
model kit [mŏd/l kĭt/] 232–9

woodworking kit [wo͝od/wür/kĭng kĭt/] **232**–14
Kit [kĭt] **117**
kitchen [kĭch/ən] **46**–5, **83**–15
kitchen timer [kĭch/ən tī/mər] **78**–18
A KITCHEN [ə kĭch/ən] **54**
Kitchen [kĭch/ən] **185**
KITCHEN UTENSILS [kĭch/ən yo͞o tĕn/səlz] **78**
kite [kīt] **225**–2
kitten [kĭt/n] **215**–10
kiwi [kē/wē] **68**–22
knee [nē] **106**–20
knee-highs [nē/hīz/] **91**–12
knee pads [nē/pădz/] **179**–19
knife [nīf] **55**–4, **83**–30
carving knife [kär/vĭng nīf/] **78**–12
multi-use knife [mŭl/tē yo͞os/nīf/, mŭl/tī–] **226**–20
paring knife [për/ĭng nīf/] **78**–16
steak knife [stāk/ nīf/] **83**–29
**knit** [nĭt] **233**–F
knitting needles [nĭt/ĭng nēd/lz] **233**–23
knit top [nĭt/ tŏp/] **88**–7
knob [nŏb] **194**–22, **194**–24
doorknob [dör/nŏb/] **53**–12
knuckle [nŭk/l] **106**–17
koala [kō ä/lə] **217**–47
lab [lăb] **5**–15
lab coat [lăb/ kōt/] **93**–33
Lab [lăb] **195**
label [lā/bəl]
mailing label [mā/lĭng lā/bəl] **183**–41
nutrition label [no͞o trĭ/shən lā/bəl] **122**–8
prescription label [prĭ skrĭp/shən lā/bəl] **112**–4
warning label [wör/nĭng lā/bəl] **112**–8
**label** [lā/bəl] **9**–V
Labour Day [lā/bər dā/] **22**–13
lace [lās] **99**–9
shoelaces [sho͞o/lā səz] **94**–24
ladder [lăd/ər] **178**–2
ladle [lā/dl] **78**–7
ladybug [lā/dē bŭg/] **214**–26
lake [lāk] **204**–13
lamb [lăm] **70**–14
lamb chops [lăm/ chŏps/] **70**–15
lamb shanks [lăm/ shăngks/] **70**–13
Lamb [lăm] **70**
lamp [lămp] **56**–15, **58**–25
lampshade [lămp/shād/] **56** ✦, **58**–26
**land** [lănd] **160**–K
landlord [lănd/lörd/] **51**–27
landmarks [lănd/märks/] **220**–3
landscape [lănd/skāp/] **220**–1
landscape designer [lănd/skāp/ dĭ zī/nər] **176**–5
LANDSCAPING AND GARDENING
[lănd/skā/pĭng ən gärd/nĭng] **176**
languages [lăng/gwĭ jəz] **189**–13
language arts [lăng/gwĭj ärts/] **189**–9
lantern [lăn/tərn] **226**–22, **239**–12
laptop [lăp/tŏp/] **196**–16
large [lärj] **96**–4, **96**–5
laser printer [lā/zər prĭn/tər] **183**–19
lashes [lăsh/əz]
eyelashes [ī/lăsh/əz] **106**–11
last [lăst]
last name [lăst/ nām/] **4**–4
last week [lăst/wēk/] **20**–18
late [lāt] **19**–24
latex gloves [lā/tĕks glŭvz/] **93**–34
**laugh** [lăf] **44**–A
laundromat [lön/drə măt/] **128**–1
laundry [lön/drē] **101**–1
laundry basket [lön/drē băs/kət] **101**–2
laundry detergent [lön/drē dĭ tür/jənt] **101**–8
LAUNDRY [lön/drē] **101**
Laundry Room [lön/drē ro͞om/] **50**
lawn [lön] **53**–26
lawn mower [lön/ mō/ər] **176**–6
lawyer [lö/yər] **168**–36
defence lawyer [dĭ fĕns/ lö/yər] **141**–4
**lay** [lā] **178**–B
layer cake [lā/ər kāk] **81**–33
LCD projector [ĕl/sē/dē/ prə jĕk/tər] **6**–6, **235**–29
leader [lē/dər] **176**–4
leaf / leaves [lēf] / [lēvz] **210**–6, **211**–6
leaf blower [lēf/ blō/ər] **176**–2
leaking [lē/kĭng] **62**–3
**learn** [lürn] **40**–E
Learning New Words [lür/nĭng no͞o/ würdz/] **8**
lease [lēs] **48** ✦, **51**–28
leather [lĕdh/ər] **98**–6
leather jacket [lĕdh/ər jăk/ət] **90**–4
**leave** [lēv] **11**–O, **38**–N, **82**–J, **160**–J, **171**–P
leaves / leaf [lēvz] / [lēf] **210**–6, **211**–6
leaf blower [lēf/ blō/ər] **176**–2
lecture [lĕk/chər] **122**–9
left [lĕft] **25**–1, **154**–8, **155**–C
legal [lē/gəl]
legal pad [lē/gəl păd/] **183**–38
LEGAL SYSTEM [lē/gəl sĭs/təm] **141**
Leg and Foot [lĕg/ ən fo͝ot/] **106**
leggings [lĕg/ĭngz] **90**–12
Legislative Assembly [lĕ/jəs lā/tĭv ə sĕm/blē] **139**–20
Member of the Legislative Assembly
[mĕm/bər əv dha lĕ/jəs lā/tĭv ə sĕm/blē] **139**–21
legs [lĕgz] **70**–21, **105**–9
leg of lamb [lĕg/ əv lăm/] **70**–14
lemonade [lĕm/ə nād/] **84**–3
lemons [lĕm/ənz] **68**–7
**lend** [lĕnd] **26**–C
length [lĕngkth] **17**–18, **96**–17
**lengthen** [lĕngk/thən] **100**–A
lens / lenses [lĕnz] / [lĕnz/əz] **115**–8, **235**–23
leopard [lĕp/ərd] **217**–36
**let out** [lĕt/ owt/] **100**–C
letter [lĕt/ər] **134**–13
letter carrier [lĕt/ər kăr/ē ər] **134**–20
letterhead [lĕt/ər hĕd/] **183**–42
lettuce [lĕt/əs] **69**–1
level [lĕv/əl] **172**–1, **180**–29
librarian [lī brër/ē ən] **133**–9
library [lī/brër ē] **5**–17, **125**–15
library clerk [lī/brër ē klürk/] **133**–1
library patron [lī/brër ē pā/trən] **133**–3
LIBRARY [lī/brër ē] **133**
licence [lī/səns]
driver's licence [drī/vərz lī/səns] **40**–4, **136**–9
driver's licence number
[drī/vərz lī/səns nŭm/bər] **136**–11
licence plate [lī/səns plāt/] **136**–12, **158**–12
marriage licence [măr/ĭj lī/səns] **41**–8
**renew** a licence [rĭ no͞o/ ə lī/səns, –nyo͞o/–] **136** ✦
taxi licence [tăk/sē lī/səns] **152**–22
Licence [lī/səns] **137**
licensing clerk [lī/sən sĭng klürk] **136**–3
LICENSING OFFICE [lī/sən sĭng ŏfəs] **136–137**
lid [lĭd] **78**–24
lieutenant governor [lĕf tĕ/nənt gŭ/ vər nər] **139**–21
life [līf]
lifeguard [līf/gärd/] **225**–19
lifeguard station [līf/gärd/ stā/shən] **225**–21
life preserver [līf/sā/vĭng dĭ vīs/] **225**–20
life vest [līf/ vĕst/] **161**–25, **226**–14
wildlife [wīld/ līf/] **220**–2
LIFE [līf] **212–213**
LIFE EVENTS AND DOCUMENTS
[līf/ ĭ vĕnts/ ən dŏ/kyə mənts] **40–41**
**lift** [lĭft] **11**–E
light [līt] **23**–14, **97**–28
brake light [brāk/ līt/] **158**–14
daylight saving time [dā/līt/ sā/vĭng tīm/] **19**–25
flashlight [flăsh/līt/] **146**–14
hazard lights [hăz/ərd līts/] **159**–36
headlight [hĕd/ līt/] **158**–7
light blue [līt/ blo͞o/] **24**–11
light bulb [līt/ bŭlb/] **56** ✦
light fixture [līt/ fĭks/chər] **55**–18
light source [līt/ sörs/] **194**–19
light switch [līt/ swĭch/] **58**–27
night light [nīt/ līt/] **37**–27
porch light [pörch/ līt/] **53**–13
streetlight [strēt/līt/] **148**–3
string lights [strĭng/ lītz/] **239**–18
tail light [tāl/ līt/] **158**–13
traffic light [trăf/ĭk līt/] **128**–8
work light [würk/ līt/] **181**–44
lightning [līt/nĭng] **13**–17
lily [lĭl/ē] **211**–26
limbs [lĭmz] **106** ✦, **210**–3
limes [līmz] **68**–8
limit [lĭ/mət] **154**–4
limo / limousine [lĭ/mō] / [lĭ/mə zēn] **156**–11
line [līn] **73**–11
assembly line [ə sĕm/blē līn] **175**–6
clothesline [klōz/līn/] **101**–9
curved line [kürvd/ līn/] **193**–23
headline [hĕd/līn/] **133**–7
line cook [līn/ ko͝ok/] **93, 185** ✦
line segment [līn/ sĕg/mənt] **193**–20
line supervisor [līn/ so͞o/pər vī zər] **175**–4
parallel lines [pă/rə lĕl līnz/] **193**–25
perpendicular lines [pür/pən dĭk/yə lər līnz/] **193**–24
straight line [strāt/ līn/] **193**–22
linen [lĭn/ən] **98**–2
linen closet [lĭn/ən klŏz/ət] **57** ✦
liner [lī/nər]
eyeliner [ī/lī/nər] **109**–36
Lines [līnz] **193**

lingerie [län/zhə rā/, –jə–] **91** ✦
links [lĭnkz] **197**–10
lion [lī/ən] **213**–33, **216**–2, **217**–38
lip [lĭp] **106**–5
lipstick [lĭp/stĭk/] **109**–38
Liquid Measures [lĭk/wəd mĕzh/ərz] **75**
liquids [lĭk/wədz] **61**–21, **179**–8
list [lĭst] **67**–14
**listen** [lĭs/ən] **6**–C, **118**–C, **174**–K
listing [lĭst/ĭng] **48**–1
litres [lē/tərz] **75**
litter [lĭ/tər] **148**–2
**litter** [lĭ/tər] **219**–L
little [lĭt/l] **23**–1
Little League [lĭt/l lēg/] **229** ✦
**live** [lĭv] **140**–H
LIVE [lĭv] **52**
live music [lĭv/ myōō/zĭk] **84**–1
liver [lĭv/ər] **70**–7, **107**–40
livestock [lĭv/stŏk/] **177**–15
living room [lĭv/ĭng rōōm/] **47**–12
LIVING ROOM [lĭv/ĭng rōōm/] **56**
lizard [lĭz/ərd] **213**–40
llama [lö/mə] **217**–27
**load** [lōd] **101**–C
loading dock [lō/dĭng dŏk/] **175**–15
loaf [lōf] **74**–10, **74**–22
meatloaf [mēt/lōf/] **81**–31
loafers [lō/fərz] **95**–30
Lobby [löb/ē] **50**
lobster [löb/stər] **71**–10
local call [lō/kəl köl/] **15**–31
lock [lŏk] **51**–34, **159**–25
locksmith [lŏk/smĭth/] **62**–11
**lock** [lŏk] **143**–E
locker [lö/kər] **5**–11, **50**–17
locket [lŏk/ət] **95**–35
Logging on and Sending Email
[lög/ĭng ön/ ən sĕnd/ĭng ē/māl] **197**
lonely [lōn/lē] **42**–17
long [lŏng] **96**–18
long distance call [lŏng/dĭs/təns köl/] **15**–32
long hair [lŏng/ hër/] **33**–3
long-sleeved [lŏng/slēvd/] **96**–14
long underwear [lŏng/ ŭn/dər wër/] **91**–3
**look** [lŏŏk]
**look** at [lŏŏk/ ăt/, –ət] **49**–H, **157**–A
**look** for [lŏŏk/ för/] / [lŏŏk/ fər] **133**–B, **173**–C
**look** in [lŏŏk/ ĭn] **173**–B
**look up** [lŏŏk/ ŭp] **8**–A
loonie [lōō/nē] **26**–5
loop [lōōp] **99**–29
loose [lōōs] **97**–30
lose [lōōz] **229** ✦
loss [lös] **115**–2
lost child [löst/ chīld/] **144**–1
lotion [lō/shən] **37**–13, **108**–9
loud [lowd] **23**–11
loungewear [lownj/wër/] **91** ✦
love [lŭv] **40**–H, **42**–18
loveseat [lŭv sēt/] **56**–1
low [lō] **97**–31
low-cut socks [lō/kŭt/ sŏks/] **91**–10
low-fat milk [lō/făt/ mĭlk/] **81**–42
lower back [lō/ər băk/] **107**–29
lozenges [lŏz/ən jəz] **113**–30
luggage [lŭg/ĭj] **161**–18
luggage cart [lŭg/ĭj kärt/] **184**–8
lug wrench [lŭg/ rĕnch/] **158**–22
lumber [lŭm/bər] **178**–17
Lunch [lŭnch] **80**
lung [lŭng] **107**–39
machine [mə shēn/]
answering machine [ăn/sər ĭng mə shēn/] **14**–17
ATM (Automated Teller Machine) [ā/tē/ĕm/] /
[ö/tə māt ĭd tē/lər mə shēn/] **132**
fax machine [făks/ mə shēn/] **183**–21
machine operator [mə shēn/ ŏp/ə rā tər] **168**–37
machine screw [mə shēn/ skrōō/] **180**–32
sewing machine [sō/ĭng mə shēn/] **98**–13
sewing machine operator
[sō/ĭng mə shēn/ ŏp/ə rā/tər] **98**–14
vending machine [vĕnd/ĭng mə shēn/] **152**–9
Machine [mə shēn/] **98, 132**
magazine [măg/ə zēn/, măg/ə zēn/] **133**–5
magazine holder [măg/ə zēn/ hōl/dər] **56**–23
magnet [măg/nət] **195**–36
magnolia [măg nōl/yə] **210**–8
mail
air mail [ër/māl/] **134**–5
junk mail [jŭnk/ māl/] **135** ✦
mailboxes [māl/bŏk/səz] **50**–11, **53**–1, **128**–13, **135**–10
overnight / next day mail
[ō/vər nīt/ / nĕkst/ dā/ māl/] **135** ✦
registered mail [rĕj ĭst ərd māl/] **134**–4
surface mail [sür/fəs māl/] **134**–6
**mail** [māl/] **135**–D
mailer [mā/lər] **183**–40
mailing [mā/lĭng]
mailing address [mā/lĭng ə drĕs/, ă/drĕs] **134**–22
mailing label [mā/lĭng la/bəl] **183**–41
main office [mān/ ŏ/fəs] **5**–12
MAINTAINING A CAR [mān/tā nĭng ə kär/] **157**
maintenance [mān/tn əns] **184**–23
maitre d' [mā/trə dē/] **185**–11
make [māk] **156** ✦
**make** [māk]
**make** a deposit [māk/ ə dĭ pŏz/ət] **132**–B
**make** a disaster kit [māk/ ə dĭz/ăs tər kĭt/] **146**–B
**make** a mortgage payment
[māk/ ə mör/gəj pā/mənt] **49**–L
**make** an offer [māk/ ən ö/fər] **49**–I
**make** a wish [māk/ ə wĭsh/] **240**–B
**make** copies [māk/ kŏp/ēz] **171**–D
**make** dinner [māk/ dĭn/ər] **39**–Q
**make** eye contact [māk/ ī/ kŏn/tăkt] **174**–J
**make** furniture [māk/ für/nĭ chər] **170**–G
**make** lunch [māk/ lŭnch/] **38**–F
**make** progress [māk/ prŏ/grəs] **10**–G
**make** small talk [māk/ smöl/tök] **12**–B
**make** the bed [māk/dhə bĕd/] **60**–F
maker [mā/kər]
dressmaker [drĕs/mā/kər] **100**–1
dressmaker's dummy [drĕs/mā/kərz dŭ/mē] **100**–2
homemaker [hōm/mā/kər] **168**–33
Makeup [māk/ŭp] **109**
makeup remover [māk/ŭp rĭ mōōv/ər] **109**–42
making [mā/kĭng] **232**–13
MAKING ALTERATIONS [māk/ĭng öl/tə rā/shənz] **100**
MAKING CLOTHES [māk/ĭng klōz/] **98–99**
Making an Emergency Call
[mā/kĭng ən ĭ mür/jən sē köl/] **15**
Making a Phone Call [mā/kĭng ə fōn/ köl/] **15**
male [māl] **4**–17
mall [möl] **126**–7
MALL [möl] **130–131**
mallet [măl/ət] **180**–2
mammals [măm/əlz] **209**–10
Mammals [măm/əlz] **213**
MAMMALS [măm/əlz] **216–217**
manager [măn/ĭ jər] **50**–8, **72**–8
account manager [ə kownt/ măn/ĭ jər] **132**–9
office manager [ö/fəs măn/ĭ jər] **182**–8
Manager [măn/ĭ jər] **92**
mane [mān] **217**–51
manoeuvre [mə nōō/vər] **117**–18
mangoes [măng/gōz] **68**–21
manicurist [mă/nə kyōō/rĭst] **168**–38
man / men [măn] / [mĕn] **30**–1, **30**–4
doorman [dör/măn/] **184**–1
mantle [măn/təl] **56**–11
manual [măn/yōō əl] **117**–2
Manual Transmission [măn/yōō əl trănz mĭsh/ən] **159**
**manufacture** [măn/yə făk/chər] **175**–B
map [măp] **7**–12, **155**–12
Map [măp] **13**
maple [mā/pəl] **210**–12
Maps [măps] **155**
MAPS [măps] **155**
March [märch] **21**–27
margarine [mär/jər ən] **72**–20
marigold [măr/ə gōld/] **211**–13
MARINE LIFE, AMPHIBIANS, AND REPTILES
[mə rēn/ līf/ ăm fĭb/ē ənz ən rĕp/tīlz] **212–213**
mark [märk] **190**–12, **190**–13, **190**–15
postmark [pōst/märk/] **134**–24
markers [mär/kərz] **7**–17, **7**–24, **154**–17
market [mär/kət] **222**–6
supermarket [sōō/pər mar/kət] **127**–18
MARKET [mär/kət] **66–67**
marriage licence [măr/ĭj lī/səns] **41**–8
married couple [măr/ēd kŭ/pəl] **35**–20
Mars [märz] **205**–4
martial arts [mär/shəl ärts/] **228**–11
mascara [mă skăr/ə] **109**–39
mashed potatoes [măsht/ pə tā/tōz] **81**–23
mask [măsk] **239**–11
catcher's mask [kăch/ərz măsk/] **231**–15
diving mask [dī/vĭng măsk/] **225**–6
face mask [fās/ măsk/] **93**–32
oxygen mask [ŏk/sĭ jən măsk/] **161**–24
particle mask [pär/tĭ kəl măsk/] **179**–14
ski mask [skē/ măsk/] **90**–15
surgical mask [sür/jĭ kəl măsk/] **93**–36
ventilation mask [vĕnt/əl ā/shən măsk/] **92**–7

masking tape [măs/kĭng tāp/] **181**–53
mat [măt] **57**–5, **57**–28
placemat [plās/măt] **55**–11
**match** [măch] **9**–T
matches [măch/əz] **146**–16, **226**–21
matching [mă/chĭng] **28**–3
Material [mə tïr/ē əl] **98**
materials [mə tïr/ē əlz] **98** ✦, **179**–7
Materials [mə tïr/ē əlz] **179**
maternity [mə tür/nə tē]
maternity dress [mə tür/nə tē drĕs/] **88**–5
maternity store [mə tür/nə tē stör/] **131**–19
math [măth] **189**–10
MATHEMATICS [măth/ə măt/ĭks] **192–193**
Math Operations [măth/ ŏp/ə rā/shənz] **192**
Math Problem [măth/ prŏb/ləmz] **192**
mattress [mă/trəs] **58**–20
May [mā] **21**–29
mayonnaise [mā/ə nāz/, mā/ə nāz/] **79**–23
mayor [mā/ər] **139**–22
meadow [mĕd/ō] **204**–20
measles [mē/zəlz] **111**–5
measure [mĕzh/ər] **100**–17, **181**–45
**measure** [mĕzh/ər] **17**–C
Measurement [mĕzh/ər mənt] **17**
MEASUREMENTS [mĕzh/ər mənts] **17, 75**
Measures [mĕzh/ərz] **75**
Measuring Area and Volume
[mĕ/zhər ĭng ër/ē ə ən vŏl/yəm, –yōōm] **193**
meat [mēt] **66**–2
meatballs [mēt/bölz] **81**–27
meatloaf [mēt/lōf/] **81**–31
Meat [mēt] **70, 76**
MEAT AND POULTRY [mēt/ n pōl/trē] **70**
mechanic [mə kăn/ĭk] **166**–8
Mechanic [mə kăn/ĭk] **158**
medical [mĕd/ĭ kəl]
medical chart [mĕd/ĭ kəl chärt/] **121**–24
medical emergency bracelet
[mĕd/ĭ kəl ĭ mür/jən sē brās/lət] **117**–3
medical exam [mĕd/ĭ kəl ĭg zăm] **122**–1
medical records technician
[mĕd/ĭ kəl rĕkərdz tĕk nĭsh/ən] **168**–39
medical waste disposal
[mĕd/ĭ kəl wāst/ dĭ spō/zəl] **121**–31
MEDICAL CARE [mĕd/ĭ kəl kër/] **118**
MEDICAL CONDITIONS [mĕd/ĭ kəl kən dĭsh/ənz] **111**
MEDICAL EMERGENCIES [mĕd/ĭ kəl ĭ mür/jən sēz] **116**
Medical Procedures [mĕd/ĭ kəl prə sē/jərz] **118**
Medical Specialists [mĕd/ĭ kəl spĕ/shə lĭsts] **120**
Medical Technician [mĕd/ĭ kəl tĕk nĭsh/ən] **93**
Medical Warnings [mĕd/ĭ kəl wör/nĭngz] **112**
medication [mĕd/ə kā/shən] **112**–3, **112** ✦,
**113**–18, **121**–20
Medication [mĕd/ə kā/shən] **113**
medicine cabinet [mĕd/ə sən kăb/ə nət] **57**–22
medium [mē/dē əm] **96**–3
meet [mēt] **222**–6
**meet** [mēt] **49**–G, **49**–R
meeting [mē/tĭng]
meeting place [mē/tĭng plās/] **146**–1
meeting room [mē/tĭng rōōm/] **184**–25
MEETING AND GREETING [mē/tĭng ən grē/tĭng] **2–3**
melons [mĕl/ənz] **68**–19
watermelons [wö/tər mĕl/ənz] **68**–18
Member of Parliament [mĕm/bür əv pär/lə mĕnt]
**138**–9
Member of the Legislative Assembly
[mĕm/bər əv dha lĕ/jəs lā/tĭv ə sĕm/blē] **139**–21
membrane [mĕm/brān] **194**–6
memory card [mĕm/ə rē kärd/] **235**–20
men / man [mĕn] / [măn] **30**–1, **30**–4
doorman [dör/măn/] **184**–1
men's store [mĕnz/ stör/] **130** ✦
Men's Underwear [mĕnz/ un/dər wër/] **91**
menu [mĕn/yōō] **82**–7, **197**–8
menu bar [mĕn/yōō bär/] **197**–1
MENU [mĕn/yōō] **80–81**
Mercury [mür/kyə rē] **205**–1
merge [mürj] **154**–10
mess [mĕs] **64**–8
message [mĕs/ĭj] **14**–18, **14**–19
messenger [mĕs/ən jər] **168**–40
meter [mē/tər] **62**–14, **129**–25, **152**–23
metre stick [mē/tər stĭk] **181**–16
mice / mouse [mīs] / [mows] **63**–28, **196**–15, **215**–18
microphone [mī/krə fōn/] **234**–18
microprocessor [mī/krō prŏ/sĕ sər] **196**–4
Microscope [mī/krə skōp/] **194**
**microwave** [mī/krə wāv/] **77**–T
microwave oven [mī/krə wāv/ ŭv/ən] **54**–13
middle [mĭd/l] **25**–2
middle-aged [mĭd/l ājd/] **32**–2
middle initial [mĭd/l ĭ nĭsh/əl] **4**–3
middle school [mĭd/l skōōl/] **188**–3
mid-length [mĭd/lĕnth] **96**–17
midnight [mĭd/nīt/] **18**–21
midwives [mĭd/wīvz] **120** ✦
Military [mĭ/lə tër ē] **138**
MILITARY SERVICE [mĭ/lə tër ē sür/vəs] **138–139**
milk [mĭlk] **66**–5, **81**–42
milkshake [mĭlk shāk/] **79**–14
**milk** [mĭlk] **177**–C
millilitres [mĭl/ə lētərz] **75**
millimetre [mĭl/ə mē/tər] **17**–14
mini [mĭn/ē] **96**–15
mini-blinds [mĭn/ē blīndz/] **58**–8
minivan [mĭn/ē văn/] **156**–8
minister [mĭ/nə stər] **138**–5, **199**–7
prime minister [prīm/ mĭn/ĭ stər] **198**–3
minutes [mĭn/əts] **18**–2
mirror [mïr/ər] **57**–18
full-length mirror [fōōl/lĕnth mïr/ər] **58**–6
rear-view mirror [rïr/vyōō/ mïr/ər] **159**–35
side-view mirror [sīd/vyōō/ mïr/ər] **158**–3
**misbehave** [mĭs/bĭ hāv/] **44**–B
**miss** the bus [mĭs dhə bŭs/] **152** ✦
missing [mĭs/ĭng] **97**–40
mittens [mĭt/nz] **90**–10
**mix** [mĭks] **77**–R
mixed berries [mĭkst/ bĕr/ēz] **81**–36
mixer [mĭk/sər] **54**–25
mixing bowl [mĭk/sĭng bōl/] **54**–28, **78**–31
mobile [mō/bil] **59**–5
mobile home [mō/bəl hōm/] **52**–7
model [mŏd/l] **156** ✦, **168**–41
model kit [mŏd/l kĭt/] **232**–9
model trains [mŏd/l trānz/] **233**–27
modern [mŏ/dərn] **199**–2
moist towelettes [moyst/ tow/əl ĕts] **146**–12
moisturizer [moys/chə rī/zər] **108**–9
mole [mōl] **32**–16
molecule [mŏl/ĭ kyōōl/] **195**–27
monarch [mŏ/nərk, mŏ/närk/] **199**–4
Monday [mŭn/dā] **20**–9
MONEY [mŭn/ē] **26**
monitor [mŏn/ə tər] **196**–11
arrival and departure monitors
[ə rī/vəl ən dĭ pär/chər mŏn/ə tərz] **161**–7
baby monitor [bā/bē mŏn/ə tər] **59**–7
vital signs monitor [vī/təl sīnz mŏn/ə tər] **121**–26
monkey [mŭng/kē] **217**–28
month [mŭnth] **20**–3
Months of the Year [mŭnths/ əv dhə yïr/] **21**
moon [mōōn]
crescent moon [krĕs/ənt mōōn/] **205**–10
full moon [fōōl/ mōōn/] **205**–12
new moon [nōō/ mōōn/] **205**–9
quarter moon [kwör/tər mōōn/] **205**–11
Moon [mōōn] **205**
moose [mōōs] **216**–1
mop [mŏp] **61**–6
**mop** [mŏp] **60**–D
morning [mör/nĭng] **18**–15
mosque [mŏsk] **126**–5
mosquito [mə skē/tō] **214**–22
motel [mō tĕl/] **126**–12
moth [mŏth] **214**–21
mother [mŭdh/ər] **34**–3, **35**–22
grandmother [grăn/mŭdh/ər, grănd/–] **34**–1
motherboard [mŭdh/ər börd/] **196**–5
mother-in-law [mŭdh/ər ĭn lö/] **34**–10
stepmother [stĕp/mŭdh/ər] **35**–26
MOTION [mō/shən] **153**
motorcycle [mō/tər sī/kəl] **150**–4
mountain [mown/tn]
mountain biking [mown/tn bī/kĭng] **226**–8
mountain lion [mown/tn lī/ən] **216**–2
mountain peak [mown/tn pēk/] **204**–14
mountain range [mown/tn rānj/] **204**–15
Mountain time [mown/tn tīm/] **19**–30
mouse / mice [mows] / [mīs] **63**–28, **196**–15, **215**–18
moustache [mŭs tăsh] **33**–5
mouth [mowth] **104**–7
mouthwash [mowth/wŏsh/] **109**–25
Mouth [mowth] **106**
**move in** [mōōv/ ĭn/] **48**–F
**move out** [mōōv/ owt/] **48** ✦
movement [mōōv/mənt] **199**–16
mover [mōō/vər] **168**–42
movies [mōō/vēz] **222**–2
movie theatre [mōō/vē thē/ə tər] **126**–6
Movies [mōō/vēz] **237**
Moving In [mōō/vĭng ĭn] **49**
moving van [mōō/vĭng văn/] **156**–18
**mow** [mō] **176**–A

mower [mō/ər] **176**–6
mozzarella cheese [mōts/ə rē lə chēz/] **71**–29
MP3 player [ĕm/pē/thrē/ plā/ər] **234**–2
mudslide [mŭd/slīd/] **144**–6
muffin [mŭf/ən] **79**–16, **80**–5
muffler [mŭf/lər] **158**–16
muffs [mŭfs] **179**–16
mug [mŭg] **55**–7
mugging [mŭg/ĭng] **142**–11
**multiply** [mŭl/tə plī] **192**–C
multi-use knife [mŭl/tē yōōs/ nīf/, mŭl/tī–] **226**–20
mumps [mŭmps] **111**–7
murder [mür/dər] **142**–12
muscle [mŭs/əl] **107**–32
mushrooms [mŭsh/rōōmz/] **69**–27
music [myōō/zĭk] **64**–3, **189**–16
  live music [līv/ myōō/zĭk] **84**–1
  music store [myōō/zĭk stör/] **130**–1
  world music [würld/ myōō/zĭk] **237**–32
Music [myōō/zĭk] **237**
MUSIC [myōō/zĭk] **238**
musician [myōō zĭsh/ən] **168**–43
mussels [mŭs/əlz] **71**–13, **212**–17
mustard [mŭs/tərd] **79**–22
mystery [mĭs/tə rē] **237**–20
nachos [nō/chōz] **79**–7
nail [nāl] **180**–34
  fingernail [fĭng/gər nāl/] **106**–18
  nail clipper [nāl klĭp/ər] **109**–31
  nail polish [nāl pŏl/ĭsh] **109**–33
  nail salon [nāl sə lŏn/] **130**–3
  toenail [tō/nāl/] **106** ✦
name [nām] **4**–1, **4**–2, **4**–4
  name tag [nām/ tăg/] **92**–15
napkin [năp/kĭn] **55**–10, **83**–26
narrow [năr/ō] **97**–35
nasal [nā/zəl]
  nasal congestion [nā/zəl kən jĕs/chən] **110**–7
  nasal spray [nā/zəl sprā/] **113**–32
National Assembly [nă/shə nəl ə sĕm/blē] **139**–20
NATIONAL PARKS [nă/shə nəl pärks/] **220–221**
natural [năch/rəl/, năch/ər əl/]
  natural gas [năch/rəl găs/] **218**–3
  natural materials [năch/rəl mə tïr/ē əlz] **98** ✦
NATURE CENTER [nā/chər sĕn/tər] **208–209**
nature program [nā/chər prō/grăm] **236**–7
Navigating a Webpage [nă/və gā/tĭng ə wĕb/pāj] **197**
navy [nā/vē] **138**–14
navy blue [nā/vē blōō/] **28**–5
near [nïr] **25** ✦
neck [nĕk] **96**–8, **96**–10, **104**–3
  crewneck [krōō/nĕk] **96**–7
  necklaces [nĕk/lə sĕz] **95**–10
  turtleneck [tür/tl nĕk/] **96**–9
needle [nēd/l] **98**–17, **100**–10, **210**–10, **233**–23
needle plate [nēd/l plāt/] **98**–18
negative integers [nĕ/gə tĭv ĭn/tə jərz] **192**–1
**negotiate** [nĭ gō/shē āt/] **157**–D
neighbourhood [nā/bər hŏŏd/] **128** ✦
nephew [nĕf/yōō] **34**–19
Neptune [nĕp/tōōn] **205**–8
nervous [nür/vəs] **42**–10
nest [nĕst] **209**–12
net [nĕt] **226**–17
  hairnet [hër/nĕt/] **93**–25
**network** [nĕt/würk/] **173**–A
Neutral Colours [nōō/trəl kŭl/ərz] **24**
neutron [nōō/trŏn] **195**–32
new [nōō]
  new job [nōō/ jŏb/] **172**–3
  new moon [nōō/ mōōn/] **205**–9
  New Year's Day [nōō/ yïrz/ dā/] **22**–9
Newfoundland time [nōō/fən lənd tīm/, –fənd–] **19**–34
news [nōōz]
  newspaper [nōōz/pā/pər] **133**–6
  news program [nōōz prō/grăm] **236**–1
  newsstand [nōōz/stănd/] **128**–12
newt [nōōt] **212**–26
New Words [nōō/ würdz/] **8**
next [nĕkst]
  next day mail [nĕkst/ dā/ māl/] **135** ✦
  next to [nĕkst/ tōō, –tə] **25**–10
  next week [nĕkst/ wēk/] **20**–20
nickel [nĭk/əl] **26**–2
niece [nēs] **34**–18
night [nīt] **18**–20
  nightclub [nīt/klŭb/] **223**–12
  nightgown [nīt/gown/] **91**–25
  night light [nīt/līt/] **37**–27
  nightshirt [nīt/shürt/] **91**–28
  nightstand [nīt/stănd/] **58**–23
  night table [nīt/ tā/bəl] **58**–23
nine [nīn] **16**
nineteen [nīn/tēn/] **16**
nineteenth [nīn/tēnth/] **16**
ninetieth [nīn/tē əth] **16**
ninety [nīn/tē] **16**
  90° angle [nīn/tē də grē/ ăng/gəl] **193**–26
ninth [nīnth] **16**
nipple [nĭp/əl] **37**–2
no [nō]
  no left turn [nō/ lĕft/ türn] **154**–8
  no exit [nō/ ĕg/zĭt] **154**–6
  no parking [nō/ pär/kĭng] **154**–11
noise [noyz] **64**–5
noisy [noy/zē] **23**–11
noon [nōōn] **18**–16
  afternoon [ăf/tər nōōn/] **18**–17
north [nörth] **155**–1
NORTH AMERICA AND CENTRAL AMERICA
  [nörth/ ə mĕr/ə kə ən sĕn/trəl ə mĕr/ə kə] **200–201**
nose [nōz] **104**–6, **110**–17
  revolving nosepiece [rə vŏl/vĭng nōz/pēs] **194**–15
not [nŏt]
  **do not drink** [dōō/ nŏt/ drĭnk] **112**–F
  **do not enter** [dōō/ nŏt/ ĕn/tər] **154**–2
  **do not operate** [dōō/ nŏt/ ŏp/ər āt/] **112**–E
  **do not take** [dōō nŏt/ tāk/] **112**–D
  **don't be** late [dōnt/ bē/ lāt/] **174**–E
  **don't litter** [dōnt/ lĭt/ər] **219**–L
  **don't smoke** [dōnt/ smōk/] **114**–G
  not working [nŏt/ wür/kĭng] **62**–1
note [nōt] **183**–39
  footnote [fŏŏt/nōt/] **190**–10
  notebook [nōt/bŏŏk/] **7**–27
  notebook paper [nōt/bŏŏk/ pāp/ər] **7**–28
  spiral notebook [spī/rəl nōt/bŏŏk/] **7**–29
novel [nŏ/vəl] **133**–16
November [nō vĕm/bər] **21**–35
nuclear energy [nōō/klē ər ĕn/ər jē] **218**–8
nucleus [nōō/klē əs] **194**–7, **195**–29
**numb** [nŭm] **119**–C
number [nŭm/bər]
  access number [ăk/sĕs/ nŭm/bər] **14**–16
  apartment number [ə pärt/mənt nŭm/bər] **4**–6
  cellphone number [sĕl/ fōn/ nŭm/bər] **4**–12
  chequing account number
    [chĕk/ĭng ə kownt/ nŭm/bər] **132**–14
  driver's license number
    [drī/vərz lī/səns nŭm/bər] **136**–11
  even numbers [ēv/ən nŭm/bərz] **192**–4
  odd numbers [ŏd/ nŭm/bərz] **192**–3
  phone number [fōn/ nŭm/bər] **4**–11, **15**–30
  prescription number
    [prĭ skrĭp/shən nŭm/bər] **112**–5
  savings account number
    [sā/vĭngz ə kownt/ nŭm/bər] **132**–11
  SKU number [ĕs/kā/yōō/ nŭm/bər] **27**–5
  social insurance number
    [sō/shəl ĭn shür/ əns nŭm/bər] **4**–15
Numbers [nŭm/bərz] **16**
NUMBERS [nŭm/bərz] **16**
Numerals [nōō/mər əlz] **16**
numerator [nōō/mər ā/ tər] **192**–5
nurse [nürs] **118**–8, **168**–44
  nurse practitioners [nürs/ prăk tĭ/shən ərz] **120** ✦
  registered nurse (RN) [rĕj/ə stərd nürs/] / [är/ĕn/]
    **120**–10
  registered practical nurse (RPN) [rĕj/ə stərd
    prăk/tə kəl nürs/] / [är/pē/ĕn/] **120**–11
  surgical nurse [sür/jĭ kəl nürs/] **120**–9
**nurse** [nürs] **36**–B
Nurse [nürs] **93**
nursery [nür/sə rē]
  nursery rhymes [nür/sə rē rīmz/] **37**–22
  nursery school [nür/sə rē skōōl/] **188**–1
nursing [nür/sĭng] **120**–12
  nursing assistant [nür/sĭng ə sĭs/tənt] **120**–12
  nursing home [nür/sĭng hōm/] **52**–12
Nursing Staff [nür/sĭng stăf/] **120**
nutrition label [nōō trĭ/shən lā/bəl] **122**–8
nuts [nŭts] **73**–36, **180**–36
nylon [nī/lŏn] **99**–12
oak [ōk] **210**–17, **210**–24
**obey** [ō bā/] **140**–D
objective [əb jĕk/tĭv] **194**–16
oboe [ō/bō] **238**–3
observatory [əb zür/və tör/ē] **205**–21
**observe** [əb zürv/] **195**–C
obstetrician [ŏb/stə trĭsh/ən] **120**–2
obtuse angle [ŏb/tōōs ăng/gəl] **193**–27
occupational therapist
  [ŏk/yə pā/shən əl thĕr/ə pĭst] **168**–45
OCCUPATIONS [ŏk/yə pā/shənz] **166–169**
ocean [ō/shən] **204**–6, **225**–1
o'clock [ə klŏk/] **18**–6

October [ŏk tō/bər] **21**–**34**
octopus [ŏk/tə pəs] **212**–**9**
odd numbers [ŏd/ nŭm/bərz] **192**–**3**
odometer [ō dŏm/ə tər] **159**–**28**
off [ŏf]
**clear off** [klïr/ ŏf/] **10**–**I**
**drop off** [drŏp/ ŏf/] **38**–**G**
gas shut-off valve [găs/ shŭt/ŏf vălv/] **146**–**4**
**get** off [gĕt/ ŏf/] **153**–**J**
**take off** [tāk/ ŏf/] **109**–**Q**
**turn off** [türn/ ŏf/] **11**–**P**, **160**–**I**, **174**–**G**, **219**–**G**
**offer** [ŏ/fər] **12**–**D**
office [ŏ/fəs] **164**–**3**
driver licensing office [drī/vər lī sən sĭng ŏf/əs] **136**–**137**
main office [mān/ ŏ/fəs] **5**–**12**
office building [ŏ/fəs bĭld/ĭng] **124**–**2**
office manager [ŏ/fəs măn/ĭ jər] **182**–**8**
office supply store [ŏ/fəs sə plī/ stör/] **127**–**21**
post office [pōst/ ŏ/fəs] **125**–**11**
post office box (PO box) [pōst/ ŏ/fəs bŏks/] / [pē/ō bŏks/] **135**–**9**
**run** for office [rŭn/ fər ŏ/fəs] **139**–**A**
Office [ŏ/fəs] **51**
OFFICE [ŏ/fəs] **134**–**135, 182**–**183**
Office Equipment [ŏ/fəs ĭ kwĭp/mənt] **183**
officer [ŏ/fə sər] **161**–**17**, **168**–**48**
Office Skills [ŏ/fəs skĭlz/] **171**
OFFICE SKILLS [ŏ/fəs skĭlz/] **171**
Office Supplies [ŏ/fəs sə plīz/] **183**
Office Visit [ŏ/fəs vĭ/zət] **119**
official [ə fĭsh/əl] **139**–**32**, **229**–**6**
oil [oyl] **73**–**31**, **218**–**6**
oil gauge [oyl/ gāj/] **159**–**29**
oil paint [oyl/ pānt/] **233**–**19**
oil spill [oyl/ spĭl/] **218**–**17**
ointment [oynt/mənt] **113**–**24**, **117**–**11**
OK [ō kā/] **154**–**5**
old [ōld] **31**–**9**, **31**–**10**
omelette [ŏm/lət, ŏ/mə lət] **76**–**12**
on [ŏn] **25**–**9**
**get** on [gĕt/ ŏn] **153**–**I**
**go** on [gō/ ŏn] **173**–**K**
on-the-job training [ŏn dhə jŏb/ trā/nĭng] **172**–**7**
on the left [ŏn dhə lĕft/] **25**–**1**
on the right [ŏn dhə rīt/] **25**–**3**
on time [ŏn tīm/] **19**–**23**
**overdose** on drugs [ō/vər dōs/ ŏn drŭgz/] **116**–**K**
**put on** [pŏŏt/ ŏn/] **87**–**B**, **108**–**D**, **109**–**P**
**try on** [trī/ ŏn/] **95**–**C**
**turn on** [türn/ ŏn/] **11**–**B**
once a week [wŭns/ə wēk/] **20**–**22**
oncologist [ŏn/kŏ lə jĭst/] **120**–**5**
one [wŭn] **16**
five after one [fīv/ ăf/ tər wŭn/] **18**–**7**
one billion [wŭn/ bĭl/yən] **16**
one eighth [wŭn/ ātth/, –āth/] **17**–**5**
one-fifteen [wŭn/fĭf/tēn/] **18**–**9**
one-forty [wŭn/för/tē] **18**–**12**
one-forty-five [wŭn/för/tē fīv/] **18**–**13**
one fourth [wŭn/ förth/] **17**–**4**
one half [wŭn/ hăf/] **17**–**2**
one hundred [wŭn/ hŭn/drəd] **16**
one hundred dollars [wŭn/ hŭn/drəd dŏl/ərz] **26**–**11**
one hundred one [wŭn/ hŭn/drəd wŭn/] **16**
100 percent [wŭn/ hŭn/drəd pər sĕnt/] **17**–**8**
one hundredth [wŭn/ hŭn/drəth] **16**
one hundred thousand [wŭn/ hŭn/drəd thow/zənd] **16**
one million [wŭn/ mĭl/yən] **16**
one o'clock [wŭn/ ə klŏk/] **18**–**6**
one-oh-five [wŭn/ō fīv/] **18**–**7**
one-size-fits-all [wŭn/sīz fĭts/öl] **96**–**6**
one-ten [wŭn/tĕn/] **18**–**8**
one third [wŭn/ thürd/] **17**–**3**
one-thirty [wŭn/thür/tē] **18**–**11**
one thousand [wŭn/ thow/zənd] **16**
one thousandth [wŭn/ thow/zənth] **16**
one-twenty [wŭn/twĕn/tē] **18**–**10**
one way [wŭn/ wā/] **154**–**3**
one-way trip [wŭn/wā/ trĭp/] **152**–**16**
one whole [wŭn/hōl/] **17**–**1**
quarter after one [kwör/tər ăf/tər wŭn/] **18**–**9**
ten after one [tĕn/ ăf/tər wŭn/] **18**–**8**
twenty after one [twĕn/tē ăf/tər wŭn/] **18**–**10**
onions [ŭn/yənz] **69**–**19**, **69**–**20**
onion rings [ŭn/yən rĭngz/] **79**–**4**
online [ŏn/līn/]
online catalogue [ŏn/līn/ kă/tə lŏg] **133**–**11**
online course [ŏn/līn/ körs/] **172**–**8**
online shipping [ŏn/līn/ shĭ/pĭng] **135**–**11**
only [ōn/lē] **154**–**7**
On the Airplane [ŏn/ dhe ër/plān/] **161**
**open** [ō/pən] **6**–**G**, **143**–**F**
opener [ō/pən ər] **54**–**14**, **78**–**1**, **146**–**8**
Opening an Account [ō/pə nĭng ən ə kownt/] **132**
opera [ŏp/rə] **223**–**11**, **236**–**5**
**operate** [ŏp/ə rāt/] **112**–**E**, **170**–**H**
Operating Room [ŏp/ə rā/tĭng rōōm/] **121**
operating table [ŏp/ə rā/tĭng tā/bəl] **121**–**40**
Operations [ŏp/ə rā/shənz] **192**
operator [ŏp/ə rā/tər] **14**–**21**, **98**–**14**, **168**–**37**
ophthalmologist [ŏf/thəl mŏl/ə jĭst] **120**–**7**
opinion [ə pĭn/yən] **44**–**3**, **140**–**2**
opossum [ə pŏs/əm, pŏs/əm] **216**–**13**
opponent [ə pō/nənt] **139**–**26**
optician [ŏp tĭsh/ən] **130**–**9**
optometrist [ŏp tŏm/ə trĭst] **115**–**6**
orange [ör/ənj] **24**–**4**
oranges [ör/ən jəz] **68**–**5**
orangutan [ə răng/ə tăng/, –tăn/] **217**–**41**
orchard [ör/chərd] **177**–**10**
orchid [ör/kĭd] **211**–**19**
order [ör/dər] **185**–**1**
order picker [ör/dər pĭk ər] **175**–**10**
**order** [ör/dər] **82**–**D**
orderly [ör/dər lē] **120**–**16**
Ordinal Numbers [ör/dn əl nŭm/bərz] **16**
organ [ör/gən] **238**–**20**
organic [ör gă/nĭk] **84**–**2**
organisms [ör/gə nĭzmz] **194**–**1**
**organize** [ör/gə nīz/] **171**–**L**, **191**–**G**
organizer [ör/gə nī/zər] **183**–**49**
ornament [ör/nə mənt] **239**–**15**
Orthodontics [ör/thə dŏn/tĭks] **119**
orthodontist [ör/thə dŏn/tĭst] **119**–**5**
orthopaedists [ör/thə pē/dĭsts] **120** ✦
Other Instruments [ŭdh/ər ĭn/strə mənts] **238**
otter [ŏt/ər] **213**–**35**
ounce [owns] **75**–**1**
out [owt] **62**–**2**
**blow out** [blō/ owt/] **240**–**C**
**check out** [chĕk/ owt/] **133**–**C**
**cross out** [krŏs/ owt/] **9**–**R**
**eat** out [ēt/ owt/] **82** ✦
**fill out** [fĭl/ owt/] **173**–**J**
**get** out of [gĕt/ owt/ əv] **153**–**F**
**let out** [lĕt/ owt/] **100**–**C**
**move out** [mōōv/ owt/] **48** ✦
outfit [owt/fĭt] **88** ✦
out of focus [owt/ əv fō/kəs] **235**–**33**
out-of-town contact [owt/əv town kŏn/tăkt] **146**–**2**
**run out** of gas [rŭn/ owt/ əv găs/] **162**–**E**
**take out** [tāk/ owt/] **9**–**Y**, **60**–**Q**, **82** ✦
**work out** [würk/ owt/] **230**–**N**
OUTDOOR RECREATION [owt/dör rĕk/rē ā/shən] **226**
outlet [owt/lĕt, –lət] **58**–**28**, **159**–**42**
outlet cover [owt/lĕt kŭv/ər] **181**–**46**
OUTSIDE THE BODY [owt/sīd/ dhe bŏ/dē] **106**–**107**
oven [ŭv/ən] **54**–**15**, **54**–**20**
oven cleaner [ŭv/ən klē/nər] **61**–**3**
over [ō/vər] **76**–**11**, **153**–**B**
overalls [ō/vər ölz/] **88**–**6**
over-bed table [ō/vər bĕd/ tā/bəl] **121**–**21**
overcoat [ō/vər kōt/] **90**–**2**
overexposed [ō/vər ĭk spōzd/] **235**–**34**
overflowing [ō/vər flō/ĭng] **63**–**18**
overhead compartment [ō/vər hĕd/ kəm pärt/mənt] **161**–**13**
overhead projector [ō/vər hĕd/ prə jĕk/tər] **7**–**16**
overjoyed [ō/vər joyd/] **43** ✦
overnight mail [ō/vər nīt/ māl/] **135** ✦
over-the-counter medication [ō/vər dhə kown/tər mĕd/ə kā/shən] **113**–**18**
**overdose** [ō/vər dōs/, ō/vər dōs/] **116**–**K**
Over-the-Counter Medication [ō/vər dhə kown/tər mĕd/ə kā/shən] **113**
owl [owl] **214**–**5**
owner [ō/nər] **166**–**11**, **175**–**1**
oxfords [ŏks/fərdz] **95**–**29**
oxygen mask [ŏk/sĭ jən măsk/] **161**–**24**
oysters [oy/stərz] **71**–**14**
Pacific time [pə sĭf/ĭk tīm/] **19**–**29**
pacifier [păs/ə fī/ər] **37**–**24**
pack [păk] **74**–**9**, **117**–**13**, **235**–**26**
backpack [băk/păk/] **94**–**18**, **226**–**15**
**pack** [păk] **49**–**M**, **162**–**A**
package [păk/ĭj] **74**–**8**, **74**–**20**, **134**–**17**
packaged food [păk/ĭjd fōōd/] **146**–**10**
PACKAGING [păk/ə jĭng] **74**
packer [păk/ər] **175**–**8**
packing tape [păk/ĭng tāp/] **183**–**32**
pad [păd]
bumper pad [bŭm/pər păd/] **59**–**4**
changing pad [chānj/ĭng păd/] **59**–**2**
foam pad [fōm/ păd/] **226**–**13**

heating pad [hē/tĭng păd/] **113**–13
ink pad [ĭnk/ păd/] **183**–46
knee pads [nē/ pădz/] **179**–19
legal pad [lē/gəl păd/] **183**–38
shoulder pads [shōl/dər pădz/] **231**–20
steel-wool soap pads [stēl/wŏŏl/sōp/ pădz/] **61**–5
sterile pad [stĕr/əl păd/] **117**–6
pail [pāl] **37**–7, **61**–7, **225**–8
pain [pān] **42**–11, **115**–3
pain reliever [pān rĭ lē/vər] **113**–26
paint [pānt] **181**–25, **232**–10, **233**–19
paintbrush [pānt/brŭsh/] **181**–22, **233**–20
paint tray [pānt/ trā] **181**–51
paint roller [pānt/ rō/lər] **181**–23
**paint** [pānt] **49**–P, **178**–A, **233**–E
painter [pān/tər] **168**–46
Painter [pān/tər] **92**
painting [pān/tĭng] **56**–9
pair of scissors [pĕr/ əv sĭz/ərz] **100**–16
paisley [pāz/lē] **96**–26
pallet [pă/lət] **175**–13
palm [pŏm] **106**–15, **210**–14
pan [păn] **54**–24
bedpan [bĕd/ păn/] **121**–28
cake pan [kāk/ păn/] **78**–26
dustpan [dŭst/ păn/] **61**–17
frying pan [frī/ĭng păn/] **78**–5
pancakes [păn/kāks/] **80**–7
pie pan [pī/ păn/] **78**–28
roasting pan [rō/stĭng păn/] **78**–13
saucepan [sŏs/păn/] **78**–25
pancreas [păng/krē əs] **107**–45
panda [păn/də] **217**–43
pane [pān] **178**–16
panel [păn/əl] **234**–7
Panel [păn/əl] **159**
panther [păn/thər] **217**–42
panties [păn/tēz] **91**–13
pants [pănts] **87**–12
security pants [sĭ kyŏŏr/ə tē pănts/] **93**–22
training pants [trā/nĭng pănts/] **37**–11
work pants [würk/ pănts/] **92**–5
pantyhose [păn/tē hōz/] **91**–18
papayas [pə pī/əz] **68**–20
paper [pā/pər]
construction paper [kən strŭk/shən pā/pər] **232**–12
copies of important papers
[kŏ/pēz əv ĭm pört/ənt pā/pərz] **146**–20
newspaper [nōōz/pā/pər] **133**–6
notebook paper [nōt/bŏŏk/ pā/pər] **7**–28
paper clip [pā/pər klĭp/] **183**–31
paper cutter [pā/pər kŭt/ər] **183**–22
paper dolls [pā/pər dŏlz/] **233**–28
paper shredder [pā/pər shrĕd/ər] **183**–24
paper towels [pā/pər tow/əlz] **54**–3
sandpaper [sănd/ pā/pər] **181**–56
toilet paper [toy/lət pā/pər] **57**–19, **146**–13
wallpaper [wŏl/ pā/pər] **59**–8
parade [pə rād/] **239**–1
paragraph [păr/ə grăf/] **190**–3
parakeet [păr/ə kēt/] **215**–15
parallel lines [păr/ə lĕl/ līnz/] **193**–25
parallelogram [păr/ə lĕl/ə grăm/] **193**–33
paramedic [pĕr ə mĕd/ĭk] **116**–2, **121**–32
parasites [păr/ə sīts/] **111**–13
parcel post [pär/səl pōst/] **134**–6
parentheses [pə rĕn/thə sēz/] **190**–19
PARENTING [pĕr/ən tĭng] **36–37**
Parents [pĕr/ənts] **34**
parent-teacher conference
[pĕr/ənt tē/chər kŏn/frəns] **22**–5
paring knife [pĕr/ĭng nīf/] **78**–16
park [pärk] **223**–10
park ranger [pärk/ rāng/jər] **220**–5
**park** [pärk] **129**–E
parka [pär/kə] **90**–9
PARK AND PLAYGROUND [pärk/ ən plā/grownd/] **224**
parking [pär/kĭng] **128**–6, **154**–11, **154**–12
parking attendant [pär/kĭng ə tĕn/dənt] **184**–3
parking garage [pär/kĭng gə rŏzh/] **124**–1
parking meter [pär/kĭng mē/tər] **129**–25
parking space [pär/kĭng spās/] **50**–18, **128**–5
PARKS [pärks] **220–221**
parliament [pär/lə mĕnt]
Member of Parliament
[mĕm/bür əv pär/lə mĕnt] **138**–9
Parliament of Canada [pär/lə mĕnt əv kăn/ə də] **138**–6
parochial school [pə rō/kē əl skōōl/] **5** ✦
parsley [pär/slē] **69**–28
part [pärt] **33**–4
**participate** [pär tĭ/sə pāt/] **10**–B
particle [pär/tĭ kəl]
particle board [pär/tĭ kəl börd/] **181**–20
particle mask [pär/tĭ kəl măsk/] **179**–14
Partner [pärt/nər] **8**
parts [pärts] **175**–5
Parts of a Bird [pärts/ əv ə bürd/] **214**
PARTS OF A CAR [pärts/ əv ə kär/] **158–159**
Parts of a Fish [pärts/ əv ə fĭsh/] **212**
Parts of a Flower [pärts/ əv ə flow/ər] **211**
Parts of an Essay [pärts/ əv ən ĕs/ā] **190**
Parts of a Phone [pärts/ əv ə fōn/] **14**
Parts of a Sewing Machine
[pärts/ əv ə sō/ĭng mə shēn] **98**
Parts of a Tree [pärts/ əv ə trē/] **210**
party [pär/tē] **64**–2
pass [păs] **161**–20
passbook [păs/bŏŏk/] **132**–10
passport [păs/pört/] **41**–10
**pass** [păs] **10**–E, **137**–G, **230**–G
passenger [păs/ən jər] **150**–2, **161**–15
past [păst] **155**–E
pasta [päs/tə] **67**–12
pasta salad [päs/tə săl/əd] **80**–20
paste [pāst]
toothpaste [tōōth/pāst/] **109**–23
pastrami [pə strŏ/mē] **71**–23
path [păth] **208**–3, **224**–3
Path [păth] **172**
patient [pā/shənt] **118**–6, **121**–18
patio [păt/ē ō] **53**–16
patio furniture [păt/ē ō für/nĭ chər] **53**–19
patron [pā/trən] **82**–6, **133**–3
pattern [păt/ərn] **99**–22
patterns [păt/ərnz] **96**
**pause** [pŏz] **235**–E
paw [pŏ] **216**–22
pay [pā]
paycheque [pā/chĕk/] **165**–14
payroll clerk [pā/rōl klürk/] **165**–10
pay stub [pā/ stŭb/] **165**–11
**pay** [pā]
**pay** a late fine [pā/ ə lāt/ fīn/] **133**–E
**pay** attention [pā/ ə tĕn/shən] **147**–D
**pay back** [pā/ băk/] **26**–D
**pay** cash [pā/ kăsh/] **27**–A
**pay for** [pā/ för/] **27**–G
pay phone [pā/ fōn] **15**–25, **129**–23
**pay** the application fee
[pā/ dhe ăp/lə kā/shən fē/] **137**–C
**pay** the bill [pā/ dhe bĭl] **82**–I
**pay** the rent [pā/ dhe rĕnt/] **48**–E
Pay [pā] **27**
PBX (private branch exchange)
[pē/ bē/ ĕks/] / [prī/vət brănch ĕks chānj/] **182**–13
peaceful assembly [pēs/fəl ə sĕm/blē] **140**–3
peaches [pē/chəz] **68**–10
peacock [pē/kŏk/] **214**–14
peak [pēk] **204**–14
pearls [pürlz] **95**–39
pears [pĕrz] **68**–4
peas [pēz] **69**–21
pedal [pĕd/əl] **159**–45, **159**–46
pedestrian [pə dĕs/trē ən] **128**–14
pedestrian crossing [pə dĕs/trē ən krŏ/sĭng] **154**–13
pediatrician [pē/dē ə trĭsh/ən] **120**–4
**peel** [pēl] **77**–K
peeler [pē/lər] **78**–15
peephole [pēp/hōl/] **51**–32
pelvis [pĕl/vəs] **107**–50
pen [pĕn] **7**–22
pencil [pĕn/səl] **7**–20, **109**–34
pencil eraser [pĕn/səl ĭ rā/sər] **7**–21
pencil sharpener [pĕn/səl shär/pə nər] **7**–23, **183**–26
penguin [pĕng/wĭn] **214**–11
peninsula [pĕ nĭn/sə lə] **204**–7
penny [pĕn/ē] **26**–1
PEOPLE [pē/pəl] **32**
pepper [pĕp/ər] **55**–13, **69**–7, **69**–29
percent [pər sĕnt/]
50 percent [fĭf/tē pər sĕnt/] **17**–10
100 percent [wŭn/ hŭn/drəd pər sĕnt/] **17**–8
75 percent [sĕv/ən tē fīv/ pər sĕnt/] **17**–9
10 percent [tĕn/ pər sĕnt/] **17**–12
25 percent [twĕn/tē fīv/ pər sĕnt/] **17**–11
Percents [pər sĕnts/] **17**
Percussion [pər kŭsh/ən] **238**
perfume [pür/fyōōm/, pər fyōōm/] **108**–6
perimeter [pə rĭ/mə tər] **193**–43
period [pïr/ē əd] **190**–11
periodicals [pïr/ē ŏd/ĭ kəlz] **133**–4
periodic table [pïr/ē ŏd/ĭk tā/bəl] **195**–26
**perm** [pürm] **33**–B
permanent resident card
[pür/mə nənt rĕ/zə/dənt kärd] **40**–2
peroxide [pə rŏk/ sīd] **117**–9

perpendicular lines [pür/pən dĭk/yə lər līnz/] **193**–24
person [pür/sən]
  appliance repair person
    [ə plī/əns rĭ për/ pür/sən] **166**–4
  businessperson [bĭz/nəs pür/sən] **166**–12
  bus person [bŭs/ pür/sən] **185**–13
  counterperson [kown/tər pür/sən] **79**–17
  delivery person [də lĭv/ə rē pür/sən] **167**–21
  electronics repair person
    [ē lĕk trŏn/ĭks rĭ për/ pür/sən] **167**–24
  repair person [rĭ për/ pür/sən] **62**–10
personal CD player [pür/sə nəl sē/dē/ plā/ər] **234**–5
PERSONAL HYGIENE [pür/sə nəl hī/jēn] **108–109**
PERSONAL INFORMATION
  [pür/sə nəl ĭn/fər mā/shən] **4**
pesticide poisoning [pĕs/tə sīd/ poy/zə nĭng] **218**–16
pests [pĕsts] **62** ✦
pet [pĕt]
  pet food [pĕt fo͞od/] **72**–5
  pet store [pĕt stör/] **130**–6
petals [pĕt/lz] **211**–8
petition [pə tĭ/shən] **148**–5
petroleum [pə trō/lē əm] **218**–6
Pets [pĕts] **215**
pharmacist [fär/mə sĭst] **112**–1
pharmacy [fär/mə sē] **128**–4
PHARMACY [fär/mə sē] **112–113**
Phase of the Moon [fāz/ əf dhə mo͞on/] **205**
Phillips screwdriver [fĭl/ĭps skro͞o/drī/vər] **180**–31
phlebotomist [flĭ bŏ/tə mĭst] **121**–29
phone [fōn]
  automated phone system
    [ö/tə māt ĭd fōn/ sĭs/təm] **14**–23
  cellphone holder [sĕl/ fōn/ hōl/dər] **94**–15
  cellphone kiosk [sĕl/ fōn/ kē/ösk] **131**–22
  cellphone number [sĕl/ fōn/ nŭm/bər] **4**–12
  cellular phone [sĕl/yə lər fōn/] **14**–8
  cordless phone [körd/ləs fōn/] **15**–24
  headphones [hĕd/ fōnz/] **6**–8, **234**–4
  Internet phone call [ĭn/tər nĕt/ fōn/ köl/] **14**–20
  microphone [mī/krə fōn/] **234**–18
  pay phone [pā/ fōn/] **15**–25, **129**–23
  phone bill [fōn/ bĭl/] **15**–28
  phone jack [fōn/ jăk/] **14**–3
  phone line [fōn/ līn/] **14**–4
  phone number [fōn/ nŭm/bər] **4**–11, **15**–30
  smart phone [smärt/ fōn/] **15**–27
Phone [fōn] **14**
Phone Bill [fōn/ bĭl/] **15**
Phone Call [fōn/ köl/] **15**
photo [fō/tō] **58**–3, **136**–4
  digital photo album [dĭ/jə təl fō/tō ăl/bəm] **235**–32
  funny photo [fŭn/ē fō/tō] **206**–2
  photo album [fō/tō ăl/bəm] **235**–31
  photocopier [fō/tə kŏp/ē ər] **183**–23
  serious photo [sïr/ē əs fō/tō] **206**–3
photographer [fə tŏg/rə fər] **206**–1
PHOTOGRAPHY [fə tŏg/rə fē] **234–235**
photosynthesis [fō/tō sĭn/thə səs] **194**–10
physical [fĭz/ĭ kəl]
  physical education [fĭz/ĭ kəl ĕ jə kā/shən] **189**–17
  physical therapist [fĭz/ĭ kəl thĕr/ə pĭst] **115**–12
  physical therapy [fĭz/ĭ kəl thĕr/ə pē] **115**–11
physically challenged [fĭz/ĭ klē chăl/ənjd] **32**–10
physician assistant [fĭz/ĭ shən ə sĭs/tənt] **168**–47
physicist [fĭz/ĭ sĭst/] **195**–33
Physics [fĭz/ĭks] **195**
pi (π) [pī] **193**–46
piano [pē ăn/ō] **238**–14
pick [pĭk] **108**–15
pickaxe [pĭk/ăks/] **178**–21
picker [pĭ/kər] **175**–10, **178**–5
pickle [pĭk/l] **80**–11
**pick up** [pĭk/ ŭp/] **6**–I, **11**–E, **38**–M, **112** ✦
pickup truck [pĭk/ŭp trŭk/] **156**–12
**picnic** [pĭk/nĭk] **224**–D
picnic table [pĭk/nĭk tā/bəl] **224**–8
picture [pĭk/chər]
  picture book [pĭk/chər bo͝ok/] **133**–12
  picture dictionary [pĭk/chər dĭk/shə nër ē] **7**–31
  picture frame [pĭk/chər frām/] **58**–4
pie [pī] **81**–35
  pie pan [pī/ păn/] **78**–28
pier [pïr] **225**–18
pierced [pïrst]
  pierced ear [pïrst/ ïr/] **32**–17
  pierced earrings [pïrst/ ïr/ĭngz] **95**–36
pig [pĭg] **215**–2, **215**–14
pigeon [pĭj/ən] **214**–15
pile [pīl] **53**–25
pill [pĭl] **113**–21
pillow [pĭl/ō] **56**–2, **58**–11
  pillowcase [pĭl/ō kās/] **58**–14
pilot [pī/lət] **161**–11
pin [pĭn] **95**–38
  bobby pins [bŏb/ē pĭnz/] **108**–21
  clothespin [klōz/ pĭn/] **101**–10
  pin cushion [pĭn/ ko͝osh/ən] **100**–13
  pushpin [po͝osh/pĭn/] **183**–35
  rolling pin [rō/lĭng pĭn] **78**–30
  safety pin [sāf/tē pĭn/] **37**–9, **100**–14
  straight pin [strāt pĭn/] **100**–12
pine [pīn] **210**–9
  pine cone [pīn/kōn/] **210**–11
pineapples [pī/năp/əlz] **68**–23
pink [pĭnk] **24**–7
pipe [pīp] **158**–15, **181**–17
  pipe wrench [pīp rĕnch/] **181**–47
**pitch** [pĭch] **230**–A
pizza [pēt/sə] **79**–10
place [plās] **146**–1
  fireplace [fīr/plās/] **56**–13
  placemat [plās măt/] **55**–11
  place of birth [plās/ əv bürth/] **4**–14
  place setting [plās/ sĕt/ĭng] **83**–17
PLACES TO GO [plā/səz tə gō/] **222–223**
PLACES TO LIVE [plā/səz tə lĭv/] **52**
plaid [plăd] **96**–22
plain [plān] **97**–33
plains [plānz] **204**–19
plan [plăn] **186**–4
**plan** [plăn] **146**–A
plane [plān] **144**–3, **150**–8, **181**–57
Planets [plăn/əts] **205**
Planning a Career [plă/nĭng ə kə rēr/] **172**
**plant** [plănt] **176**–E, **177**–A, **219**–N
plants [plănts] **208**–5
  houseplant [hows/plănt/] **56**–4, **211**–27
Plants [plănts] **210**
PLANTS [plănts] **210**
plaque [plăk] **119**–12
plastic [plăs/tĭk]
  plastic storage bags [plăs/tĭk stör/ĭj băgz] **72**–25
  plastic storage container
    [plăs/tĭk stör/ĭj kən tā/nər] **78**–4
  plastic utensils [plăs/tĭk yo͞o tĕn/ səlz] **79**–19
  plastic wrap [plăs/tĭk răp/] **72**–24
plate [plāt] **55**–1
  bread-and-butter plate [brĕd/n bŭt/ər plāt/] **83**–19
  dinner plate [dĭn/ər plāt/] **83**–18
  licence plate [lī/səns plāt/] **136**–12, **158**–12
  salad plate [săl/əd plāt/] **83**–20
  vanity plate [vă/nə tē plāt/] **136** ✦
platform [plăt/förm/] **152**–7
platter [plăt/ər] **55**–20
platypus [plăt/ĭ pəs, –po͝os/] **217**–48
play [plā] **223**–8
  play area [plā/ ër/ē ə] **130**–11
  playground [plā/grownd/] **50**–3
**play** [plā] **235**–B
  **play** an instrument [plā/ ən ĭn/strə mənt] **238**–A
  **play** cards [plā/ kärdz/] **233**–H
  **play** games [plā/ gāmz/] **232**–B
  **play** with [plā/ wĭth/] **36**–M
player [plā/ər] **229**–5
  CD player [sē/dē plā/ər] **159**–38
  DVD player [dē/vē/dē/ plā/ər] **56**–7, **234**–10
  MP3 player [ĕm/pē/thrē/ plā/ər] **234**–2
  personal CD player [pür/sə nəl sē/dē plā/ər] **234**–5
  portable cassette player
    [pör/tə bəl kə sĕt/ plā/ər] **234**–6
  portable DVD player
    [pör/tə bəl dē/vē/dē/ plā/ər] **234**–11
  video player [vĭd/ē ō plā/ər] **197**–11
PLAYGROUND [plā/grownd/] **224**
pliers [plī/ərz] **180**–7
plugs [plŭgz] **179**–15, **234**–16
plumber [plŭm/ər] **63**–20
plums [plŭmz] **68**–13
plunger [plŭn/jər] **181**–50
plywood [plī/wo͝od/] **178**–18
p.m. [pē/ĕm/] **18**–5
pneumatic drill [no͞o măt/ĭk drĭl/] **178**–9
poached eggs [pōcht/ ĕgz/] **76**–9
PO box (post office box) [pē/ō bŏks/] /
  [pōst/ ö/fəs bŏks/] **135**–9
pocket [pŏk/ət] **100**–7
podium [pō/dē əm] **206**–5
poinsettia [poyn sĕt/ē ə, –sĕt/ə] **211**–24
point [poynt] **17**–7,
  endpoint [ĕnd/poynt/] **193**–21
pointer [poyn/tər] **197**–12
poison [poy/zən] **116**–J
  poison ivy [poy/zən ī/vē] **210**–25
  poison oak [poy/zən ōk/] **210**–24
  poison sumac [poy/zən so͞o/măk, –sho͞o/–] **210**–23

poisoning [poy/zən ïng] **218**–16
poisonous fumes [poy/zən əs fyōōmz/] **179**–3
polar bear [pō/lär bër] **216**–7
poles [pōlz] **226**–18, **231**–25
police [pə lēs/]
police officer [pə lēs/ ö/fə sər] **141**–1, **168**–48
police station [pə lēs/ stā/shən] **124**–6
polish [pöl/ĭsh] **61**–8, **109**–33
**polish** [pöl/ĭsh] **60**–E, **109**–O
political [pə lĭ/tĭ kəl]
political campaign [pə lĭ/tĭ kəl kăm pān/] **139**–25
political movement [pə lĭ/tĭ kəl mōōv/mənt] **199**–16
political party [pə lĭ/tĭ kəl pär/tē] **139** ✦
polka-dotted [pō/kə dŏt/əd] **96**–21
pollution [pə lōō/shən] **218**–11, **218**–14
Pollution [pə lōō/shən] **218**
polo [pō/lō] **229**–15
polo shirt [pō/lō shïrt/] **92**–14
poncho [pŏn/chō] **90**–19
pond [pŏnd] **204**–21
pool [pōōl] **51**–22, **184**–22, **228**–2
pool service [pōōl/ sür/vəs] **184**–21
pool table [pōōl/ tā/bəl] **50**–15
pop [pŏp] **73**–34, **79**–11, **237**–25
pop-up ad [pŏp/ŭp] **197**–9
porch light [pörch/ līt/] **53**–13
porcupine [pör/kyə pīn/] **216**–11
Pork [pörk] **70**
pork chops [pörk/ chŏps/] **70**–10
porpoise [pör/pəs] **213**–30
port [pört] **196**–7
airport [ër/pört/] **151**–10
portable [pör/tə bəl]
portable cassette player
[pör/tə bəl kə sĕt/ plā/ər] **234**–6
portable DVD player
[pör/tə bəl dē/vē/dē/ plā/ər] **234**–11
portable TV [pör/tə bəl tē/ vē/] **234**–8
porter [pör tər] **160**–1
positive integers [pŏ/zə tĭv ĭn/tə jərz] **192**–2
post [pōst] **134**–6
postcard [pōst/kärd/] **134**–16
postmark [pōst/märk/] **134**–24
post office [pōst/ ö/fəs] **125**–11
post office box (PO box) [pōst/ ö/fəs bŏks/] /
[pē/ō bŏks/] **135**–9
Xpresspost [ĕk/sprĕs/ pōst] **134**–2
postage [pō/stĭj] **135** ✦
postal [pō/stəl]
postal clerk [pō/stəl klürk/] **135**–7
postal forms [pō/stəl förmz/] **134**–19
postal code [pō/stəl kōd] **4**–9
postal scale [pō/stəl skāl/] **183**–27
postal worker [pō/stəl wür/kər] **169**–49
POST OFFICE [pōst/ ö/fəs] **134–135**
pot [pŏt] **54**–16, **78**–6
pot holders [pŏt hōl/dərz] **78**–29
teapot [tē/pŏt/] **55**–16
potatoes [pə tā/tōz] **69**–17
baked potato [bākt/ pə tā/tō] **81**–25
mashed potatoes [măsht/ pə tā/tōz] **81**–23
potato chips [pə tā/tō chĭps/] **73**–35
potato salad [pə tā/tō săl/əd] **80**–19
sweet potatoes [swēt/ pə tā/tōz] **69**–18
potty seat [pŏt/ē sēt/] **37**–12
pouch [powch] **217**–52
Poultry [pōl/trē] **70, 76**
POULTRY [pōl/trē] **70**
pound key [pownd/ kē/] **14**–7
**pour** [pör] **82**–C
powder [pow/dər] **37**–14, **108**–4, **109**–41
power [pow/ər] **218**–2, **218**–5
power cord [pow/ər körd/] **196**–2
power outlet [pow/ər owt/lĕt] **159**–42
power sander [pow/ər săn/dər] **180**–11
pox [pŏks] **111**–6
practical [prăk/tə kəl] **120**–11
prairie dog [prër/ē dög/] **215**–22
**praise** [prāz] **36**–J
pregnant [prĕg/nənt] **32**–15
**preheat** [prē/hēt/] **77**–A
premier [prē/myër, –mër] **139**–17
preparation [prĕ/pə rā/shən] **185**–4
PREPARATION [prĕ/pə rā/shən] **76–77**
**prepare** [prĭ/për] **174**–A
prep cook [prĕp kŏŏk] **93**
PREPOSITIONS [prĕp/ə zĭsh/ənz] **25**
PREPOSITIONS OF MOTION
[prĕp/ə zĭsh/ənz əv mō/shən] **153**
preschool [prē/skōōl/] **188**–1
**prescribe** medication [prĭ skrib/mĕd/ə kā/shən] **112** ✦
prescription [prĭ skrĭp/shən] **112**–2
**pick up** a prescription
[pĭk/ ŭp/ə prĭ skrĭp/shən] **112** ✦
prescription label [prĭ skrĭp/shən lā/bəl] **112**–4
prescription medication
[prĭ skrĭp/shən mĕd/ə kā/shən] **112**–3
prescription number [prĭ skrĭp/shən nŭm/bər]
**112**–5
present [prĕz/ənt] **94** ✦, **240**–3
presentation [prĕ/zən tā/shən] **182**–6
president [prĕz/ə dənt] **199**–5
press [prĕs] **78**–11
**press** [prĕs] **15**–B, **15**–D
presser foot [prĕs/ər fŏŏt/] **98**–19
pressure [prĕsh/ər] **111**–14, **118**–9
**pretend** [prĭ tĕnd/] **233**–G
Prewriting [prē/rī/tĭng] **191**
price [prīs] **27**–2, **27**–3, **27**–7
price tag [prīs tăg/] **27**–1
prime minister [prīm/ mĭn/ə stər] **138**–3, **198**–7, **199**–7
principal [prĭn/sə pəl] **5**–4
print [prĭnt] **96**–23
**print** [prĭnt] **4**–C, **171**–I
printer [prĭn/tər] **169**–50, **196**–17
inkjet printer [ĭnk/jĕt prĭn/tər] **183**–18
laser printer [lā/zər prĭn/tər] **183**–19
Priority Courier [prī ör/ə tē kōō rē ər] **134**–1
prism [prĭz/əm] **195**–35
prisoner [prĭz/nər] **141**–15
private school [prī/vət skōōl/] **5** ✦
Problem [prŏb/ləm] **192**
problems [prŏb/ləmz] **115**–1, **192**–11
Problems [prŏb/ləmz] **115, 119**
PROBLEMS [prŏb/ləmz] **62–63**
Procedures [prə sē/jərz] **117, 118**
PROCEDURES [prə sē/jərz] **146–147**
processed cheese [prō/sĕst chēz/] **71**–26
Process [prō/sĕs] **191**
processor [prō/sĕ sər] **54**–26
Processor [prō/sĕ sər] **92**
produce section [prō/dōōs sĕk/shən] **72**–2
product [prŏd/ŭkt] **192**–9
Products [prŏd/ŭkts] **72, 73**
program [prō/grăm]
children's program [chĭl/drənz prō/grăm] **236**–9
nature program [nā/chər prō/grăm] **236**–7
news program [nōōz/ prō/grăm] **236**–1
shopping program [shŏp/ĭng prō/grăm] **236**–10
sports program [spörtz/ prō/grăm] **236**–11
**program** [prō/grăm] **170**–I
Programs [prō/grămz] **236**
projector [prə jĕk/tər] **6**–6, **7**–16, **235**–29
promotion [prə mō/shən] **172**–4
proof of insurance [prōōf/ əv/ĭn shŏŏr/əns] **136**–8
**proofread** [prōōf/rēd/] **191**–I
**protect** [prə tĕkt/] **143**–D
protector [prə tĕk/tər] **196**–1
proton [prō/tŏn] **195**–31
proud [prowd] **43**–21
province [prŏv/ins] **4**–8, **198**–1
provincial capital [prə vĭn/shəl kă/pət əl] **139**–19
Provincial Government [prə vĭn/shəl gŭ/vərn mənt] **139**
prunes [prōōnz] **68**–26
pruning shears [prōō/nĭng shïrz/] **176**–9
psychiatrist [sī kī/ə trĭst, sə–] **120**–8
PUBLIC SAFETY [pŭb/lĭk sāf/tē] **143**
public school [pŭb/lĭk skōōl/] **5** ✦
PUBLIC TRANSPORTATION
[pŭb/lĭk trăns/pər tā/shən] **152**
**pull** [pŏŏl] **119**–F, **224**–A
pullover sweater [pŏŏl/ō/vər swĕt/ər] **88**–3
pulse [pŭls] **122**–A
pumps [pŭmps] **95**–26
Punctuation [pŭngk/chōō ā/shən] **190**
puppy [pŭp/ē] **215**–12
**purchase** [pür/chəs] **94**–A
purifier [pyŏŏ/rə fī/ ər] **113**–14
purple [pür/pəl] **24**–6
purses [pür/səz] **94**–2, **94**–14
**push** [pŏŏsh] **224**–B
pushpin [pŏŏsh/pĭn/] **183**–35
**put** [pŏŏt] **9**–X
**put away**
[pŏŏt/ə wā/] **9**–Z, **60**–G
**put down** [pŏŏt/ down/] **6**–J
**put** in coolant [pŏŏt/ ĭn kōō/lənt] **157**–I
**put on** [pŏŏt/ ŏn/] **87**–B, **108**–D, **109**–P, **135**–C
**put** on hold [pŏŏt/ ŏn hōld/] **171**–N
**put** the utilities in your name
[pŏŏt/ dhe yōō tĭl/ə tēz ĭn yər nām/] **49**–O
puzzle [pŭz/əl] **59**–17
pyjamas [ pə jăm/əz, –jŏm/–] **91**–24
pyramid [pïr/ə mĭd] **193**–39
quarter [kwör/tər] **26**–4
quarter after one [kwör/tər ăf/tər wŭn/] **18**–9

1/4 cup [kwör/tər kŭp/] **75**–8
quarter moon [kwör/tər mo͞on/] **205**–11
quarter to two [kwör/tər tə to͞o/] **18**–13
3/4 sleeved [thrē/ kwör/tər slēvd/] **96**–13
question mark [kwĕs/chən märk/] **190**–12
Quick and Easy Cake [kwĭk/ ən ē/zē kāk/] **77**
quiet [kwī/ət] **23**–12
quill [kwĭl] **216**–25
quilt [kwĭlt] **58**–16
quilt block [kwĭlt/ blŏk/] **232**–15
**quilt** [kwĭlt] **232**–C
quotation [kwō tā/shən] **190**–9
quotation marks [kwō tā/shən märks/] **190**–15
quotient [kwō /shənt] **192**–10
rabbit [răb/ət] **215**–13
raccoon [ră ko͞on/] **216**–16
**race** [rās] **230**–S
racing [rā/sĭng] **228**–19
rack [răk] **98**–16
dish rack [dĭsh/ răk/] **54**–5
roasting rack [rō/stĭng răk/] **78**–14
towel rack [tow/əl răk/] **57**–15
racquet [răk/ət] **231**–2
racquetball [răk/ət bŏl/] **228**–12
radiation [rā/dē ā/shən] **218**–15
radiator [rā/dē ā/tər] **158**–19
radio [rā/dē ō] **102**–6, **159**–37, **179**–22
radioactive materials
[rā/dē ō ăk/tĭv mə tïr/ē əlz] **179**–7
radiologist [rā/dē ŏl/ə jĭst] **120**–6
radishes [răd/ĭ shəz] **69**–4
radius [rā/dē əs] **193**–35
rafting [răf/tĭng] **226**–2
rags [răgz] **61**–9
rail [rāl] **59**–10
railroad crossing [rāl/rōd krö/sĭng] **154**–14
rain [rān] **218**–13
rain boots [rān/ bo͞ots/] **90**–20
raincoat [rān/kōt/] **90**–18
rainforest [rān/ för/əst] **204**–1
raining [rā/nĭng] **13**–11
**raise** [rāz] **6**–A
raisins [rā/zənz] **68**–25
rake [rāk] **176**–8
**rake** [rāk] **176**–C
ranch [rănch] **52**–10
rancher [răn/chər] **177**–22
Ranch Hand [rănch hănd/] **92**
RANCHING [răn/chĭng] **177**
R&B [är/n bē/] **237**–28
range [rānj] **204**–15
ranger [rān/jər] **220**–5
rash [răsh] **110**–10
raspberries [răz/bër/ēz] **68**–15
rats [răts] **63**–27, **215**–17
rattle [răt/l] **37**–26
rattlesnake [răt/l snāk/] **213**–38
raw [rö] **70**–24
ray [rā] **212**–11
razor [rā/zər] **109**–27
razor blade [rā/zər blād/] **109**–28
reaction [rē/ăk shən] **116**–E
**read** [rēd]
**proofread** [pro͞of/rēd/] **191**–I
**read** the card [rēd/ dhe kärd/] **135**–G
**read** the definition [rēd/ dhe dĕ/fə nĭ/shən] **8**–B
**read** the paper [rēd/ dhe pā/pər] **39**–V
**read** to [rēd/ to͞o] **36**–N
Reading a Phone Bill [rē/dĭng ə fōn/ bĭl/] **15**
reality show [rē ă lə tē shō/] **236**–6
rear-view mirror [rïr/vyo͞o/ mïr/ər] **159**–35
receipt [rĭ sēt/] **27**–6
**receive** [rĭ sēv/] **135**–F
receiver [rĭ sē/vər] **14**–1
reception area [rĭ sĕp/shən ër/ē ə] **182**–15
receptionist [rĭ sĕp/shə nĭst] **118**–2, **164**–5, **169**–51, **182**–14
reclined seat [rĭ klīnd/ sēt/] **161**–27
**record** [rĭ körd/] **195**–D, **235**–A
records [rĕk/ərdz] **168**–39
RECREATION [rĕk/rē ā/shən] **226**
recreational vehicle (RV)
[rĕk/rē ā/shən əl vē/ə kəl] / [är/vē/] **156**–10
Recreation Room [rĕk/rē ā/shən ro͞om/] **50**
recruiter [rə kro͞o/tər] **172**–14
rectangle [rĕk/tăng/gəl] **193**–29
**recycle** [rē sī/kəl] **60**–B, **219**–C
recycling bin [rē sī/klĭng bĭn/] **61**–2
red [rĕd] **24**–1
red hair [rĕd/ hër/] **33**–15
redwood [rĕd/wo͝od/] **210**–18
**redecorate** [rē dĕk/ə rāt/] **48** ✦
**reduce** [rĭ do͞os/] **219**–A
referee [rĕf/ə rē/] **229**–6
reference librarian [rĕf/rəns lī brër/ē ən] **133**–9
refrigerator [rĭ frĭj/ə rā/tər] **54**–9
refund [rē/fŭnd] **97** ✦
reggae [rĕ gā/] **237**–31
register [rĕj/ə stər] **73**–15
**register** [rĕj/ə stər] **157**–F
registered nurse (RN)
[rĕj/ə stərd nürs/] / [är/ĕn/] **120**–10
registration [rĕj/ə strā/shən]
registration sticker
[rĕj/ə strā/shən stĭk/ər] **136**–13
registration tag [rĕj/ə strā/shən tăg/] **136**–13
regular price [rĕg/yə lər prīs/] **27**–2
regulations [rĕ gyə lā/shənz] **164**–6
relatives [rĕ lə tĭvz] **44**–6
**relax** [rĭ lăks/] **39**–U
relieved [rĭ lēvd/] **42**–15
reliever [rĭ lēv/ər] **113**–26
religion [rĭ lĭ jŭn] **140**–1
religious holiday [rĭ lĭj/əs hŏl/ə dā/] **22**–7
**remain** [rē/mān] **147**–E
remarried [rē măr/ēd] **35**–24
remote [rĭ mōt/] **234**–9
**remove** [rĭ mo͞ov/] **109**–Q, **132**–G
remover [rĭ mo͞o/vər] **109**–42
**renew** a license [rĭ no͞o/ ə lī/səns, –nyo͞o/–] **136** ✦
rental agreement [rĕn/təl ə grē/mənt] **51**–28
Rental Office [rĕn/təl ö/fəs] **51**
Renting an Apartment [rĕn/tĭng ən ə pärt/mənt] **48**
repair [rĭ për/] **166**–4, **167**–24
repair person [rĭ për/ pür/sən] **62**–10
**repair** [rĭ për/] **170**–J
REPAIRS [rĭ përz/] **62–63**
repellent [rĭ pĕl/ənt] **226**–23
**replace** [rĭ plās/] **157**–K
**report** [rĭ pört/] **143**–J, **143**–K
reporter [rĭ pör/tər] **169**–52
representative [rĕ/prĭ zĕn/tə tĭv] **167**–20
Reptiles [rĕp/tïlz] **213**
REPTILES [rĕp/tïlz] **212–213**
**request** [rĭ kwĕst/] **12** ✦
Requirements [rĭ kwïr/mənts] **140**
rescue [rĕs/kyo͞o] **145**–20
rescue breathing [rĕs/kyo͞o brē/dhĭng] **117**–16
resource centre [rē/sörs sĕn/tər] **172**–9
Resources [rē/sörs/səz, rĭ sör/səz] **219**
respirator [rĕs/pə rā/tər] **179**–13
Responding [rĭ spŏn/dĭng] **191**
Responsibilities [rĭ spŏn/sə bĭl/ə tēz] **140**
RESPONSIBILITIES [rĭ spŏn/sə bĭl/ə tēz] **140**
restaurant [rĕs/tə rŏnt] **125**–14, **128**–10
RESTAURANT [rĕs/tə rŏnt] **79, 82–83**
Restaurant Dining [rĕs/tə rŏnt dī/nĭng] **185**
Restaurant Kitchen [rĕs/tə rŏnt kĭ/chən] **185**
restrooms [rĕst/ ro͞omz/] **5**–9
results [rĭ zŭltz/] **139**–27
resuscitation [rĭ sə sə tā/shən] **117**–17
retail clerk [rē/tāl/ klürk/] **169**–53
**retire** [rĭ tïr/] **41**–O
return [rĭtürn/] **73**–16
return address [rĭ türn/ ə drĕs/, –ă/drĕs] **134**–21
**return** [rĭ türn/] **27**–H, **133**–D
REUNION [rē yo͞on/yən] **44–45**
**reuse** [rē yo͞oz/] **219**–B
**revise** [rĭ vīz/] **191**–J
Revising [rĭ vī/zĭng] **191**
revolving [rĭ vŏl/vĭng]
revolving door [rĭ vŏl/vĭng dör/] **184**–2
revolving nosepiece [rĭ vŏl/vĭng nōz/pēs/] **194**–15
**rewind** [rē wīnd/] **235**–C
**rewrite** [rē rīt/] **191**–J
rhinoceros [rī nŏs/ər əs] **217**–30
ribbon [rĭ/bən] **99**–30
ribs [rĭbz] **70**–5, **76**–2
rib cage [rĭb/ kāj/] **107**–48
rice [rīs] **67**–10, **81**–30, **177**–1
**ride** [rīd] **129**–D
rider [rī/dər] **152**–3
riding [rī/dĭng] **226**–9
right [rīt] **25**–3, **155**–B
right angle [rīt/ ăng/gəl] **193**–26
right turn only [rīt/ türn/ ōn/lē] **154**–7
Rights [rīts] **140**
ring [rĭng] **37**–25, **79**–4, **95**–40
clip-on earrings [klĭp/ŏn ïr/ĭngz] **95**–37
pierced earrings [pïrst/ ïr/ĭngz] **95**–36
**rinse** [rĭns] **108**–F
ripe [rīp] **68**–30
ripped [rĭpt] **97**–41
ripper [rĭ/pər] **100**–18
rise [rīz] **127**–13
sunrise [sŭn/rīz/] **18**–14

river [rĭv′ər] **155**–10, **204**–3
RN (registered nurse) [är′ĕn′] / [rĕj′ə stərd nürs′] **120**–10
road work [rōd′ würk′] **154**–16
Road Worker [rōd′ wür′kər] **92**
roast [rōst] **70**–1
  roast beef [rōst bēf′] **71**–21
  roast chicken [rōst chĭk′ən] **81**–22
  roasted turkey [rō′stəd tür′kē] **76**–4
  roasting pan [rō′stĭng păn′] **78**–13
  roasting rack [rō′stĭng răk′] **78**–14
robe [rōb] **91**–29
robin [rŏb′ən] **214**–16
**rock** [rŏk] **36**–D
rock concert [rŏk′ kŏn′sərt] **222**–5
rocking chair [rŏk′ĭng chër′] **37**–21
rock [rŏks] **208**–6, **237**–23
Rodents [rōd′nts] **215**
RODENTS [rōd′nts] **215**
rollers [rō′lərz] **33**–19, **181**–23
rolling pin [rō′lĭng pĭn′] **78**–30
rolls [rōlz] **74**–11, **74**–23, **80**–17
romance [rō′măns] **237**–16
Roman Numerals [rō′mən nōō′mər əlz] **16**
roof [rōōf] **46**–1
roof garden [rōōf′ gär′dn] **50**–4
roofer [rōō′fər] **62**–8
room [rōōm]
  baby's room [bā′bēz rōōm′] **47**–10
  ballroom [bŏl′ rōōm′] **184**–26
  banquet room [băn′kwət rōōm′] **185**–14
  bathroom [băth′rōōm′] **46**–4
  bedroom [bĕd′rōōm′] **46**–2
  conference room [kŏn′frəns rōōm′] **182**–4
  dining room [dī′nĭng rōōm′] **82**–1
  dining room chair [dī′nĭng rōōm′ chër′] **55**–8
  dining room table [dī′nĭng rōōm′ tā′bəl] **55**–9
  dish room [dĭsh′ rōōm′] **83**–13
  guest room [gĕst′ rōōm′] **184**–13
  kids' bedroom [kĭdz′ bĕd′rōōm′] **47**–9
  living room [lĭv′ĭng rōōm′] **47**–12
  meeting room [mē′tĭng rōōm′] **184**–25
  roommates [rōōm′măts′] **64**–1
  room service [rōōm′ sür′vəs] **184**–17
  storeroom [stör′rōōm′] **185**–5
Room [rōōm] **50, 118, 121**
ROOM [rōōm] **56**
rooster [rōō′stər] **215**–7
roots [rōōts] **210**–5, **211**–3
rope [rōp] **224**–4, **226**–19
rose [rōz] **211**–15
rotary [rō′tə rē]
  rotary card file [rō′tə rē kärd′ fīl′] **183**–44
  rotary cutter [rō′tə rē kŭt′ər] **232**–16
rotten [rŏt′n] **68**–32
round trip [rownd′ trĭp′] **152**–17
route [rōōt] / [rowt]
  bus route [bŭs′ rōōt, –rowt] **152**–1
  escape route [ĕs′kāp rōōt, –rowt] **146**–3
  evacuation route [ĭ văk′yōō′ā shən rōōt, –rowt] **146**–5
router [row′tər] **180**–12
ROUTINES [rōō tēnz′] **38–39**
rubber [rŭb′ər]
  rubber band [rŭb′ər bănd′] **183**–34
  rubber gloves [rŭb′ər glŭvz′] **61**–4
  rubber mat [rŭb′ər măt′] **57**–5
ruffle [rŭ′fəl] **58**–17
rug [rŭg] **58**–22
ruler [rōō′lər] **17**–13
rules [rōōlz] **64**–7
Rules [rōōlz] **190**
**run** [rŭn] **11**–D
  **run** across [rŭn′ə krŏs′] **153**–G
  **run** around [rŭn′ə rownd′] **153**–H
  **run** for office [rŭn′ fər ŏ′fəs] **139**–A
  **run out** [rŭn′owt′] **162**–E
runner [rŭ′nər] **185**–15
rural area [rŏŏr′əl ër′ē ə] **52**–4
RV (recreational vehicle) [är′vē′] / [rĕk′rē ā′shən əl vē′ə kəl] **156**–10
rye bread [rī′ brĕd′] **71**–20
sad [săd] **43**–19
safety [sāf′tē] **37**–19, **92**–4, **159**–53
  safety boots [sāf′tē bōōts′] **179**–20
  safety deposit box [sāf′tē dĭ pŏz′ət bŏks′] **132**–7
  safety glasses [sāf′tē glăs′əz] **92**–10, **179**–10
  safety goggles [sāf′tē gŏg′əlz] **179**–11
  safety pin [sāf′tē pĭn′] **37**–9, **100**–14
  safety rail [sāf′tē rāl′] **59**–10
  safety regulations [sāf′tē rĕ′gyə lā′shənz] **164**–6
  safety vest [sāf′tē vĕst′] **92**–4
  safety visor [sāf′tē vī′zər] **179**–12
Safety [sāf′tē] **76**
SAFETY [sāf′tē] **76–77, 143, 179**
Safety Equipment [sāf′tē ĭ kwĭp′mənt] **179**
Safety Hazards and Hazardous Materials [sāf′tē hăz′ərdz ən hăz′ər dəs-mə tïr′ē əlz] **179**
sailboat [sāl′bōt′] **225**–3
sailing [sā′lĭng] **227**–8
salad [săl′əd]
  chef's salad [shĕfs′ săl′əd] **80**–14
  dinner salad [dĭn′ər săl′əd] **80**–15
  fruit salad [frōōt′ săl′əd] **80**–21
  pasta salad [päs′tə săl′əd] **80**–20
  potato salad [pə tā′tō săl′əd] **80**–19
  salad bar [săl′əd bär′] **79**–24
  salad fork [săl′əd förk′] **83**–27
  salad plate [săl′əd plāt′] **83**–20
  spinach salad [spĭ′nĭch săl′əd] **80**–13
Salad Dressings [săl′əd drĕ′sĭngz] **80**
Salads [săl′ədz] **80**
salamander [săl′ə măn′dər] **212**–27
salami [sə lä′mē] **71**–24
SALE [sāl] **102–103**
sales [sālz]
  sale price [sāl′ prīs′] **27**–3
  sales clerk [sālz′klürk′] **94**–3
  sales tax [sālz′ tăks′] **27**–8
Salesperson [sālz′pür′sən] **92**
salmon [săm′ən] **71**–3
  salmon steak [săm′ən stāk′] **71**–4
salon [sə lŏn′] **130**–3, **131**–18
salt and pepper shakers [sölt′ n pĕp′ər shā′kərz] **55**–13
same [sām] **23**–15
SAME AND DIFFERENT [sām′ ən dĭ′frənt, –dĭ fə rənt] **28–29**
samples [săm′pəlz] **84**–5
sand [sănd] **225**–23
  sandbox [sănd′bŏks′] **224**–15
  sandcastle [sănd kăs′əl] **225**–12
  sand dune [sănd dōōn′] **204**–5
  sandpaper [sănd′pā′pər] **181**–56
sandals [săn′dlz] **88**–9
sander [săn′dər] **180**–11
sandwich [săn′wĭch, –sănd′–] **79**–5, **80**–10, **80**–12
sanitation worker [săn′ə tā′shən wür′kər] **169**–54
satellite [săt′əl īt′] **205**–20
  satellite dish [săt′əl līt′ dĭsh′] **53**–6
satisfied [săt′ĭs fīd′] **42**–6
Saturday [săt′ər dā′] **20**–14
Saturn [săt′ərn] **205**–6
saucepan [sös′păn′] **78**–25
saucer [sö′sər] **83**–25
sausage [sö′sĭj] **70**–12, **80**–2
**sauté** [sö′tā, sō tā′] **77**–E
**save** [sāv] **219**–E
saving [sā′vĭng] **19**–25
savings account number [sā′vĭngz ə kownt′ nŭm′bər] **132**–11
saw [sö] **180**–9
  hacksaw [hăk′sö′] **180**–5
  jigsaw [jĭg′sö′] **180**–10
saxophone [săk′sə fōn′] **238**–5
**say** [sā] **2**–A, **3**–L, **4**–A
scaffolding [skăf′əl dĭng] **178**–4
scales [skālz] **57**–27, **72**–3, **135**–8, **155**–7, **195**–41, **212**–3
  postal scale [pō′stəl skāl′] **183**–27
scallions [skăl′yənz] **69**–20
scallops [skăl′əps, skŏl′–] **71**–12, **212**–19
**scan** [skăn] **171**–H
scanner [skăn′ər] **183**–20
scared [skërd] **43**–23
scarf / scarves [skärf] / [skärvz] **95**–12
  winter scarf [wĭn′tər skärf′] **90**–5
scenery [sē′ nə rē] / [sēn′rē] **162**–2
schedule [skĕj′ōōl, –ōō əl] **152**–4
**schedule** [skĕj′ōōl, –ōō əl] **171**–J
school [skōōl] **126**–9
  adult school [[ə dŭlt′–, ăd′ŭlt skōōl′] **188**–8
  elementary school [ĕl′ə mĕn′trē skōōl′] **188**–2
  grade school [grād skōōl] **188**–2
  high school [hī′ skōōl′] **188**–4
  junior high school [jōōn′yər hī′ skōōl′] **188**–3
  middle school [mĭd′l skōōl′] **188**–3
  nursery school [nür′sə rē skōōl′] **188**–1
  parochial school [pə rō′kē əl skōōl′] **5** ✦
  preschool [prē′skōōl] **188**–1
  private school [prī′vət skōōl′] **5** ✦
  public school [pŭb′lĭk skōōl′] **5** ✦
  school bus [skōōl′ bŭs′] **156**–21
  school crossing [skōōl′ krŏ′sĭng] **154**–15
  technical school [tĕk′nĭ kəl skōōl′] **188**–5
  vocational school [vō kā′shə nəl skōōl′] **188**–5

SCHOOL [skōōl] **5, 10, 11**
School Registration Form
[skōōl/ rĕj/ə strā/shən förm/] **4**
SCHOOLS AND SUBJECTS
[sklōōz ən sŭb/jəkts] **188–189**
science [sī/əns] **189**–11
SCIENCE [sī/əns] **194–195**
Science Lab [sī/əns lăb/] **195**
scissors [sĭz/ərz] **33**–20, **100**–16
scoop neck [skōōp/ nĕk/] **96**–10
score [skör] **10**–3, **229**–1
scorpion [skör/pē ən] **214**–30
scrambled eggs [skrăm/bəld ĕgz/] **76**–7
scraper [skrā/pər] **181**–52
screen [skrēn] **6**–2, **196**–11, **235**–30
big-screen TV [bĭg/skrēn/ tē/ vē/] **50**–14
fire screen [fīr/ skrēn/] **56**–12
flat screen TV [flăt/ skrēn/ tē/vē/] **234**–7
screen door [skrēn/ dör/] **53**–15
sunscreen [sŭn/skrēn/] **108**–7, **225**–10
screener [skrēn/ər] **160**–5
screening area [skrē/nĭng ër/ē ə] **160**–4
screw [skrōō] **180**–32, **180**–33
Phillips screwdriver [fĭl/ĭps skrōō/drī/vər] **180**–31
screwdriver [skrōō/drī/vər] **180**–30
scroll bar [skrōl/bär/] **197**–15
**scrub** [skrŭb] **60**–K
scrubs [skrŭbz] **93**–31
scrub brush [skrŭb/ brŭsh/] **61**–20
surgical scrub cap [sür/jĭ kəl skrŭb/ kăp/] **93**–35
surgical scrubs [sür/jĭ kəl skrŭbz/] **93**–38
scuba [skōō/bə]
scuba diving [skōō/bə dī/vĭng] **227**–12
scuba tank [skōō/bə tăngk/] **225**–5
sea [sē]
sea anemone [sē/ ə nĕm/ə nē] **212**–24
sea horse [sē/ hörs/] **212**–13
sea lion [sē/ lī/ən] **213**–33
sea otter [sē/ ŏt/ər] **213**–35
seashell [sē/shĕl/] **225**–24
sea urchin [sē/ ür/chən] **212**–21
seaweed [sē/ wēd/] **225** ✦
Sea Animals [sē/ ăn/ə məlz] **212**
SEAFOOD AND DELI [sē/fōōd/ ən dĕ/lĭ] **71**
seal [sēl] **213**–34
Sea Mammals [sē/ măm/əlz] **213**
seam ripper [sēm/ rĭp/ər] **100**–18
search [sürch]
search and rescue team
[sürch/ ən rĕs/kyōō tēm/] **145**–20
search box [sürch/ bŏks/] **197**–5
search engine [sürch/ ĕn/jən] **197**–6
SEARCH [sürch] **173**
SEASONAL CLOTHING [sē/zə nəl klō/dhĭng] **90**
Seasons [sē/zənz] **21**
seat [sēt]
back seat [băk/ sēt/] **159**–54
car safety seat [kär/ sāf/tē sēt/] **37**–19
child safety seat [chīld/ sāf/tē sēt/] **159**–53
front seat [frŭnt/ sēt/] **159**–51
loveseat [lŭv/ sēt/] **56**–1
potty seat [pŏt/ē sēt/] **37**–12
reclined seat [rĭ klīnd/ sēt/] **161**–27
seat belt [sēt/ bĕlt/] **159**–52
upright seat [ŭp/rīt/ sēt/] **161**–28
**seat** [sēt] **82**–B
second [sĕk/ənd] **16**
Second Floor [sĕk/ənd flör/] **50**
seconds [sĕk/əndz] **18**–3
section [sĕk/shən] **72**–2
security [sĭ kyŏŏr/ə tē]
security camera [sĭ kyŏŏr/ə tē kăm/rə] **50**–19
security gate [sĭ kyŏŏr/ə tē gāt/] **50**–16
security guard [sĭ kyŏŏr/ə tē gärd/] **132**–5, **169**–55
security pants [sĭ kyŏŏr/ə tē pănts/] **93**–22
security screener [sĭ kyŏŏr/ə tē skrē/nər] **160**–5
security shirt [sĭ kyŏŏr/ə tē shürt] **93**–20
Security Checkpoint [sĭ kyŏŏr/ə tē chĕk/poynt/] **160**
Security Guard [sĭ kyŏŏr/ə tē gärd/] **93**
sedan [sə dăn/] **156**–1
**see** [sē] **106**–A
seed [sēd] **211**–1
seedling [sēd/lĭng] **211**–4
**seek** [sēk] **114**–A, **147**–H
see-saw [sē/sö/] **224**–16
**select** [sə lĕkt/] **196**–B
self-checkout [sĕlf/ chĕk/owt] **73**–10, **133**–10
**sell** [sĕl] **170**–K
semi [sĕm/ī] **156**–15
semicolon [sĕm/ē kō/lən] **190**–18
Senate [sĕn/ət] **138**–8
senator [sĕn/ə tər] **138**–10
**send** [sĕnd] **197**–I
**send in** [sĕnd/ ĭn] **173**–H
Sending a Card [sĕn/dĭng ə kärd/] **135**
Sending Email [sĕn/dĭng ē/māl/] **197**
senior [sēn/yər]
senior citizen [sēn/yər sĭt/ə zən] **30**–5
senior housing [sēn/yər howz/ĭng] **52**–11
Senses [sĕn/səz] **106**
sentence [sĕn/tns] **190**–2
**Sentence** [sĕn/tns] **141**–F
**separate** [sĕ/pə rāt/] **76**–B
September [sĕp tĕm/bər] **21**–33
sequins [sē/kwĭnz/] **99**–33
Serious Medical Conditions
[sïr/ē əs mĕd/ĭ kəl kən dĭsh/ənz] **111**
serious photo [sïr/ē əs fō/tō] **206**–3
**serve** [sürv] **139**–D, **230**–P
**serve** the meal [sürv/ dhə mēl/] **82**–F
Serve [sürv] **76**
server [sür/vər] **82**–8, **83**–9, **169**–56, **185**–8
service [sür/vəs]
customer service [kŭs/tə mər sür/vəs] **97** ✦
customer service representative
[kŭs/tə mər-sür/vəs rĕ/prə zĕn/tə tĭv] **167**–20
guest services [gĕst/ sür/vəs əz] **130**–12
pool service [pōōl/ sür/vəs] **184**–21
room service [rōōm/ sür/vəs] **184**–17
SERVICE [sür/vəs] **138–139, 185**
serving bowl [sür/vĭng bōl/] **55**–21
**set** [sĕt] **10**–A, **33**–C, **82**–A
**set up** [sĕt/ ŭp/] **173**–I
sunset [sŭn/sĕt/] **18**–18
setting [sĕ/tĭng] **83**–17
settlers [sĕt/lürz] **198**–2
seven [sĕv/ən] **16**
seventeen [sĕv/ən tēn/] **16**
seventeenth [sĕv/ən tēnth/] **16**
seventh [sĕv/ənth] **16**
seventieth [sĕv/ən tē əth] **16**
seventy [sĕv/ən tē] **16**
75 percent [sĕv/ən tē fīv/ pər sĕnt/] **17**–9
**sew** [sō] **98**–A, **98**–B, **170**–L
sewing [sō/ĭng]
sewing machine [sō/ĭng mə shēn/] **98**–13
sewing machine operator
[sō/ĭng mə shēn/ ŏp/ə rā/ tər] **98**–14
Sewing Machine [sō/ĭng mə shēn/] **98**
Sewing Supplies [sō/ĭng sə plīz/] **100**
sex [sĕks] **4**–16
shade [shād] **225**–13
lampshade [lămp/shād/] **56** ✦, **58**–26
shadow [shă/dō/] **109**–35
shake [shāk]
milkshake [mĭlk/shāk/] **79**–14
**shake** [shāk] **3**–J, **174**–I
shakers [shā/kərz] **55**–13
shampoo [shăm pōō/] **108**–10
shanks [shănks] **70**–13
shaper [shā/pər] **91**–15
Shapes [shāps] **193**
**share** [shër] **8**–M
Sharing and Responding
[shër/ĭng ən rĭ spŏn/dĭng] **191**
shark [shärk] **212**–4
sharpener [shär/pən ər] **183**–26
shave [shāv]
aftershave [ăf/tər shāv/] **109**–30
**shave** [shāv] **109**–M
shaver [shā/vər] **109**–26
shaving cream [shā/vĭng krēm/] **109**–29
shears [shïrz] **176**–9
sheep [shēp] **215**–6
sheet [shēt]
cookie sheet [kŏŏk/ē shēt/] **78**–27
dryer sheets [drī/ər shēts/] **101**–5
fitted sheet [fĭt/əd shēt/] **58**–12
flat sheet [flăt/ shēt/] **58**–13
shelf [shĕlf] **54**–2
shell [shĕl]
seashell [sē/shĕl/] **225**–24
Shellfish [shĕl/fĭsh/] **71**
shelter [shĕl/tər] **52**–13
shield [shēld]
windshield [wĭnd/shēld/] **158**–1
windshield wipers [wĭnd/shēld wī/pərz] **158**–2
shift [shĭft] **159**–50
shin [shĭn] **106**–21
shin guards [shĭn/ gärdz/] **231**–13
shingles [shĭng/gəlz] **178**–20
**ship** [shĭp] **175**–D
shipping clerk [shĭp/ĭng klürk/] **175**–14
shirt [shürt] **86**–1
nightshirt [nīt/shürt/] **91**–28
polo shirt [pō/lō shürt/] **92**–14

security shirt [sĭ kyŏŏr/ə tē shürt/] **93**–20
sports shirt [spörts/ shürt/] **88**–4
T-shirt [tē/shürt/] **86**–4
work shirt [würk/ shürt/] **92**–2
shock [shŏk] **116**–B, **116**–F
shoes [shōōz] **86**–7, **87**–13, **95**–32
shoe department [shōō/ dĭ pärt/mənt] **95**–7
shoelaces [shōō/lās əz] **94**–24
shoe store [shōō/ stör/] **130**–10
SHOES AND ACCESSORIES
[shōōz/ ən ĭk sĕs/ə rēz] **94–95**
shoot [shōōt] **211**–5
**shoot** [shōōt] **230**–H
shop [shŏp]
barbershop [bär/bər shŏp/] **129**–19
beauty shop [byōō/tē shŏp/] **130** ✦
coffee shop [kö/fē shŏp/] **126**–11
doughnut shop [dō/nŭt shŏp/] **129**–17
gift shop [gĭft/ shŏp/] **130** ✦, **184**–5
ice cream shop [īs/ krēm shŏp] **131**–16
**shop** [shŏp] **28**–A, **143**–H
Shop [shŏp] **100**
SHOP [shŏp] **80–81**
shoplifting [shŏp/lĭf/tĭng] **142**–8
shopping [shŏp/ĭng]
shopping basket [shŏp/ĭng băs/kət] **73**–9
shopping list [shŏp/ĭng lĭst/] **67**–14
shopping mall [shŏp/ĭng möl/] **126**–7
shopping program [shŏp/ĭng prō/grăm] **236**–10
SHOPPING [shŏp/ĭng] **27**
shore [shör] **204**–12
short [shört] **32**–6, **96**–16
short hair [shört/ hër/] **33**–1
short-order cook [shört/ör/dər kŏŏk/] **185**–1
short-sleeved [shört/slēvd/] **96**–12
**shorten** [shört/ən] **100**–B
shorts [shörts] **89**–25, **91**–4
shoulder [shōl/dər] **105**–13
shoulder bag [shōl/dər băg/] **94**–17
shoulder blade [shōl/dər blād/] **107**–28
shoulder-length hair [shōl/dər lĕngkth/ hër/] **33**–2
shoulder pads [shōl/dər pădz/] **231**–20
shovel [shŭv/əl] **176**–7, **178**–22
show [shō] **236**–4, **236**–6, **236**–8
**show** [shō] **137**–B, **160**–C
shower [show/ər]
shower cap [show/ər kăp/] **108**–1
shower curtain [show/ər kür/tn] **57**–14
shower gel [show/ər jĕl/] **108**–2
shower head [show/ər hĕd/] **57**–13
stall shower [stöl/ show/ər] **57** ✦
shredder [shrĕ/dər] **183**–24
shrimp [shrĭmp] **71**–11, **212**–18
shut [shŭt] **146**–4
shuttle [shŭt/l] **152**–19, **205**–19
sick [sĭk] **42**–12
homesick [hōm/sĭk/] **43**–20
side [sīd] **76**–10
sideburns [sīd/bürnz/] **33**–7
side-view mirror [sīd/vyōō/ mïr/ər] **158**–3
Side Salads [sīd/ săl/ədz] **80**
sidewalk [sīd/wök/] **129**–24
sign [sīn] **4**–D
street sign [strēt/ sīn/] **129**–26
vacancy sign [vā/kən sē sīn/] **50**–7
vital signs monitor [vīt/l sīnz/ mŏn/ə tər] **121**–26
**sign** [sīn] **48**–D
signal [sĭg/nəl]
strong signal [strŏng/ sĭg/nəl] **14**–11
turn signal [türn/ sĭg/nəl] **158**–6, **159**–34
weak signal [wēk/ sĭg/nəl] **14**–12
signature [sĭg/nə chər] **4**–19
SIGNS [sīnz] **154**
silk [sĭlk] **98**–5
**simmer** [sĭm/ər] **77**–P
**sing** [sĭng] **36**–O, **238**–B
single [sĭng/gəl]
single father [sĭng/gəl fö/dhər] **35**–23
single mother [sĭng/gəl mŭdh/ər] **35**–22
sink [sĭnk] **54**–4, **57**–25
Sirius [sïr/ē əs] **205** ✦
sister [sĭs/tər] **34**–5, **35**–27
sister-in-law [sĭs/tər ĭn lö/] **34**–16
stepsister [stĕp/sĭs/tər] **35**–29
sitcom (situation comedy)
[sĭt/kŏm/] / [sĭch/ōō ā/shən kŏm/ə dē] **236**–2
**sit down** [sĭt/ down/] **6**–F
site [sīt] **126**–2
sitter [sĭt/ər] **166**–9
situation comedy (sitcom)
[sĭch/ōō ā/shən-kŏm/ə dē] / [sĭt/kŏm/] **236**–2
six [sĭks] **16**
six-pack [sĭks/păk/] **74**–9, **74**–21
6-year-old boy [sĭks/yïr ōld/boy/] **31**–9
sixteen [sĭks/tēn/] **16**
sixteenth [sĭks/tēnth/] **16**
sixth [sĭksth] **16**
sixtieth [sĭks/tē əth] **16**
sixty [sĭks/tē] **16**
Sizes [sī/zəz] **96**
**skate** [skāt] **230**–U
skates [skāts] **231**–9, **231**–10
skateboard [skāt/börd/] **224**–7
skateboarding [skāt/bör/dĭng] **228**–13
skating [skā/tĭng] **227**–4, **227**–5, **227** ✦, **228**–10
**ski** [skē] **230**–V
skiing [skē/ĭng] **227**–1, **227**–3
water skiing [wö/tər skē/ĭng] **227**–7
skill inventory [skĭl/ ĭn/vən tör/ē] **172**–12
Skills [skĭlz] **171**
SKILLS [skĭlz] **170, 171, 174**
skin [skĭn] **107**–31
skinless [skĭn/ləs] **70** ✦
skirt [skürt] **87**–10
skis [skēz] **231**–24
ski boots [skē/ bōōts] **231**–26
ski hat [skē/ hăt/] **90**–11
ski mask [skē/ măsk/] **90**–15
ski poles [skē/ pōlz/] **231**–25
skull [skŭl] **107**–47
skunk [skŭngk] **216**–15
SKU number [ĕs/kā/yōō/ nŭm/bər, skyōō/] **27**–5
sky [skī] **209**–9
skyscraper [skī/skrā/pər] **127**–13
slacks [slăks] **87**–12
sledding [slĕd/ĭng] **227**–6
sledgehammer [slĕj/hăm/ər] **178**–23
sleeper [slē/pər] **91**–27
sleeping bag [slē/pĭng băg/] **226**–12
Sleepwear [slēp/wër] **91**
SLEEPWEAR [slēp/wër] **91**
sleepy [slē/pē] **42**–3
sleeve [slēv] **100**–6
long-sleeved [lŏng/slēvd/] **96**–14
short-sleeved [shört/slēvd] **96**–12
sleeveless [slēv/ləs] **96**–11
3/4 sleeved [thrē/kwör/tər slēvd/] **96**–13
slender [slĕn/dər] **32**–9
**slice** [slīs] **77**–C
slide [slīd] **194**–3, **224**–13
mudslide [mŭd/slīd/] **144**–6
sliding glass door [slī/dĭng glăs/ dör/] **53**–18
sling [slĭng] **113**–19
slip [slĭp] **91**–22, **91**–23, **132**–4
slippers [slĭp/ərz] **91**–26
slippery floor [slĭ/pər ē flör/] **179**–6
slow [slō] **23**–4
small [smöl] **96**–1, **96**–2, **97**–37
small town [smöl/ town/] **52**–3
smart phone [smärt/ fōn/] **15**–27
**smell** [smĕl] **106**–C
**smile** [smīl] **2**–D
smock [smŏk] **93**–26
smog [smŏg] **218**–11
smoggy [smö/gē] **13**–14
**smoke** [smōk] **114**–G
smoke detector [smōk/ dĭ tĕk/tər] **51**–29
smoked turkey [smōkt/ tür/kē] **71**–25
Snack Foods [snăk/ fōōdz/] **73**
snail [snāl] **212**–22
snake [snāk] **213**–39
rattlesnake [ră/təl snāk] **213**–38
snap [snăp] **99**–26
**sneeze** [snēz] **110**–B
snorkelling [snör/kə lĭng] **227**–11
snow [snō]
snowboard [snō/börd/] **231**–23
snowboarding [snō/bör/dĭng] **227**–2
snowstorm [snō/störm/] **13**–23
snowing [snō/ĭng] **13**–12
soap [sōp] **57**–4, **61**–5, **108**–3
soap dish [sōp/ dĭsh/] **57**–3
soap opera [sōp/ ŏp/rə] **236**–5
sober [sō/ bər] **143** ✦
soccer [sŏk/ər] **229**–12
soccer ball [sŏk/ər böl/] **231**–12
social [sō/shəl]
Social Insurance Number card
[sō/shəl in shŏŏr/ əns nŭm/bər kärd/] **40**–5
social insurance number
[sō/shəl in shŏŏr/ əns nŭm/bər] **4**–15
social worker [sō/shəl wür/kər] **169**–57
socks [sŏks] **86**–6
ankle socks [ang/kəl sŏks/] **91**–7
crew socks [krōō/ sŏks/] **91**–8
dress socks [drĕs/ sŏks] **91**–9

low-cut socks [lō/kŭt sŏks/] **91**–10
Socks [sŏks] **91**
sofa [sō/fə] **56**–18
sofa cushions [sō/fə koo/shənz] **56** ✦
soft [sŏft] **23**–6
softball [sŏft/bŏl/] **229**–10
softener [sŏ/fən ər] **101**–6
software [sŏft/wër/] **167**–18, **196**–10
soil [soyl] **208**–2
solar [sō/lər]
solar eclipse [sō/lər ĭ klĭps/] **205**–16, **205** ✦
solar energy [sō/lər ĕn/ər jē] **218**–1
Solar System and the Planets [sō/lər sĭs/təm ən dhə plăn/əts] **205**
soldier [sōl/jər] **169**–58
sole [sōl] **94**–21
solid [sŏl/əd] **96**–19
Solids [sŏl/ədz] **193**
solution [sə loo/ shən] **192**–14
**solve** [sŏlv] **170**–M
son [sŭn] **34**–15
grandson [grăn/sŭn/, grănd/–] **34** ✦
son-in-law [sŭn/ĭn lŏ/] **34** ✦
sore throat [sör/ thrōt/] **110**–6
**sort** [sört] **101**–A
soul [sōl] **237**–28
soup [soop] **72**–18, **80**–16
soup bowl [soop/ bōl/] **83**–21
soup spoon [soop/spoon/] **83**–32
Soup [soop] **77**
sour [sow/ər] **84**–4
sour cream [sow/ər krēm/] **72**–21
Sources [sör/səz] **218**
sous chef [soo/ shĕf/] **185**–6
south [sowth] **155**–3
sovereign [sŏv/rĕn] **138**–1
soybeans [soy/bēnz/] **177**–3
space [spās] **50**–18, **128**–5
space shuttle [spās/ shŭt/əl] **205**–19
space station [spās/ stā/shən] **205**–18
Space [spās] **205**
Space Exploration [spās/ ĕk/splə rā/shən] **205**
spades [spādz] **233**–30
spaghetti [spə gĕt/ē] **81**–26
spare tire [spër/ tīr/] **158**–23
sparrow [spăr/ō] **214**–7
spatula [spăch/ə lə] **78**–19
**speak** [spēk] **170**–N
speakers [spē/kərz] **50**–5, **206**–4, **234**–14
Special [spĕ/shəl] **80**
Specialists [spĕsh/ə lĭsts/] **120**
speed limit [spēd/ lĭm/ət] **154**–4
speedometer [spĭ dŏm/ə tər] **159**–27
speed skating [spēd/skā/tĭng] **227** ✦
**spell** [spĕl] **4**–B
sphere [sfïr] **193**–42
spider [spī/dər] **214**–29
spill [spĭl] **218**–17
spinach [spĭn/ĭch] **69**–11
spinach salad [spĭn/ĭch săl/əd] **80**–13
spinal column [spī/nəl kŏl/əm] **107**–49
spiral notebook [spī/rəl nōt/book/] **7**–29
splint [splĭnt] **117**–14
sponge [spŭnj] **61**–19
sponge mop [spŭnj/ mŏp/] **61**–6
spoon [spoon] **55**–5, **78**–9
soup spoon [soop/spoon/] **83**–32
tablespoon [tā/bəl spoon/] **75**–7
teaspoon [tē/spoon/] **75**–6, **83**–31
**spoon** [spoon] **77**–F
sports [spörts]
sports car [spörts/ kär/] **156**–4
sports coat [spörts/ kōt/] **89**–14
sports jacket [spörts/ jăk/ət] **89**–14
sports program [spörts/ prō/grăm] **236**–11
sports shirt [spörts/ shŭrt/] **88**–4
sport-utility vehicle (SUV) [spört/ yoo tĭl/ə tē vē/ĭ kəl] / [ĕs/yoo/vē/] **156**–7
SPORTS [spörts] **228, 229, 230, 231**
SPORTS EQUIPMENT [spörts/ ĭ kwĭp/mənt] **231**
SPORTS VERBS [spörts/ vürbz/] **230**
sprained ankle [sprānd/ ăng/kəl] **110**–18
spray [sprā] **108**–12, **113**–32
spray gun [sprā/ gŭn/] **181**–21
spray starch [sprā/ stärch/] **101**–12
spread [sprĕd]
bedspread [bĕd/sprĕd] **59**–11
spring [sprĭng] **21**–37, **58**–19
sprinkler [sprĭng/klər] **53**–22
square [skwër] **193**–30
squash [skwŏsh] **69**–24
squeegee [skwē/jē] **61**–15
squid [skwĭd] **212**–7
squirrel [skwür/əl] **215**–21
stadium [stā/dē əm] **126**–1
staff [stăf] **185** ✦
Staff [stăf] **120**
stage [stāj] **194**–17
stage clips [stāj/ klĭps/] **194**–21
stain [stān] **181**–24
stained [stānd] **97**–42
stairs [stërz] **50**–10
stairway [stër/wā/] **50**–10
stall shower [stŏl/ show/ər] **57** ✦
stamps [stămps] **134**–18, **134**–23, **183**–47
stand [stănd] **152**–18
checkstand [chĕk/stănd/] **73**–12
newsstand [nooz/stănd/] **128**–12
nightstand [nīt/stănd/] **58**–23
**stand** [stănd] **141**–D
**stand up** [stănd/ ŭp/] **6**–D
standard time [stăn/dərd tīm/] **19**–26
**staple** [stā/pəl] **171**–F
stapler [stā/plər] **183**–28
staples [stā/pəlz] **183**–29
star [stär] **205**–13
starfish [stär/fĭsh/] **212**–16
star key [stär/ kē/] **14**–6
starch [stärch] **101**–12
**start** [stärt] **12**–A, **40**–B, **230**–R
starting point [stär/tĭng poynt/] **162**–1
starving [stär/vĭng] **43** ✦
**state** [stāt] **15**–G, **195**–A
statement [stāt/mənt] **132**–16
station [stā/shən]
bus station [bus/ stā/shən] **124**–7
fire station [fīr/ stā/shən] **125**–12
gas station [găs/ stā/shən] **125**–10
gas station attendant [găs/ stā/shən ə tĕn/dənt] **162**–3
lifeguard station [līf/gärd/ stā/shən] **225**–21
police station [pə lēs/ stā/shən] **124**–6
space station [spās/ stā/shən] **205**–18
station wagon [stā/shən wăg/ən] **156**–6
subway station [sŭb/wā/ stā/shən] **151**–11
Station [stā/shən] **152**
stationery [stā/shə nër/ ē] **183**–42
**stay** [stā]
**stay away** [stā ə wā/] **147**–I
**stay** fit [stā fĭt/] **114**–E
**stay** on the line [stā ŏn dhə līn/] **15**–H
**stay** on well-lit streets [stā ŏn wĕl lĭt/ strēts/] **143**–B
Stay Well [stā wĕl/] **114**
steak [stāk] **70**–2, **81**–24
broiled steak [broyld/ stāk/] **76**–3
halibut steak [hăl/ə bŭt stāk] **71**–6
salmon steak [săm/ən stāk/] **71**–4
steak knife [stāk/ nīf/] **83**–29
**steal** [stēl] **142** ✦
**steam** [stēm] **77**–D
steamed vegetables [stēmd/ vĕj/tə bəlz] **81**–32
steamer [stē/mər] **78**–3
steel [stēl]
steel toe boots [stēl/ tō/ boots/] **92**–6
steel-wool soap pads [stēl/wool/ sōp/ pădz/] **61**–5
steering wheel [stïr/ĭng wēl/] **159**–26
stems [stĕmz] **211**–9
step [stĕp]
stepbrother [stĕp/brŭdh/ər] **35**–30
stepdaughter [stĕp/dö/tər] **35** ✦
stepfather [stĕp/fŏ/dhər] **35**–25
stepladder [stĕp/lăd/ər] **61**–13
stepmother [stĕp/mŭdh/ər] **35**–26
steps [stĕps] **53**–3
stepsister [stĕp/sĭs/tər] **35**–29
stereo system [stër/ē ō sĭs/təm] **56**–8
sterile [stër/əl]
sterile pad [stër/əl păd/] **117**–6
sterile tape [stër/əl tāp/] **117**–7
stethoscope [stĕth/ə skōp/] **118**–10
stewing beef [stoo/ĭng bēf/] **70**–3
stick [stĭk] **231**–11, **232**–11
drumsticks [drŭm/stĭks/] **70**–23
lipstick [lĭp/stĭk/] **109**–38
stick shift [stĭk/ shĭft/] **159**–50
yardstick [yärd/stĭk/] **181**–16
sticker [stĭk/ər] **102**–3, **136**–13
sticky notes [stĭk/ē nōts/] **183**–39
**stir** [stür] **77**–O
stir-fried beef [stür/frīd/ bēf/] **76**–6
stitches [stĭch/əz] **117**–15
stock clerk [stŏk/ klürk/] **169**–59
stockings [stŏk/ĭngz] **91**–17
stomach [stŭm/ək] **107**–41
stomach ache [stŭm/ək āk/] **110**–4
stop [stŏp] **129**–16, **151**–13, **154**–1
**stop** [stŏp] **155**–D

Stop [stŏp] **152**
stopped up [stŏpt/ ŭp/] **63**–19
storage [stör/ĭj] **72**–25, **78**–4
storage locker [stör/ĭj lŏk/ər] **50**–17
store [stör]
bookstore [bŏŏk/stör/] **130**–4
candy store [kăn/dē stör/] **131**–17
card store [kärd/stör/] **130**–7
convenience store [kən vēn/yəns stör/] **128**–3
department store [dĭ pärt/mənt stör/] **131**–13
electronics store [ē lĕk trŏn/ĭks stör/] **131**–20
furniture store [für/nĭ chər stör/] **126**–8
hardware store [härd/wër/ stör/] **148**–4
home improvement store
[hōm/ ĭm prōōv/mənt stör/] **127**–20
jewellery store [jōō/lə rē, jōō/əl rē stör/] **130**–2
maternity store [mə tür/nə tē stör/] **131**–19
men's store [mĕnz/ stör/] **130** ✦
music store [myōō/zĭk stör/] **130**–1
office supply store [ö/fəs sə plī/ stör/] **127**–21
pet store [pĕt/ stör/] **130**–6
shoe store [shōō/ stör/] **130**–10
toy store [toy/ stör/] **130**–5
video store [vĭd/ē ō stör/] **129**–20
Store [stör] **99**
STORE [stör] **72–73**
storeroom [stör/rōōm/] **185**–5
storey [stör/ē]
two-storey house [tōō stör/ē hows] **52** ✦
storm [störm] **13**–19
hailstorm [hāl/störm/] **13**–21
snowstorm [snō/störm/] **13**–23
storm door [störm/ dör/] **53**–10
thunderstorm [thŭn/dər störm/] **13**–16
story [stör/ē]
action story [ăk/shən stör/ē] **237**–19
adventure story [ăd vĕn/chər stör/ē] **237**–19
horror story [hör/ər stör/ē] **237**–17
science fiction story [sī/əns fĭk/shən stör/ē] **237**–18
stove [stōv] **54**–18, **226**–16
**stow** [stō] **160**–G
straight [strāt] **155**–A
straight hair [strāt/ hër/] **33**–9
straight line [strāt/ līn/] **193**–22
straight pin [strāt/ pĭn/] **100**–12
strainer [strā/nər] **78**–22
straw [strö] **79**–18
strawberries [strö/bĕr/ēz] **68**–14
straw hat [strö/ hăt/] **90**–23
stream [strēm] **204** ✦
street [strēt] **150**–5, **155**–8
streetlight [strēt/līt/] **148**–3
street sign [strēt/ sīn] **129**–26
street vender [strēt/ vĕn/dər] **129**–29
STREETS [strēts] **126–127**
strep throat [strĕp/ thrōt/] **111**–4
stress [strĕs] **115**–4
**stretch** [strĕch] **230**–M
stretcher [strĕch/ər] **121**–33
string [strĭng]
string beans [strĭng/ bēnz/] **69**–8
string lights [strĭng/ līts/] **239**–18
string of pearls [strĭng/ əv pürlz/] **95**–39
Strings [strĭngz] **238**
striped [strīpt] **96**–20
stripper [strĭ/pər] **181**–42
stroller [strō/lər] **37**–18
strong signal [strŏng/ sĭg/nəl] **14**–11
stub [stŭb] **165**–11
stucco [stŭk/ō] **178**–15
student [stōōd/nt] **6**–5
**study** [stŭ/dē] **10**–D, **137**–A
STUDYING [stŭ/dē ĭng] **8–9**
stuffed animals [stŭft/ ăn/ə məlz] **59**–15
style [stīl/] **88** ✦
Styles [stīlz] **96**
STYLES [stīlz] **96**
stylist [stī/lĭst] **167**–31
SUBJECTS [sŭb/jəkts/] **188–189**
**submit** [səb mĭt/] **48**–C
substitute [sŭb/stə tōōt/] **79**–20
**subtract** [səb trăkt/] **192**–B
suburbs [sŭb/ürbz] **52**–2
subway [sŭb/wā/] **151**–12
subway car [sŭb/wā/ kär/] **152**–6
subway station [sŭb/wā/ stā/shən] **151**–11
Subway Station [sŭb/wā/ stā/shən] **152**
Succeed [sək sēd/] **10**
SUCCEEDING IN SCHOOL [sək sē/dĭng ĭn skōōl/] **10**
suede [swād] **99**–8
sugar [shŏŏg/ər] **73**–30
sugar bowl [shŏŏg/ər bōl/] **55**–14
sugar-free [shŏŏg/ər frē/] **122**–7
sugar substitute [shŏŏg/ər sŭb/stə tōōt/] **79**–20
suit [sōōt] **87**–11
bathing suit [bā/dhĭng sōōt/] **90**–26
business suit [bĭz/nəs sōōt/] **88**–11
jumpsuit [jŭmp/sōōt/] **93**–24
three-piece suit [thrē/pēs/ sōōt/] **88** ✦
wet suit [wĕt/ sōōt/] **225**–4
suite [swēt] **184**–16
sum [sŭm] **192**–7
sumac [sōō/măk] **210**–23
summer [sŭm/ər] **21**–38
sun [sŭn] **209**–8
sunblock [sŭn/blŏk/] **108**–8, **225**–10
sunburn [sŭn/bürn/] **110**–14
sunflower [sŭn/flow/ər] **211**–10
sunglasses [sŭn/glăs/əz] **90**–27
sunrise [sŭn/ rīz] **18**–14
sunscreen [sŭn/skrēn/] **108**–7, **225**–10
sunset [sŭn/ sĕt] **18**–18
Sunday [sŭn/dā] **20**–8
sunny [sŭn/ē] **13**–9, **76**–10
superintendent [sōō/prĭn tĕn/dənt, sōō/pər ĭn–] **50**–8
supermarket [sōō/pər/ mär/kət] **127**–18
**supervise** [sōō/pər vīz/] **170**–O
supervisor [sōō/pər vī/zər] **165**–8, **175**–4
Supplies [sə plīz/] **100, 183**
SUPPLIES [sə plīz/] **61, 180–181**
supply [sə plī/] **127**–21
supply cabinet [sə plī/ kăb/ə nət] **182**–1
support [sə pört/] **179**–18
support group [sə pört/ grōōp/] **115**–15
supporter [sə pör/tər] **91**–6
Supreme Court of Canada
[sə prēm/ kört/ əv kăn/ə də] **138**–11
surface mail [sür/fəs māl] **134**–6
surfboard [sürf/börd/] **225**–16
surfer [sür/fər] **225**–15
surfing [sür/fĭng] **227**–9, **227**–10, **227** ✦
surgeon [sür/jən] **121**–36
Surgeon [sür/jən] **93**
surge protector [sürj/ prə tĕk/tər] **196**–1
surgical [sür/jĭ kəl]
surgical cap [sür/jĭ kəl kăp/] **121**–37
surgical gloves [sür/jĭ kəl glŭvz/] **121**–39
surgical gown [sür/jĭ kəl gown/] **93**–37, **121**–38
surgical mask [sür/jĭ kəl măsk/] **93**–36
surgical nurse [sür/jĭ kəl nürs/] **120**–9
surgical scrub cap [sür/jĭ kəl skrŭb/ kăp/] **93**–35
surgical scrubs [sür/jĭ kəl skrŭbz/] **93**–38
Surgical Assistant [sür/jĭ kəl ə sĭs/tənt] **93**
surprised [sər prīzd/, sə–] **43**–30
suspenders [sə spĕn/dərz] **94**–1
suspense [sŭs/pĕns] **237**–20
SUV (sport-utility vehicle) [ĕs/yōō/vē/] /
[spört/ yōō tĭl/ə tē vē/ĭ kəl] **156**–7
**swallow** [swäl/ō] **116**–J
swap meet [swŏp/ mēt/] **222**–6
sweat [swĕt]
sweatpants [swĕt/pănts/] **89**–23
sweatshirt [swĕt/shürt/] **89**–22
sweater [swĕt/ər] **28**–2, **87**–14
cardigan sweater [kär/də gən swĕt/ər] **88**–2
pullover sweater [pŏŏl/ō/vər swĕt/ər] **88**–3
**sweep** [swēp] **60**–J
sweet potatoes [swēt pə tā/tōz] **69**–18
sweets [swēts] **84**–8
**swim** [swĭm] **230**–L
swimsuit [swĭm/sōōt/] **90**–26
swimming [swĭm/ĭng]
swimming pool [swĭm/ĭng pōōl/] **51**–22
swimming trunks [swĭm/ĭng trŭngks/] **90**–22
**swing** [swĭng] **230**–Q
swings [swĭngz] **224**–11
Swiss cheese [swĭs/ chēz/] **71**–27
switch [swĭch] **58**–27
swollen finger [swō/lən fĭng/gər] **110**–16
swordfish [sörd/fĭsh/] **71**–5, **212**–10
symbol [sĭm/bəl] **155**–5
SYMPTOMS AND INJURIES
[sĭmp/təmz ən ĭn/jə rēz] **110**
synagogue [sĭn/ə gŏg/] **127**–16
synthetic materials [sĭn thĕ/tĭk mə tïr/ē əlz] **98** ✦
syringe [sə rĭnj/] **118**–12
syrup [sĭr/əp, sür/–] **113**–29
system [sĭs/təm]
fuel injection system
[fyōō/əl ĭn jĕk/shən sĭs/təm] **158**–17
stereo system [stĕr/ē ō sĭs/təm] **56**–8
SYSTEM [sĭs/təm] **141**
tab [tăb] **197**–7
table [tā/bəl]
changing table [chān/jĭng tā/bəl] **59**–1
coffee table [kō/fē tā/bəl] **56**–19

dining room table [dī/nĭng ro͞om/ tā/bəl] **55**–9
end table [ĕnd/ tā/bəl] **56**–14
examination table [ĭg zăm/ə nā/shən tā/bəl] **118**–7
folding card table [fōl/dĭng kärd/ tā/bəl] **102**–4
night table [nīt/ tā/bəl] **58**–23
operating table [ŏp/ə rā/tĭng tā/bəl] **121**–40
over-bed table [ō vər bĕd/ tā/bəl] **121**–21
periodic table [pïr/ē ŏd/ĭk tā/bəl] **195**–26
picnic table [pĭk/nĭk tā/bəl] **224**–8
pool table [po͞ol/ tā/bəl] **50**–15
tablecloth [tā/bəl klöth/] **55**–12
tablespoon [tā/bəl spo͞on/] **75**–7
table tennis [tā/bəl tĕn/əs] **228**–14
tray table [trā/ tā/bəl] **161**–21
turntable [türn/tā/bəl] **234**–12
tablet [tăb/lət] **113**–22, **113**–27
**tackle** [tăk/əl] **230**–F
taco [tö/kō, tăkō] **79**–8
tags [tăgz] **92**–15, **136**–13
tail [tāl] **216**–24
tail light [tāl/ līt/] **158**–13
tailor [tā/lər] **100**–3
tailpipe [tāl/ pīp/] **158**–15
**take** [tāk]
**do not take** with dairy products [do͞o nŏt/ tāk/ wĭth dër/ē prŏd/ŭkts] **112**–A
**take** a bath [tāk/ ə băth/] **108**–B
**take** a break [tāk/ ə brāk/] **11**–H
**take** a citizenship test [tāk/ ə sĭt/ə zən shĭp tĕst/] **140**–I
**take** a driver education and training course [tāk/ ə drī/vər ĕj/ə kā/shən ən trā/nĭng körs/] **137**–F
**take** a message [tāk/ ə mĕs/ĭj] **171**–Q
**take** a nap [tāk/ ə năp/] **53**–A
**take** a picture [tāk/ ə pĭk/chər] **206**–B
**take** a seat [tāk/ ə sēt/] **6**–F
**take** a shower [tāk/ ə show/ər] **38**–C, **108**–A
**take** a tour [tāk/ ə to͞or/] **220**–A
**take** a written test [tāk/ ə rĭt/ən tĕst] **137**–D
**take** care of children [tāk/ kër/ əv chĭl/drən] **170**–P
**take** cover [tāk/ kŭv/ər] **147**–J
**take** dictation [tāk/ dĭk/tā shən] **171**–K
**take in** [tāk/ ĭn] **100**–D
**take** medicine [tāk/ mĕd/ə sən] **114**–D
**take** notes [tāk/ nōts/] **10**–C
**take off** [tāk/ öf/] **109**–Q, **160**–J
**take** one hour before eating [tāk/ wŭn/ ow/ər bĭ för/ ē/tĭng] **112**–B
**take out** [tāk/ owt/] **9**–Y, **60**–Q, **82** ✦
**take** ownership [tāk/ ō/nər shĭp/] **49**–K
**take** temperature [tāk/ tĕm/prə chər] **118**–B
**take** the bus to school [tāk/ dhə bŭs/ tə sko͞ol/] **38**–H
**take** the car to a mechanic [tāk/ dhə kär/ tə dhə mə kăn/ĭk] **157**–C
**take** the children to school [tāk/ dhə chĭl/drən tə sko͞ol/] **38**–G
**take** the order [tāk/ dhē ör/dər] **82**–E
**take** with food [tāk/ wĭth fo͞od/] **112**–A
**take** X-rays [tāk/ ĕks/rāz/] **119**–B
Taking a Flight [tā/kĭng ə flīt/] **160**
Taking a Test [tā/kĭng ə tĕst/] **10**
TAKING A TRIP [tā/kĭng ə trĭp/] **162–163**
Taking Care of Your Car [tā/kĭng kër/ əv yər kär/] **157**
TAKING CARE OF YOUR HEALTH [tā/kĭng kër əv yər hĕlth/] **114–115**
talk [tök]
talk show [tök/ shō/] **236**–4
talk therapy [tök/ thër/ ə pē] **115**–13
**talk** [tök]
**talk** about [tök ə bowt/] **174**–L
**talk** on the phone [tök/ ŏn dhə fōn/] **15**–C
**talk** to friends [tök/ tə frĕndz/] **173**–A
**talk** to the teacher [tök/ tə dhə tē/chər] **6**–B
tall [töl] **32**–4
tambourine [tăm/bə rēn/] **238**–17
tan [tăn] **24**–18
tangerines [tăn/jə rēnz/] **68**–9
tank [tăngk] **158**–10, **225**–5
tank top [tăngk/ tŏp/] **89**–24
tanker [tăng kər] **156**–20
tape [tāp]
clear tape [klër/ tāp/] **183**–30
correction tape [kə rĕk/shən tāp/] **183**–37
duct tape [dŭkt/ tāp/] **181**–49
electrical tape [ē lek/trĭ kəl tāp/] **181**–43
masking tape [măs/kĭng tāp/] **181**–53
packing tape [păk/ĭng tāp/] **183**–32
sterile tape [stër/ əl tāp/] **117**–7
tape measure [tāp mĕzh/ər] **100**–17, **181**–45
target [tär/gət] **231**–7
**taste** [tāst] **106**–D
tattoo [tă to͞o/] **32**–18
tax / taxes [tăks] / [tăks/əz] **27**–8
taxi [tăk/sē] **150**–3
**hail** a taxi [hāl/ ə tăk/sē] **152** ✦
taxi driver [tăk/sē drī/vər] **152**–21
taxi licence [tăk/sē lī/səns] **152**–22
taxi stand [tăk/sē stănd/] **152**–18
TB (tuberculosis) [tē/bē/] / [to͞o bür/kyə lō/səs] **111**–15
TDD (telecommunication device for the deaf) [tē/dē/dē/] / [tĕl/ə kə myo͞o nə kā/shənz də vīs/ för dhə dĕf] **15**–26
tea [tē] **79**–12, **81**–39, **81**–40
teacup [tē/kŭp] **55**–6
teapot [tē/pŏt/] **55**–16
teaspoon [tē/spo͞on/] **75**–6, **83**–31
**teach** [tēch] **170**–Q
teacher [tē/chər] **5**–8, **6**–4, **22**–5
teacher's aide [tē/chərz ād/] **5**–16
team [tēm] **145**–20, **229**–3
TEAM SPORTS [tēm/ spörts/] **229**
technical school [tĕk/nĭ kəl sko͞ol/] **188**–5
technician [tĕk nĭsh/ən]
computer technician [kəm pyo͞o/tər tĕk nĭsh/ən] **167**–19, **182**–12
medical records technician [mĕd/ĭ kəl rĕk/ərdz tĕk nĭsh/ən] **168**–39
Technician [tĕk nĭsh/ən] **93**
teddy bear [tĕd/ē bër/] **37**–23
teen / teenager [tēn] / [tē/nā/jər] **31**–11
teething ring [tē/dhĭng rĭng/] **37**–25
teeth / tooth [tēth] / [to͞oth] **106**–7
toothache [to͞oth/āk/] **110**–2
toothbrush [to͞oth/brŭsh/] **57**–23, **109**–22
toothbrush holder [to͞oth/brŭsh/ hōl/dər] **57**–24
toothpaste [to͞oth/pāst/] **109**–23
telemarketer [tĕl/ə mär/kə tər] **169**–60
TELEPHONE [tĕl/ə fōn/] **14–15**
Telephone Skills [tĕl/ə fōn/ skĭlz/] **171**
telescope [tĕl/ə skōp/] **205**–23
television / TV [tĕl/ə vĭzh/ən] / [tē/vē/] **56**–6
big-screen TV [bĭg/skrēn/ tē/vē/] **50**–14
flat panel TV [flăt/ păn/əl tē/vē/] **234**–7
flat screen TV [flăt/ skrēn/ tē/vē/] **234**–7
portable TV [pör/tə bəl tē/vē/] **234**–8
teller [tĕl/ər] **132**–1
Teller [tĕl/ər] **132**
Telling Time [tĕ/lĭng tīm/] **18**
temperature [tĕm/prə chər] **110**–8
temperature gauge [tĕm/prə chər gāj/] **159**–30
Temperature [tĕm/prə chər] **13**
ten [tĕn] **16**
ten after one [tĕn/ ăf/tər wŭn/] **18**–8
ten dollars [tĕn/ dŏl/ərz] **26**–8
10 percent [tĕn/ pər sĕnt/] **17**–12
ten thousand [tĕn/ thow/zənd] **16**
10-year-old girl [tĕn/yïr ōld/ gürl/] **31**–10
tenant [tĕn/ənt] **50**–6
TENANT MEETING [tĕn/ənt mē/tĭng] **64–65**
tennis [tĕn/əs] **228**–15
table tennis [tā/bəl tĕn/əs] **228**–14
tennis court [tĕn/əs kört/] **224**–6
tennis racket [tĕn/əs răk/ət] **231**–2
tennis shoes [tĕn/əs sho͞oz/] **95**–32
tent [tĕnt] **226**–10
tenth [tĕnth] **16**
Terminal [tür/mə nəl] **160**
termites [tür/mīts] **63**–22
term [türm] **139** ✦
Terms [türmz] **199**
terrified [tĕr/ə fīd/] **43** ✦
test [tĕst] **121**–30
test booklet [tĕst/ bo͝ok/lət] **10**–1
testing area [tĕs/tĭng ër/ē ə] **136**–2
test tube [tĕst/ to͞ob/] **195**–42
Test [tĕst] **10**
text [tĕkst]
textbook [tĕkst/bo͝ok/, tĕks/-] **7**–25
text box [tĕkst/ bŏks/, tĕks/-] **197**–13
text message [tĕkst/ mĕs/ĭj, tĕks/-] **14**–19
**thank** [thăngk] **12**–E, **174**–N
Thanksgiving [thăngks gĭv/ĭng] **22**–14
theatre [thē/ə tər] **126**–6, **127**–23
theft [thĕft] **142**–9
therapist [thër/ ə pĭst] **115**–12, **115**–14, **168**–45
therapy [thër/ ə pē] **115**–11, **115**–13
thermal undershirt [thür/məl ŭn/dər shürt/] **91**–2
thermometer [thər mŏm/ə tər] **118**–11
thick [thĭk] **23**–7
thighs [thīz] **70**–22, **106**–19
thimble [thĭm/bəl] **100**–15
thin [thĭn] **23**–8, **32**–9
THINGS [thĭngz] **23**
**think** [thĭnk] **191**–E
third [thürd] **16**

Third Floor [thürd/ flör/] **50**
thirsty [thür/stē] **42**–2
thirteen [thür/tēn/] **16**
thirteenth [thür/tēnth/] **16**
thirtieth [thür/tē əth] **16**
thirty [thür/tē] **16**
35 mm camera
[thür/tē fīv/ mĭl/ə mē/tər kăm/rə] **235**–21
this week [dhĭs/ wēk/] **20**–19
thorn [thörn] **211**–29
thread [thrĕd] **99**–23, **100**–11
three [thrē] **16**
three-piece suit [thrē/pēs/ sōōt/] **88** ✦
3-ring binder [thrē/ rĭng/ bīn/dər] **7**–27
3/4 sleeved [thrē/kwör/tər slēvd/] **96**–13
three times a week [thrē/ tīmz/ ə wēk/] **20**–24
throat [thrōt] **107**–35, **110**–6, **111**–4
throat lozenges [thrōt/ lŏz/ən jəz] **113**–30
through [thrōō] **153**–K
**throw** [thrō] **230**–C
**throw away** [thrō/ ə wā/] **11**–N
**throw up** [thrō/ ŭp/] **110**–E
throw pillow [thrō/ pĭl/ō] **56**–2
thumb [thŭm] **106**–16
thunderstorm [thŭn/dər störm/] **13**–16
Thursday [thürz/dā] **20**–12
tick [tĭk] **214**–27
ticket [tĭk/ət] **152**–15, **161**–19
ticket agent [tĭk/ət ā/jənt] **160**–3
ticket window [tĭk/ət wĭn/dō/] **152**–12
tidal wave [tīd/l wāv/] **145**–17
tide [tīd] **225** ✦
tie [tī] **88**–12, **89**–16, **92**–13, **229** ✦
**tie** [tī] **86**–A
tiger [tī/gər] **217**–39
tight [tīt] **97**–29
tights [tīts] **91**–19
tile [tīl] **57**–12, **178**–11, **178**–C
time [tīm]
Alaska time [ə lăs/kə tīm/] **19**–28
arrival time [ə rī/vəl tīm/] **161** ✦
Atlantic time [ət lăn/tĭk tīm/] **19**–33
Central time [sĕn/trəl tīm/] **19**–31
daylight saving time [dā/līt/ sā/vĭng tīm/] **19**–25
departure time [dĭ pär/chər tīm/] **161** ✦
Eastern time [ē/stərn tīm/] **19**–32
Hawaii-Aleutian time
[hə wī/ē ə lōō/shən tīm/] **19**–27
Mountain time [mown/tn tīm/] **19**–30
Newfoundland time
[nōō/fən lənd tīm/, –fənd–] **19**–34
on time [ŏn/ tīm/] **19**–23, **161**–29
Pacific time [pə sĭf/ĭk tīm/] **19**–29
standard time [stăn/dərd tīm/] **19**–26
three times a week [thrē tīmz/ ə wēk/] **20**–24
time clock [tīm/ klŏk/] **165**–7
Time [tīm] **18**
TIME [tīm] **18–19**
timer [tī/mər] **78**–18
Times of Day [tīmz/ əv dā/] **18**
Time Zones [tīm/ zōnz/] **19**
tire [tīr] **158**–5, **158**–23, **162**–F
tired [tīrd] **43**–32
title [tīt/l] **133**–14, **190**–5
toad [tōd] **212**–28
toast [tōst] **80**–4
toaster [tō/stər] **54**–6
toaster oven [tō/stər ŭv/ən] **54**–15
today [tə dā/] **20**–5
toddler [tŏd/lər] **31**–8
toe [tō] **92**–6, **94**–23, **105**–10
toenail [tō/nāl/] **106** ✦
Tofu [tō/fōō/] **77**
toggle bolt [tŏg/əl bōlt/] **180**–38
to-go box [tə gō/ bŏks/] **82**–5
toilet [toy/lət] **57**–21
toilet brush [toy/lət brŭsh/] **57**–20
toilet paper [toy/lət pā/pər] **57**–19, **146**–13
token [tō/kən] **152**–10
tomatoes [tə mā/tōz] **69**–6
tomorrow [tə mör/ō] **20**–6
tongs [tŏngz] **78**–23, **195**–44
tongue [tŭng] **106**–8
too [tōō]
too big [tōō/ bĭg/] **97**–38
too expensive [tōō/ ĭk spĕn/sĭv] **97**–44
too small [tōō/ smöl/] **97**–37
tool belt [tōōl/ bĕlt/] **92**–3
TOOLS AND BUILDING SUPPLIES
[tōōlz/ ən bĭl/dĭng sə plīz/] **180–181**
toonie [tōō/nē] **26**–6
tooth / teeth [tōōth] / [tēth] **106**–7
toothache [tōōth/āk/] **110**–2
toothbrush [tōōth/brŭsh/] **57**–23, **109**–22
toothbrush holder [tōōth/brŭsh/ hōl/dər] **57**–24
toothpaste [tōōth/pāst/] **109**–23
top [tŏp] **88**–7, **89**–24
torn [törn] **97**–41
tornado [tör nā/dō] **145**–15
torso [tör/sō/] **106** ✦
tortoise [tör/təs] **213**–42
total [tōt/l] **27**–9
totebag [tōt/ băg/] **94**–19
**touch** [tŭch] **106**–E
towel [tow/əl]
bath towel [băth/ tow/əl] **57**–16
dish towel [dĭsh/ tow/əl] **61**–22
hand towel [hănd/ tow/əl] **57**–17
paper towels [pā/pər tow/əlz] **54**–3
towel rack [tow/əl răk/] **57**–15
towelettes [tow/əl ĕts] **146**–12
tower [tow/ər] **196**–3
town [town] **52**–3, **146**–2
town car [town/ kär/] **152**–20
townhouse [town/hows/] **52**–6
tow truck [tō/ trŭk/] **156**–14
toy [toy]
toy chest [toy/ chĕst/] **59**–16
toy store [toy/ stör/] **130**–5
Toys and Games [toyz/ ən gāmz/] **59**
track [trăk] **5**–21, **152**–14
track and field [trăk/ ən fēld/] **228**–18
tractor [trăk/tər] **177**–9
tractor trailer [trăk/tər trā/lər] **156**–15
traffic light [trăf/ĭk līt/] **128**–8
TRAFFIC SIGNS [trăf/ĭk sīnz/] **154**
tragedy [trăj/ə dē] **237**–14
trailer [trā/lər] **156**–15, **156**–17
train [trān] **150**–7, **233**–27
training [trā/nĭng] **172**–2, **172**–5, **172**–7
training pants [trā/nĭng pănts/] **37**–11
Training [trā/nĭng] **172**
Train Station [trān/ stā/shən] **152**
**transcribe** [trăn skrīb/] **171**–C
transfer [trăns für/, trăns/fər] **152**–5
**transfer** [trăns für/, trăns/fər] **171**–O
**translate** [trănz/lāt] **8**–C
translator [trănz/lā/tər] **168**–35
Transmission [trănz mĭsh/ən] **159**
Transportation [trăns/pər tā/shən] **152**
TRANSPORTATION [trăns/pər tā/shən] **150–151, 152**
**travel** [trăv/əl] **41**–P
travel agency [trăv/əl ā/jən sē] **131**–14
tray [trā] **55**–17, **83**–10
paint tray [pānt trā] **181**–51
tray table [trā tā/bəl] **161**–21
Tree [trē] **210**
trees [trēz] **208**–1, **239**–16
TREES AND PLANTS [trēz/ ən plănts/] **210**
trench coat [trĕnch/ kōt/] **90**–21
triangle [trī/ăng/gəl] **193**–32
tricycle [trī/sĭ kəl] **224**–12
trigonometry [trĭg/ə nŏm/ə trē] **192**–18
**trim** [trĭm] **176**–B
trip [trĭp] **152**–16, **152**–17
tripe [trīp] **70**–8
tripod [trī/pŏd] **235**–25
trombone [trŏm bōn/] **238**–10
trout [trowt] **71**–1
trowel [trow/əl] **176**–10, **178**–13
truck [trŭk] **150**–6
dump truck [dŭmp/trŭk/] **156**–19
fire truck [fīr/ trŭk/] **144**–10
garbage truck [gär/bĭj trŭk/] **127**–22
hand truck [hănd/ trŭk/] **175**–11
pickup truck [pĭk/ŭp trŭk/] **156**–12
tow truck [tō/ trŭk/] **156**–14
truck driver [trŭk/ drī/vər] **169**–61
TRUCKS [trŭks] **156**
trumpet [trŭm/pət] **238**–11
Trunk [trŭngk] **158**
trunk [trŭngk] **158**–11, **210**–4, **217**–49
swimming trunks [swĭm/ĭng trŭngks/] **90**–22
**try on** [trī/ŏn] **95**–C
T-shirt [tē/shürt/] **86**–4
tsunami [sōō nä/ mē/, tsōō–] **145**–17
tub [tŭb]
bathtub [băth/tŭb/] **57**–2
tuba [tōō/bə] **238**–12
tube [tōōb] **74**–12, **74**–24, **195**–42
tuberculosis (TB)
[tōō bür/kyə lō/səs] / [tē/bē/] **111**–15
Tuesday [tōōz/dā] **20**–10
tulip [tōō/ləp] **211**–11
tuna [tōō/nə] **71**–7, **72**–19, **212**–8
tuner [tōō/nər] **234**–13

turbulence [tür/byə ləns] **161**–22
turkey [tür/kē] **70**–17, **239**–10
roasted turkey [rōs/təd tür/kē] **76**–4
smoked turkey [smōkt/ tür/kē] **71**–25
turn [türn] **154**–5, **154**–7, **154**–8
turn signal [türn/ sĭg/nəl] **158**–6, **159**–34
turnstile [türn/stīl/] **152**–8
turntable [türn/tā/bəl] **234**–12
**turn** [türn]
**turn in** [türn/ ĭn/] **191**–M
**turn** left [türn/ lĕft/] **155**–C
**turn off** [türn/ öf/] **11**–P, **160**–I, **174**–G, **219**–G
**turn on** [türn/ ön/] **11**–B
**turn** right [türn/ rīt/] **155**–B
turnips [tür/nəps] **69**–16
turquoise [tür/koyz, –kwoyz] **24**–9
turtle [tür/tl] **213**–43
turtleneck [tür/tl nĕk/] **96**–9
tusk [tŭsk] **217**–50
tuxedo [tŭk sē/dō] **89**–17
TV Programs [tē/vē/ prō/grămz] **236**
TV / television [tē/vē/] / [tĕl/ə vĭzh/ən] **56**–6
big-screen TV [bĭg/skrēn/ tē/vē/] **50**–14
flat panel TV [flăt/ păn/əl tē/vē] **234**–7
flat screen TV [flăt/ skrēn/ tē/ vē/] **234**–7
portable TV [pör/tə bəl tē/vē/] **234**–8
tweezers [twē/zərz] **117**–4
twelfth [twĕlfth] **16**
twelve [twĕlv] **16**
twentieth [twĕn/tē əth] **16**
twenty [twĕn/tē] **16**
twenty after one [twĕn/tē ăf/tər wŭn/] **18**–10
twenty dollars [twĕn/tē dŏl/ərz] **26**–9
twenty-first [twĕn/tē fürst/] **16**
twenty-five [twĕn/tē fīv/] **16**
25 percent [twĕn/fīv/ pər sĕnt/] **17**–11
twenty-four [twĕn/tē för] **16**
twenty-one [twĕn/tē wŭn/] **16**
twenty-three [twĕn/tē thrē/] **16**
twenty to two [twĕn/tē tə too/] **18**–12
twenty-two [twĕn/tē too/] **16**
twice a week [twīs/ ə wēk/] **20**–23
twig [twĭg] **210**–1
twins [twĭnz] **28**–1
two [too] **16**
two dollars [too dŏl/ərz] **26**–6
2-door car [too/dör kär/] **156**–2
two-storey house [too/stör/ē hows/] **52** ✦
two-way radio [too/wā rā/dē ō] **179**–22
2 x 4 (two by four) [too/ bī/ för/] **181**–19
**type** [tīp] **170**–R, **196**–A
**type** a letter [tīp/ə lĕt/ər] **171**–A
**type** the message [tīp/ dhə mĕs/ĭj] **197**–E
**type** the subject [tīp/ dhə sŭb/jĕkt] **197**–D
**type** your password [tīp/ yər păs/würd/] **197**–A
Types of Health Problems [tīps/ əv hĕlth/ prŏb/ləmz] **115**
Types of Job Training [tīps/ əv jŏb/ trā/nĭng] **172**
Types of Material [tīps/ əv mə tïr/ē əl] **99**
Types of Math [tīps/ əv măth/] **192**
Types of Medication [tīps/ əv mĕd/ə kā/shən] **113**
Types of Movies [tīps/ əv moo/vēz] **237**
Types of Music [tīps/ əv myoo/zĭk] **237**
Types of TV Programs [tīps/ əv tē/vē/ prō/grămz] **236**
ugly [ŭg/lē] **23**–22
umbrella [ŭm brĕl/ə] **90**–17, **225**–14
umpire [ŭm/pīr] **229** ✦
uncle [ŭng/kəl] **34**–8
uncomfortable [ŭn kŭmf/tə bəl, –tər–] **42**–9
unconscious [ŭn/kŏn/shəs] **116**–A
under [ŭn/dər] **25**–11, **153**–A
long underwear [lŏng/ ŭn/dər wër] **91**–3
thermal undershirt [thür/məl ŭn/dər shürt] **91**–2
underexposed [ŭn/dər ĭk spōzd/] **235**–35
underpants [ŭn/dər pănts/] **91**–14
undershirt [ŭn/dər shürt/] **91**–1
**underline** [ŭn/dər līn/] **9**–S
Under the Hood [ŭn/dər dhə hood/] **158**
Underwear [ŭn/dər wër/] **91**
UNDERWEAR AND SLEEPWEAR [ŭn/dər wër/ ən slēp/wër/] **91**
**undress** [ən drĕs/] **36**–E
unfurnished apartment [ŭn/für nĭsht ə pärt/ mənt] **48**–4
uniform [yoo/nə förm/] **88**–10, **231**–16
Unisex Socks [yoo/nə sĕks/ sŏks/] **91**
Unisex Underwear [yoo/nə sĕks/ ŭn/dər wër] **91**
universal remote [yoo/nə vür/səl rĭ mōt/] **234**–9
UNIVERSE [yoo/nə vürs/] **205**
university [yoo/nə vür/sə tē] **188**–7
university degree [yoo/nə vür/sə tē də grē/] **41**–7
university residence [yoo/nə vür/sə tē rĕz/ə dəns] **52**–8
**unload** [ŭn lōd/] **101**–E
**unpack** [ŭn păk/] **49**–N
unravelling [ŭn răv/əl ĭng] **97**–43
unripe [ŭn rīp/] **68**–31
unscented [ŭn sĕn/təd] **108** ✦
**unscramble** [ŭn skrăm/bəl] **9**–W
up [ŭp]
**buckle up** [bŭk/əl ŭp/] **36**–L
**clean up** [klēn/ ŭp/] **147**–L
**cut up** [kŭt/ ŭp/] **77**–I
eggs sunny-side up [ĕgz/ sŭn/ē sīd/ ŭp/] **76**–10
**get up** [gĕt/ ŭp/] **38**–B
**hang up** [hăng/ ŭp/] **15**–D, **101**–H
**look up** [look/ ŭp/] **8**–A
**pick up** [pĭk/ ŭp/] **6**–I, **11**–E, **38**–M
pop-up ad [pŏp/ ŭp ăd/] **197**–9
**set up** [sĕt/ ŭp/] **173**–I
**stand up** [stănd/ ŭp/] **6**–D
stopped up [stŏpt/ ŭp/] **63**–19
**throw up** [thrō/ ŭp/] **110**–E
**wake up** [wāk/ ŭp/] **38**–A
**walk** up [wŏk/ ŭp/] **153**–C
upright seat [ŭp/rīt/ sēt/] **161**–28
upset [ŭp sĕt/] **43**–28
upstairs [ŭp/stërz/] **51** ✦
Uranus [yoor/ə nəs, yoo rā/nəs] **205**–7
urban area [ür/bən ër/ē ə] **52**–1
urchin [ür/chən] **212**–21
URL [yoo/är/ĕl/] **197**–4
USB port [yoo/ĕs/ bē/ pört/] **196**–7
**use** [yooz]
**use** a cash register [yooz/ə kăsh/ rĕj/ə stər] **170**–S
**use** a credit card [yooz/ə krĕ/dət kärd/] **27**–B
**use** a debit card [yooz/ə dĕ/bət kärd/] **27**–C
**use** a gift card [yooz/ ə gĭft/ kärd/] **27**–E
**use** deodorant [yooz/dē ō/dər ənt] **108**–C
**use** energy-efficient bulbs [yooz/ ĕn/ər jē ĭ fĭ/shənt bŭlbz] **219**–H
**use** punctuation [yooz/ pŭngk/choo ā/shən] **190**–C
Used Car [yoozd/ kär/] **157**
used clothing [yoozd/ klō/dhĭng] **102**–2
utensils [yoo tĕn/səlz] **79**–19
utility / utilities [yoo tĭl/ə tē] / [yoo tĭl/ə tēz] **48**–5, **156**–7
U-turn [yoo/türn/] **154**–5
vacancy sign [vā/kən sē sīn/] **50**–7
vacation [vā kā/shən] **22**–6
vaccination [văk/sə nā/shən] **114** ✦
vacuum [văk/yoom]
vacuum cleaner [văk/yoom klē/nər] **61**–10
vacuum cleaner attachments [văk/yoom klē/nər ə tăch/mənts] **61**–11
vacuum cleaner bag [văk/yoom klē/nər băg/] **61**–12
**vacuum** [văk/yoom] **60**–H
valley [văl/ē] **204**–18
valuables [văl/yə bəlz, –yə wə–] **132**–8
valve [vălv] **146**–4
van [văn] **156**–13, **156**–18
vandalism [văn/də lĭz/əm] **142**–1
vanity plate [vă/nə tē plāt/] **136** ✦
variable [vër/ē ə bəl] **192**–12
vase [vās, vāz, vŏz] **55**–23
vault [vŏlt] **132**–6
VCR [vē/sē/är/] **102**–7
veal cutlets [vēl/ kŭt/ləts] **70**–6
Vegetable [vĕj/tə bəl] **77**
vegetables [vĕj/tə bəlz] **66**–8, **72**–27, **81**–32
vegetable garden [vĕj/tə bəl gär/dn] **53**–27, **177**–14
vegetable peeler [vĕj/tə bəl pē/lər] **78**–15
VEGETABLES [vĕj/tə bəlz] **69**
vegetarian [vĕj/ə tër/ē ən] **70** ✦
vehicles [vē/ĭ kəlz] **156**–7, **156**–10
vein [vān] **107**–37
velcro [vĕl/krō] **99**–29
velvet [vĕl/vət] **99**–10
vending machine [vĕn/dĭng mə shēn/] **152**–9
vendors [vĕn/dərz] **84**–7, **129**–29
ventilation mask [vĕnt/əl ā/shən măsk/] **92**–7
Venus [vē/nəs] **205**–2
verdict [vür/dĭkt] **141**–14
vertebrates [vür/ tə brəts] **194**–12
vest [vĕst] **89**–15
down vest [down/ vĕst] **90**–14
life vest [līf/ vĕst/] **161**–25, **226**–14
safety vest [sāf/tē vĕst] **92**–4
veterinarian [vĕt/ər ə nër/ē ən] **169**–62
vice principal [vīs/ prĭn/sə păl] **5**–5
victim [vĭk/təm] **142**–10
Victoria Day [vĭk/tō/rĭ/ə dā] **22**–11
video [vĭd/ē ō]
videocassette [vĭd/ē ō kə sĕt/] **133**–18
video game console [vĭd/ē ō gām/ kŏn/sōl/] **232**–3

video game controller
[vĭd/ē ō gām/ kŏn trōl/ər] **232**–4
video player [vĭd/ē ō plā ər] **197**–11
video store [vĭd/ē ō stör/] **129**–20
**videotape** [vĭd/ē ō tāp/] **240**–A
view [vyo͞o]
rearview mirror [rïr/vyo͞o/ mïr/ər] **159**–35
sideview mirror [sīd/vyo͞o/ mïr/ər] **158**–3
village [vĭ/lĭj] **52**–3
vine [vīn] **210**–22
vineyard [vĭn/yərd] **177**–16
violence [vī/ləns, vī/ə–] **142**–4
violet [vī/ə lət, vī/lət] **24**–8, **211**–23
violin [vī/ə lĭn/] **238**–6
virus [vī/rəs] **111**–17
vise [vīs] **180**–26
vision [vĭ/zhən]
vision exam [vĭ/zhən ĭg zăm/] **136**–6
vision problems [vĭ/zhən prŏb/ləmz] **115**–1
Visit [vĭ/zət] **119**
visor [vī zər] **179**–12
visually impaired [vĭzh/ wəlē ĭm pērd/] **32**–11
vital signs monitor [vīt/l sīnz/ män/ə tər] **121**–26
vitamins [vī/tə mənz] **113**–17
v-neck [vē/nĕk/] **96**–8
vocational [vō kā/shə nəl]
vocational school [vō kā/shə nəl sko͞ol/] **188**–5
vocational training [vō kā/shə nəl trā/nĭng] **172**–5
voice message [voys mĕs/ĭj] **14**–18
volcanic eruption [vŏl kăn/ĭk ĭ rŭp/shən] **145**–16
volleyball [vŏl/ē bŏl/] **229**–14, **231**–3
Volume [vŏl/yəm, –yo͞om] **75, 193**
volunteer [vŏl/ən tïr/] **121**–17
**volunteer** [vŏl/ən tïr/] **41**–Q
**vomit** [vŏm/ət] **110**–E
**vote** [vōt] **140**–A
waffles [wŏ/fəlz] **80**–8
wages [wā/jĭz] **165**–12
wagon [wă/gən] **156**–6
waist [wāst]
waist apron [wāst/ ā/prən] **93**–30
waistband [wāst/bănd/] **100**–5
**wait** [wāt] **94**–B, **128**–B, **170**–T
waiter [wā/tər] **82**–8
head waiter [hĕd/wā/tər] **185**–12
waiting area [wā/tĭng ër/ē/ă] **182**–16
Waiting Room [wā/tĭng ro͞om/] **118**
waitress [wā/trəs] **83**–9
wait staff [wāt/ stăf/] **185** ✦
**wake up** [wāk/ ŭp/] **38**–A
walk [wŏk] **53**–2
crosswalk [krŏs/wŏk/] **128**–15
walk-in freezer [wŏk/ĭn frē/zər] **185**–3
**walk** [wŏk]
**walk** a dog [wŏk ə dŏg/] **129**–F
**walk** down [wŏk/ down/] **153**–D
**walk** to class [wŏk/ tə klăs/] **11**–C
**walk** up [wŏk/ ŭp/] **153**–C
**walk** with a friend [wŏk/ wĭth ə frĕnd/] **143**–A
walker [wŏ/kər] **113**–11
wall [wŏl] **56**–10, **194**–5
drywall [drī/wŏl/] **178**–19
wallpaper [wŏl/pā/pər] **59**–8
wallet [wŏ/lət] **94**–13
walrus [wŏl/rəs] **213**–32
war [wör] **199**–10
warehouse [wër/hows/] **175**–7
warm [wörm] **13**–4
warm clothes [wörm/ klōz/] **146**–6
warning label [wör/nĭng lā/bəl] **112**–8
Warnings [wör/nĭngz] **112**
wash [wŏsh]
mouthwash [mowth/wŏsh/] **109**–25
washcloth [wŏsh/klŏth/] **57**–6
**wash** [wŏsh]
**wash** clothes [wŏsh/ klōz/] **219**–K
**wash** hair [wŏsh/ hër/] **108**–E
**wash** the dishes [wŏsh/ dhə dĭsh/əz] **60**–M
**wash** the windows
[wŏsh/ dhə wĭn/dōz] **60**–I
washer [wŏ/shər] **50**–12, **101**–3, **180**–37
dishwasher [dĭsh/wŏsh/ər] **54**–8, **185**–2
washing [wŏ/shĭng] **61**–21
washrooms [wŏ/sh ro͞omz] **5**–9
wasp [wŏsp] **214**–17
waste [wāst] **121**–31, **218**–12
wastebasket [wāst/băs/kət] **57**–26
watch [wŏch] **94**–16
**watch** [wŏch] **39**–X, **147**–C
water [wŏ/tər] **209**–13, **225**–1
body of water [bŏd/ē əv wŏ/tər] **204** ✦
bottled water [bŏt/ld wŏ/tər] **146**–11
cold water [kōld/ wŏ/tər] **57**–10
hot water [hŏt/ wŏ/tər] **57**–9
hot water bottle [hŏt/ wŏ/tər bŏt/l] **113**–15
watercolour [wŏ/tər kŭl/ər] **233**–21
waterfall [wŏ/tər fŏl/] **204**–2
water fountain [wŏ/tər fown/tn] **224**–9
water glass [wŏ/tər glăs/] **83**–22
watermelons [wŏ/tər mĕl/ənz] **68**–18
water pollution [wŏ/tər pə lo͞o/shən] **218**–14
water polo [wŏ/tər pō/lō] **229**–15
water skiing [wŏ/tər skē/ĭng] **227**–7
**water** [wŏ/tər] **176**–F
WATER SPORTS [wŏ/tər spörts/] **227**
wave [wāv] **145**–17, **225**–17
**wave** [wāv] **2**–F
wavy hair [wā/vē hër/] **33**–10
way [wā]
hallway [hŏl/wā/] **184**–18
one way [wŭn/ wā/] **154**–3
one-way trip [wŭn/wā/ trĭp/] **152**–16
two-way radio [to͞o/wā/ rā/dē ō] **179**–22
wrong way [rŏng/ wā/] **154**–2
Ways to Conserve Energy and Resources
[wāz/ tə kən sürv/ ĕn/ər jē n rē/sör/səz,
–rĭ sör/səz] **219**
Ways to Get Well [wāz/ tə gĕt/ wĕl/] **114**
Ways to Pay [wāz/ tə pā/] **27**
Ways to Serve Eggs [wāz/ tə sürv/ ĕgz/] **76**
Ways to Serve Meat and Poultry
[wāz/ tə sürv/ mēt/ n pōl/trē/] **76**
Ways to Stay Well [wāz/ tə stā/ wĕl/] **114**
Ways to Succeed [wāz/tə sək sēd/] **10**
weak signal [wēk/ sĭg/nəl] **14**–12
WEATHER [wĕdh/ər] **13**
Weather Conditions [wĕdh/ər kən dĭsh/ənz] **13**
Weather Map [wĕdh/ər măp/] **13**
webcam [wĕb/kăm/] **196**–12
Webpage [wĕb/pāg/] **197**
website address [wĕb/sīt ə drĕs/] **197**–4
wedding [wĕ/dĭng] **22**–2
Wednesday [wĕnz/dā] **20**–11
weed [wēd]
seaweed [sē/ wēd/] **225** ✦
weed whacker [wēd/ wăk/ər] **176**–12
**weed** [wēd] **176**–G
week [wēk] **20**–15
last week [lăst/ wēk/] **20**–18
next week [nĕkst/ wēk/] **20**–20
once a week [wŭns/ ə wēk/] **20**–22
this week [dhĭs/ wēk/] **20**–19
three times a week [thrē/ tīmz/ ə wēk/] **20**–24
twice a week [twīs/ ə wēk/] **20**–23
weekdays [wēk/dāz/] **20**–16
weekend [wēk/ĕnd/] **20**–17
Week [wēk] **20**
weigh [wā] **75**–B
weight [wāt] **32**–8
Weight [wāt] **32, 75**
weightlifting [wāt/lĭf/tĭng] **228**–16
weights [wāts] **231**–22
WEIGHTS AND MEASUREMENTS
[wāts/ ən mĕzh/ər mənts] **75**
welder [wĕl/dər] **169**–63
well [wĕl] **42**–14
Well [wĕl] **114**
west [wĕst] **155**–2
western [wĕs/tərn] **237**–15
wet [wĕt] **101**–17
wetsuit [wĕt/ so͞ot/] **225**–4
whacker [wăk/ər] **176**–12
whale [wāl] **213**–29
wheat [wēt] **177**–2
wheat bread [wēt/ brĕd/] **71**–19
wheel [wēl] **159**–26
wheelbarrow [wēl/băr/ō] **176**–3
wheelchair [wēl/chër/] **113**–9
wheel cover [wēl/ kŭv/ər] **158**–9
whisk [wĭsk] **78**–21
whiskers [wĭs/kərz] **216**–20
white [wīt] **24**–14
whiteboard [wīt/börd/] **6**–3
white bread [wīt/ brĕd/] **71**–18
whole salmon [hōl/ săm/ən] **71**–3
wide [wīd] **97**–36
widow [wĭd/ō] **41** ✦
widower [wĭd/ō ər] **41** ✦
width [wĭdth, wĭtth] **17**–20
wife [wīf] **34**–12
ex-wife [ĕks/ wīf/] **35** ✦
former wife [för/mər wīf/] **35** ✦
wild [wīld] **215** ✦
wildlife [wīld/līf] **220**–2
willow [wĭl/ō] **210**–13
win [wĭn] **229** ✦

wind [wĭnd]
windbreaker [wĭnd/brā/kər] **90**–24
wind power [wĭnd/ pow/ər] **218**–2
windshield [wĭnd/ shēld/] **158**–1
windshield wipers [wĭnd/shēld/wī/pərz] **158**–2
windsurfing [wĭnd/sür/fĭng] **227**–10, **227** ✦
window [wĭn/dō] **47**–11, **56**–17, **136**–7
drive-through window [drīv/thrōō/ wĭn/dō] **128**–11
ticket window [tĭk/ət wĭn/dō] **152**–12
window pane [wĭn/dō pān/] **178**–16
windy [wĭn/dē] **13**–18
wine glass [wīn/ glăs/] **83**–23
wing [wĭng] **70**–20, **214**–1
winter [wĭn/tər] **21**–40
winter scarf [wĭn/tər/skärf/] **90**–5
WINTER AND WATER SPORTS
[wĭn/tər ən wö/tər spörts/] **227**
**wipe** [wīp] **60**–O
wipers [wī/pərz] **158**–2
wipes [wīps] **37**–15, **61**–23
wire [wīr] **181**–13
wire stripper [wīr/ strĭp/ər] **181**–42
wireless headset [wīr/ləs hĕd/sĕt] **14**–14
wiring [wīr/ĭng] **186**–7
**withdraw** [wĭdh drö/, wĭth–] **132**–F
witness [wĭt/nəs] **141**–11
wolf [wŏŏlf] **216**–4
woman [wŏŏm/ən] **30**–2
women [wĭ/mən] **30**–3
Women's Socks [wĭ/mənz sŏks/] **91**
Women's Underwear [wĭ/mənz ŭn/dər wër/] **91**
wood [wŏŏd] **178**–18
plywood [plī/wŏŏd] **178**–17
redwood [rĕd/wŏŏd] **210**–18
wood floor [wŏŏd/ flör/] **58**–21
woodpecker [wŏŏd/pĕk/ər] **214**–8
wood screw [wŏŏd/ skrōō/] **180**–33
wood stain [wŏŏd/ stān/] **181**–24
woodworking kit [wŏŏd/wür/kĭng kĭt/] **232**–14
wooden spoon [wŏŏd/n spōōn/] **78**–9
Woodwinds [wŏŏd/wĭndz/] **238**
wool [wŏŏl] **61**–5, **98**–3
word [würd] **190**–1
word problem [würd/ prŏ/bləm] **192**–11
Words [wördz] **8**
work [würk/] **121**–30, **154**–16
workbook [würk/bŏŏk/] **7**–26
work gloves [würk/ glŭvz/] **92**–17, **179**–17
work light [würk/ līt/] **181**–44
work pants [würk/ pănts/] **92**–5
work shirt [würk/ shürt/] **92**–2
**work** [würk] **8**–I, **10**–J, **38**–K
WORK [würk] **186**–**187**
Work Clothes [würk/ klōz/] **88**
worker [wür/kər]
careful worker [kër/fəl wür/kər] **179**–2
careless worker [kër/ləs wür/kər] **179**–1
childcare worker [chīld/kër wür/kər] **166**–16
construction worker
[kən strŭk/shən wür/kər] **178**–1
dockworker [dŏk/wür/kər] **167**–23
factory worker [făk/tə rē wür/kər, –trē] **175**–3
food preparation worker
[fōōd/ prĕp ə rā/shən wür/kər] **185**–4
garment worker [gär/mənt wür/kər] **167**–29
postal worker [pō/stəl wür/kər] **169**–49
sanitation worker [săn/ə tā/shən wür/kər] **169**–54
social worker [sō/shəl wür/kər] **169**–57
Worker [wür/kər] **92**, **93**
working [wür/kĭng]
not working [nŏt/ wür/kĭng] **62**–1
woodworking kit [wŏŏd/wür/kĭng kĭt] **232**–14
Working with a Partner [wür/kĭng wĭth ə pärt/nər] **8**
Working with Your Classmates
[wür/kĭng wĭth yər klăs/māts/] **8**
**work out** [würk/ owt/] **230**–N
WORKPLACE [würk/ plās/] **164**–**165**
WORKPLACE CLOTHING
[würk/ plās/ klō/dhĭng] **92**–**93**
world [würld]
world languages [würld/ lăng/gwĭ jəz] **189**–13
world music [würld/ myōō/zĭk] **237**–32
WORLD MAP [würld/măp/] **202**–**203**
WORLD HISTORY [würld hĭs/tə rē] **199**
worm [würm] **212**–23
worried [wür/ēd] **42**–13
wrap [răp] **72**–24
**wrap** [răp] **240**–F
wrench [rĕnch] **158**–22, **181**–47, **181**–48
wrestling [rĕs/lĭng] **228**–17
wrinkled [rĭng/kəld] **101**–19
wrist [rĭst] **106**–14
wristwatch [rĭst/wŏch/] **94**–16
**write** [rīt]
**write** a cheque [rīt/ ə chĕk/] **27**–D
**write** a cover letter [rīt/ ə kŭv/ər lĕt/ər] **173**–G
**write** a final draft [rīt/ ə fī/nəl drăft/] **191**–L
**write** a first draft [rīt/ ə fürst/ drăft/] **191**–H
**write** a note [rīt/ ə nōt/] **135**–A
**write** a resume [rīt/ ə rĕ/zə mā/] **173**–F
**write** a thank-you note
[rīt/ ə thăngk/ yōō nōt/] **174**–O
**write** back [rīt/ băk/] **135**–H
**write** on the board [rīt/ ön dhə börd/] **6**–E
writer [rī/tər] **169**–64
Writing and Revising [rī/tĭng ən rĭ vī/ zĭng] **191**
Writing Process [rī/tĭng prŏ/sĕs] **191**
Writing Rules [rī/tĭng rōōlz] **190**
wrong way [röng/ wā/] **154**–2
Xpresspost [ĕk/sprĕs/ pōst] **134**–2
Xpresspost bubble envelope
[ĕk/sprĕs/ pōst bŭ/bəl ĕn/və lōp/] **134**–3
xylophone [zī/lə fōn/] **238**–15
yard [yärd]
courtyard [kört/ yärd/] **51**–21
yardstick [yärd/stĭk/] **181**–16
YARD [yärd] **53**
yarn [yärn] **233**–22
year [yïr] **20**–4, **31**–9, **31**–10
Year [yïr] **21**
yellow [yĕl/ō] **24**–2
yesterday [yĕs/tər dā/] **20**–7
yield [yēld] **154**–9
yoga [yō/gə] **122**–4
yogourt [yō/gərt] **72**–22
young [yŭng] **32**–1
Your First License [yər fürst/ lī/səns] **137**
YOUR HEALTH [yər hĕlth/] **114**–**115**
zebra [zē/brə] **217**–35
zero [zïr/ō] **16**
zipper [zĭp/ər] **99**–25
Zones [zōnz] **19**
zoo [zōō] **222**–1
zoom lens [zōōm/ lĕnz/] **235**–23
zucchini [zōō kē/nē] **69**–25

**Continents**


Africa [ăf/rĭ kə] **202–5**
Antarctica [ănt ärk/tĭ kə, –är/tĭ–] **202–7**
Asia [ā/zhə] **202–4**
Australia [ō strāl/yə] **202–6**
Europe [yŏŏr/əp] **202–3**
North America [nörth/ ə mĕr/ə kə] **200–201, 202–1**
South America [sowth/ ə mĕr/ə kə] **202–2**


**Countries and other locations**


Afghanistan [ăf găn/ə stăn/] **203**
Albania [ăl bā/nē ə] **203**
Aleutian Islands [ə lōō/shən ī/ləndz] **200, 203**
Algeria [ăl jïr/ē ə] **203**
American Samoa [ə mĕr/ə kən sə mō/ə] **202**
Andaman Islands [ăn/də mən ī/ləndz] **203**
Angola [ăng gō/lə] **203**
Argentina [är/jən tē/nə] **202**
Armenia [är mē/nē ə] **203**
Australia [ō strāl/yə] **202–6**
Austria [ō/strē ə] **203**
Azerbaijan [ăz/ər bī jŏn/] **203**
Azores [ā/zörz] **202**
Baffin Island [băf/ən ī/lənd] **200**
Bahamas [bə hŏ/məz] **200, 202**
Bahrain [bä rān/] **203**
Bangladesh [bäng/glə dĕsh/, băng/–] **203**
Banks Island [bănks/ ī/lənd] **200**
Belarus [bē/lə rōōs/, byĕl/ə–] **203**
Belgium [bĕl/jəm] **203**
Belize [bə lēz/] **201, 202**
Benin [bə nïn/, –nēn/] **203**
Bermuda Islands [bər myōō/də ī/ ləndz] **200, 202**
Bhutan [bōō tăn/] **203**
Bolivia [bə lïv/ē ə] **202**
Bosnia [bŏz/nē ə] **203**
Botswana [bŏt swŏ/nə] **203**
Brazil [brə zïl/] **202**
Brunei [brōō nī/] **203**
Bulgaria [bŭl gër/ē ə] **203**
Burkina Faso [bər kē/nə fä/sō] **203**
Burma [bür/mə] **203**
Burundi [bŏŏ rōōn/dē] **203**
Cambodia [kăm bō/dē ə] **203**
Cameroon [kăm/ə rōōn/] **203**
Canada [kăn/ə də] **200, 202**
Canary Islands [kə nër/ē ī/ ləndz] **203**
Cape Verde [kāp/ vürd/] **202**
Central African Republic [sĕn/trəl ăf/rĭ kən rĭ pŭb/lĭk] **203**
Chad [chăd] **203**
Chile [chïl/ē] **202**
China [chī/nə] **203**
Colombia [kə lŭm/bē ə] **202**
Comoros [kŏm/ə rōz] **203**
Congo [kŏng/gō] **203**
Cook Islands [kŏŏk/ ī/ləndz] **202**
Corsica [kör/sĭ kə] **203**
Costa Rica [kōs/tə rē/kə] **201, 202**
Croatia [krō ā/shə] **203**
Cuba [kyōō/bə] **201, 202**
Cyprus [sī/prəs] **203**
Czech Republic [chĕk/ rĭ pŭb/lĭk] **203**
Democratic Republic of the Congo [dĕm/ə krăt/ĭk rĭ pŭb/lĭk əv dhə kŏng/gō] **203**
Denmark [dĕn/märk] **203**
Devon Island [dĕv/ən ī/lənd] **200**
Djibouti [jĭ bōō/tē] **203**
Dominican Republic [də mïn/ĭ kən rĭ pŭb/lĭk] **201, 202**
Ecuador [ĕk/wə dör/] **202**
Egypt [ē/jĭpt] **203**
Ellesmere Island [ĕl/əs mïr/ ī/lənd] **200**
El Salvador [ĕl săl/və dör/] **201, 202**
Equatorial Guinea [ē/kwə tör/ē əl gïn/ē, ĕk/wə–] **203**
Eritrea [ĕr/ə trē/ə] **203**
Estonia [ĕ stō/nē ə] **203**
Ethiopia [ē/thē ō/pē ə] **203**
Federated States of Micronesia [fĕ/də rā/təd stāts/ əv mī/krə nē/zhə] **203**
Fiji [fē/jē] **203**
Finland [fĭn/lənd] **203**
France [frăns] **203**
Franz Josef Land [frănz/ yō/səf lănd/] **203**
French Guiana [frĕnch/ gē ăn/ə, –ŏ/nə] **202**
French Polynesia [frĕnch/ pŏl/ə nē/zhə] **202**
Gabon [gă bōn/] **203**
Galápagos Islands [gə lō pə gōs ī/ləndz] **202**
Gambia [găm/bē ə] **203**
Georgia [jör/jə] **203**
Germany [jür/mə nē] **203**
Ghana [gŏ/nə] **203**
Greater Antilles [grā/tər ăn tïl/ēz] **201**
Greece [grēs] **203**
Greenland [grēn/lənd, –lănd/] **200, 202**
Guam [gwŏm] **203**
Guatemala [gwŏ/tə mŏ/lə] **201, 202**
Guinea [gïn/ē] **203**
Guinea-Bissau [gïn/ē bĭ sow/] **203**
Guyana [gī ăn/ə] **202**
Haiti [hā/tē] **201, 202**
Hawaiian Islands [hə wī/ən ī/ləndz] **200, 202**
Hispaniola [hĭs/pən yō/lə] **201**
Honduras [hŏn dŏŏr/əs] **201, 202**
Hong Kong [hŏng/ kŏng/] **203**
Hungary [hŭng/gə rē] **203**
Iceland [īs/lənd] **203**
India [ĭn/dē ə] **203**
Indonesia [ĭn/də nē/zhə] **203**
Iran [ĭ rŏn/, ĭ răn/] **203**
Iraq [ĭ rŏk/, ĭ răk/] **203**
Ireland [īr/lənd] **203**
Israel [ĭz/rē əl, –rā–] **203**
Italy [ĭt/l ē] **203**
Ivory Coast [īv/rē kōst/] **203**
Jamaica [jə mā/kə] **201, 202**
Japan [jə păn/] **203**
Jordan [jör/dn] **203**
Kazakhstan [kä/zək stăn/] **203**
Kenya [kĕn/yə, kēn/–] **203**
Kiribati [kïr/ə băs/] **203**
Kuwait [kōō wāt/] **203**
Kyrgyzstan [kïr/gĭ stăn/] **203**
Laos [lows] **203**
Latvia [lăt/vē ə] **203**
Lebanon [lĕb/ə nŏn] **203**
Lesotho [lə sō/tō, –sōō/tōō] **203**
Lesser Antilles [lĕ/sər ăn tïl/ēz] **201, 202**
Liberia [lī bïr/ē ə] **203**
Libya [lĭb/ē ə] **203**
Lithuania [lĭth/ōō ā/nē ə] **203**
Luxembourg [lŭk/səm bürg/] **203**
Macedonia [măs/ə dō/nē ə] **203**
Madagascar [măd/ə găs/kər] **203**
Madeira Islands [mə dïr/ə ī/ləndz] **203**
Malawi [mə lŏ/wē] **203**
Malaysia [mə lā/zhə] **203**
Maldives [mŏl/dēvz] **203**
Mali [mŏ/lē] **203**
Malta [mŏl/tə] **203**
Marshall Islands [mär/shəl ī/ləndz] **203**
Mauritania [mör/ə tā/nē ə] **203**
Mauritius [mö rĭsh/əs] **203**
Mexico [mĕk/sĭ kō/] **200, 201, 202**
Moldova [mŏl dō/və] **203**
Monaco [mŏn/ə kō/] **203**
Mongolia [mŏng gō/lē ə] **203**
Montenegro [mŏn/tə nē/grō] **203**
Morocco [mə rŏk/ō] **203**
Mozambique [mō/zəm bēk/] **203**
Namibia [nə mĭb/ē ə] **203**
Nepal [nə pŏl/] **203**
Netherlands [nĕdh/ər ləndz] **203**
New Caledonia [nōō/ kăl/ə dō/nē ə] **203**
New Zealand [nōō/ zē/lənd] **203**
Nicaragua [nĭk/ə rŏ/gwə] **201, 202**
Niger [nī/jər] **203**
Nigeria [nī jïr/ē ə] **203**
Northern Mariana Islands [nördh/ərn mə/rē ă/nə ī/ləndz] **203**
North Korea [nörth/ kə rē/ə] **203**
Norway [nör/wā] **203**
Oman [ō măn/] **203**
Pakistan [păk/ə stăn/] **203**
Palau [pə low/] **203**
Panama [păn/ə mŏ/] **201, 202**
Papua New Guinea [păp/yōō ə nōō/ gïn/ē] **203**
Paraguay [păr/ə gwī/, –gwā/] **202**
Peru [pə rōō/] **202**
Philippines [fĭl/ə pēnz/, fĭl/ə pēnz/] **203**
Poland [pō/lənd] **203**
Portugal [pör/chə gəl] **203**
Puerto Rico [pwër/tə rē/kō, pör/tə–] **201, 202**
Qatar [kă/tär, kə tär/] **203**
Romania [rō mā/nē ə, rōō–] **203**
Russia [rŭsh/ə] **203**
Rwanda [rōō ŏn/də] **203**
Samoa [sə mō/ə] **202**
Saudi Arabia [sow/dē ə rā/bē ə] **203**
Senegal [sĕn/ə gŏl/] **203**
Serbia [sür/bē ə] **203**
Seychelles [sā shĕlz/, –shĕl/] **203**
Sierra Leone [sē ër/ə lē ōn/, –lē ō/nē] **203**
Singapore [sĭng/ə pör/] **203**
Slovakia [slō vä/kē ə] **203**
Slovenia [slō vē/nē ə] **203**
Society Islands [sə sī/ə tē ī/ləndz] **202**

Solomon Islands [sŏl′ə mən ī′ləndz] **203**
Somalia [sə mŏ′lē ə] **203**
South Africa [sowth′ ăf′rĭ kə] **203**
South Georgia [sowth′ jör′jə] **202**
South Korea [sowth′ kə rē′ə] **203**
Spain [spān] **203**
Sri Lanka [srē′ lăng′kə, shrē′–] **203**
Sudan [so͞o dăn′] **203**
Suriname [so͞or′ə nŏ′mə] **202**
Svalbard [svŏl′bərd] **203**
Swaziland [swŏ′zē lănd′] **203**
Sweden [swēd′n] **203**
Switzerland [swĭt′sər lənd] **203**
Syria [sĭr′ē ə] **203**
Tahiti [tə hē′tē] **202**
Taiwan [tī′wŏn′] **203**
Tajikistan [tə jĭk′ə stăn′] **203**
Tanzania [tăn′zə nē′ə] **203**
Tasmania [tăz mā′nē ə] **203**
Thailand [tī′lănd′, –lənd] **203**
Togo [tō′gō] **203**
Tonga [tŏng′gə] **202**
Tunisia [to͞o nē′zhə] **203**
Turkey [tür′kē] **203**
Turkmenistan [türk mĕn′ə stăn′] **203**
Uganda [yo͞o găn′də] **203**
Ukraine [yo͞o′krān, yo͞o krān′] **203**
United Arab Emirates [yo͞o nī′təd ăr′əb ĕm′ər əts] **203**
United Kingdom [yo͞o nī′təd kĭng′dəm] **203**
United States of America
[yo͞o nī′təd stāts′ əv ə mĕr′ə kə] **200, 202**
Uruguay [yo͞or′ə gwī′, –gwā′] **202**
Uzbekistan [o͞oz bĕk′ə stăn′] **203**
Vanuatu [vă′no͞o ă′to͞o] **203**
Venezuela [vĕn′ə zwā′lə] **202**
Victoria Island [vĭk′tör ē ə ī′lənd] **200**
Vietnam [vē′ĕt nŏm′, –năm′] **203**
Wake Island [wāk′ ī′lənd] **203**
Western Sahara [wĕs′tərn sə hăr′ə] **203**
Yemen [yĕm′ən] **203**
Zambia [zăm′bē ə] **203**
Zanzibar [zăn′zə băr] **203**
Zimbabwe [zĭm bŏb′wā] **203**

**Bodies of water**
Arctic Ocean [ärk′tĭk ō′shən] **200, 203**
Atlantic Ocean [ət lăn′ tĭk ō′shən] **200, 202–203**
Baffin Bay [băf′ən bā′] **200, 202**
Baltic Sea [bŏl′tĭk sē′] **203**
Beaufort Sea [bō′fərt sē′] **200**
Bering Sea [bër′ĭng sē′] **200**
Black Sea [blăk′ sē′] **203**
Caribbean Sea [kăr′ə bē′ən sē′, kə rĭb′ē ən–] **201**
Caspian Sea [kăs′pē ən sē′] **203**
Coral Sea [kör′əl sē′] **203**
Gulf of Alaska [gŭlf′ əv ə lăs′kə] **200, 202**
Gulf of California [gŭlf′ əv kăl′ə förn′yə] **200**
Gulf of Mexico [gŭlf′ əv mĕk′sĭ kō′] **200, 202**
Hudson Bay [hŭd′sən bā′] **200, 202**
Indian Ocean [ĭn′dē ən ō′shən] **203**
Labrador Sea [lăb′rə dör′ sē′] **200**
Mediterranean Sea [mĕd′ə tə rā′nē ən sē′] **203**
North Atlantic Ocean [nörth′ ət lăn′tĭk ō′shən] **202**
North Pacific Ocean [nörth′ pə sĭf′ĭk ō′shən] **202, 203**
North Sea [nörth′ sē′] **203**
Pacific Ocean [pə sĭf′ĭk ō′shən] **200, 202, 203**
Philippine Sea [fĭl′ə pēn′ sē′] **203**
Red Sea [rĕd′ sē′] **203**
South Atlantic Ocean [sowth′ ət lăn′tĭk ō′shən] **203**
Southern Ocean [sŭdh′ərn ō′shən] **203**
South Pacific Ocean [sowth′ pə sĭf′ĭk ō′shən] **202, 203**

**The United States of America**
**Capital:** Washington, D.C. (District of Columbia)
[wŏ′shĭng tən dē′sē′] **200**

**Regions of the United States**
Mid-Atlantic States [mĭd′ət lăn′tĭk stāts′] **201**–10
Midwest [mĭd′wĕst′] **201**–9
New England [no͞o′ ĭng′glənd] **201**–11
Pacific States [pə sĭf′ĭk stāts′] **201**–7
Rocky Mountain States [rŏk′ē mown′tn stāts′] **201**–8
South [sowth] **201**–13
Southeast [sowth′ēst′] **201**–13
Southwest [sowth′wĕst′] **201**–12
West Coast [wĕst′ kōst′] **201**–7

**States of the United States**
Alabama [ăl′ə băm′ə] **200**
Alaska [ə lăs′kə] **200, 202**
Arizona [ăr′ə zō′nə] **200**
Arkansas [är′kən sŏ′] **200**
California [kăl′ə förn′yə] **200**
Colorado [kŏl′ə răd′ō, –ra′dō] **200**
Connecticut [kə nĕt′ĭ kət] **200**
Delaware [dĕl′ə wër′] **200**
Florida [flŏr′ə də] **200**
Georgia [jör′jə] **200**
Hawaii [hə wī′ē] **200**
Idaho [ī′də hō′] **200**
Illinois [ĭl′ə noy′] **200**
Indiana [ĭn′dē ăn′ə] **200**
Iowa [ī′ə wə] **200**
Kansas [kăn′zəs] **200**
Kentucky [kən tŭk′ē] **200**
Louisiana [lo͞o ē′zē ăn′ə] **200**
Maine [mān] **200**
Maryland [mër′ə lənd] **200**
Massachusetts [măs′ə cho͞o′səts] **200**
Michigan [mĭsh′ĭ gən] **200**
Minnesota [mĭn′ə sō′tə] **200**
Mississippi [mĭs′ə sĭp′ē] **200**
Missouri [mə zo͞or′ē] **200**
Montana [mŏn tăn′ə] **200**
Nebraska [nə brăs′kə] **200**
Nevada [nə văd′ə, –vŏ′də] **200**
New Hampshire [no͞o′ hămp′shər] **200**
New Jersey [no͞o′ jür′zē] **200**
New Mexico [no͞o′ mĕk′sĭ kō′] **200**
New York [no͞o′ yörk′] **200**
North Carolina [nörth′ kăr′ə lī′nə] **200**
North Dakota [nörth′ də kō′tə] **200**
Ohio [ō hī′ō] **200**
Oklahoma [ō′klə hō′mə] **200**
Oregon [ör′ĭ gən] **200**
Pennsylvania [pĕn′səl vān′yə] **200**
Rhode Island [rōd′ ī′lənd] **200**
South Carolina [sowth′ kăr′ə lī′nə] **200**
South Dakota [sowth′ də kō′tə] **200**
Tennessee [tĕn′ə sē′] **200**
Texas [tĕk′səs] **200**
Utah [yo͞o′tŏ] **200**
Vermont [vər mŏnt′] **200**
Virginia [vər jĭn′yə] **200**
Washington [wŏ′shĭng tən] **200**
West Virginia [wĕst′ vər jĭn′yə] **200**
Wisconsin [wĭs kŏn′sən] **200**
Wyoming [wī ō′mĭng] **200**

**Canada**
**Capital:** Ottawa [ŏt′ə wə] **201**

**Regions of Canada**
Atlantic Provinces [ət lăn′tĭk prŏv′ən səz] **201**–6
British Columbia [brĭt′ĭsh kə lŭm′bē ə] **201**–2
Northern Canada [nör′dhərn kăn′ə də] **201**–1
Ontario [ŏn tër′ē ō′] **201**–4
Prairie Provinces [prër′ē prŏv′ən səz] **201**–3
Québec [kwĭ bĕk′] **201**–5

**Provinces of Canada**
Alberta [ăl bür′tə] **200**
British Columbia [brĭt′ĭsh kə lŭm′bē ə] **200**
Manitoba [măn′ə tō′bə] **200**
New Brunswick [no͞o′ brŭnz′wĭk] **200**
Newfoundland and Labrador
[no͞o′fən lənd ən lă′brə dör′] **200**
Northwest Territories [nörth′wĕst′ tër′ə tör′ēz] **200**
Nova Scotia [nō′və skō′shə] **200**
Nunavut [no͞o′nə vo͞ot′] **200**
Ontario [ŏn tër′ē ō′] **200**
Prince Edward Island [prĭns′ ĕd′wərd ī′lənd] **200**
Québec [kwĭ bĕk′] **200**
Saskatchewan [să skăch′ə wŏn] **200**
Yukon [yo͞o′kŏn] **200**

**Mexico**
**Capital:** Mexico (City) [mĕk′sĭ kō′ (sĭt′ē)] **201**

**Regions of Mexico**
Chiapas Highlands [chē ă′pəs hī′ləndz] **201**–18
Gulf Coastal Plain [gŭlf′ kō′stəl plān′] **201**–16
Pacific Northwest [pə sĭf′ĭk nörth′wĕst] **201**–14
Plateau of Mexico [plă tō′ əv mĕk′sĭ kō′] **201**–15
Southern Uplands [sŭdh′ərn ŭp′ləndz] **201**–17
Yucatan Peninsula
[yo͞o′kə tăn′ pə nĭn′sə lə, yo͞o′kə tŏn′–] **201**–19

**States of Mexico**
Aguascalientes [ä′gwəs kăl yĕn′tās] **201**
Baja California Norte [bŏ′hŏ kăl′ə förn′yə nör′tā] **200**
Baja California Sur [bŏ′hŏ kăl′ə förn′yə so͞or′] **200**
Campeche [kăm pē′chē] **201**
Chiapas [chē ă′pəs] **201**
Chihuahua [chĭ wŏ′wŏ] **200**
Coahuila [kō′ə wē′lə] **200**

Colima Michoacán [kə lē/mə mē/chō ə kăn/] **201**
Distrito Federal [dĭ strē/tō fĕd/ə răl/] **201**
Durango [do͝o răng/gō] **201**
Guanajuato [gwă/nə hwă/tō] **201**
Guerrero [gə rĕr/ō] **201**
Hidalgo [hĭ dăl/gō] **201**
Jalisco [hə lĭs/kō, –lēs/–] **201**
México [mĕk/sĭ kō/, mĕ/hē kō] **201**
Morelos [mö rĕl/ōs] **201**
Nayarit [nă/yə rēt/] **201**
Nuevo León [nwā/vō lā ōn/] **200**
Oaxaca [wə hă/kə] **201**
Puebla [pwĕb/lə] **201**
Querétaro [kə rĕt/ə rō/] **201**
Quintana Roo [kēn tă/nə rō/] **201**
San Luis Potosí [săn/ lo͞o ēs/ pō/tə sē/] **201**
Sinaloa [sē/nə lō/ə] **200**
Sonora [sə nör/ə] **200**
Tabasco [tə băs/kō] **201**
Tamaulipas [tă/mow lē/pəs] **201**
Tlaxcala [tlă skă/lə] **201**
Veracruz [vĕr/ə kro͞oz/, –kro͞os/] **201**
Yucatán [yo͞o/kə tăn/, –tŏn/] **201**
Zacatecas [ză/kə tā/kəs] **201**

# Research Bibliography

The authors and publisher wish to acknowledge the contribution of the following educators for their research on vocabulary development, which has helped inform the principals underlying OPD.


Burt, M., J. K. Peyton, and R. Adams. *Reading and Adult English Language Learners: A Review of the Research.* Washington, D.C.: Center for Applied Linguistics, 2003.

Coady, J. "Research on ESL/EFL Vocabulary Acquisition: Putting it in Context." In *Second Language Reading and Vocabulary Learning,* edited by T. Huckin, M. Haynes, and J. Coady. Norwood, NJ: Ablex, 1993.

de la Fuente, M. J. "Negotiation and Oral Acquisition of L2 Vocabulary: The Roles of Input and Output in the Receptive and Productive Acquisition of Words." *Studies in Second Language Acquisition* 24 (2002): 81–112.

DeCarrico, J. "Vocabulary learning and teaching." In *Teaching English as a Second or Foreign Language,* edited by M. Celcia-Murcia. 3rd ed. Boston: Heinle & Heinle, 2001.

Ellis, R. *The Study of Second Language Acquisition.* Oxford: Oxford University Press, 1994.

Folse, K. *Vocabulary Myths: Applying Second Language Research to Classroom Teaching.* Ann Arbor, MI: University of Michigan Press, 2004.

Gairns, R. and S. Redman. *Working with Words: A Guide to Teaching and Learning Vocabulary.* Cambridge: Cambridge University Press, 1986.

Gass, S. M. and M.J.A. Torres. "Attention When?: An Investigation Of The Ordering Effect Of Input And Interaction." *Studies in Second Language Acquisition* 27 (Mar 2005): 1–31.

Henriksen, Birgit. "Three Dimensions of Vocabulary Development." *Studies in Second Language Acquisition* 21 (1999): 303–317.

Koprowski, Mark. "Investigating the Usefulness of Lexical Phrases in Contemporary Coursebooks." *Oxford ELT Journal* 59(4) (2005): 322–32.

McCrostie, James. "Examining Learner Vocabulary Notebooks." *Oxford ELT Journal* 61 (July 2007): 246–55.

Nation, P. *Learning Vocabulary in Another Language.* Cambridge: Cambridge University Press, 2001.

National Center for ESL Literacy Education Staff. *Adult English Language Instruction in the 21st Century.* Washington, D.C.: Center for Applied Linguistics, 2003.

National Reading Panel. *Teaching Children to Read: An Evidenced-Based Assessment of the Scientific Research Literature on Reading and its Implications on Reading Instruction.* 2000. http://www.nationalreadingpanel.org/Publications/summary.htm/.

Newton, J. "Options for Vocabulary Learning Through Communication Tasks." *Oxford ELT Journal* 55(1) (2001): 30–37.

Prince, P. "Second Language Vocabulary Learning: The Role of Context Versus Translations as a Function of Proficiency." *Modern Language Journal* 80(4) (1996): 478-93.

Savage, K. L., ed. *Teacher Training Through Video - ESL Techniques: Early Production.* White Plains, NY: Longman Publishing Group, 1992.

Schmitt, N. *Vocabulary in Language Teaching.* Cambridge: Cambridge University Press, 2000.

Smith, C. B. *Vocabulary Instruction and Reading Comprehension.* Bloomington, IN: ERIC Clearinghouse on Reading English and Communication, 1997.

Wood, K. and J. Josefina Tinajero. "Using Pictures to Teach Content to Second Language Learners." *Middle School Journal* 33 (2002): 47–51.

LIBRARY
COLLEGE